More Army Blue

MORE ARMY BLUE

The Uniform of Uncle Sam's Regulars 1874-1887

John P. Langellier

Schiffer Military History
Atglen, PA

DEDICATED TO

Bill Bentham, D.V.M., Donald E. Kloster, John F. Sukey

"England has its Grenadiers.
France has its zoo-zoos,...
The U.S.A. never changes they say;
But continually wears the blues..."

Edward Harrigan
The Regular Army Oh!

Book Design by Ian Robertson.

Library of Congress Catalog Number: 00-111768

Printed in China.
ISBN: 0-7643-1310-X

We are interested in hearing from authors with book ideas on related topics.

Published by Schiffer Publishing Ltd.
4880 Lower Valley Road
Atglen, PA 19310
Phone: (610) 593-1777
FAX: (610) 593-2002
E-mail: Schifferbk@aol.com.
Visit our web site at: www.schifferbooks.com
Please write for a free catalog.
This book may be purchased from the publisher.
Please include $3.95 postage.
Try your bookstore first.

In Europe, Schiffer books are distributed by:
Bushwood Books
6 Marksbury Avenue
Kew Gardens
Surrey TW9 4JF
England
Phone: 44 (0) 20 8392-8585
FAX: 44 (0) 20 8392-9876
E-mail: Bushwd@aol.com.
Free postage in the UK. Europe: air mail at cost.
Try your bookstore first.

CONTENTS

FOREWORD

The development of an altogether new uniform for troops of the United States Army, a few years after the Civil War, in many ways reflected the national mood of a war-weary country bent upon change and reaching its God-given destiny. It was an age of expansionism and dawning of great industry. The country was taking on muscle in preparation for its emergence as a world power, and assuming a leading role in the community of nations. Yet, despite the burgeoning international independence, the armies of Europe still registered powerful influences on the international political scene. One subtle manifestation of this sway was the style of clothing adopted by the United States government for its soldiers.

The story of how it all happened has never been told so well or so comprehensively. In this volume, sequel to the author's highly praised *Army Blue: The Uniform of Uncle Sam's Regulars, 1848-1873*, John P. Langellier continues the story of the evolution of American army uniforms during a critical period that saw experimentation and innovation finally surmount conservatism to produce some of the more practically functional and aesthetically appealing martial clothing in American history. It was a time when the United States Army's principal duties lay in manning the nation's coastal defenses, overseeing the Reconstruction governments in the states of the former Confederacy (through 1877 in some cases), and dealing with Indians from remote stations of the trans-Mississippi frontier. The period witnessed the gradual demise of Brigadier General Montgomery C. Meigs' timeworn administration of the Quartermaster Department (1861-1882)—the end of a system once caught up in frustration of wartime politics, mismanaged contracts, and outright fraud (although largely cleaned up after the war), and the dawning change under his successor, Brigadier General Samuel B. Holabird, who during his administration (1883-1890) reformed existing system deficiencies.

Initially working as deputy quartermaster general under Meigs, Holabird steadily emerged as a leader in his own right. He eventually spearheaded the development and adoption of new specification standards for uniforms, then streamlined and institutionalized their production during the years when the nation stood poised for entry into the twentieth century.

Montgomery C. Meigs served as the U.S. Army's quartermaster general from 1861 until his retirement in 1882. During his long tenure in office he was a model of economy and ethics, although he tended to be tradition-minded and reluctant to accept major changes. He wears the uniform of a major general of the style adopted in 1851, and that remained almost unaltered until 1902. The only departure from the norm are the two stars of his brevet (honorary) rank, instead of the more common shoulder straps with gold embroidered border and silver stars on a dark blue background. LC

While Holabird's personality attributes, presence, and authority fostered rapid change, especially after he succeeded to Meigs' position, his vision did not exactly take hold overnight. Langellier's treatise goes beyond the overview to discuss how experiments, trials, tests, and modifications influenced virtually every facet of quartermaster clothing production from headgear to footwear. Thoughts, opinions, and recommendations, both solicited and unsolicited, came from general officers in lofty War Department offices, as well as from lowly privates serving at isolated frontier outposts to help formulate the decisions affecting these articles during what is now commonly (yet shortsightedly) termed the "Indian wars" period. The breadth of Langellier's research, coupled with his years of accumulated expertise in the study of historical army uniforms, is evident throughout, and together make this book the most thorough and precise accounting that the topic has ever received. Beyond good reading and good history, it will serve as an invaluable reference for museum curators, archaeologists, material culturalists, historians, military collectors, students, and antiquarians because of the accurate and inclusive treatment that it affords. In sum, John Langellier has herein produced an original masterpiece of documentation (both manuscript and photographic) and an informed interpretation that will likely stand as a permanent cornerstone for the study of American military uniforms of the late nineteenth century. Enjoy!

Jerome A. Greene
Historian and Staff Curator
National Park Service
Denver, Colorado

In 1883, Samuel B. Holabird would become quartermaster general. Like his predecessor Meigs, he was dedicated, but in contrast, he tended to be more flexible in his thinking about what type of garb should be provided by his department for the common soldier. He appears in the 1872-pattern dress uniform for a field grade (major through colonel) officer in the Quartermaster Department, complete with the chapeau de bras. USAMHI

ACKNOWLEDGMENTS & ABBREVIATIONS

Over the more than two decades it took to assemble the materials for this book I was assisted by numerous individuals, who either shared their personal collections, or made available materials in various public institutions in this country and Canada. Many of these generous people, or their organizations, are listed below. I would be remiss, however, if I did not single out four friends who did so much to make this study possible. I cannot adequately express my gratitude to Gordon Chappell, Kurt Cox, Jerome Greene, and Glen Swanson for all they did to facilitate this project.

In addition to these colleagues, I want to acknowledge Dr. Vincent Transano, the command historian of the U.S. Navy Facilities Engineering Command, for taking time to comment on early drafts of this study. So, too, do I owe Rita Amendola, Casey Barthelmess, Donald Kloster, Dr. Howard G. Lanham, Robert "Sandy" Sanders, Peter Scarafiotti, Nicky Sperry, Don Troiani, and Edward Vebell thanks for helping me secure a number of key photographs and artifacts that enhanced this publication. I also am obliged to Peter Schiffer and his able colleagues at Schiffer Military History, most particularly Robert Biondi and Ian Robertson, for making every effort to produce a quality book from my manuscript and cache of images. Finally, I am indebted to my wife, Deanna, and our daughter, Erica, who patiently weathered this undertaking as I disappeared night after night to complete *More Army Blue....* I sincerely hope that the final product in some small way repays all the support I received while undertaking this venture.

Abbreviations

Pictorial Sources

AHS	Arizona Historical Society, Tucson, AZ
AMWH	Autry Museum of Western Heritage, Los Angeles, CA
BB	Bill Bentham, D.V.M.
BH	B. William Henry
BP	Brian Pohanka
BU	Brown University Library, Anne S.K. Brown Military Collection, Providence, RI
CBF	Christian Barthelmess Family
CECSM	Civil Engineer Corps and Seabee Museum, Port Hueneme, CA
CF	Chuck Fowler
CSPM	Colorado Springs Pioneer Museum, Colorado Springs, CO
D&BM	Dan and Barb Miller
DM	Douglas C. McChristian
DJM	Donald J. McGee
DPL	Denver Public Library, Western History Collection, Denver, CO
DS	Don Spaulding
EB	Brigadier General Edward Burka, M.D., USAR (Ret.)
ES	Eric A. Saul
FAM	Frontier Army Museum, Ft. Leavenworth, KS
FDNHS	Ft. Davis National Historic Site, Ft. Davis, TX
FLNHS	Ft. Laramie National Historic Site, Torrington, WY
FSHM	Ft. Sam Houston Museum, San Antonio, TX
GC	Gordon S. Chappell
GL	George M. Langellier, Jr.
GM	Greg Martin
GS	Glen Swanson
HO	Hayes Otoupalik
HP	Herb Peck, Jr.
JB	Jack Blades
JG	Jerome A. Greene
JL	Joshua Landish
JM	James M. May III
KC	Kurt Hamilton Cox
KSHS	Kansas State Historical Society, Topeka, KS
LACMNH	Los Angeles County Museum of Natural History, Seaver Center, Los Angeles, CA
LC	Library of Congress, Washington, DC
LBBNM	Little Bighorn Battlefield National Monument, Crow Agency, MT
LDSA	Church of Jesus Christ of Latter Day Saints Archives, Salt Lake City, UT
MHS	Montana Historical Society, Helena, MT
MK	Mark Kasal
MM	Michael J. McAfee, Ph.D.
MNH	Museum of Nebraska History, Lincoln, NE
NA	National Archives, College Park, MD
NAC	National Archives of Canada, Ottawa, Ontario
NPS	National Park Service

NYSDMNA	New York State Department of Military and Naval Affairs, Albany, NY
OFN	Old Ft. Niagara, Niagara, NY
PAC	Public Archives of Canada, Ottawa, Ontario
RB	Robert G. Borrell, Sr.
RD	Ray Darida
SACS	San Antonio Conservation Society, San Antonio, TX
SDSHS	South Dakota State Historical Society, Pierre, SD
SHSND	State Historical Society of North Dakota, Bismarck, ND
SI	Smithsonian Institution, Museum of American History, Military History Collections, Washington, DC
SIT	A Stitch in Time, Hoisington, KS
TC	Tojhusmuseet, Copenhagen, Denmark
TT	Thomas Trevor
UKL	University of Kansas, Spencer Library, Lawrence, KS
UPM	Union Pacific Museum, Omaha, NE
USA	U.S. Army (Former Presidio Army Museum Collection) Presidio of San Francisco, CA
USACHH	U.S. Army Chaplain Historical Holding, Ft. Monmouth, NJ
USACM	U.S. Cavalry Museum, Ft. Riley, KS
USAMHI	U.S. Army Military History Institute, Carlisle Barracks, PA
USAMNCO	U.S. Army Museum of the Non-commissioned Officer, Ft. Bliss, TX
USAQM	U.S. Army Quartermaster Museum, Ft. Lee, VA
WAM	Watervliet Arsenal Museum, Watervliet, NY
WC	Wes Clark
WPM	West Point Museum, United States Military Academy, West Point, NY
WSHS	State Historical Society of Wisconsin, Madison, WI
WSM	Wyoming State Museum, Cheyenne, WY
WR	Walt Redling

End Notes

AG	Adjutant General
AGO	Adjutant General's Office
AGUSA	Adjutant General United States Army
A&NJ	*Army and Navy Journal*
ARSW	*Annual Report of the Secretary of War*
Br.	Branch
CCF	Consolidated Correspondence Files
Cir.	Circular
GO	General Orders
HQA	Headquarters of the Army
IGUSA	Inspector General United States Army
NA	National Archives, Washington, DC
OQMG	Office of the Quartermaster General
LR	Letters Received
LS	Letters Sent
RG	Record Group, National Archives
RUSACC	Records of U.S. Army Continental Commands
USAMHI	U.S. Army Military History Institute, Carlisle Barracks, PA
WD	War Department

INTRODUCTION

After the American Civil War ended, widespread dissatisfaction spread relating to the U.S. Army uniform. The desire for change in this area characterized a prevalent mind set for change among many officers, ranging from sweeping recommendations about military policy and tactics, most brilliantly championed by Colonel Emory Upton, to less notable, minor goals.[1] Politics, both within and without the military, fiscal considerations, and tradition versus pragmatism all formed parts of a complex equation.

There were those, such as the commanding general of the army, William Tecumseh "Cump" Sherman, and the quartermaster general, Montgomery C. Meigs, who stood as bastions of the status quo.[2] But these venerable veterans, both professional soldiers and graduates of West Point, faced formidable challengers, including a rising star who never attended the military academy, Nelson A. Miles, and even one of Meigs' successors, a reform-minded quartermaster officer by the name of Samuel B. Holabird. Egos and economics came into play when military men took sides as to what the proper outfit would be for the small, far flung force of regulars.

Rufus Zogbaum, a prominent illustrator-writer for pictorial newspapers of the late Victorian and early Edwardian eras, succinctly summarized the matter:

> The subject of what to wear always seems to be a vexed question in our little army, and the advantages of this or that pattern of coat or cap are discussed over and over again in all departments of the service, from headquarters of the general commanding the army to the barracks of a one-company post on the remote frontier.[3]

In this simple statement, Zogbaum came to the heart of the matter. What follows is an attempt to demonstrate the validity of these observations, as well as to provide details about what the soldier and his officer actually wore, which on more than one occasion was at odds with the officially sanctioned uniform found in orders and regulations. Indeed, during more than a quarter of a century after the Civil War, the U.S. Army demonstrated that in a democracy, even the military was not a slave to higher authority. Personal initiative came from many quarters, making the American soldier of this period, like his counterparts from other times, highly individualistic. This trait, sometimes referred to as "Yankee ingenuity," both taxed the martial hierarchy, while at the same time demonstrated a particular strength of the common soldier then and now.

Yet, during the decades immediately following the Civil War, the uniform evolved into a distinct entity, one that came to be associated with the nation the soldiers who wore it served. Gradually, as the sur-

Public Law 181 of July 25, 1866, supplemented by General Orders No. 75, War Department, September 5, 1866, created the position of general in the United States Army, which among other things was indicated by four silver stars on shoulder straps and epaulets, as Ulysses S. Grant depicts in one of his final portraits taken in uniform. MM

On March 4, 1868, after Ulysses S. Grant became president of the United States, William T. Sherman assumed the mantle of commanding general of the U.S. Army. From that time through late 1872 he wore four stars, and the special uniform indicating his position as the top military man of the time, with twelve buttons in each row grouped in sets of four. After the publication of General Orders No. 92, War Department, October 26, 1872, however, he would don a new style of shoulder strap with two silver stars flanking the arms of the United States, as seen here. LC

Emory Upton poses in the dress uniform of a lieutenant colonel of the First U.S. Artillery, indicated by his 1872-pattern officer's shoulder knots that were to have scarlet backgrounds on the pads and a silver embroidered regimental number flanked by silver oak leaves to indicate his unit and rank. USAMHI

plus articles on hand left over from the vast Union army disappeared from the supply chain, so too did the thinking that had created it. What followed was a period of mixing government issue with field expedients, especially during the campaigns of the 1870s. But by the mid- to late 1880s, the soldier in both garrison and under combat conditions tended to rely less on ad hoc solutions, and leaned more toward acceptance of what the government provided, albeit with modifications in a number of instances. The transitional years between 1874 and 1887, consequently, are a worthy subject for study.

NOTES

1 For more on this acclaimed military visionary read, Stephen Ambrose, *Upton and the Army* (Baton Rouge: Louisiana State University, 1964). For additional context on the subject of change in the post-Civil War martial establishment consult, Donna M.E. Thomas, "Army Reform in America: The Crucial Years, 1876-1881," (Unpublished Ph.D. Dissertation, Department of History, University of Florida, 1980).

2 Meigs spent more than four decades in the military, much of it as quartermaster general, a post he held since the early days of the Civil War through retirement on February 6, 1882. The sixty-five year old Meigs then was succeeded briefly by Sherman's father-in-law, Colonel D.H. Rucker, who remained just long enough to be confirmed as a brigadier general so that he could retire at the higher rank. In turn, during early 1882, Colonel Rufus Ingalls followed Rucker. He, too, retired shortly thereafter, serving little more than a year. On July 1, 1883, he also applied for retirement, thereby opening the way for Samuel B. Holabird to be his replacement. Holabird assumed office effective from that date through June 16, 1890. Erna Risch, *Quartermaster Support of the Army: A History of the Corps, 1775-1939* (Washington, DC: Office of the Quartermaster General's Office, 1962), 514.

3 Rufus Fairchild Zogbaum, "Army Uniform," *Harper's Weekly* (May 4, 1895), 417.

Three cavalrymen depict the transitional nature of the uniform during the 1870s. The trooper standing with his arms at the sides of his sky blue kersey trousers wears a modified Civil War vintage four button sack coat with exterior pocket added, while the other dapper dandy standing with a cigar on the right appears in an 1872-pattern pleated blouse. The seated man evidently has opted for an 1874-pattern enlisted blouse. All of the trio sport 1872-pattern forage caps with insignia correct for cavalrymen. AMWH

1

"The present uniform is good enough," 1872-1880

Soon after the outbreak of the Civil War, Brigadier General Montgomery C. Meigs filled the vacant office of quartermaster general of the U.S. Army. President Abraham Lincoln had selected him to assume the post that many others sought, including an especially formidable candidate, William T. Sherman.

Meigs would remain the quartermaster general until retirement in 1882, but often he looked back with pride on the days of fighting between the North and South. In fact, during a time of widespread confusion and considerable graft, he deserved praise for his ethical and able performance of difficult duties. After that conflict, however, he tended toward protectiveness of the Quartermaster Department and its reputation.[1]

Indeed, even in the face of a strong grassroots movement to replace the uniform of the late war with new patterns, Meigs staunchly championed the old uniform that had served Billy Yank. The new commanding general of the army, none other than Meigs' former competition, Sherman, was inclined to agree. Nevertheless, the winds of change ultimately grew strong enough to whisk away former martial fashions and replace them with updated designs.[2]

This turn of affairs came about after the promulgation of Special Orders No. 260, Headquarters of the Army, July 3, 1871, established a board of officers to review the army regulations in their entirety, a requirement that stemmed from the many lessons of the late war that caused considerable revision of such areas as tactics, weapons, and accoutrements.[3] Inspector General of the Army Randolph B. Marcy presided over this body that would take the initiative to ponder the matter of the uniform as one of its many areas of consideration. In fact, one major outcome of this group's deliberations was General Orders No. 92, War Department, October 26, 1872, which set forth a new uniform that was to replace the styles worn previously (see Appendix A for the complete text of this order).[4]

Despite Meigs' earlier efforts to stem the tide of revisionists, once the new order was released, he reacted in his characteristic professional manner and attempted to provide the replacement outfit as rapidly as possible. As one example, he instructed a subordinate to "visit one or more of the establishments in Philadelphia where small work is turned out by the band saw, and ascertain by trial if the band saw can be applied to cutting out garments for the army." He went on to propose: "It

Left: Lieutenant Colonel Custer's 1872-pattern officer's helmet with gilt metal eagle plate surmounted by the proper silver regimental numeral superimposed on the shield. SI

Opposite: Lieutenant Colonel George A. Custer has placed his helmet on a table next to him. The remainder of his outfit is the 1872-pattern finery of a field grade officer of cavalry, although the gold lace ornamentation on his cuffs is far larger than that called for by regulations of the time. The prescribed width was 1/4 inch, but in Custer's case the lace is approximately 1/2 inch. Custer's manner of draping his gold chest cords is also non-regulation. GS

Thomas French appears in the finery adopted in 1872 for mounted company grade officers (lieutenants through captains), in this case as a captain of the Seventh U.S. Cavalry. BP

Captain George Yates of the Seventh U.S. Cavalry wore this 1872-pattern helmet with his full dress kit. Photograph by Michael O'Donnell. NYSDMNA

Left: Detail of the side vent and gold cord band on an officer's 1872-pattern dress helmet. This example belonged to First Lieutenant William W. Cooke, Seventh U.S. Cavalry. CSPM

This example of an officer's 1872-pattern mounted helmet, made by Horstmann of Philadelphia, lacks the required regimental numeral on the front plate. A large leather washer supports the yellow cavalry horsehair plume, allowing it to cascade gracefully over the felt body. There is no tassel on the left side, unlike many officers' helmets of the period. USACM

Second Lieutenant Robert G. Carter was commissioned to the Fourth U.S. Cavalry upon graduation from the United States Military Academy in 1870. He appears in the 1872-pattern dress uniform of a company grade officer of that branch. The breast cord is of the gold wire that was commonly seen during the early 1870s. He had draped the cords in a non-regulation manner to suit his own tastes. NA

An 1872-pattern company grade officer's dress coat as indicated by seven buttons in each row and two gold lace ornaments on each cuff. These are the regulation 1/4 inch width. JG

may be found better to use a metal saw blade and a knife edge rather than saw teeth. This you can determine after examination and trial."[5] Meigs concluded that the then present method of cutting out garments probably was not as effective as the use of the band saw or band cutter.[6]

Indeed, earlier he had observed that without cutting machines "the supply of new uniforms to the Army would have been much slower, somewhat more costly, and no better" than those assembled through other means. He went on to state: "When a large quantity of clothing of one pattern is wanted speedily, the machine cuts it more cheaply, more quickly, and quite as well as it can be done by hand." Meigs continued, "Cutting machines for military clothing have been used for many years in Europe, and their general adoption, like that of the power-loom, of the sewing machine, and other machines for cheapening manufacture, is only a question of time." He went on to defend the mechanization, noting that comparing the work of the cutter to hand production demonstrated the machines' increased speed and they were more economical. Additionally, he claimed, "Without the machine the Department would have been at the mercy of combinations among" the men previously employed as hand-cutters, who might increase their prices when an emergency or other situation arose to their advantage.

Meigs wanted to avoid this possibility as much as take a step toward more cost-effective operations. He thus concluded his remarks, which had been prompted by an adverse letter sent by representatives of the Garment Cutters Society of the City of Philadelphia (an early union), in no uncertain terms: "The government in this matter moves only with the times, and the workmen will doubtless find, with the increase of manufacture, that there is still room for all who are industrious and skilful to earn an honest living."[7]

Based on Meigs' positive attitude, two cutters were obtained, one invented by A. Warth and the other produced by Band Knife Company.

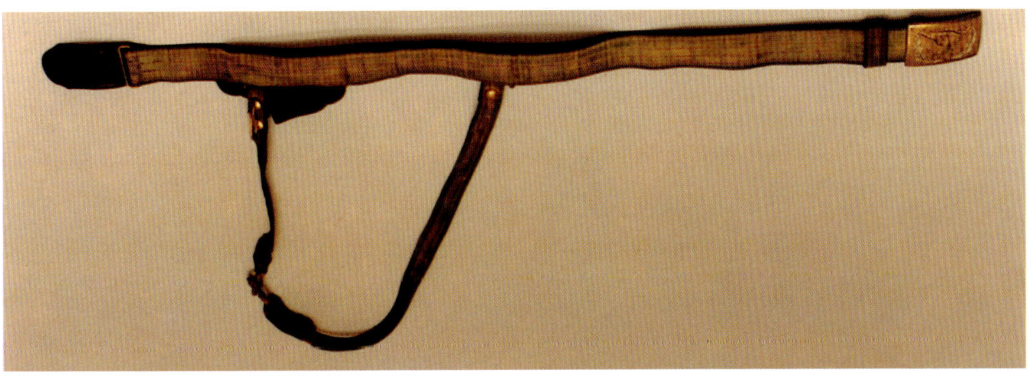

In 1872 three gold lace stripes were sewn to the cuffs of field grade (majors through colonels) dress coats, and a dress belt with solid bullion also was prescribed as another means to distinguish this goup of officers. Photograph by Glen Swanson. GS

Seventh U.S. Cavalry Captain Thomas M. McDougall wore this dress shoulder knot of a style that prevailed from the late 1870s onward. The gold cord is distinctly different from that on the earliest knots. Photograph by Glen Swanson. GS

Variant of an 1872-pattern cavalry officer's shoulder knot. Rather than being outlined in gold wire cord only, a row of contrasting gold embroidery thread has been added. WSM

After a year the results were hailed as beneficial, and better than projected when the equipment first was obtained. With the Warth machine, for instance, up to a thousand pairs of trousers had been cut out per day. The Band Knife version allowed cloth for 400 pairs to be turned out, and could slice through 140 thicknesses of cotton drill. This meant the "machines more than paid for themselves in labor saving."[8] Later Meigs sought to increase the machine's effectiveness by adding a flexible shaft of the type he had observed while visiting the 1876 Centennial Exposition in Philadelphia.[9]

As an aside, this international fair was held in honor of the United States' first one hundred years of nationhood. It brought together technology from all over the world. Meigs' organization was represented with displays of "clothing and equipage, and of wagons, ambulances, and other military material provided by the Quartermaster's Department" that was "placed in the Government Building at the Centennial Exposition." In recognition of this effort, the exposition's commissioners presented the department a medal and a certificate.[10]

Although Meigs simultaneously displayed the work of his department with pride to the public while pursuing increased efficiency through employing up-to-date methods at manufacture, he elsewhere demonstrated a less practical, but more humanistic side. When the Philadelphia firm of Pollack and Jacobs approached officials in Washington about the manufacture of martial wear by contract to private enterprise, Meigs replied there was no work to be given out at present. He explained:

> Most of the clothing is cut out at the arsenal [using the Warth Cutter] and made up by women who have long depended upon this work for support. Uniform coats are made by tailors, the women not being able to make them up. But none are now being manufactured.

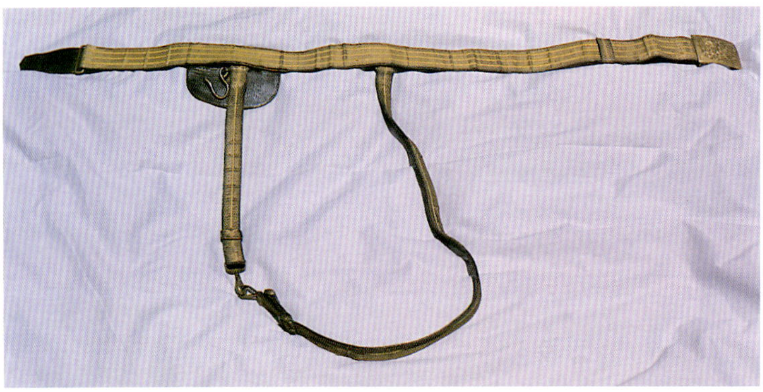

Front, back, and buckle of an 1872-pattern cavalry company grade officer's belt, distinguished by three horizontal yellow silk stripes bordered by gold wire lace. These materials were interwoven, and the colors would reflect the branch, with artillery officers displaying scarlet, infantry medium blue, and officers of the various staff corps black. This belt belonged to Edmund Luff, who received his commission in the Eighth U.S. Cavalry in 1867 and remained with the regiment through the 1890s. JM

Hook and front saber sling of Luff's cavalry company grade officer's 1872-pattern dress saber belt. JM

Above, Right: Rear sling of Luff's 1872-pattern company grade cavalry officer's dress belt. JM

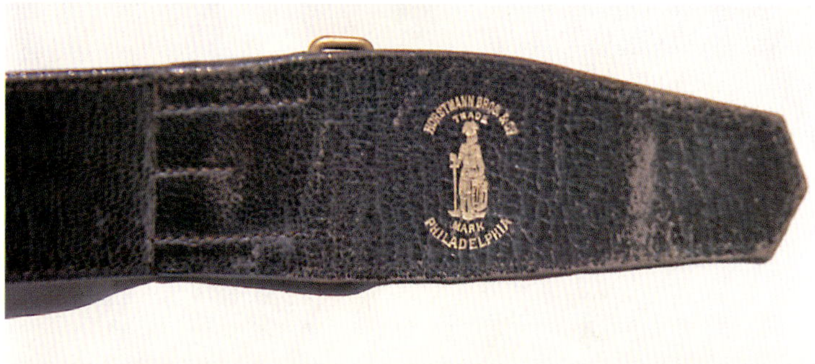

Right: Maker's trademark (Horstmann of Philadelphia) on the rear tab that went behind the heavy gilt buckle of the Luff's 1872-pattern dress saber belt. JM

When there was a press of work, the Philadelphia Depot [or arsenal, as it also was called] sometimes had to resort to contracting for the services of "some of the Clothing houses to assist. But in slack time, at the Arsenal, it is best to endeavor to distribute all the work among those poor women who are perhaps a little better paid by the U.S. than by the Clothing houses.

Meigs further interjected that this work force had been selected "from a great number for skills and for having some connection with the army. The attempt has been to give work to widows and others who have had or lost relatives in the war." Given the strong power of the Grand Army of the Republic (the Civil War veterans' national organization) and the presence of many former Union officers and enlisted men in political offices, including President U.S. Grant, Meigs' words staved off any further discussion of the manufacture process.

Protecting the needy was only one of Meigs' many concerns, however. The quartermaster general faced other obstacles in fulfilling his mission, not the least of which was a shortage of funds.[11] Nonetheless, the Quartermaster Department set about letting contracts for those items it could not manufacture.

The quartermaster general particularly seemed keen to have the pleated blouses made and sent "during the coming winter."[12] While during 1873 Meigs subsequently expressed negative comments about this article of clothing, he was anxious to place this particular item in production as soon as possible. In fact, he instructed that the pleated blouse patterns be sent with an individual skilled in cutting garments to the Jeffersonville Depot in Indiana, where they could be manufactured along with trousers.[13] This workman would have considerable labor ahead, because Meigs wanted 30,000 blouses to be furnished from there![14] One-third of these would be cut, and all materials, including thread and needle, packaged and set aside until quartermasters from the various garrisons actually made requisitions for them.[15] His goal was to have the work force mobilized and fabrication undertaken rapidly.[16] He thought that

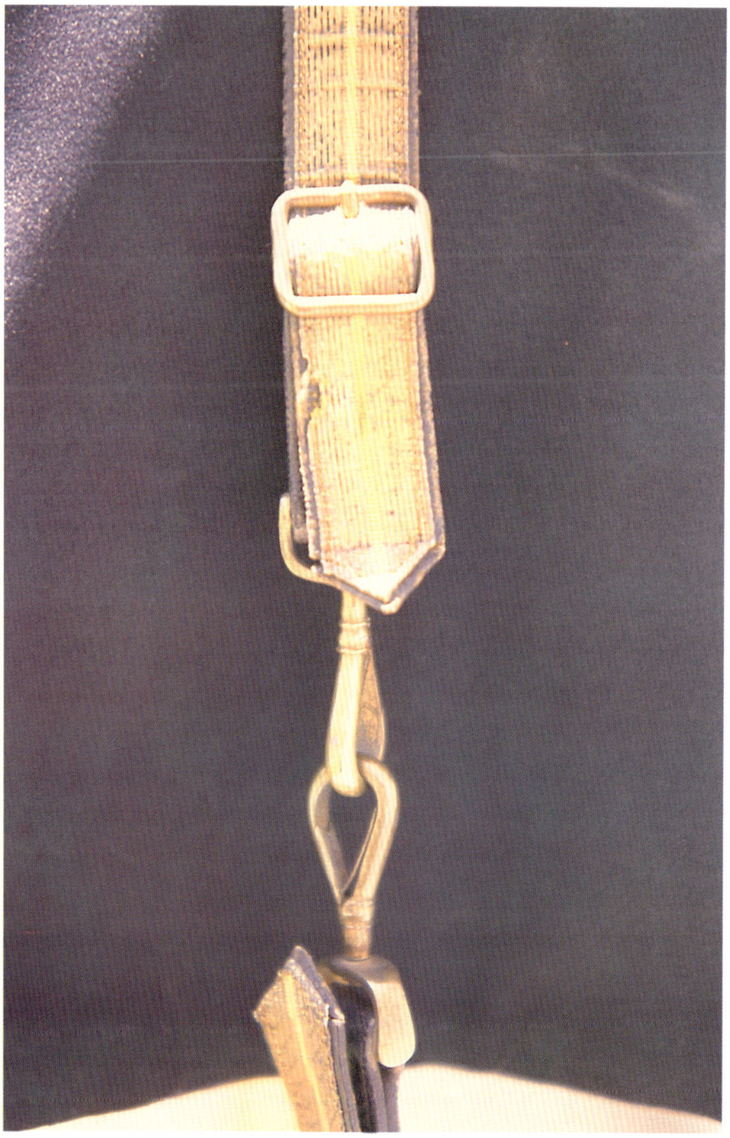

Typical gilt snap hooks used to connect the rings on the saber scabbard to the slings of an 1872 pattern officer's dress belt. JM

Regimental adjutants, aides de camp, and certain staff corps officers combined a gold cord aiguillette with the right shoulder knot of their dress uniform. First Lieutenant Cooke, as adjutant of the Seventh U.S. Cavalry wore such a rig, with the aiguillette being an integral part of the knot. LBBNM

Detail of the "pencils" at the end of Lieutenant Cooke's aiguillette—so-called because allegedly early versions of this accessory actually had pencil-lead inside so that an aide could take down orders and other communications from a superior officer. CSPM

these actions would "better suit present prevailing tastes in the army and thus avoid the recutting which it is believed, is a caprice, and not a necessity...."[17]

To expedite the work, and in order to demonstrate that the government was not at the mercy of the professional cloth cutters, Meigs authorized a contract to obtain one of the cutting machines he had observed (the model sold by Alvin Warth) as an emergency measure, which would be abandoned after the "delivery of the uniform now so urgently needed and pressed especially for posts on the Upper Missouri River."[18]

Cooke's shoulder knots with aiguillette—the centers of the pads were covered with yellow facing material, while the number denoted the regiment, and bars indicated his rank of first lieutenant. Photograph by Gordon Chappell. CSPM

This letter was telling in that it indicated the concern for delivery to remote forts, that for much of the year could only be reached with some difficulty because their lines of supply were all but cut off when the river froze and severe weather conditions set in. This prompted Meigs to indicate that "The uniform coat is the principal part of the uniform and in case of necessity be worn with the New, or even with the Old forage cap or hat."[19]

Meigs had another concern to contend with at that time, as well. His department would run out of funds early in 1873, before making up the items called for in General Orders No. 92.[20] Fabrication would be halted as a result, and the issue of new garments would reach only those posts that already had been sent advance supplies. Thereafter, old patterns were to be sent out for a considerable period, until the fiscal situation could be resolved.[21] This caused Meigs to call for lists of old stocks to be sent in for disposition until new garments were on hand.[22]

Without adequate money for this and other new uniform production, Meigs asked the chairman of the military affairs committee in the United States Senate to advance a substantial sum from the next year's appropriations to rectify the problem.[23] He likewise contacted the secretary of war, making known the need for over $397,000 to carry on this work—no mean amount for its day when a recruit made but $13 a month.[24] Meigs summarized this situation in his annual report:

> The President of the United States having adopted a new uniform for the Army, its manufacture was begun by this office. But the

appropriation made before the change of uniform, and based upon estimates looking to the use of material in store, was not sufficient to provide uniforms of the new pattern for 30,000 men. The manufacture and distribution was therefore arrested until, on the 1st of July, 1873, the appropriation of the present fiscal year became available. Nearly all the troops have now received the new uniform. The old pattern clothing stored in the Philadelphia depot, has in compliance with the law, been sold at public auction, the sales amounting to $490,094.31. The surplus of such clothing distributed at military posts throughout the country is being reported for sale as fast as the new uniform takes its place.[25]

A cost-conscious U.S. Congress likewise inhibited the original progress. These lawmakers directed during fiscal year 1874 (July 1, 1873, to June 30, 1874) that "none of the money appropriated" by them was to "be used in the purchase of hats, uniform caps, forage caps, uniform coats, uniform jackets, flannel sack coats, and unlined coats, but that these articles should be issued from the supply on hand known as old pattern; and that none of these articles enumerated should be purchased until those on hand are exhausted."[26]

Meigs noted an inequity in this requirement in that the prices set for the old pattern as charges against the clothing accounts of men who drew these items were many times higher than the rate articles fetched at auction. The quartermaster general listed the amounts set by the government versus prices realized at auction to make his point. On one hand the army deducted $5.50 for a uniform coat: $2.13 for a lined four button and $1.77 for an unlined one; $4.11 for cavalry and light artillery jackets; $1.20 for a pair of bootees; and $2.07 for a pair of boots, whereas at an October 1873 sale in Philadelphia the same goods brought the following returns: $.76 1/2 per coat; $.82 for the lined sack and $.49 for unlined sacks; $.47 1/2 for shell jackets; $1 per pair of bootees; and $1.90 for a pair of boots. Meigs rightly judged this discrepancy to be unfair to the enlisted man.[27]

Rear of the 1872-pattern officer's dress coat with aiguillette attached to the shoulder knot. NA

In this photograph Cooke has removed all indications of rank from his 1872-pattern officer's dress coat, having buttoned it open to reveal its velvet lined collar and his white bow tie. The metal clips on his shoulder are to hold his 1872-pattern shoulder knots. LBBNM

To make matters worse, lawmakers in Washington directed that money accumulated from surplus sales would be deposited with the Treasury Department as general funds, rather than being credited to the War Department for military use, as had been the practice prior to 1872. What this meant was the quartermaster general's efforts to dispose of old items caused a loss of revenue of nearly one million dollars for his department during the fiscal year when the new uniform was adopted. Insufficiency of funds resulting from these circumstances meant commanders had to contact the Clothing and Equipment Branch at Philadelphia directly to ascertain whether they could obtain any of the desired articles they needed to clothe their troops.[28]

All these factors made it difficult for Meigs and his subordinates to make inroads into providing the new kit as he underscored in an 1874 letter:

> In obedience to this law, you will make no further issue of the new uniform corresponding with that above named [hats, uniform caps, forage caps, uniform coats, uniform jackets, flannel sack coats, and unlined coats], including campaign hats with the exception of the helmets of light artillery. There being none of the old dress caps for

General Orders No. 67, War Department, June 25, 1873, stated that aiguillettes for aides, adjutants, and certain staff officers "could be made separate," in order to be worn with "the coat underneath the knot by means of a strap or tongue passing through the lower fastening of the knot." JB

First Lieutenant George W. Baird served as regimental adjutant of the Fifth U.S. Infantry from 1871 through 1879, a position that is indicated by his aiguillette. Baird's 1872-pattern infantry officer's dress cap with white cock feathers is visible on the table between the lieutenant and his wife. FAM

that branch of service on hand, the helmets will be supplied to the light artillery.[29]

Thus, requests for forage cap covers, pompons, campaign hats, and the like all had to be considered on an individual basis. In the instances of dress helmets and dress caps, the requests often were honored.[30] In many other cases where the 1872-pattern was being sought, however, the answer regularly was disappointing. Many officers learned that the new items they requested were not on hand, or would only be issued under certain conditions. For instance, the commander of Company B, Sixteenth U.S. Infantry was informed that campaign hats were reserved for troops serving on the frontier only.[31] Given that this regiment served in Texas, this caveat presented no problem. Conversely, the same officer likewise was told that no cap covers could be obtained, nor could pompons be furnished, because the latter items were to be issued with the dress cap, and not separately.[32]

Another group singled out to receive old patterns exclusively were Indian scouts. These Native Americans, who since July 1866 had been permitted to enlist for six month periods as auxiliaries and scouts, were to receive articles from stock, which were to "be legally exempted from sales" and issued to those Apaches, and others who had joined Uncle Sam.[33]

Despite such hurdles, one of Meigs' subordinates, Captain Jonathan Rodgers, the military storekeeper in charge of operations at Philadelphia, shared his superior's pride in the 1872 uniform. He touted: "It is, in quality, appearance, and workmanship, vastly superior to the old. None but good cloth has been used, and prices paid for making it have been sufficient to insure good work. The patterns are all better than formerly used, and if the Army complains, the Quartermaster need feel no remorse." Captain Rodgers added: "The new uniform" was "in the process of manufacture, and will shortly be issued."

While he asserted the helmet included in the new issue appealed to him as "the most sightly headgear I have ever seen...," he listed some short-comings that would have to be rectified later. Specifically, Rodgers pointed out the fur felt of the shell was "almost too light; the disk on the crown should be broader to bear the strain of the spear, plume, and socket, and the binding should be heavier and broader."[34]

Nor was Rodgers the only one to ponder improvements on the original designs. Most notably, Inspector General Marcy continued to review samples of new patterns, including uniform coats and trousers. The latter item still required refinement, as Marcy pointed out. While they appeared well made, he wanted stitching around the buttons to strengthen the cloth, and approved Captain Rodgers' advice to issue 500 pairs for trial.

Additionally, Marcy learned that there was no authority to make up trousers with the type of pockets and without a waistband as called for by the 1872-board.[35] The reason for this stemmed from the secretary of war's decision that trousers of the old pattern were to be continued in production "in view of the great increase in the cost" in adopting the new pattern. The added expense for making up the required number of foot trousers according to the 1872-board's wishes was approximately

An 1872-pattern infantry company grade officer's dress coat with shoulder knots, aiguillettes, and dress belt with blue stripes alternating with gold. JB

A first lieutenant of the Twenty-fifth U.S. Infantry with his shoulder knots atop the 1872-pattern company grade officer's dress coat. JB

$35,100, along with another $20,475 for mounted trousers of the design that called for the discontinuance of the previous side-seam pockets.[36] Further, certain sizes existed in sufficient quantity that manufacture of new trousers was prohibited until the stock was considerably diminished or exhausted.[37]

Less weighty matters were shared with the secretary of war as well. For example, he was asked to approve a new chevron, in this case for farriers. This was a horseshoe, an appropriate symbol for the trade of this specialist that was essential to the mounted service. The secretary permitted the introduction of the new insignia.[38]

A special designation for musicians, however, was denied. First Lieutenant Ira Quinby of the Eleventh U.S. Infantry learned that trouser stripes for his company musicians were not provided by the quartermaster.[39] Although the practice of applying such stripes to the trousers of bandsmen and company musicians seemed to have been carried out unofficially for some years, no authorization existed for this custom until the 1880s.

Lieutenant Michael L. Courtney of the Twenty-fifth Infantry aired another concern. He reported a problem experienced by his doughboys, and the following solution: "The sky blue facings, trimmings, and insignia of rank of enlisted men should be of better material, those furnished the past year fading on exposure to the sun."[40] Given that Courtney's command was serving at Ft. Stockton, Texas, this criticism was no doubt valid. In fact, the fading problem continued as a source of adverse commentary for many years to come.[41]

A pair of 1872-pattern Twenty-fifth U.S. Infantry officer's shoulder knots. The background material was medium blue, although some very early examples had light blue backgrounds. JB

What cannot be ascertained from Lieutenant Courtney's correspondence was whether these dress coats were of the new pattern or simply old 1858-pattern enlisted frock coats that had been faced with the 1872-

First Lieutenant James H. Bradley's 1872-pattern knots signified his rank and his regiment, the Seventh U.S. Infantry. Photograph by Glen Swanson. GS

The background of 1872-pattern staff officers' knots were to be dark blue. According to the original scheme set in place in July 1872, the corps were represented by old English letters as follows: A.D., Adjutant General's Department; I.D., Inspector General's Department; J.A. (as seen here-the gold leaves to designate a major), Bureau of Military Justice (Judge Advocate's Department); S.S., Signal Service; Q.D., Quartermaster's Department; S.D., Subsistence Department; M.D., Medical Department; P.D., Pay Department; E.C., Engineer Corps; and O.D., Ordnance Department. General Orders No. 107, War Department, December 14, 1872, altered this plan to a certain degree by calling for a solid shield of silver for the Adjutant General's Department, a silver metal castle for engineer officers, and a silver embroidered shell and flame for ordnance officers. These were the same basic insignia worn on the front of the forage cap, as well, although engineers had a gold wreath around their devices, while the other two corps did not. EB

Front and rear view of 1872-pattern shoulder knots worn by Colonel Nelson A. Miles of the Fifth U.S. Infantry. Note the maker's label. WC

pattern tails, cuffs, and collar "flashes." These altered garments were to be issued at reduced prices to those infantrymen and others who cared to draw these garments in lieu of new-made ones.[42]

Converting 1858-pattern coats continued for several years as indicated by two representative letters from 1876. One from First Lieutenant L.S. Ames, Second U.S. Infantry, called for facings for forty coats of the old pattern, which were to be converted.[43] At McPherson Barracks, Georgia, Major John Belcher requested facing for thirty-eight of the 1858-pattern frock coats so that infantrymen at that post might alter these into a facsimile of the 1872-pattern.[44] From the Twenty-fourth Infantry Captain John Clous asked what the price of facings were for retrimming old pattern frock coats, and he also inquired about the charges and the number of yards of cord for each flannel sack coat, possibly meaning converting old four-button blouses into an imitation of the new 1874-pattern five-button blouse.[45] Even then, once the soldier acquired

Right: Company grade infantry officer's 1872-pattern dress belt with the proper blue silk striping bordered by gold. Belts for artillery company grade officers would have displayed scarlet striping, and for second lieutenant through captains of the various staff corps, black striping. Photograph by Kurt Cox. JB

the coat and facings items he had the additional cost of paying a tailor in his unit to alter the garment.

Not only were some 3,314 infantry 1858-pattern infantry coats sent to the depot a Ft. Leavenworth, Kansas, to be distributed in the Military Division of the Missouri, where presumably they would be converted either into dress wear or some form of field and garrison item, but also seventeen cavalry musicians' 1855-pattern jackets and 3,849 regular cavalry enlisted shell jackets were to be shipped, thereby indicating that 1872-pattern dress coats still were not being worn universally.[46] To demonstrate the state of flux that was then ongoing, small quantities of 1872-pattern dress coats simultaneously had been provided to Ft. Leavenworth, but only for non-commissioned staff officers or support branches, i.e., commissary sergeants, hospital stewards, and ordnance enlisted personnel. Curiously, cavalry dress helmets with all their components were on hand, as were substantial quantities of dress caps and insignia for all branches, including infantry but excluding engineers.[47] From this one may infer that the helmet in some instances was being combined with the old shell jacket, just as the 1872-pattern caps were being mixed with converted dress coats. Indeed, so many caps and helmets were on hand at Ft. Leavenworth that requests for more had been halved, whereas no mention was made of new cavalry coats.[48]

Similarly light (horse) artillerymen at Ft. Adams, Rhode Island, were to receive the old pattern shell jacket with scarlet trim that was to be worn unaltered, presumably in tandem with the 1872-pattern dress helmet in lieu of the 1872-pattern dress coat. What is more, their heavy artillery comrades at that post continued to draw the 1858-pattern frock, which then would be converted with the proper facings.[49]

In 1877 old pattern infantry coats and facings were recommended for foot soldiers, including three of the old style infantry musicians' coats with trim that differed greatly from the "herringbones" applied to the chests of the 1872-pattern dress coat for bandsmen, all for Post #2 Little Bighorn River (later Ft. Custer, Montana Territory), as well as at Ft. Buford, Dakota Territory, and Ft. Ellis, Montana Territory. By this time, the cavalry commander at the latter post sought new pattern dress coats for his troopers, but even then it turned out the 1855-pattern shell jacket was provided instead.[50] In like manner, doughboys with a company of the Second Infantry at Jefferson Barracks, Missouri, were to be sent facings to apply to the old coats.[51]

Rear views of an 1872-pattern officer's dress belt buckle and the tab that went behind the buckle. Note the detail of the lace, indicating the wearer was a company grade officer of infantry. Photograph by Kurt Cox. JB

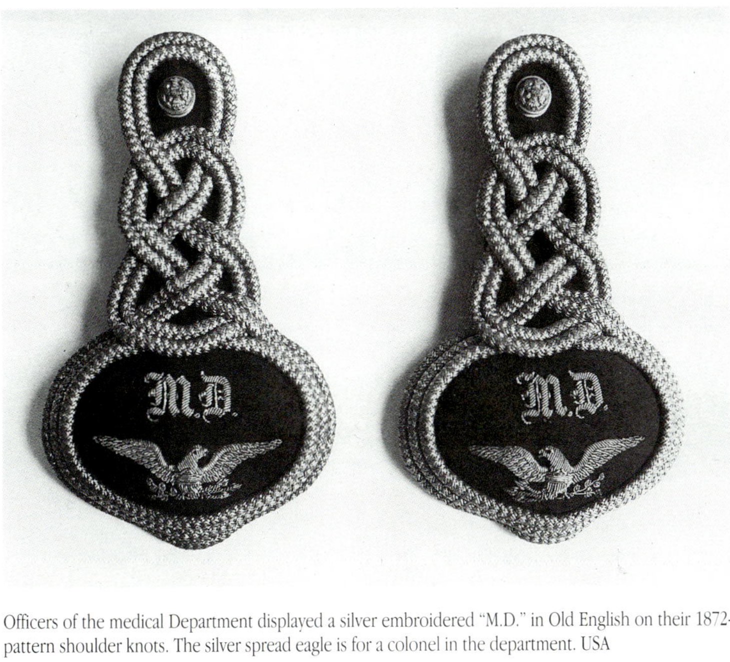

Officers of the medical Department displayed a silver embroidered "M.D." in Old English on their 1872-pattern shoulder knots. The silver spread eagle is for a colonel in the department. USA

An infantry second lieutenant in the company grade full dress uniform prescribed from 1872 through 1879. His trousers are light blue, and regulations called for them to be decorated with 1 1/2 inch dark blue cloth leg stripes for infantry officers. The sword is the correct M1860 Staff and Field type. GS

Not all foot troops were being issued frock coats for alteration, as evidenced by the fact that according to the commanding officer of Ft. Niagara, New York, the men of the Third U.S. Artillery serving there were in the new uniform, which afforded "great satisfaction."[52] Even so, two years later the garrison, which had changed to men of the Seventh U.S. Infantry, included four-button sack coats, although there were overcoats and buffalo overshoes of the new pattern, as well, plus the folding campaign hat with hat cords. The last item was unusual in that it was only supposed to be issued to troops serving on campaign, and not to Eastern garrisons.[53]

At another military reservation in New York state, Allegheny Arsenal, Lieutenant Marcus Lyon reported all the enlisted Ordnance Department personnel in his command were in new coats.[54] Earlier in the year Major George A. Gordon requested new pattern dress coats for the cavalrymen at Camp Supply, Indian Territory. Presumably these were issued, as mounted coats were not being made from converted 1858-pattern enlisted frock coats. As such, some cavalry and light artillery soldiers were receiving the 1872-pattern dress coat by this time.[55] What all this meant was a mixture of old and new articles that produced a motley appearance for much of the 1870s.

The effect was not entirely popular. For instance, from the Department of Texas, Colonel Ranald Mackenzie petitioned that none of the pleated blouses, old sack coats, or shell jackets be issued to his troopers of the Fourth U.S. Cavalry. He was informed that orders required these old pattern items to be supplied until stocks were expended.[56]

In another case Meigs responded to observations made by Captain Augustus C. Robinson. The quartermaster general succinctly outlined his department's policy:

> You are informed that limited appropriations, and therefore very limited stock of clothing and special provisos attached to appropriation laws, have caused delay. Had there been a stock of the new

Front view with and without cock feathers of an 1872-pattern infantry officers' dress cap, which remained regulation until replaced by a helmet in 1881. SI

Side views of an 1872-pattern infantry officer's dress cap. Photographs by Glen Swanson. WC

Detail of Colonel Nelson A. Miles' 1872-pattern dress cap with cock feather removed to show the sheet brass reinforcement at the top front of the cap that helped hold the feathers in place. Photograph by Glen Swanson. WC

Interior maker's label of one of Miles' 1872-pattern officer's caps. WC

Regulation tulip (plume staff) for the officer's 1872-pattern dress cap that held the cock feathers upright. Photograph by Glen Swanson. GS

Front of the 1872-pattern heavy artillery officer's dress cap with scarlet cock feathers in place. JG

Second Lieutenant Tasker H. Bliss of the First U.S. Artillery typifies the 1872 through 1879 dress for company grade officers of the heavy artillery. Field grade officers differed little from this look, except for the fact that their belts were of solid bullion lace and their coats featured three gold lace ornaments on each cuff, rather than the two for lieutenants and captains. USAMHI

According to the uniform regulations of 1872, general officers were to wear epaulets with their dress uniforms. A single 1 1/2 inch diameter star denoted a brigadier general, as seen here (opposite page); two stars (one 1 1/2 and the other 1 1/4 inch) set off major generals; three stars (two the sizes called for in the case of a major general and the third with a 1 1/16 inch diameter) represented the lieutenant general (Phillip H. Sheridan); and two 1 1/2 inch stars flanking the Arms of the United States was called for on the epaulets of the general commanding the U.S. Army at the time—William T. Sherman. Glen Swanson Photograph. WC

> uniforms on hand, the estimates would have been filled when received. But last year there was no money to accumulate a stock ahead, and this year issue of new is prohibited by law. This Office has done the best possible under the circumstances, and regrets legislation which embarrasses the supplying of the Army, and causes suffering, and consequently discontent and grumbling.[57]

The quartermaster for the Department of Arizona was informed of this predicament, as well, when he learned old patterns "of certain items of clothing" were to be sent for issue rather than the ones prescribed by the 1872-board. This included vintage forage caps, uniform hats, insignia, sack coats, uniform jackets (shell jackets), and coats, all of which were being sent to the troops in the department.[58]

While Meigs admitted that issuing old items was "distasteful to the soldiers" under the law of June 16, 1874, he had no choice in the matter.[59] This particularly was so given the amount of inventory on hand, that included 15,121 uniform coats, 13,138 flannel sack coats, 119,995 cavalry and artillery jackets, plus footgear worth a total of $223,000 at the prices established in 1871, when these items were the current issue. To sell them at auction would fetch only a fraction of their assigned value, he noted. Thus, many articles that were on hand had to be sent in lieu of new ones.[60]

Desirous of complying with the law and making do with what was available, quartermaster personnel even wanted to know what stocks remained at various supply points. For example, a request was sent to

Japanned tin canister holding William T. Sherman's General of the Commanding Army epaulettes. WC

Detail of the stars and Coat of Arms on Sherman's epaulettes. Glen Swanson Photograph. WC

the Department of the Missouri to ascertain what sizes of all old uniform coats and blouses for all branches were in the Ft. Union, New Mexico Territory, inventory, one of the major distribution points for the Southwest.[61]

Ever mindful of his charge to protect the government's property and to economize, Meigs took yet another step. He requested data on what items in the inventory had been treated with the Cowles moth-proofing method that had been contracted for on a broad experimental basis. He wanted specifics as to what garments had been subjected to this process, and the costs attendant to this undertaking.

Following a similar course, Meigs wished to learn more about a British process for inhibiting moth damage. He had heard of an experiment conducted in England using a heat process to suppress these destructive insects, and was curious as to the results.[62]

Even while Meigs made overtures to protect the goods on hand, he did not cease his efforts to procure new articles as needed. For one thing, during the summer of 1874 he granted authority to buy 20,000 pairs of Berlin gloves, so-called after the commercial name for the cloth used to fabricate them.[63] The quartermaster general further gave permission to purchase 150 red horsehair plumes and a like number of light artillery cords, bands, top pieces, and sockets, plus 1,000 yellow cavalry plumes, 500 scrolls and rings, 500 eagles, 500 top pieces and sockets, 500 yellow cords and bands, 1000 side buttons, 1500 infantry pompons, and 500 heavy artillery pompons.[64]

Detail of attachments for the epaulettes on the shoulder of Sherman's dress coat. Glen Swanson Photograph. WC

Sherman's dress frock coat with three sets of four buttons each designated for the general commanding the U.S. Army. Only Grant and Sherman were authorized such a coat. Glen Swanson Photograph. WC

Left: Sherman's dress coat with epaulettes, red Moroccan leather sword belt, and buff silk sash in place. The latter accessory could be worn "scarf style" by officers above the rank of brigadier general. Glen Swanson Photograph. WC

Below Left: After the promulgation of General Orders No. 11, Headquarters of the Army, February 12, 1877, sashes could be worn either around the waist or for those "above the rank of Brigadier General...across the body from the left shoulder to the right side. The sash may be of buff silk and gold thread." Artist Henry Ogden depicted General William T. Sherman and Major General John M. Schofield as central figures in this illustration wearing their sashes according to this order. A brigadier general in the background has on the sash around the waist as was required for that grade. Officers below brigadier general wore no sashes after 1872, as the other officers in this illustration disclose. GS

Detail of the "bullions" (tassels) on Sherman's buff silk sash. Glen Swanson Photograph. WC

Brigadier General George Crook preferred rugged civilian garments to the regulation dress uniform for his grade. Nonetheless, he appears here in full regalia, complete with chapeau de bras—which was to be worn by all officers except those in the combat arms—heavy gold embroidered sword belt, epaulets bearing one large silver star on each to indicate his rank, and the double breasted frock coat with eight pairs of staff officers' buttons, according to regulations. Major generals wore nine buttons grouped in threes on each side of their double breasted coats, while a lieutenant general had ten buttons in each row, on the breast, the upper and lower ones grouped by threes and the middle ones grouped by fours. Finally, for a general the coat would have two rows of buttons placed by fours for a total of twelve buttons in each row. GS

Even then, those units that had received items conforming to the 1872 regulations found the issue a mixed blessing, as represented by the experience of one company of infantry at Ft. Yuma, California. An officer reporting from this remote post commented:

> So far as I am able to judge since the new clothing has been issued, the troops are well clothed. I would recommend, however, that issuing officers be required to be more careful in filling estimates to supply the number of sizes required. The clothing issued to Co. G, 23rd Inft., except in about 1/2 dozen cases, had to be recut and made new, and the dress caps, nearly all of them new of the largest sizes, so that the men now wear them with capes inside the linings to make them fit. I believe, however, that this will be remedied by the plan of issue now proposed and indications in the last instructions with regard to the issue of clothing.[65]

There were other problems besides inappropriate sizes being sent to the field. Lieutenant Colonel Richard I. Dodge of the Twenty-third Infantry shared another consideration, at least for officers. He indicated, "in various places (after slight and inadequate description)" General Orders No. 92 simply described certain items as "'according to pattern.'" This resulted in the Twenty-third's officers receiving "from tailors, hatters & c. articles of dress scarcely any two of which are alike or according to the same pattern, yet all claim to be after pattern in the Quartermaster General's Office." Dodge, therefore, requested regimental commanders be furnished with accurate descriptions of these articles.[66]

The quartermaster general's office reacted with a request for specifications of many of the items that were to be worn by officers. The reply came from J.R. Ackerman, who had furnished a number of prototypes to the 1872-board.[67] These were as follows:

> Full dress coat for officers of the ranks of colonel, lt. colonel, and major. Adopted 1872.
>
> Frock coat of dark blue broad cloth. Double breasted buttoning to the throat, two rows of buttons on the breast, nine buttons in each row placed at equal distances from one another. The buttons to be what is known as 'coat size' and placed five inches from eye to eye at top of the lapel, swelling over the chest making the distance over the fullest part of the chest six inches from eye to eye and running down to the buttons at the bottom of lapel, at the waist, to width of four inches from eye to eye.
>
> The skirt of coat to extend from two thirds to three quarters of the distance from the top of the hip to the bend of the knee. Pockets in pleats behind. The pleats to have 'side edges' nine and one-half (9 1/2) inches and four (4) buttons on coat behind, namely two (2) on the waist seam at top of pocket pleat and two (2) on the bottom of the 'side edges.'

This chapeau de bras with its original japanned tin carrying case belonged to Nelson A. Miles. WC.

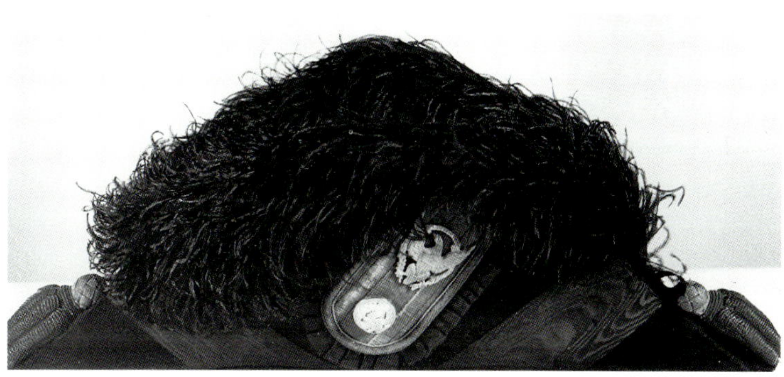

This chapeau de bras had a more horizontal aspect along its bottom edge compared to Miles' hat, which was more curved. Such variations were common during the decades immediately following the Civil War. WSHS

Nelson A. Miles' Medal of Honor. This is the 1862-pattern adopted by the U.S. Army during the Civil War. The style remained in use until a new design was adopted in 1896. This was the only medal permitted in the early 1870s for wear with the dress uniform, although officers sometimes of their own volition added symbols of veterans' organizations. WC

This staff corps lieutenant has tucked his chapeau de bras under his right arm. The belt is the correct 1872-pattern staff officers' version of gold lace with three black silk stripes running around it horizontally. Trousers for generals and staff officers were to be without welt or stripes, and match the dark blue color of their coat. The medal is that of the Loyal Legion of the United States, a veterans' organization of the era, and as such was not regulation, but sometimes added as a matter of individual preference. SACS

The coat to have a standing collar from one to two inches in height—fastening in front with a hook & eye, and the slope backwards at an angle of thirty (30) degrees, on each side. The corners of the collar to be rounded.

The sleeves of the coat to terminate in a cuff stitched down, three inches in depth, to close at the hand with three (3) buttons and button holes. The bottom button to be placed one (1) inch from bottom of sleeve. The top one three and one-quarter (3 1/4) inches from bottom of sleeve and one-quarter inch above top of cuff—the middle button midway between the top and bottom one.

The cuffs to be ornamented with three double stripes of gold lace or braid running up the sleeve parallel to the front edge and at right angles with the bottom of sleeve, each double stripe is to terminate in a point within which is a small button known as 'vest size', which shall be one-quarter inch below the top of the point, and on a horizontal line with the top button with which the cuff closes—all buttons used on sleeves to be of the small 'vest size.'

The double stripes of gold braid are to be placed the outer edges of each distant from one another one-half inch, and between the inner edges of each double stripe there is to be a 'light' of one-eighth inch in width.

The collar and cuffs to be of same material as the coat.

Buttons according to the arm of the service for which they are intended.

For captains, lst lt & 2nd lt

The same as above excepting there shall be seven buttons on each side of breast instead of nine and two double stripes of gold braid on each cuff instead of three.

The undress coat for <u>all</u> officers of the Army is as follows: To be of dark blue serge broadcloth, or beaver 'sack shaped'—slightly shaped to the figure.

To be single breasted buttoning with five buttons placed at equal distances from one another, from the throat down to the line of the waist. The collar is to be turned down, fastening in front with a hook and eye. The edges of the collar and coat to be braided with black braid, silk or mohair, laid on flat. The braid to be one half inch in width. Extending backward from each button hole is to be placed a double stripe of black braid, silk or mohair, turned at the center and to form a 'herringbone loop.' At the top button the distance from the eye of the button to the outer edge of the loop is six inches, gradually decreasing at each button until at the button at the waist, where the distance from the eye of the button to the outer

Acting Assistant Surgeon Victor Biart cradles his M1840 Medical Department sword. The dark blue background on his shoulder knots bear "M.D." in silver embroidered old English letters, flanked by a silver bar to indicate his rank as a first lieutenant, whereas two bars designated a captain, gold oak leaves a major, silver oak leaves a lieutenant colonel, and a silver spread eagle a colonel. The same symbols were used on shoulder straps to signify rank. A second lieutenant had no symbol until 1917, when the gold bar was adopted. FAM

edges of the loop is five inches. There is to be a 'light' one-eighth of an inch between the double stripes of braid where they approach the front edges of the coat.

The coat is to extend one-third to one-half the distance from the hip to the bend of the knee.

It is slit up the sides, directly over the outside seam of the trousers, to the waist as to admit of the sword belt being under the coat and enable the wearer to wear the sword 'hooked up' with the belt so worn. The edges of the these slits are to be bound with the flat one-half inch braid same as the other edges of the coat.

The side seams of the coat are to have a double stripe of black braid terminating at the armhole seams on the shoulder in the 'herring-bone' loop the same as the ornaments on the breast.

The cuffs of coat is (sic) to be closed with three buttons & holes, same as full dress coat. The sleeve is to be ornamented with a double knot of braid—the bottom of which knot is to be three inches from the bottom of the sleeve, and the braid comprising which is to extend all around the sleeve and form a cuff.

The braid used for the ornaments of the chest, side seams, and sleeves is to be black silk or mohair—one-quarter inch in width.

The buttons on breast of undress coat to be regular coat size, those on the cuffs, vest size.

Overcoat

For all but General Officers

Dark blue beaver close fitting frock surtout with a cape, detachable at pleasure. Cape to fall to the tip of the fingers when the arm and hand is extended. The skirt of the coat to extend for mounted officers half way between the knee and the ankle; for dismounted officers three inches below the knee.

The coat for all officers is to have seven buttons on the breast arranged same as a full dress coat; four buttons behind with wide edges same as full dress coat. There is no button on the sleeves.

In this November 1873 image Lieutenant Colonel George Custer wears no headgear at all, while many of his fellow officers on the steps of his quarters at Ft. Abraham Lincoln, Dakota Territory, have replaced their dress helmets with an array of head dress. For instance, both Captain William Thompson (seated to the right leaning against the banister) and First Lieutenant James Calhoun (seated to the rear in the center) have on forage caps. In Calhoun's case the cap has a water resistant removable cover. Other officers also have opted for forage caps, including Captain John S. Poland of the Sixth U.S. Infantry (in the back row seated to the left of a civilian named Charles Thompson, who wears a black hat). Poland has not yet obtained the new 1872-pattern dress coat, but instead continues to wear the single-breasted company grade officer's frock coat of the Civil War and pre-Civil War eras. In the center front row, Captain George W. Yates demonstrates a preference for a non-regulation fur cap. Two more members of the group, Second Lieutenant Benjamin Hodgson (to Custer's immediate left) and Captain Thomas M. McDougall (in the back row far left) have on yet one more non-regulation style headpiece—British-inspired "pillbox" caps. LBBNM

In this circa 1875 portrait Second Lieutenant John W. Martin of the Fourth U.S. Cavalry not only had donned a pillbox cap instead of the dress helmet, but also has taken his dark officer's blue cape with black velvet collar to the photographer's studio to add dash to his portrait. NA

Second Lieutenant Frank U. Robinson retained his breast cord, but set aside his dress helmet for an 1872-pattern officer's forage cap with gold embroidered crossed sabers and silver embroidered number "2" for the Second U.S. Cavalry. USAMHI

Rank is indicated by a single knot near the edges of the sleeve composed of black silk-braid, one-eighth inch in width. For a colonel 5 braids
" Lt.Col. 4"
" Maj 3"
" Captain 2"
" lst Lt 1"
" 2nd Lt none"
The edges of the overcoat to be stitched without braid.
Trousers
For all officers of the staff and staff corps—dark blue doeskin same color as coat without welt, cord, or stripe.
For all other officers of the line—Infantry Artillery, Cavalry, & c. sky blue doeskin with stripe one and one half inches in width sewed down to the outer seam. Edges of stripe to be welted. Stripes on trousers to be the same color as facings of the respective arms of the service excepting infantry which will be dark blue, same color as the coat.

The quartermaster department also faced the challenge of drafting a better specification for the basic cloth used in the manufacture of enlisted uniforms, given that material on hand was deemed as inferior or

Left: Lieutenant Mason M. Maxon's circa 1875 pillbox cap bears his regimental insignia of the Tenth U.S. Cavalry. Photograph by Gordon Chappell. FDNHS

A second lieutenant of heavy artillery likewise has opted for the chasseur type forage cap adopted in 1872 as regulation in place of the dress cap with scarlet cock feathers. The crossed gold embroidered cannons indicated the branch, while the background of the shoulder knot pads were scarlet for artillery. BH

Typically, the forage cap was worn with the 1872-pattern officer's blouse, as Captain Myles Moylan, commanding officer of Company A, Seventh U.S. Cavalry, exhibits in this photo. According to regulations, shoulder straps were to be worn with this jacket at all times. Straps had yellow backgrounds for cavalry, scarlet for artillery, medium blue for infantry, and dark blue for the various staff corps. Captain Moylan also has added a pale waistcoat and watch fob. Officers were permitted vests of dark blue or cream color by regulations. GS

in such poor condition as to render it useless. The negative opinion of the kersey in stock for trousers especially was problematical, prodding a quest for an improved standard. During August 1874 a standard was drafted for better cloth. Several months later, cloth samples of dark blue cloth and sky-blue kersey made from these specifications were delivered to Meigs from contractors per the instructions of the secretary of war on October 3, 1874. Meigs recommended a board of officers to review the samples, as well as to examine cloth already on hand "with the view to select a standard therefrom, if suitable fabrics are found in store." Meigs suggested that the Board view the material for suitability of campaign wear, "and not select too fine and costly a material." In this Meigs felt: "The cloth for Army use should be strong and warm rather than fine and smoothly finished." A copy of the secretary's instructions was attached directing a contract for 100,000 yards of 6/4 kersey would not be let until a standard was adopted, and all bidders were furnished samples.[68]

Almost simultaneously, Meigs informed both the Jeffersonville Depot and the Philadelphia Depot to "use certain dark blue cloth & sky blue kersey, unsuitable for making into garments, for lining Great Coats, in lieu of woolen blankets heretofore used for that purpose." In turn, the old pattern blankets on hand at the Indiana facility were to "be kept for issue to prisoners, and for saddle blankets."[69]

As a captain of infantry, the shoulder straps on Malcolm McArthurs' 1872-pattern officer's blouse would have consisted of a medium blue background bordered by gold embroidery and displaying two silver bars at each end of the strap. GS

Front, rear, and three-quarter views of an 1872-pattern officer's blouse for a lieutenant colonel in the staff corps. Photograph by Edward Vebell. DS

This new pattern was one adopted on August 5, 1874, as a replacement for earlier issue shirts, which were found "to shrink very much and to irritate the skin," thereby prompting the men "to purchase many shirts from civilians...."[75] The lack of uniformity this caused was to be halted as stocks of the old shirts neared exhaustion.

The pullover garment had a small rolling collar and separately applied cuffs, each of which was held by a tinned iron button. Three more tinned iron buttons measuring 17/32 of an inch each were used to secure the neck and the two inch by eleven inch plait that covered the shirt's placket. There was a fourth one on the neck band, as well, to allow for a tighter fit if desired. The body was two piece with drop shoulders and relatively long tails that could be tucked deeply into the trousers so as not to ride up on the wearer. The whole was made of "gray shirting flannel," which when new had a sort of modeled blue-gray cast.[76] The first issue shirts came in only one weight of cloth.[77] By 1876, the shirt itself was considered adequate, but the single heavy weight was not. As a result, a lighter weight also was provided for in that year, so that shirts subsequently came in two grades of heaviness.[78]

Even then, this item was not the last word on the subject, but something closer to what the troops wanted would be provided by serendipity. In 1875, quartermaster officials pondered what to do with a stock of nearly 18,000 yards of blue flannel that was considered to be of no use for blouses or other purposes. Meigs had a sample shirt made of the material and sent it to the secretary of war with hopes that this official would give his blessing to the item, which the quartermaster general wanted to have issued in lieu of the gray twill shirt to troops in the

New dress uniforms also were prescribed for enlisted men in 1872. Caps with pompons (described in official specifications as "pear-shaped") were to be worn by foot troops (white for infantry, scarlet for heavy artillery, and the like), while mounted troops were to have plumed helmets (yellow for cavalry, scarlet for light artillery, and orange for Signal Service). GS

Right side of an 1872-pattern cavalry enlisted dress helmet. Bands, cords, and plume were yellow for this branch, while they were scarlet for light artillery and orange for Signal Corps troops. SI

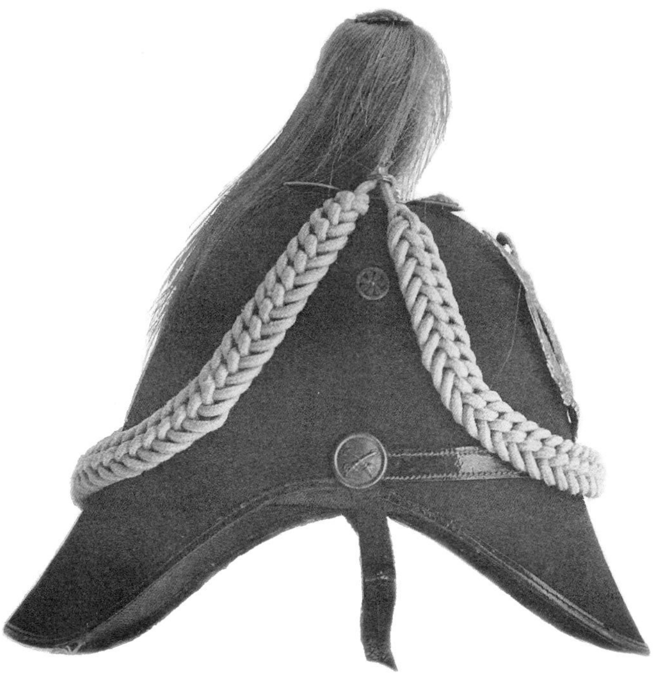

Right profile of an 1872-pattern cavalry trooper's helmet, in this case from Sergeant William Williams of the Seventh U.S. Cavalry. The black japanned pinwheel ventilator is clearly evident. LBBNM

Dakota, Wyoming, Montana, and Idaho Territories. If sold at auction, the material would bring only a minimum price, but if used for shirts Meigs felt "that the troops will be glad to get them in the localities named." This would be an economic boon and an acceptable substitute to the gray flannel shirt for the troops in the colder northern outposts, concluded Meigs, who said that the only cost would be the labor to make them, and this could be accomplished after the new fiscal year beginning July 1, 1875.[79] The secretary of war approved of the money saving proposal, and Meigs changed his target to starting production before the end of the fiscal year. These were to be produced in the same sizes and proportions as the gray flannel item, and the use of wide cotton tape sewed to the inside of the collar and yoke was required to keep the new shirt from shrinking.[80] Based on this style, 10,000 of the limited run item were turned out, then issued, with the response that "in the field this shirt is a comfortable and convenient garment."[81] For instance, Lieutenant Alfred Morton, serving at Ft. Laramie, Wyoming Territory, recommended that the blue shirt become the standard rather than the gray flannel one.[82] Two captains of the Fourth Infantry serving in the West, Oddment M. Coats of Company C and Samuel P. Ferris of Company I, summed up the key reasons why this shirt was a boon, in that it was "comfortable and convenient."[83]

Although such efforts to address perceived shortcomings in military clothing were being carried out, individual letters to the editor of the *Army and Navy Journal* or to Washington officials continued to express varied concerns.[84] Nonetheless, no systematic analysis of the clothing issued and worn by troops was available. That situation changed with the publication of General Orders No. 6, War Department, Adjutant General's Office, January 29, 1875.[85] Among other things, this document put the question of the uniform to the field, with the Surgeon General's Office once again taking the lead as it did nearly a decade earlier, when in 1868 it had provided an influential report compiled by Lieutenant Colonel Alfred A. Woodhull of the Medical Department.[86] Dozens of responses from military surgeons and line officers went to considerable lengths in expressing sentiments related to the topic. Several examples serve to chart the numerous concerns that existed relative to the matter.

Colonel Henry Hunt, a member of the board that was largely responsible for the 1872 uniform regulations, was one of those who replied in detail. From Ft. Adams, Rhode Island, the artillery officer opened with good marks when it came to the dress cap and uniform coat, which he viewed as "suitable in character and sufficient in quantity." He made a similar comment about the 1872-pattern forage cap. That was not the case for the helmet, however, a piece of headgear that he asserted was:

The 1872-pattern enlisted mounted dress helmet was issued with cords and bands of one-piece, as opposed to the two-piece cords and bands for mounted officers. Photograph by Gordon Chappell.

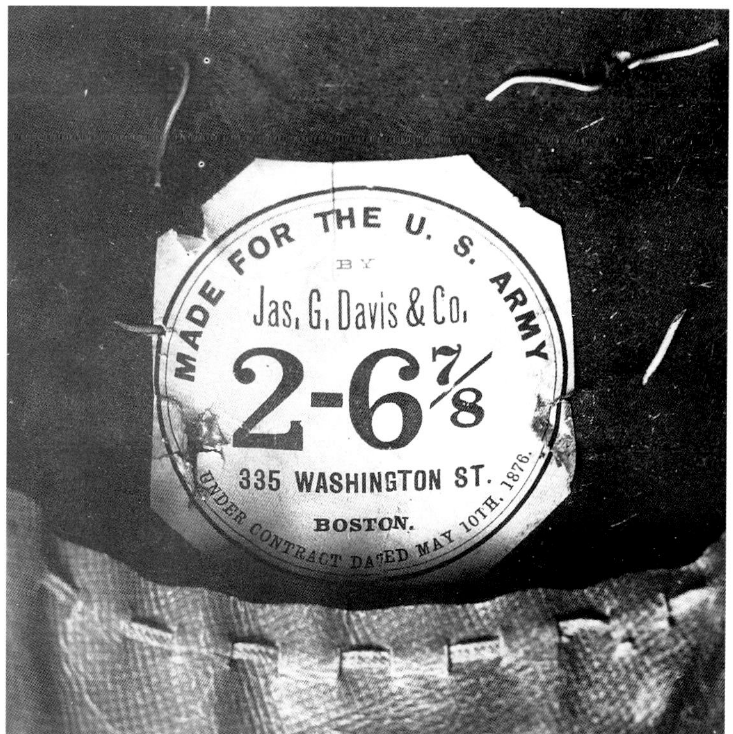

Interior of an 1872-pattern mounted dress helmet with contractor's label inside, and a portion of the sweatband showing. CF

Because the cords were one-piece when issued, the mounted soldier had difficulty extracting himself from the helmet, as seen in this portrait of Private Stanilaus Roy, a member of Company A, Seventh U.S. Cavalry, who would receive the Medal of Honor for his actions at the Little Bighorn. GS

> not according to the model selected by the board of 1870. The visor is unnecessarily large and awkward, and has not the military style of the model. The horse hair plume is unnecessarily large, awkward, heavy, and long—one-third the amount of horse hair and of shorter length would answer the purpose much better than the present pattern. The model was more erect and the plume sat better than the one actually issued. The model was that of the English horse-guards.

Hunt went on to indicate that he had issued orders for the great coat "always to be worn on duty, dress or undress, and by all men outside their quarters, between retreat and reveille." Little wonder then that he praised this "excellent garment," but went on to point out that as with coats and trousers the garment was "liable...to be cut down in length and breadth to suit individual tastes." Hunt would have none of this, emphasizing:

> It should be required that the skirts should come down to near the ankle in no case even for the tallest men to be more than 10 inches from the ground. The coat should be long enough to wear over the belts and at northern posts lined throughout. An adjustable hood should be issued with the coat or separately, especially in the northern half of the country and in all cold regions." Finally, he encouraged the issue of a second great coat in the third year of enlistment and stable frocks for every year of a soldier's enlistment.

Another cold weather item, "arctic shoes" were seen "as necessary as greatcoats, especially on the sea coast when snow always becomes slush soon after falling," as was the case at Hunt's coastal artillery fortress. Many of the artillerymen bought their own, but all should be provided them by the government, he insisted.

Other footwear mentioned by Hunt included stockings, which he concluded "should be made of wool." Likewise, the new pattern shoe was good, but did not take into account the "variety in shapes" of feet. This meant that adjustments "should be made for width of foot, high and low insteps; larger or smaller feet," and other characteristics.

Hunt had little to recommend the pleated blouse, which he declared "was originally furnished for fatigue purposes, in cases where the men would otherwise go in shirt sleeves." Old light artillery or cavalry mounted jackets (shell jackets) seemed more suitable "in lieu of one of the [pleated] blouses for undress wear and drills."[87]

The colonel did not like the old pattern trousers, either. While those of new material were improvements, there needed to be three pairs issued per year and "stringent regulations...issued that both coat and trousers should be sufficiently loose to be comfortable...." He wanted the

Front and rear views of Sergeant William William's 1872-pattern mounted dress coat. The chevrons were custom made from facing material, rather than the issue type. Photograph by Kurt Cox. LBBNM

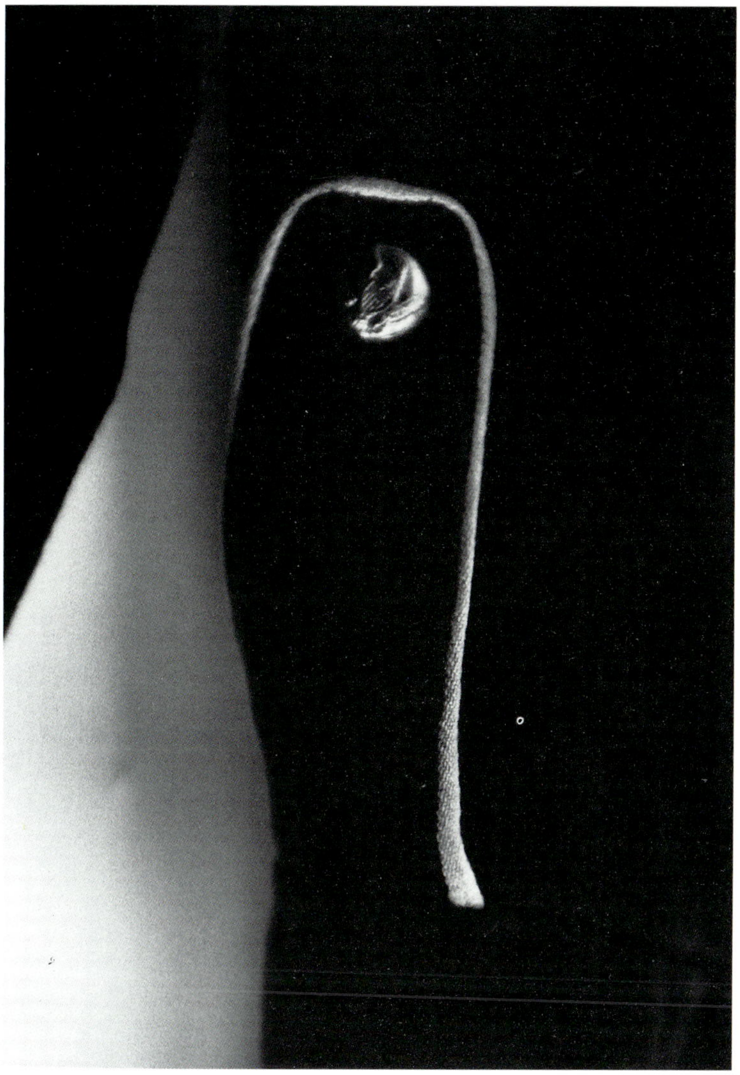

Detail of belt loop for an 1872-pattern enlisted dress coat. In 1872, after the first mounted coats were made and issued, it was learned that these appendages were placed in such a way as to interfere with the wearing of the saber belt on the right side where the saber was slung. This required local alterations to correct the problem. Subsequent production by the Quartermaster Department resulted in a different placement of the straps so that there would be a proper configuration, allowing the belt to be worn without hindrance. LBBNM

An 1872-pattern cavalry enlisted dress coat with the horseshoe device for a farrier, which was adopted in September 1874. SI

The interior skirts of some of the first 1872-pattern enlisted dress coats were lined with a light yellow Italian cloth, but this was changed to a darker lining on coats made soon thereafter. KC

Inspector General's Department to make this a special concern as they went about their duties at military posts around the country. He cited the opinion of his post surgeon as to why this was important. The doctor contended:

> It is a very general practice among soldiers, approved often by their officers, in having coats and trousers altered to fit them, to have them made of such scanty proportions as to injure their military appearance, detract from their comfort and durability, and perhaps to be detrimental to the health of the wearer.[88]

Colonel Hunt's comments were not the only ones to be voiced. Many others spoke out as well, including from Camp Sheridan, Nebraska, where Captain A. Sutorius of the Third Cavalry indicated the clothing worn by his command was "comparatively good." Unfortunately, he reported the uniform items were in varying colors and textures, "some being lighter both in color and quality." He went on to request two great-coats and four stable frocks per annum as an increase over the table of allowance.[89]

At Camp Douglas, Utah Territory, Colonel Jonathan Smith thought "The men should be provided with rubber arctics," because six months of the year either snow or mud was on the ground in that garrison.[90] The post surgeon agreed with Colonel Smith as to the requirement for rubber arctic shoes for the winter, and also suggested that gaiters be adopted by foot troops. Moreover, he exhorted that trousers "be cut narrow at

The 1872-pattern mounted musician's dress coat with regulation yellow worsted herringbone chest trim. This particular example includes the chevrons of a chief trumpeter—three bars, an arc, and a bugle, as adopted in June 1873. SI

Regimental bandsmen often were decked out in finery that differed from the regulation outfit issued to the rank and file, such as this specially-made cavalry dress coat with ornamentation applied to the chest of facing in a design reminiscent of Civil War musicians' coats and jackets. JG

the bottom, so as to allow the gaiters to fit the ankle neatly." Additionally, the doctor alluded to the successful use of leggings during the Civil War, which when not obtained by troops led to the tucking of trowser legs into the stockings as a field expedient.[91]

From Pineville, Louisiana, Captain William Penrose of the Third U.S. Infantry acknowledged the unmade uniform coats and trousers were of good quality, "but those made up were apparently the same as the old issue and are of *inferior quality*." He wanted an increased allowance unless overalls and jackets were furnished because of numerous fatigues and work projects required of the men. The captain also thought one pair of gloves per month was more realistic. Further, he was not a strong supporter of blue, contending their were better colors, and called for white pants, jackets, and straw hats for his command because the summers were "*so long* and *hot*." In fact, he felt a "*blue jeans jacket* is durable, comely and economical."[92]

Ft. Ellis, Montana's Major Nelson B. Sweitzer judged four shirts a year were required, and the "quality of those now issued is miserable and on account of the small number and poor quality the men are required to buy from stores." What was needed were two great-coats per enlistment, the skirts of which required linings so they afforded poor protection against the "cold weather common to this country." He wanted six, not two, stable frocks per five years, as well as two pairs of overalls the first year and one pair each year thereafter, rather than the five issued. Both of these garments were pronounced good quality, though. Arctic or buffalo shoes in the quantity of at least one pair per year were another must. Conversely, only three ponchos rather than six seemed adequate. Likewise, the forty pairs of white Berlin gloves were too many—only thirty-two being required, whereas woolen mittens should be doubled from ten to twenty and an improved quality adopted. This was because, the major indicated, the poor caliber of the government issue forced soldiers to buy gloves or mittens themselves to make up for the shortcomings of those provided by Uncle Sam.[93]

Meigs was sensitive to the fact that soldiers had to revert to their own meager resources for winter wear at many posts, especially those that fell below the demarcation line for issue of special fur garments—42° latitude. This meant that troops in southern Michigan, northern Ohio, Pennsylvania, and other inclement areas of the country, not only in the Midwest and East, but the Southwest, as well, such as New Mexico, where high elevations often brought low temperatures in winter, were excluded from obtaining fur protective clothing, unless they elected to pay for such items themselves.[94]

This dividing line did not cause concern for troops at the northerly installation of Ft. Pembina, Dakota Territory, where Captain Loyd Wheaton of the Twentieth U.S. Infantry made his report. Given the post's location, the captain's men could draw winter gear, but he concluded the allowance for Arctic overshoes should be doubled from two to four pairs.[95]

As to another item, uniform coats, he found them becoming in appearance, but defective in that they:

> were cut too wide, and when the coat is sufficiently long in the waist and sleeves it is too large otherwise. Most enlisted men are young, and from the amount of active duty required, are seldom of large girth about the waist. It is better that the coats be too large than too small, as the loose coats can be fitted by the company tailors.

While the blouse also was an improvement over the old sack coat, it inevitably was too large at the neck and waist, and the plaits were "distasteful to the men." It seemed "essential that the ordinary undress of the soldier should not only be serviceable, but that it should look well. The blouse is not suitable in the respect of looking well," he remonstrated. So, too, did the trousers fit poorly and were of inferior quality. When sufficiently long for the soldier, the waist was too large, the seat baggy, and the legs were too wide.

Shirts likewise received an inferior rating. What is more, Wheaton proposed a new kind of shirt, one of "heavy dark-blue material, shrunk before making." This would allow troops in hot climate to "march in their shirt sleeves and still be uniform in appearance." Because the men tended to do this anyway, Wheaton must have rationalized that rather than condemn the non-military practice, it should be sanctioned and made more consistent.

The upshot was to call for the abolishment of the campaign hat or reduction of its brim size and improvement of its material. Discontinuance of the blouse also was suggested, and "a close fitting sack coat, same length as the present blouse, hooking close at the neck, with turn down collar; close in front with eight buttons and to have no 'piping'" was put forth. The captain further felt the "greatcoat should be lined with denser material than blankets and have a wool lined collar." By reducing the issue of uniform coats to five, the resultant savings could be expended on sealskin caps with ear flaps. Replacing the mitten pattern with one of heavy cloth or skin that had a gauntlet wrist was yet another suggestion.

Finally, Captain Wheaton spoke of several types of new headgear. On one hand he decried the campaign hat as "a failure in every respect." He damned it as "unserviceable, hot, uncomfortable, hideous in appearance, and of worthless material." The brim he found "too wide." In addition, "after the hat has been worn a week, the brim falls down all around when not hooked up, and prevents sight. If hooked up the hat is no more protection against the sun than a cap." On the Black Hills Expedition the hats of the infantry were full of holes after ten days marching. When the expedition returned, at the end of sixty days, more than three-fourths of the hats had been patched with pieces of canvas and worn out trousers in order that they might be kept on the head. "Upon a march, the infantry soldier, if not prevented by his company commander, will attempt to improve the campaign hat by cutting off a part of the brim. A more worthless piece of head covering than the campaign hat I have never seen as a soldier. It is not suitable."

In more positive tones he praised the forage cap, which he said was "of good material, a neat and comfortable head dress for a mild climate and ordinary wear." Some of the caps, however, had visors that were of insufficiently thick leather. "In this latitude (49°), it is not practical to wear in the field, during winter," any of the head dress issued. Consequently, the men all wore "fur or woolen caps purchased of traders or made by themselves." He also wrote in positive terms about the dress

Christian Barthelmess became the drum major of the Sixth U.S. Cavalry in late 1878 and donned this uniform that was a combination of an 1872-pattern field grade officer's coat with the old style epaulets and an aiguillette on the right shoulder. He also has added a baldric. His headgear is a forage cap with gold braid trim. CBF

August Lutz, Company A, Fifth U.S. Cavalry, in the 1872-pattern dress uniform for mounted trumpeters. He has cut the cords from his helmet and added a tassel to the bands to make it possible for him to remove the headpiece while retaining the breast cords. Such modifications characterized individual initiatives taken by the rank and file. Also note his regulation light cavalry saber with leather saber knot, the Colt .45 caliber revolver on the table next to the helmet, and the reinforcing (extra layer of cloth applied to Lutz' trouser inseams) as called for in the case of mounted troops. JG

This cavalry musician must have been a member of the regimental band, because of the 1 inch sergeant stripes on his trousers and the chevrons on his dress coat, which would not be worn by a company trumpeter of the period. He holds his 1872-pattern dress helmet with one-piece cords and bands. D&BM

While trousers often were worn over the tops of the boots, Private Gustave Korn, Seventh U.S. Cavalry, has tucked the legs into the boots and is ready for mounted service. He holds the reins of Comanche, the venerated Little Bighorn survivor. LBBNM

cap, a piece of headgear he saw as an improvement over the old hat. It was both "serviceable and appropriate for full dress, excepting during the winter in this latitude," he stated.[96]

Colonel Henry Clitz, in command of the Tenth U.S. Infantry from his headquarters at Ft. McKavett, Texas, likewise thought the dress cap to be "well made, durable, light, comfortable".[97] The commanding officer at Ft. Riley, Kansas, Lieutenant Colonel Joseph Whistler, chimed in that the cap was an improvement over the hat formerly worn by his Fifth Infantry doughboys, and in the Twenty-fifth U.S. Infantry Colonel George Andrews mentioned it was "suitable for its purpose."[98] From Lebanon, Kentucky, the Sixth U.S. Infantry's Captain Charles E. Morse rated the dress cap's "quality excellent, color good, well-made, and durable." While the pompon was excellent, as well, its color was poor, and instructions were needed as to how to clean the white, which soiled easily.[99] At Baton Rouge Barracks, Assistant Surgeon Clarence Ewen diagnosed the ventilator in the dress cap's crown as "worthless." He urged that a summer helmet with a ring inside to promote circulation of air should be provided instead.[100]

Advice from another post in the Southeast, Key West Barracks, Florida, was more general. There Major Clermont L. Best, Sr. of the Fourth Artillery, reflected:

> The dress of the U.S. Army, besides a uniformity throughout as nearly as possible consistent with climatic extremes, should be one of simplicity and usefulness. Superfluous articles, for which there is no positive or practical use should be excluded. Officers will recollect how during the late war everything that was not indispensably useful disappeared. And today with exception of the Artillery garrisoning the seacoast defenses, the Army is in a state of chronic warfare of some kind or another. Hence the soldier should be dressed and prepare for the field at short notice.

In that light, the cap and dress coat seemed unneeded. Rather the new blouse, with the addition of shoulder scales, could serve for dress and field wear.

Major Best went on to question:

> However desirable entire uniformity of dress may be, can it be proper for extremes of climate? Should the same number of ounces of clothing be adapted to Arctic cold and tropical heat? I think not. The object of clothing is to protect the human system against warmth as well as cold, and in connection color is worthy of consideration as well as texture. White is considered by analyzation [sic] the best protection against heat—blue and black ranking last in order.

In those cases where the climate was "oppressive" the major leaned toward a blouse "of gray or other light metallic color, lighter in texture, and the blue woolen pants replaced by an article of strong white linen." Linen conducts heat much better than wool, while the latter has double the power of absorbing perspiration and odors in such a manner as to dry out more quickly and be less pungent. Nevertheless, he felt the flannel shirts and drawers should be issued in all areas, but "lighter in tex-

Civil war surplus accoutrements were mixed with the new 1872-pattern uniform for some years, the carbine sling and saber belt dating from the earlier period, while one of several versions of the M1874 Dyer carbine pouches is placed at the rear of the uniform, as one example of the new items of equipment adopted in the early 1870s. ES

In 1872 a new patented method of producing chevrons was adopted, whereby a piece of facing material in the branch color was chain stitched with silk thread to form stripes. This example is for a sergeant major of cavalry. AMWH

ture for the lower regions," as well as a forty percent cotton mix to wool. He desired a lighter forage cap with more air space at the top for Southern posts.[101]

Another respondent, Assistant Surgeon W.E. Buchanan at Ft. Brown, Texas, expressed thoughts about headgear, as well. He found "The present style of head covering is in my opinion, entirely unfit for this climate and would recommend a straw or felt hat of light texture and color. The double caped overcoat, now furnished, is of no use in this climate, as a general thing there are but a few days in the year when the overcoat is required, when one with a single cape is quite heavy and warm enough."[102]

Colonel Joseph H. Potter, the commander at Ft. Brown, Texas, went further in that he wanted an increase in the allowance of stockings, drawers, blankets, and forage caps. He also found: "The campaign hat objectionable in many respects and...entirely unsuited to this climate. I am of the opinion that this article of clothing should not be issued in this climate or any other. I would recommend a straw or felt hat for summer and the forage cap for winter wear in this section of the country."[103]

From Ft. Quitman, Texas, Acting Assistance Surgeon B. Alexander concluded: "The dress of a soldier having great influence upon his health the clothing as determined by regulation (with a few exceptions) [is]

Some non-commissioned officers favored "gull wing" chevrons of facing cloth cut out individually in lieu of the regulation style, as exemplified by the dress coat worn by Sergeant Williams of the Seventh U.S. Cavalry. LBBNM

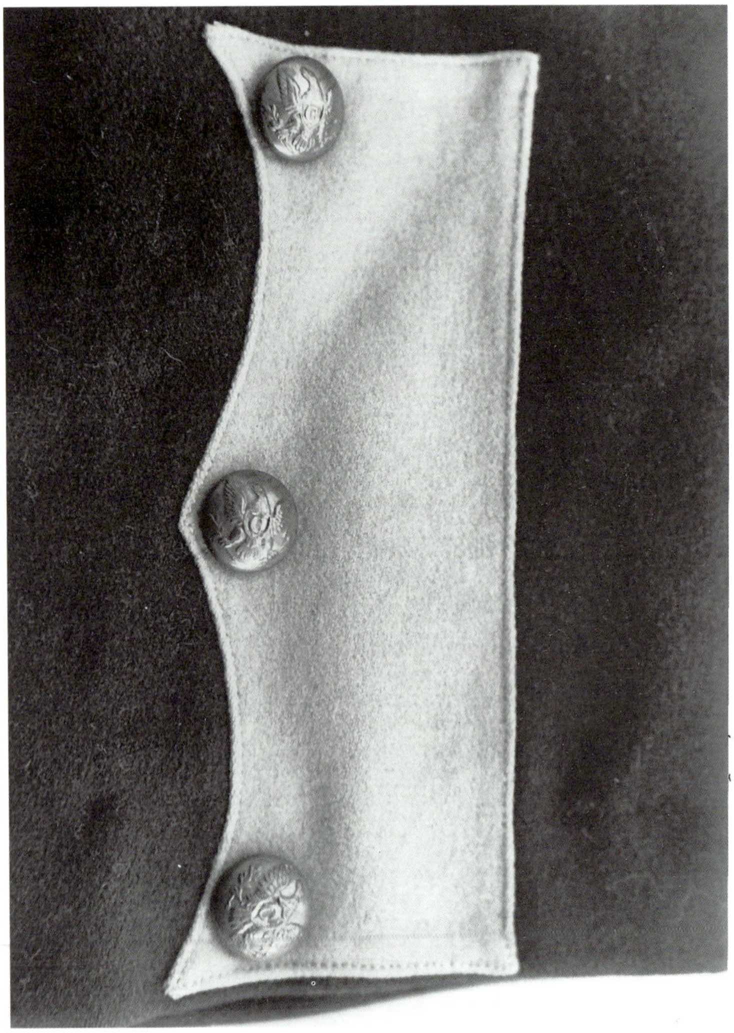

Sergeant Williams further deviated from regulations by adding officers' cavalry buttons with a "C" in the shield to his coat in place of the plain enlisted button. LBBNM

sufficient in quantity and well adapted." He went on to write: "The great-coat is perhaps the most important article of dress for the soldier, especially in countries liable to great vicissitudes of temperature and to sudden cold and winds. The great-coat now in use is well adapted for its purpose." He recommended no change for the blouse and dress coat. He did point out that trousers, while:

> well adapted for the winter season did not serve troops in warm climates who should be supplied with trousers of chintz or some such material—I mean something that is very light, and yet of such a colour as will not require to be as frequently washed as white would. I am aware that trousers of a lighter texture, but of the same material as now worn, are to be issued, but such cloth I think would not wear well, and would cause the soldier additional expense, without fully answering the purpose.

In conclusion, the doctor prescribed rubber clothing for rainy weather. He also called for a straw hat for wear during the "summer months in all Southern climates."[104]

Captain George Shorkley responded from Ft. Craig, New Mexico Territory, that except for stockings, enlisted clothing of the new pattern were good, however, the allowance of stockings, trowsers, and drawers was insufficient. Additionally, "The pattern of Dress Coat is faulty in that the waist is too short, for the size of the body—to explain a No. 1 Coats (sic) fits a man 5 feet 5 inches but is too short in the waist and the loops for the belt need changing; about one half of the dress coats in garrison have been altered by the tailors to fit the men either in belt straps at hips, waist or neck." He went on to state, "The old pattern blouses are issued and used, none of the last new pattern have been received at the Post."[105]

Also from Ft. Craig, New Mexico Territory, Acting Assistant Surgeon J. Frazer Boughter set down a lengthy list of observations. He stated:

> The new shako is certainly an improvement over the old dress hat, it is light, weighs but *seven and a half* (7 1/2) ounces, has sufficient height above the hair and is ventilated by openings at the top, its peak is horizontal, a moderate curve would perhaps be better to shade the eyes; it is liked by the men very much.
>
> The campaign hat is for the purpose designed very serviceable, but for the Southwest, where the heat of the summer is excessive, it would certainly be better to have the color a gray or light drab, as next to white, grey gives the greatest protection from the direct solar rays, and black the least.

Typical buttons of the 1850s through the mid-1880s, excavated from Major Marcus Reno's first engagement site of the Battle of Little Bighorn. Those without letters on the breast of the eagles were enlisted issue, while the ones bearing a "C" for cavalry were officers' patterns, but used by some enlisted men who purchased them to customize their uniforms. GS

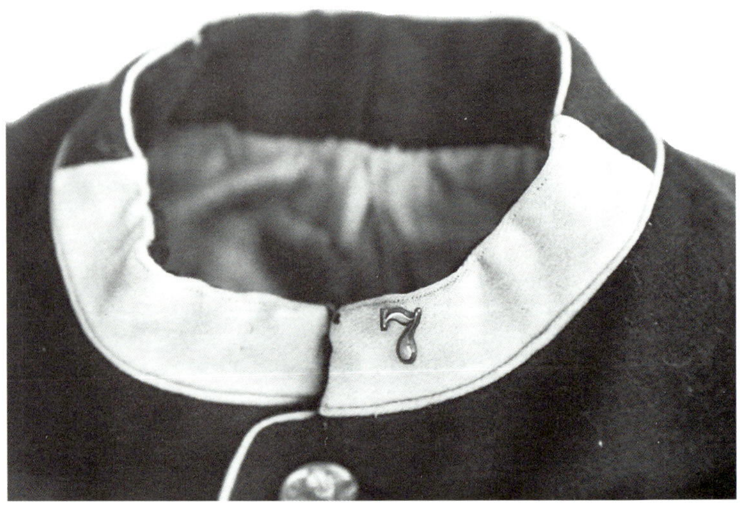

The standard version of the enlisted 1872-pattern dress coat had facing material trim, as Sergeant Williams' coat does. One of the stamped brass regimental numbers that were to appear on both sides of the collar, however, is missing. LBBNM

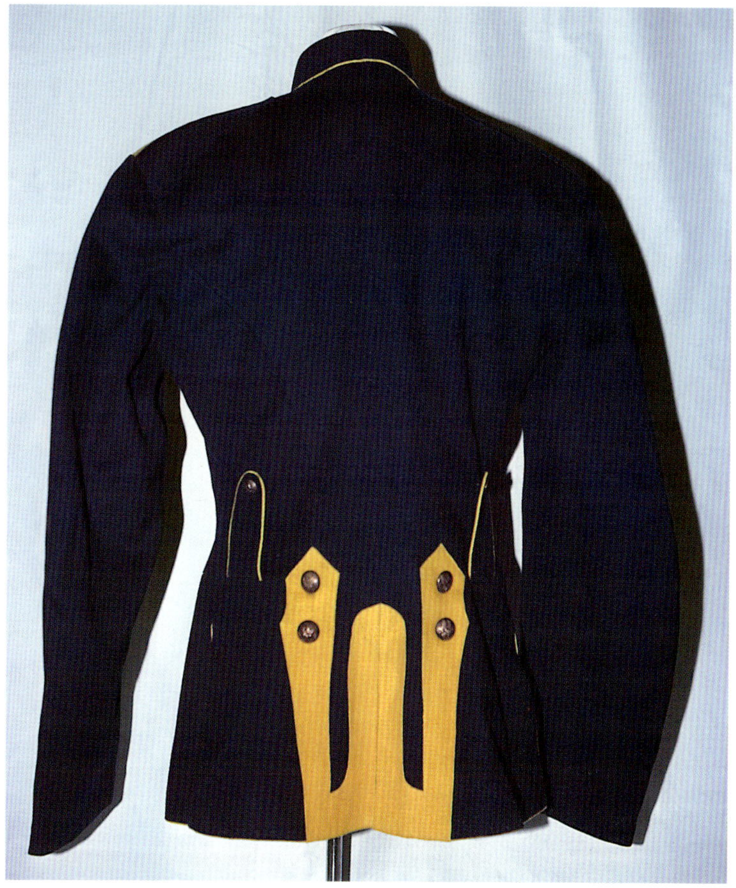

Rear view of an 1872-pattern enlisted cavalry dress coat including belt loops. The latter appendage had to be relocated after it was discovered the original placement on the first coats produced interfered with the wearing of the saber belt. SI

Left: Stamped 1/2 inch sheet brass numeral for the Ninth U.S. Cavalry on the collar of the 1872-pattern cavalry enlisted uniform coat. GS

The cost of this hat complete ($2.64) is high, but it must be considered that the material from which it is manufactured is excellent. The forage cap is in every respect a great and marked improvement over the old and miserable cap heretofore issued, the new one has all the requisites of a good cap, the material (dark blue) is good, the cap does not touch the hair; it would perhaps be an advantage in this climate to have the cap perforated on the top with several small openings, before being issued. The forage cap covers are good.
The uniform coat, of which four (4) sizes are now issued, is good; the average quality of the cloth very good, the color is durable, the lining strong, the blue facings are well sewed on, the improvement in appearance is great, the most marked being the doing away with the shoulder scales or epaulets, allowing the garment to be loose round the neck, over the shoulders and across the chest.
Regarding the sizes now issued the most common complaint is that the waist is not low enough, frequently requiring the straps at the sides for the belt to be lowered several inches. The trousers as now issued are in a great many respects very inferior, the color is not uniform, it is very common to see many shades of the sky blue cloth in one company, this being very noticeable, the material (sky blue cloth) is not generally good, to the eye the texture is not uniform nor as close as it should be, the 'tearing power' is not known. They vary greatly in weight, of woolen cloth the heavier the substance is in a given batch the better. They very seldom fit a soldier when first issued.

Doctor Boughter went on to observe the thirteen pairs issued over a five-year enlistment was not adequate because of the inferior material. Further, he decried: "The slovenly and injurious manner soldiers have of using a belt or strap to support their trousers should be positively prohibited, braces would be the best way of supporting them and should be issued, made of some elastic but durable material." Additionally, he pronounced the white woolen shirt best for garrison and gray for campaigns, and advocated flannel as the best material for shirts, and thought three per year was insufficient.

He continued:

The blouse as now issued is good and comfortable as regards the purpose for which a blouse is intended for a soldier, viz: a garment in which none of the muscles are constricted, and a free play of all the muscles of the shoulder, chest and arm is allowed, so he may make, unimpeded, any movement or exertion required of him, the present one is admirably adapted.

On the surface the blouse seemed admirable, but its drawbacks far outweighed its merits in that: "The plaits are objected to as they collect the dust and make it very difficult to keep the blouse clean. In this country where high winds (with much dust) prevail it is certainly an objection. Most of the men stitch the plaits down which presents a neater appearance."

Side and rear views of an 1872-pattern Signal Corps private's dress coat. Collar insignia never were prescribed for this coat, unlike those worn by other branches. SI

Still not through with his remarks, the surgeon indicated: "The great coat is good, the double cape a great addition, the only objection is a want of uniformity in the color of the sky blue cloth from which they are manufactured as many shades being observable as in the trousers."

He believed the need existed to have more than one issued for each five years at northern posts, while the rubber blanket was "a most valuable part of the soldier's outfit." Finally, white Berlin gloves were good and ample in number (eight pairs per year).[106]

Assistant Surgeon John Vance at Ft. Wingate, New Mexico Territory, made some similar remarks to those of his colleague at Ft. Craig, as well as added other findings, such as one related to "The helmets worn by the cavalry." These he wrote, "are too heavy for comfort weighing about 18 oz. Each." Conversely, he thought the caps for winter wear were satisfactory.

On the other hand, the "quality of cloth for dress coats and pants (new pattern)" was "loose in texture with a long nap collecting lint and dirt." This made the garments produced from this material difficult to keep clean. Otherwise it was suitable for the New Mexico climate.

The blouse once more was denounced as:

> very unpopular among the men. They call it the 'charcoal mans dress and 'formless frock.' The wearer of such garb is supposed to belong to the laboring classes. No soldier cares to be seen in such a dress. The plaits in front are not corded or stitched, and they refuse to lie flat and regular, giving them too much the appearance of an unstarched shirt bosom. To give them a neat front many of the men have the plaits stitched down. The new blouse is more expensive than the old, and this makes it less popular.

For this reason, the old pattern four-button blouse was "preferred to the new style" with pleats. And again an old complaint surfaced in that: "All the ready made pants issued to the troops require more or less alteration to make them fit the wearer. The saddle pieces of cavalry pants require to be re-adjusted and their bottoms modified."

So, too, did "Pants cut out, but not made up," require "cutting again, which necessitates further waste of cloth; and when they are made up and washed, are found to shrink so much, that they cannot be worn; reflecting on the cutter who did not properly sponge the cloth. It would be more economical to issue the cloth in bolt, or pattern."

For winter the doctor counseled "buffalo overshoes would be a great comfort." He followed with a suggestion for overcoats, many of which had "no lining in the capes. I learn that there is a large quantity of an inferior quality of army blanket in the clothing depot, which would make excellent lining, and I would recommend that one of the blankets be issued to each soldier for the purpose of lining his over coat." Finally, the good doctor wanted "none but colored woolen undershirts" to be issued to the troops at his post.[107]

Captain George W. Chilson, who commanded a troop of the Eighth Cavalry at Ft. Wingate, New Mexico Territory, was less verbose than Surgeon Vance. He did make some succinct points, nonetheless. Most notably he maintained: "The helmets are unwieldy. A helmet after the style of the Prussian Helmet made with a skeleton of light spring steel and covered with some black water-proof material is recommended, the plume to be dispensed with and a spike substituted."

He found the shirts generally good, with the white woolen serving best for garrison and the gray one for campaign. Flannel (wool) was seen as the best material in either case, and for all underclothing, with a

Private Will C. Barnes of the Signal Corps holds his dress 1872-pattern helmet with orange plume and bands. He has severed the cords from the helmet so that it can be removed when not being worn. The belt and oval brass U.S. plate are Civil War vintage for foot troops, despite the fact that Signal Corps enlisted personnel had mounted style helmets and dress coats. NA

difference in weight being employed relative to climate. The issue of three per year was not adequate because of the rough washing by laundresses, and the fact that the men tended not to have the shirts mended when damage was done.

As far as "The *sack coat*," it was "not considered suitable for a soldier. The old sack coat or else one similar to that now worn by officers (without trimmings) would be preferable." He ended with a rhetorical question: "Could more pains be taken to keep companies supplied with good tailors the un-made trowsers now issued, would it is thought answer every purpose."[108]

Captain Joseph Boyd Campbell, Fourth Artillery, at Ft. Sitka, Alaska Territory, judged the quality of clothing generally good, but opted for better linings. An exception to his positive remarks once more was the plaited blouse, a garment that was "universally disliked, for the reason that it is unbecoming, almost to deformity, if it does not fit; its construction renders it difficult and expensive to alter, and for like reasons it fits very few men when issued." Thus, as others had stated, the old Civil War sack was preferred. Also, Campbell's men requested that chevrons should be worn upon the blouse, and a pair should be allowed for each

The enlisted 1872-pattern light artillery uniform resembled the cavalry dress uniform, except that all trim was to be scarlet. USAQM

The distinctive red and white flags device of the Signal Corps from 1864 through 1891. These were worn on the left arm above the elbow for privates of the second class, and on both arms above the elbow for privates of the first class. Non-commissioned officers placed them above the chevrons. AHS

one issued. This comment was made because while the non-commissioned officers traditionally had worn their rank on the sleeves of the blouse, regulations at that point still did not mention this practice.

Overcoat chevrons, however, were called out in regulations, but they were hidden by the cape. The recommendation for their relocation above the cuff rather than above the elbow was the solution that Campbell provided. He also noted that "owing to the great variety of the service chevrons, it is impractical to draw them. They should be obtained through the company commanders and the money values increased to thirty five cents and fifty cents respectively for those indicating service in war; one set to be allowed for every dress coat."

As for head dress, he portrayed "the forage caps" as "poor in quality." They were "seldom accurately marked as to size. The cap covers are all one size, and of so poor a quality as to be almost useless." To eliminate this defect Campbell wanted every cap to "be furnished from the factory with its cover, and should be issued as one." He opined:

> the old style cap with slanting visor and falling crown, as made for officers, was a much more becoming head dress for men in ranks, and a more comfortable one withal. Men would prefer to pay more for a cap if they could truly secure a good article. A cheap cap destroys beyond anything the personal appearance of a man no matter how well he may otherwise be dressed. The regimental number should be removed from the collar of the dress coat and it, the company letter, and badge of the arm of service should be worn upon the caps. The soldier's identity would in those respects then, always be known.[109]

Side buttons on light artillery 1872-pattern enlisted helmets bore crossed cannon, while those for cavalry and signal troops had crossed sabers. GS

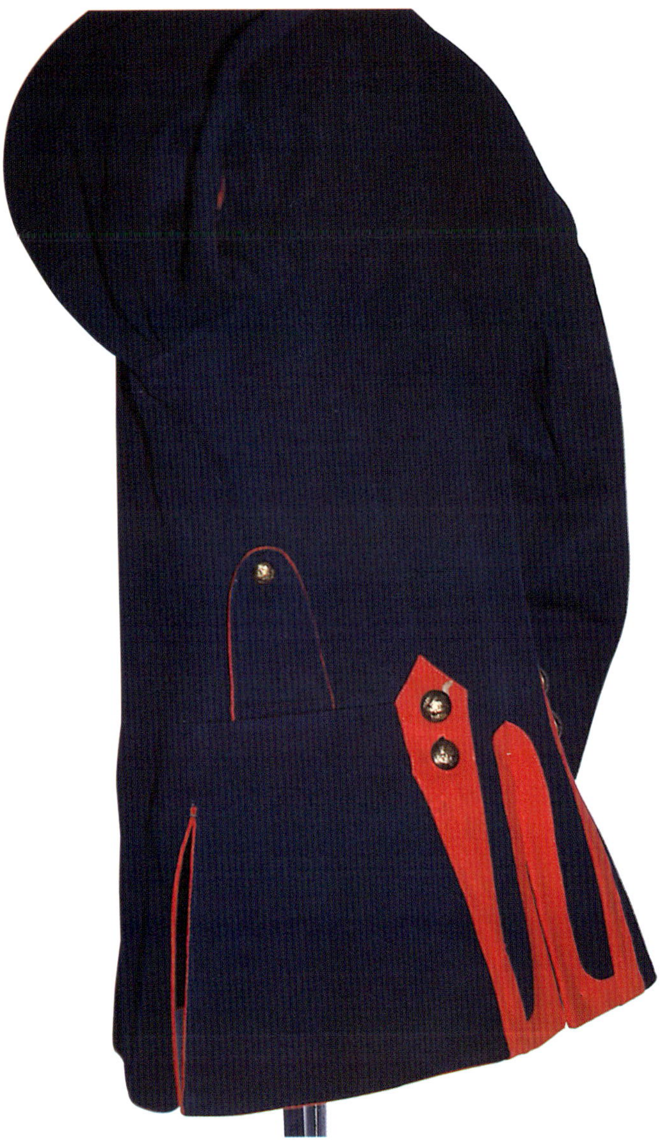

A side view of an 1872-pattern light artillery dress coat shows the side slit and belt loop. In addition to adjustments to the position of the belt loops, the length of the waist for 1872-pattern mounted dress coats also was required to secure a proper fit. This reconfiguration was revised from time to time during the 1870s, until final measurements were settled upon. SI

Surgeon Thomas Andrew McParlin conveyed his ideas to Colonel Nelson A. Miles at Ft. Leavenworth, Kansas. He sagely summarized some of the main pitfalls of the American soldier's kit as provided by the government:

> We attempt to have one uniform for officers and for men for dress, (and subject to modification) for undress, fatigue, for marches, campaigns, for winter and for summer, for the tropics, and the gulf stations, and for those on the 49th° North latitude—as at Pembina, and the Canada frontier, is impractical and unwise: it would be cruel if carried out by a martinet, and costly in human life, or health, as in money. The officer (and the soldier) in all countries, take special pride in a handsome dress, suitable for dress occasions, receptions, parades, occasions of etiquette and ceremony, where other services are represented home or foreign; and for such, and other proper garrison duties, a stylish uniform is needed.

McParlin saw the pre-Mexican War dress as a good example of dress wear, but without the heavy, hot padding. He believed that loose clothing was just the thing to maintain coolness in the heat and to allow layering against the cold. Further, roll collars were more desirable than stand collars. Gray soft felt campaign hats were promoted, as were "Glengarry Scotch" caps with "ear flaps and a waterproof falling flap behind."

When it came to the brass screw shoes that were issued, McParlin recorded the field experience of the Fifth Infantry against the Cheyenne, Comanche, and Kiowa. During these campaigns, the shoes were destroyed. The surgeon championed strong ankle boots for foot soldiers instead.

The rapid deterioration of the campaign hat was equally troublesome. This headgear supposedly "soon wore out, and fell to pieces," thereby requiring the men "to patch or sew the parts together again, but the material was very poor, easily torn, and insusceptible of any proper repairs. In such a state of affairs, the men would soon be without any protection to the head, against the solar heat, or the elements generally."

As for the great coat, it was "suitable for northern stations," but too heavy for southern climates. It absorbed "too much wet" and dried very slowly once it became moist. McParlin wanted "two varieties...made;

of a heavy and light cloth; and material kept available for making them waterproof."[110]

If cold weather required special clothing, so did hot weather conditions. Major John Milton Brannan knew his First Artillery gunners at Ft. Barrancas, Florida, needed relief from heat and humidity. As others had indicated, the right headgear was especially important. Brannan believed, "...straw hats are absolutely necessary in this climate from May lst to October 31st and should be issued to troops."[111]

Another artillery officer posted to the South, Major Henry Abner Allen, expanded on this idea. With Raleigh, North Carolina, "experiencing eighty to ninety degrees" many days during the "summer and sometimes even higher," Allen exhorted: "the propriety, if possible, of issuing to the enlisted men white trousers, and jackets, and also straw hats, to be worn on fatigue, and in general on all except full dress duty. The hats I think are especially necessary and should be worn on sentinel duty."[112]

These and many other observations were reiterated and published under the imprint of the surgeon general. The report reached the conclusion:

> It is probably not possible to devise a uniform which will serve for both Arizona and Minnesota, and accordingly it is found that officers serving in the south recommend the side of thinner, and those in the north of thicker and warmer articles than those allowed by regulations. Practically, the soldier purchases much clothing from traders in order to protect himself against extremes of temperature, which cannot be done by the exclusive use of articles furnished by the Government.[113]

The 1872-pattern dress cap for heavy artillery had a scarlet wool pompon and worsted trim, along with a stamped sheet brass eagle and crossed cannon. The 5/8 inch regimental number and battery letter sometimes were added, but were not mandatory until the release of General Orders No. 8, Headquarters of the Army, February 8, 1877. Engineer enlisted men wore the same cap, but with a brass castle on the front and a white topped red pompon. SI

Front and three-quarter views of an 1872-pattern heavy artillery musician's dress coat with herringbone chest trim. This particular example includes the chevrons of the principal musician—three bars and a bugle device in scarlet facing material. SI

Detail of the heavy artillery cap pompon with the brass wire that was inserted into a reinforced slot at the front of the piece of headgear. All pompons were to be of the same pattern, but dyed in the appropriate branch color. RB

An 1872-pattern coat for a sergeant major of heavy artillery. SI

A heavy artillery battery at Ft. Niagara, New York, includes the first sergeant (at the head of the company), who is armed with an M1840 non-commissioned officer's sword, and to his left the two company musicians hold M1840 musicians' swords. The remainder of the men carry Springfield "trapdoor" rifles. OFN

Neither this young bandsmen of the Third U.S. Artillery Regiment, with his special trefoil trim on the dress coat, nor his older comrade with a pair of service chevrons on each cuff wear any unit identification on their caps. Stamped sheet brass regimental numbers, however, are attached to the collars, in compliance with regulations. RB

This represented one of the reasons, according to the report, why enlisted men did not draw their full allowance of clothing, preferring instead to use the funds saved from their allotment to procure suitable articles form private sources. In this light, the surgeon general's office concurred with "the wishes of the majority of officers and men" who desired to be furnished "two distinct kinds of clothing"—one for cold weather and another warm weather, "and that each be of the best quality." The document went on to list the gist of responses from the field. Drawers were needed in two weights, and a new pattern that the Quartermaster Department proposed was advocated as a replacement for the then current pattern. Better quality stockings and two weights of shirts of a material that did not shrink or irritate the skin were urged. An increased allowance of shirts also was deemed necessary, a point made as well for the stable frock, which was distributed to the troops one per year, rather than two per year that was seen as more realistic. So, too, were mittens and fur caps with ear flaps required. Next, a replacement for the "universally condemned" campaign hat was high on the list of improvements, as was the dress helmet, which was thought to be "too heavy, and has too steep a visor," thereby causing headaches to the wearer. Similarly, the pleated blouse was rejected as being wholly unpopular in that it gathered dust and was difficult to keep clean. Finally, blanket-lined great coats were pronounced insufficiently warm, thus sheepskin or buffalo overcoats, which would be temporarily given to the men as weather and climate dictated, were sought.[114]

(Left) A private of heavy artillery 1872-pattern dress coat has five enlistments in peacetime stripes indicating twenty-five years of service. Rather than being applied separately, as was the common practice, these are made from one piece of cloth, and black silk chain stitching outlines the material to create the stripes. The coat on the left is the 1872-pattern for a Corps of Engineers' private. The collar was supposed to display a brass castle device on each side until 1884. Photograph by Glen Swanson. GS

Brass castle insignia for the 1872-pattern Engineer Corps enlisted dress coat collar. Specifications called for the height of the battlements to be 3/8 inch; of center tower, 1/2 inch; of side towers, 5/8 inch each; breadth at base and top, 1 inch. JG

This litany of shortcomings helped provide a catalyst for change, and in some situations simply reinforced new directions that the Quartermaster Department had already taken. One notable instance of this latter course was the resolution to abandon the unpopular pleated jacket for "a different pattern blouse from that now in the hands of the troops," a decision authorized by the secretary of war on February 27, 1874.[115]

There were two prototypes turned out, one lined and the other unlined. These were examined and approved by the head of the War Department. Based on these models, a March 1874 directive called for three standard samples to be made for each arm of the service and then sealed to serve as the models for all future fabrication. One was to go to the quartermaster general's office, one set was to be retained at the Philadelphia Depot, and the last set was to be shipped to Jeffersonville. Further, no more of the pleated blouses were to be made thereafter, although all old pattern blouses on hand were to be issued. After that, when it became "necessary to manufacture blouses to fill orders..." only the new pattern were to be made.[116] Even in the wake of these encouraging words, however, "it was not deemed advisable to commence the change until those [old pattern pleated blouses] on hand had been disposed of."[117]

In the meantime, the streamlined blouse's basic appearance was spelled out in Circular No. 27 issued by the War Department on the day the secretary of war had given his nod to the garment that was to serve for "fatigue purposes, general wear, and on field service." It was similar to the old Civil War sack coat in some respects, but its roll collar had an edging made from worsted "cord of the color of the uniform coat fac-

Engineer private's dress uniform of the 1872-pattern, complete with red and white pompon on the cap. USAQM

This example of an engineer first sergeant's 1872-pattern dress coat clearly illustrates the white silk chain stitch on the chevrons that was distinct to this branch. Black thread formed the chevrons for non-commissioned officers in other arms of the service and corps, except in the case of hospital stewards. SI

Engineer Corps battalion quartermaster sergeant chevrons of scarlet with white silk chain stitching. The same chevrons were used in the cavalry, infantry, and artillery for regimental quartermaster sergeants, but of yellow, sky blue, and scarlet stitched with black silk, respectively. AMWH

ings." This meant the collar was edged in yellow for cavalry, light blue for infantry, scarlet for artillery and engineers, gray for commissary sergeants, orange for signal enlisted men, and emerald green for hospital stewards. The same cord trimmed the cuffs, forming an inverted "V" similar to the old 1858-pattern enlisted frock coat with a single vest size eagle button at the back where the trim was gathered at the seam, although some examples had two or three buttons as ornamentation. The lower front edge of the coat had a less pronounced curve than the old sack coat. Additionally, it was a more form fitted garment in that it was comprised of four panels, including two at the back, rather than a single panel as the old Civil War veteran had been. Also, the blouse continued to be single breasted, as was it 1860s' predecessor, but closed "with five buttons on the breast, same as worn on the uniform coat," rather than the previous four. At first, existing dark blue flannel was used for the item that came in unlined and lined versions. The latter type originally was to use blue flannel on hand as lining that was deemed inferior for the blouses or coats, but the new gray shirt flannel was ultimately adopted when the old material was determined to be unavailable. In turn, the sleeves were lined with unbleached muslin. There were to be two interior slash pockets at the breast, as well.[118]

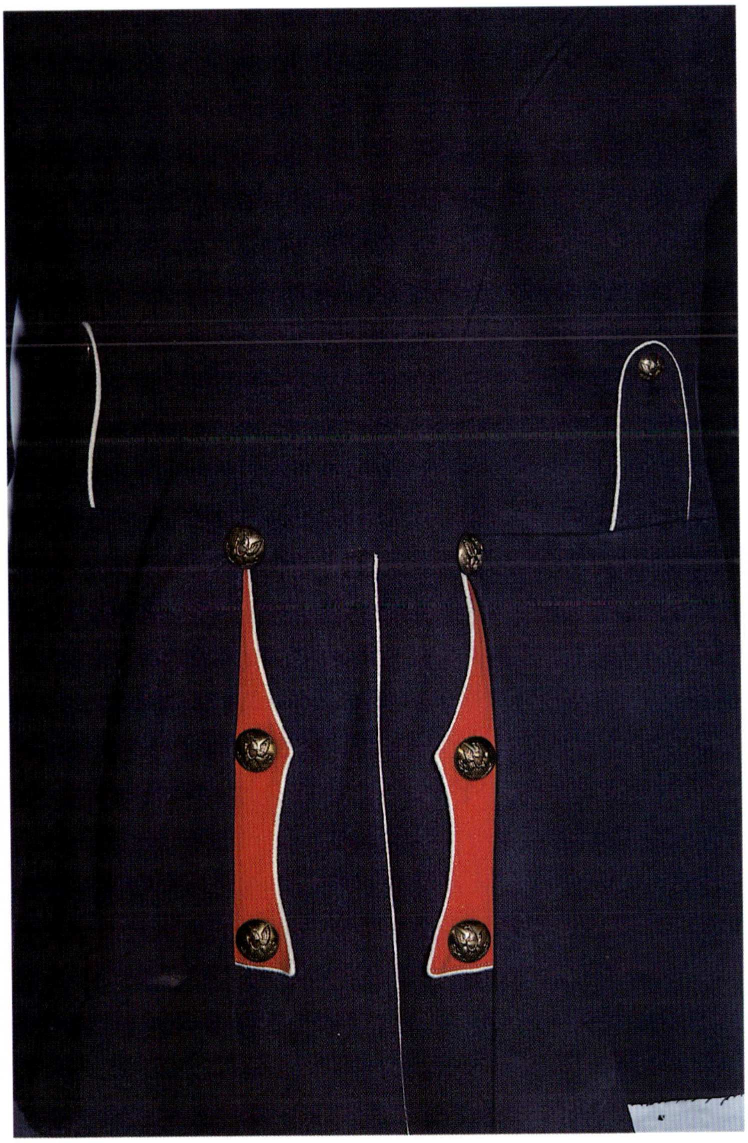

Rear of an 1872-pattern Engineer Corps enlisted dress coat with belt loops, which were piped in white while the tail flashes were scarlet piped in white. SI

According to General Orders No. 92, War Department, September 26, 1872, service chevrons were to be worn on the dress coat, below the elbow. This order also stated service in war was to be "indicated by a white stripe on each side of the chevron for Artillery, and a red stripe for all other corps, the stripe to be one-eighth of an inch wide." The center of service in war stripes was the color of the wearer's branch in which he was enlisted during the Civil War. In this case, the medium blue represented infantry. The coat is for a soldier in the Corps of Engineers, because of the scarlet facings with white piping. SI

General Orders No. 107, War Department, December 14, 1872, specified that hospital stewards would wear a cap with emerald green worsted braid and a pompon of the same color. A gilt wreath with white metal letters "U.S." in the center also was called for by this order. SI

Yellow thread also was used on hospital steward's chevrons. It is unclear whether these were to be worn specifically with the enlisted blouse, or were a variant that also could be sewn to the dress coat. AMWH

Following a parallel course, the quartermaster went on to assure that an improved design for the forage cap had been produced and approved on November 9, 1874. As for the campaign hat, the original manufacturer was being contacted to obtain a report as to what course of action might be taken to acquire a more durable material. Further, as of 1873 single-breasted dismounted great coats had been furnished with a detachable large outer cape of the same sky-blue kersey, this expedient being seen as adequate until stocks of the old pattern were exhausted, at which time double-breasted mounted overcoats would be made up for all troops. The interim garment was deemed "admirable" and had the added option of the extra outer cape being "detached and worn separately in mild weather."[119]

As for footgear, on April 19, 1872, the Quartermaster Department submitted brass-screwed boots and shoes to the secretary of war as samples of improved standards with a request that he permit a board to convene to review the merits of these items. The secretary concurred, and subsequently the board proposed 3,000 pairs of boots and 2,000 pairs of shoes be manufactured "for trial in active service...."[120]

During 1874 the interdepartmental correspondence related to the footgear with screw-fastened soles was considerable, beginning with orders for 3,250 pairs of bootees in sizes 8 through 10.[121] From the field, responses generally were positive, but haste in issue and defects in the attaching screws caused quartermaster personnel to take steps so that these problems would not be repeated.[122]

The quartermaster general further indicated that another element of footwear—stockings—had been addressed.[123] The quantity had been increased, but a better standard was yet to be adopted. The Pacific Woolen Mills of San Francisco was producing some new samples with the idea that this would become the new standard. Thereafter, Meigs thought a fresh supply of the improved type would be bought in the next fiscal year.

If patterns for enlisted uniforms were being rethought so soon after the promulgation of the 1872 regulations, could changes in the officers' outfit be far behind? Rumors to this effect caused acting quartermaster general Colonel Rufus Ingalls, joined by Commissary General R. MacFeely, to inquire:

> Having heard that it is contemplated to make some modifications to the Uniform of officers of the Army, we respectfully submit the following recommendations:

Some hospital steward's 1872-pattern dress coats were made with emerald green piping, but the standard that ultimately was adopted had emerald green facings with white trim and white stitching on the half chevrons. No collar devices were prescribed until 1882. SI

That epaulettes be substituted for shoulder knots in the uniform for all officers of the Staff Department.

That the insignia of rank and Maltese cross in silver, be worn on the epaulettes by officers of the Quartermaster Department; and the insignia of rank and a silver crescent be that of the Subsistence Department.

That officers of the Quartermaster Department wear buff colored ostrich feathers on the chapeau, and those of the Subsistence Department near grey ostrich feathers.

That aigiulettes be worn by officers of all the Staff Departments.

That all officers of the Staff Departments wear on the trousers a stripe like that designed for officers of the Topographical Engineers on page 195 of the Army Regulations of 1847.

That the gold lace be removed from the sleeves of the coat. That the sack coat be made without slits, and that the belt be worn on the outside; also that the braid be removed from the sack coat.

That a Maltese cross be placed on the shield on the button for the Qr.Mr. Department; and a crescent for the Subsistence Department.[124]

Even as these two officers were communicating their ideas General Orders No. 96, War Department, November 19, 1875, already had provided for one of their requests. This order called for the officers' sack-coat thereafter to be made without slashes at the hips and to be "without braid." The former modification meant that the sword belt and sword could no longer be worn under the blouse, but instead was to be worn outside the coat.

This reduced the cost of the garment and brought it more in line with the cut of the enlisted blouse. Of course, the material was finer, while other differences set it apart from the issue item for the rank and file, such as officer's buttons designating the arm of service, shoulder straps, and three small buttons on each cuff (some enlisted men, however, had additional buttons on their cuffs occasionally, as period photographs indicate). Not a few officers also took the order to mean the black braid on the sleeves, chest, and rear of the jacket were to be discontinued, but not the edging on the collar and around the outer seams. As such, some officers elected to wear a coat trimmed with flat braid, as surviving specimens and portraits of the era demonstrate.

General Orders No. 96 also made other pronouncements, including granting permission for officers "to wear a plain dark-blue body coat with the button designating their respective corps, regiments, or department without any other mark or ornament upon it." While this garment was "not to be considered as a dress for any military purpose," another prescription of General Orders No. 96 was the new practice that infantry officers were to sport a crossed rifles insignia as a replacement for the hunting horn device.[125] This same order changed the enlisted insignia for infantry to sheet brass stamped crossed rifles, as well, except for musicians who were to retain the traditional hunting horn.[126] Moreover, the order clarified the wearing of cap insignia, a matter of some confusion since the new uniform regulations of 1872 went into force.[127]

In this regard General Order No. 96 of 1875 added a new scheme by calling for the placement of company letters and regimental num-

Ordnance Sergeant Leodegar Schnyder wore a tailor-made coat, as some other staff non-commissioned officers opted to do. His buttons are officers' models for the Ordnance Corps, and the chevrons made of facing cloth cut out to form both the rank devices and his service stripes. The brass collar insignia are placed at a slight angle because of the rather short height of Schnyder's collar. FLNHS

Post commissary sergeant's uniform with white piping and cadet gray facings. The 1873 general order that established this outfit called for the points of the white metal crescents on the cap, collar, and the cloth insert above the chevrons to be worn "in the same vertical line," although until the mid-1880s, the points were in a horizontal line. Note that the crescent was cadet gray to match the chevrons. USAQM

bers, where applicable. In all instances save for musicians, the number of the regiment was to go above the crossed sabers, rifles, or crossed cannons insignia, and letter of the company or battery below the insignia. Field musicians and bandsmen were to bear the number of the regiment in the crook of the bugle and the company letter above the crook. Further, engineer rank and file were to display the company letter above the brass castle. This arrangement was called for in the case of not only the forage cap, but also the dress cap for foot troops.

As far as the new infantry insignia, not everyone received the news about change favorably. One veteran perhaps responded for others when he penned his discontent about "the time honored bugle" that was "to be done away with. Now we have 'crossed rifles without bayonets.' 'Yes, but that is so much more appropriate for infantry.' That's so, and by the same token let's give the engineers crossed quills, nibs upward, or if they prefer, a pick and a spade. For what do they have to do with castles, unless they are in the air?"[128]

Regardless of this less than enthusiastic reception, the new rifle insignia went into effect.[129] It was to be, "when issued,...charged at two cents each," in accordance with General Orders No. 21, War Department, March 21, 1876. The order also indicated "The letter of the company will be placed in the *lower* angle, and the number of the regiment in the *upper* angle, of the cap-badge for enlisted men of infantry."

Quartermaster Specification No. 8, adopted on May 31, 1876, further clarified the appearance of these insignia.[130] Although enlisted cap insignia had been well defined as to the manufacture, apparently some individuals still required further illumination when it came to the arrangement on the cap for enlisted men in all arms. This led to the release of General Orders No. 8, Headquarters of the Army, February 8, 1877.[131] General Orders No. 8 read in part:

> Hereafter the cap-badges, numbers of regiments, and letters of companies will be worn by enlisted men of the Army in the following manner, viz:
> *For Light Artillery and Cavalry soldiers*—the numbers of their regiments in the upper, and the letters of their companies in the lower, angles of the badges of their respective arms upon the forage caps; the helmets and trimmings according to the pattern now worn.
> *For Ordnance Sergeants and soldiers*—the 'shell and flame' on dress and forage caps.

Official sealed standard of the 1872-pattern post ordnance sergeant coat with white piping as authorized in 1873. SI

All other enlisted men serving with the Ordnance Corps wore the same 1872-pattern uniform coat as issued to post ordnance sergeants. Originally, these were trimmed in crimson only, although white piping soon was incorporated in this instance, as well. This example is for a corporal. These personnel were stationed at various arsenals, such as the one at Watervliet, New York. SI

For Hospital Stewards—the letters 'U.S.' in white metal, inclosed by wreath, on dress and forage caps.
For Commissary Sergeants—crescent in white metal, the points in a vertical line, on dress and forage caps.
For Engineers—the castle, with letter of company, above it, on dress and forage caps.
For Artillery—crossed cannon, with number of the regiment in upper, and letter of company in lower, angles, on dress and forage caps.
For Infantry—the crossed rifles, with the numbers of the regiment and the letters of company placed as for Artillery, upon the dress and forage caps.
For Field and Band Musicians—bugle, with numbers of regiment on the center, and the letters of the company above the bugle. [This did not apply to the cavalry, whose trumpeters and bandsmen continued to wear crossed sabers.]
The cap trimmings for enlisted men of all arms and corps to be yellow metal, unless otherwise specified.

While no doubt remained as to the proper placement of enlisted insignia on headgear, the fragile nature of these devices was a cause for different consideration. Because branch devices, letters, and numbers had been provided separately prior to the mid-1890s, and also due to the rather weak attachments on the back of the various cap insignia, the items tended to fall off the headgear. This prompted a number of soldiers to strengthen their cap insignia by inventive means. A few enterprising individuals brazed the components together, or reinforced them in various ways. Such an arrangement could be used for not only the forage cap, but also the 1872-pattern dress cap for foot troops.

Captain John Mendenhall, an artillery officer posted in the San Francisco area, went so far as to suggest that the cap ornaments furnished his Fourth Artillery gunners at Pt. San Jose, California, had fastenings that were "very poor...." The captain thought "if small staples were put on and firmly they would last much longer."[132]

An infantry officer, Captain Augustus Corliss, went so far as to propose crossed rifles with the "number, and letter" attached "in solid form, so that they might be fastened to the cap by means of one loop."[133]

General Orders No. 38, War Department, March 20, 1873, set forth the uniform for the newly created post commissary sergeant's position. Among other articles, an 1872-pattern dress cap with white metal crescent, brass eagle, cadet gray pompon, and cadet gray worsted trim was called for. It should be noted that all other enlisted dress caps had stamped sheet brass insignia, save for hospital stewards. JG

Although the dress coats made in 1872 for post ordnance sergeants were trimmed in crimson only, by the following year specifications were changed to crimson piped in white, as this official Quartermaster Department photograph of the 1872-pattern post ordnance sergeant dress uniform indicates. Trouser stripes were to be of 1 1/4 inch wide crimson facing material. USAQM

The captain was told that this design would be frail and would increase the likelihood of breakage. Moreover, the manufacturing cost was deemed prohibitive.

Although the problem of enlisted cap insignia design was not resolved until the mid-1890s, this matter was not as much discussed as was another outgrowth of the 1872 regulations—the folding hat. This item was based on the Mexican War era Andrew's hat that had been revisited by the 1868 board and the Woodhull Report. The prototype subsequently selected by the 1872 board was made by R. Warnock & Co., but others bid on the contract to provide the 10,000 hats called for by the quartermaster.[134] In the meantime, Philadelphia hatter P. Herst had furnished Langdon C. Easton, the chief quartermaster officer at the depot in that city, with a sample hat, which was then sent along to Meigs. Meigs examined the Warnock and Herst prototypes and pronounced the pattern on hand from the board as "plain" in comparison to the Herst sample, which he described as having a "velvet" finish.[135] Nevertheless, Meigs confessed he was not a hat expert, and while he thought the Herst example was "better finished and likely to keep cleaner than the Board hat, and I think it may be received, so far as appearance goes, as fully equal," he still was not convinced as to "the important question of durability and wear." Consequently, he recommended that Easton "get the best expert advice and aid in inspection" before selecting between the two hats.[136]

Perhaps Easton followed this prescription, because a contract was not issued for nearly a month. When it was made, the award went to Herst, who bid $2.83 1/2 for each hat with cords and tassels.[137] Just after this agreement, however, the contractor discovered he could not obtain cords on the open market for the hat as supposed, artillery ones being the only ones that had been released as surplus in quantities.[138] This finding was minor, in that sufficient quantities were in stock at the depots to make delivery without cords acceptable, although the ones for infantry tended to be very faded, a factor that seemed of little consequence, because the hats were "only to be worn on fatigue duty and on campaign or marches."[139] Herst thus received an order for 10,000 hats without cords at $2.80 each.[140]

The official Quartermaster Department sealed pattern for the commissary sergeant's dress coat had white crescent points upward for the chevrons, despite specifications to the contrary. This was but one of several disconnects between official standards and articles as actually issued or worn. SI

Rear of an 1872-pattern commissary sergeant's coat. JG

Absence of cords, which after all were worn at the individual initiative of the soldiers, and as such not necessarily a common practice, was a minor drawback when compared to the hat itself. This piece of headgear became a matter of considerable debate. Even loyal quartermaster officer John Rodgers proposed an abbreviated brim. He observed the standard hat, after wear in the field, became very pliable. Then, because of the weight associated with the broad brim, it tended to droop "down in an uncomfortable and unsightly manner over the neck and face of the wearer."[141] Easton then forwarded an improved model for Meigs to examine.[142] This began several years of deliberation on this matter that led to the adoption of a new pattern in 1876.

William O. Taylor, a Seventh Cavalry trooper who had to wear this hat on rugged campaign service, summed up the reason why this headpiece ultimately was replaced. Taylor rightly recollected the old black campaign hat had:

> a very wide brim that had hooks and eyes on it, front and rear so that it might be made to appear in shape at least like a chapeau of a Major General, but the handling that it got and the rain and wind gave it an appearance unlike anything I ever saw on the head of a man. Some of the Companies like L, F, and C, refused to wear them and purchased out of private funds, a hat of much better shape and quality. Owing to the cheap material and its great width the brim of my hat had become separated from the crown for nearly one half the way round, and in consequence I was sometimes looking over the brim and sometimes, under it.[143]

From another source, Major Charles E. Compton, who commanded Ft. Dodge, Kansas, came a report from a member of the Fifth Infantry, Captain Edmond Butler. The captain again presented a familiar scenario—the issue hats were not durable. Compton sent this complaint on to Rodgers at Philadelphia. Rodgers rebutted that the hats furnished to the men of the Fifth Infantry met government standards, and that there should be no grounds for dissatisfaction. He, therefore, suggested that some of the supposedly faulty hats be sent to Philadelphia for examination by experts.

Butler complied, as well as furnished an affidavit from eight of his men indicating that the hats became unserviceable after only 120 hours of wear. Rodgers and his experts could not accept this, and retorted that it was not possible for the headgear to degenerate after such a brief period. Thus, he dismissed the whole matter as "groundless."

Not to be put off, Butler secured forty-four testimonials from enlisted men and several from officers at his post backing up the discontent with the hat based upon poor serviceability. By this point the secretary of war entered the picture with a directive that all commanding officers furnish responses to the adequacy of the uniform items being issued, including the campaign hat.[144]

Despite his youthful appearance, this sergeant of Company E, Second U.S. Infantry, has completed one five-year enlistment, as indicated by the service chevron on the lower sleeve of his 1872-pattern dress coat. His uniform is an excellent representation of the 1872 regulations for the infantry enlisted full dress uniform. USAMHI

The Fifth U.S. Infantry private with his Napoleonic stance, and his seated comrade, a company musician, also offer a representative view of the 1872-pattern as first issued for doughboys, including the surplus 1858-pattern 1 inch stamped sheet brass company letters on their forage caps and Civil War style shoes, or brogans. In the former instance, General Orders No. 92, War Department, October 26, 1872, called for the badge of the corps or the letter of the company (in the case of combat arms) to be the only adornment. FAM

The sealed sample of the 1872-pattern infantry regimental quartermaster uniform coat. Collar numerals were called for to indicate the regiment. These were to be of stamped sheet brass and measure 1/2 inch in height. SI

1872-pattern infantry pioneer uniform coat. SI

Responses were soon forthcoming. For the most part, reactions to "the campaign-hat" were adverse, and this head dress was "universally condemned because of its poor material" In the face of such criticism Rodgers still did not relent. He contended the shape of the hat, not the materials used to make it, was the problem. To rectify the situation the original makers of the standard hat, Warnock and Company, were to examine the matter once again, in theory to secure "as durable a hat as possible."[145]

Consequently, in 1875, the deputy quartermaster general, Lieutenant Colonel Judson D. Bingham, announced: "steps are now being taken to procure hats satisfactory to the Army."[146] Meigs himself pursued one of the paths to reach this goal when he requested assistance from Sir Edward Thornton, England's Minister to the United States, in obtaining "samples of cloth-covered cork helmets worn by Her Britannic Majesty's troops in tropical climates such as India."[147]

Securing examples of foreign patterns was by no means a new concept, nor was the quest for a cooler version of headgear for summer months. Previously, however, the solution to beat the heat often was a civilian straw hat or boater, as had been the case at the Ft. Monroe Artillery School in the late 1850s, and by orders in the Department of Texas and much farther north in the Department of the Platte, both in the early 1870s.[148]

While straw hats continued to be sanctioned as optional for hot climates for years to come, the English-inspired cork helmet constituted a parallel effort that indicated the continued dual track of reliance on foreign models of headgear versus homegrown American solutions.[149] Indeed, Secretary of War William Belknap ultimately permitted the purchase of 100 British imports complete with *puggree* (cloth band) for experimental issue to troops in the Arizona Territory, although previously he had declined such a request by Meigs. After the Medical Department supported the concept, Belknap made a favorable ruling, and authorized the purchase of the experimental helmets.[150]

These items, replete with puggree, cost $3.50. They were received in San Francisco, and distributed to certain troops in Southern California and Arizona.[151] After a suitable period, responses proved less than enthusiastic—the verdict, the helmets were too heavy and insufficiently ventilated.[152]

Despite this criticism, the quest for a summer helmet did not end there. Such a piece of headgear going back as early as the "Ventilated or Eastern Hat" discussed and illustrated in the Woodhull Report found continued advocates. This meant that West Point cadets would be provided with a version of the helmet produced by the New York firm of Henry V. Allien, in compliance with General Orders No. 121, War Department, December 22, 1877.[153] By the following year, 100 similar helmets were sent to Ninth Cavalry troopers for trial in Texas, while similarly Ft. Monroe's garrison was to receive 250 helmets.

Although the summer helmet did not end with this preliminary issue, the matter became a sidebar compared to the quest for a better campaign hat. Even while the first summer helmets were being tested, Warnock personnel had revisited the content of the folding hat and reported that a different formula should be used, one that would be more expensive, but in theory more substantial. Both Warnock and P. Herst made up samples using the new specifications. Meigs thought the latter firm produced a better version, the former contractor turning out what he considered an ungainly, stiff rendition. Consequently, he opted for the Herst hat, and requested a tandem trial of 100 of these items were distributed for field study alongside the summer helmets sent to the Department of Arizona—a move that was approved on September 18, 1875.[154]

With efforts to improve the folding hat running concurrently with trials for a cork helmet, Quartermaster General Meigs sought another course of action. In October 1875 one of his subordinates requested that a board be convened to deliberate over some key matters of uniform issue, including "the best pattern of a campaign hat for the Army."[155] This suggestion was carried out through Special Order No. 264, War Department, December 27, 1875, with Brevet Major General Daniel H. Rucker presiding.[156]

Even while the members met, Meigs informed the group that 100 experimental hats of a new model had been sent to Arizona for field tests.[157] This effort proved of no consequence, however, because the board

Rear of an 1872-pattern infantry enlisted uniform dress coat. SI

Right: 1872-pattern infantry musician's dress coat, in this case for a principal musician, as designated by chevrons with a trumpet over three stripes, a chevron introduced in 1872. SI

never received information about the hat's performance during their session.[158] Nevertheless, the group launched into the subject in depth, submitting a report that presented their own findings:

> The board is of the opinion that the Campaign Hat for the Army should be soft, pliable, of light-weight, firm texture and the greatest possible durability that can be obtained for a reasonable price.
>
> With this view the board has procured information from all available sources in regard to the manufacture and component materials of the various hats of the character named fabricated for Army and commercial purposes. Experts in the manufacture of hats of all kinds have been examined and their opinions obtained.
>
> There appear to be two distinct kinds or classes of felt hats:—one made from fur and one made from wool.
>
> Those manufactured from fur are of a vast variety of qualities ranging from very low to very high prices according to the quality and kind of material. It is, however, generally conceded that no fur hat, that will give good service, can be manufactured, except for the better quality of furs and at a price varying from $2.50/100 to $3.00/100 each. If from the best quality of furs, the prices would range much higher.
>
> Whether made from fur or from wool, no inspection can exactly determine the particular material or materials from which made, so that in any case, much reliance must be placed on the integrity of the manufacturer. No positive test can be applied save actual wear. It is, however, thought by the Board that there will be less opportunity for imposition in the manufacture of wool hats, while the cost of the material being much less, there will be less inducement in that direction.
>
> From all the information the Board has been able to obtain, wool hats of the best grade will give equal service with the best grade of fur hats. This has been attested, even by prominent hatters engaged exclusively in the manufacture of fur hats. Severe tests were also instituted by the Board with satisfactory results.
>
> In view of all these facts, and the greatly decreased cost to the soldier, together with the large saving to the government, the Board is induced to recommend felt hats made of wool for issue to the enlisted men of the Army.
>
> The pattern recommended for adoption has been sent to the office of the Quartermaster General, duly sealed for identification. It is a plain black, velvet finished, hat. similar to the fatigue hat worn by officers during the late war; with crown 5 1/2 inches high, and brim 2 3/4 inches wide, for medium sized hats, the edge of the brim turned over and stitched, without binding; with a revolving ventilator in each side 3 1/2 inches above the brim; and with japanned sweat leather.
>
> For all purposes of the service it is believed that black is the most desirable color.

A musician in the Twenty-first U.S. Infantry with the correct worsted herringbones of light blue on the chest of his 1872-pattern uniform coat and the regulation stamped sheet brass numerals on the collar. GS

A specially modified 1872-pattern dress coat for a regimental infantry musician. JG

It is further recommended that the campaign hat for officers be of the same color and pattern as that for enlisted men, either fur or wool as may be preferred by the individual officer. If of fur, the brim need not be turned over or bound. A sample hat of fur, duly sealed, has also been sent to the Quartermaster General's Office.[159]

The Board's wishes were to be carried out, although it is somewhat of a puzzle why a challenge did not arise about the color.[160] Many officers of the era had sought a light colored or drab hat.[161] Clearly the board championed black, perhaps under the false assumption that the ventilator fans, a feature previously called for in the case of the 1872-pattern infantry and heavy artillery officer's dress caps, would address that need.

Wasting little time, 100 sample hats were ordered to be sent to San Francisco, and from there distributed for testing in Arizona.[162] After many months these were pronounced to be an improvement over the folding hat, and proved more popular than the British style helmet. With that, on June 14, 1876, specifications were approved for the Board's proposed campaign hat.[163] Once again, the hat's actual issue lagged behind its official adoption. Not until April 1877 did the first disbursement take place.[164] Even then it was made clear that hats only were to be "supplied to troops in the field or on the frontier, as required by existing numbers."[165] In all other cases, the folding hat continued to be offered, in the main to officers, but also even to military prisoners, a group that was so supplied until 1881. These were to be altered by cutting down the large brim and reblocking the crown in such a manner as to approximate the 1876-pattern hat.[166] As time passed, the reworked hats and those that remained as first made in the early 1870s were removed from the inventory and provided for sale to various entities, including the "extra Inauguration Police" in Washington, D.C., and military surplus dealers of the era.[167]

In 1878, Ft. Douglas, Utah Territory's Fourteenth U.S. Infantry Regimental band set aside traditional caps for foot troops and were provided with 1872-pattern mounted dress helmets. Their coats were modified by the addition of Austrian knots on the cuffs and fringed cloth epaulets. BH

In addition to the new campaign hat adopted, the board considered many other far-ranging topics related to uniforms. Among the items was the summer helmet.[168] Additionally, the requirement for issue winter headgear was addressed, along with the need for fur gauntlets and Arctic overshoes, as were recommendations for the lengthening of the tongues of issue shoes; improved patterns for great coats and trousers; an adjustment to the cut of the collars and waists of dress coats; an improved means of relaying measurements when ordering coats for the troops; and a new system of supplying clothing to the field.[169]

Uniform regulations called for regimental bands "to wear the uniforms of their Regiments or Corps," but commanding officers could "make such additions of ornaments" as they judged proper. Colonel Miles' Fifth U.S. Infantry was one such example, in that the uniform coats had white facings with red piping, as did the trouser's stripes, while the caps bore a large spread eagle and feathered plume in lieu of the pompon. Cloth epaulets and aiguillettes completed the ensemble, as depicted in two portraits taken in Leavenworth, Kansas, around 1875. FAM

Throughout the 1870s the band of the United States Military Academy continued to wear the dress cap, but these were trimmed in white. White belts and special white trim also were applied to the dress coat, while long white worsted aiguillettes and lyre devices on the coat collar added further decoration. USAMHI

The interior lining of an 1872-pattern enlisted uniform coat, which was substantially padded, also shows the quartermaster's inspector's stamp that indicates the size (no. 3) and the fiscal year when it was added to the Philadelphia depot's inventory. SI

Starting with the matter of winter headgear, the 1876 board recommended a sealskin cap, a prescription that likewise was heeded and made official on May 23, 1876, which simply read: "To be made of the 'wool seal' skin, with ear flaps, cape, and vizor, according to pattern. Sizes same as for dress and forage caps."[170] (Unfortunately, the pattern piece evidently did not survive.) On the same day specifications for fur gauntlets were adopted, as well as another accessory for cold weather wear.[171] By the end of the month, a specification for wool mittens likewise was to be provided as a concession against Jack Frost.[172]

Shortly after that, on June 22, 1876, the Quartermaster Department's clothing bureau let a preliminary contract for 2,000 fur caps. The award went to Edmund R. Lyon of Philadelphia.[173] Purchase of gauntlets and mittens would follow, with the former articles being sent to posts in the extreme north at two pairs per man per year, while troops at other garrisons were to be given the mittens.[174]

As another means to cope with intensely frigid conditions, the Board advocated Arctic overshoes, or "snow excluders," as both "warmer and more serviceable" than privately purchased buffalo moccasins, or the 1862 and 1873 patterns of buffalo overshoes, which had been tried previously. The Board also concluded the new footgear ideally were to be two sizes larger than the shoe or boot worn by the soldier.[175] The result was footgear made of waterproof black tweed uppers with heavy felt lining. The lower section, including the heel and sole, as well as the top edge of the snow excluders, were of vulcanized rubber. These weighed approximately three pounds per pair. They fastened with a strap and buckle at the front. To further ensure a tight seal, the tongue was completely formed to the entire upper section so as to keep out moisture.[176]

With winter wear being better attended to, another matter of considerable discussion also was addressed—trousers. This was a protracted bone of contention because of cut and materials that were condemned as both inferior in quality and erratic in color. Thus, the news that the supply of kersey for trousers had been consumed must have pleased many critics.[177] On February 12, 1876, the Board expressed the opinion that this garment, likewise, could be "improved, at but a very slight additional cost."[178] The recommended pattern for both foot and mounted trousers were to differ from the old style "in having frog-mouth pockets, watch pocket, strap and buckle on the back, a slight spring at the foot, and no waist band."[179] In other words, the design first suggested by the 1872 board was revived.

In fact, prototypes had been furnished by Captain Rodgers in November 1874 "made without the waist-band and with pockets in front opening at the top as contemplated in the change of uniform published

In warmer months, when the cadet corps donned white trousers, so also did the West Point band. FAM

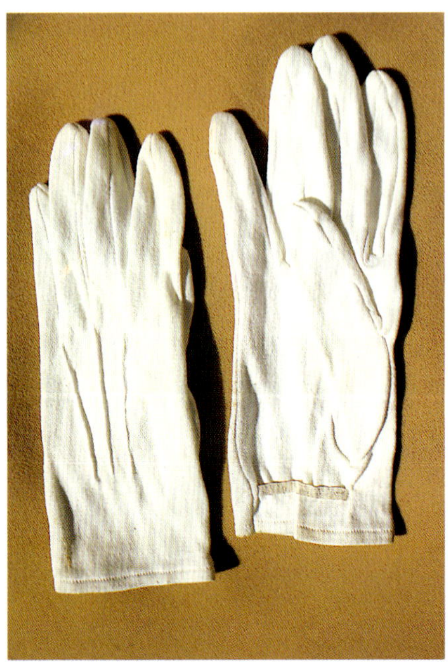

White Berlin gloves formed a regular part of the dress uniform after the adoption of the accessories in 1872. JB

Every member of this infantry company at Ft. Lyons, Colorado, has on the Berlin gloves with their 1872-pattern dress uniform. The drummer and bugler on the far left wear hunting horn insignia on their caps, the original badge for infantrymen according to the 1872 uniform regulations. General Orders No. 96, War Department, November 19, 1875, however, reserved this device for infantry field and band musicians, while introducing crossed rifles for all other doughboys. USAMHI

Representative contract label inside the sweatband of an 1872-pattern enlisted forage cap. JG

in General Orders No. 92...." These Rodgers said could "be made without increased expense." For that reason, he advocated the fabrication of 500 pairs for trial. By December 2, Colonel Easton had shipped off samples to Quartermaster General Meigs, along with some new dress coats made of the new blue cloth adopted earlier in 1874. On January 4, 1875, Meigs replied that the trousers were well made, but he further suggested that stitching should be added around the buttons, just as Inspector General Marcy had proposed the previous year. With this minor addition, Meigs gave his blessing to the 500 trial trousers, requiring that officers whose commands received the items would report their observations to the quartermaster general's office after troops had worn them. One of the responses from Captain Robert F. Scott, whose Company F, Third U.S. Artillery, had tried out ten pairs, probably echoed the general positive reaction summarizing: "The new trousers are more acceptable and more serviceable than those formerly issued. The pattern gives great satisfaction and in quality of cloth" was an advancement over the previous article.

With this background, and supplies of old stocks at last decreasing sufficiently, on March 25, 1876, the Quartermaster Department officially adopted the awaited trousers.[180] These garments were "to be made of sky-blue kersey, loose and without plaits, and a cut without waistband." Even so, the fact that their back rose to a goodly height, and also was fitted out with a cloth back belt with twin pronged buckle, meant that the trousers could be snugly adjusted to each wearer. Additionally, six buttons of tin with four holes in the center, through which they would be sewn to the trousers, were spaced on each side, along with two in the rear and two in the front at the waist for suspenders, an accessory not yet issued to the men, but that they could buy if they so desired. These suspender buttons were of the same type as on the flannel shirt (11/16 inch diameter), while five smaller ones in tin, with a 17/32 inch diam-

Left: General Orders No. 67, War Department, June 25, 1873, modified the original requirement for enlisted insignia, and called for the badge of the corps and letter of company to be worn in front of the forage cap by enlisted men of artillery, infantry, cavalry, and engineers. This meant crossed cannon, a hunting horn, crossed sabers, or a turreted castle was to be combined with the small stamped sheet brass company letter (5/8 of an inch high) adopted as standard to replace the large Civil War letters. As such, the example depicted in this photograph of an 1872-pattern enlisted forage cap was for a cavalrymen in Troop D. Above: Side view of an 1872-pattern enlisted forage cap. JG

The exception to General Orders No. 67 was for enlisted men serving on Ordnance Corps companies. They were to wear the stamped brass bomb and shell only, without company letter, just as post ordnance sergeants did. JG

(Left) An 1872-pattern infantry cap with the hunting horn device issued to all infantrymen, until 1875, when that insignia was to be worn by musicians only. (Right) An 1872-pattern infantry enlisted cap with stamped sheet brass crossed rifles per General Orders No. 96 of 1875. Photograph by Gordon Chappell.

eter, closed the fly. On mounted trousers another pair of buttons were applied to the inside of each cuff for the purpose of securing a strap (somewhat like modern ski pants); thereby the trousers could be kept in position within the boot top, while the trooper was mounted. The material for the strap was not specified, however, nor were its dimensions, because it was up to the soldier to obtain his own fasteners. Under the circumstances, it seems few cavalrymen employed them, but reinforcing or "saddling pieces" on the inseams and seats continued to be included for mounted troops. Evidently, the ample ends of the legs, which were "to spread well over the boot or shoe," were adequate to keep the trousers from moving up the leg of both mounted and dismounted soldiers alike.

Two front pockets with curved openings at the top were provided, and a watch pocket with pinked upright flap was positioned on the right side at the very top of the waist. A lining of eight ounce cotton duck in natural colors (not dyed or bleached) fortified the waist. This material also was used to make the inside of the front pockets and watch pocket.

For mounted trousers 1 5/6 yards of kersey was the average amount of cloth required, in contrast to 1 3/8 yards on average for dismounted pairs, the reinforcement making up the difference between the two quantities. The remainder of the materials required included 4/5 yard of unbleached muslin or drilling; 7/100 yard of colored jeans; 12/25 ounces of thread; and 7 suspender buttons. The number of fly buttons was 5 for foot trousers and 13 for mounted trousers, the additional buttons being those required for the inside of the cuffs.[181]

General officers and staff officers were to have dark blue cloth versions, with no welt or stripe.[182] Officers of artillery, cavalry, and infantry were to carry on the tradition of 1 1/2 inch wide stripes welted at the edges, which ran down each outer seam in facing cloth of scarlet, yellow, and dark blue, respectively. Further, these line officers were to wear light blue cloth of the color for enlisted men.[183]

This last requirement was important in that an improved sky-blue kersey had been adopted on May 23, 1876, to replace the 1874 standard. Eventually, this new cloth would be used to make 1876-pattern enlisted trousers (presumably the standard kersey adopted in 1874 was

Top and side views of the 1872-pattern infantry enlisted cap. Note the black japanned metal ventilator that supposedly helped air circulation. CF

According to General Orders No. 21, War Department, March 20, 1876, the crossed rifles were to be worn with the regimental number above and company letter below their intersection for all enlisted infantrymen serving within a company, save for the musicians, as the private does in a circa 1875 studio portrait. He also has on the belt for the M1872 infantry brace system with the support straps removed. WSM

Another infantry private in the 1872-pattern dress uniform likewise has the regimental number and company letter on his cap, along with the brass collar numbers for his regiment, all according to regulations. MM

used for the first pairs fabricated). Accordingly, Quartermaster Specification No. 63 introduced the light quality refined kersey.[184]

Moreover, a heavier quality standard for kersey had been prescribed. For the most part, this weightier kersey ultimately was meant as the fabric for the new great coat that the board asked to be introduced in 1876.[185] Outwardly, the overcoats resembled their mounted predecessor, which had been adopted in basic form in 1851. The fact that they were to be made from a superior quality kersey was one indication of the differences that existed between the garments introduced in 1876 and those that were issued prior to that time.[186]

Among other things, it was double breasted with five 1854-pattern large coat buttons in each row like the mounted overcoat of yore, but in this case all troops were thereafter to have the same garment. Under its 5 inch deep falling collar, a long matching cape reached to the sleeve ends, and was attached by eight to ten vest-sized buttons, thereby making it possible to detach this item for separate wear, unlike the permanently attached ones from earlier times. Five inch cuffs could be turned down over the hands if need be, but usually were worn turned up, these being of matching material. A belt at the back, which could be taken in or let out by means of two large 1854-pattern enlisted coat buttons, was one more element that remained similar to past designs. Inside, dark blue twilled flannel served as a lining from the shoulder to the top of where the skirt was slit. A pair of inside pockets on each side of the chest opened horizontally. Although the coat represented a refinement over previous types, only large sizes were to be produced at first, smaller

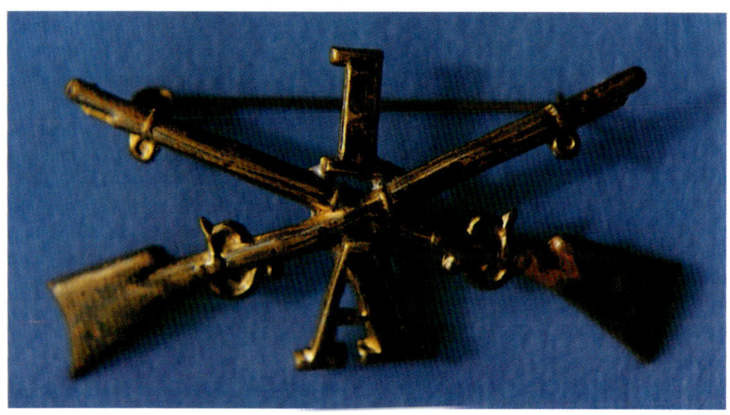

The proper arrangement of number and letter for infantry enlisted men, except for musicians, called for by General Orders No. 21 of March 20, 1876. Because the wire backings on the cap insignia were fragile, some individuals had the components brazed together, and even occasionally added a sturdy pin back attachment as seen here. TT

General Orders No. 21 also called from cavalry troopers to wear the regimental number above their crossed sabers and the company letter below. Again, the elements have been attached, including by two small rings to hold the "D" on the saber scabbards, thus allowing the letter to swing free. A pin back likewise has been provided to this custom insignia for a member of the Sixth U.S. Cavalry, Company D. TT

Sky blue kersey trousers of the cut used during the Civil War remained regulation after the adoption of the 1872-pattern uniform, despite a thwarted effort to change the design. This pair is for an infantry sergeant, with the regulation 1 inch dark blue stripe of facing cloth down each outer seam. SI

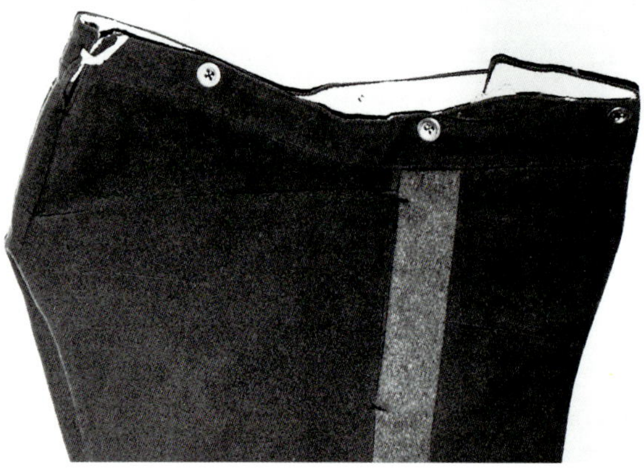

A pair of commissary sergeant's trousers of the 1873-1876 period with the correct 1 1/4 inch cadet gray leg stripes. A detail of the waistband (above) shows the watch pocket on the right side cut in a slight arc with a piece of matching cloth in an inverted arc above. SI

sizes of old stocks existing in such quantities that general issue did not begin until the summer of 1878.[187]

Nor were these new overcoats the last word related to this subject. Since 1872 the chevrons for infantry non-commissioned officers were of a light blue that essentially was so close in hue to the sky-blue kersey as to be nearly invisible. To rectify this situation, General Orders No. 21, War Department, March 20, 1876, replaced the light blue chevrons stitched in black with dark blue chevrons stitched in white, for overcoats only.[188] This was a departure from the norm in that previously all chevrons, save those for engineers, had black stitching. These were to be worn only on the overcoats, the sky blue types being retained for the dress coat. Even then, the more visible stripes were only apparent when the cape of the coat was worn buttoned back over the shoulders. Otherwise the cape obscured the chevrons, which were worn above he elbows, not only for the infantry, but for all other branches of service, as well.

Further, General Orders No. 21 sanctioned a long-standing tradition. For the first time since 1872, "Chevrons similar to those prescribed for the uniform-coat" were to be worn "by non-commissioned officers upon the sleeves of their blouses." While in point of fact most corporals and sergeants did so on a widespread basis judging from photographic evidence from the Civil War and after, this practice was not authorized by prior regulations, but merely was a well established custom.[189] Thus, the new orders gave credence to a long-standing, non-regulation convention.

One last task assigned by the Board, the provision of clear cut standards, had long been a concern. Both the Board and Meigs were disconcerted over the disparity of the uniform that often differed from one officer to the next. Consequently, the quartermaster general commissioned Captain Rodgers to contact Philadelphia for the purpose of hav-

Construction of the watch pocket and placement of suspender buttons on trousers varied, as one indication that each garment was sent with all cloth components cut out, along with thread and buttons to be assembled by individual seamstresses (many of whom were family members of veterans) before being returned to the quartermaster depots for issue. A certain number of trousers also were sent out to military posts unassembled, so that they could be made up by local enlisted tailors, who received a fixed fee for the work they performed for their comrades. Moreover, the rear of enlisted trousers had a "V" notch and two small hand sewn reinforced holes for a draw string as a means to snug up trousers to fit the wearer. Suspenders, which had to be purchased privately because none were issued at this time by the army, also held the trousers in place, although "braces" were not to be worn in a manner that was visible, i.e. without a coat or jacket, because such an appearance generally was considered gauche by Victorian era officers. SI

ing the sealed patterns on hand there to be loaned to the quartermaster general's office, where they could be examined as the basis for drafting detailed descriptions.[190]

Once Rodgers had the items in hand, he set himself to work. In the process he pointed out that the officer's dress cap's body was too lightweight, "and the cloth covering" was not properly applied in that "the seam joining the crown and sides should be under the gold braid." Rodgers provided samples of what he deemed more proper, one from Horstmann and one from Bent & Bush. He considered the latter specimen "the most acceptable for a standard—the plume excepted, which is too large." The captain preferred "a medium between" the Bent & Busch cock feathers and the plume on the quartermaster standard.[191]

Rodgers also addressed the helmet worn by officers, and provided a sketch with its measurements "for about a size 3" in order to "give a better idea of the shape than the written description." He used the illustration to underscore the point that:

> the helmets first made by Bent & Bush were of a different shape from the standard, although it was the intention to follow it as closely as possible form the description [meaning the original written specification]. The shell of the standard helmet for officers is not sufficiently *stiff*, and the proportion of gum shellac used in making [it] should be increased so as to give the helmet sufficient body or stiffness to bear the weight of its ornaments and trimmings.

As for those trimmings, Captain Rodgers again detailed what the well turned out officer should have as follows:

> *Eagle:*—Of yellow metal, gilt; pattern same as in coat of arms of the United States, with national shield on breast; head surmounted by scroll with motto "E Pluribus Unum" in relief letters. Scroll extending downwards and outwards and joining olive branch and arrows in talons of eagle. Whole height, 4 1/2 inches; greatest width, between tips of wings, 4 inches. Secured to helmet by wire stems.
> *Top piece and plume-socket:*—Of yellow metal, gilt. Base or foot a cross piece made convex to fit the top of helmet; ends of arms mitre shaped and fastened to helmet by ornamental buttons. Length between points of opposite arms, 5 1/4 inches. Arms at widest part 1 1/4 inches. Edges grooved and beveled. Sphere one inch in diameter, on base, surmounted by short neck with ring, (neck 1/2 inch, ring 5/8 inch diameter) from which is raised an inverted conical tube representing rays and displaying on front an heraldic eagle the head of which is surmounted by a star, in relief. Diameter of tube at top one inch; height, (including sphere at bottom) three inches. The plume held in position at top of socket by a brass pin 4 3/4 inches long having ornamental head, and a small brass disc. This pin enters through the socket top piece, the shell of helmet and concave

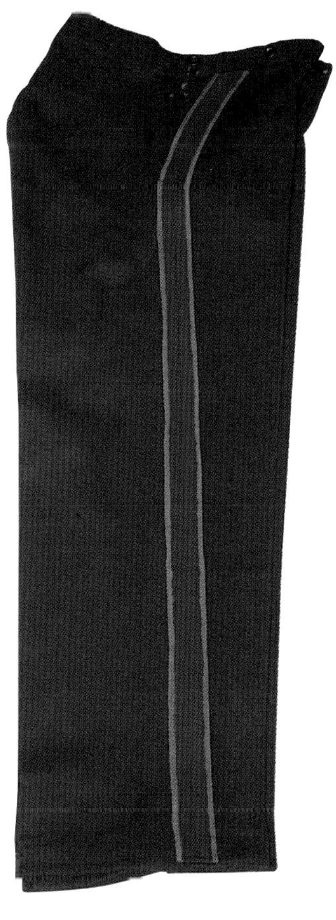

Uniform regulations in 1872 singled out trousers for Engineer Corps enlisted men, stating that they would be based upon a pattern in the Quartermaster General's Office (a phrase repeated in the 1882 regulations). It is possible that these trousers were the same sky-blue kersey as for other enlisted men, but that the leg stripes for non-commissioned officers were of worsted scarlet edged in white tape as revealed by a pair in the National Museum of American History's military collections. This observation is supposition, however. SI

Inexplicably, another pair of 1872-pattern trousers in the Museum of American History collection has double 1/2 inch yellow stripes affixed, which in 1883 were approved for all musicians. Prior to this time, some trumpeters had taken it upon themselves to add such adornment to their trousers, and it is possible the Quartermaster Department had this pair made up as a preliminary to official sanction of the practice. Note the reinforcing material on the seat, which was applied of matching fabric all the way down to the cuffs on the garment. Also evident are two of the buttons on the inside of the cuff, four of these fasteners being sewn stoutly in place on each cuff interior so that straps could be attached and worn under the instep to keep the legs from riding up on horse soldiers. SI

The sky-blue kersey foot trousers of the 1861 through 1876 period illustrated in an official image from the Quartermaster Department. USAQM

brass disc (1 7/8 inches in diameter) on the inside and is secured by a brass thumb nut.

Scrolls and rings: Of yellow metal, gilt, placed at sides near top, between the arms of the top piece. The scroll (or button) is ornamented to correspond with the fastenings of top piece and is 3/4 of an inch in diameter; small eye and ring (1/2 inch in diameter) in centre to hold cords and bands; stem to enter shell of helmet and fasten on the inside.

Leather straps attached to four buttons sewn inside each cuff could be made or obtained by individuals to hold their trousers in place–a feature that had particular application to mounted troops. This example was worn with a pair of dark blue trousers by a Quartermaster Department officer. EB

Side Buttons: (worn on each side just above the lower edge of Helmet). Of yellow metal, gilt, 7/8 of an inch in diameter, according to arm of service; edges beveled and grooved, surface slightly convex and chased; secured to helmet as scrolls are. Designs for Cavalry and Signal Service crossed sabers; for Light Artillery crossed cannons.

Hair Plumes:—Of good horse hair, dyed, to droop over back and sides of Helmet; woven and sewed together at one end and fastened to brass eyelet [here he made a sketch to illustrate his meaning] for socket piece. Length of plume 14 inches [13 was penciled above lightly] Colors: light yellow for cavalry, orange for Signals Corps and scarlet for Lt. artillery.

Cords and bands:—Of gold-thread cord. 2 1/2 lines; the bands loop plaited and fastened to rings and scrolls at sides and festooned on front and back of helmet. The front festoon falls to the upper edge of visor and the rear one to a corresponding depth behind. The loop plaiting is about one [3/4 written above, which was the specification actually adopted] inch wide. At left ring and scroll a pendant tassel of sixty or seventy fringes where the cords are fastened. Gilt cords about 5 feet 8 inches long with two netted slides of about 3/4 inch diameter; aiguillette (2 3/4 in. diameter) and tassels at each end of cord.[192]

While some minor rewording appeared in the final version, one item that would be left out of the published specification was the mention of the Signal Service.[193] In its immediate post-Civil War configuration, only the chief of the signal corps' uniform was mentioned, although the 1872 regulations did indicate the use of knots for full dress with Old English "SS" embroidered on them, but nothing else was said about officers in this organization, who in the beginning were detailed from other branches for a period of time, rather than being assigned to the arm on a permanent basis.[194] Thus, Rodgers was preemptive in his including a helmet for the dress uniform of these signal subalterns.

Although premature in this instance, Rodgers' descriptions contained some details that would be overcome by events. Most notably he went to considerable lengths when it came to the 1872-pattern campaign hat, an article that was soon destined to be discontinued. Nonetheless, his comments were useful in explaining the appearance of this short-lived piece of headwear. He recorded:

> The crown of the fatigue hat is more lens shaped so as to fold with crease in centre lengthway of the hat. His brim turns up at each side and is hooked at the outer edges in front and rear of body of hat, thus giving the outline a sweep nearly semi-circular from extreme front to extreme point of rear. The brim is flat and is 4 1/2 inches wide—outer edges slightly concave where the hook and eyes are sewed.[195]

He ended with a mention that the band was 1 1/4 inches wide. Rodgers also included three sketches showing the hat folded, unfolded, and from the underside.

Rodgers likewise treated another item that was destined for replacement, in that he provided a drawing of the gold embroidered bugle for

Above: Civil War surplus 1851-pattern sky blue kersey foot soldier's overcoats were modified in 1873 by adding a second longer cape, then issued to enlisted men for several years thereafter. SI

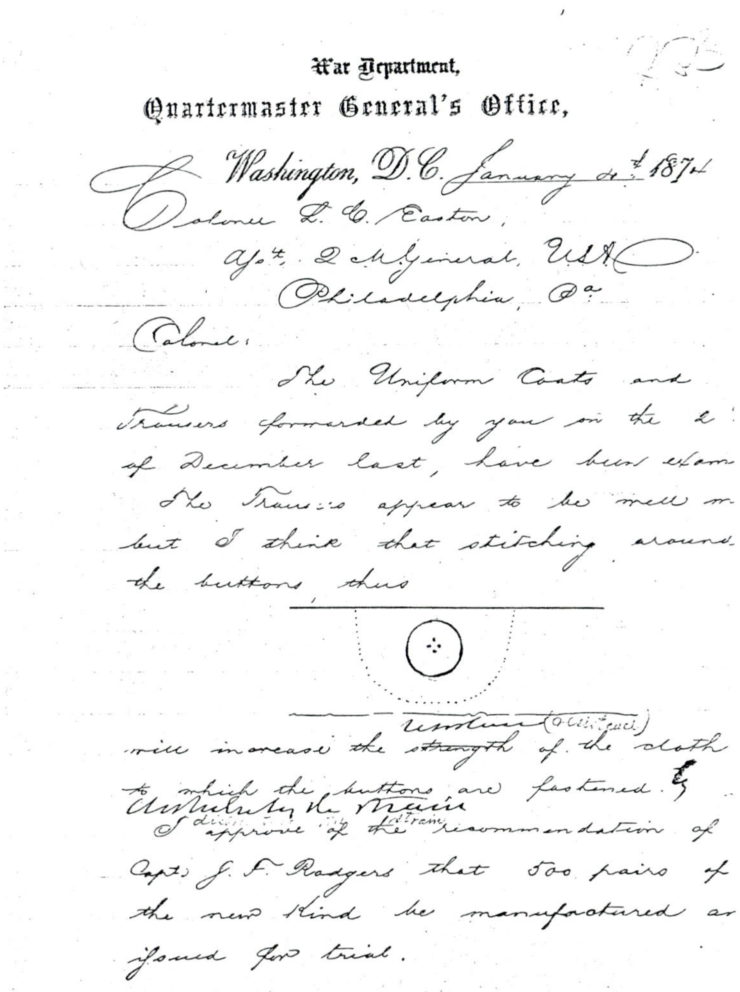

War Department,
Quartermaster General's Office,
Washington, D.C. January 2d 1874
Colonel L. C. Easton,
Asst. Q. M. General, USA
Philadelphia, Pa.
Colonel:
The Uniform Coats and Trousers forwarded by you on the 2 of December last, have been exam[ined]. The Trousers appear to be well m[ade] but I think that stitching around the buttons, thus
[sketch]
semicircle
will increase the strength of the cloth to which the buttons are fastened. & I approve of the recommendation of Capt. J. F. Rodgers that 500 pairs of the new kind be manufactured and issued for trial.

In 1874 Quartermaster General Meigs called for the buttons on the waistband and fly to be reinforced by extra stitching in the form of a semicircle. This was but one example of the level of detail he oversaw relative to the manufacture of military clothing. NA

Sky blue enlisted trousers of the 1872-1876 period for privates and musicians who wore no stripes; only corporals and various ranks of sergeants had leg stripes along the outer seams. SI

Front, side, and rear view of the double-breasted 1851-pattern mounted overcoat. These were in short supply after the Civil War, but existing stocks were issued to troops for several years, and almost the same design was revived in 1876, using kersey conforming to the specifications adopted in 1874. By 1878 they began to be provided to the enlisted men. Both the 1851 and 1876-pattern greatcoats had long unlined capes, were double-breasted with five 1854-pattern enlisted brass buttons in each row, and had double thickness of material at the ends of the sleeves, which rose to form a cuff approximately 5 inches in depth. The 1876 version also had sleeves with a slightly enlarged circumference to facilitate layering them over other garments. TC

infantry officers' forage and dress caps, which had been changed in 1875 to the now well known crossed rifles device. He also provided a picture of the artillery crossed cannons for officers in gold embroidery, which indicated how the regimental number was worked into the circle where the two guns bisected. Additionally, he jotted a few words about the device that was placed above these insignia on the dress cap, outlining its appearance as: "gold embroidered eagle with shield on breast, surmounted by thirteen stars—size as follows from top of stars to end of tail 1 3/8 inches, width from tip of wings 1 1/2 inches; tips of wings joined by arc of rays."[196]

Additionally, Rodgers strongly urged:

> In publishing an order descriptive of officers' uniforms strict compliance with its terms should be required and commanding officers and inspectors general directed to see that the uniforms worn conform accurately to the description, otherwise the individual tastes and caprices of officers will continue when indulged and uniformity can never be secured."[197]

Although Rodgers' goal of "strict compliance" was never achieved entirely, his efforts to define the officers' kit did bear fruit, ultimately being released, albeit in an edited form, along with colored lithographs (originally prepared for a limited edition quartermaster publication, then reprinted in the *Annual Report of the Secretary of War* for 1876). Indeed, Rodgers' efforts were included in this publication in response to

The 1876-pattern overcoat was the old style mounted overcoat, but issued to all troops, and made of the new 1874 specification of kersey. USAQM

According to the 1872 regulations: "On the frontier and campaign, officers may wear the soldier's overcoat, with insignia of rank on the sleeve." The Seventh Cavalry's Captain Frederick Benteen elected to follow this course, but added what appears to be a bear fur collar to the standard mounted coat. GS

Because the color of infantry chevrons was so close to that of the sky-blue kersey for overcoats, they virtually were invisible when worn on these cold weather garments. Consequently, new dark blue chevrons with white silk chain stitching were adopted for infantry non-commissioned officers in accordance with General Orders No. 21, War Department, March 29, 1876. The inserts for first sergeants and principal musicians were to be white, although this specimen for a first sergeant employs the logenze in sky-blue of the type worn with the coat chevron. It may be an unadopted prototype or a custom made insignia. General Orders No. 21 also was the first official reference to chevrons being worn on blouses. Prior to this directive, non-commissioned officers regularly did so, but without authorization by the army. JG

the 1875 board's wishes to do so in order to address the complaints of "the want of uniformity in the uniform of officers of the Army."[198]

One description not found in Rodgers' preliminary work, but contained in the published version was a description of the officers' dress cap that was spelled out as:

> ...felt shell, covered with indigo-blue cloth; 3 1/2 inch high in front; 4 1/2 high on sides; 6 1/2 inches high over the swell of the back; crown 5 1/2 inches long by 5 inches wide; revolving ventilator in crown; gold-wire braid 1/8 of an inch wide around the lower edge and around the crown at top also, from top to bottom, at each side and back; patent leather vizor unbound; patent leather chin-strap 1/2 of an inch wide with gilt slide; gilt side or chin strap buttons, vest size, according to arm of service [I for infantry and A for artillery in center of shield, respectively]; japanned or goatskin sweat-leather, silk lining; plume-socket of leather on inside at front with metallic guard at opening at top and front edge of crown; gold-embroidered eagle with shield on breast, surmounted by thirteen stars in silver; length from top of stars to end of tail, 1 3/8 inches; width from tip to tip of wings, 1 1/2 inches; tips of wings joined by an arc of rays; embroidered badge of arm or corps in front [crossed rifles of gold

Another Seventh Cavalry officer, Captain Thomas Weir, likewise has adapted an enlisted overcoat, but has removed the cape and added black astrakhan for increased warmth. GS

for infantry and gold embroidered crossed cannons for artillery]; bottom of badge to be even with top of chin strap.[199]

Rodgers made some other comments, as well, one being that he felt the cuffs of officers' coats should measure 3 1/2 inches rather than 3 inches. He also preferred 1/2 inch gold lace that would be "raised and stuffed" similar to some European armies and American militia uniform trim, rather than the flat 1/4 inch lace that had been called for in regulations. These he thought should be "3 1/2 inches long instead of 3 inches as at present."[200] Although the change was approved, it seems that the requirement to have the lace "stuffed and raised so as to be 1/8 inch wide when finished" was ignored by most if not by all officers.[201] In part, this action officially recognized the departure from regulations by some officers of the early 1870s who elected to have wider ornamentation applied to their dress coats.[202]

Rodgers further felt the braid allowed for the overcoats of general officers, as edging was an excellent idea for all officers, rather than the stitching called for in quartermaster instructions. The captain declared both officers and tailors saw the merit of such braid in helping to keep the edges from fraying. He thought a 1/2 inch wide braid sewn flat "around the front and bottom edges of" the coat, cape, and collar was desirable.[203] On this topic he eventually was overruled.

Finally, he expressed the view that "exact shades of cloths for coats and trowsers should be established by sample." This was particularly desirable for the material worn by line officers, as there was a likelihood of tailors using a "variety of shades of sky-blue."[204]

For the most part, Rodgers' enumeration of officers' wear received widespread distribution in the form of the *Annual Report of the Secretary of War* for 1876 (see Appendix B for a reprint). Relative to this matter, in that same year the Quartermaster Department began a practice aimed at clearing up ambiguities in the manufacture of uniform components. The means to this end was the publication of uniform specifications, beginning on May 31, 1876. From that time, and over the next three years, these specifications "simply were identified by title and date." Then, in 1879, they were also numbered in the sequence in which they were adopted, a convention that continued until February 1914.[205]

Among the many specification that were to be published in 1876 were those for facing material to trim dress coats, and from which chevrons were produced, as well as trousers' stripes, as of May 31:

> To be made six-quarter (6/40 of a yard wide, of beat American fleece-wool, free from shoddy, flocks, or other impurities; twilled; all wool, dyed in the following colors, viz: sky-blue; dark-blue; scarlet, yellow, crimson, orange, gray, emerald-green, and white.
> To contain sixty-four (64) threads in the chain, sixty (60) threads in the filling to the square inch, and to weigh sixteen (16) ounces to the linear yard.

Similarly, chevrons made from this facing material were delineated on May 26, 1876 as Specification No. 12 to indicate rank for all non-commissioned officers irrespective of the arm of service. These were to:

> be made of cloths the color of the facings on their respective uniform coats (except that those for great coats be of dark-blue for

So, too, has Brigadier General George Crook converted an enlisted kersey overcoat by adding a fur collar for wear on campaign in 1876. The blanket he leans on the standard gray 1873-pattern blanket with the letters U.S. worked into the center with heavy dark blue thread. USAMHI

Left: Officers also had a dark blue overcoat with detachable cape, which in general outline resembled that worn by the enlisted men. Colonel Nelson Miles has altered his coat by adding a thin strand of fur. He also has procured a fur cap for winter campaigning. GS

Infantry.) The bars to be divided by a heavy stitching of No. 8 silk, and the upper and lower edges to be finished or bound with similar stitching,

White silk stitching for Engineers and for great coats Infantry; black for all others.

The arms of the chevrons bars to be six (6) to seven (7) inches long, to be the arcs of a circle of about twenty-five (25) inches radius, and to meet at angle of about ninety-six (96) degrees. Distance between extreme outer ends about nine (9) inches.

One chevron to be worn on each sleeve of the uniform coat and great coat, above the elbow, the point downward.

Designs for Chevrons.—For a Sergeant Major, three (3) bars and an arc of three bars.

For a Quartermaster Sergeant, three (3) bars and a tie of three (3) bars.

For a Principal Musician, three (3) bars and a bugle of the pattern worn on caps.

Front view of an 1872-pattern overcoat worn by officers below the grade of brigadier general, with or without the detachable cape worn. This specimen is attributed to Colonel Nelson A. Miles. Photograph by Glen Swanson. WC

Rear view of an 1872-pattern officer's overcoat. The placement of the buttons was the same as for the officer's dress coat. Buttons were also of the same type as worn by the officers on their dress coats, depending on their arm of service or corps. Photograph by Glen Swanson. WC

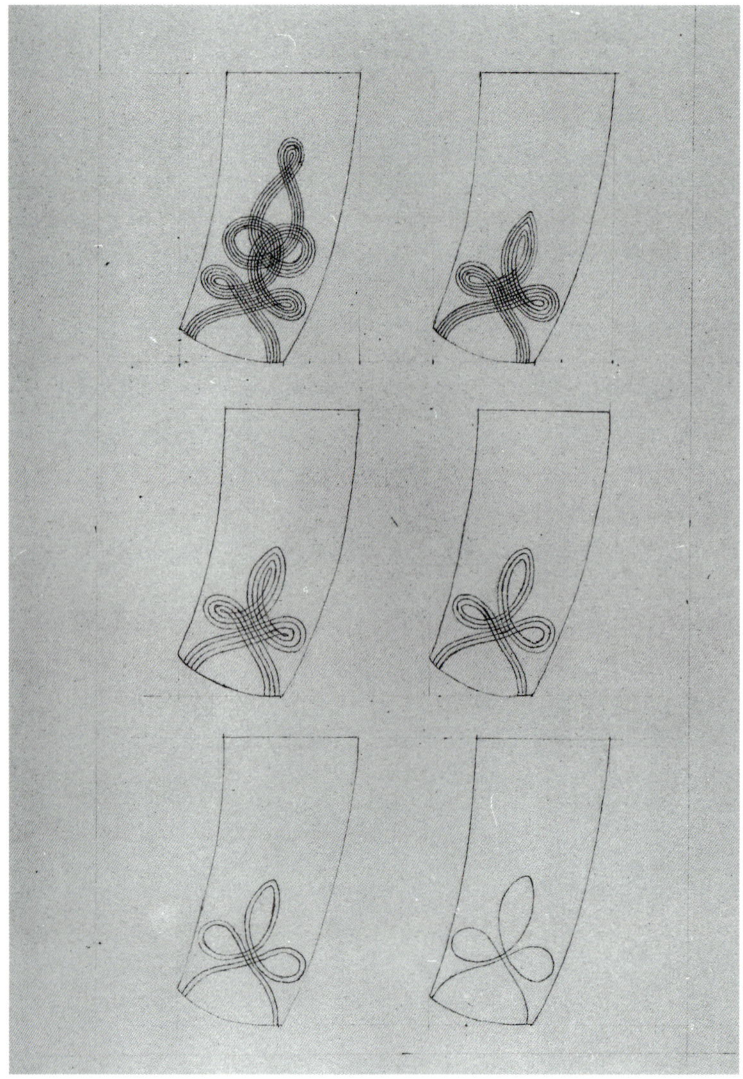

Rank on officers' overcoats was displayed by flat black silk braid in five rows ending in a double knot for generals, five strands for colonels, four strands for lieutenant colonels, three strands for majors, two strands for captains, one strand for first lieutenants, and plain for second lieutenants. NA

For an Ordnance Sergeant, three (3) bars and an outlined star.
For a Commissary Sergeant, three bars and a crescent.
For a Hospital Steward, a half-chevron of emerald green cloth, one and three-fourths (1 3/4) inch wide, piped with yellow cloth, running obliquely downward from the outer to inner seam of the sleeve, and at an angle of about thirty (30) degrees to the horizontal, and in the center a 'Caduceus' two (2) inches long, the head of toward the outer seam on the sleeve.
For a First Sergeant, three (3) bars and a lozenge, white lozenge for Engineers.
For a Battalion or Company Quartermaster Sergeant, three (3) bars and a tie of one (1) bar.
For a Sergeant, three (3) bars.
For a corporal, two (2) bars.
*For a Saddler Sergeant, three (3) bars and a saddler's broad knife, handle upward. Knife of the following dimensions: Handle one and three-quarters (1 3/4) inch long, three-quarters (3/4) inch wide near top, five-eighths (5/8) inch near blade; blade one and one-eighth (1 1/8) inch deep in center; from point to point of blade, three and one-quarter (3 1/4) inches; center of edge one and one-quarter (1 1/4) inch above lower angle of chevron.
*For a Pioneer, two crossed hatchets of cloth, same color and material as the facings on the uniform coat, to be sewed to the sleeve above the elbow, in the place indicated for a chevron, (those for a Corporal to be just above and resting on the chevron.) the head of the hatchet upward, its edge outward, and to be of the following dimensions, viz: Handle, four and one-half (4 1/2) inches long, one-quarter (1/4) to one-third (1/3) of an inch wide; hatchet two (2) inches long, on (1) inch wide at edge.
*For a Farrier, horseshoe, same color and material as the facings on the uniform coat, with toe piece one and three-quarters (1 3/4) inch long, one-half (1/2) inch deep, and two heel pieces one-half (1/2) by three-quarters 3/4) inch each of *gray* cloth. Four (4) nail holes, showing the underlying blue coat-cloth, on each side of the shoe, at equal distances from each other. To be worn above the elbow, heels pointing downward. Dimensions of horseshoe: three-quarters (3/4) of an inch wide, four and one-half (4 1/2) inches long from outer edge of the toe piece to a line between extreme points of heels; between outer lines across center, three and three-quarter (3 3/4) inches; between extreme points of heels, two (2) inches.
To indicate service, a diagonal half chevron one-half (1/2) inch wide, extending from seam to seam, the front end nearest the cuff, one and one-half (1 1/2) inch above the cuff; to be the same color as the facings, except for Engineers, which shall be white. Service in war will be indicated by a white stripe on each side of the chevron, for Artillery, and a red stripes for all other corps. The stripe to be one-

Nelson Miles' sleeve braid of five strands as the colonel of the Fifth U.S. Infantry. Photograph by Glen Swanson. WC

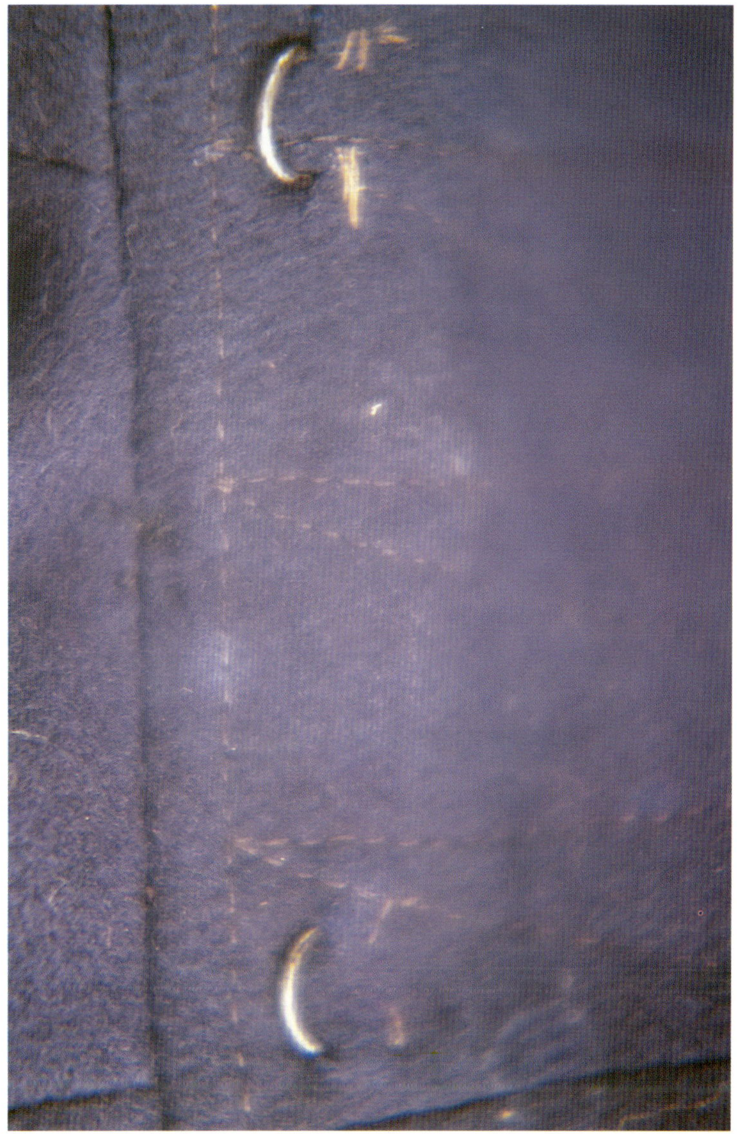

Black japanned eyelets cold be fastened with corresponding hooks on the lower front panel of the 1872-pattern officer's overcoat to keep the garment's skirts from blowing in windy weather. GS

In this January 1877 field photograph all the officers pictured, save Colonel Miles, who stands in the center in his 1872-pattern officer's overcoat, have obtained heavy fur garments as they face the twenty below zero cold of Cantonment Tongue River in today's Montana. All appear to wear various types of fur headgear. NA

One of Nelson Miles' fur field caps. WC

eighth (1/8) of an inch wide. Distance between each service chevron one-quarter (1/4) of an inch.

In great coat chevrons, Infantry, for First Sergeant, Principal Musician, and Pioneer, the center design as described above shall be of white cloth.

Signal Service device, two (2) embroidered signal flags crossed, each three-quarters (3/4) of an inch square, bearing in the center a square one-quarter (1/4) of an inch. One flag white with red inner square, the other red with white inner square. Flags and square bullion edged; staff three inches long, with silver spears, made upon a piece of dark blue coat-cloth three (3) inches square, with the corners rounded off. To be worn by non-commissioned officer above the chevrons, by privates of the first class on both sleeves above the elbow, and by privates of the second class on the left sleeve only.

In 1877 the U.S. Army at last bought a quantity of buffalo overcoats for the use of troops in extreme cold climates. These would be handed out to the men during the winter season, then returned to the local quartermaster for cleaning and storage once the weather improved. While the forage cap could be worn with the coat, it usually was combined with headgear made of fur. JG

A member of the Twenty-fifth U.S. Infantry in a buffalo coat. No standard pattern was adopted, but examples tended to resemble the basic garment seen here. HP

In 1876 the Quartermaster Department let a contract for sealskin caps and gauntlets. Two years later, muskrat versions, as seen here, were obtained instead, this fur being considered more impervious to damaging moisture. JG

NOTE—Chevrons marked (*) require to be made on groundwork of dark-blue cloth.

While relatively detailed, the specifications left out chief trumpeters, nor were they clear on which way the crescent was to be oriented on the commissary sergeant chevron. Also, it was not noted whether the signal devices were mirror images, and if so was the red flag or the white flag to be worn toward the front of the sleeve? What is more, while company or battalion quartermaster sergeants were provided for in this outline, the actual presence of these men in a unit probably never materialized, and the appointment of pioneers also was limited.[206]

Conversely, a more thorough description of the metallic insignia for uniform coats, caps, and helmets was released on May 31, 1876. Coat ornaments were of particular note.[207] According to Quartermaster Specification No. 8 these were to be of No. 28 stamped sheet brass. Those for infantry, cavalry, and artillery troops were to have beveled edges and measure 1/2 inch long (as opposed to 5/8 inch for cap numerals). A pair of brass wires were soldered to the back of the numbers so that they could be attached to the collar.

For engineers a castle with three towers was called for. The height of the battlements were to measure 3/8 inch, 1/2 inch for the center tower, and 5/8 inch heights for the side towers. The breadth at the top and base was to be 1 inch. Once again these were to fasten to the coat collar by means of two small wires soldered to the back of the castle.

A 1/2 inch diameter shell with a 1/2 inch flame above, the greatest width of the latter being near the base where it met the shell being 3/4 inch was the design for ordnance enlisted personnel. Two wires were provided on the rear for attachment to the collar.

Finally, for commissary sergeants the only non-brass insignia was mentioned. This was to be a 1 inch crescent of white metal, with the height of the arc measuring 9/16 inch and the center measuring 1/4 inch. Although not stated, these were to be worn with their points upward.

Another missing reference was to collar insignia for signal corpsmen and hospital stewards. Regulations and specifications never mentioned any collar device for the 1872-pattern dress coat of the former group, while the latter medical enlisted men would not be told that they would wear collar ornaments until 1882.

But these were only some of the minor kinks that had to be worked out in bringing the 1872 regulation uniform to fruition. Even as the Quartermaster Department dealt with such matters, one article, regardless of how close it came to the standards set for it, was seen as without merit. This was the rain cover for the forage cap.

Another official recognition of the need for foul weather gear came with the adoption of buffalo overshoes. A low-topped style was tried shortly after the Civil War (top), but was replaced by the 1873-pattern with a higher top (bottom) that rose above the ankle, thereby offering additional protection from the cold. USAQM

A more advanced design came about with the issue of canvas and rubber 1876-pattern arctic overshoes. USAQM

Civil War style brogans remained in vogue (top) for several years as footwear for dismounted troops. A new boot design was adopted for mounted troops (bottom) in 1872, which featured brass screwed soles that were made on lasts conforming more closely to the shape of the foot than the previous model. USAQM

New shoes also were produced beginning in 1872 (top) with patented brass screws to affix the soles to the uppers. The boot of the 1860s era (bottom) with sewn soles would be issued until supplies were exhausted, then replaced by the screwed sole model. USAQM

An officer in Texas put it this way:

In obedience to circular letter H:120 S. from your office, I have the honor to report that in my opinion, it would be very conducive to the comfort of the men and economical to the government to issue cotton trousers instead of Cap Covers, to enlisted men where the mercury in the sun rises to 165 F. (Solar heat.)[208] The departmental commander in Texas, Brigadier General E.O.C. Ord indicated that this opinion was not the only one in support of white trousers rather than the cap covers, but he was informed that "an arsenal supply of cotton trousers would cost ten times as much as cap covers."[209]

Veteran western campaigner Brigadier General George Crook likewise thought cap covers could be discarded.[210] The Quartermaster Department also realized the marginal worth of the accessory, as well, and would drop it from the inventory in 1877.[211]

Crook's preferences for protection against the elements ran to more practical solutions, as his aide, Captain John Bourke, recounted during

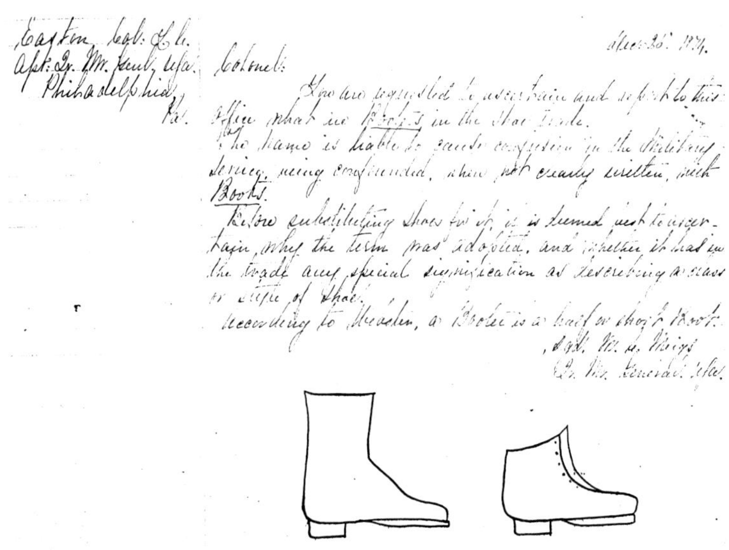

Easton, Col: L. C.
Asst: Qr. Mr. Genl, USA.
Philadelphia,
Pa.

Dec: 26. 1874.

Colonel:

You are requested to ascertain and report to this Office what is Bootees in the Shoe Trade.

The name is liable to cause confusion in the Military Service, being confounded, when not clearly written, with Boots.

Before substituting shoes for it, it is deemed right to ascertain, why the term was adopted, and whether it has in the trade any special signification as describing a class or style of shoe.

According to Webster, a Bootee is a half or short Boot.

Sgd. M. C. Meigs
Qr. Mr. General, USA.

As part of efforts to arrive at suitable footgear in the 1870s, it is questionable what the difference in terminology was concerning shoes and bootees, as evidenced by this original letter from 1874 with accompanying sketches. NA

An 1874-pattern gray flannel (actually brown and blue thread mixture) shirt and 1875-pattern drawers. The shoes are of the 1872-pattern. USAQM

Front, back, and detail of the neck lining of an 1874-pattern flannel shirt, in this case one produced at the Jeffersonville Depot in Indiana during fiscal year 1875-1876, in size 2, as indicated by the stamping. SI

the summer campaign of 1876, when a large field force headed into the Northern Plains to drive those Indians on to reservations who had elected to remain free and follow their traditional nomadic ways.[212] On this foray the general wore: "boots of Government pattern, number 7; trousers of brown corduroy, badly burned at both ends; shirt of brown, heavy woollen; blouse of the old army style; hat, a brown kossuth of felt, ventilated at the top."[213]

Another officer with George Crook, Charles King, contrasted that officer with the other general on the 1876 campaign, Alfred H. Terry, in a passage that epitomized the two extremes when it came to campaign wear:

> General Terry, as became a brigadier, was attired in the handsome uniform of his rank; his staff and his line officers...were all in neat regimentals, so that shoulder straps were to be seen in every direction. General Crook, as became an old campaigner and frontiersman, was in rough hunting rig, and in all his staff and line there was not a complete suit of uniform.[214]

Thus Crook was not the only one to adopt mufti, as indicated by King's description of his own garb in 1876. Speaking of himself in third person, King related:

> ...the Mexican spurs on the heels of that officer instantly click together as he stands to attention to his chief. A motley garb is that of the same staff official; a dark blue shirt like that of his senior, a belt supporting a revolver and hunting knife; buckskin breeches, heavily beaded and fringed, thrust into legs of cavalry boots, the feet whereof have long since been worn away and are now replaced by Indian moccasins.[215]

Although King's self-portrait appeared in one of the numerous novels he wrote after a medical retirement from the military in 1879, this was no flight of fancy. In fact, King posed for a candid photograph in 1876 with his company commander in the outfit he verbally depicted, complete with "garish buckskin pants."[216]

Nor was King alone in his departure from regulations when it came to the field uniform. Many officers elected to obtain civilian articles of clothing, with bibbed-front shirts both plain or adorned in some manner often being favored. Buckskin trousers or the prescribed sky-blue wool with additional reinforcing of canvas in the inseams also were not uncommon among those who held commissions.[217]

In turn, the rank and file in Crook's column mostly wore a conglomerate of old and new issue items. There were four-button sack coats from the Civil War, old cavalry "shell" jackets, and the 1858-pattern enlisted frock coat, the last two items of surplus often being modified from the way the soldier received them.[218] Even the unpopular pleated

Two privates of the Seventh U.S. Cavalry, Timothy Donnelly (right) and George Walker (left), wear 1872-pattern enlisted forage caps sans insignia, and kersey trousers, while Donnelly has on an 1874-pattern shirt with a square cut, rather than pointed cut construction at the end of the slit where it pulls over the head. He also has added a civilian belt to in order to support his trousers. There were no belt loops on trousers, however, until late in the nineteenth century, and then only on khaki garments. GS

blouse might be pressed into service by "wise soldiers wearing out old clothing rather than current issue," while a few men, among whom perhaps several were recruits who had no outdated or worn clothing to take to the field, possibly opted for the 1874-pattern blouse.

Again King recorded this propensity, making note of "the contrast between the appearance of the new-comers and that of the score of soldiers who have been through campaigns...." King continued: "Among the latter hardly a vestige of regulation uniform is to be seen."[219] John Finerty, a newspaper correspondent with the expedition, phrased it more simply: "On an Indian campaign little attention is paid to uniform."[220]

As for headgear, enlisted personnel availed themselves of everything from Civil War "bummer's" caps, 1872-pattern forage caps, an occasional regulation folding hat, but more likely than not an array of privately purchased slouch hats in black, brown, drab, white, and whatever hue might be on hand for those with the cash, including straw renditions. Some men attempted to maintain a certain martial appearance when they opted for civilian headgear by adding hat cords for a bit of color, or more than likely to help "preserve a hat's size...."[221]

The 1874-pattern flannel shirt, in this instance tucked into the overalls prescribed for mounted enlisted men for stable duty from 1872 through much of the remainder of the nineteenth century. USAQM

Another pair of Seventh Cavalry troopers, First Sergeant John Ryan (standing) and Sergeant William Capes (seated), wear the issue kersey trousers with 1 inch yellow leg stripes to indicate their status as sergeants, but neither of the men have on the issue shirt. In fact, Capes has elected to buy a civilian "miner's," or fireman's style shirt, so-called because of their fairly widespread use by individuals in these occupations. He has added crossed embroidered sabers to the collar and edging around the collar and bib front, much as some officers in the regiment did. Ryan's 1872-pattern forage cap bears the old large style stamped sheet brass crossed sabers originally intended for the 1858-pattern hat. Above these is either the company letter or perhaps the regimental number. GM

The white stable frock was worn with overalls for mounted troops as they groomed their horse, cleaned stalls, and the like, in order to preserve their wool uniforms from soiling during such tasks. The same basic design had been in use since before the Civil War, and remained relatively unchanged for decades. USAQM

The 1872 regulations also provided for engineer enlisted men to have overalls of white cotton, which covered the entire body from neck to ankles as a fatigue outfit. USAQM

Sometimes even sleeve garters were procured, or leather thongs used to keep the rather voluminous kersey trousers gathered near the ankle. Some infantrymen even "adopted the practice of tucking their trouser bottoms into their socks" in the era before leggings had been issued.[222]

But others besides Crook's followers took to the field that fateful summer of 1876, most notably the Seventh Cavalry under Lieutenant Colonel George Armstrong Custer. Once again, officers tended to eschew all or part of the regulation outfit, Custer being dressed in a "buckskin coat and breeches and black slouch hat" according to First Lieutenant Charles A. Varnum, an officer in the regiment who survived the Little Bighorn battle.[223] A first sergeant with Company M of the Seventh, John Ryan, echoed Varnum, and further stated Custer wore high top cavalry boots, while his brother Thomas Ward Custer was dressed similarly with a broad brimmed hat, buckskin jacket, and trousers.[224]

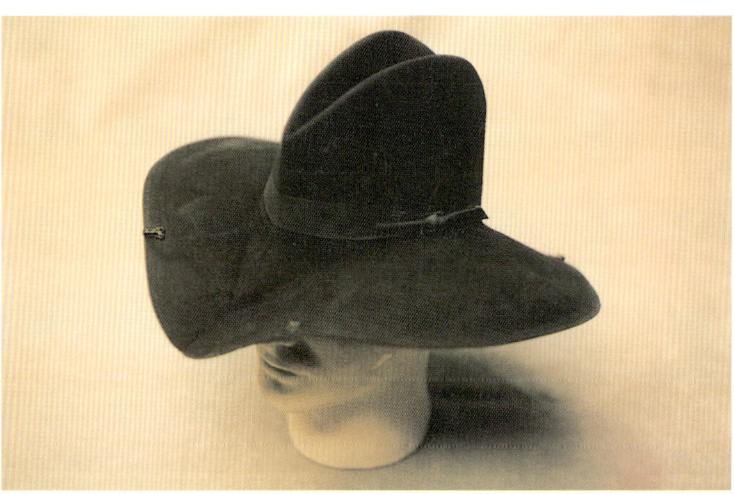

A black folding campaign hat was all the rage for enlisted men, or so it was believed when higher authorities prescribed it in 1872. Black japanned hooks and eyes kept the brim in position like a chapeau, or could be loosened to allow the brim to be worn down as protection, in theory at least, against the elements. GS

Civil War surplus hat cords could be added to the 1872-pattern and subsequent campaign hats. They were scarlet for artillery, blue for infantry, yellow for cavalry, and intermixed buff and green for hospital stewards. JG

First Lieutenant Edward Godfrey, another officer of the Seventh who was spared, concurred with Ryan, but added details about others who preferred garments made from hides. He recorded Captain George Yates, along with First Lieutenants James Calhoun, Algernon Smith, James Porter, and W.W. Cooke (the regimental adjutant) took a page from their lieutenant colonel's book and wore buckskin jackets, as Captain Myles Keogh sometimes did.[225] Godfrey underscored, however, that none of these men had on buckskin trousers. Instead, they all wore kersey trousers, presumably with the 1 1/2 inch yellow stripes down the outer seams that set them apart as officers. The one exception was Lieutenant Henry Harrington, who tugged on "white canvas trousers, with fringe on the outer seams." He combined this with the "blue blouse," presumably either the 1872-pattern or the newer 1875-pattern, although various types of dark blue civilian sack coats were not uncommon on the frontier at that time.[226] Indeed, Assistant Surgeon (equivalent to a captain) George Lord, along with Second Lieutenants James Sturgis and William Van W. Reily, "wore the blue."[227] Lieutenant Varnum went so far as to assert: "Officers and men wore the blue blouse as a general thing."[228] This last point was an important one, in that field uniforms frequently deviated from the regulation, unlike most European armies of the era.

That was not the case for Major Marcus Reno, who testified that he rode into battle in the regulation officer's blouse.[229] The major also stated that he was one of those who availed himself of the opportunity to buy a broad brimmed straw hat, which a trader at the mouth of the Rosebud offered for sale at "25 or 50 cents," these having "no band, but they were a very good shelter from the sun."[230] Perhaps Lieutenant Varnum acquired one of these hats, as well.[231] Certainly he "was in a soldier's blue shirt." Presumably this meant one of the 10,000 navy blue flannel ones produced in 1875. Years later, he did not recollect anyone wearing "fancy shirts".[232] This contrasted to some extent with Godfrey's statement that: "All of the officers wore the dark blue shirt with rather wide falling collar, which when the blouse was worn, was over the blouse collar; most of them had cross-sabers, and 7, like the old cap ornament, worked in white or yellow silk on the points of the collar."[233] Based on photographs depicting Seventh Cavalry officers in shirts adorned not only in this manner, but also with contrasting tape trim, Godfrey's declaration seemed to ring more true. George Custer had long favored such an article of clothing dating back to his early career, and some of his subordinates apparently followed his lead.[234] Moreover, the unofficial use of branch insignia on shirt collars presaged a similar practice that was authorized in army regulations early in the next century, albeit with metallic ornaments rather than those that were of thread worked into the shirt collar.

Returning to Varnum's memory, his statement was at odds with Godfrey's in yet another detail—the color of Custer's hat. While both agreed it had a broad brim, Godfrey distinctly remembered a rather low crown affair "very similar to the cowboy hat" that was of a "whitish gray".[235] Varnum contended it was black.[236]

Peter Thompson, a private with Company C agreed with Godfrey. He disclosed Custer was in a "cream colored hat..., the brim of which was turned up on the right side and fastened by a small hook and eye to its crown. This gave him opportunity to sight his rifle while riding."[237] Photographs show Custer wearing both dark and light hats, including one with an upturned brim on one side, therefore, it is difficult to tell which version is correct for the fateful day of the Little Bighorn engagement.[238]

One thing Varnum and Godfrey were in accord about, though, was the fact that some officers selected leggings rather than boots, either of canvas or buckskin.[239] This accessory was but one reflection of the "great latitude" Varnum indicated that was allowed to officers in the field. Headgear was another example of this, with Varnum pointing out: "Officers purchased their own and [they] were either brown or black, with black predominating. The shapes were irregular; some were rolled up on both sides, other just flat, and others turned the brim up in front giving a Napoleonic appearance."[240]

Interestingly enough, the 1872-pattern folding hat could be configured in all these ways, and was worn by officers and men alike, although Second Lieutenant Winfield Scott Edgerly tossed his aside at some point during the fighting, but could not remember what he put on in its place thereafter.[241]

Another leftover from the Civil War, the four-button enlisted sack coat continued to be issued well into the 1870s for field and garrison wear. USAQM

Front and rear views of the four-button sack coat, which became a mainstay after its adoption in the late 1850s. TC

Less data is available on the rank and file in the Seventh Cavalry. Lieutenant Godfrey professed: "Nearly all the men wore the blue, but many, perhaps most of them, had their trousers reinforced with white canvas on the seat and on the legs from the knees halfway up," thereby signifying the "saddlepieces" that were sewn to the issue mounted trousers evidently were not substantial enough to stand the wear and tear of campaigning, or foot trousers had been fortified for horseback service.[242] Lieutenant Varnum insisted "The men wore the garments issued by the Quartermaster, & were generally clothed alike." This included the short boots in vogue during the 1860s through 1870s, which "the men either stuffed their trousers into...or wore the trousers long, over the boots...." Antithetically, they did not ride with gauntlets, these items being neither issued at that time (despite the erroneous recollection by Varnum that they were), nor worn by those who might have bought civilian riding gloves of some sort. The lieutenant explained: "The day was very hot, and gloves of any sort were undoubtedly thrust into the saddle bags before the action. It is practically impossible to handle a carbine with gloves on."[243]

The lieutenant repeated, "There was little variation in dress amongst the men," and in this light he believed troopers "apparently...wore an issue campaign hat...." He did allow that regulations were not as strict in 1876 as they would be later. What is more, in the post-Civil War era there were numerous changes afoot, which meant "uniform matters were topsy-turvy."[244]

As a matter of fact, the men probably took similar courses of action to those who went with Crook, employing old enlisted nine-button frock coats, shell jackets, and pleated blouses, modifying them as they saw fit by removing trim or replacing stand collars with roll collars, and whatever other refurbishment they deemed expedient.[245] Indeed, enlisted participants in the campaign tended to demonstrate that they were not clones. As an example of individualism, Trooper George W. Glease (real name George W. Glenn) was on his third enlistment when he rode to the Little Bighorn. He related on the way up the Rosebud River he was shown "a white wool hat, with crossed sabers and a brass letter 'C'" belonging to an enlisted man who presumably had been killed. Glenn did not know

The infantryman at the right with fixed bayonet wears a four-button sack coat and "bummer's" cap of Civil War vintage, while the other infantryman in the center background has donned the new 1872-pattern enlisted forage cap and a nine-button pleated blouse, which was yet another 1872 innovation for enlisted men. NAC

to whom this unique piece of headgear belonged, but another man, Sergeant Daniel Kanipe of Company C, shed light on the mystery:

> [Nathan] Short wore a light hat with the cross sabers drawn on the front of it with the number '7' between the sabers....It was a common thing for the men to mark their equipment with their initials for identification. There were very few men from the company who marked their hats as Short did, but I recall very well that he had marked his in this manner. The soldiers all had their hats marked, but usually inside."[246]

Knipe further pointed out that each trooper was assigned a number for his gear, Short's being "50." When the body was found by scouts from Crook's column, the gear was marked with that number.[247]

Of course, Short was but one of 268 members of the Seventh Cavalry who perished on that campaign. After the unit's defeat at Little Bighorn, officials in Washington reacted quickly. Public sentiment ran high. The non-reservation Indians responsible for besting the command and its flamboyant commander had to be brought to bay. The military mobilized. "Custer Avengers" rode forth by the hundreds.

Meigs quickly realized the seasoned veterans and new recruits bound for the field would have to be supplied. One of his first responses related to this new set of circumstances came two months after the Little Bighorn disaster. He instructed the head of Jeffersonville Depot to send 142 shirts in size 2, and 27 lined blouses in size 4 to Ft. Abraham Lincoln—Custer's former headquarters. Meigs indicated the urgency in that he required that if no gray flannel shirts were available, dark blue flannel ones should be sent to the Department of Dakota. Meigs anticipated other requirements from Jeffersonville in the near future. Consequently, he closed his letter with instructions that production of 5,000 lined blouses should be carried out "of such sizes and for such arms of the service" that were likely "to be needed."

At the same time Meigs told his representatives at Philadelphia to furnish 180 campaign hats (folding pattern), as well as 13 forage caps, 27 lined infantry blouses, 250 pairs of trousers, 7 pairs of infantry corporals' chevrons, 302 pairs of shoes, 13 pairs of unmade trousers, and 40 pairs of gloves (size 11) to the same garrison.[248] This was just the tip of the iceberg, in that the quartermaster general revealed that clothing had been sent for 2,500 cavalry troopers to Ft. Lincoln and the Cheyenne Depot earlier in the month![249]

Compounding the challenge faced by Meigs' department, some of the troops heading for the field did so while cold temperatures faced them. Crook's troops, for instance, had set out during the winter of 1876,

As evident in this circa 1875 picture, John Briody, a corporal in Company F, Seventh U.S. Cavalry, has opted to convert the roll collar of an old style four-button sack by adding what seems to be a velvet covering. He also had a convenient exterior breast pocket tailored into the blouse. GS

The 1872-pattern pleated nine-button jacket proved unpopular due to the fact that it was difficult to keep neat and clean. It was also relatively expensive to produce. Piping on the collar, yoke, and cuffs indicated the wearer's branch, in this case light blue for infantry. SI

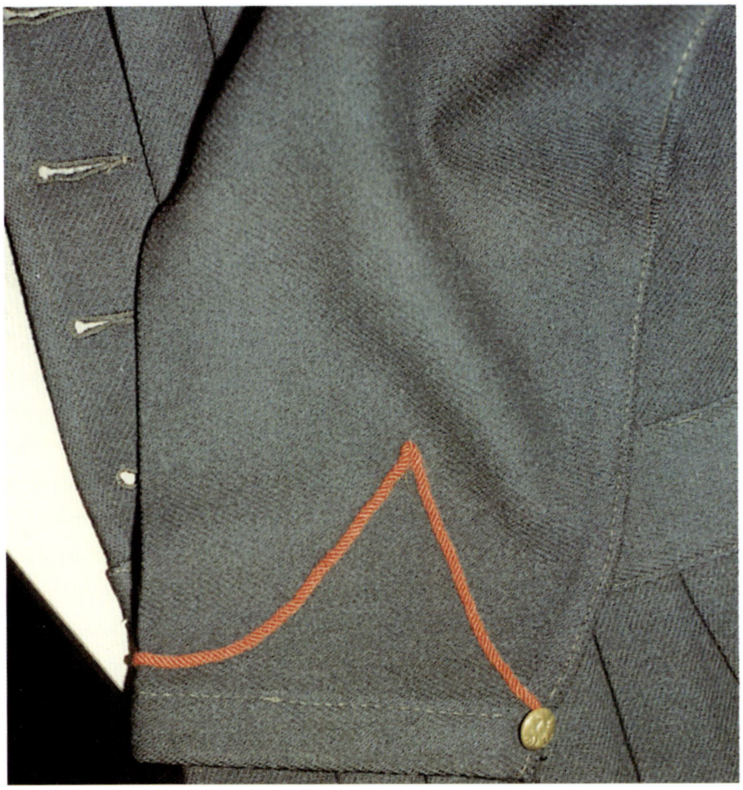

Cuff piping on an 1872-pattern blouse was scarlet for engineers and artillerymen, yellow for cavalrymen, green for hospital stewards, gray for commissary sergeants, crimson for ordnanace personnel, and orange for signalmen. Photograph by Kurt Cox. SI

and had to be prepared for the frigid weather.[250] So would others who came after the ill-fated summer campaign. For them Meigs advocated issue of cloth-lined great coats and provision of overshoes.[251] He went on to underscore that 200 buffalo overcoats ought to be purchased, "as for some years past none have been issued."[252]

The quartermaster general followed up with a requisition for the thousands of pairs of buffalo overshoes stored at the depot in Omaha. These were to be shipped along with the cloth lined greatcoats. The two hundred buffalo coats, which Meigs sought for men on "guard service," were to be bought from suppliers "in the Northwest, or if not there" they might be available from Eastern markets.[253]

Nor was this the end of the matter, in that rather than returning to their permanent quarters, as was customary, military authorities were determined to campaign during the winter against the Plains Indians despite the weather. By way of example, Colonel Miles, after tracking down Sitting Bull's band in October 1876, remained in action with his Fifth Infantry and portions of the Twenty-second Infantry. Ignoring temperatures that plummeted in some instances to fifty below zero, Miles and his doughboys plowed through deep snows and endured great privations in order to capture Crazy Horse. Their presistence ultimately helped wear down the famed Oglala, who surrenderd in May 1877.[254]

What this meant for the Quartermaster Department was the requirement to provide clothing capable of withstanding the rigors of a potentially dreadful winter war. To this end Meigs wanted the estimates for clothing needs as soon as possible, along with recommendations for the time it would take to send the orders and the route of shipment proposed. He went on to caution: "The stock of clothing being very limited, great care should be exercised to avoid accumulation at the various posts."[255]

What is more, Quartermaster General Meigs expressed his concerns to the commanding general of the army, writing:

> There is it seems to me danger of great suffering, perhaps disaster, to troops attempting a winter campaign in the region of the Black Hills, and of the Big Horn and Yellowstone. The climate is cold at best, and the elevated plains are subject to fierce storms of wind and drifting snow during which the thermometer sinks below zero, and the exposure is like that of the Arctic regions.
>
> The various Arctic exploring expeditions have generally escaped loss of life or limb but they owe this mainly to their being dressed as Esquimaux are, enveloped in furs. Moreover they travel on foot. If cavalry are to operate in this region this winter, it appears they should be fortified by being clothed in furs. The buffalo affords the best fur available to us for this purpose, and buffalo coats, overalls and shoes should be provided.[256]

Meigs closed with the acknowledgement that while the garrison at the Tongue River Cantonment (later to become Ft. Keogh, Montana) had received proper gear for the season, those troops on the march had not. He realized the holding of good weather to that time made it "difficult to induce soldiers to carry the burden of these warm wrappings, which also in a degree retard their movements, yet their necessity is shown by experience."[257]

Recognizing that the special winter gear was not the property of the soldier, Meigs asked that the men with Miles be allowed "to hold and use" the warm articles of clothing until they were "no longer needed." The secretary of war had heard this entreaty, and made it clear that the men would not be charged for the items, so long as they were restored to the quartermasters after the winter campaign.

Not one to set back and observe, Meigs continued his initiatives by procuring three sample pairs of felt boots from C.E. Mayer of Berlin, Ontario, with the express purpose of sending these on to Sherman. He wanted the lieutenant general to decide whether this protective footgear should be bought in quantity from Canada for the units in the Department of the Platte, where the winter campaign was being waged.[258]

Even with the adoption of the pleated blouse in 1872, old style uniforms continued to be pressed into field service by enlisted men. For instance, all or part of the worsted yellow tape sometimes was removed from 1855-pattern cavalry enlisted jackets, and the stand collars modified to roll collars for campaign use during the late 1860s through the mid-1870s. GS

Front and rear views of the 1872-pattern enlisted blouse. SI

A favorable reply prompted quick action. Sixty dozen pairs were purchased from Jacob Shantz, another Berlin, Ontario, outfitter. These were to be provided to the troops for the duration of the bad weather, then returned by the men to quartermaster stores when Spring brought an end to their use.[259]

Blankets to relieve not only the men, but livestock, too, likewise were being sent to the front.[260] All the old pattern ones, in fact, were slated for use as horse covers.[261]

The quartermaster general persisted, ordering that 1,000 additional pairs of sealskin gloves should be obtained for the soldiers in the Dakotas, along with at least that many caps. Unfortunately, his subordinates could not fill such an order for at least ninety to one hundred days in the Philadelphia market, so he turned to his operatives in San Francisco to see if they could successfully place the order through contractors on the West Coast.[262]

In fact, this situation was a difficult one, and depot personnel at Philadelphia could not procure 454 sealskin caps they had hoped to provide. Given the season was growing too late to ship the caps to the troops on the Tongue River, the order was canceled.[263]

The shortage of sealskin was not lamented by some individuals, however, who based on experience found that this material became brittle after being exposed to moisture. Although more than 6,000 of the caps alone were bought during fiscal year 1877, their deterioration caused another fur, muskrat, to be designated as a replacement.[264]

Once manufacture of the muskrat cap began in earnest during the late 1870s, the basic design with its ear flaps, cape, and visor, and brown cotton chintz or silesia lining would remain in vogue into the early twentieth century.[265] As in the past, it was to be issued temporarily to the men when higher authority thought conditions warranted severe winter gear.[266]

Additionally, in 1878, muskrat gauntlets began to phase out other types of fur that had been informally employed. According to specifications adopted on March 12, 1879, they would be made of muskrat outer shells with a lining of lamb's fleece inside of the hands. Cuffs were to be lined, too, but in blue or red cloth (flannel), and "be at least 5 inches deep," although most surviving specimens are closer to 4 inches in depth. The cuffs were to be of "sufficient fullness to admit" the ends of the sleeves of the dress coat or blouse. Palms were to be of buckskin.[267]

Even as sealskin was being replaced, the extreme cold faced by some troops had caused a return to acquisitions of buffalo overcoats, beginning in 1877, and continuing well into the 1900s.[268] In 1876, when Miles took to his winter war, he asked Meigs for such coats, only to discover that just three of these garments remained in stock. These bad tidings set Miles into motion, and buffalo robes were rounded up locally by the men and fashioned into overcoats by troops from the Sixth U.S. Infantry then stationed at Ft. Buford, Dakota Territory. These long, bulky garments with their "high rolling collars," along with locally improvised leggings, mittens, and the like, helped sustain the men during the bitter winter.[269] Although never formally covered by specifications,

The 1872-pattern pleated field blouse and folding hat are worn here by Private Howard Weaver, Troop A, Seventh Cavalry. Neither item was particularly popular with the troops. GM

for the next several years buffalo overcoats were obtained, probably from suppliers who made civilian models. They tended to follow a model that was double-breasted, closing with five large buttons of hard rubber. Army blue flannel often was used to line the slash pockets, which were located one on each side. The remainder of the lining was a heavy brown cotton twill, although the earlier versions pressed into service by Miles' men may have been blanket lined. Ankle length was the norm.[270]

One more experiment that derived from the considerable field experience being gained in this period also came about, in this instance during 1877. This was the fabrication of 10,000 shirts of a modified design. In essence, this was little more than the gray flannel shirt with its collar removed, a practice that many enlisted men previously initiated, and that had been requested for trial by Lieutenant Colonel William French.[271] This prompted the deputy quartermaster general, Judson Bingham, to acknowledge, "Inquiry having shown that this habit [cutting off of the collars] was general, shirts are now made without collars."[272] Consequently, in 1878, the gray flannel collarless shirt became the norm, at least for the next three years. The specifications adopted on January 16, 1878, called for a shirt made:

> of Army standard gray shirting flannel. Loose, with shoulder yoke, collar band, and one (1) plait two (2) inches wide, and about twelve (12) inches in front. Collar band to be about seven-eighths (7/8) of an inch deep. Two buttons and button-holes in front plait, one at the end of collar band, and one at each wristband. The yoke to be lined with gray flannel, same quality as shirt is made of. A slit eight (8) inches long, at the lower edge of each side seam, rounded off at the two front edges. To be four (4) sizes.

The next year, 1878, brought about a less practical proposed addition to the basic issue—a cravat. This suggestion was rejected, but permission remained for men to purchase cravats or other forms of neckties if they pleased, but not for wear with the uniform while on duty.[273]

Although the idea to spruce up the uniform with a cravat was not embraced in 1878, in that year a more important action was taken. The United States Congress enacted legislation that provided for enlisted men to be promoted to officers, a possibility that for the most part was restricted to the Signal Service. Nonetheless, the Quartermaster Department offered a contingency for "Meritorious non-commissioned officers of the Army recommended" for advancement. If they passed their examinations, the "candidates for promotion" would receive a certificate from the adjutant general. Further, they could add "a single stripe of gilt lace similar to that worn by commissioned officers on each sleeve" to the cuffs of their uniform coats, so long as they remained in "the specially honorable position of 'candidate.'" This was according to General Orders No. 62, War Department, Headquarters of the Army, August 16, 1878, that went on to indicate if a man passed the age of eligibility for a commission (thirty years), he still could display the dis-

An infantry corporal has combined his 1872-pattern pleated blouse with an 1872-pattern forage cap. The headgear bears the crossed rifle insignia adopted for the infantry rank and file in 1875. Wearing old and new articles simultaneously was common throughout much of the Victorian era. DM

The negative response to the 1872-pattern folding hat and pleated blouse eventually brought about the discontinuance of these items. This resulted in the adoption of the 1874-pattern blouse, a more streamlined garment, with five buttons down the front and one at each cuff. Piping on the collar and cuffs of the same worsted yarn as on the pleated blouse denoted the branch, such as yellow for cavalry. JG

tinctive candidate's stripe on the left sleeve only. No known examples or photographs depict this device, thereby seeming to demonstrate the infrequency in which this congressional nod to potential upward mobility for the rank and file actually was exercised.[274]

Conversely, this same legislation did pave the way for Signal Service officers to be added to the military rolls, albeit as permanent second lieutenants, a situation that remained in place until the 1890s. General Orders No. 86, Headquarters of the Army, December 3, 1878, nevertheless provided for more than just these junior officers in theory, at least, by designating their uniform as follows:

> By direction of the Secretary of War, the uniform and dress of officers of the Signal Corps will be the same as that for the Chief Signal officer, the usual distinction being made for the grades. The distinctive insignia on the cap and shoulder-knot will be according to the pattern deposited in the office of the Chief Signal Officer.

One other matter of securing equity, and for that matter uniformity, was initiated in 1878. Prior to that year, military storekeepers in the Quartermaster Department wore the old single-breasted frock coat and shoulder straps. This must have rankled them, and made them feel somewhat like second class citizens, but General Orders No. 23, Headquarters of the Army, May 14, 1878, ended this predicament by bringing them in line with all others of their rank. Thereafter, they were to be garbed in the same manner as assistant quartermasters, with the rank of captain. That is, they would have the double-breasted frock coat with seven buttons in each row, shoulder knots bearing the gold embroidered letters "Q.D." in Old English, and the chapeau de bras with dark trousers bearing no stripes or welt.

There were lined and unlined versions during the first production years of the 1874-pattern blouse. The former articles were given extra warmth by the addition of material inside the blouse, which at first essentially was the same as for the field shirt of logwood and indigo dyed thread that produced a sort of blue-gray hue. FAM

The cord on the cuffs of the 1874-pattern blouse was applied in a like manner to that of its predecessor. As before, scarlet identified artillery personnel and engineers, orange signalmen, and so forth. The skirts were slightly rounded at the front, and one button was to be applied to each cuff. SI

Even as provisions were made for the opening up of the officer's corps to more than just graduates of the United States Military Academy, and bringing military storekeepers in line with the rest of his commissioned comrades, Meigs was sounding a familiar drumbeat. Despite supposed objections to the clothing provided by his department, he indicated to the editor of the *Army and Navy Journal* that 75,000 shirts, 55,000 pairs of drawers, 100,0000 pairs of stockings, and 50,000 blouses had been allowed by appropriations for the fiscal year ending June 30, 1877. Over the previous twelve months 69,757 shirts, 89,264 pairs of drawers, and 120,048 pairs of stockings, along with 38,623 sack coats and blouses had been sent to the rank and file. This was not a sign of dissatisfaction to Meigs, but the result of success. As was the replacement of the plaited blouse adopted in 1872, "which proved unsatisfactory to the soldiers, and they avoided drawing it, preferring the old style used during the war." In its place, after stocks of this disliked garment had been exhausted, Meigs pointed out his department had brought into being "a blouse of a style somewhat resembling that in the war, but improved in cut, shapes, and workmanship." He concluded with the claim that this item gave good satisfaction.[275]

Although these words were a bit self-congratulatory, to Meigs' credit, despite his reservations about the uniform adopted in 1872, and through many difficulties in making the patterns sanctioned in that year, he and his department finally had replaced the Civil War vintage clothing with new garments throughout. In the process, quartermaster personnel had upgraded a number of items, and replaced a few found wanting (most notably the pleated blouse and folding hat), and on occasion had bowed to field soldiers, who had long clamored for an outfit that was both martial in appearance, but above all practical and durable.

Yet there were those who were not as satisfied as Meigs as to the perfect state of soldiers' clothing. This was apparent when yet a third board was called into being during the 1870s. On the surface, this body's directive set forth in Special Orders No. 244, War Department, November 11, 1878, did not address the issue of clothing. Instead, this order stemmed from a recommendation by the chief of ordnance, Stephen Benet, for a representative group of field officers of infantry to meet in order "to consider the whole subject of intrenching knives, intrenching bayonets, trowel bayonets, and intrenching tools for the United States service, and to recommend to the Secretary of War what device should be adopted, either in lieu of, or in addition to, the present triangular bayonet."[276] Although this was a very specific task, once the board assembled, presided over by "Bear Coat" (Colonel Nelson Miles of the Fifth U.S. Infantry), they, like the 1871-72 board, expanded their horizons.[277] This course of action would have far ranging consequences after the board reported its deliberations in 1879.

Consequently, following a half dozen years of halting starts and setbacks, the uniform promised in 1872 had reached most of the rank

This infantryman has on the 1874-pattern blouse with sky blue cord on the collar and cuffs, and the bugle insignia that was regulation until 1875. He wears the Palmer brace yoke system with Hagner No. 2 cartridge boxes. USAMHI

Sergeant Daniel A. Kanipe, Company C, Seventh U.S. Cavalry, has combined his 1874-pattern enlisted blouse with sharply creased mounted kersey trousers and his forage cap to provide the typical look of a trooper in garrison during the mid- to late 1870s. LBBNM

The 1874-pattern blouse was to have five buttons on the front, one on each cuff, and cord in the branch color on the collar and cuffs, yet the Twentieth U.S. Infantry private in the foreground on the left side of a .50 caliber Gatling gun at Ft. McKean, Dakota Territory, has added extra buttons to his cuff and removed the sky blue cord. So, too, have the two infantry privates in the background had their cord removed. Conversely, the first sergeant on the right side of the Gatling, Hugh Hynds, has trim on his cuffs and three buttons, as well. His garment is a modified four-button sack coat with an external pocket added. The other sergeant in the background, resting on a spare wheel, has opted for an old 1858-pattern frock coat that has been reconfigured as a blouse. In such cases the trim might be removed and the collar turned down. This was also done to cavalry mounted "shell jackets" in some instances. All the doughboys have changed over to the crossed rifle insignia adopted in 1875, except First Sergeant Hynds, who still wears a large stamped brass hunting horn of the type adopted for the 1858-pattern hat. SHSND

A pair of infantry privates pose in 1874-pattern enlisted blouses with sky blue piping on the collar and cuffs, while the crossed rifle insignia appear on their forage caps as called for in 1875. TT

The privates in this picture have donned the 1874-pattern blouse with the 1872-pattern forage cap, although the caps bear smaller non-regulation sabers in three of the four cases that were private purchases. The small brass company letters are regulation size, however, as of 1872, although not until the middle of the decade did general orders clarify wearing these unit identifications. The blouse worn by the man on the left, Musician George Penwell, has three buttons on the cuff, rather than the one that was typical of these garments as delivered by Quartermaster General's Department as the standard. Photographic evidence, however, frequently depicts the three cuff button decoration. Penwell also has added double 1/2-inch stripes, apparently applied to a piece of dark cloth and then sewn to the trousers. LBBNM

General Orders No. 96 of November 19, 1875, not only called for enlisted men of infantry, but also officers to adopt the crossed rifles insignia on or before June 1, 1876. For officers, the rifles were to be gold embroidery with the regimental number in silver embroidery above, and no company letter, as seen here for a member of the Twenty-fifth U.S. Infantry. JB

Side view 1872-pattern officer's forage cap. JB

Left: Another example of an 1872-pattern officer's forage cap, in this case one that belonged to Major Marcus Reno of the Seventh U.S. Cavalry. Photographs of Reno in this piece of headgear indicate that he wore it without the traditional leather chin strap, as just one example of personal preference taking precedent over regulations for officers and enlisted men alike in the 1870s. Photograph by Glen Swanson. WC

and file of the U.S. Army. After this lengthy transition period from Civil War garb to the new outfit, the outcome was disappointing to some, thereby leading to persistent calls for further reform. The Board headed by Colonel Miles would serve as a major catalyst for this movement. After being called into session, these officers went far beyond the original scope proposed by the chief of ordnance.[278]associates made a broad review of both subjects.

They likewise were provided some existing prototypes, including two pleated blouses made up in the late 1860s for a previous board.[279] Additionally, they examined specimens of foreign uniforms provided by the Quartermaster Department from the museum in Philadelphia, including several French items ranging from great coats, to trousers, uniform coats, and jackets.[280] A Swiss dress cap, and a Spanish dress cap with two havelocks were furnished, too. When more European examples were requested, the secretary of war indicated it was impractical to go abroad to collect additional pieces.[281]

Although travel to Europe was denied, Meigs thought it would be instructive if the board members visited the depots at Philadelphia and Jeffersonville, where they could inspect the materials on hand. Because some of the group had served in the field after the June 16, 1874, law that mandated the issue of old inventory items before new articles could be provided, they could personally compare the remaining items that had been the source of many complaints in contrast to "the material and style of clothing now made [that] all have been improved since the old stock was bought...."[282]

With this mass of materials in front of them, and based upon their own considerable experiences, along with input from others, the board set about its task. For example, they leaned toward a dark blue shirt instead of the gray one that had been the mainstay. This may have been in response to Meigs' forwarding of a late 1878 circular letter from his department, along with some of the shirts made of surplus Civil War blue flannel that had been issued "in 1874 or 1875, which were very much liked." Meigs thought that "shirts of that pattern or something near it should be adopted."[283]

In due course a report on the dark blue shirt provided by Lieutenant George Patterson of the Fourteenth Infantry also was furnished to Miles and his colleagues, followed by yet another study discussing the merits of this garment.[284] To confirm the evidence that the blue shirt should

Officers' dress caps also were to bear the crossed rifles and regimental numbers after General Orders No. 96 was published, as Colonel Miles' cap did. Photograph by Glen Swanson. WC

The white cock feathers have been removed from this Seventeenth U.S. Infantry dress cap of Malcolm McArthur to show the crossed rifles insignia prescribed in 1875. The 1872-pattern coat is a field grade officer's with the knots of a major of the Eleventh U.S. Infantry. Photograph by Glen Swanson. GS

Other prescriptions found in General Orders No. 96 of 1875 were the discontinuance of black braid and the elimination of the slit at the hips on officers' blouses. This representative 1875-pattern officer's blouse is for a cavalry captain. WC

replace the gray one, the Board sought the surgeon general's opinion as to which of the two colors "would be most conducive to health and would be least injurious when impacted into wounds."[285]

With the response that the dark hue was no more problematical than the lighter one as far as infection, the Board had all the evidence needed in support of the efficacy of the dark blue shirt. And when a fellow officer from the field recommended "an outer garment or stable frock" for infantrymen to wear on fatigue duties, they were supportive, as well. Samples of overalls in blue drilling and unbleached cotton were sent from the quartermaster general, who likewise stated that cavalry and artillery stable frocks and overalls, as well as engineer overalls could be supplied for review, should the Board wish.[286]

Another request from a serving officer, First Lieutenant Cyrus Earnest, who wrote from Ft. Yuma, California, was considered, too. This company grade officer of the Eighth U.S. infantry proposed a duck or flannel "simple, well fitting single breasted sack coat with outside, side pockets to correspond with a like double breasted blouse for officers." This style would, according to the lieutenant, "secure freedom, ease or

Detail of a cavalry captain's 1875-pattern blouse revealing the fact that the design was to be devoid of braid. WC

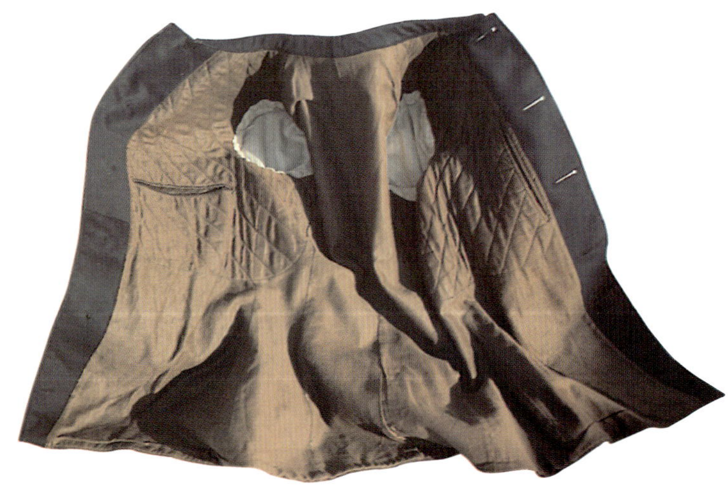

Linings of officers' blouses varied greatly depending on the tailor and budget of the individual. WC

The second lieutenant on the left retains the 1872 pattern officer's blouse with black braid, while his comrade, who gazes down on the lady in the feathered hat, wears an 1875-pattern blouse, which was to be made without slashes at the hip, and also wears the shoulder straps of a first lieutenant in one of the staff corps. GS

A Fifth U.S. Cavalry officer, First Lieutenant William E. Almy, has on an 1875-pattern officer's blouse with black braid bordering the edge and collar. Some officers opted to include such trim on their jackets, even after the chest frogging and sleeve ornamentation had been discontinued. FAM

convenience on campaign or in garrison...."[287] Several versions were made up with outside pockets in the skirts, inside pockets in the breast, two outside pockets in the breast, and a like number on the outside, and one with outside pockets alone. Captain Rodgers expressed the opinion, however, that:

> Outside pockets will probably prove a failure in blouses, especially skirt pockets in so light a fabric, being liable to tear out at the corners. With the belt on, a man is almost certain to tear them if he attempts to put his hands in. Breast pockets (outside) are less objectionable on this ground, but without giving any special advantage over the inside ones they will increase the cost of making about 25 cents each....[288]

Whether or not these factors influenced the Board, they did not suggest a blouse without pockets, but did advocate a white blouse for enlisted men with white braid chevrons for those of non-commissioned officers, and white trousers without stripes for all the rank and file.[289] Further, they asked for the waists of enlisted dress coats to be lengthened by one inch, just as the previous board had requested.[290]

The Board's other proposals for clothing were wide sweeping and varied.[291] They wanted the infantry facing to be changed to white from sky-blue, in that the latter shade faded, while the traditional branch color for dragoons, orange, was asked for to designate cavalry, while the yellow that had been worn by cavalrymen was to be exchanged with Signal Service personnel.[292]

As far as footgear, the Board championed a return to sewed soles rather than the screwed patterns that had been the rage during the 1870s, the latter styles being damned because the brass fasteners worked their

Example of an 1875-pattern officer's blouse, in this case for a first lieutenant of infantry, with the black mohair trim on the collar and outer edges. Another custom feature is a loop sewn to the left side of material that matches the blouse, to help support the sword belt, an accoutrement that was to be worn outside the jacket per General Orders No. 96 of 1875, whereas previously regulations called for it to be worn under the blouse. ES

A board of officers convened by Special Orders No. 264, War Department, December 27, 1875, requested that the flat gold lace cuff ornaments on the officer's dress coat be changed from the previous 1/4 to a 1/2 inch width, and that this was to be "raised and stuffed so as to be 3/8 of an inch wide when finished." This is an example of the padded cuff design for a company grade officer. EB

way through the leather and into the feet of the wearer.[293] Hoping to rectify this defect, the Board considered a "great number of letters and reports" related to the subject and concluded:

> These show that the shoes now issued are the cause of frequent and, it is believed, well-founded complaints. These complaints are due in a measure to the pattern of the shoe, which is made on incorrect principles and is such as to contract the foot, and compress the toes to the screw fastening, which frequently wound the foot, and as conductors of heat and cold, subject the wearer to annoyance and at times suffering.[294]

While the Board admitted the present shoes are no doubt "the most durable that have been issued for many years," their many shortcomings made them:

> objectionable for reasons herein given, and the board therefore recommends that the shoes be of the pattern known as English Waukanphast shoe, to be sewed and of black leather, with bellow tongue and eyelets and hooks for lacing; the height of the shoe to be 6 inches and of the heel 3/4 inch, according to pattern submitted.[295]

This pattern was a sample reviewed by the board, and that had been obtained from the London-based Waukanphast and Co., which held a patent for their shoes in the United States since 1869.[296] Furthermore, the Board wanted an improved boot design of black leather that was of the "same pattern as the shoe, the leg to extend well up and cover the knee in front, the top of the leg sloping downward and backward so as not to interfere with the motion of walking."[297]

A captain of the Quartermaster Department's shoulder knot worn with this coat also exemplifies the type of gold cord that was typical by the mid-1870s. EB

The remainder of the dress coat for officers prescribed in 1876, with the exception of the padded gold lace, was identical to the prior model, as evidenced by this specimen for a captain of the Quartermaster Department made around 1876. EB

An 1872-pattern field grade mounted officer's coat, in this case for a major of the Seventh U.S. Cavalry, reveals that some officers had flat gold braid added to their cuffs, which was broader than the original 1/4 inch width spelled out in the 1872 regulations. WC

In 1876, a new campaign hat was called for to be worn by officers and enlisted men alike. This article was made of black wool and turned up at the outer edge of the brim, then stitched back onto itself. GS

Detail of non-regulation wide flat gold lace on a field grade officer's dress coat of the 1872-pattern. WC

Leggings, long a subject of discussion, also were proposed, with brown canvas being the favored material. So were two weights of stockings and undergarments dependent on season and climate.

Other items related to coping with environmental conditions included a blanket-lined canvas overcoat for issue to troops in extremely cold climates, these being seen as a means of doing away with buffalo overcoats that were increasingly more expensive as the once seemingly limitless bison herds began to dwindle to the point of near extinction. In addition to the cost of buffalo coats, they were bulky and subject to absorbing moisture, which in frigid weather proved a major drawback.[298]

In a related matter, the Board leaned toward an ulster overcoat that Major General John M. Schofield had been requesting for officers, except generals, as a replacement for the style adopted in 1872.[299] Similarly, they thought a lining of facing material in branch colors was appropriate for the capes of enlisted great coats to add both warmth, as well as a means of encouraging branch cohesiveness. Some men had informally done this on their own initiative and out of pocket, and the custom seemed worthy of official approval.

Besides making improvements for cold weather, the Board gave consideration to the problem of soaring temperatures, as noted not only with a proposal for a white sack coat and trousers, but also for the universal issue of white cork helmets to all enlisted men.

Finally, a helmet for foot troops to do away with the "objectionable" shako, of an improved design that also would be adopted for mounted troops in lieu of the steep visor version ushered in during 1872, was promoted. The mounted men would continue to sport plumes, however, while the dismounted soldiers would wear a spike.

Interestingly enough, rather than just respond via internal communications to the recommendations made by the Board, their study was

One of the features of the 1876-pattern campaign hat was a device known as a "Brasher spinner," after the individual who patented the item. This inside view shows the means of attachment of the metal spinner, one being set into each side of the crown. The idea was that air would circulate better by means of these small fan blades. Unfortunately, the invention was not very successful. A portion of the leather sweatband also is shown. GS

This pair of 1876-pattern trousers for a commissary sergeant have the correct facing cloth leg stripe, in this case of 1 1/4 inch wide cadet gray. SI

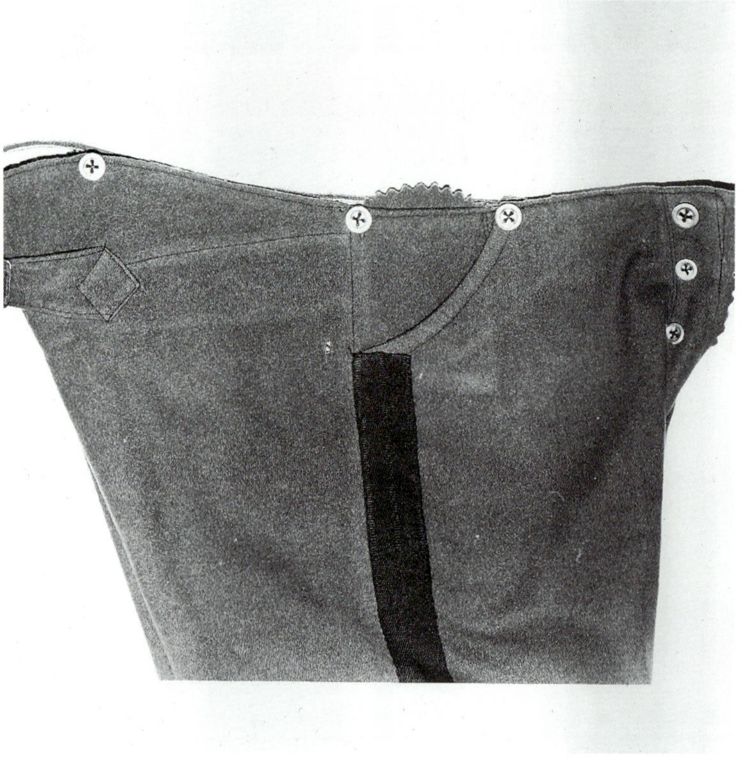

The same Board of officers who advocated the adoption of the new campaign hat also suggested another style of trousers, which likewise were adopted in 1876. For the most part they were to conform to the design that originally had been considered for wear when the 1872 uniform was prescribed, but were deemed to be too expensive to produce. They were made without a waistband, but had a high back, a watch pocket inserted into the top right seam, "frog-mouth" pockets on each side at the hips, and a short cloth belt in the rear with brass buckle to secure the garment to the wearer. This example is for a sergeant of infantry. Note that the trouser stripe is not made from the regulation dark blue facing material cloth, however, but is of the worsted tape found on 1861-pattern trousers. This may be an early attempt to replace infantrymen's stripes with a more substantial material. SI

published as General Orders No. 76, Headquarters of the Army, July 23, 1879, with commentary from the report and remarks by General Sherman. Both economics and a conservative frame of mind colored the general's response. He went down the list presented by the Board, sometimes responding with a brief authorization or in many cases a simple disapproval. In several instances he elected to editorialize, demonstrating his strong bias for the pre-1872 pattern, a reactionary predilection, a bent toward certain prerogatives remaining in the hands of commanding officers, and even reliance on individual initiative of the common soldier, as is evident in the following excerpt from General Orders No. 76:

> 30. The Schofield ulster overcoat, according to specifications and plates.
> *Disapproved.*
> 31. That the capes of the soldier's overcoat be lined with flannel of the color of the facings of the corps.
> *Approved.*
> 32. The adoption of a canvas overcoat lined with cloth for issue to the troops in extremely cold and wet climates.
> *Approved.*
> 33. A rearrangement of the ornaments on the sleeves and collar of the dress coat, according to plates.
> *Disapproved.*—Changes to the uniform should be very rare, because the ornaments are solely designed to indicate the corps and the rank of the wearer. The uniform worn during the civil war became familiar to every man, woman, and child in the country, and should *never* have been changed; and if any change is now attempted it should be back toward that then worn and made historic.

Rear view of an 1876-pattern pair of sky-blue kersey trousers. The semi-circular piece on the seat is part of the saddling that ran down the inside of the trousers to the cuffs as a means of reinforcement for pairs worn by mounted troops. Foot soldiers did not require this additional cloth. SI

The sleeve ornaments, except soldier's chevrons, might be removed at once without cost or detriment, as superfluous. No collar ornamentations are advisable at all. The shoulder-strap is distinctive, and should remain unchanged, and *always* worn. I further prefer that 'Captains and under' should wear the single-breasted coat, 'Majors and over' the double-breasted; but as this change [to a double-breasted coat for all officers in 1872] was made against my advice I will not renew it.

The shoulder-strap as now universally understood shows the rank and corps of the wearer and should remain unchanged. Brevet rank might be indicated by a badge, worn when exercising brevet rank and removed when the lineal or exact rank only is claimed.

34. That the dress coats for enlisted men be made one inch longer in the waist than at present for all sizes.

Approved.

35. That shoulder-straps on the officer's sack coat should be abolished; that the sleeves should be ornamented with black silk braid, and that the insignia of rank be worn on each end of the collar.

Disapproved.—The shoulder-strap should never be omitted on any kind of 'uniform.' Collar ornaments are historically offensive.

36. The color of the pantaloons of all commissioned officers be dark blue.

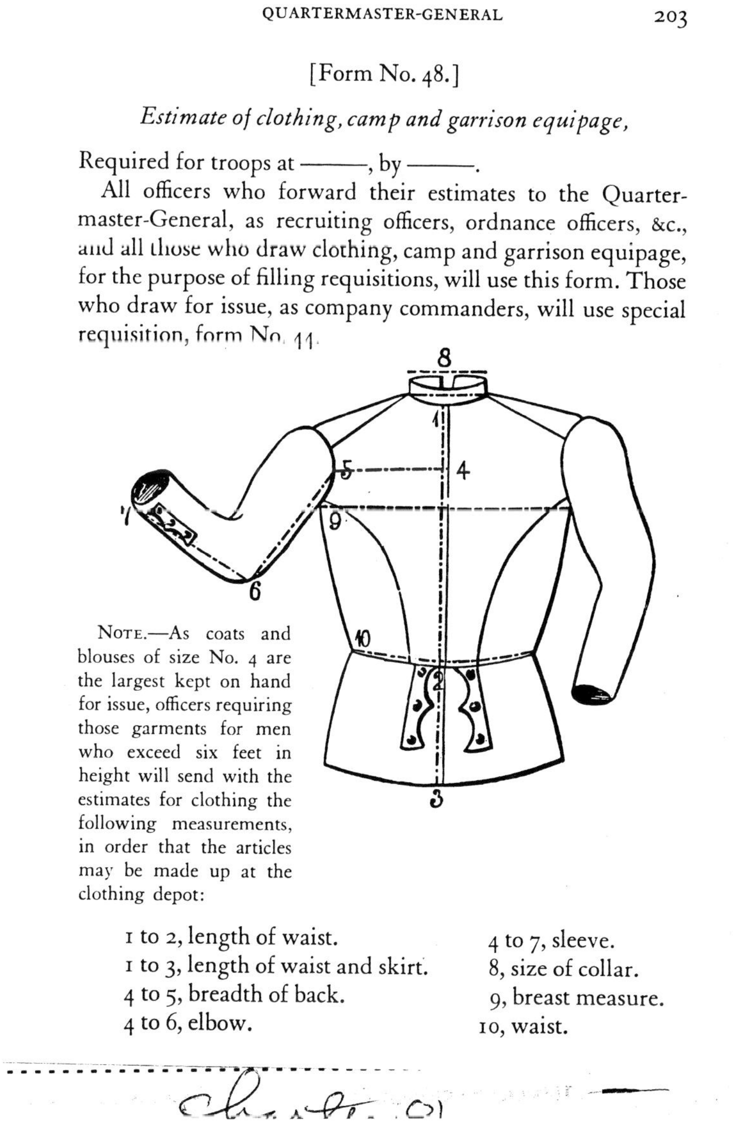

QUARTERMASTER-GENERAL 203

[Form No. 48.]

Estimate of clothing, camp and garrison equipage,

Required for troops at ———, by ———.

All officers who forward their estimates to the Quartermaster-General, as recruiting officers, ordnance officers, &c., and all those who draw clothing, camp and garrison equipage, for the purpose of filling requisitions, will use this form. Those who draw for issue, as company commanders, will use special requisition, form No. 11.

NOTE.—As coats and blouses of size No. 4 are the largest kept on hand for issue, officers requiring those garments for men who exceed six feet in height will send with the estimates for clothing the following measurements, in order that the articles may be made up at the clothing depot:

1 to 2, length of waist.
1 to 3, length of waist and skirt.
4 to 5, breadth of back.
4 to 6, elbow.
4 to 7, sleeve.
8, size of collar.
9, breast measure.
10, waist.

The Board that called for the introduction of the new hat and trousers also succeeded in having a new form produced to facilitate ordering proper sizes of coats for their men. As of 1876 these were to be used by officers when making requisitions. ARSW, *1876*

Tenth U.S. Cavalry Sergeant E.D. Gibbon exhibits two items that resulted through actions of the 1876 board, the campaign hat with "Brasher" spinner ventilators, which he holds in his left hand, and mounted reinforced trousers, in this case with the correct 1-inch leg stripes in yellow facing material as called for in the case of cavalry sergeants. His vest, shirt, and watch chain are private purchase civilian items. In turn, his 1874-pattern b louse is customized in that the trim was to be on the collar only, yet it appears that he has added non-regulation worsted braid all the way around the garment's edges. Note that no chevrons appear on the sergeant's sleeves. Although non-commissioned officers traditionally wore stripes to indicate their rank above the elbow, not until General Order No. 21 of March 21, 1876 was the practice sanctioned in writing. FAM

A brigadier general's dress coat with epaulets, sash around the waist, and sword belt of red Russian leather with three rows of gold embroidery was regulation from 1872 through 1902. WC

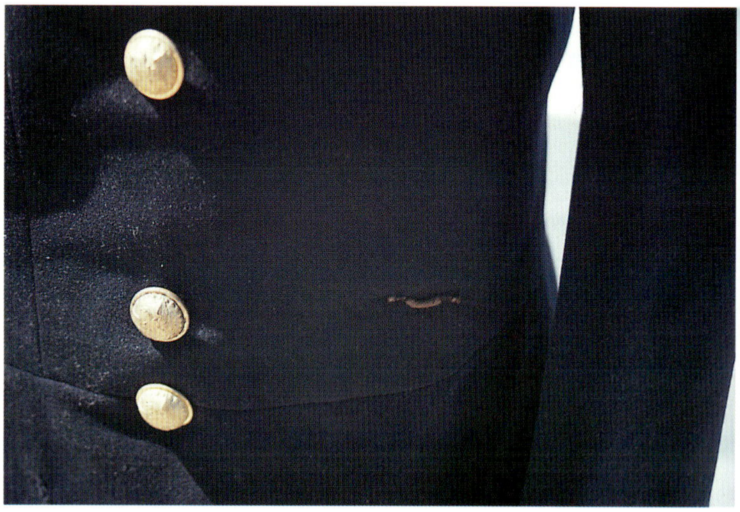

Close up of Brigadier General Nelson A. Miles' 1872-pattern frock coat (Miles was promoted to brigadier general in December 1880) discloses a custom appendage on the right side near the waist to help hold the sash and belt in place. WC

Disapproved.—Officers in line of battle should have the same color of pantaloons as the troops. Especially should this be so when the troops wear white pants, as in the case of the Corps of Cadets.
37. The facings of the Cavalry be orange, the Infantry white, and the Signal Corps yellow.
Disapproved.—The present 'facings' of all the arms of service are now well understood and sufficiently distinctive.
38. The adoption of helmets of pattern submitted for all persons in the line of the Army.
Disapproved.—The present uniform is good enough—helmets for mounted troops, hats [he meant caps] for foot troops.
39. A summer uniform for all officers and enlisted men, to consist of a white cork helmet, a white sack coat and pantaloons.
Disapproved.—I prefer commanding officers of posts be authorized to allow. in hot weather, their officers and men to buy white pants, using their present uniform blue flannel sack coat and a straw hat. These can be universally procured at cheap rates.
40. Brown canvas leggings.
Disapproved.—It is better for troops to improvise these out of old canvas and tents than to make them an article of manufacture and issue by the quartermaster.

Detail of four of the general staff buttons on a brigadier general's double breasted dress coat. These were grouped in pairs, with a total of eight buttons in each row. WC

Detail of the regulation dress belt plate, belt, and sash for general officers. WC

Miles' general officer's red Russian leather dress belt, plate, and its japanned tin carrying case. WC

41. Shoes of prescribed pattern.
Recommended for manufacture at the Leavenworth [military] prison and experimental trial by marching troops. There is no article of dress so valuable and material to the soldier as the shoe or boot, and it is not deemed wise to prescribe any fixed patterns, but to allow the Quartermaster's Department to manufacture the shoes for the Army of the very best materials and of the best patterns possible, almost regardless of cost. there is no necessity of adopting any shoe as *uniform.* Soldiers should be permitted to buy any kind of shoe they please with their own money.
42. Boots of pattern prescribed.
Same remarks as for 'shoes.'
43. Two grades of under-clothing, to suit varied climates.
Approved as to shirts and socks, but not as to drawers.
44.Substitution of blue flannel shirts for the gray ones now used.
Approved.
45. Changes in the patterns of under-clothing.
Approved.
46. Changes recommended in the allowance of clothing.
This is already subject to the discretion of the Secretary of War, who must be guided by the annual appropriation bill.
47. The coats and pantaloons to be issued 'cut and made up,' or 'cut and unmade,' as called for by requisition.
This is already done, and can be increased in practice if the experience of the Clothing Bureau warrants it. It is a question of economy alone.

Although many of the recommendations of the Miles Board had been rejected by General Sherman, with the passage of time a number of the suggestions made by these officers and endorsed by many others

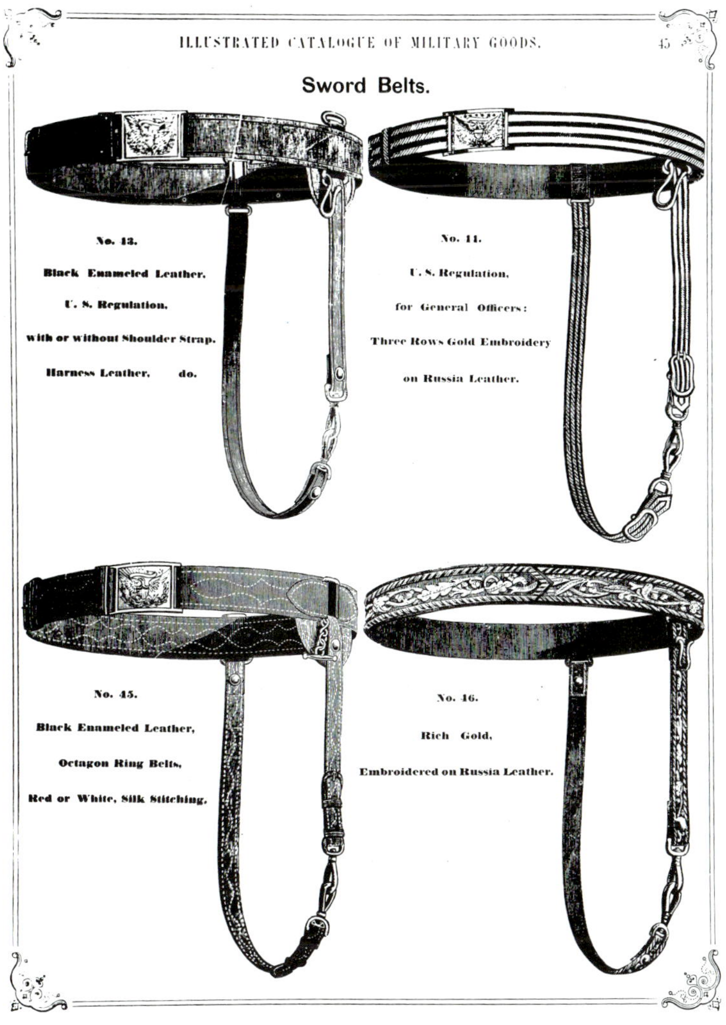

This Civil War catalog from military supplier Schuyler, Hartley and Graham demonstrates that the Russian leather belt with three rows of gold embroidery and another optional "rich gold embroidery" belt without buckle were available to general officers before the release of the 1872 uniform regulations, and continued to be obtainable for years thereafter. KC

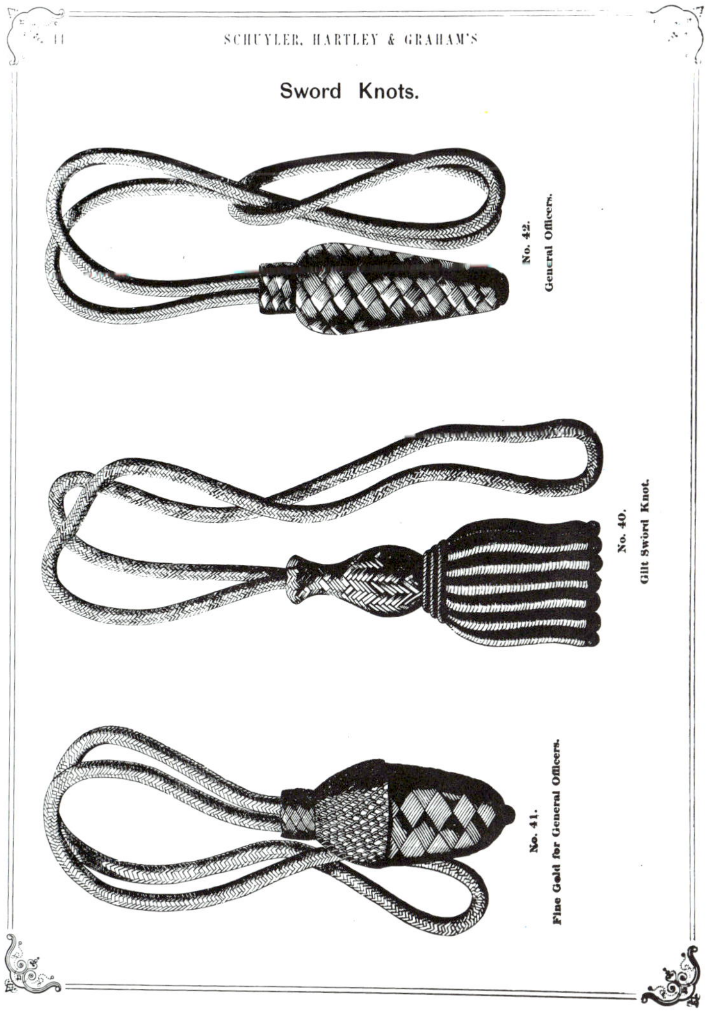

Two versions of sword knots authorized for general officers appear on the left and right of yet a third option that could be bought by all officers. KC

The regulation sword and saber knot for all field grade and company officers in gold lace, and a more expensive alternative. KC

ultimately would come to pass.[300] In the meantime, disappointed military men turned to various military periodicals to express their displeasure at the commanding general's restrained stand.

P.J. Cooney, a soldier at Ft. Verde, Arizona Territory, was one of those who directed a letter to the editor. He contended that "formerly the money allowance for clothing was much larger, which enabled us to save sufficient pay for altering...." The decrease of the cash allotment, however, meant the soldiers had to pay out of their "pockets what the Government expressly agrees to furnish." While Cooney admitted "great improvements have been made in the last few years, both in the material and make of our clothing," it seemed "impossible to fit a company of men without having the measure of each man separately, which would be impracticable, owing to the large extent of territory our Army is scattered over...." He thought the answer was to issue the cloth and pay company tailors to produce the clothing.[301]

An officer serving in the Lone Star State stated his case for the disallowed "summer uniform of white sack coat and white trousers and either white straw hat or white cork helmet," all of which he viewed as "an absolute necessity in Texas." The fact that the government failed to provide such critical items and left it to the rank and file to buy articles for their comfort in torrid heat was appalling to the critic who signed his letter "100 deg. in the shade."[302]

A third article echoed the concept that the government had violated its compact with the soldiery by failing to provide proper clothing. Of course, this was a difficult task given the problem of widely varied climatic conditions, but the equipment board had made a genuine effort to address these diverse requirements. Further, the writer pointed out that civilian sportsmen had access to a great many articles that would be suitable for adoption by the military, including waterproof canvas overcoats and leggings. A new system was called for that would allow for purchase of practical articles from manufacturers who already had found solutions to durable, weather resident clothing.

Finally, another Texas-based writer thought that a grassroots campaign should be launched to demonstrate to Sherman that a large number of officers were in support of a summer uniform.[303] Yet a third writer was even more blunt. He bitterly commented:

> If the Board of young, energetic, and experienced officers, appointed for the purpose by the War Department recommends certain important and necessary changes in the uniforms of the officers and soldiers of the Army, is it not something like a grandmother dictating to a young society lady how to dress, for the General of the Army to order officers to dress in old and obsolete styles, and to disapprove of the Board's modern idea of comfort and neatness in uniforms?

Major generals had three groups of three buttons in each row on their coats, making nine in each row total. The collars and cuffs were to be of dark blue velvet, as they were for other general officers. WC

Major generals wore gold epaulets with two silver embroidered stars. A typical pair is seen here with the front and back shown, along with the japanned tin carrying case. WC

There were a number of methods for attaching the epaulets to a general officer's dress coat, such as this option, in this case for Miles' general officer's coat. WC

Japanned tin carrying case for a chapeau de bras. WC

> Why are the soldiers ordered to purchase their summer clothing and straw hats from the traders when the Government contracts with the soldier to supply his clothing?[304]

In the face of such pressure, Sherman partially retreated, inasmuch as the cork helmet was permitted for general issue in areas where climate dictated. Indeed, the Quartermaster Department, while indicating that the 100 trial helmets sent to Arizona Territory in 1875 had been declined by some troops and adversely commented upon by those who did receive them, nevertheless pressed ahead with development of that piece of headgear.[305] A substitute for the facing material that had been used to cover early versions of the helmet issued at Ft. Monroe, Virginia, and elsewhere, was seen as too costly. Meigs wanted a less expensive substitute in a light color, perhaps a pale gray because he preferred it "for the sake of coolness" and because this color would "not soil or become shabby so soon as white." As another means of keeping the helmet's appearance from deteriorating, the quartermaster general even thought it would be desirable for a removable cover to be tried, "if possible, in order that it may be taken off and be washed when soiled."[306]

Neither gray or a removable encasement would be adopted, but white drilling, which was washable and which had been used with success by the British, was seen as a workable compromise. Meigs thus asked the secretary of war if helmets destined for Ft. Monroe could employ this material.[307] While facing materials was to remain the standard for the gunners at the artillery school, at least for the moment, Meigs nevertheless pressed the case for drilling, which could be whitened with chalk rubber.[308] He had two samples made, one with the finer material that would cost $3.41 per unit, and the other with drilling that

General officers and staff officers wore chapeau de bras. The cockade was to go on the right side, and the front point of the hat was to be angled slightly to the wearer's left. WC

Captain Frederick Benteen's 1872-pattern folding hat, which is shown closed, had ribbon edging around the brim that was not found on enlisted models. When closed, this type of headgear resembled a chapeau de bras. GS

First Lieutenant Edward S. Godfrey wears an officer's version of the 1872-pattern folding campaign hat with the 1872-pattern officer's blouse. Godfrey has partially opened his broad-brimmed piece of headgear and angles it so that the hat somewhat resembles a bicorne of the Napoleonic era. USAMHI

Detail of the acorn tips found on officers' hat cords for those below the rank of brigadier general. The cords were to be intermixed black and gold thread, while gold thread versions were authorized for all general officers. MK

could be procured for $2.50 a helmet. These were sent to the secretary for further consideration.[309]

While this exchange about the summer helmet for the Ft. Monroe garrison took place and set the stage for wider distribution of the summer helmet, Meigs' department faced other considerations resulting from the Miles Board. As in the past, experimentation and the passage of time formed key parts of the equation as quartermaster personnel attempted to provide some of the new items that Sherman had permitted.

Even then, as of late June 1879 Meigs had not received authority from the secretary of war to produce any of the items that the Board had requested, nor could he because the fiscal year was coming to an end. Under the circumstances, he would have to wait for the appropriations for the new fiscal year to begin the process of providing the new issue.[310]

The one exception to this, of course, was the discontinuance of gold lace ornamentation on officers' dress coats. Because officers paid

Some officers substituted various civilian headgear for use in the field, such as this black slouch hat that has been militarized by the addition of a velvet oval with gold embroidered crossed sabers and a silver regimental number, along with officer's hat cords. WC

In a Seventh U.S. Cavalry field mess during the 1874 Black Hills Expedition, both privately purchased slouch hats and two examples of the 1872-pattern officers' campaign hat are evident with broad brim hooked up. One of the officers in the folding hat seated from left has his dark trousers carefully reinforced in the seat with a light-colored material, probably canvas. Also of interest are the brogans that have been substituted for the more commonly preferred boots of cavalrymen. LBBNM

At the Little Heart River near Ft. Abraham Lincoln, George Custer and several fellow officers take an outing during July 1875. Most Civil War vintage articles have been replaced by more up to date military or civilian items, such as buckskin jackets and wide brimmed planter's or slouch hats. NA

for all their own uniforms, they did not have to await government funding. More to the point, implementation of this directive was simple, and could be done for free by careful removal of the lace from the cuffs, which many officers evidently did in due course. Thereafter, new coats would be made without the additional trim, cutting the cost of purchase slightly.

Another pronouncement, which was not related to General Orders No. 76, but effected a small number of individuals living on officers' row, was the adoption of a shoulder strap for chaplains. Originally, these military clergyman had a very indistinct black slouch hat, trousers, and a nine button frock coat without any martial designation, although the single-breasted frock did have black mohair frogging similar to that found on 1872-pattern officers' blouses. With the promulgation of General Orders No. 10, Headquarters of the Army, February 13, 1880, however, the secretary of war permitted chaplains to "wear on the uniform coat prescribed in General Orders No. 92, of 1872, a shoulder-strap of black velvet, with a shepherd's crook of frosted silver on the center of the strap." The order further allowed the wearing of a black cord on the outer seam of the trousers, although this would be barely visible in that the trousers were of black cloth, as well.

While these two minor items for officers were being introduced, another form of distinction was adopted, not only for officers, but also for the rank and file. This was for marksmen of all ranks, who in 1880 were granted a pair of 3/4 inch square buttons in sterling silver representing a target. Designed to be worn on both sides of the blouse collar, these devices were presented to men who scored a minimum of eighty percent at 200 yards, when firing from a standing position, and at 300 yards kneeling, as well as seventy percent at 600 yards.[311]

It is of note that by fall 1881 additional efforts had been made by the Ordnance Department, then headed by Stephen Vincent Benet, to expand upon the marksmanship recognition program. To this end, Benet ordered designs for impressive medals as prizes to recognize the top

One of George Custer's buckskin jackets, which he had adopted in lieu of regulation field dress since the later 1860s. SI

In this depiction of George Custer (center figure, laying in the grass), other officers and civilians, taken on August 13, 1874, a wide array of campaign clothing is evident. The combination of civilian and military items particularly is noteworthy, and was common during the time. For example, Custer (lying down, center) and Captain William Ludlow (first on left) wear buckskins. Both Captain Ludlow and Lieutenant Tom Custer (third from left) wear leggings. Many have donned civilian's shirts, including the bib-front style that was popular with firemen, frontiersmen, and other non-military men of the period, as well as several officers. Eleven of the twenty-nine officers in the photo wear the 1872-pattern campaign hat, eight have selected the 1872-pattern forage cap, and the remaining men wear civilian slouch hats. Most have tied a neckerchief or scarf around their neck, while almost all have decided upon regulation trousers. GS

A number of fellow Seventh U.S. Cavalry officers elected to follow Custer's choice of buckskin jackets, including Second Lieutenant Henry W. Harrington, whose jacket is seen here. WPM

Another photograph from the 1876 campaign on the northern Plains shows officers of the Third U.S. Cavalry in the Black Hills. Most leaned toward light colored civilian slouch hats, but a wide array of 1872 and 1875-pattern officers' blouses, civilian jackets, and non-regulation field shirts again make the point that uniformity was not common during campaigning of the 1870s. NA

marksmen in the army. These were to be provided by Tiffany of New York, then cast by the U.S. Mint in Philadelphia.[312]

While these efforts were underway in the Ordnance Department, the Quartermaster Department concentrated on another form of distinction—service chevrons, long a means for enlisted personnel to display their status as veterans, were made available free of charge. Previously, these "hash marks" had been provided as part of the allowances for clothing, thereby meaning that the soldiers who drew them had funds subtracted from their annual allotment.[313]

Many other items were available from Quartermaster Department, although not given out as gratis. Nevertheless, the department continued its efforts to make use of supplies on hand for the rank and file, and to provide reduced costs of issue when possible. This included alteration of 3,913 of the folding pattern hats that still were in storage, at a cost of $.15 per unit.[314] Cutting down the brims and a slight reblocking was far less expensive than purchasing new 1876-pattern campaign hats, although the troops no doubt would have preferred the newer model.

Additional articles remaining in inventory also were to be sent to posts to fill requisitions before new versions would be released. Besides old campaign hats, coats, jackets, and sack coats were distributed, but

Brigadier General George Crook, near the head of the column in his light colored civilian jacket (most probably of canvas), poses with Captain James "Teddy" Egan and men of Company K, Second U.S. Cavalry in Custer City, Montana, in September 1876. Most of the troopers appear to have on 1872-pattern folding hats and 1874-pattern blouses. SDSHS

The two Sixth U.S. Cavalry officers (standing in the back row left and center) posted to Ft. Apache, Arizona Territory, in the mid-1870s also demonstrate that dark colored slouch hats were worn, sometimes with insignia applied. The same officer has bought a double breasted civilian coat to which he added regulation buttons, while his comrade is more regulation in an 1872-pattern officer's forage cap and 1875-pattern officer's blouse. NA

these items were falling in numbers, and some components, such as hat feathers, could be sold because they no longer formed part of the uniform.[315] Further items continued to be disposed of when they were condemned because of poor condition and other reasons. This included 1858-pattern hats, Civil War surplus rubber blankets, and ponchos, old wool blankets, and approximately 30,000 great coats of outdated patterns.[316]

In fact, through various means some old pattern items were no longer available. Among the articles that were not on hand was the great coat, at least in size 4, thereby making it possible for Meigs to have new ones made based upon the pattern worked up in May 1879.[317] Originally, these probably did not have capes lined in facing material, because of difficulty in obtaining suitable fabric for this purpose was experienced just as it had been when efforts were made earlier in the decade to produce the 1872 dress coats and chevrons.[318]

Time was of the essence so far as Meigs was concerned, because troops were deploying to the mountains of Colorado against the Utes as winter approached. In the high altitudes, the quartermaster general approved purchase on the open market of whatever might be required to keep hardships for the troops to the minimum. This was an old story as Meigs narrated:

> The small appropriations granted by Congress for clothing and equipage for several years past has reduced us to a system of living from hand to mouth, have depleted our depots and storehouses, so that we have not lately been able to keep up a working stock.[319]

Meigs attempted to rectify this situation, but could not move the congressional committee on appropriations to add funds. With the coming of winter, his department again had to "spend freely the money saved by years of enforced economy...to prevent much suffering at the beginning of the campaign."[320]

On several other occasions Meigs made known his tale of woe. For instance the quartermaster general lamented to the commanding general of the Military Division of the Pacific:

> For several years past, Congress has, for reasons conducive to the Committee on Appropriations, cut down on appropriations for clothing and equipage of the Army to the closest margin, which has emptied the depots of the Quartermaster Department of all working stock.
>
> The old clothing left over at the end of the War has become obsolete, been used as far as possible, been transferred under laws for that purpose to the National Home for Disabled Volunteers, and much of it has been injured by moths, until finally only the garments of smaller sizes remained, and orders now do not allow what little remains to be issued to the troops who have greatly objected to its use.
>
> All these causes have completely exhausted our working stock. But while this has been explained to members of the Committee in charge of Army bills, the desire to distinguish their service by economy in military expenditures has been so strong as to prevent the granting of the appropriations needed to put this Department again in a proper position to supply the Army promptly at all times and under all emergencies.[321]

Meigs went on to explain how the law prevented contracts from being let in advance of appropriations. Once funds were on hand, it took considerable time for the bid process to operate, especially because con-

In the early 1870s First Lieutenant Joseph A. Sladen of the Fourteenth U.S. Infantry resembled a cowhand more than an officer in his pullover shirt decorated with light colored cloth tape and light slouch hat. Indeed, except for the M1851 eagle belt plate, no other military items are obvious. Even the saddlebags and holster are of civilian make. USAMHI

First Lieutenant William W. Robinson models a miner's shirt, which was favored by a number of officers during the 1870s. Moreover, embroidered crossed sabers and the number "7" have been worked into both sides of the collar, special features that had been used in the Seventh U.S. Cavalry starting in the 1860s. GS

tractors, once selected, had to set up their production every time a new specification was introduced. Then, too, the higher standards for cloth that had been adopted, resulted in more rejections of yard goods because manufacturers found it very difficult to meet the requirements.

Meigs wished the situation would change during the forthcoming winter, because the national elections had been decided. As a result, he hoped that "we may find more liberal disposition in Congress, and may succeed in getting a special allowance for replenishing our exhausted stock."

Not trusting this matter to fate, Meigs approached the secretary of war with a request that Congress be asked for one million dollars to set things right. The practice of drawing on surplus from the Civil War no longer was possible. In spite of many precautions, materials had suffered from the elements, time, and insects.[322] With nothing left on the shelves, the money was needed to prevent suffering by the troops. Meigs pleaded: "Though a rich and prosperous Nation, our Army has no reserve of clothing, and waits for its manufacture from day to day. We are living from hand to mouth."[323] He concluded by pointing out that appropriations had shrunk while prices had risen for goods. This large infusion of cash was needed to set thing right.

In the meantime, Meigs' organization continued to provide whatever it could from items on hand. One of the articles that could be sent out for the men on campaign was the gray flannel shirt, which by this point was made in two grades.[324] Meigs admitted that "neither of them" were proper "for a warm climate," while only one of them was "heavy enough for the winter climate of the extreme north." The material continued to be coarse, as well, leading him to favor a navy blue flannel garment that would be less "harsh and irritating to the skin," and that would be produced in weights that would be appropriate in different climatic conditions.

Here Meigs was in concert with the Miles Board, and his support set Captain Rodgers in motion. First, the captain made a report on blue flannel in stock and also had several model shirts prepared that included double-breasted versions, one with and one without collar, and another single-breasted type with detachable plastron "such as are worn by firemen & c."[325]

Not only did he intend to have shirts that would meet ranges in temperature, but also he indicated trousers would be made in a weight

Officers of the Fifth and Twenty-second U.S. Infantry, along with a contract surgeon and other inhabitants of Cantonment Tongue River, Montana Territory, during the winter of 1876-77 seem universal in their acceptance of kersey trousers, but headgear and blouses run the gamut from regulation to civilian styles. FAM

E.A. Pier, a soldier with the Fifth U.S. Infantry, Company F in the 1870s, offers another example of the non-regulation garb worn on campaign by enlisted men and officers alike. USAMHI

that would be suitable for posts in warm climates or cold conditions, depending on their locations.[326] This scheme was laudable, but not always practical. When urgency arose for trousers to be delivered to several posts in Texas, for instance, rather than wait for lighter ones to be made the Quartermaster Department substituted heavy kersey ones as an expedient, because the latter type already were on hand.[327]

Whether the heavier cloth was well received cannot be ascertained, but one thing that is known was occasional complaints about trousers in general persisted. What was not clear was whether these were items from old stocks or new patterns, causing Quartermaster Department officials to ask for samples from one board of survey to ascertain this information.[328] Even then, Meigs saw a use for old pattern trousers, even those that might be patched. These he thought could be issued to military prisoners. For this group, Meigs asserted: "All that is necessary is that they be warm and protected from the weather and decently covered."[329]

Regardless of weight, the color of trousers presented a challenge, in that Meigs indicated: "Experience had shown it is difficult to secure uniformity in the color of sky-blue kersey." Consequently, "many thousand yards have been rejected on account of color alone...."[330] For this reason, he told Captain Rodgers at the Philadelphia Depot to inquire into substituting dark blue for both trousers and greatcoats. He reminded the captain that dark blue had been the regulation for trousers at least when the Civil War erupted, but scarcity of the cloth and the high costs of indigo dye caused the lighter hue to be adopted.

With the emergency passed, Meigs believed "that officers and troops generally have a preference for dark blue," so despite the fact that light blue had been worn by the Union as it "gained its victories, and suffered its losses in Mexico and the rebellious States," he did not "think it right to lead manufacturers into what seems in fact a trap." He concluded:

> Slight differences in shade of color which are important in the uniform, of the Army, are of no consequence in commercial dealings with the general public and the manufacturer's bid without appreciating the difficulty of matching a precise shade of color and the importance of perfect uniformity and correspondence in the clothing bought in different years, and made of cloth manufactured in different seasons, and at different places from the Atlantic to Pacific shores.[331]

Having conceded all these factors, Meigs was displaying a willingness to depart from tradition for the sake of practicality. This was somewhat out of keeping with his basic philosophy, therefore, when Rodgers

In this informal 1878 group photograph taken in Montana Territory, most of these Fifth U.S. Infantry enlisted personnel have on either the gray flannel 1874-pattern shirt or some form of blouse, including possibly four button sack coats and 1874-pattern jackets. Forage caps, hats purchased from sutlers or other civilian sources, and perhaps some 1876-pattern issue wool campaign hats are evident. NA

With double-barrel shotgun in hand, a Fifth U.S. Infantry soldier returns from foraging during 1878, as his outfit camps in the Yellowstone Valley, Montana Territory. The headgear may be some sort of cloth sportsman's cap, or an early civilian version of the summer helmet. NA

All the privates in this picture of cavalry serving in Arizona Territory during the 1870s manifest the individualistic touches that were common during this decade, when variety was the watchword. Some use old Civil War four button sack coats; one man wears a pleated 1872-pattern blouse, but most have on the 1874-pattern blouse. There are 1872-pattern folding hats, an 1872-pattern forage cap with protective cover, privately purchased slouch hats, and perhaps an 1876-pattern issue campaign hat or two. There is even a man in a striped civilian shirt and a bandanna, the latter article resembling the ubiquitous Hollywood convention infrequently seen in actual photographs of the period. To his right is another trooper, who may have on the experimental campaign shirt made of dark blue flannel issued in limited quantities during the summer of 1875. The other visible shirts are either the 1874-pattern in gray wool, or maybe even the gray flannel shirt without collar that was tried briefly in 1878 and adopted as official during the following year. USAMHI

Detail of the Jeffersonville Depot stamp, indicating this specimen of the collarless gray flannel shirt was a size 2 made during fiscal year 1877-78. SI

replied with a recommendation to retain sky-blue for over coats and trousers, but in the future bidders should be forewarned about specific, and strict requirements for conformity to specifications, including exact color matches, the quartermaster general must have been pleased.[332] With that the status quo remained. The two-tone look continued on for decades to come.

Conversely, Meigs' department was not yet willing to close the books on old pattern uniforms still deemed serviceable. For one thing, 1858-pattern infantry frockcoats continued to be issued with new facings cut out and sent to the local garrisons for alteration. This practice remained in vogue at least on a limited basis through mid-1879, where infantrymen in Texas were among the foot soldiers still in old patterns that were converted to an approximation of the 1872-pattern dress coat.[333]

Simultaneously, their comrades in the cavalry were expected to continue with the outdated 1855-pattern mounted jacket, causing some grumbling at Ft. Concho and Ft. McKavett, Texas, about the "rotten blouses" they were forced to wear. Ostensively, the complaint was made that these shell jackets were fashioned from a heavier wool than the 1872-pattern cavalry dress coat, thereby making them uncomfortable at these posts located in a torrid zone. The local answer to the problem was to ship offending garments for the buffalo soldiers at Ft. Davis, which was considered to be a cooler climate.[334]

By disposing of the jackets, this made it possible for the other two garrisons to apply for new 1872-pattern cavalry dress coats. Meigs might have been suspicious of the motives that resulted in this transaction. Perhaps the Texas troopers wanted to circumvent the requirement that still remained when it came to wearing old patterns until the supply had been depleted. This might be the reason why the quartermaster general sent a communique to Captain Rodgers, who was to make a comparison of the weight of shell jacket material to that of the dress coat. The verdict was that the cloth in both articles of clothing "weighed exactly the same per linear yard," and in fact the jacket's overall weight was less

Front and rear views of the collarless gray flannel shirt adopted in 1878. SI

In late 1879 the Quartermaster Department gave consideration to the making of a new style of shirt. Several models were considered, including one inspired by firemen, as this sketch from December 11, 1879, official correspondence indicates. NA

In search of a more martial summer looking head dress, during the late 1870s British-inspired cork helmets were issued to the garrison of the artillery school at Fort Monroe, Virginia, and experimentally to some troops in the Southwest. The band and artillerymen of the former post paraded in early examples of these helmets during the late 1870s. USAMHI

Straw hats were permitted when commanding officers received approval for men in their command to buy such items for warm weather wear. This hospital steward (as indicated by the caduceus half chevrons and 1 1/4 inch emerald green leg stripes) in Wyoming Territory has put aside issue headgear to avail himself of such a straw hat. WSM

because the garment only extended to the waist and did not have the tails of the dress coat. In this light, when word came from Ft. Brown, Texas, that a board of survey called for the disposal of such jackets, the answer was that the items were serviceable and were required to be worn as "the full dress uniform" by law.[335] This meant that troops of cavalry along the border with Mexico evidently continued to combine the dress helmet with the shell jacket well into the late 1870s.

Even those units furnished the new dress coats were not always content. An inspection at Ft. Missoula, Montana Territory was used as an example of "the universal complaint" about the shortness of the waists, the conclusion being reached that the man used as the model for the garment was "short bodied," so "when a man of a different build" wore it the waist of the coat was nearer the "armpits than the waist." The same criticism was leveled at the belt loops, which were "generally so placed that they are either to high or too low to answer the purpose for which they were designed."[336]

At Ft. Vancouver, Washington Territory, another inspection revealed "all dress coats are too short waisted and trousers are made up without regard to prescribed model. This is not infrequently the case throughout the Army."[337] While the matter was referred to quartermaster personnel responsible for supplying Ft. Vancouver, the official stand from Meigs' department was that uniform coats made within the past three years (1877-80) were not defective because the pattern had been altered to lengthen the waist.[338]

Such a state of affairs did not last indefinitely. The rank and file received a Christmas present of sorts when the announcement came late in December 1879 that thereafter "none but articles of the new pattern will be furnished by the Quartermaster Department...."[339] It must have given Meigs a certain sense of satisfaction to retire examples of items made "obsolete by the adoption of new standards." He wanted specimens of all the items thus rendered passé to be preserved at the department's museum in Philadelphia, particularly the plaited blouse and the folding hat.[340]

Meigs could not resist one parting salvo about these items. He wanted an annotation to be made with these two pieces "showing that they were not adopted on recommendation of the Q.M. Dep't, but they

Early enlisted helmets were covered in white facing material for the garrison at Ft. Monroe and cadets at the United States Military Academy, but by 1880 this material was reserved for officers. As such, this is an 1880-pattern summer helmet for an infantry officer, as so indicated by crossed rifles side buttons. CECSM

A drill covered helmet finally was settled upon for enlisted men and adopted as standard in 1880. Commonly, the cloth was white, but in 1882 1,000 were made in off white versions on a trial basis, because they were less conspicuous in the field as a target for the enemy. These also did not show soiling as readily as the issue white helmet. Nevertheless, white continued to be the norm until khaki-covered helmets were adopted in the wake of the Spanish American War. RB

were devised by the Medical Department of the Army." He then expanded his commentary:

> The records of this office show that on the 25" of October 1870, the Surgeon General of the Army forwarded to the Quartermaster General a copy of the printed report upon the uniform and clothing of the Army, made by Bvt. Lt. Col. Alfred A. Woodhull...January 31, 1868, from which appears (pp. 8, 9, & 12) that the folding campaign hat and plaited blouse were highly recommended. These articles were finally adopted by the Secretary of War in July 1872, upon recommendation of the Board of Officers who revised the uniform of the Army.[341]

Even before Meigs exorcised these demons, he had been considering some articles of the uniform himself. Before Sherman's negative reaction, Meigs particularly pursued a pet project, the subject of a dress helmet. He had obtained samples of ones worn by the German military and offered to show them to the commanding general, if there was interest. Among the specimens were a Prussian dragoon and a Prussian artillery helmet, both of which were sent to Jeffersonville for its museum.[342] There also was a guard's dragoon helmet and an infantry helmet, which Meigs had sent to the Philadelphia collection, while he retained a cuirassier model in his own office.[343] With that, the subject of the dress helmet was ended for the moment, the dress cap being retained for foot soldiers and the old helmet with elongated rear visor remaining regulation for mounted troops.[344]

Early in the next year, however, considerable momentum developed for several of the other items launched by the Miles Board. For one thing, the summer helmet was to be distributed on a wider basis after a specification was produced in May 1880, followed the next month by a contract with Horstmann Brothers and Company, which were among the first 6,000 cork helmets made for general issue to the rank and file.[345] Late in the year General Orders No. 72, Headquarters of the Army, November 4, 1880, made it clear that the helmets were to be "supplied only to troops serving in extremely hot climates, in the first and third years of their enlistments, and those only in lieu of the campaign hat." This last restriction was disdainful, thereby adversely impacting on the acceptance of the helmet by troops who had habitually worn some form of slouch hat as the preferred field head dress.

This same general order listed prices for all articles of clothing, including reduced costs for old pattern great coats and trousers made of the kersey adopted prior to November 14, 1874. This was important in that the production of the new overcoat with lined capes in branch colors was stalled until the appropriation was made for the next fiscal year, that is to say, not until after July 1, 1880.[346]

While waiting for funding, the Quartermaster Department established specifications for the new great coat on February 6, followed by one for appropriate flannel to line the capes so that a contract eventually could be let for this cloth.[347] This was after a brief exchange to ascertain what color the lining for infantry capes was to be.[348] While facings were sky-blue, such a lining was thought to "mar the appearance of capes, or give the appearance of not being lined at all." Additionally, there was the problem of matching the facing color to that of the kersey. The use of dark blue lining, the same color as used for trouser stripes for infantry non-commissioned and commissioned officers, as well as for the infantry overcoat chevrons, was proposed. This proposition was allowed and incorporated into the final specifications.[349]

The Miles Board also proved successful in their recommendation to eliminate the gold lace on the cuffs of officers' coats. General Sherman concurred, and his permission to discontinue this trim was given in General Orders No. 76, Headquarters of the Army, July 23, 1879, which stated that after January 1, 1880, the ornamentation no longer was to be worn. This second lieutenant of the Tenth U.S. Cavalry has obeyed the directive, but retains the 1872-pattern helmet, in this case a variant with the foot of the plume bases running fore and aft rather than crosswise. Such helmets seemed to have been produced by the firm of Baker and McKenney. NA

All this effort was fine in principal, but in reality the money was not in the coffers to proceed rapidly. Political machinations in Congress still kept a tight grip on quartermaster operations as Meigs pointed out in an exchange with a fellow officer in March 1880.[350] What this meant was the soldier in the field still fell victim to whatever was available in the supply system. For instance, immediately after enlisting in September 1880, Private Charles Parker indicated that he received no overcoat, but only was given a blanket. Once he reported to his first duty station, Ft. Shaw, Montana Territory, the local quartermaster gave him one of the old double-caped infantry great coats that had been pressed into service beginning in 1871. He recalled, "It reminded me of the old-time London cabby as featured in some of Dicken's works. Arctic overshoes, heavy with two leather straps, were issued, and for field service and in very cold weather gauntlets and caps with ear flaps of muskrat, and buffalo overcoats were issued."[351]

The fur articles mentioned by Private Parker were those that had long been in service either officially or unofficially, and that continued to be popular among some military men of the era despite the leanings of the 1879 board toward a canvas substitute. First Lieutenant George B. Davis, Fifth U.S. Cavalry, was one who extolled the virtues of items produced from buffalo, writing:

> I have the honor to submit the following reports with reference to the Buffalo Fur Caps and gloves issued by the Quartermaster Department.
>
> Both Caps and Gloves have now been in my company for several months and seem to give entire satisfaction to the enlisted men. They are stronger and more durable than the muskrat cap & glove. They are better made, and are of much better material.
>
> I see no reason why, with proper and reasonable care, the articles should not be at least twice as durable as the old pattern caps and gloves.
>
> There is a minor defect in the manufacture of the gloves which I desire to call to the attention of the Quartermaster General. The gloves are lined with cloth, which are, in many cases, I find to be of inferior quality and sewn to wear out. This defect is an important one, but one which can be easily remedied. It is, I am convinced clearly a defect in the material or manufacture of either articles.[352]

Such enthusiasm may have prompted one quartermaster officer involved with the process of supply to ask for "information and guidance" relative to future purchases of buffalo caps and gauntlets.[353] This was a particularly astute question in that the 1879 board's canvas overcoats were about to be provided on a significant scale, some 2,500 destined to be purchased with money available after July 1, 1880, for distribution to the Great Plains. The idea was to furnish the coats in quantities that would presumably be ample for soldiers in Montana and the Dakotas.[354]

In short order Meigs decided to speed up the project. He permitted materials for the coats to be paid for out of money left on hand from the fiscal year ending June 30, 1880.[355] The main component was to be white duck, according to the original sample. The 2,500 to be made based on this prototype were be of the same material.[356] By August 18, 1880, however, Captain Rodgers completed the specifications for the "Miles overcoat," the material was to be dyed blue.[357] The exact shade is not known, however, but the lining was the twenty-two ounce sky-blue kersey, which may indicate that the outer color was the same or near this shade. Other aspects of the garment were more clearly indicated. A hood with blue worsted cords and tassels, presumably as draw strings, was included, as was a sixty-inch-long cord and tassel at the neck. Originally, seven rubber buttons were to close the front of the coat, and two more were attached to the belt at the back.[358]

Whatever its final appearance, the overcoat débuted in 1880, but did not meet with widespread acceptance. The men tended to prefer the old buffalo coats, thereby ending the life of this experimental item.[359]

This was not his intent, however, as Meigs informed the secretary of war. The idea was for the canvas greatcoat to replace the kersey model altogether, while the buffalo overcoat would continue to be provided "for troops exposed at posts as sentinels or in other duties involving great exposure."[360] These would remain government property as they had in the past, and be temporarily provided to the troops who needed them, while the canvas overcoat would be issued permanently and charged against the soldier's annual clothing allowance.

At least one anonymous individual would have concurred with this plan, as indicated by a reference in an 1880 *Army and Navy Journal* article, which noted the Boston *Advertiser* gave favorable marks to a canvas overcoat fabricated by N.B. Harwood & Co. of Minneapolis. Waterproof overcoats like those available from the Minnesota-based firm, preferably of a blue color obtained from a fast dye, "or, if not, brown or gray; the coats to have large outside pockets with flaps..." seemed just the thing, especially if linings "of heavy woolen stuff" were provided. The commentary also promoted jackets and leggings of the same material as ideal, the latter item being knee-length for foot troops and would reach "half-way above the knee" for mounted troops. Rather than obtain these items based on awarding a contract to a low bidder or acquired from one of the quartermaster depots, the author of this piece suggested purchases on the open market, stating: "the only fixed prin-

Second Lieutenant Herbert G. Squiers of the Seventh U.S. Cavalry also combined the 1872-pattern helmet and the dress coat with plain cuffs per General Orders No. 76. Once again, the helmet is the variation with the plume staff base running fore and aft. GS

ciple being that the articles so purchased shall conform to the standard color and style prescribed by a Board of Officers who shall meet every two years for this purpose."[361]

This unsigned essay broached a topic of some concern to many military men of the period. The government's contract system and employment of labor for its own facilities had been a subject of discussion. The issue was significant enough to bring about the convening of a board of officers to examine the matter. Meigs chaired the conclave, but in the end, nothing really came of the assembly. Instead, the members merely rehashed many disputed points of army administration that characterized the days of the bureau system before a centralized general staff structure was introduced early in the twentieth century.

Although far from perfect, the old system of supply remained in place, with reasonable success. One change was the provision of footgear, which, following General Sherman's declaration, began to be manufactured at Ft. Leavenworth, Kansas, by military prisoners. During fiscal year 1879 the operation was set up, but by the time the year ended (June 30, 1880), some 16,158 pairs of shoes remained to be made to fill the original production quota. Adding to the workload, another 30,000 pairs of boots and 25,000 pairs of shoes were called for in fiscal year 1880. With shortfalls continuing, the quartermaster general adjusted the numbers and expressed his intention to let contracts after the next appropriation cycle to make up for any differences.[362]

Part of the problem stemmed from delays in delivery of the materials needed to fabricate footgear at the prison. A proposal was made that this stumbling block be eliminated by allowing the officer in charge of the Ft. Leavenworth's disciplinary facility to purchase the leather needed for the manufacturing process. This Meigs opposed, stating that the officers in Kansas had not the experience of those at the Eastern depots, nor did they have access to the correct marketplace to secure goods of the best quality and most reasonable prices.[363]

Even then, the Quartermaster Department did not have sufficient funds to facilitate the continued footgear production at Ft. Leavenworth, much less "properly clothe the troops" generally, because, as he noted, "there being now a deficiency in flannel for the manufacturing of Blouses, and which it will be impossible to purchase at the present time."[364] This age old predicament, coupled with the "manifestly inferior" product being turned out at the prison in comparison to the footwear formerly obtained through contracts, prompted Meigs to call for outside inspection of the fruits of Ft. Leavenworth's inmate labor. Any items not meeting the rigid standard would be clearly stamped and provided for use of military convicts not only at Ft. Leavenworth, but also at Alcatraz and post guardhouse occupants throughout the army.[365]

This last mentioned part of Meigs' scheme raised another matter. Prison labor was not trained or skilled in the production of footwear, and more to the point, their work was not free. Indeed, the men had to be fed and clothed, as well as were paid a small fee for their efforts. In fiscal year 1880, for instance, that amount totaled $18,699.60, of which $8,692.53 were charges for clothing and equipment.[366] There were other costs, too, such as repair of equipment used in shoe making.[367]

These were but minor expenditures when compared to the contracts let during the same period ranging from 1,300 dress 1872-pattern helmets, 5,000 dress caps, 13,000 wool 1876-pattern campaign hats, 7,500 muskrat caps, 7,500 pairs buffalo gauntlets, 10,000 pairs woolen mittens, 8,000 pairs Arctic overshoes, and 15,000 forage caps, as just part of successful bids reported in July 1880, right after the new fiscal year began.[368] The last mentioned item, which cost the government just under $.61 each, were to be acquired from Horstmann Bros. & Co. of Philadelphia. Interestingly, that frequent supplier of goods to the army asked permission to print the company name and address in the sweatband of the forage caps they produced, a detail often seen in specimens of military headgear from the period.[369]

While quartermaster personnel dealt with contractors, they had other matters to address that resulted from General Orders No. 76. One important element remained to be provided by Meigs' organization—the blue flannel shirt. Soon after the commanding general had approved this item, Meigs provided the secretary of war with some background on the subject. He narrated:

> In the year 1875 there being a surplus from the war supply of dark blue flannel, not heavy or good enough for Blouses, it was by authority of the War Department made up into blue flannel shirts and issued to the Army at the price which the grey flannel shirts were then issued.

General Orders No. 76 of 1879 allowed capes for enlisted overcoats to be lined in flannel of the color used as facing for uniform coats. This added extra warmth and contributed to unit identification. The same order sanctioned an experimental blanket lined canvas overcoat. According to the *Annual Report of the Secretary of War* for fiscal year 1881, these were to be made of 7 yards of blue dyed canvas lined with 3 5/9 yards of sky-blue kersey. There were ten rubber buttons, five in each row, and two cords and tassels, all of which were attached to the front of the coat as closures. In a sketch made for a Canadian newspaper in October 1881, Captain Jacob F. Kent, of the Third U.S. Infantry in command of Ft. Shaw, Montana Territory, posed in what probably was one of the overcoats, or a variation with shawl collar based on the design advocated by Miles and his board. PAC

Chaplain Edward A. Horton wears the single-breasted nine button black frock coat with "herring-bone" loops prescribed in 1872, along with the shoulder straps adopted for these martial clergymen under General Order No. 10 of February 13, 1880. USACHH

> The soldiers like the new garment. The supply of this material has all but been exhausted. The late Board on Army Equipment recommended that dark blue flannel shirt be substituted for the grey flannel shirts now issued (page 20 GO No. 76 ser. 1879.)
>
> The General of the Army approved this recommendation (page 38 of the order, subject 44) and the Secretary of War on 19" July last, directed that this and other recommendations be carried out and that no changes be made at any time which would involve an expenditure not clearly within existing appropriations and directing further that great care be taken to avoid a deficiency. (page 41 of the Order referred to.)

Meigs went on to state: "This shirt is not a necessity. It is like many other garments which might be devised, one which many soldiers, if they could get it for nothing, will like to have."[370] Under the circumstances, Meigs did not "think it prudent or wise to add this unnecessary garment to the list of clothing...."[371] His chief reason was cost, and he enclosed a memorandum from Captain Rodgers to demonstrate the point. The cost to make the gray flannel shirt was $1.77 versus that for the blue flannel shirt at $3.18 each. The difference of $1.41 between the two designs resulted from the higher price of dark blue flannel at $1.44 per yard, which was a fifty percent increase over gray shirting material. Rodgers calculated that to supply the whole army of 25,000 men with the four shirts per annum they were allowed would result in an additional expenditure of $141,000 more for the blue over the gray shirt.

Whether Meigs was motivated purely by a sense of strict economy imposed upon him by law, or spurred on by other reasons, such as not wanting to expend his already limited resources on an item he did not readily support, cannot be determined. For the time being, however, he had his way. When the Quartermaster Department received requests for the dark blue flannel shirt, the reply was none would be furnished. Those who needed such garments had only one option, to draw gray ones instead.[372] Even a recommendation from one of his own subordinates, Major R.N. Batchelder, who was in charge of quartermaster operations at the San Francisco Depot, was denied authority to fabricate shirts made with sleeves of a design that differed from the sealed pattern. In this instance, it was not price. Rather, Meigs could not abide such a request in that he felt: "Uniformity in the uniform clothing of the Army is desirable and no changes should be made without decided advantage." Meigs "did not see such in the suggestion to justify a change in the existing standard," thus he opted for the status quo.

Although he could block one of his underlings from making changes, the quartermaster general could not stave off the commands of his superiors. Consequently, when he learned that higher authority wanted the new blue flannel shirt to become regulation, he abandoned his former stance and ordered specifications to be drawn up for light and heavy quality dark blue wool flannel to be drawn up in advance of a foreseen need to advertise for such cloth.[373]

Meigs was not about to let this subject pass without having one last word, provoking him to write General Sherman as 1880 neared an end. He acknowledged the general's letter of December 13 concerning desired changes in the dress of the army, but made it known that this action would prove costly. For this reason, he asked Sherman to at least review some of the fiscal ramifications that would arise should the costly dark blue flannel shirt replace the gray one, and a knit undershirt be substituted for the woven flannel one being issued at the time. He repeated his lament of the difficulty experienced "in getting sufficient appropriations" in the past, and although he was requesting a half million dollar appropriation through the secretary of war to alleviate the many shortages in the stocks, he seemed less than enthusiastic about adding more expenses.

Sherman was unmoved. It seemed that he had relented from his determined stand that the uniform was good enough. So it was that a few days after Christmas 1880 Meigs dutifully furnished a draft general order to Sherman, along with the financial impact if such changes were inaugurated. Interestingly, by this time, Meigs had acquiesced, coming to the conclusion that "the increased cost was quite insignificant."[374]

This was a fascinating turn of events because not only did the draft order include the blue flannel overshirt, but also dress caps were done

The shoulder strap with silver embroidered shepherd's crook and gold border that was to distinguish chaplains beginning in 1880 and continuing through 1888. USACHH

away with, a helmet replacing the cap for dismounted men, and a new helmet design in general being adopted that would supplant the 1872-pattern for mounted troops.

Amazingly, both the old warhorses, Sherman and Meigs, had put aside their conservative, highly independent points of view to bow to the winds of change. Had these proud veterans finally given in to the young lions who called for reform? It would seem so, if only from a letter Meigs sent to Sherman during December 1880 in which he asked permission "to trouble" the man who brought total war to the South with "a little question of Helmets for officers."

First he stated the facts. The helmet for the cavalry and mounted artillery officers was of felt, weighing 19 1/2 ounces versus the shako for infantry and heavy artillery officers of pasteboard covered in cloth that was 7 1/4 ounces. He then revealed:

> The helmets asked for by officer in the printed petition are those recommended by the Miles Board. They are of cork covered with cloth and weight as follows: for mounted officers 17 1/2 ounces.
>
> The present white standard cork helmet for officers and men in hot climate, which is now worn without trimmings, weights 7 1/2 oz.
>
> You have signified that you will approve a black felt helmet, properly ventilated, as soon as one can be invented that don't [sic] weigh down the wearer. As the outward appearance of the officers Helmet as an article of uniform is all that directly concerns the Government (the officer pay and pay for their own helmets and other head gear which is not manufactured or furnished by the Government) will it not be sufficient to adopt some pattern and color, leaving the material to be selected by each officer himself?
>
> The Miles Board recommended cork, and the printed petition asked for this. There is a difference of 2 oz. in weight between the Cavalry officers felt helmet, and the cork helmet recommended by the Miles Board. If officers generally desire the change, will it not be well to indulge them?[375]

Here was the key; Meigs was willing to concede to the majority, and even added that a helmet for the rank and file would be in order should all line officers be granted permission to wear one. He concluded that while the white cork helmet without trimmings was best for hot climates, the entire matter should move forward with "actual trials and experience of the officers" themselves, whom Meigs believed would "probably develope [sic] the most satisfactory material and pattern." In closing, Meigs had some sample helmets forwarded to Sherman for inspection.[376]

With that, the die was cast. Soon officers and men alike would receive word that the energetic officers of the Miles Board had triumphed over entrenched higher authority.

NOTES

1 Russell F. Weigley, *Quartermaster General of the Union Army: A Biography of M.C. Meigs* (New York: Columbia University Press, 1959), offers excellent insights into the personality of this influential figure.

2 Gordon Chappell, *The Search For The Well-Dressed Soldier, 1865-1890* (Tucson: Arizona Historical Society, 1972), 1-15, presents a useful review of the post-Civil War criticism of the uniform worn during the 1860s, and many suggestions of replacements for it. Also, John P. Langellier, *Army Blue: The Uniform of Uncle Sam's Regulars, 1848-1873* (Atglen, PA: Schiffer Military History, 1998), 183-277, adds background relative to the adoption of new uniform regulations in 1872.

3 Douglas C. McChristian, *The U.S. Army in the West, 1870-1880: Uniforms, Weapons, and Equipment* (Norman: University of Oklahoma Press, 1995), 1-143, provides a succinct overview of the new weapons and accoutrements being issued through 1873, as well as the transition from the Civil War uniform to the new 1872-patterns.

4 There were some important additions and changes to this basic document in both 1872 and 1873. These included General Orders No. 97. War Department, November 8, 1872, which read: "The new sword for foot officers, prescribed by General Orders No. 92, Adjutant General's Office, 1872, will be supplied with two scabbards, one *nickel plated*, to be worn with the dress, and one browned, with the undress uniform."
In addition, General Orders No. 38 War Department, March 20, 1873, set out provisions in response to an act creating the position of commissary sergeants, whose uniform were to be the "same as ordnance, except as follows: Facings stripes, pompon, and chevron, to be cadet gray stead of crimson. Crescent (points up) of same color as chevron and above it, instead of a star. Distinctive badge for coat collar, hat, and cap, to be a crescent of white metal, points in same vertical line." Hereinafter, these documents will be referred to as GO No., WD, date.

5 M.C. Meigs to J.F. Rodgers, November 24, 1874, Letters Sent, Clothing Branch, Book B, 1874, Office of the Quartermaster General, Record Group 92, National Archives. M.C. Meigs to J.A. Ekin, December 7, 1874, ibid., also expressed the quartermaster general's interest in improved mechanization of clothing production for the military. Hereinafter references from this source will be cited as follows: Name of correspondents, date, LS, Clothing Br., Book, Vol., or Pt., year, OQMG, RG92, NA.

6 In the *Annual Report of the Secretary of War, 1876*, Vol. I, 127-8, (hereafter referred to as *ARSW*, date, volume, and page) Meigs pointed out that "an endless band saw...with a keen, smooth edge instead of saw-teeth, has been placed in each depot. This machine readily cuts out 130 thicknesses of cloth and very much diminishes the work of cutting out such articles as can be handled in bulk on a table, such as beds sacks, overalls, stable-frocks, and colored facings for uniform coats." Meigs also indicated that an Alvin Warth cloth-cutting machine with one inch feed had been bought for $2,525 and installed at Philadelphia, where it was used to cut out pieces for coats, trousers, and other woolen items. He ended with a comment that Jeffersonville had been upgraded with steam power capabilities years earlier, and that Philadelphia now had steam heating as well, thereby putting an end to the dangerous use of stoves.

7 M.C. Meigs to Owen Lamb and Others, February 5, 1874, Combined Correspondence Files, Box 1170, OQMG, RG92, NA. For the original letter that sparked Meigs' reply see, Owen Lamb, B.J. Murray, H. Miles, Thomas Butler, F.G. Lupton, and William Lindsay to M.C. Meigs, January 5, 1874, ibid. Hereafter the abbreviation CCF will be used in conjunction with information from this source.

8 M.C. Meigs to J.A. Ekin, August 4, 1876, LS, Clothing Br., Book B, 1876, ibid.

9 M.C. Meigs to D.H. Rucker, October 6, 1876, ibid. Meigs likewise had read an article in the September 23, 1876 issue of *Scientific American* about a Russian-made "'napameter' for testing the endurance of military cloth." One of these inventions was at the Exposition, and Meigs wanted it examined and tried, if possible, to ascertain whether the machine had value for the Quartermaster Department. M.C. Meigs to D.H. Rucker, September 18, 1876, ibid. After that, approval to expend funds on one of the machine for Jeffersonville was given. M.C. Meigs to D.H Rucker, January 9, 1877; M.C. Meigs to D.H. Rucker, January 25, 1877; and M.C. Meigs to J.A. Ekin, January 30, 1877, Book A, 1877, ibid.

10 *ARSW, 1876*, Vol. I, 128. The department also had requested funds to present a display of foreign uniforms per a State Department request for these items to be exhibited. Rufus Ingalls to Secretary of War, December 2, 1875, Book B, 1875, ibid. Among the other costs involved was a small contract for the repainting of two drums by Horstmann. M.C. Meigs to D.H. Rucker, February 10, 1877, Book A, 1877, ibid. When the displays ended the quartermaster general's office requested a list of the items furnished along with recommendations for disposition of the material. Endorsement J.D. Bingham to D.H. Rucker, March 16, 1877, ibid. In the end, materials belonging to private citizens, which had been borrowed for the exhibition, were to be returned to the owners, while the items the army furnished were to be sent to the Philadelphia Depot. M.C. Meigs to D.H. Rucker, March 26, 1877, ibid. This latter material was incorporated into Schuylkill Arsenal's museum where "a quite complete set of past and present U.S. Army uniforms on lay figures" could be viewed since the establishment of this collection soon after the Civil War ended. M.C. Meigs to Frank Leslie, March 30, 1877, ibid. A contemporary description of this facility is found in "Clothing For Soldiers," Philadelphia *Inquirer* (January 7, 1888), 1. Many of the items from this collection now are in the Smithsonian Institution's Museum of American History.
Besides the historical materials, current sealed samples were maintained at Philadelphia and usually the other general depots to ensure conformity to specifications in manufacture. One example of a lengthy list of such pattern material is found in, M.C. Meigs to L.C. Easton, April 15, 1875, LS, Clothing Br., Book A, 1875, OQMG, RG92, NA. This shipment contained light artillery, cavalry, and signal helmets and components; dress caps for enlisted personnel in all branches and arms with insignia and pompons; campaign hat cords for commissary sergeants, cavalry, infantry, artillery, ordnance department; and hospital stewards; a campaign hat; a forage cap; dress coats for privates, a hospital steward, and a commissary sergeant; dress coats for musicians of cavalry, infantry, artillery, engineers, and signal service; a pair of buffalo overshoes; a pair of stockings; a pair of mittens; a pair of Berlin gloves; a pair of Arctic buckle shoes; a pair of Arctic snow excluder shoes; a half dozen lined blouses one for each branch and arm; a half dozen unlined blouses, one for each branch and arm; a stable frock; a pair of cavalry overalls; and a pair of engineer overalls, or in other words, nearly the complete gamut of the 1872 regulation uniform.

11 M.C. Meigs Endorsement to Secretary of War, December 30, 1876, Book B, 1876, ibid.

12 *ARSW, 1873*, Vol. I, 120 and 151. Not until eleven months later were funds forthcoming to so that widespread issue of the new uniform could begin anew. *ARSW, 1874*, Vol. I, 151.

13 M.C. Meigs to J.A. Ekin, October 10, 1872, LS, Clothing Br., Pt. 2, 1872, OQMG, RG92, NA. The material used for lining the original blouses is unknown, although later specifications were clear and may give some indication of the first garments made.

14 Located on the Ohio River in Indiana, the depot began operations during the Civil War, as one of many aspects of expansion required to supply the vast Union Army during that conflict. Two brief articles provide background. W.T. Williams, "History of Jeffersonville Quartermaster Intermediate Depot," *Quartermaster Review* V No. 4 (January-February 1926), 10-20; and C.S. Hamilton. "Jeffersonville Intermediate Depot History and Functions," *Quartermaster Review* VII No. 1 (July-August 1927), 3-9. The primary depot that predated Jeffersonville and continues in operation in another form today was along the banks of the Schuylkill River (thus the name Schuylkill Arsenal) in Philadelphia. For a synopsis read, L.C. Baird, "The Philadelphia Quartermaster Intermediate Depot," *Quartermaster Review* VI, No. 6 (May-June 1927), 18-23. These were the two main facilities, although there were general depots at New York and Washington, DC as well. Later, San Francisco and St. Louis would become locations for general depots as well. Risch, *Quartermaster Support of the Army*, 457.

15 M.C. Meigs to L.C. Easton, August 26, 1872, LS, Clothing Br., Pt. 2, 1872, OQMG, RG92, NA.

16 M.C. Meigs to C.H. Hoyt, August 26, 1872, ibid.

17 M.C. Meigs to D.H. Rucker, August 13, 1872, ibid.

18 M.C. Meigs to E.A. Goodwin, August 7, 1872, General & Misc. Correspondence, Vol. A, 1872, ibid.

19 M.C. Meigs to L.C. Easton, September 10, 1872, LS, Clothing Br., Pt. 2, 1872, ibid.

20 M.C. Meigs to L.C. Easton, September 5, 1872, ibid.

21 M.C. Meigs to Secretary of War, October 8, 1872, ibid.

22 M.C. Meigs to L.C. Easton, January 3, 1873, Book A, 1873, ibid.; M.C. Meigs to J.A. Ekin, January 3, 1873, ibid.; and M.C. Meigs to D.H. Rucker, January 4, 1873, ibid.

23 M.C. Meigs to A.J. Perry, September 19, 1872, Pt. 2, 1872, ibid. As one indication of the long period of issuing pre-1872 items Captain G.M. Bascom at Baton Rouge, Louisiana was told that hats, forage caps, uniform coats, uniform jackets, flannel sack coats, and trousers in sizes 1 and 2 were being sent of old patterns to clothe the foot soldiers in that area, with the projection "that next year the infantry can be supplied with new uniforms throughout." R. Ingalls to G.M. Bascom, September 22, 1875, Book B, 1875, ibid. Even with this hopeful prediction, during late summer 1876, Meigs reiterated that "all serviceable old pattern hats, uniform caps, forage caps, uniform coats, uniform jackets, flannel sack coats lined and unlined, should be retained and issued as required by law." He also stated that all other articles of old pattern clothing, except hat cords and tassels were obsolete, and should be sold at auction at any posts where these surplus items were on hand. M.C. Meigs to Chief Quartermaster Division of the Pacific, November 16, 1876, Book B, 1876, ibid. He later requested a general order to be issued stipulating that all posts issue the specifically designated old pattern items that were still serviceable. M.C. Meigs to AGUSA, September 15, 1876, ibid.

24 M.C. Meigs to John Logan, Book A, 1873, ibid.

25 M.C. Meigs to Secretary of War, February 25, 1873, ibid.

26 *ARSW, 1873*, Vol. I, 120-1.

27 Ibid., 152 3. Other correspondence underscored this situation. For instance Major Judson David Bingham instructed Acting Assistant Quartermaster at Plattsburg Barracks, NY that the appropriation bill required "the issue of the old pattern uniform hats, forage caps, uniform coats, & sack coats, until the stock on hand in the Qr.Mrs. Dept. shall have become exhausted." As such, only a few of the items of the new pattern could be furnished. J.D. Bingham Endorsement to Acting Assistant Quartermaster, Plattsburg Barracks, NY, July 9, 1874, LS, Clothing Br., Book B, 1874, OQMG, RG92, NA. Again, according to, Major Judson David Bingham to Captain Charles Alexander Alligood, July 9, 1874, ibid., old stocks to be used up first, so that the previous patterns were being sent of fatigue clothing. This meant that the eagles, which had been requested for the dress caps for distribution to troops in South Carolina, were not going to be sent because "the caps are not supplied at present." Bingham essentially repeated this mantra when he turned down a request for new pattern forage caps. Old ones were being sent instead. Major Judson David Bingham to Lieutenant John Wesley Dillenback, July 9, 1874, ibid. Finally, Brigadier General Montgomery C. Meigs to Major Langdon Cheves Easton, July 11, 1874, ibid., cited the appropriation bill and instructed: "In obedience to this law, you will make no further issue of he new uniform corresponding with that above named [hats, uniform caps, forage caps, uniform coats, uniform jackets, flannel sack coats, and unlined coats], including campaign hats with the exception of the helmets of light artillery. There being none of the old dress caps for that branch of service on hand, the helmets will be supplied to the light artillery."
Helmet components were being procured too, as would be dress caps in 1874 and thereafter. For instance, 500 sets of bands and cords along with 500 horsehair plumes were ordered for light artillerymen, and 1000 yellow plumes along with 500 sets of bands and cords and 1000 side buttons were ordered for cavalrymen late in 1874. At the same time 1,500 infantry dress cap pompons and 500 heavy artillery pompons were to be purchased. J.D. Bingham to L.C. Easton, November 10, 1874, ibid. By the next year a contract for some 3,125 dress caps went to Horstmann at $1.96 1/2 each. Ex. Doc. No. 95, 44th Cong. lst sess., June 2, 1875. Early the next year Captain Rodgers recommended 15,000 more infantry dress caps and 800 cavalry helmets should be bought all for the posts along the Upper Missouri River. February 25, 1876, Letter No. 294, LR, OQMG, 1876, RG92, NA. For a good sample of the types of contracts being let, at least for head dress consult, Edgar M. Howell, *United States Army Headgear* 1855-1902 (Washington, DC: Smithsonian Institution, 1975), 89-90.

28 M.C. Meigs to Secretary of War, September 29, 1874, LS, Clothing Br., Book B, 1874, OQMG, RG92, NA.

29 Risch, *Quartermaster Support of the Army*, 497. For more on Meigs' views relative to other government legislation and requirements consult, ibid., 344; 346; and 498-9.

30 J.D. Bingham Endorsement to Adjutant General of the Army, January 2, 1874, Book A, 1874, OQMG, RG92, NA. M.C. Meigs to Secretary of War, June 25, 1874, LR, Office of the Secretary of War, RG107, reiterated that old pattern clothing articles were being shipped for distribution to the troops, yet surplus sales continued, thereby possibly leading to shortages. Consequently, Meigs wanted permission to make new items at least in those cases where "only such particular sizes of garments are exhausted and will be manufactured according to the new pattern." Nonetheless, he acknowledged "those sizes of the old pattern on hand that are serviceable, under the requirement of the law, must be issued." H.I. Crosly to M.C. Meigs, July 7, 1874, LS, Clothing Br., Book B, 1874, OQMG, RG92, NA. For additional information on the old pattern clothing still on hand, and its proposed value and costs, see February 18, 1874, ibid.

31 M.C. Meigs to L.C. Easton July 11, 1874, ibid. In this same letter Meigs wanted to know what units had previously been sent the new uniform, with the exception of those on the Upper Missouri. Elsewhere Meigs instructed the quartermaster at the St. Louis Arsenal (Depot) in Missouri to sell all the items from the Civil War on hand except for serviceable trousers, flannel shirts, and stocking. These three items of the old pattern were to be issued to the troops in lieu of new patterns. M.C. Meigs to D.J. Young, May 22, 1874, Book A, 1874, ibid.

32 For instance, contracts for helmets for Signal Service personnel and various helmet insignia were awarded to Horstmann in 1875, as were pompons. Bent and Bush likewise had contracts for pompons for the 1872-pattern enlisted dress cap and some helmet components. R. Ingalls to Secretary of War, June 4, 1875, Book A, 1875, ibid. The Bent and Bush contract not only included dress caps, but both 1872-pattern forage cap covers and mounted dress helmets, also. M.C. Meigs to A.D. Schenck, April 16, 1875, ibid. The same letter provided names of other contractors, such as John Mundell & Co., of Philadelphia for boots and shoes with brass screws; P. Herst for folding campaign hats; C.W. Waller & Company and L.J. Phillips & Co., both for forage caps; and wool mittens from J.B. Brinton. What is more, although foot soldiers were to have dress caps with pompons, when a request for 1872-pattern mounted helmets was made for the regimental band of the Fourteenth U.S Infantry at Ft. Dou glas, Utah Territory, the order was filled. J.D. Bingham to D.H. Rucker, January 20, 1876, Book, A, 1876, ibid. Because regulations permitted regimental commanders to add "such ornamentations as they deem proper" to the uniform of bands, this request was not only in line, but also would be paid for from non-appropriated funds, thereby costing the government nothing. This money came from the officers and soldiers themselves, and was obtained through various levies and practices.
As a further example of new items that were furnished, the insignia for the cap worn by enlisted men in the Ordnance Department, plus the collar brass required for the 1872-pattern dress coat,, were shipped to Benecia, California. J.D. Bingham to D.H. Rucker, August 25, 1876, Book B, 1876, ibid. Artillerymen at Ft. Warren, Massachusetts likewise were supplied with heavy artillery caps, pompons, and insignia, along with Berlin gloves, two musicians' dress coats and fifty-nine dress coats for privates, the last two articles perhaps being altered 1858-pattern frock coats with new facings, but possibly the new 1872-pattern instead. M.C. Meigs to D.H. Rucker, September 2, 1876, ibid.

33 J.D. Bingham to Commander Company B, Sixteenth Infantry, January 7, 1874, ibid.

34 Ibid. In another instance, J.D. Bingham to J.G. Leife, January 6, 1874, ibid., reiterated that only men posted to the frontier could draw the campaign hat, not those serving at such stations as Jackson Barracks, Louisiana, where Leife's command provided the garrison.

35 The practice of providing uniform components to Indian scouts, as well as Indian prisoners of war, continued for decades, with outdated articles often being the mainstay in these instances. based on photographic evidence. For examples see, John Langellier, *American Indians in the U.S Armed Forces, 1866-1945* (London: Greenhill Books, 2000). Also occasionally clothing was provided for American Indians held as prisoners of war, such as those incarcerated at Ft. Marion in San Augustine, Florida. M.C. Meigs to Secretary of War, February 24, 1877, LS, Clothing Br., Book A, 1877, OQMG, RG92, NA.
There were other uses for surplus military clothing. For instance, under a congressional act of Febuary 3, 1873, Civil War issue items could be condemned if unsuitable for use by active duty personnel, and then transferred to the National Home for Disabled Volunteers under a congressional act of June 18, 1874. See for instance, R. Ingalls to Secretary of War, October 9, 1875, Book B, 1875; and M.C. Meigs to All Depots, February 27, 1877, Book A, 1875, ibid.
On occasion, military surplus was used to clothe victims of various natural disasters. For example, when a wide area of Nebraska and Kansas was ravaged by grasshoppers, boots, shoes, uniform coats, sack coats, caps, hats, jackets, and great coats of the old pattern were made available. J.D. Bingham to B.C. Card, February 15, 1875, 1875, ibid. This use helped reduce old stocks, thereby making the day when new patterns could be issued draw closer. J.D. Bingham to L.H. Pelouse, February 15, 1875, ibid.
Another small quantity of surplus items, in this case 1,000 outdated overcoats, were condemned. in early November 1875. These were to be given to residents of Virginia City, Nevada Territory, where a major fire had ravaged the community, leaving many in need of clothing for the coming winter. *ARSW, 1876*, Vol. I, 126.

36 Unless otherwise indicated, all the above information from Rodgers was taken from, *ARSW, 1873*, Vol. I, 152.

37 R.B. Marcy to L.C. Easton, January 4, 1874, LR, Entry 2182, Box 76, OQMG, RG92, NA.

38 J.D. Bingham to R.B. Marcy, January 2, 1874, LS, Clothing Br., Book A, 1874, OQMG, RG92, NA.

39 J.D. Bingham to Captain Charles Morse, January 3, 1874, ibid.

40 The large stock of sizes no. 1 and 2 of foot trousers along with size no. 1 of mounted trousers at Jeffersonville Depot was another reason why new patterns were not provided, a prohibition being instituted not "to manufacture more of these sizes at present." M.C. Meigs to J.F. Rodgers, October 25, 1872, CCF, Box 1170, ibid.

41 J.D. Bingham to L.C. Easton, September 11, 1874, Book B, 1874, LS, Clothing Br., ibid. Despite the approval for this device, not until 1883 did published regulations mention them as an item of issue. William K. Emerson, *Chevrons: Illustrated History an Catalog of U.S. Army Insignia* (Washington, DC: Smithsonian Institution, 1983), 60, this being but one example of the fact that quartermaster "depots did not always supply all chevrons prescribed and, at times, issued unauthorized chevrons."

42 J.D. Bingham to Ira Quinby, February 26, 1874, Book A, 1874, LS, Clothing Br., OQMG, RG92, NA. It should be noted that the old worsted trouser stripes for noncommissioned offices had been replaced by the 1872 regulations with ones of facing cloth, a point that evidently had escaped some officers as inferred from a letter to Captain John H. Calif, commanding a battery of the Second Artillery at Fort Monroe, Virginia. J.D. Bingham to J.H. Calif, October 8, 1875, Book B, 1875, ibid. The captain also was informed that his men were foot troops, and as such they could not have mounted great coats, but the old dismounted great coat with extra cape attached as had been provided for in 1871.

43 Extract of Report of Lieutenant M.L. Courtney, August 7, 1874, Book B, 1874, ibid.

44 While fugitive dyes plagued Meigs' department, so also did obtaining facing material in the wake of the 1872-pattern uniform coat's adoption. At first, none of this fine cloth was readily available. For this reason Meigs instructed: "Quietly ascertain where you can find a stock of facing cloth and new trimmings, and prepare to purchase on telegraphic instructions to that effect." M.C. Meigs to Secretary of War, August 28, 1872, Pt. 2, 1872, ibid., expressed the concern that "The facing cloth is to be found in this country only in small quantities, and all that was found on inquiry has been purchased and the rest of the cloth necessary to complete 30,000 uniforms has been ordered from Messrs Horstmann Bros. as the quickest way of procuring it from abroad." This meant it was highly unlikely that supply of the new uniform could be made by December 1, 1872, but efforts would be made to supply as many of the remote posts as possible by then. Previously Meigs had contacted a military supplier to ascertain whether the firm could provide facing cloth in scarlet, white, crimson, sky-blue, yellow, red, and emerald green, requesting that samples be provided. M.C. Meigs to Shannon, Miller and Crane, August 12, 1872, ibid. Also see, M.C. Meigs to L.C. Easton, August 2, 1872, ibid.; M.C Meigs to W.B. Baker, October 24, 1872, ibid.; and L.C. Easton to Quartermaster General, October 29, 1872, LR, AGO, RG94, for more on the problem of facing material supply, and indicating Easton had obtained trim for only 1,000 cavalry coats and 600 artillery from Horstmann. A bit more was expected in a week.

45 *ARSW, 1874*, Vol. I, 152-3.

46 February 14, 1876, Letter No. 250, LR, 1876, OQMG, RG92, NA.

47 February 14, 1876, Letter No. 264, ibid.

48 September 23, 1876, Letter No. 1359, ibid. The costs for coats and facings were to be $5.92 for infantrymen, which was approximately half that of an 1872-pattern dress coat. J.D. Bingham to J.M. Thompson, September 23, 1875, LS, Clothing Br., Book B, 1875, ibid. The charge for the 1858-pattern coat alone was $5.55. R. Ingalls to Inspector General of the Army, July 21, 1875, ibid. Although the charge to the soldier remained $5.92 with facings and a coat, according to R. Ingalls to G. Barret, September 22, 1875, ibid. this price was for infantry and heavy artillery coats only. Those for engineers, ordnance personnel, hospital stewards, and commissary sergeants were $6.24. R. Ingalls to AGUSA, September 23, 1875, ibid.

49 R. Ingalls to S. VanVliet, July 21, 1875, ibid.

50 J.D. Bingham to J.A. Ekin, August 11, 1875, ibid. This same letter revealed that over 6,000 1874-pattern lined blouses and more nearly 2,500 unlined 1874-pattern blouses for infantry, cavalry, ordnance personnel, commissary sergeants, and hospital stewards, were in fact available for issue. These had been shipped from Jeffersonville in response to a previous question as to the quantities required by branch. J.D. Bingham to J.A. Ekin, July 20, 1875, ibid.

51 J.D. Bingham to S. VanVliet, August 11, 1875, ibid.

52 J.D. Bingham to D.H. Rucker, August 11, 1875, ibid.

53 J.D. Bingham to J.L. Eckerson, August 29, 1876, Book B, 1876, ibid.

54 J.D. Bingham to D.H. Rucker, April 9, 1877; J.D. Bingham to J.A Ekin, April 10, 1877; and J.D. Bingham to Chief Quartermaster Military Division of the Missouri, April 10, 1877, Book A, 1877, ibid. The April 9 letter also indicated 107 sealskin caps, 75 pairs of sealskin gauntlets, 75 infantry dress caps, 76 of the new wool campaign hats, 70 blanket lined overcoats, and 500 pairs of Berlin gloves were among the other items being shipped to Post #2. Another piece of correspondence indicated that this same garrison was to receive 60 hat cords and 235 gray flannel shirts of the heavy twilled material. J.D. Bingham to J.A. Ekin, April 9, 1877, ibid. This all was in keeping with the continued requirement to issue old patterns until the inventory was depleted or the articles no longer serviceable, with the exception of shoes and blankets, a charge that was underscored by M.C. Meigs to Chief Quartermaster Military Division of the Missouri, March 15, 1877, ibid.

55 J.D. Bingham to D.H. Rucker, March 14, 1877, Book A, ibid.

56 G.A. DeRussy to AGUSA, September 15, 1874, Post LS, No. 1874/83, Old Ft. Niagara MSS Collections.

57 G.A. DeRussy to Assistant Adjutant General, September 20, 1876, Post LS, No. 1876/49, ibid.

58 April 2, 1876, Letter No. 553, LR, OQMG, RG92, NA.

59 January 16, 1876, Letter No. 184, ibid.

60 R. Ingalls to R.S. Mackenzie, August 31, 1875, LS, Clothing Br., Book B, 1875, ibid.

61 M.C. Meigs to Captain A.C. Robinson, Ft. Sill, August 21, 1874, Book B, 1874, ibid. By the next year, much of the inventory of old pattern items was reduced considerably, or completely used up at Philadelphia and Leavenworth, but thousands of uniform coats, jackets, and blouses still were on the rolls at Jeffersonville. J.D. Bingham to L.H. Pelouse, February 15, 1875, Book A, 1875, ibid.

62 J.D. Bingham to Major R.G. Chandler, September 2, 1874, ibid.

63 *ARSW, 1876*, Vol. I, 127.

64 M.C. Meigs endorsement to Secretary of War, September 29, 1874, LS, Clothing Br., Book B, 1874, OQMG, RG92, NA.

65 J.D. Bingham endorsement to Captain G.C. Smith, Military Division of the Missouri, November 25, 1874, ibid.

66 J.D. Bingham to L.C. Easton, September 3, 1874, ibid; and M.C. Meigs to S. VanVliet, June 17, 1871, Pt. 1, 1871, ibid. For further details on this experiment consult a January 1873 report relative to George A. Cowles Company's contract to protect woolen items through chemical treatment of the cloth or clothing, see M.C. Meigs to O.E. Michaelis, September 11, 1872, Pt. 1, 1872, ibid.; Secretary of War to Quartermaster General, July 10, 1872, Abstract from Register of War Office, 1872, even numbers, Office of the Secretary of War, RG107, NA; and Microfilm Collections, Heraldry, Box 83, U.S. Army Military History Institute, Carlisle Barracks, PA. *ARSW, 1873*, Vol.I, 121, noted $350,000 had been appropriated and "expended for the treatment of woolen and cotton material in store...,in order to render it proof against moth and mildew." An additional $100,000 was being sought to complete the process, but by fiscal year 1876, funds were no longer available for this project, but instead workers in the employ of the Philadelphia Depot were to carry out moth prevention treatments. *ARSW, 1876*, Vol. I, 127.

67 M.C. Meigs to J.A. Ekin, September 29, 1874, LS, Clothing Br., Pt. 2, 1874, OQMG, RG92, NA, addresses the subjection of materials and sealskin to high temperatures as a means of killing moths and their eggs.

68 M.C. Meigs to L.C. Easton, August 19, 1874, ibid. Quartermaster Specification No. 23 for this item read: "Made of strong white cotton known commercially as 'Berlin cotton wool.' Gored between the fingers. Three (3) welts stitched along the back of hand. A white elastic band, one-fourth (1/4) inch wide, about one (1) inch long, fastened to the inner side of the wrist. Stitched hem around the wrist. To be of three sizes: No. 9, 10, and 11. Adopted May 31, 1876." As early as 1873 George Armstrong Custer required his Seventh U.S. Cavalry troopers to wear the white gloves "or light colored gauntlets" at guard mount in full dress without overcoats. He likewise man dated that top boots would not be worn by the men or officers when "on dismounted duty." Special Order No. 76, November 17, 1873, Headquarters Seventh Cavalry, Ft. Abraham Lincoln, DT, Records US Army Mobile Units, 1821-1942, RG391, NA.

69 J.D. Bingham to L.C. Easton, November 10, 1874, LS, Clothing Br., Book B, 1874, OQMG, RG92, NA.

70 J.D. Bingham to L.C. Easton July 9, 1874, "Abstract from Annual Report of Capt. Charles Wheaton, 23rd Inf. Ft. Yuma, CA," June 22, 1874, ibid.

71 Lieutenant Colonel Richard I. Dodge to Adjutant General, October 18, 1874, CCF, Box 1170, ibid. Also see, Adjutant General to Quartermaster General, October 24, 1874, and endorsements, LR, Clothing Br., Book B, 1874, ibid.

72 J.R. Ackerman's Sons to M.C. Meigs, November 5, 1874, ibid.

73 L.C. Easton, August 19, 1874, LS, Clothing Br., Book B, 1874, ibid, indicated standards for dark blue cloth and sky-blue kersey were available as the basis on which future contracts were to conform. M.C. Meigs to L.C. Easton, August 21, 1874, ibid., stated that there was to be some adjustment of the first specifications as suggested by Easton in a telegram. On that same day the modified specifications were approved.

74 M.C. Meigs to Secretary of War, October 21, 1874, ibid.

75 M.C. Meigs to J.A. Ekin, October 12, 1874; and M.C. Meigs to L.C. Easton October 12, 1874, ibid. This information was repeated in a report issued by the Surgeon General which read: "The stock of inferior blankets used for the purpose of lining greatcoats is now nearly exhausted, and hereafter such coats will be lined with dark-blue or sky-blue kersey, similar to that used for the manufacture of coats and trousers." Previously, blanket-lined overcoats had been permitted in early 1871 for posts "north of the forty-second degree of north latitude." *Circular No. 8 Report on Hygiene of the United States Army With Descriptions of Military Posts and Circular No. 9 Report of the Surgeon General on the Transport of Sick and Wounded by Pack Animals* (New York: Sol Lewis, 1974), liii.

76 According to ibid., liii, the kersey and dark blue cloth standards adopted in 1874 were based upon recommendations of a board of officers called by Special Orders No. 241 in 1874 to deliberate on the subject. The specifications were similar to early drafts prescribed in August, but of stouter breaking strains. For the earlier specifications see: M.C. Meigs to L.C. Easton, August 19, 1874, LS, Clothing Br., Book B, 1874, OQMG, RG92, NA; and M.C. Meigs to L.C. Easton August 21, 1874, ibid. Specifications for these two materials are found in Appendix D along with select other specifications not covered in the text. *U.S. Army Uniforms and Equipment, 1889* (Lincoln: University of Nebraksa Press, 1986), is another highly useful source for specifications as they had evolved by the late 1880s, and its foreword by Jerome A. Greene is also most informative.

77 M.C. Meigs to L.C. Easton, January 21, 1875, LS, Clothing Br., Book A, 1875, OQMG, RG92, NA.

78 M.C. Meigs to L.C. Easton, November 14, 1874, ibid.

79 M.C. Meigs Telegram to Donald McLennan, November 13, 1874, ibid. By the next year the kersey began to be delivered but Meigs noted that its quality was not to his liking in certain instances, and he instructed his work force not to use any material that was "not equal to the standard." M.C. Meigs to Secretary of War, April 28, 1875, Book A, 1875, ibid.. This matter did not preclude sales of old pattern kersey, nor did it impede the making of trousers of the new material, which commenced in the spring, but which would probably not be available for issue until July 1875. J.D. Bingham to Leonard Myers, February 15, 1875; and J.D. Bingham to I.F. Riley, April 23, 1875, ibid. Later in the summer of 1875 John Dodson & Co., represented by his agents Wilson & Bradbury, would be successful in landing a contract for more sky-blue kersey. M.C. Meigs to Secretary of War, August 14, 1875, ibid. Some two years later production was in full swing with the quartermaster general even requiring an another 20,000 yards of the sky-blue kersey to be added to an existing contract. M.C. Meigs to D.H. Rucker, January 23, 1877, Book A, 1877, ibid.

80 M.C. Meigs to J.A. Ekin, July 11, 1874, Book B, 1874, ibid.

81 *Report on Hygiene of the United States Army*, xlix and lii.

82 R. Ingalls to A.R. Eddy, July 12, 1875, LS, Clothing Br., Book, B, 1875, OQMG, RG 92, NA, stated 200,000 yards of the twilled gray shirting flannel was to be bought at $.39 per yard from Mission and Pacific Woolen Mills. J.D. Bingham to Propietors Mission & Pacific Woolen Mills, September 23, 1875, ibid., announced that this San Francisco company had won the contract.

83 J.D. Bingham to A.R. Eddy, July 12, 1875, ibid.

84 McChristian, *The U.S. Army in the West*, 170. It is interesting to note that many of the early quartermaster inventories of the period carried listings for shirting material and blouse lining, yet when specimens are compared, the cloth is the same. Perhaps the blouse lining came in wider bolts, and in this instance was accounted for separately. Later, however, when blue shirting flannel became the norm, a distinct blouse lining came into being.

As far as weights of shirt material, correspondence indicated troops serving in warm climates could be issued the lighter fabric on special order from the quartermaster general's office, while soldiers posted at all other garrisons were to wear the heavy flannel version. As such, orders for both weights were placed. M.C. Meigs to J.A. Ekin, February 1, 1877, LS, Clothing Br., Book A, 1877, OQMG, RG 92, NA.

85 M.C. Meigs to Secretary of War, April 15, 1875, Book A, 1875, ibid.

86 M.C. Meigs to J.A. Ekin, May 18, 1875, ibid. The goal of June 30 for fabrication was set along with the notice that if more than the original quantity could be produced, the quartermaster general wanted to be contacted to consider the option. This same piece of correspondence indicated that 2,000 stable frocks and 5,000 pairs of cavalry overalls were to be made during the same period at Jeffersonville, the two items being produced from a stock of shelter tents that were stored at that depot. M.C. Meigs to J.A. Ekin, May 19, 1875, ibid.

87 *ARSW, 1876*, Vol. I, 126. See also, *ARSW, 1875*, Vol. I, 231.

88 A. Morton, July 31, 1876, Letter No. 1347, LR, 1876, OQMG, RG92, NA.

89 C.M. Coats and S.P. Ferris, Endorsements, July 28, 1875, Ft. Fetterman, Wyoming Territory Records, April 1874-July 1880, Wyoming State Museum.

90 McChristian, *The U.S. Army in the West*, 148-65, capsulizes many of the criticisms leveled at U.S. Army clothing of the 1874 through 1877 period.

91 Among other things this directive instructed commanders "in consultation with their medical officers" to prepare "a report on the clothing and accoutrements now issued and used by enlisted men of the Army, with regard to their sufficiency, suitability to their purpose, and quantity, and their effects, if any on the health of the wearers...."

92 See, Chappell, *The Search for the Well-Dressed Soldier*, 13.

93 Hunt thought the shell jacket "would add to the appearance of the men and utilize a large quantity of material" that already was in stock. The colonel likewise mentioned that the five-button 1874-pattern blouse had been received by this time, too, and was much preferred to the pleated 1872-pattern. Later in the text, this matter will be discussed in greater length. Henry Hunt to AGUSA, March 13, 1875, Microfilm Copies 666, Roll 436, LR, AGO Correspondence, February-March 1875, RG94, NA.

94 Ibid. What Dr. John Campbell suggested was trousers like those adopted in the mid-1850s in which "the body was attached to the waistband in plaits, or gatherings which insured abundant freedom of movement for the muscle and joint." What the surgeon referred to was the "chasseur" pattern that was introduced in 1854, but discontinued three years later. For examples see, Langellier, *Army Blue*, 75-6

95 Captain A. Sutorius to AGUSA March 12, 1875, Microfilm Copies 666, Roll 436, LR, AGO Correspondence, February-March 1875, RG94, NA.

96 Colonel Jonathan Smith to AGUSA, March 19, 1875, ibid.

97 Surgeon Edward Vollum to Post Adjutant, March 17, 1875, ibid.

98 Captain William Penrose to AGUSA March 20, 1875, ibid.

99 Major N.B. Sweitzer to AGUSA, March 15, 1875, ibid. It should be noted that woolen mittens began to be issued in the early 1870s, as will be noted elsewhere in this chapter. The commanding officer at Ft. Niagara, New York, found these to be "insufficient" and wanted the palms to "be strengthened with buckskin, or sheepskin." He also recommended that the double-caped overcoat adopted in 1871 "be issued exclusively to the troops at this northern station. They should be lined with blue cloth." G.A. DeRussy to AGUSA, Post LS, No. 1875/30, Old Ft. Niagara, New York MSS Collection.

100 M.C. Meigs to AGUSA, November 28, 1874, LS, Clothing Br., Book B, 1874, OQMG, RG92, NA. In this same letter Meigs also sought funds generated by the sale of uniforms to be credited to his clothing and equipment accounts, rather than being turned over to the paymaster general and from there to the national treasury.

101 In June 1875, First Lieutenant Paul Harwood, acting assistant quartermaster at Ft. Pembina expressed another point of view concerning the winter kit. He recommended a fur cap, moccasins, and "a superior fur glove or gauntlet" be provided his unit similar to the types worn by the Canadian Light Infantry at Ft. Garry, Manitoba, just sixty miles to the north. There the soldiers of Queen Victoria presented "a fine appearance so far as their winter outfit compared to our [U.S.] men who present a motley array in caps made of a variety of fur without regard to uniformity in shape or kind of material." R. Ingalls to B.C. Card, October 21, 1875, ibid. Harwood's observations prompted Quartermaster Department officials to ask permission to obtain a sample of the moccasins, fur cap, and gauntlets or gloves worn by the Canadian Light Infantry for study in as much as this was but one of several "complaints received from officers stationed at posts in high northern latitudes" where woolen garments did not suit the purposes of protecting the troops from the cold. R. Ingalls to Secretary of War, October 2, 1875, ibid. Ultimately, Canadian suppliers would provide some fur items for issue to U.S. troops.

102 Captain Loyd Wheaton to AGUSA, March 10, 1875, Microfilm Copies 666, Roll 436, LR, AGO Correspondence, February-March 1875, RG94, NA.

103 H. Clitz to AGUSA, March 5, 1875, ibid..

104 1875, ibid.

105 C.E. Morse to AGUSA, March 15, 1875, ibid.

106 C. Ewen to Post Adjutant, March 10, 1875, ibid.

107 Major C.L. Best to AGUSA, March 13, 1875, ibid.

108 Assistant Surgeon W.E. Buchanan to Post Adjutant Ft. Brown, Texas, February 24, 1875, ibid.

109 Colonel J.H. Potter, Twenty-fifth Infantry to AGUSA, March 15, 1875, ibid.

110 Acting Assistant Surgeon B. Alexander, Ft. Quitman, Texas to Captain Charles Bentzoni, March 15, 1875, ibid.

111 Captain George Shorkley, Ft. Craig, New Mexico Territory to AGUSA, March 20, 1875, ibid.

112 Acting Assistant Surgeon J. Frazer Boughter, Ft. Craig, New Mexico Territory to Post Adjutant March 18, 1875, ibid.

113 Assistant Surgeon John Vance Lauderdale to Commanding Officer Ft. Wingate, New Mexico Territory, March 15, 1875, ibid.

114 Captain George W. Chilson to Adjutant General USA, April 22, 1875, Ft. Wingate, New Mexico Territory, ibid.

115 Joseph Boyd Campbell to AGUSA, April 8, 1875, ibid.

116 Surgeon Thomas Andrew McParlin to Colonel Nelson A. Miles, March 5, 1875, ibid.

117 Major John Milton Brannan to AGUSA, February 18, 1875, Roll 435, ibid.

118 Major Henry Abner Allen to AGUSA, March 2, 1875, ibid.

119 *Report on Hygiene of the United States Army*, xlvii-xlix.

120 Despite this requisite at that time no buffalo overcoats were on hand, although some 999 blanket-lined ones were in storage at Ft. Leavenworth, Kansas as substitutes. M.C. Meigs to D.H. Rucker, February 14, 1874, LS, C&E Br., Book A, 1874, OQMG, RG92, NA.

121 *Report on Hygiene of the United States Army*, l.

122 M.C. Meigs to L.C. Easton, March 2, 1874, CCF, Box 82, OQMG, RG92, NA. Sometimes permission was given for lined blouses to be made in lieu of unlined ones depending on the needs of troops in the field. M.C. Meigs to J.A. Ekin, January 5, 1877, LS, Clothing Br., Book A, 1877, ibid.

123 H. Crosby Chief Clerk, Quartermaster Department Endorsement to Adjutant General USA, March 25, 1878, Microfilm Copies 666, Roll 436, LR, AGO Correspondence, February-March 1875, RG94, NA.

124 J.D. Bingham to J.A. Ekin, November 20, 1876, LS, Clothing Br., Book B, 1876, OQMG, RG92, NA, revealed that owing to the fact that no inferior dark blue flannel was on hand at Philadelphia some 28,653 yards of gray shirting material was to be sent to Jeffersonville, where the 1874-pattern blouses were to be made.

125 Not until Quartermaster Specification 13 was adopted on March 12, 1879, did a printed description of the blouse appear for the lined blouse and as Specification No. 14 for the unlined blouse, both of which are reprinted in Appendix D.

126 *Report on Hygiene of the United States Army*, l.

127 Ibid, li.

128 M.C. Meigs to L.C. Easton, August 21, 1874, LS, Clothing Br., Pt. 2, 1874, OQMG, RG92, NA. This did not mean that new footgear was immediately available on a widespread basis given that in the last months of 1874 there were some 52,346 pairs of boots and 7,458 pairs of bootees of old patterns in stock for issue. M.C. Meigs to the Secretary of War, September 29, 1874, ibid. Other discourses as to the pros and cons of metallic fastenings for soles are found in M.C. Meigs to C. Cole, October 27, 1874, ibid.; M.C. Meigs to L.C. Easton, October 28, 1874, ibid.; M.C. Meigs to Buckingham and Hecht, November 10, 1874, ibid., M.C. Meigs to Hecht Bros., Co., November 10, 1874, ibid.; M.C. Meigs to Wm. Sellers & Co., November 11, 1874, ibid.; and M.C. Meigs to Secretary of War, December 8, 1874, ibid.

Late in 1874 the quartermaster general addressed a broader issue relative to footgear. He asked for a clarification of what the term "bootee" meant in the shoe trade, because the use of the word was "liable to cause confusion in the Military Service, being confounded, when not clearly written, with boots. The idea was to substitute the word shoe to avoid this problem, but Meigs wanted make certain that this would not present difficulties when contracts were let on the open market. He himself cited Webster's definition of a bootee as "a half or short boot" and included a sketch of a bootee versus shoes, as he understood these items to be. M.C. Meigs to L.C. Easton, December 26, 1874, ibid.

129 One officer with the Twenty-fifth Infantry criticized the poor performance of the brass screwed shoes issued to his doughboys, this being a typical reaction to the footgear. L.B. Quinby to Chief Quartermaster, Department of Texas, December 29, 1874, ibid. The contractor supposedly corrected such defects as noted by Meigs in 1875, who asked that four pairs of the shoes and four pairs of the boots all with improved brass screws be forwarded to him for inspection and to be sealed as standards. M.C. Meigs to R. Ingalls, April 16, 1875, ibid. Just over a month later Meigs was told by an officer in the Ordnance Department that after a fair test he found the shoes he had been sent almost a year earlier "to be the best shoes the government ever has issued...." O.E. Michaelis to Quartermaster General, May 18, 1875, ibid. As far as quantity Meigs believed troops drew "more boots and shoes" than were "necessary or allowed by regulations, for the reason that the soldier knows that this office will keep him shod, and he can sell the excellent boots and shoes he receives at much higher prices, than he is charged by the Government." M.C. Meigs to AGUSA, August 25, 1876, Book B, 1876, ibid. Whether this was true or not is unknown, but the point to be made is Meigs' claim of the superiority of the footgear provided by his department. Sidney B. Brinckerhoff, *Boots and Shoes of the Frontier Soldier* (Tucson: Arizona Historical Society Museum Monograph No. 7, 1976), delves into the subject of military footgear for the last quarter of the nineteenth century. As such, this topic is only briefly treated in the remainder of the present study.

130 The specifications for stockings finally settled upon were adopted on June 4, 1877 as Specification No. 21. These were to be "good super-pulled wool and fine medium or X fleece wool, and to be mixed in the proportions of forty to fifty per cent (40 to 50%) of black and fifty to sixty per cent (50 to 60%) of white, according to the shade required. They were to weigh three pounds to a dozen pairs when finished, and the legs, which were ribbed, were to measure "not less than fourteen (14) inches long; the feet to be of three (3) sizes, viz: 9 1/2, 10 1/2, and 11 1/2 inches," the size of which were "to be plainly stamped on the toe of each stocking." See Appendix D for complete details.

131 Colonel R. Ingalls to Inspector General R.B. Marcy, November 20, 1875, Book A, Clothing Br., LS, OQMG, RG92, NA. Marcy indicated he was not disposed toward making a change in the uniform of quartermaster general, and probably had no desire to see a change at all within the Quartermaster Department. R.B. Marcy to M.C. Meigs, May 1, 1876, Letter No. 563, Register LR, 1876, OQMG, ibid. Even at this late date Marcy continued to serve as the arbiter for uniform changes. although it was four years after the regulations board had disbanded. His department likewise provided oversight to assure that the regulations were being followed and items were properly distributed, as indicated in an inspector general report made N.H. Davis, which Marcy transmitted to Meigs. January 10, 1876, Letter No. 51, ibid.

132 In spite of the change, it appears that an order for 10,000 bugles was almost placed by accident until D.H. Rucker noticed the error, and questioned whether the bid requested from contractors actually was to be for dress cap eagles. Telegram, March 9, 1878, Letter No. 348, LR, OQMG, RG92, NA.

133 Rufus Ingalls to D.H. Rucker, January 24, 1876, Book A, 1876, LS, Clothing Br., Book A, 1876, ibid., stated the secretary of war had approved crossed rifles marked as sample "B." On January 6, advertisement was made for bids to produce 35,000 of the new insignia.

134 In this regard, originally, GO No. 92, WD, October 26, 1872, stated the forage cap would bear the "badge of the corps or letter of company" on the forage cap, and likewise included only the statement that the dress cap would have "trimming of yellow metal, according to pattern." By the following year, GO No. 67, WD, June 25, 1873, provided additional details whereby the dress cap for engineers would bear a brass castle and company letter and those for the Ordnance Department would display the shell and flame in brass. Furthermore, the forage cap was to have "the badge of Corps and letter of Company" on the front for artillery, infantry, cavalry, and engineer enlisted personnel, and once more the men of the Ordnance Department would have the shell and flame.

135 *A&NJ*, December 25, 1875, 322.

136 In early January the secretary of war approved the crossed rifles insignia, selecting sample number 2 from what probably were several choices. Consequently, a contract for 35,000 pairs was to be let on the open market. R. Ingalls to D.H. Rucker, January 24, 1876, LS, Clothing Br., Book A, 1874, OQMG, RG92, NA.

137 A reprint of these specifications are found in, John Langellier, *Hats Off: U.S. Army Head Dress, 1872-1912* (Atglen, PA Schiffer Military History, 1999), 34-5.

138 Also in that year general officers above the rank of brigadier were permitted "at their option, to wear the sash across the body from the left shoulder to right side." These sashes could be buff silk or gold thread. GO No. 11, HQA, February 12, 1877. Prior to the 1872 uniform regulations, all officers were required to have sashes, with those of general officers being in buff silk and the line offices in crimson silk, and those for medical officers in emerald green silk. All were to be worn around the waist and tied at the left hip, except for the officer of the day who wore the sash "scarf fashion," in other words in the same manner as being allowed by GO No. 11 for major generals and above.

139 T.J. Sperry, "1872 Insignia Expedient Attachment Devices," *Military Collector and Historian* XLI No. 1 (Spring 1989): 43-45, offers examples of this practice.

140 Captain John Mendenhall to Chief Quartermaster Department of California, January 21, 1876, LR, OQMG, RG92, NA.

141 J.D. Bingham to Captain A.W. Corliss, April 9, 1877, ibid.

142 Ibid.; and J.D. Bingham to D.H. Rucker, March 9, 1877, ibid. In another exchange, a like-minded officer was told his scheme to improve the fastening of cap insignia was also too costly. M.C. Meigs to Lieutenant R.D. Potts, March 8, 1877, ibid. Also, M.C. Meigs to R.N. Potts, March 8, 1879, ibid., continued to assert that the cost of improving cap ornaments was prohibitive.

143 M.C. Meigs to L.C. Easton, August 9, 1872, and M.C. Meigs to D.H. Rucker, August 13, 1872, LS, Clothing Br., Pt. 1, 1872, OQMG, RG92, NA; Horstmann Brothers & Co. to L.C Easton, August 3, 1872, and P. Herst to L.C. Easton, August 5, 1872, CCF, Box 1170, ibid.

144 L.C. Easton to M.C. Meigs, September 16, 1872, Pt. 2, 1872, ibid., and Endorsement M.C. Meigs, September 17, 1872, to ibid.

145 Easton, September 18, 1872, Pt. 1, 1872, ibid.

146 Contract with P. Herst, Phila., October 19, 1872, Quartermaster Contracts, ibid.

147 P. Herst to L.C. Easton, October 24, 1872, CCF, Box 1170, ibid.

148 L.C. Easton to Quartermaster General, November 1, 1872, ibid.; and J.D. Bingham to L.C. Easton, November 23, 1872, LS, Clothing Br., Pt. 2, 1872, ibid.

149 P. Herst to L.C. Easton, November 7, 1872, CCF, Box 1170, ibid.; and R. Allen to L.C. Easton, November 22, 1872, ibid.

150 J.F. Rodgers to L.C. Easton, November 12, 1872, LR, Philadelphia Depot, Box 56, ibid.

151 Endorsement 1, L.C. Easton, November 14, 1873, LS, Clothing Br., Pt. 2, 1873, ibid.

152 James S. Hutchins, "The Army Campaign Hat of 1872," *Military Collector and Historian* XVI No. 3 (Fall 1964): 65-73, outlines the hat's promises, pitfalls, and uses.

153 William O. Taylor, *With Custer on the Little Bighorn* (New York: Viking, 1996), 155. Previous to this time, however, Taylor's commanding officer, George Custer, ordered: "Felt hats differing in color or materially in shape from the regulation campaign hat, will not be worn by officers or men of this command." Circular No. 52, Headquarters Detachment 7th Cavalry, May 22, 1873, General and Special Orders and Circulars Issued by General Custer's Detachment, April 1873-September 1873, Vol. 2, Records of U.S. Army Mobile Units, 1821-1942, RG391, NA. This order was ignored by many, including Custer himself! Custer also dictated guard mount was to be performed in full dress, and without overcoats, while white Berlin gloves or light colored gauntlets could be worn. In the latter instance, the gauntlets would have to be purchased by individuals because none were issued until the mid 1880s to the troops. Conversely, he prohibited top boots for officers and men on dismounted duty. Special Order No. 76, Headquarters Battalion 7th Cavalry, November 19, 1873, ibid. Another critic, a first lieutenant who transferred to the Seventh Cavalry to fill a vacancy left by the debacle at Little Bighorn, experienced the shortfalls of the folding hat first hand in 1877. He decried how it lost its shape after exposure or use so that the brim soon drooped down "like a pair of elephant ears." Ezra B. Fuller, "Recollections of an Old Cavalryman," *Journal of the United States Cavalry Association* XXVI (January 1916), 417.

154 Howell, *United States Army Headgear 1855-1902*, 55, summarizes this series of exchanges found in May 5, 1875, CCF (Proceedings) OQMG, RG92, NA. M.C. Meigs to Secretary of War, May 5, 1875, LS, Clothing Br., Book A, 1875, ibid., repeats this lengthy discussion of the deterioration of the folding hat and lists all the men from the Fifth U.S Infantry who attested to this problem. Also see J.D. Bingham to Captain S. Ovenshine, March 20, 1875, ibid., which indicated that the acting assistant quartermaster at the Cheyenne Agency likewise reported troops who received the campaign hat from him considered the headdress unsuited for the purpose intended. Of forty hats issued, within three weeks of field wear, only about a half dozen remained in good shape. He maintained: "The brims tear off, the crowns come out, the hooks and eyes soon pull off and the wide brim then becomes a hinderance to the men in marching and in using the rifle." In response, Bingham requested the deteriorated hats to be sent to the quartermaster general's office for inspection.

155 GO No. 6, WD, January 29, 1875. A summary of the responses was published in *Report on Hygiene of the United States Army*, xlvii-liii. For complete copies of the replies from this extensive survey obtain, Microfilm 666, Rolls 435 and 436, LR, AGO Correspondence, February-March 1875, RG94, NA.

156 *Report on Hygiene of the United States Army*, xlix.

157 Ibid., l.

158 *ARSW, 1875*, Vol. I, 230.

159 Gordon Chappell, *Summer Helmets of the U. S. Army, 1875-1910* (Cheyenne: Wyoming State Museum, 1967), 7. This monograph remains one of the most useful references on the topic of the summer helmet. For Meigs' letter requesting samples, see, M.C. Meigs to Sir Edward Thornton, March 6, 1875, LR, Microfilm 666, Roll 440, AGO, RG94, NA.

160 Cir. No. 10, Headquarters, Department of Texas, July 7, 1871. GO No. 30, Headquarters, Ft. Laramie, Wyoming Territory, June 18, 1872, authorized local commanders to allow their men to purchase straw hats, but this meant the soldier had to do so out of his meager pay. During the summer of 1876, Major Marcus Reno indicated that he and some other officers of the Seventh U.S. Cavalry bought broad-brimmed straw hats without bands from a trader who brought a supply with him via riverboat. These cost between $.25 and $.50 each, and provided "Very good shelter from the sun." W.A. Graham, ed., *Official Record of a Court of Inquiry convened...upon request of Major Marcus A. Reno...to investigate his conduct at...the Little Bighorn, June 25-26, 1876* (Pacific Palisades, CA: 1951), 509. Another Custer subaltern, Second Lieutenant Charles A. Varnum, supposedly saw one officer who had a straw hat, presumably acquired from the same trader. John P. Everett, "Bullets, Boots, and Saddles. Being Personal Recollections of Men Who Took Part in the Battle of the Big Horn in Montana Territory June 25, 1876, as Told to John P. Everett," The *Sunshine Magazine* IX (September 1930), 5.

161 Light colored wool hats also were obtained by the men from their own funds. Perhaps the best known examples were those worn by the men who rode with Custer on

the ill-fated 1876 summer campaign. Custer himself wore a broad brimmed version, for instance. W.A. Graham, *The Custer Myth* (Mechanicsburg, PA: Stackpole Books, 1995), 346. Another individual recalled he saw "white hats, brown, hats, black hats, all kinds of hats except the Service hat." *A&NJ*, September 15, 1877, 90. Recollections from the same campaign recorded a white wool trooper's non-regulation hat being spotted near the Rosebud by some of Brigadier General George Crook's men that had crossed sabers and a brass "C" or had the saber insignia drawn on the front along with the Seventh Cavalry's numeral. McChristian, *The U.S. Army in the West*, 286, citing Walter Camp's field notes of the 1876 campaign.

162 Meigs had asked for the authority to procure 200 helmets for trial, and sent a sample to the secretary of war. At first, Secretary of War William Belknap declined the request because of fiscal constraints. Shortly thereafter, Meigs returned to the secretary with a second recommendation to have the surgeon general review the British model just received through Sir Edward Thornton, such a helmet being a possible substitute "in view of the failure of the campaign hat." See, M.C. Meigs to Secretary of War, March 13, 1875, LR, Microfilm 666, Roll, 440, AGO, RG94, NA, and lst Endorsement, March 18, 1875, along with M.C. Meigs to Secretary of War, 1875, and Endorsements 2 and 3, June 1, 1875, and June 26, 1875, ibid.; and R. Ingalls to R. Allen, June 28, 1875, LS, Clothing Br., Book B, 1875, OQMG, RG92, NA; and R. Ingalls to R. Saxton, June 28, 1875, ibid., indicated 100 British style helmets were being sent to Arizona, after being made up based on the sample sent to Colonel Rufus Saxton.

163 R. Ingalls to R. Allen, June 28, 1875; S. VanVliet to Quartermaster General, October 4, 1875 and 3rd Endorsement, ibid.

164 Howell, *U.S. Army Headgear, 1855-1902*, 73. First Lieutenant George Wilson, a Twelfth U.S. Infantry officer at Ft. Mohave, Arizona Territory, wanted to know how to distribute the helmets and hats to troops for trial. March 31, 1876, Letter No. 493, LR, OQMG, RG92, NA. Thereafter reports from the field did not flood the quartermaster general's office. In fact, nothing was heard by early 1876. R. Ingalls to J.G.C. Lee, January 27, 1876, LS, Clothing Br., Book A, 1876, ibid. Later on, a memorandum noted that in October 1875, when the 100 summer helmets were sent for trial to Arizona, "some of the troops declined to receive them; others reported adversely on them." After that it appeared "these helmets" were "distributed to various posts of the Military Division of the Pacific, and you are now requested to collect them at the San Francisco Depot and report their condition...." M.C. Meigs to Chief Quartermaster, Military Division of Pacific, May 21, 1879, Book A, 1879, ibid.

165 Several years later Meigs was asked to comment on the cadet helmet in response to a request for them to be provided by the Quartermaster Department and likewise fitted out with spike and chinchain as officers' models were. He replied his department did not supply clothing to the corps of cadets. Additionally, he indicated there were no cadet helmets in the Quartermaster Department's stocks. Nonetheless, Meigs saw "no objection to the cadets wearing these trimmings on their white summer helmets. I think that on duty their use adds to the beauty of the uniform." But for "off duty," he encouraged, "They wear the helmets instead of forage cap as being cooler and safer in the hot midsummer air of West Point and without trimmings." M.C. Meigs to AGUSA, June 10, 1881, Book B, 1881, ibid.

166 Chappell, *Summer Helmets of the U.S. Army, 1875-1910*, 7.

167 Howell, *United States Army Headgear, 1855-1902*, 56.

168 Acting Quartermaster General to Adjutant General, October 2, 1875, CCF (Proceedings), OQMG, RG92, NA.

169 The other members were Lieutenant Colonel Henry M. Black, Eighteenth Infantry; Lieutenant Colonel Willliam B. Royall, Third Cavalry; Captain Abram C. Wildrick, Third Artillery; and Captain James G.C. Lee, assistant quartermaster, who served as the Board's recorder.

170 R. Ingalls to D.H. Rucker, January 17, 1876, LS, Clothing Br., Book A, 1876, ibid.

171 *United States Army Headgear, 1855-1902*, 57.

172 D.H. Rucker to M.C. Meigs, with endorsements and enclosures, June 9, 1876, CCF (Proceedings), OQMG, RG92, NA.

173 During May, Meigs contacted the depot in Philadelphia informing the personnel there of the approval of the new hat by the secretary of war. He indicated he would send the hat to them and wanted three more prepared accompanied by standards so that these could be distributed to the purchasing depots. May 11, 1876, Register of LR, Philadelphia Depot, ibid. Early in June, Major James Jackson Dana at the Philadelphia Depot asked for precise specifications for the hat. June 8, 1876, ibid. A few days later the quartermaster general transmitted sample hats, which served as the approved sealed pattern along with specifications, these going to Ekin and Rucker. June 14, 1876, ibid. Previously, the firm of John T. Waring & Co. of Yonkers, NY, said they would furnish the required specifications along with samples and express them to Philadelphia. June 6, 1876, ibid. Ultimately this maker would receive the first contract for 15,000 hats at $1.25. Cords, which were in stock from the Civil War, would be charged at an additional $.07, when issued with the hat. M.C. Meigs to D.H. Rucker, June 20, 1876, LS, Clothing Br., Book A, 1876, ibid.

174 In one case a order even was placed for a white campaign hat, but Meigs made it known that none were furnished by the Quartermaster Department. Only the black regulation hat was provided. M.C. Meigs to Chief Quartermaster, Military Division of the Missouri, June 26, 1879, Book A, 1879, ibid.

175 R. Ingalls to S. VanVliet, September 21, 1875; and R. Ingalls to R. Allen, September 21, 1875, LS, Clothing Br., Book B, 1875, ibid.

176 Once the specifications had been completed, the secretary of war approved them, as well as the adoption of the hat. M.C. Meigs to J.A. Ekin, June 14, 1876, Book B, 1876, ibid. M.C. Meigs to D.A Rucker, June 14, 1876, ibid., repeated this message and returned the sample hat as the sealed pattern, along with another hat furnished by P. Herst & Son, that had been rejected. Also see, June 9, 1876, Letter No. 1163; June 15, 1876, Letter No. 1211, Register of LR, Philadelphia Depot, 1875, ibid; and *ARSW, 1877*, Vol. I, 265. In order to have a record of the standard, a request for permission was made to hire a photographer to provide four photos of the campaign hat. J.D. Bingham to D.H. Rucker, September 6, 1876, LS, Clothing Br., Book B, 1876, OQMG, RG92, NA.

177 According to *ARSW, 1876*, Vol. I, 129, the first lot of 1876-pattern hats were contracted for after the folding model had "proved a failure". The new hats were based on the standard samples that were in the depots, and an initial 15,000 were "purchased and are being issued for trial." It appears the first 3,500 1876-pattern hats were sent to the Omaha Depot, presumably for issue to the troops serving on the Upper Missouri and the Great Plains. J.D. Bingham to D.H. Rucker, April 7, 1877, LS, Clothing Br., Book A, 1877, OQMG, RG92, NA.

178 M.C. Meigs to Lieutenant Charles Cresson, September 14, 1876; endorsement on letter to Chief Quartermaster, Department of Arizona to Chief Quartermaster, Military Division of Pacific, October 31, 1876, Book B, 1876; M.C. Meigs to Chief Quartermaster, Military Division of Missouri, October 31, 1876, Book B, 1877; M.C. Meigs to D.H. Rucker, April 7, 1877, Book A, 1877; M.C. Meigs to Chief Quartermaster, Military Division of Pacific, June 2, 1877, Book A, 1877; all in LS, Clothing Br., ibid. When a question was asked from the garrison at Angel Island, California, if general prisoners were to receive the 1876-pattern campaign hat, the response was negative. M.C. Meigs endorsement to AGUSA, January 3, 1877, Book A, 1877, ibid.

179 Assistant Adjutant General to the Commanding Officer, Ft. Sanders, Wyoming Territory, October 5, 1878, Ft. Sanders Document File, RUSACC, RG393, NA; and J.D. Bingham to D.H. Rucker, September 25, 1879, LS, Clothing Br., Book B, 1879, OQMG RG92, NA, instructed that 700 campaign hats were to be altered for military prisoners at Ft. Leavenworth, Kansas. Also see, Howell, *United States Army Headgear, 1855-1902*, 59. According M.C. Meigs to D.H. Rucker, July 14, 1880, LS, Clothing Br., Book B, 1880, OQMG, RG92, NA, some 3,913 hats of the 1872-pattern were permitted to be altered at an estimated cost of $.15 each.

180 *ARSW, 1879*, Vol. I, 64.

181 R. Milliasent to Commanding Officer, Ft. Sanders, Wyoming, October 5, 1878, Ft. Sanders Document File, RUSACC, RG393, NA, was one of several form letters prepared requiring all the old pattern folding campaign hats to be returned to Captain Rodgers in Philadelphia. This decision from September 23, 1878, signaled the death knell for the unpopular headpiece. J.D. Bingham to D.H. Rucker, September 25, 1879, Book B, 1879; and M.C. Meigs telegram to D.H. Rucker, February 26, 1881, Book A, 1881, both in LS, Clothing Br., OQMG, RG92, NA, offer information relative to disposal of the hat.

182 In regard to the summer helmet see, J.G.C. Lee to Quartermaster General, January 26, 1876, LR, ibid., which asked if any reports had been received from Arizona relative to the cork helmets and new hat design trial pieces that had been sent for testing in that command. R. Ingalls to J.G.C. Lee, January 27, 1876, LS, Clothing Br., Book A, 1876, ibid., noted the Board still had not received reports from Arizona relative to the trial campaign hats and cork helmets. Elsewhere a Twelfth Infantry officer at Prescott, Arizona Territory wanted instructions as to how to issue thirty hats and thirty helmets to the garrison at Camp Mohave. George Wilson to Quartermaster General, March 31, 1876, LR, OQMG, ibid.

Ingalls also wanted to know if Lee had received the summer helmet submitted by F.A. Goodhue of New York, for the group's consideration. This question came in response to Goodhue's correspondence relative to the matter of the helmets he previously had left with the quartermaster general's office. F.G. Goodhue to Quartermaster General, January 25, 1876, ibid. The Board also considered some other options, including a patented hat from John Case that had been passed to D.H. Rucker, who presided over the Board. War Department to Quartermaster General, January 27, 1876, ibid.

183 Vol. I, 128-9. Others were interested in the means of procurement beside the board as indicated by inquiry form an officer of the U.S. Marine Corps, who probably wanted to compare how the army went about this process with the policy of the marines. R. Ingalls to J.S. Broome, October 8, 1875, LS, Clothing Br., Book B, 1875, OQMG, RG92, NA. In terms of the Board's interest in issuance a lengthy draft circular offered ample instructions to the field. J.D. Bingham to L.C. Easton, January 21, 1875, Book A, 1875, ibid.

Moreover, *ARSW, 1876*, Vol. I, 204-5, noted the Board sought the lengthening of the enlisted dress coat waists "from three-eighths or an inch to three-quarters of an inch according to size" and wanted the patterns for the coat collars, which they found to be ill-fitting, readjusted as well. The complaint of poor fitting necks and too short waists could be traced to as early as 1873, but nothing substantial was done about these shortcomings until the 1875 board called for the problems to be addressed. For background consult, Langellier, *Army Blue*, 266. As further assurances of proper fit, the same board was instrumental in having a new form provided to the field (Form 48) that included a sketch of the coat with the various measurement points clearly illustrated. What is more, the number of sizes would ultimately be increased.

While separate from the board's undertakings, the manner in which the rear facings were attached to the tail of the light artillery dress coat had been raised as a concern and its general appearance reviewed. A template was made indicating it was identical to that for the cavalry, as were the remaining specifications for the coat. B.H. Richard to Quartermaster General, April 16, 1876, Box 1170, CCF, OQMG, RG92, NA; and April 17, 1876, Letter No. 773, Register of LS, Philadelphia Depot, 1876, ibid. Later the quartermaster general wanted to inspect an artillery uniform coat and a complete set of patterns for uniform coats. M.C. Meigs to D.H. Rucker, March 23, 1877, LS, Clothing Br., Book A, 1877, bid.

184 Quartermaster Department Specification No. 7, May 23, 1876. According to Register LR, Philadelphia Depot, March 23, 1876, File 579, ibid, these sealskin caps, along with gauntlets were approved for troops at northern posts.

185 According to specifications these gauntlets were to be of three sizes, 9, 10, and 11, with cuffs of at least five inches, "and of sufficient fullness to admit the cuff of dress-coat or blouse." The palms were to be buckskin. According to Register of LR, Philadelphia Depot, ibid, March 24, 1876, four caps and four pairs of gauntlets were "to be procured and sent to the quartermaster general's office with specifications, to be sealed samples." May 3, 1876, ibid. This letter revealed a pair of sealskin gauntlets and a cap of that material had been forwarded to the Philadelphia Depot for safe keeping and as the model for future contracts. Less than two weeks later Rodgers' letter regarding the specification was received in Philadelphia as indicated by May 19, 1876, LR, File 989, ibid. May 23, 1876, File 1040, ibid., noted the specifications for fur caps and gauntlets had been received from Rodgers. May 25, 1876, ibid., indicated the specifications were approved for both items. Several days later Major J.J. Dana forwarded a letter from Captain Rodgers referring to the specifications for the caps and gauntlets, and stated that "blue black seal" or "pup seal" were the names the trade commonly used to designate the type of fur being called for to make these items. Ibid., June 2, 1876. J.D. Bingham to D.H. Rucker, August 26, 1876, LS, Clothing Br., Book B, 1876, ibid., also carried references to the sealskin gauntlets.

186 Quartermaster Specification No. 24, adopted May 31, 1876, stated these mittens were to be made of "pure gray woolen yarn, doubled and twisted; thumb and forefinger formed." They were to come in sizes 10, 11, and 12 inches in length. Further, that in each dozen pairs made, there would be five of the smallest, four of the medium, and three of the largest size, "and to weigh two and one-quarter (2 1/4) pounds" presumably per dozen. Five years previously mittens had been adopted as part of GO No. 9, WD, February 8, 1871, and standards were adopted for them on July 3, 1873, according to the *Report on Hygiene of the United States Army*, liii, but their exact design is unknown.McChristian, *The U.S. Army in the West*, 176.

187 Howell, *United States Army Headgear 1855-1902*, 77-8.

188 *ARSW, 1876*, Vol. I, 170.

189 Randy Steffen, *The Horse Soldier, 1776-1943*, Vol. II (Norman: University of Oklahoma Press, 1979), 136 and 140.

190 Brinckerhoff, *Boots and Shoes of the Frontier Soldier*, 9-11, provides excellent illustrations of the winter footgear of the early 1870s and a concise account of the adoption of these items. Further, three pairs of the Arctic overshoes and three pairs of sealskin gauntlets were posted on April 25, 1876 from the quartermaster general, along with written specifications and the notation that the footgear should weight three pounds ten ounces, not three pounds 16 ounces, as stated in the original specifications. May 8, 1876, File No. 901, Register of LR, Philadelphia Depot, OQMG, RG92, NA. Later, word was sent that the secretary of war approved the sealed sample. Specifications were sent to the depot in Philadelphia as well. May 17, 1876, File No. 964, ibid.

The snow-excluders had been selected over a "buckle-gaiter" pattern cold weather footgear, both of which had been purchased on a limited basis and issued for trials in 1874. These were found to be "as good in cold, dry weather as the buffalo overshoes, and are much better in wet weather." This meant that Meigs judged one or the other style would ultimately do away with the buffalo overshoes. *Report on Hygiene of the United States Army*, liii. For other representative correspondence from the board see, Entry 1011, LR, OQMG, RG92, NA, Letter Nos. 416, 441, 464, 527, 535, and 941.

191 Captain Samuel Ovenshine, who had been part of the outspoken commentators in opposition to the folding hat also provided a pair of trousers that he found to be poorly dyed. The response was the party line. Quartermaster Bingham informed Captain Ovenshine "no similar complaints" had reached the Clothing Branch of the Quartermaster General's Department, although "occasionally the want of uniformity of color has been reported." J.D. Bingham, to S. Ovenshine, August 14, 1875, LS, Clothing Br., Book B, 1875, ibid.

192 Rucker to M.C. Meigs, with endorsements and enclosures, June 9, 1876, CCF (Proceedings), OQMG, RG92, NA, which includes Rucker's February 15, 1876 letter to Meigs. Also see February 6, 1876, Letter 235, LR, ibid, as well a Letter Nos. 245, 281, and 393, from this same source.

193 Report of Board for "Improvements of Uniform Trousers," February 12, 1876, CCF, Box 1170, ibid.

194 The forgoing was based on enclosures from J.F. Rodgers to L.C. Easton, November 30, 1874 along with related endorsements, CCF, Box 76, ibid. It should be noted that after theses deliberations the recording secretary asked permission to have photographs taken of the articles of uniform considered by the 1875-6 board because no drawings were available. Captain J.G.C. Lee to Quartermaster General, April 5, 1876, LR, ibid.

195 R. Ingalls to D.H. Rucker, March 25, 1876, LS, Clothing Br., Book A, 1876, ibid.; and *ARSW, 1876*, Vol. I, 129-30. Also see, GO No. 82, WD, November 14, 1878, for the final announcement of the adoption of the trousers recommended by the 1875-6 board. As early as february 1877 the new trousers began production, with an order for 6,000 mounted trousers. Thereafter they gradually phased out the old pattern as routinely was the case when new items were adopted. M.C. Meigs to D.H. Rucker, February 27, 1877, LS, Clothing Br., Book A, 1877, OQMG, RG92, NA. This same letter called for a contract to procure 134,000 pairs of Berlin gloves, in addition to a quantity ordered previously.

196 McChristian, *The U.S. Army in the West*, 170. As to this traditional saddling for mounted troops, the quartermaster general stated: "the seams in the inside of the legs and seat are turned outward, instead of inside, as in the case of the outer seams of the legs." This prevented "the men from removing the re-inforcement when worn out, and wearing the trousers without it." As such, Meigs ordered: "You will cause all mounted trousers to be made hereafter with the seams turned down on the inside." M.C. Meigs to D.H. Rucker, November 20, 1876, LS, Clothing Br., Book B, 1876, OQMG, RG92, NA.

In another instance, the deputy quartermaster general, Lieutenant Colonel J.D. Bingham had tried "a pair of infantry trousers, and after four months wear on horse-back" he stated they showed little sign of wear. From this experiment he concluded the mounted trousers with reinforcement were unnecessary. He went on to state that he also wore the brass screwed shoes during that same period. Again he was pleased, stating he could not "praise them too much." J.D. Bingham to M.C. Meigs, LR, 1876, ibid. Despite the former comment, reinforcing remained the norm for mounted trousers well into the twentieth century.

197 Captain Rodgers emphasized the belted back would require that a buckle be added to this the list of materials for making the trousers approved by the Acting Quartermaster General Rufus Ingalls on March 25, 1876. April 12, 1876, File No. 720, Register of LR, Philadelphia Depot, ibid. Previously, one pair of the trousers for foot troops and one for mounted troops were sent to the Philadelphia Depot as sealed standards, and for the purpose of producing specifications. March 28, 1876, File No. 601, ibid. As another matter of refinement, in order to reinforce buttons, stitching was to en circle buttons on the waistband. M.C. Meigs to L.C. Easton, Box 76, CCF, ibid; and J.D. Bingham to L.C. Easton, January 4, 1875, LS, Clothing Br., Book A, 1875, ibid. New standard samples were produced almost immediately to conform to this adjustment. J.D. Bingham to D.H. Rucker, January 6, 1875, ibid.

198 Later one manufacturer asked for elucidation on the subject of trousers for engineer officers. The reply was that these would be of dark blue cloth without welt or stripe. J.D. Bingham to Jonathan Wanamaker, March 6, 1877, Book A, 1877, ibid. This was a reasonable question in that there were enlisted engineer troops, and Engineer Corps officers commanded them, meaning that their trousers were distinctly different in color from the sky-blue of the rank and file. Years later, the engineer enlisted men would have the color of their trousers changed to dark blue to conform with those worn by their officers.

199 For a contemporary commentary on the subject of trousers from a cavalry officer of the era see, *A&NJ*, April 14, 1877, 578.

200 March 27, 1876, File No. 603, Register of LR, Philadelphia Depot, OQMG, RG92, NA, contains a request for specifications and blanks for both kersey cloth and woolen stockings. May 26, 1876, File No. 1067, ibid., noted the standard sample of sky-blue kersey, light quality and its specifications had been received at the depot for safe keeping. Previously, the "great diversity of shades of kersey now being received from contractors" was decried, therefore the new standards were welcomed by those who wanted uniformity. J.F. Rodgers to Office of Quartermaster General, February 19, 1876, Letter No. 266, LR, ibid. Later that year two samples of kersey were provided for the quartermaster general's office as well as a sample of the shirting flannel. D.H. Rucker to Office of the Quartermaster General, April 13, 1876, Letter No. 481, ibid.

201 Members of the Board were not the only ones interested in a replacement for the former pattern of great coat. For example see, Captain F. Mears to AGUSA, January 15, 1876, as forwarded to Office of the Quartermaster General, February 1, 1876, Letter No. 166, ibid. Also see, ibid., Letter Nos. 167 and 241.

202 The Board's secretary furnished the group's views on the improvement of the overcoat. J.G.C. Lee to Office of Quartermaster General, February 15, 1876, Letter No. 241, ibid. Also refer to Letter Nos. 167, ibid., for related information. By April three great coats conforming to the sealed sample were sent to Philadelphia. D.H. Rucker to Office of the Quartermaster General, April 13, 1876, Letter No. 480, ibid; and according to May 2, 1876, File No. 889, Register of LR, Philadelphia Depot, ibid., one of the overcoats was on hand as the model for the making of all future great coats.

203 McChristian, *The Army in the West*, 172.

204 R. Ingalls to D.N. Rucker, January 6, 1876, LS, Clothing Br., Book A, 1876, OQGM, RG92, NA, noted the inspector general's request to the secretary of war to have dark blue chevrons prescribed for the overcoats of infantrymen had been approved. Later Rucker forwarded to Inspector General Marcy samples of two chevrons from Rodgers in dark blue and suggested that these be adopted with the dividing bars being made of white stitching that would show up whereas the black stitching usually employed would not. J. Rodgers to D.N. Rucker, January 15, 1876, LR, OQMG, ibid. This was followed by the requirement for two pairs of each non-commissioned infantry chevrons to be made as the patterns for overcoats. R. Ingalls to D.N. Rucker, January 21, 1876, Book A, 1876, LS, Clothing Br., ibid.

205 Rodgers seemed to have developed a slightly modified version of non-commissioned officers' chevrons that he evidently meant to replace the first style adopted in 1872, or to serve for blouses as indicated in GO No. 21. On January 10, 1876 he submitted samples for a first sergeant "made with only sufficient ground to afford space for the lozenge" and two other samples of chevrons, which probably followed a similar scheme of using less blouse and coat cloth, as possible new standards. If they were approved, he would have complete sets made up "for the other arms of the service and for ordnance and commissary sergeants...." D.N. Rucker to R. Marcy, January 11, 1876, LR, ibid.

206 J.F. Rodgers to R. Saxton, April 8, 1875, Box 1170, CCF, ibid.

207 J.F. Rodgers, June 9, 1875, CCF (Hats), Box 137, ibid.

208 Ibid.

209 To compare Rodgers' draft relative to the helmet versus its final form consult, *ARSW, 1876*, Vol. I, 170, and 227-8, or from a more readily available source obtain the reprint of the helmet specification in the definative work by Gordon Chappell, *Brass*

Spikes and Horsetail Plumes: A Study of the U.S. Army Dress Helmet, 1872-1904 (Gettysburg: Thomas Publications, 1997), 7-8.

210 Not until June 20, 1878, did Congress provide for the appointment of two sergeants from the ranks of the Signal Service to be elevated to the rank of second lieutenant as a recognition of their "services by the promise of a military career." In addition, two years later, "the Signal Corps was advanced to equality of consideration with other staff corps, and its chief was given the rank of brigadier-general." Theo F. Rodenbough and William L. Haskin, eds., *The Army of the United States: Historical Sketches of Staff and Line With Portraits of Generals-in-Chief* (New York: Argonaut Press, 1966), 148.

211 J.F. Rodgers, June 9, 1875, CCF (Hats), Box 137, OQMG, RG92, NA.

212 Ibid.

213 Ibid.

214 *ARSW, 1876*, Vol. I, 129.

215 Ibid., 120-1.

216 J.F. Rodgers, June 9, 1875, CCF (Hats), Box 137, OQMG, RG92, NA.

217 *ARSW, 1876*, Vol. I, 129.

218 Lieutenant Colonel George Custer was one of those who modified his dress coat with larger lace as indicated by a surviving coat at the Little Bighorn Battlefield National Monument, and from photographs of the period. For a comparison of Custer's coat to those of some of his fellow Seventh Cavalry officers, see Kurt Hamilton Cox, *Custer and His Commands: From West Point to Little Bighorn* (London: Greenhill Books, 1999), 38-40; 44-6; 48; 51; 53-4; 56-7; and 59.

219 J.F. Rodgers, June 9, 1875, CCF (Hats), Box 137, OQMG, RG92, NA.

220 Ibid.

221 William K. Emerson, "Guides for Military Research," *Trading Post* XXXVI No. 2 (January-March 1977): 4. By 1880 Philadelphia was supplied with 100 printed copies of each specification that had been adopted to that time so that the depot could use them when making contracts and conducting other related business. A book also was furnished so that one copy of each specification could be inserted and an index made for this material. Thereafter, new specifications could be added and the index updated. S.B. Holabird to D.H. Rucker, October 13, 1880, LS, Clothing Br., Book , 1880, OQGM, RG92, NA.

222 Section 1100 of the Revised Statues provided that artillery batteries were to have a quartermaster sergeant, as did Section 1103 for cavalry companies, and Section 1107 for infantry companies, but according to GO No. 99, HQA, December 5, 1868, men serving in the heavy artillery or the infantry were deemed "unnecessary under the present circumstances of the Army" and therefore were "not appointed except by official authority from the Adjutant General's Office. Nonetheless, sample chevrons for company quartermaster sergeants had been made up, including for Ordnance Department and Signal Service non-commissioned officers, but these were not intended for issue. Rather, they were to be placed on file as prototypes in the event the grade was required. In the meantime, the depots were not to be sent examples, but instead they all were retained at the quartermaster general's office. This information was transmitted to Marcy, who continued to play an influential role in such decisions. J.D. Bingham to J.A. Ekin, April 17, 1875, LS, Clothing Br., Book A, 1875, OQMG, RG92, NA. The charge to the soldier for chevrons and related devices were as follows: \$.55 for signal crossed flag devices; chevrons for sergeants were \$.25 per pair; corporals \$.20 per pair; farriers \$.75 per pair; chief trumpeters \$.60 per pair; hospital stewards \$.75 per pair; and all other chevrons \$.50 per pair. M.C. Meigs to J.A. Ekin, March 22, 1877, Book A, 1877, ibid.

223 Specifications for the various cap and helmet ornaments are found in Langellier, *Hats Off*, 34-5, and therefore not repeated here.

224 According to the Quartermaster Specification adopted on May 31, 1876, the 1872-pattern cap-cover was to be "Made of enameled or glazed muslin; bottom edge bound with narrow braid. Shape and sizes to correspond with, and fit closely over, the different sizes of forage-caps....A button-hole stayed with cloth, on each side near the bottom, for the cap-buttons."

One other accessory with an even longer history was the M1840 non-commissioned officers sword, which in response of Ordnance Memorandum No. 19, was deleted as an item of issue to company sergeants. GO No. 77, WD, August 6, 1875. Although this vintage badge of first sergeants was dispensed with, those infantrymen who were issued trowel bayonets on a trial basis were to wear these combination weapons-tools in the scabbard, "excepting when it is required to be fixed for use as a weapon." GO No. 53, WD, April 19, 1875. This meant that the bulky bayonet scabbard for the trowel device formed part of the uniform when under arms, being worn on the left side of the black leather waist belt.

225 Post Commander, Ft. Concho, Texas to Assistant AGUSA, August 20, 1876, Post Returns, Ft. Concho, Texas, RG371, NA.

226 M.C. Meigs to E.O.C. Ord, December 15, 1876, LS, Clothing Br., Book B, 1876, OQMG, RG92, NA. In this same message Meigs further pointed out the surgeon general's stance articulated in 1870 "'that woolen goods of proper thickness for soldiers' uniforms and clothing are more suitable protection and healthful than those made of any other material.'" Another officer, who served in San Antonio, Texas and held a contrary point of view recommended pith helmets and white trousers for summer climates. W.J. Daggart to M.C. Meigs, July 14, 1876, LR, ibid. Even though the items were not favored, during the summer of 1876, 117 of them were shipped along with forage caps to troops of the Ninth Cavalry in the West, thereby reflecting continued efforts by the quartermaster department to have the articles in the hands of the troops rather than in stock. J.D. Bingham to D.H. Rucker, August 30, 1876, LS, Clothing Br., Book B, 1876, ibid.

227 George Crook to Quartermaster General, November 2, 1876, Letter No. 1544, LR, 1876, ibid.

228 *ARSW, 1877*, Vol. I, 241.

229 In December of 1875 the commissioner of Indian affairs sent an ultimatum to the Lakota and Northern Cheyenne to proceed to their respective reservations, or be considered hostile. Sitting Bull, Crazy Horse, and many other individuals refused, with leader after leader and band after band departing the reserves for the unceeded territory loosely defined in the 1868 Treaty of Ft. Laramie as "that country north of the North Plate River and east of the Bighorn Mountains." These actions promoted the Interior Department to turn the matter over to the War Department.

In response, Brigadier General George Crook assembled a field force at Ft. Fetterman, Wyoming Territory, as one of three expeditions sent out against the "free roamers". His men would march north, while Colonel John Gibbon with elements of the Second Cavalry and Seventh Infantry proceeded eastward from Ft. Ellis, Montana Territory. A third prong of this converging army was headed by Brigadier Alfred Terry, who set out westward from Ft. Abraham Lincoln, Dakota Territory, with troops that included Lieutenant Colonel George Custer and the Seventh Cavalry. All these contingents had but one goal—locate the Indians and drive them back to the confines of the reservations. For an excellent overview of the 1876 summer operations read, John S. Gray, *Centennial Campaign: The Sioux War of 1876* (Norman: University of Oklahoma Press, 1988).

230 John G. Bourke, *On The Border With Crook* (New York: Charles Scribner's Sons, 1891), 201. Elsewhere Crook's men took a page from their leader. For example, in the Southwest Third Cavalry troopers with Crook pressed their white canvas stable uniforms into service or bought commercial hunting togs. Although unseemly, these nonetheless served the purpose intended for rugged field duty. Ibid., 212.

Crook's expedition was not only covered by Bourke's writings, but also by other authors as well, along with a good pictorial record from the camera of Stanley J. Morrow. These images reveal much about the uniform worn into the field during the large scale operations launched against the Plains Indians in the summer of 1876. For a useful source that reprints Marrow's nineteenth century photographs along with a concise accompanying text read, Paul L. Hedren, *With Crook in the Black Hills: Stanley J. Morrow's 1876 Photographic Legacy* (Boulder, CO: Pruett Publishing Company, 1985).

231 Charles King, *Campaigning With Crook and Stories of Army Life* (New York: Harper and Brothers, 1890), 81-2. In another recollection King presented Crook as: "Simple as a frontiersman in his dress, he was most at ease in the worn old shooting suit; and in sixteen years of association with him in the field—from the Gila [River in Arizona] to the Yellowstone, in the garrisons of various departments, as his guest at his happy fireside; in frequent visits at his headquarters—never did I see him in the uniform of his rank until he lay garbed for the grave." Charles King, "George Crook," War *Papers read Before the Commandary of the State of Wisconsin, Military Order of the Loyal Legion of the United States*, Vol. I, 267.

232 Charles King, *Captain Blake* (Philadelphia: Lippincott, 1891), ix.

233 Hedren, *With Crook in the Black Hills*, 62. This photograph is reprinted by Hedren and clearly shows the uncanny resemblance between King and his fictional alter ego in the novel *Captain Blake*. King's fiction was noted for its attention to detail and accuracy, points that made him popular among army officers who read the dozens of military-based novels and short stories, many of which had been taken from his own career. For more on King's widespread acceptance for verisimilitude consult, Oliver Knight, *Life and Manners in the Frontier Army* (Norman: University of Oklahoma Press, 1978). In fact, King's non-fiction work, *Campaigning With Crook*, 82, indicated that he and other members of the Fifth Cavalry "had fallen back upon our comfortable, old Arizona scouting-suits, and were attired in deerskin, buckskin, flannels, and other nondescript items so that an outsider "could not have told officer from private. It may have been suitable as regarded Indian campaigning, but was undeniably slouchy and border-ruffianish." Although somewhat defensive about the appearance, King nonetheless was no different from his commanding officer in his "old shooting coat, an indescribable pair of trousers, a straw hat minus ribbon or binding, a brim ragged as the edge of a saw and a crown without a thatch." Ibid., 120.

234 Hedren, *With Crook in the Black Hills*, 69-70.

235 Wilmot P. Sanford, a private in the Sixth U.S. Infantry at Ft. Buford, Dakota Territory, bought three of the old frock coats, for instance, and had one converted to a field blouse. Michael D. Hill and Ben Innis, eds., "The Ft. Buford Diary of Private Sanford, 1876-1877," *North Dakota History* LII No. 3 (Summer 1985): 346-7. This alteration could have been accomplished in a number of ways, such as by removing the standing collar and replacing it with a rollover type, or through cutting down the skirts to the hips. "usually with the front corner rounded like a sack coat. The cuffs sometimes were altered by removing the overlay of cloth with the decorative braid, leaving them plain." McChristian, *The U.S. Army in the West*, 151. Refashioning the short twelve-button mounted jacket was in vogue as well. Collars were cut off and replaced, and trim removed to create a more functional, less conspicuous garment. What this meant is that during the 1870s a "mélange of blouses in the ranks exasperated company commanders and contributed to a most un-uniform army." Ibid., 151.

236 Hedren, *With Crook in the Black Hills*, 68. It is telling that some 1,149 four-button sack coats were supplied to Crook's expedition versus 102 pleated blouses and only 80 of the 1874-pattern five button blouses. M.I. Ludington to Adjutant General, Department of the Platte, August 4, 1876, Letters and Telegrams Received, Circulars and Orders Ft. Fetterman, Wyoming, Wyoming Territory Records, Wyoming State Museum.

237 King, *Captain Blake*, ix. For other descriptions of the 1876 campaign garb by this keen observer read, Charles King, *Marion's Faith* (Philadelphia: Lippincott, 1889),

138-9, and 154-5. King's field outfit in Arizona was much the same, as an indication of fairly widespread efforts by officers and some enlisted men to provide a more serviceable campaign dress than that offered by the army. Writing about duty in the Southwest he represented his kit as "...a motley dress made up of collections from the troop and trader's store—a combination costume of blue flannel shirt, bandanna kerchief, trousers with machine made saddle piece, Tonto [Apache] moccasins and leggings, fringed gauntlets and a broadbrimmed white felt hat...." Charles King, *An Apache Princess* (New York: Grossett and Dunlap, 1903), 146-7. A decade later, artist Fredric Remington's illustrations, based on personal observations in Arizona Territory, were remarkably similar to King's descriptions.

238 John F. Finerty, *War-Path and Bivouac* (Chicago: M.A. Donohue, 1890), 52.

239 Hedren, *With Crook in the Black Hills*, 69.

240 Ibid., 69.

241 E.M. Coughlin to Dwight Franklin, August 23, 1933, Glen Swanson Collection. Coughlin assisted Varnum, who was then in his advanced years, by answering correspondence on behalf of the elderly Seventh Cavalry veteran. He relayed Varnum's answers to a number of questions sent by Franklin, who at the time was in the process of preparing an illustration of the Custer fight. Some of Varnum's recollections were clouded with the passage of time, but for the most part paralleled other eye witness accounts.

242 Ryan's statements first appeared in the Hardin, Montana *Tribune* on June 22, 1923. They were reprinted in W.A. Graham, *The Custer Myth* (Mechanicsburg, PA: Stackpole Books, 1953), 346-7. First Sergeant Ryan likewise noted that the men wore "high topped boots, going into the engagement, and when we found the bodies of the men, we found nearly all of the lower parts of their boots near the bodies, the legs of the boots being cut off and carried away by the Indians." These probably were reused as soles for moccasins or refashioned into other items such as knife scabbards. Ibid., 347.

243 Edward S. Godfrey to E.S. Paxson January 16, 1896, and reprinted first in Albert J. Partoll, ed., *After the Custer Battles: Sources of Northwest History No. 29* (Missoula: Montana State University, 1939), 3, and subsequently in Graham, *The Custer Myth*, 345-6. According to ibid., 365, Private George C. Barry of the Seventh Infantry came unto the scene with Terry's column and saw First Lieutenant Donald McIntosh's body still clad in a buckskin shirt or jacket that had the officer's name in it. McIntosh's brother-in-law, First Lieutenant Francis Gibson, was able to identify the remains only by his uniform and a gutta purcha button, presumably worn on a non-regulation shirt, which must have been distinct. Daniel O. Magnussen, ed., *Peter Thompson's Narrative of the Little Bighorn Campaign 1876 (Glendale, CA: The Arthur H. Clark Co., 1974)*, 251.

244 Graham, *The Custer Myth*, 345-6.

245 Ibid., 346.

246 E.M. Coughlin to Dwight Franklin, August 23, 1933.

247 Graham, *Official Record of a Court of Inquiry*, 511.

248 Ibid., 509. In the so-called "valley fight." Reno's hat was lost or tossed aside, possibly after the scout Bloody Knife was killed and his gore spattered the major in the face. By the time he was on Reno Hill, he had pressed a kerchief into service as head covering. Magnussen, *Peter Thompson's Narrative*, 228.

249 Everett, "Bullets, Boots, and Saddles," 5.

250 E.M. Coughlin to Dwight Franklin, August 23, 1933.

251 Graham, *The Custer Myth*, 345.

252 Robert M. Utley, ed., *Life in Custer's Cavalry: Diaries and Letters of Albert and Jennie Barnitz, 1867-1868* (New Haven: Yale University Press, 1977), 139-40, contains a July 25, 1868, journal entry from Jennie Barnitz, spouse of a Seventh Cavalry captain. Elizabeth Custer advised Mrs. Barnitz "to get some heavy shirts for the field" to send with Captain Barnitz. Mrs. Custer even provided patterns and loaned one of Lieutenant Colonel Custer's shirt, which she had made, as a sample. That day Jennie Barnitz went to town and bought the flannel, setting to work on cutting out the cloth for shirts the next day in order to "make them out once." In fact, the finished product closely resembled shirts worn by Custer. Compare for instance the portrait taken in Leavenworth, Kansas of Captain Albert Barnitz in 1868 in Cox, *Custer and His Commands*, 32, with those of his commanding officer in D. Mark Katz, *Custer in Photographs: A Visual Portrait of one of America's Most Intriguing Civil War Heroes* (New York: Bonanza Books 1985), 103-4, and a surviving speci men attributed to Custer in James S. Hutchins, *Boots & Saddles at the Little Bighorn* (Ft. Collins, CO: The Old Army Press, 1976), 22. Nor were such items restricted to the Seventh Cavalry alone, as indicated by the portrait of Second Lieutenant Edwin P. Andrus, Fifth U.S. Cavalry reprinted in ibid., 19. Additionally, less than a half dozen years after the battle, another survivor of Little Bighorn, Captain Thomas M. McDougall, said that Cooke, Smith, and Custer's younger brother, as well as some other officers wore "white felt hats, so that the General was not distinguishable from other officers except by those who knew him personally." This mimicking also extended to "buckskin suits", McDougall remarked. *AN&J*, February 26, 1881, 611.

253 Graham, *The Custer Myth*, 345.

254 E.M. Coughlin to Dwight Franklin, August 23, 1933.

255 Magnussen, *Peter Thompson's Narrative*, 146. Private Thompson went on to say Custer rode in shirt sleeves, having removed his buckskin jacket and tied it to the rear of his saddle in the heat of the day. Custer's trousers, stated Thompson, were "tucked into his boots." Ibid., 145-6.

256 Private Charles Windolph mirrored Godfrey's description of Lieutenant Colonel Custer's field kit in his oral recounting from decades after Little Bighorn. "I can almost see him in my mind's eye. He was wearing a broad western hat, with low crown and wide brim. It was grayish in color." Frazier and Robert Hunt, *I Fought With Custer: The Story of Sergeant Windolph* (New York: Charles Scribner's Sons, 1947), 54. Did the old soldier have an extraordinary memory over a half century after the event, or was he assisted by the Hunts, to whom he told his story, and who no doubt would have been familiar with Godfrey's writings? For contemporary images of Custer in both light and dark headgear see, Cox, *Custer and His Commands*, 37-8, and 63.

257 Godfrey mentioned canvas leggings and Wellington boots for some officers. Graham, *The Custer Myth*, 346. Varnum stated: "The wearing of buckskin leggings was optional in the field." E.M. Coughlin to Dwight Franklin, August 23, 1933.

258 Ibid.

259 Hutchins, *Boots & Saddles at the Little Bighorn*, 16 and 72-3, n16.

260 Graham, *The Custer Myth*, 346. An officer (Charles A. Woodruff) with another element of the pincer moving to apprehend the Plains Indians who refused to be driven onto the reservation substantiated this ad hoc practice recording: "You could tell the kind of flour we used by reading the brand on the sacks used for reseating our trou sers." This observer also spoke of how "In warm weather we went in our shirt sleeves, in cold weather put on our overcoats." Charles A. Woodruff, "Battle of the Bighole," *Contributions to the Historical Society of Montana* VII (191): 99. It can be surmised that the same essentially was true for Custer's command. In fact, Godfrey reminisced because the day of the Custer fight "was warm" only a few of the participants wore "any kind on blouse." Partoll, *After the Custer Battle*, 3.
Although it was summer, the evenings and mornings could be chilly. This meant the men hauled their kersey overcoats with them, and when not needed could roll the garments up and pack them on their saddles. In one case, Private Thompson found another use for great coats. On Reno Hill he folded up one to make a pillow for a mortally wounded comrade, then used his own to provide a makeshift shelter from the sun for the stricken trooper. Magnussen, *Thompson's Narrative of the Little Big horn*, 225.

261 E.M. Coughlin to Dwight Franklin, August 23, 1933. Varnum concluded this statement with the incorrect recollection that: "Gauntlets were a regular issue at this time." They would not be until well into the 1880s. See Chapter 2 for details.

262 Ibid.

263 Hutchins, *Boots & Saddles*, 4.

264 Kenneth Hammer, ed., *Custer in '76: Walter Camp's Notes on the Custer Fight* (Provo, UT: Brigham Young University Press, 1976), 137. There even are hints that forage caps, including old "bummer's caps" were taken into the field, as some archeological recoveries imply, as well as Varnum's suggestion that a few of these caps were clapped on the heads of some of the Seventh Cavalry's personnel. E.M. Coughlin to Dwight Franklin, August 23, 1933.

265 Hammer, *Custer in '76*, 137.

266 M.C. Meigs to J.A. Ekin, August 24, 1876, LS, Clothing Br., Book B, 1876, OQMG, RG92, NA.

267 M.C. Meigs to D.H. Rucker, August 24, 1876, ibid.

268 M.C. Meigs to J.D. Bingham, August 24, 1876, ibid. Another exchange revealed 382 gray flannel shirts, 72 blue shirts, 37 sack coats, 503 unlined infantry blouses and 213 lined infantry blouses were being sent to the Cheyenne Depot, in this instance presumably for Crook's column that trudged out of Ft. Fetterman, Wyoming Territory in autumn 1876,. J.D. Bingham to J.A. Ekin, September 19, 1876, ibid.

269 Men with Crook's column out of Ft. Fetterman had cloth caps trimmed with fur and provided with ear flaps; foul weather gauntlets; Indian moccasins with cork soles that could be covered by buffalo overshoes with the fur on the inside; and all manner of overcoats ranging from bear, beaver, and buffalo, to canvas ones that were lined with blanket material, which had been bought by form a supplier in St. Paul Minnesota. Bourke, *On the Border With Crook*, 251-3. Some of these items were supplied by the government; other items were procured by individuals. Chappell, *Search for the Well-Dressed Soldier*, 29

270 These would have been the old pattern overcoats, and not the ones recommended by the 1875 board, as was noted in one communication to an officer in St. Louis that "no new pattern great coats can be supplied until those of the old pattern on hand shall have been issued." J.D. Bingham to C.C. Cresson, November 11, 1876, LS, Clothing Br., Book B, 1876, OQMG, RG92, NA.

271 M.C. Meigs to Secretary of War, September 4, 1876, LS, Clothing Br., ibid.

272 M.C. Meigs to S.B. Holabird, September 4, 1876, ibid.

273 Jerome A. Greene, *Yellowstone Command: Colonel Nelson A. Miles and the Great Sioux War* (Lincoln: University of Nebraska Press, 1991), offers a superb recounting of this campaign.

274 M.C. Meigs to Chief Quartermaster Division of the Missouri, January 22, 1877, LS, Clothing Br., Book A, 1877, ibid.

275 M.C. Meigs to W.T. Sherman, October 9, 1876, Book B, 1876, ibid.

276 277 Meigs to AGUSA, March 28, 1877, ibid.

278 M.C. Meigs to S.B. Holabird, October 13, 1876, ibid.

279 M.C. Meigs to S.B. Holabird, October 21, 1876, ibid.

280 Telegrams, H.C. Hodges to S.B. Holabird, October 19, 1876, ibid; and H.C. Hodges to J.A. Ekin, October 19, 1876, ibid.

281 J.D. Bingham to Chief Quartermaster, Division of the Missouri, October 30, 1876, ibid. First Lieutenant H.C. LaPoint, a Second Cavalry officer posted to Camp Brown, Wyoming Territory, was one of those who availed himself of the old blankets that could be used as horse covers. Endorsement J.D. Bingham to A. Barret, January 29, 1877, Book A, 1877, ibid. These could not be substituted as saddle blankets, however, those articles being supplied by the Ordnance Department as spelled out in J.D. Bingham to H.J. Nowlan, August 14, 1877, Book B, 1877, ibid.

282 M.C. Meigs to S.B. Holabird, October 13, 1876, ibid.

283 J.D. Bingham to J.M. Marshall, February 7, 1877, Book A, 1877, ibid.
284 Howell, *United States Army Headgear*, 78.
285 T.J. Sperry "Winter Clothing on the Northern Plains," *Military Collector and Historian*, XLIV No. 3 (Fall 1992): 116; and McChristian, *The Army in the West*, 175-6, describe the cap well. The former article attributes its adoption to the so-called Miles Board of 1878-9.
286 This was in keeping with GO No. 9, WD, February 8, 1871, which the Quartermaster Department wanted to be revised to allow for blanket lined or cloth lined overcoats, overshoes, and mittens, all to be provided to the troops as departmental commanders found necessary, then returned when climatic conditions improved. J.D. Bingham to AGUSA, February 4, 1875, LS, Clothing Br., Book A, 1875, OQMG, RG92, NA. When not in use quartermasters customarily kept the fur items in sealed petroleum paper. These packets were to be unwrapped during the period between the middle of June and the middle of September, every ten days so they could be subjected to a thorough "heating and brushing" then rewrapped until the items were called for by the commanders of departments. J.D. Bingham to A.C. Ayers, February 23, 1877, Book A, 1877, ibid.
287 Specification No. 25, March 12, 1879.
288 *ARSW, 1878*, Vol. I, 241. As to the longevity of the buffalo overcoat, an article written decades after their adoption indicated these coats were "almost priceless...in as much as they cannot be replaced. They were purchased in the early days when buffalo herds roamed the plains...and when procured were the cheapest and best overcoats obtainable." Each year, at the end of winter, they had been stored away carefully, thereby lasting for a considerable time. In fact, troops participating in the Siberian Expedition at the conclusion of World War I wore buffalo coats, and the article went on to say that men of the third battalion of the Fourth U.S. Infantry stationed at Ft. Lincoln, North Dakota were to be issued coats for the coming winter of 1927-8, even though some of the aged garments were "from 50 to 60 years old...." *Winners of the West*, January 30, 1928, 6.
289 Hill and Innis, "The Fort Buford Diary": 28-9; and 32.
290 Jerome A. Greene, "The U.S. Army Buffalo Overcoat and M1883 Canvas Blanket-Lined Overcoat on the Northern Plains Frontier, 1876-1891," *Military Collector and Historian* XLIV No. 2 (Summer 1992): 73-75; and Sperry, "Winter Clothing on the Northern Plains" ibid.: 117-19, concisely address the buffalo overcoat.
291 M.C. Meigs to Secretary of War, March 3, 1877, LS, Clothing Br., Book A, 1877, OQMG, RG92, NA. The secretary of war gave his blessing to the idea, and 6,000 collarless shirts were made to send to the Military Division of the Missouri, 2,000 others went to the Military Division of the Atlantic, and the final 2,000 were shipped to the Military Division of the Pacific, where the would then be distributed to various commands and directions given for opinions to be provided as to their reception by the soldiers. M.C. Meigs to J.A. Ekin, March 11, 1877, ibid.
292 *ARSW, 1878*, Vol. I, 331.
293 September 21, 1878, OQMG, 1878, Microfilm Collections, Box 83, USAMHI, Carlisle Barracks, PA. The scheme called for officers to obtain a seventeen to twenty-one inch long by approximately one and one-eighth inch wide black silk necktie with a stiff canvas inner, that would be held in place by a strap and buckle arrangement. Enlisted men were to don one of black Italian cloth with a slate-colored jean back of approximately the same size as that prescribed for officers, and that also used a similar attachment. The Austrian-inspired accessory was not approved however.
294 Emerson, *Chevrons*, 108, indicates that the mark for candidates for promotion were described in slightly more detail in 1889 as a "double stripe running the length of the cuff, pointed at the end, with a small button below the point of the stripe." These were to be 1/4 inch wide with a space between the stripes of 1/8 inch. Those for the dress coat were gilt and those for the blouse and overcoat were to be of facing material in the wearer's branch color. As an indication of the rarity of these items, the same source points out that only four pairs of lace and thirty pairs of cloth stripes were in the inventory in 1900. Nevertheless, the same practice continued into the early twentieth century, even after the adoption of the 1902-pattern uniform.
The general orders that permitted the candidate stripe was a follow on to GO No. 37, WD, June 19, 1878, that set forth the basic principles embodied in the law permitting non-commissioned officers to be promoted to second lieutenants. By 1890, the program was extended to all unmarried enlisted men, who met certain criteria, rather than just non-commissioned officers. Even then, promotions were few under this plan. For a brief overview refer to, Ernest F. Fisher, Jr., *Guardians of the Republic: A History of the Noncommissioned Officer Corps of the U.S. Army* (New York: Ballantine Books, 1994), 136-7.
295 M.C. Meigs to Editor, *A&NJ*, February 8, 1877, LS, Clothing Br., Book A, 1877, OQMG, RG92, NA. In that same year a tally from Meigs demonstrated that much of the old pattern had been issued or otherwise disposed of. Less than 1,700 sack coats remained in stocks of the unlined variety and only 294 lined ones. Mounted musicians' jackets had dwindled to 39, shell jackets for privates to 565, felt hats to 86, and unlined enlisted frock coats were down to 1,550. Only foot trousers and dismounted great coats, presumably some or all with the additional cape, remained in large numbers, these totaling 18,478 and 114,534 respectively. M.C. Meigs to B.F. Butler, January 31, 1877, ibid. Even at this late date Meigs told the officer responsible for supplying troops in the Dakotas to carry on issuance of old pattern items, except for blankets and shoes. M.C. Meigs to Chief Quartermaster Department of Dakota, March 15, 1877, ibid.
296 S. Benét to Secretary of War, July 3, 1878, File 7721, AGO 1878, Microcopy 666, Roll 435, AGO, RG94, NA.
297 The other members of the gathering were Colonel Ranald MacKenzie, Fourth U.S. Cavalry; Lieutenant Colonel Henry Morrow, Thirteenth U.S Infantry; Major George Sanford, First U.S. Cavalry; Captain Daniel Benham, Seventh U.S. Infantry; and Captain Joseph Sanger, First U.S. Artillery. Given that these men were not all from the infantry, and also because of the considerable field experience most of the brought to the table, it is not surprising that they broadened their scope. For brief background on these men see, McChristian, *The U.S. Army in the West*, 223-5. This same source provides ample information on the Board's recommendations for equipment. It should be noted in the interest of the present study that the board had copies of the materials used to produce the 1868 Woodhull Report, as well as all the correspondence that was generated in reply to the 1875 circular requesting medical officers and others to discuss the merits of the uniform. These are found in the National Archives microfilm collections M666, Rolls 434-439.
298 Letter S185-78, January 8, 1879, LR, Surgeon General's Office, RG112, NA.
299 M.C. Meigs to President of Board, January 14, 1879, LS, Clothing Br., Book A, 1879, OQMG, RG92, NA.
300 H. Hodges to D.H. Rucker, January 9, 1879; J.D. Bingham to D.H. Rucker, April 10, 1879, ibid.; and D.H. Rucker to President of Board, January 14, 1879, LR, Clothing Br., Letter No. 68, ibid.
301 M.C. Meigs to President of Board, January 11, 1879, ibid.
302 M.C. Meigs to AGUSA, January 27, 1879, ibid.
303 M.C. Meigs to President of Board, January 16, 1879, LS, Clothing Br., Book A, 1879, ibid.
304 J.D. Bingham to G. Patterson, February 27, 1879; and J.D. Bingham to President of Board, March 28, 1879, ibid.
305 Ibid. The surgeon general indicated to Colonel Mackenzie that there was no data that the indigo in the blue shirts would be any more harmful than the dye in the gray material. Surgeon General to General R.S. MacKenzie, February 19, 1879, ibid.
306 M.C. Meigs to N.A. Miles, January 2, 1879, LS, Clothing Br., Book A, 1879, OQMG, RG92, NA.
307 J.D. Bingham to President of Board, January 20, 1879, ibid.
308 J.F. Rodgers to J.J. Dana, January 20, 1879, ibid. After the Board disbanded some of these blouses were among the items returned to Philadelphia, including two blouses with pockets, and two blouses, one of white and one of blue. There were also four jackets (white and blue) and six pairs of trousers (white and blue), that may have been the overalls and stable frocks that had been proposed but not adopted for infantrymen. J.D. Bingham to A.F. Rockwell, April 10, 1879, ibid. All the foreign specimens and the two plaited blouses from the 1868 board (the latter two items now being preserved in the Smithsonian Institution's Museum of American History military collections) likewise were returned to the quartermaster museum in Philadelphia. J.D. Bingham to D.H. Rucker, April 10, 1879, ibid. Elsewhere it was indicated that the canvas leggings reviewed by the Board and a rubber overcoat were among the materials sent for the Philadelphia collection. H. Hodges to D.H. Rucker, October 29, 1879, Book B, 1879, ibid.
309 M.C. Meigs to J.F. Rodgers, May 9, 1879, Book A, 1879., ibid.
310 There was some confusion in the Quartermaster General Department as to what coat was to have the length increased because the Board did not have standard samples of these garments in their hands. J.D. Bingham to J.F. Rodgers, May 14, 1879, ibid. It is possible that the Board was reacting to the coats made prior to 1876 with slightly shorter waists, and that those produced after the 1875-76 board had made a like suggestion had not bee issued on a widespread basis, thereby continuing the old complaint of length.
311 Unless otherwise noted, all the recommendations of the Miles Board as outlined in the above text were treated in M.C. Meigs to J.F. Rodgers, May 9, 1879, ibid.
312 An article in *A&NJ*, November 9, 1879, 265, provides contemporary commentary on the subject of facing colors.
313 M.C. Meigs to Chief Quartermaster Military Division of the Missouri, January 27, 1879, LS, Clothing Br., Book A, 1879, OQMG, RG92, NA.
314 GO No. 76, HQA, July 23, 1879.
315 316 Brinckerhoff, *Boots and Shoes of the Frontier Soldier*,16, and n25, 46. A sketch of the "improved" shoe was provided to the board in response. M.C Meigs to D.H. Rucker, January 23, 1879, LS, Clothing Br., Book A, 1879, OQMG, RG92, NA. Other drawings relative to screwed soles and the tools used in the manufacture of this type of footwear are found in M.C. Meigs to D.H. Rucker, January 20, 1878, and M.C. Meigs to D.H. Rucker, February 21, 1879, ibid.
317 GO No. 76, HQA, July 23, 1876.
318 Some 300 trial canvas overcoats were considered, but if these could not be made up quickly Miles at least wanted a "sample together with the light colored French over coat" held at the Philadelphia Depot, so that the Board could review these items. N.A. Miles to M.C. Meigs, January 20, 1879, LR, Clothing Br., Letter No. 851, OQMG, RG92, NA. Several months later Sherman approved 100 coats to be made for trial and these were to be sent to Ft. Keogh, Montana Territory. M.C. Meigs to N.A. Miles, August 26, 1879, LS, Clothing Br., Book B, 1879, ibid.
319 Greene, "The U.S. Army Buffalo Overcoat," 72.
320 Two years earlier, Meigs had indicated that he was unaware of a general desire to do away with the dark blue, double breasted officers overcoat with gilt buttons prescribed by general orders in 1872, and he saw no "advantage in changing the perfect pattern" adopted in that year. M.C. Meigs to General of the Army, March 26, 1877, LS, Clothing Br., Book A, 1877, OQMG, RG92, NA. Evidently General Sherman shared Meigs' sentiments in that he would reject the overcoat's adoption when the board suggested it in 1879. Nonetheless, it seems Philadelphia military tailors J.R. Ackerman's Sons may have furnished an example for the board's consideration, or more probably made some prototypes of the canvas greatcoat according M.C. Meigs to J.P. Sanger, April 29, 1879, ibid.

321 The Board suggested many new items of equipment as well, which are not treated in this study about the uniform. Suffice it to say, that their recommendations in both areas, although well founded in many instances, would have been costly to produce. For instance, the new articles of clothing would require an additional $525,000 in appropriations if adopted according to M.C. Meigs to AGUSA, July 12, 1879, ibid.

322 On the surface, some of Sherman's remarks that had to do with the enlisted man securing items such as summer clothing or making leggings themselves might appear that he was unsympathetic to the rank and file. This was far from the case. Supposedly not only was he ever ready to help a needy soldier, but also almost a third of his own pay was given for the purchase of "train tickets, boots, and clothing for old comrades in arms, and he provided assistance to the widows and orphans of soldiers whenever asked." Marsha Landreth, *Great American Generals: William T. Sherman* (New York: Gallery Books, 1990), 77. Another biographer added: "In many ways, Sherman, like Winfield Scott before him, tried to hang on rather than innovate." John F. Marszalek, *Sherman: Soldier's Passion for Order* (New York The Free Press, 1993, 443. In addition to Marszalek, also review the overview of this complex man and his impact on the U.S. Army provided by R.A. Andrews, "Years of Frustration: William T. Sherman, The Army and Reform," (unpublished MA Thesis, Department of History, Northwestern University, 1968).

323 *Army and Navy Register*, July 10, 1880, 3.

324 *A&NJ*, August 23, 1879, 45.

325 *Army and Navy Register*, June 12, 1880, 6.

326 *A&NJ*, September 22, 1879, 144.

327 Ibid., November 8, 1879, 264.

328 M.C. Meigs to Chief Quartermaster, Military Division of the Pacific, May 21, 1879, LS, Clothing Br., Book A, 1879, OQMG, RG92, NA. Previously all the information the department had available on this subject had been sent to the Miles Board. M.C. Meigs to President of Board, February 1, 1879, ibid.

329 M.C. Meigs to J.F. Rodgers, March 4, 1879, ibid. A similar letter was sent to D.H. Rucker. M.C. Meigs to D.H. Rucker, March 15, 1879, ibid.

330 M.C. Meigs to Secretary of War, July 16, 1879, ibid.

331 Ibid, and M.C. Meigs to D.H. Rucker, July 18, 1879, ibid.

332 M.C. Meigs to G. Getty, August 20, 1879, ibid. At that time Colonel George Getty commanded Ft. Monroe's artillery school.

333 M.C. Meigs to N.A. Miles, June 30, 1879, ibid.

334 Douglas C. McChristian, *An Army of Marksmen: The Development of United States Army Marksmanship in the 19th Century* (Ft. Collins, CO: Old Army Press, 1981), 45; *ARSW, 1880*, Vol. I, 13.

335 R.W. Julian, *Medals of the United States Mint: The First Century 1792-1892*. Neil Harris, ed., (N.P.: The Token and Medal Society, Inc., n.d.), 337.

336 For background on service chevrons refer to, Emerson, *Chevrons*, 34; 55; 75-6; 78-9; 82; 135-8; and 211. Also refer to, S.B. Holabird to Chief Quartermaster Military Division of the Missouri, June 20, 1881, for clarification for the "campaign service chevron" followed by GO No. 60, HQA, June 6, 1882; GO No. 92, HQA, August 9, 1882; GO No. 129, HQA, November 18, 1882; and GO No. 38, HQA, June 6, 1883, for the evolution of these insignia.

337 M.C. Meigs to D.H. Rucker, July 14, 1880, LS, Clothing Br. Book B, 1880, OQMG, RG 92, NA.. The conversion of large quantities of the folding hat is one of the reasons why this piece of headgear, in its original state, is extremely rare.

338 M.C. Meigs to Chief Quartermaster Military Division of Missouri, April 28, 1879, Book A, ibid.

339 M.C. Meigs to Chief Quartermaster Military Division of Missouri, July 29, 1879, Book B; M.C. Meigs to Secretary of War, October 27, 1879, Book B; and M.C. Meigs to B.F. Butler, January 7, 1879, Book A, ibid. At that time General Benjamin "Beast" Butler was being contacted in regard to clothing for the National Soldier's Home, which was located in the Military Division of the Atlantic, where he was in command. Approximately 60,000 overcoats were kept of old patterns, but GO No. 113 issued in 1879 called for the disposal of all old overcoats. S.B. Holabird to A.H. Russell, July 13, 1880, Book B, 1880, ibid.

340 J.D. Bingham to D.H. Rucker, September 3, 1879, Book B, and M.C. Meigs to D.H. Rucker, May 19, 1879, Book A, ibid. The May letter included the pattern for great coat sleeves and collars.

341 M.C. Meigs to D.H. Rucker, July 30, 1879, Book B, ibid. As an interim measure, the quartermaster general permitted the purchase of 6,334 yards of lining flannel to complete the first lot of 1880-pattern great coats. M.C. Meigs to D.H. Rucker, August 11, 1880, ibid. By September, the requisition for overcoats to be issued to signalmen at Ft. Whipple, Virginia was put on hold for a few weeks while the purchase of lining flannel on the open market was being undertaken. This was required because no fabric was on hand, and a contract for the material was not due to be filled until October 31. S.B. Holabird to Acting Assistant Quartermaster, Ft. Whipple through Office of Chief Signal Officer, September 25, 1880, ibid. This must have been in response to a previous order for 100 great coats made in late July of which forty were to be size 1 and sixty in size 2. Other items called for in this requisition were 100 sets of horsehair plumes, cords, bands, eagles, scrolls and rings, and side buttons for the Signal Service dress helmet. Additionally, eighty dress coats, 100 crossed signal devices, and chevrons for corporals and sergeants were included. Also of interest was a large quantity of dismounted trousers, indicating that although the Signal Service enlisted men wore a mounted uniform, this did not necessarily include the mounted reinforced trousers. S.B. Holabird to J.F. Rodgers, July 8, 1880, ibid.

In another letter, a company commander with the Tenth Cavalry was informed "that owing to the scarcity of materials the Great Coats" ordered for his men "could not be furnished" immediately, but some would be sent early in December. S.B. Holabird to T.C. Lebo, November 29, 1880, ibid. Likewise, some 649 great coats, of which most were extra lined, were being sought for the Department of the Platte. M.C. Meigs to Chief Quartermaster Military Division of the Missouri, November 1, 1880, ibid. The status of overcoats requested by the recruiting officer at Buffalo, New York also was questioned. S.B. Holabird to J.F. Rodgers, November 13, 1880, ibid. Under normal circumstances each recruit was to receive one overcoat and one blanket upon enlistment. M.C. Meigs to AGUSA, November 27, 1880, ibid. Finally, of 947 great coats due the Cheyenne Depot, only a dozen were available and twenty-nine more invoiced, causing a quartermaster official to respond: "I fear serious embarrassment and complaint will result." Therefore, he requested the supply process to be speeded up as rapidly as possible. S.B. Holabird to D.H. Rucker, December 27, 1880, ibid.

342 M.C. Meigs to D.H. Rucker, October 27, 1879, ibid.

343 Ibid.

344 M.C. Meigs to Commanding General Military Division of the Pacific, November 20, 1880, ibid. Previously Meigs had sent Lieutenant General Philip H. Sheridan a nearly identical missive asking for help. M.C. Meigs to P.H. Sheridan, November 2, 1880, ibid.

345 Ibid.

346 Efforts at to waterproof and guard fabrics against moths was an ongoing but not successful battle as indicated by M.C. Meigs to Surgeon General of the Army, October 12, 1880; M.C. Meigs to Inspector General of the Army, October 22, 1880; and M.C. Meigs to Secretary of War, November 25, 1880, ibid.

347 M.C. Meigs to Secretary of War, December 16, 1880, ibid.

348 As examples, an order destined for Ft. Apache, Arizona Territory, included 190 gray flannel shirts. S.B. Holabird to A. Bannett, April 22, 1880, Book A, ibid. Artillerymen at Plattsburg Barracks, New York, also were to be sent gray shirts instead of blue ones. S.B. Holabird to C.W. Hobbs, September 3, 1880, ibid.

349 M.C. Meigs to J.F. Rodgers, August 20, 1879, Book B, ibid.

350 S.B. Holabird to D.H. Rucker, December 11, 1879, ibid.

351 M.C. Meigs to Chief Quartermaster Department of Texas, March 7, 1879, ibid.

352 J.D. Bingham to D.H. Rucker, May 17, 1879, Book A, ibid. Similarly, during the following year, when the contract for woolen stockings was "necessarily slow" in being filled, Meigs allowed cotton stockings to be substituted for shipment to garrisons in Texas. M.C. Meigs to Chief Quartermaster Military Division of Missouri, October 22, 1880, Book B, 1880, ibid. In fact, stockings were in extremely short support at the time as indicated by a telegram from M.C. Meigs to D.H. Rucker, October 28, 1880, ibid. Some 14,000 pairs were needed for the Department of Dakota, another 21,000 for the Department of Texas, 16,000 for Missouri, and 18,000 for the Department of the Platte, all of which were sought "before the winter sets in." R. Ingalls to J.F. Rodgers, August 24, 1880, ibid. This was followed by another telegram to provide 15,000 pairs that "were much needed at various posts...." Telegram M.C. Meigs to D.H. Rucker, October 28, 1880, ibid. This meant only small numbers could be supplied, such as 250 pairs of woolen stockings for Ft. Riley, Kansas, and a shipment to men at Cantonment Glendine. M.C. Meigs to D.H. Rucker, October 13, 1880; and Telegram M.C. Meigs to R. Ingalls, October 28, 1880, ibid. Another 1,545 pairs were bought for Ft. Garland, Colorado on the open market. S. VanVliet to D.H. Rucker, August 4, 1880, ibid.; while 500 pairs of woolen stocking were provided to the military prison at Ft. Leavenworth late in the year. S.B. Holabird to A.P. Blunt, December 21, 1880, ibid. In fact, it was toward the end of 1880 before 1,000 pairs of woolen stockings were forwarded to the Omaha Depot and 4,0000 pairs to the Cheyenne Depot. S.B. Holabird to Chief Quartermaster Military Division of the Missouri, November 23, 1880, ibid.

353 J.D. Bingham to Chief Quartermaster Military Division of the Missouri, February 20, 1879, ibid.

354 M.C. Meigs to Chief Quartermaster Military Division of the Missouri, October 32, 1879, Book B, ibid.

355 M.C. Meigs to J.F. Rodgers, September 21, 1879, ibid.

356 Ibid.

357 M.C. Meigs to D.H. Rucker, December 26, 1879, ibid.

358 J.D. Bingham to Acting Assistant Quartermaster, San Diego, Texas, February 4, 1879; J.D. Bingham to Chief Quartermaster Military Division of Missouri, February 4, 1879; and J.D. Bingham to W. Hughes, July 16, 1879, Book A, 1879, ibid.

By the following year a report to an officer in the Inspector General's Department showed old patterns were at rock bottom in many cases, with dismounted overcoats being the only item in relatively large numbers (nearly 80,000 coats) versus 68 mounted musicians' jacket and 64 pairs of unmade foot trousers. Other items on hand included but 42 1858-pattern musicians' frock coats and just over 5,000 frock coats for privates, presumably of various branches. There were under 5,000 shell jackets on hand as well, and less than 7,500 four-button sacks both lined and unlined. These figures did not include the stocks in San Francisco. S.B. Holabird. to E.F. Brown, December 18, 1880, Book B, 1880, ibid. In turn, San Francisco listed the following old pattern articles: 1,375 mounted great coats; 2,646 dismounted great coats; 188 musicians' frock coats; 4,613 privates' frock coats; 47 mounted musicians' jackets; 1,114 mounted jackets for privates; a combined 1,363 sack coats of lined and unlined types, most of which were the smallest sizes; 1,362 pairs of mounted trousers made and 687 unmade; 1,085 foot trousers made and 573 unmade; 1,107 lined blouses in sizes 1 and 2 only (presumably pleated blouses) and 968 unlined blouses; as well as 1,377 forage caps. M.C. Meigs to W.B. Franklin, November 25, 1880, ibid.

359 M.C. Meigs to Chief Quartermaster Department of Texas, February 12, 1879, Book A, 1879, ibid.

360 H. Hodges to J.F. Rodgers, April 19, 1879, ibid., conveyed Meigs' request for a comparison of the thickness of material used in both garments.

361 M.C. Meigs to AGUSA, April 24, 1879, ibid.

362 R.F. Hughes to Chief Quartermaster, Military Division of the Missouri, November 22, 1880, Book B, ibid. Hughes, a captain with the Third U.S. Infantry, also complained that the material of the coat, especially the facings, were anything but uniform, there being many variations from the standard.

363 E. Schriver to D.H. Rucker, August 11, 1880, ibid. Colonel Edmund Schriver was a senior member of the Inspector General's Department at the time.

364 S.B. Holabird to R.N. Batchelder, August 11, 1880, ibid., and S. VanVliet to Inspector General of the Army, May 17, 1880, Book A, ibid. A quartermaster spokesperson also indicated that the fault was with others, not the department, because troops tended to alter articles of clothing that led to them not fitting as they should. S. VanVliet to IGUSA, September 3, 1880, Book B, ibid. On occasion, department officials did acknowledge errors in manufacture, as in the case of a special order for heavy artillery dress coats for Ft. Trumball, Connecticut. M.C. Meigs to T. McCrea, September 20, 1880, ibid.

365 M.C. Meigs to AGUSA, December 20, 1879, Book B, ibid. Some of the items of the new pattern even were contracted for previously, as indicated by an extensive list found in J.D. Bingham to D.H. Rucker, August 30, 1879, Book B, 1879, ibid.

366 M.C. Meigs to D.H. Rucker, January 15, 1879, Book A, ibid.

367 Ibid.

368 M.C. Meigs to W.T. Sherman, July 18, 1879, Book B, ibid. See also, Chappell, *Brass Spikes*, 23. While Meigs was contemplating helmets, Captain G.G. Greenough of the Fourth U.S. Artillery proposed a replacement for the forage cap with a rear flap to protect the neck. While the quartermaster general thought the idea had merit he confessed: "...the feeling and tastes of the troops must be considered in all attempts to improve their clothing, and they are governed very much by the prevailing fashions of the day." He went on to indicate that with the passage of time the chasseur forage cap adopted in 1872 would become the subject of discontent and that then "public opinion will demand another change," but until that time it seemed wise to leave the matter rest. M.C. Meigs to AGUSA, August 8, 1879, LS, Clothing Br., Book B, 1879, OQMG, RG92, NA.

369 M.C. Meigs to J.A. Ekin, July 24, 1879, ibid.

370 M.C. Meigs to D.H. Rucker, July 24, 1879, ibid.

371 Six of the sample helmets from the Miles Board went to Philadelphia as well, according to H. Hodges to D.H. Rucker, October 29, 1879, Book B, ibid. Other specimens prepared for the Board likewise were went there. As further indication that the dress cap with pompon was to be continued for some time, 500 were ordered for heavy artillery and 2,000 for infantry from the firm of J.H. Wilson in late March 1879. Ex. Doc. 56, Senate, 46th Cong., 2d Sess. Supposedly nearly ninety percent of the officers who had to wear the cap were in favor of its replacement by a helmet, some 573 of them signing a petition to this effect in 1880, as just one indication of mounting pressure to change dress headgear in the wake of the 1879 board. *A&NJ*, November 20, 1880, 314.

372 Chappell, *Summer Helmets*, 11. The original specifications for the cork helmets were slated for the artillery school, based upon recommendations made by the commanding officer there, Colonel Getty. S. VanVliet to D.H. Rucker, May 15, 1880, CCF, Box 77, OQMG, RG92, NA. A few days thereafter, Meigs asked for permission to adopt this pattern as standard for the entire army. The first 500 were requested for the First Infantry as it readied itself for the heat of Texas. Meigs estimated the cost to be from \$3.00 to \$3.50 each, as opposed to the mounted dress helmet at \$3.16, the dress cap at \$1.38, and the campaign hat at \$.86. M.C. Meigs to Secretary of War, May 24, 1880, LS, Clothing Br., Book A, 1880, ibid. The secretary concurred. By late June multiple copies of printed specifications were sent out to all the depots according to letters sent by S.B. Holabird to D.H. Rucker, H.A Ekin, R. Ingalls, and L.C. Easton, June 28, 1880, ibid. A sealed sample was reviewed then sent to Philadelphia for safekeeping as the standard. M.C. Meigs to D.H. Rucker, November 15, 1880, Book B, ibid.

373 S.B. Holabird Hughes, January 9, 1880, Book A, ibid. In the meantime, cloth-lined great coats of the old pattern were on hand, but still only for issue to troops "in extreme northern latitudes." S.B. Holabird to Chief Quartermaster Military Division of the Missouri, February 9, 1880, ibid. This same information wa repeated in S.B. Holabird to L.A. Matile, September 17, 1880, Book B, ibid. Prices for the new pattern overcoats were given, including for those that were blanket lined, and those that had lined capes in GO No. 35, HQA, May 12, 1880. For more on lined overcoats for cold climates see, S.B. Holabird to Chief Quartermaster Military Division of the Missouri, February 9, 1880, LS, Clothing Br., Book A, 1880, OQMG, 92, NA. According to McChristian, *The U.S. Army in the West*, 232, two years prior to the approval for the cape lining both Meigs and Sherman, in a rare display of largesse, had concluded that capes could be lined in branch colors at such a time when stocks of the overcoats had be reduced considerably. The men had been doing this previously out of pocket, to add warmth and "an element of flare to the outfit." Ibid., 232.

374 Specification No. 9 for Great-Coats was adopted on February 6, 1880. Less than a week later, the facing material specification was instituted. S. VanVliet to D.H. Rucker, February 13, 1880, LS, Clothing Br., Book A, 1880, OQMG, RG92, NA.

375 S. VanVliet to D.H. Rucker, January 16, 1880, ibid.

376 S. VanVliet to AGUSA, January 28, 1880, Book A, ibid. Later in the year the quartermaster general asked the chief of engineers what color he wanted to line the capes for his enlisted troops. Because scarlet piped with white had been called for in regulations for the dress coat facings, it was not practical to have the two colors. Therefore, Meigs pointed out the two choices available—the scarlet of artillery or the red of light artillery. M.C. Meigs to Chief of Engineers, September 5, 1879, Book B, ibid.

377 S. VanVliet to D.H, Rucker, February 13, 1880, ibid. This letter indicated that the commissary sergeant's cape should be lined in gray, although at one point white was considered as indicated by yet a second letter sent to Rucker from VanVliet that same day. The subject of cape lining was once again a matter of commentary in the *A&NJ* as indicated by an article that appeared on January 3, 1880, 433.

378 M.C. Meigs to R. Ingalls, March 26, 1880, LS, Clothing Br., Book A, 1880, OQMG, RG92, NA.

379 As quoted in P.M. Ashburn, *History of the Medical Department of the United States Army* (Cambridge, MA: Houghton Mifflin Co., 1929), 113-4. While Arctic overshoes had been prescribed by the 1879 board, existing stocks of buffalo overshoes had to be absorbed before the moths destroyed them. M.C. Meigs to Assistant Adjutant General Military Division of Missouri, June 16, 1880, Book A, 1880; and H. Hodges to Chief Quartermaster Department of the East, October 21, 1880, LS, Clothing Br., Book B, 1880, OQMG, RG92, NA. New overshoes were ordered, however, but the original provision specified a particular brand name rather than allowing for other firms to bid on the contract with a comparable product. This fact was pointed out and advertisements for bids adjusted accordingly. M.C. Meigs to D.H. Rucker, June 23, 1880, Book A, ibid.

380 G.B. Davis to Chief Quartermaster Division of the Missouri February 14, 1880, Book A, ibid. At this time the department also was considering a heavier woolen mitten lined with lambskin. These, like fur gauntlets, muskrat caps, and buffalo overcoats, were to be returned to the local quartermaster at the end of each season. M.C. Meigs to Chief Quartermaster Military Division of the Missouri, December 21, 1880, Book B, ibid. When these trial mittens proved less than successful, Meigs instructed that some pairs faced with calfskin were to be made and distributed for review. M.C. Meigs to D.H. Rucker, May 24, 1880, Book A, ibid. It seems some of the lambskin-lined versions had been sent during actions against the Ute, along with buffalo caps and gauntlets. It was pointed out that: "The Buffalo goods were purchased last year during an emergency, it being impossible to procure sufficient muskrat to fill the demands of the then impending Ute campaign." M.C. Meigs to Assistant Adjutant General, Military Division of the Missouri, June 12, 1880, ibid.

381 S.B. Holabird to D.H. Rucker, endorsement February 14, 1880, ibid. Muskrat gauntlets and caps remained in the system at that point, along with Arctic overshoes and buffalo overcoats as indicated in M.C. Meigs to D.H. Rucker, July 14, 1880; and M.C. Meigs to Chief Quartermaster Military Division of the Missouri, July 16, 1880, Book B, ibid. The July 16 letter also indicated that buffalo overcoats were being shipped specifically to men of the Twenty-fifth U.S. Infantry, then serving in Dakota Territory, with eighty each destined for Ft. Meade and Ft. Randall, and forty for Ft. Hale. A purchase of fifty additional buffalo coats was permitted for troops going into winter camp at Glendive Creek. M.C. Meigs to Chief Quartermaster Military Division of the Missouri, October 27, 1880, ibid. Another thirty were to be bought for the camp on the Unumpohgre, and 264 muskrat caps sent from stocks. S.B. Holabird to J.F. Rodgers, October 9, 1880; and M.C. Meigs to Chief Quartermaster Military Division of the Missouri, October 9, 1880, ibid. Meigs stated that "the utmost of dispatch" had been used to fill these orders along with thousands of other caps and gauntlets sent from the various depots for the distribution in the Military Division of Missouri. Although many had been shipped out from the depots, there were many outstanding orders to be filled, and he asked: "cannot some of the Caps & Gauntlets shipped last year, be utilized during the coming season. They should last more than one season certainly." M.C. Meigs to Chief Quartermaster Military Division of the Missouri, September 29, 1880, ibid. In fact, there were some in stock, such as at Ft. Ellis, Montana Territory, but in this instance all 200 were too small to fit anyone. S.B. Holabird to R. Ingalls, December 17, 1880, ibid.

At this point muskrat caps were the norm, and generally favored by the men. Enclosure from R.P. Hughes to R. Marcy in M.C. Meigs to Chief Quartermaster Military Division of Missouri, November 29, 1880, ibid. Likewise muskrat gauntlets were the standard, although when that material became difficult to obtain, the Quarter master Department was willing to buy buffalo gauntlets as well as those of muskrat. M.C. Meigs to D.H. Rucker, June 18, 1880; M.C. Meigs to D.H. Rucker, June 19, 1880; Telegram M.C. Meigs to D.H. Rucker, June 19, 1880; M.C. Meigs to Edmund R. Lyon, June 28, 1880; and M.C. Meigs to D.H. Rucker, June 28, 1880, Book A, ibid.

All these special winter items continued to be restricted to certain "extreme northern latitudes," meaning requests for any of these articles, such as one from Ft. Leavenworth, were denied. M.C. Meigs to Chief Quartermaster Military Division of the Missouri, October 25, 1880, ibid.

382 The distribution was to be as follows: For Montana Territory, Forts Missoula, 100; Ellis, 150; Shaw, 150; Assiniboine, 250; Custer, 250; Logan, 50; Benton, 25; Keogh, 500; in the Dakotas, Abraham Lincoln, 150; Buford, 100; Meade, 250; Benton, 25; Hall, 25; Pembina, 50; Sisseton, 50; Totten, 50; Randall, 50; Sully, 100; Yates, 100; Stevenson, 50; and Cantonment Bad Lands, 25. M.C. Meigs to D.H. Rucker, June 11, 1880, Book B, ibid. The sealed sample accompanied this instruction. Unfortunately, it did not survive.

383 M.C. Meigs to D.H. Rucker, June 18, 1880, ibid.

384 S.B. Holabird to R. Ingalls, June 18, 1880, ibid.

385 M.C. Meigs to D.H. Rucker, August 18, 1880, LR, Philadelphia Depot, Letter No. 1147, ibid.

386 Specification No. 10, adopted August 18, 1880.

387 Greene, "The U.S. Army Buffalo Overcoat," 74. McChristian, *The U.S. Army in the West*, 233, states "these coats were made of a kersey-lined blue canvas outer shell, wth an attached hood. However, for reasons that remain unclear, the enlisted men did not favor the canvas coats and refused to draw them."

388 M.C. Meigs to Secretary of War, December 16, 1880, LS, Clothing Br., Book B, OQMG, RG92, NA.

389 *A&NJ*, June 12, 1880, 6.

390 Ibid., April 10, 1880, 1; and April 24, 1880, 4. In another instance, charges that the cash allowance for men had not kept pace with the costs of uniform articles, caused some adverse commentary. See for example, ibid., July 10, 1880, 3. R.P. Hughes to Chief Quartermaster Military Division of the Missouri, November 29, 1880, LS, Clothing Br., Book B, 1880, OQMG, RG92, NA, declared that the system of furnishing uniforms provoked universal complaint amongst the troops" within the division.

391 M.C. Meigs to A.P. Blunt, November 5, 1880, ibid. Blunt served as the "governor" of the Military Prison when the experiment began.

392 M.C. Meigs to Secretary of War, November 22, 1880, ibid.

393 M.C. Meigs to A.P. Blunt, November 23, 1880, ibid. Months earlier purchases of 14,000 yards of lining material for blouses was authorized to be purchased and sent to Jeffersonville. The cost was $.21 1/2 per yard from Thomas Kent's company. S. VanVliet to D.H. Rucker, August 20, 1880, ibid.

394 M.C. Meigs to Secretary of War, December 1, 1880, ibid.

395 M.C. Meigs to A.P. Blunt, June 25, 1880, Book A, ibid., This letter provided a list of clothing furnished to Ft. Leavenworth's military prisoners as well as other costs incurred to operate this penal institution, and also indicated that nearly $9,500 in clothing and equipment had been furnished the prison in 1877-8, and just over $7,000 in 1878-9. None of these amounts reflected any of the costs to supply the prison guard. M.C. Meigs to A.P. Blunt, August 17, 1880, ibid.

396 M.C. Meigs to A.P. Blunt, October 25, 1880, Book B, ibid.

397 S.B. Holabird to D.H. Rucker, July 25, 1880, Book A, ibid. In this same lengthy letter, Holabird underscored the "very urgent" need for kersey. Some 82,000 yards were ordered from Joseph Draw & Son of Newark Delaware and another 42,000 yards from J.M. Hains in New Albany, Indiana (both at $1.79 a yard), which had to be obtained to make trousers and great coats. S. VanVliet to R.N. Batchelder, August 5, 1880, ibid., listed other items and materials not included in the above correspondence, as well as acknowledging that certain items had not been bid upon, but would be acquired in due course. Among these articles were 650 dress caps, 850 pompons, 3,530 campaign hats, 3,530 forage caps, 800 cap eagles, 30 cap crescents, 50 cap wreaths and 100 letters U.S. both for hospital stewards, 100 cavalry helmet plumes, 100 cavalry helmet bands and cords, 200 pairs of scrolls and rings, 600 cavalry helmet side buttons, 50 cap insignia shells and flames, 2,000 crossed rifles, 3,000 crossed sabers, 8,600 letters, and 17,000 numbers (all for caps).
The other side of the equation, the items to be shipped to departmental quartermasters, can be found in a representative letter by S.B. Holabird to J.F. Rodgers, July 14, 1880, ibid. In a related matter, sealed samples of canton flannel, Berlin gloves, sky-blue kersey in light and heavy weights, shirting flannel in the two weights, dark blue flannel, and woolen stockings, had to be made up and adopted along with trials of fine samples of textile fabrics conducted so that cape lining specifications could be drawn up. Examples of these activities are found in: S.B. Holabird to D.H. Rucker, August 7, 1880; M.C. Meigs to R.N. Batchelder, August 9, 1880; M.C. Meigs to Scott & Bartlett, August 19, 1880; and M.C. Meigs to R.N. Batchelder, August 17, 1880, ibid.

398 anVliet to D.H. Rucker, August 4, 1880, ibid.

399 M.C. Meigs to Secretary of War, April 28, 1880, Book A, ibid.

400 Ibid. Other items that fell into this category included canvas gaiters (leggings) and a canvas suit for fatigue duty, both of which would be forthcoming in the next decade, but not during Meigs' tenure as quartermaster general. See R.P. Hughes to R.B. Marcy as enclosed in M.C. Meigs to Chief Quartermaster Military Division of the Missouri, November 29, 1880, Book B, ibid. At times, both officers and men took it upon themselves to acquire garments they believed to be important, but that were not provided by the government or were not regulation. One such case was "an exceedingly handsome blouse or fatigue coat, designed for an officer of the Fifth Cavalry. The collar was velvet, the sleeves and edges were ornamented with braid, and a single aiguilette of black cord was looped from the right to left shoulder." This item evidently was authorized by Wesley Merritt. "the colonel of the Fifth [U.S. Cavalry] who is always alive to progress and improvement...." Merritt permitted this innovation, "thereby securing for his officers a very neat and attractive undress coat." *A&NJ*, February 26, 1880. Ignoring the editorializing in this piece, individual initiative or deviations from the regulation by certain units were not uncommon in the early 1880s, following similar trends of earlier times.
In other instances, efforts to improve military clothing came from within the Quartermaster Department. By way of example Meigs sought input from two of his subordinates asking for "suggestions as to what improvement, if any, can be made in the present pattern of uniforms." Endorsement S.B. Holabird to D.H. Rucker February 10, 1880; and S.B. Holabird to Officer in Charge of Depot at San Francisco, California, February 10, 1880, LS, Clothing Br., Book A, 1880, OQMG, RG92, NA.

401 M.C. Meigs to Secretary of War, April 28, 1880, ibid.

402 S.B. Holabird to Chief Quartermaster Department of the South, August 21, 1880, Book B, ibid.

403 M.C. Meigs to R.N. Batchelder, October 28, 1880, ibid.

404 M.C. Meigs to D. H. Rucker, November 11, 1880, ibid.

405 M.C. Meigs to General of the Army, December 14, 1880, ibid.

406 M.C. Meigs to General of the Army, December 27, 1880, ibid. For all intents this draft was identical with the final version issued as GO No. 4, HQA, January 7, 1881.

407 M.C. Meigs to General of the Army, December 8, 1880, LS, CLothing Br., Book B, 1880, OQMG, RG92, NA.

408 Ibid.

409 Ibid.

410 He also took an interest in securing what he thought to be proper designs for the eagles that were to adorn these helmets, instructing one of his subordinates "to have a complete set of them modelled and when the designs are approved, to have them executed in steel, for use by the manufacturer who may be the contractor." M.C. Meigs to D.H. Rucker, December 28, 1880, ibid.

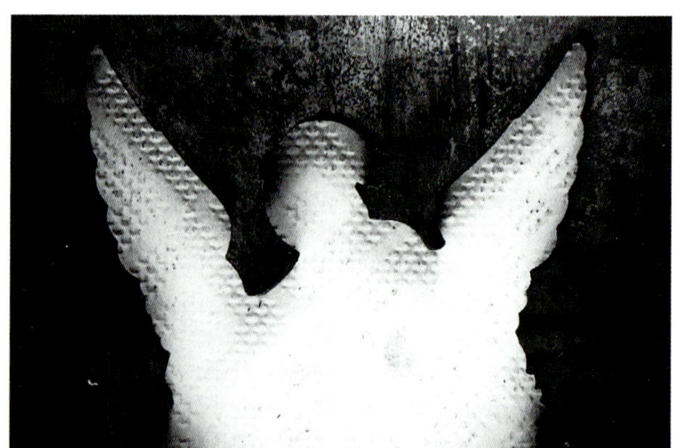

The adoption of a new dress helmet for infantry enlisted men in 1881 required new insignia, including a helmet plate, the die for which is seen here (left top)and its accompanying trimming die (right top). A new mounted dress helmet for enlisted men also was called for in 1881, but new fittings were not produced immediately, as seen by the dates on the plume's staff dies produced by R.H. Jacobus of Philadelphia under contract in 1882 (bottom left and right). RD

2

"No cause for serious complaint can be found," 1881-1884

By 1881 the Quartermaster Department set about to fulfill General Sherman's new directives for both a blue field shirt and a dress helmet.[1] In the latter instance, a helmet at last was permitted for all troops and regimental officers. This brought about the eventual discontinuance of the less than popular 1872-pattern mounted dress helmet, and also swept aside the old dress cap with cock feathers for foot officers and pompons for enlisted men. Nonetheless, the helmet style established in 1881 was in a different form than conceived of by the 1879 board.[2]

These articles were announced in General Orders No. 4, Headquarters of the Army, January 7, 1881, which provided for helmets for field officers that had plumes of buffalo-hair in white for infantry, yellow for cavalry, and red for artillery. The body was to be "of cork or other suitable material covered with black cloth, or of felt at the option of the wearer." Further, the trimmings consisted of gold cords, bands, and tassels, a top piece and plume socket, chain chin-strap and hooks, and an eagle with motto, bearing either crossed cannon, rifles, or sabers, all in gilt, to denote the arm of service. A silver number on the shield of the helmet eagle designated the officer's regiment. Helmets for all other officers of mounted troops and of Signal Corps were the same as field officers' headgear, except the color of the plume was to be orange for Signal Corps second lieutenants, the only commissioned officers in this organization except for the chief signal officer, who as a brigadier general continued to wear a chapeau. Helmets for all other officers of foot troops (second lieutenants through captain of heavy artillery and infantry) were the same, except that a spike replaced the plume, and no gold cords were worn with their head dress.[3]

Furthermore, this same general order called for helmets of mounted troops to be of black felt, with a leather chin-strap, large crossed cannon or sabers, letter of company and number of regiment, plain side buttons, and top piece and plume-socket, all of brass. The plumes of horsehair and worsted cords and bands were essentially the same as those spelled out in 1872, with yellow continuing for cavalry and scarlet for light artillery.

Helmets for all foot troops were of the same pattern and material as for mounted men, with leather chin-strap, plain side buttons, top piece, and spike, again all in brass. The trimmings were to be as follows: commissary sergeants, a crescent of white metal; hospital stewards, a wreath of brass, with letters U.S. in white metal; engineers, a castle, with letter of company; ordnance, a shell and flame; artillery, crossed cannon; infantry, crossed rifles, and letter of company and number of regiment, all in brass.

This order was to become effective for all but cavalry and light artillery troops on July 1, 1881, "or as soon thereafter as the supplies can be procured by the Quartermaster's Department; for cavalry and light batteries whenever the present stock of helmets is exhausted by issues." Even in the last mentioned instance, a plan soon came about that was designed to bring the old 1872-pattern helmets still in the inventory into approximately the same configuration as the new helmet.[4]

This process entailed the modification of the helmet bodies to conform more closely to the 1881 style by reducing the visors, especially in

Most company grade infantry officers were to have spiked helmets beginning in 1881, except those serving in a mounted capacity, such as the regimental adjutant. In that case, a white buffalo plume was to be used, as were cords and bands of gold thread. Infantry field grade officers also wore the plumed helmet with white plume. GS

Front, right side, and rear view of an 1881-pattern company grade infantry officer's helmet, in this case worn by John Leefe, a first lieutenant of the Nineteenth U.S. Infantry. The body is made of cork covered in cloth, as most surviving examples are. MK

the rear, and some reblocking. The remodeled helmets were provided to mounted troops, given that a contract for 16,000 new pattern helmets had been let previously to Raymold and Whitlock of New York on May 5, 1881, based on specifications officially established for foot troops only less than two months earlier, and which superseded the first version of the helmet, most notably differing in the matter of insignia.[5]

Despite intentions to convert stocks on hand, the appropriations for the fiscal year were exhausted, and "none of the old pattern helmets" could "be altered until appropriations for the next fiscal year" became available. Thus, instructions "to alter 10,000 of the old pattern helmet" could not be undertaken until the Quartermaster Department obtained funds for that purpose. In the meantime, the helmets at Jefferson Barracks were recalled, if not needed, so that they ultimately could be modified at Philadelphia.[6] To heighten the problem, it was revealed that the cost of alterations had been underestimated. The actual cost was to be $6.50 per dozen.[7]

Opposite: A trio of "shavetails" in the new 1881-pattern helmet. They are from left to right: Frank B. McCoy, Third U.S. Infantry; Marion R. Saffold, Thirteenth U.S. Infantry; and John M. Cunningham, Nineteenth U.S. Infantry. All wear the company grade infantry officers' dress uniform with spiked helmet, light blue trousers trimmed with dark blue 1 1/2 inch cloth leg stripes, and double-breasted dress coat with seven buttons in each row surmounted by shoulder knots that had medium blue backgrounds, on which regimental numbers were indicated in silver embroidery. FAM

Eagle plates varied from manufacturer to manufacturer for the 1881-officer's helmet, as indicated by these two specimens for infantry officers. The one on the left is the common type seen, while the one on the right was made by the firm of Henry V. Allien. Photograph by Gordon Chappell.

While the scheme to recut helmets temporarily was halted for lack of funds, other expenses were to be considered, as well, in that General Orders No. 4 had proposed on-hand supplies of devices that had been in use with the forage cap or dress cap for the new helmet. Specifications published some five months after General Orders No. 4's appearance, however, initiated a very different concept, in that the ornaments and trimmings would have to be newly fabricated. These were to consist of:

> ...a spike about three (3") inches high on a base of oak leaves, according to sample, and to be made to screw into the base of the ventilator as shown in sample.
>
> Eagle with shield and motto, and side buttons, according to pattern, for each arm of service. All to be yellow metal.
>
> The number of the regiment, or device of corps, to be in white metal and be borne on the lower half of shield on eagle's breast, according to sample.
>
> The standard sample to be followed in all respects as to shape, quality of materials, workmanship & c.
>
> To be of six (6) standard sizes, numbered one to six (1 to 6) inclusive, corresponding to the trade sizes, 6 3/4 to 7 3/8 inclusive.

With these specifications in hand and a purchase of the first foot helmets completed, the quartermaster general subsequently: "recommended the sale of all dress caps, metallic hat and cap trimmings rendered obsolete by the adoption of the new helmets." The secretary of war concurred. In due course, these items were disposed of at public auction.[8]

Not all 1881-pattern officers' helmets were of cork covered in cloth. Felt bodies were also permitted, such as this example for a company grade infantry officer. Photograph by Robert L. Sanders. JG

Company grade infantry officer's dress coat, belt, and knots conforming to regulations of 1881 through 1886, with blue striping on the dress belt and matching medium blue centers for the dress knots. FAM

Prior to this sale, General Orders No. 52, Headquarters of the Army, June 14, 1881, dispensed more details about the overlays for helmet plates, along with references to helmets for cavalry and light artillery enlisted personnel for the first time. This order indicated German silver regiment numbers or corps devices were to be affixed to the shield on the helmet eagle. Brass side buttons were to bear the device of the corps or arm of service. The top piece, plume socket, and rings all were to be brass. Horsehair plumes, and cords and bands of color of the arm of service once more were specified.

All these accessories had to be included in the estimates for the next fiscal year relative to clothing. As such, the changes made in the trimmings of the new dress helmets after the release of General Orders No. 52 for "the eagle with shield, with crossed cannons, or rifles, or sabers" would add to the annual budget. Shipping required another expenditure, as well as a challenge. At first the idea was to send the helmets made up, with the number of the regiment, or the insignia of the staff corps placed on the shield, along with the proper side buttons, cords, and other proper ornamentation to indicate the arm of service.[9] Eventually, however, this procedure was determined to be impractical, especially for mounted helmets. For the sake of convenience then, the parts ultimately were sent separately and the helmets assembled at their final destination, presumably by the men receiving them.[10]

Another result of insufficient money being available to Meigs' department restricted the number of prototypes that could be furnished of

Dress knot of a captain of the Seventeenth U.S. Infantry with the medium blue background that remained regulation until 1886. GS

Shoulder knot of a captain of the First U.S. Infantry. WSM

the 1881-pattern helmet.[11] Thus, only fifty models of the standard helmet were obtained to distribute to the various chief quartermasters around the country as samples.[12] To provide a cost effective method for quartermaster personnel around the country to maintain consistency for this new headgear, Meigs approved the expenditure of $90 for photographs of the new helmets, and had a set of prints sent to each of the depots.[13]

In this environment, it was little wonder that Meigs informed a Nineteenth U.S. Infantry lieutenant that the Quartermaster Department had no money to purchase articles of uniform for officers of the army, including the new dress helmet. He emphasized: "Officers will be as likely to purchase the issue uniform helmet which, in the opinion of the Quartermaster General will be quite good enough for anybody, to wear on frontier service, and generally in towns and cities, except on service in public ceremonies and festivals where officers desire to be particularly well dressed."[14]

Budgetary considerations also meant that cork summer helmets were not available, nor was it probable that they could be obtained because of the limited funds expected in fiscal year 1882. This news was sent to all depots.[15] In spite of this situation, considerable efforts were made to supply the First U.S. Infantry with 500 of the cork helmets, while out of a batch of 6,000 that was expected to be ordered under contract in the future, orders for the Military Divisions of the Atlantic and the Pacific were expected to be filled, along with 725 held for posts not included in these areas, and another 275 for West Point, although originally the quartermaster general had indicated his department did not provide such helmets to the cadets at Military Academy as part of its mission.[16]

This last restriction related to West Point would be lifted later, but in the meantime, pending this new supply, only "troops stationed in extremely hot climates" were to be provided with this headgear.[17] In this regard, troops at garrisons in Arizona Territory were shipped nearly 1,000 summer helmets by express during the summer of 1881.[18]

Eventually, however, by spring 1881 additional availability of helmets came about as a result of "close economy in all aspects and little reductions here and three, cutting of all margins" that resulted in a savings of $35,700. These savings were applied to the purchase of cork helmets and as a contingency for emergencies.[19]

Shoulder knot of the colonel of the twenty-second U.S. Infantry. The background is medium blue, and the eagle, as well as regimental numeral are silver embroidered. FSHM

Typical example of a heavy artillery company grade officer's 1881-pattern helmet with cork body covered in cloth. RB

Heavy artillery company grade officer with his 1881-pattern helmet. Leg stripes were 1 1/2 wide of scarlet facing material. The piece of cloth on the arm and M1860 staff and field sword are black crepe—an authorized sign of mourning. RB

Officers had the option of buying helmets made of felt, such as this less expensive Fifth U.S. Artillery company grade version available from J.H. McKenney. Photograph by Gordon Chappell.

Of course, the original limited availability of money for contracts did not apply to officers who purchased their own headgear, along with all other items of the uniform. There was some confusion whether or not the helmets were meant only for officers in the line, however, as indicated by a letter from a surgeon asking whether this head dress also was permitted for use by officers who did not wear the dress helmet, but instead donned the chapeau. The answer was that staff officers could buy the summer helmet, too, but this did not indicate that the item was to be worn with full dress in lieu of the chapeau.[20]

The helmets purchased by officers exhibited numerous variations, depending on the designs followed by the dealer from which they were obtained. In a similar instance, not all enlisted cork helmets conformed to the standard 1880-pattern. In one instance this resulted in the return of several helmets covered in facing cloth from Ft. Monroe's "Artillery School to the Philadelphia depot." Meigs indicated: "The helmets previously issued (those covered with white cloth) cannot be altered, and they differ but slightly from those of the new pattern." Because there were no cork helmets in stock and no funds to acquire new ones during fiscal year 1881, he ordered: "the cork helmets now on hand should be re-issued."[21]

An 1881-pattern dress helmet for light artillery officers, regimental adjutants, and field grade officers of artillery, along with shoulder knots of the style worn from the 1870s through the early twentieth century. The number indicates the regiment, in this instance the First U.S. Artillery. Photograph by Glen Swanson. GS

The same resource limitations resulted in the announcement that no more greatcoats could be made because the appropriations for the fiscal year were exhausted.[22] Despite this announcement, Meigs ordered funds diverted from other accounts for the production of 500 new pattern coats from materials on hand.[23] The quartermaster general went on to indicate that no more blanket lined great coats would be issued now that "an excellent overcoat, body lined with a cape in branch color flannel" had been adopted.[24]

While money for the new great coat was in short supply, not all expenditures were being denied. For instance, per the authority of the Secretary of War, the Quartermaster Department, along with the Ordnance Department, were to provide several specimens of U.S. Army uniform and equipage to be sent via the consul general of France for the French minister of war.[25]

As such, the department no doubt was pleased to furnish the French government with "a set of various articles of uniform clothing."[26] This action represented a reciprocation of similar courtesies extended by Paris in past times. Given the long tradition of modeling American uniforms on European styles, the turnabout must have been a source of pride for the Quartermaster Department.

One item that characterized a significant departure from European paradigms was the overshirt. Unlike most other martial organizations in the Western world, the U.S. Army increasingly employed this practical piece of clothing for field wear, without the blouse. In fact, General Orders No. 4 indicated that in the future only lined blouses would be sent to the troops, because the shirts could "be worn in the summer without the blouse." Additionally, the order made it clear that old gray

A light artillery company grade officer's coat of the type that was regulation from 1880 until 1903. RB

Circa 1880 shoulder knot of a captain of the First U.S. Artillery. The number and captain's bars are silver embroidery on a scarlet background. The button with eagle and shield bears an "A" for artillery, per regulations. SI

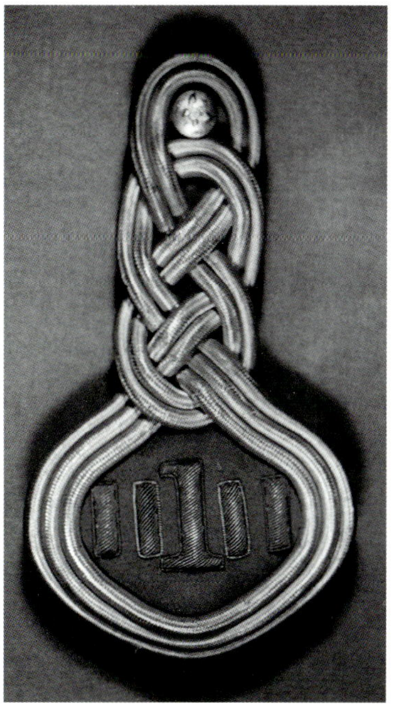

Colonel Nathan A.M. Dudely's 1880-pattern dress coat and 1881-pattern dress helmet. Photograph by Glen Swanson. JB

Colonel Nathan A.M. Dudely's dress knots as the commanding officer of the First U.S. Cavalry. JB

Right side of Captain Luff's 1881-pattern cavalry officer's helmet. JM

flannel shirts would be handed out until the supply was depleted. At that point, the blue flannel shirts, which Sherman had espoused, would be furnished "at the rate of three in the first year and two in each of the second, third, fourth, and fifth years of enlistment."[27]

Preparatory to furnishing the dark-blue shirts, remaining gray material was thereafter to be used for lining blouses, "to the extent of money allotted for making the shirts" of the old pattern.[28] Simultaneously, a pair of sample shirts were sent to General Sherman for his consideration as replacements for the gray flannel model. When he reviewed these, he expressed his idea that the shirts would be tucked into the trousers, as had been the case in the past, yet still have "the appearance of a blouse." With this in mind, Captain Rodgers was instructed "to have some other examples made piped, with brass buttons, some double, some single-breasted, similar to firemen's shirts," and added that "perhaps a sample shirt worn in the Navy" could be included. The subject was visible at the highest levels, so that his efforts were "important" and required "careful consideration."

In response Rodgers dutifully provided several options, from which the commanding general was asked to select, and to indicate his approval on the tag accompanying his choice.[29] Sherman did so, and on February 9, 1881, the final selection was officially accepted.[30] Some seven days later, Specification No. 77 provided particulars for the new shirts, along with indicating that after July 1, 1881, no more collarless gray shirts would be issued. The design followed Sherman's concept in

Captain Edmund Luff of the Eighth U.S. Cavalry removed the gold lace ornamentation from his company grade officer's dress coat and combined it with the new helmet after its adoption in 1881. JM

Cloth covered paste board carrying and shipping container for Captain Luff's helmet. JM

A more typical Japanned tin officer's helmet carrying case for the 1881 helmet. GS

Another variation on the theme, a case used by Captain John Bourke of the Third U.S. Cavalry to keep his 1881-pattern helmet from being damaged or soiled when not in use. NSM

that it was a coat style that opened all the way to the bottom, with five vest sized 1854-pattern enlisted buttons as closures. There was no lining, except a small stay at the interior of the shoulders, and no pockets or side slits, thereby presenting a blouse-like configuration per Sherman's wishes. And like the blouse, the cuffs and falling collar were trimmed with worsted cord in the color of the branch. One small detail from the specification as originally released was revised. In early April, the two buttons called for to secure the cuffs were rescinded. Instead, Meigs declared that there was to be but one small regulation button on each cuff.[31]

Having worked out this final technicality, the new shirt was ready for manufacture, although by late May it seemed that the production of this item would not be completed and ready for delivery until summer or autumn 1881.[32] In a related disclosure, the first 4,000 yards of an order for 110,000 of shirt flannel was not due from the contractor, B.Y. Pippey & Co. of New York, until July 1, while the other installments were projected through January 1882, when the final run of 20,000 yards was due to the depot at Jeffersonville.[33]

In regards to this slow progress, Meigs was anxious to have the cloth delivered as soon as it could be obtained. In an uncharacteristic departure from his usual frugality he suggested that in order to clothe the Army as soon as possible, it was better to "pay higher" prices "than to have the troops suffer."[34]

Another indication of Meigs' department being more responsive to the field soldier arose when new trouser designs were considered. Many men had found the trousers produced by the Quartermaster Department wanting, and took it upon themselves to have the government issue reworked trousers following a prevalent civilian fashion of the era. Remarkably, rather than decry the custom, quartermaster officials conceded to popular tastes.

Once more, the surrender to the will of the soldiery displayed an adjustment of the attitude within the department. In fact, the resolution to embrace the new design came in response to a petition dispatched in the form of a printed circular to the quartermaster general sent from a company commander with the Twenty-fifth U.S. Infantry, Captain Gaines Lawson, then posted to Ft. Randall, Dakota Territory, through the regimental commander and on up the chain of command, recommending "that the trousers hereafter...furnished the enlisted men be made with a 'waistband,' or of the material furnished out of which they can be made, as the trowsers that are now furnished are not strong enough around the waist to be worn without suspenders...." The petitioner concluded with the remark: "it was evidently intended by General Orders No. 4 that the pants were to be worn, especially when wearing the dark-blue flannel shirt without a blouse."[35]

The point was key in that it was considered a serious breech of etiquette for Victorian gentlemen to appear with exposed suspenders. Hollywood, to the contrary, the rank and file of the U.S. Army during

Detail of plume staff with separately applied eagle on Luff's 1881-pattern helmet, characteristic of helmets produced by Horstmann of Philadelphia. JM

Cavalry officer's plume staff with the more typical eagle and star being cast integrally with the plume staff. KSHS

this period seldom appeared as common laborers in shirt sleeves with exposed galluses.

Meigs was willing to take the matter under advisement, even if only to prevent the drawing of larger sizes of trousers than necessary so that they might be cut down by local tailors, a practice he thought was wide spread.[36] Regardless of the validity of his charges, when Sherman accepted the idea, Meigs obligingly made it known that the requested change in trouser design was in the offing.[37]

Indeed, Assistant Quartermaster S.B. Holabird shared Meigs' budgetary concerns. If trousers with springbottoms and waistbands were issued, along with a different design of pockets, cloth would not be wasted, nor would the men persist in spending money to alter their trousers according to the desired fashion. To support his viewpoint, Holabird contended "that soldiers, as a rule, draw trousers of larger sizes to enable them to cut them down for the single purpose of securing the much desired 'spring'" of the cuffs "which every enlisted man has in the trousers he wears." Ultimately, a decision was reached to adopt a style with "spring bottoms [a cuff style in fashion at the time that flared at the front], which if approved may be issued in lieu of the pattern now furnished."[38] A pair of civilian trousers were even sent to the Philadelphia Depot as a basis for a military version.

Even then, the new design was not immediately available. For instance, trousers of the old pattern, but made of new standards of kersey, were produced for the prisoners at Ft. Leavenworth in early 1882.[39] As for the rest of the troops, the new trouser design was not formally announced until General Orders No. 108, Headquarters of the Army, Sep-

Captain Edmund Luff, Eighth U.S Cavalry, in his dress coat. JM

Left: A detail of Captain Luff's breast cord indicates that the tassels are held together, as depicted in official illustrations, but which was atypical judging from extant examples and photographs of the period. JM

tember 4, 1882, called for a pattern of "sky-blue mixture, waistband 2 inches wide, to button with 1 button in front, pockets in front, opening at top."[40] This was the style approved by Sherman in 1881, but the actual specifications were not adopted until October 8, 1882. The pattern proved short-lived, however, in that by January 1884, another modification was introduced as a replacement. As such, only limited quantities of the trousers were made in 1883.

One other occurrence in 1883 related to trousers would prove more enduring. This was the mention for the first time of leg stripes for musicians. It had been customary for some time for musicians to wear double stripes on their trousers, albeit without official sanction. Even so, the illustrations accompanying the uniform regulations published in 1882 showed such stripes for company buglers and drummers. Nevertheless, not until General Orders No. 59, Headquarters of the Army, July 31, 1883, did this ambivalent situation end with a formal statement that company musicians were to have two cloth stripes the color of the facings of the arm of service measuring 1/2 inch wide each running down the outer seams of their trousers.

Even as implementation proceeded in stages, another concept was put forth by First Lieutenant G.B. Backus, an officer of the First U.S. Cavalry who served as the acting assistant quartermaster for Ft. Klamath, Oregon. The lieutenant wanted do away with "full length trousers" and replace them with "riding trousers." The latter fashion was to reach to the calf and fasten "with a cord in a manner similar to" the Canton flannels that were regulation at the time. This meant that boots were to be worn outside the trousers, rather than inside as had been the common practice. This would require boot tops to be longer and wider. Backus felt this would improve the mounted uniform and save the government money.[41]

While neither breeches nor more commodious boots were adopted immediately, such concepts ultimately would be approved. Indeed, Assistant Quartermaster General Holabird was sympathetic toward change, although he had his own views as to what constituted the ideal form of trousers. He recognized the common complaint that the 1876-pattern was ill-fitting, "especially around the waist and pelvis, and, generally, that it presents a clumsy and misshapen appearance." His remedy was a large piece of material that would lap over the front and joined at the side "with a wide strong strap to buckle and hold taut" the waist. In turn, the straps could "be attached as a draw-around immediately above the hips of the wearer," rather than by using a small strap at the rear of the trousers as had been the previous design in use. As one additional precaution, suspenders could be added, thereby resulting in "enormous comfort" and simplicity for the soldier.[42]

The breast cords were to cross on top of the right shoulder, then pass under the arm, as seen here. Sometimes they were worn under the knots, and sometimes atop them, depending on the individual officer. JM

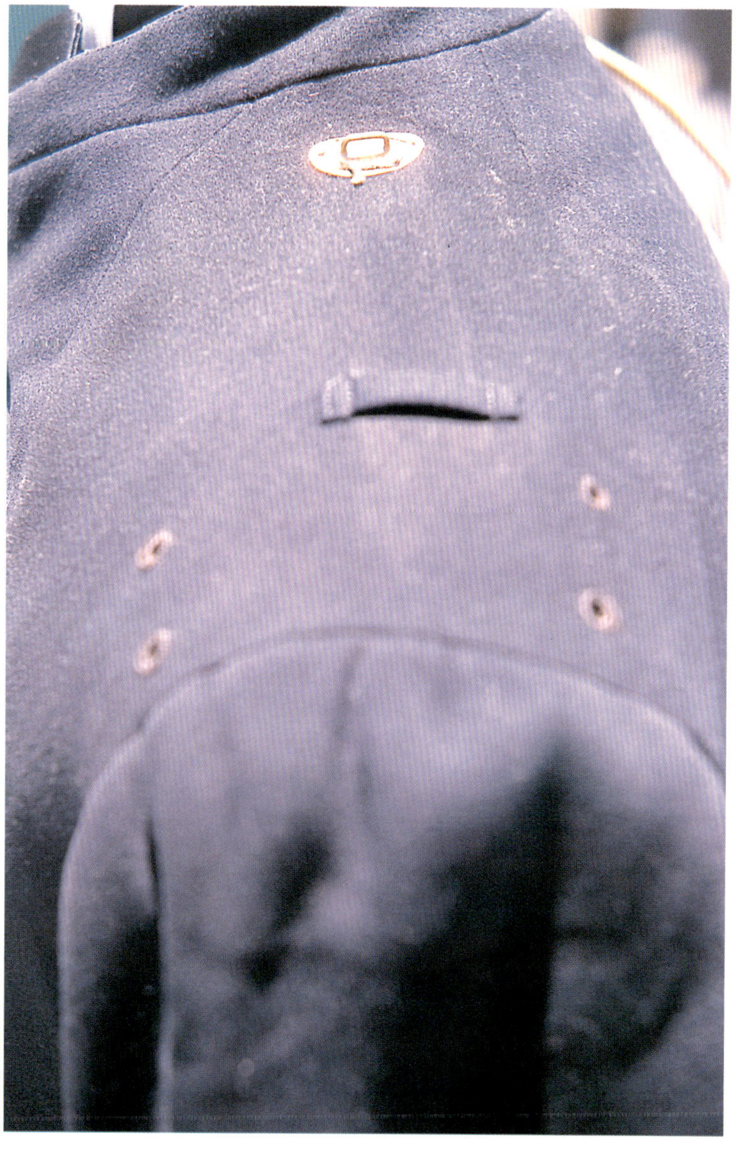

The shoulder knots were held on place by attachments strongly sewn to the coat. JM

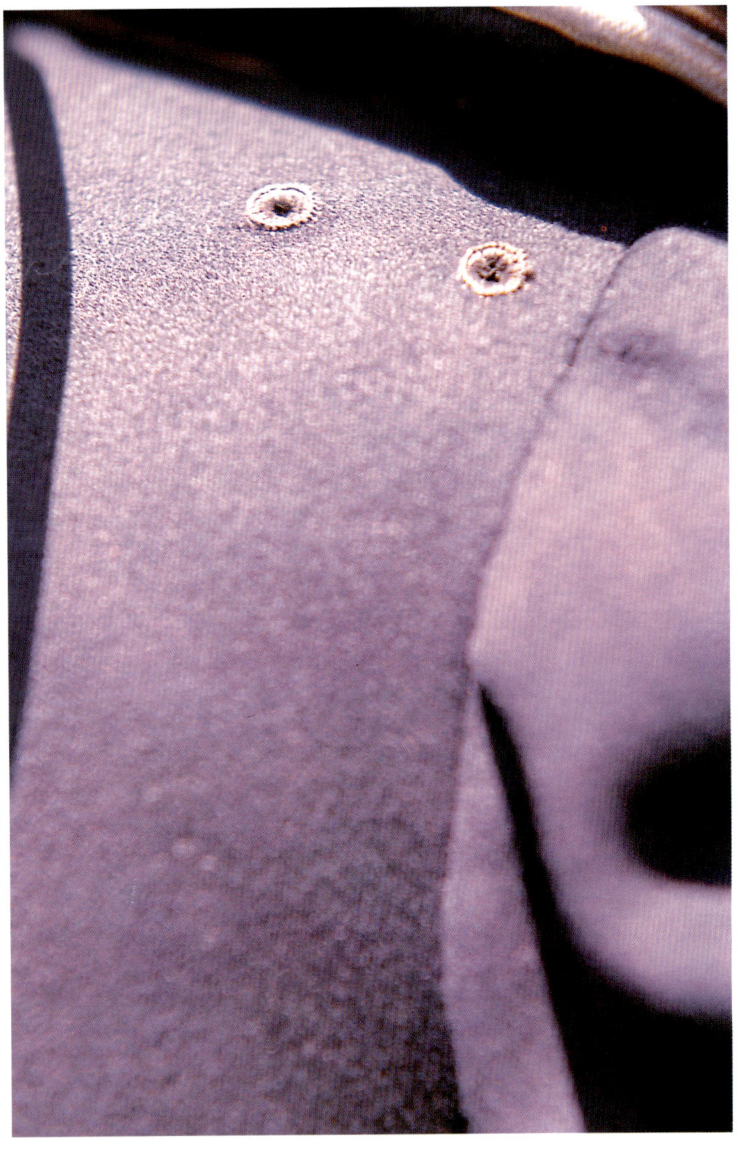

Some older coats had eyelets reinforced with thread that allowed shoulder straps to be worn when off duty in place of the shoulder knots. The straps were kept in place by strings that passed through the holes and then could be tied inside. JM

The regimental adjutant of the Second U.S. Cavalry with the aiguillettes worn on the right shoulder as was regulation. His 1881-pattern helmet, on the table next to him, bears a plate of the type made by the New York firm of Henry V. Allien. GS

Holabird also covered many other topics from head to foot in his article. He expressed very specific ideas, such as the distribution of red bandannas and "knit or woven braces" that forked "in the front so as to button to the trowsers with two buttons on each side for each brace, and one for each brace behind."[43] While his various design concepts were of interest, including the suggestion for a gray uniform in violation of the standing tradition of army blue, Holabird's most significant statement was his quest for a "good quality; well made, serviceable neat, well fitting, and attractive" uniform.[44] He was passionate about this goal, concluding:

> It is well to remember that in the uniform of the soldier the interest and hopes of millions may yet be centered, and it must keep pace with national requirements. A uniform is characteristic of a people. It is an outgrowth of National character. It may be impoverished and rendered mean in appearance for a time, but too many men have already died in it, to have it totally ignored or neglected, and too many men still wear it equally ready to dye it anew with their blood in the service of their country. Let us then endeavor to throw an interest around it, to build it up, to make it a source of pride of the wearer, and an indication of National power wherever seen.[45]

With these lofty objectives being voiced, and Holabird destined to assume the mantle of quartermaster general, over the next several years the army uniform would be revitalized. Consequently, through the remainder of the 1880s, change was constant, albeit sometimes subtle.

Even as a new day was dawning, Meigs was nearing retirement. He did so in early February 1882, after an army career of some forty-six years![46] As a fitting finale to his long career, just a few months before his return to civilian life, in November 1881, closing preparations for the publication of color lithographs of the uniform accompanied by pertinent regulations were being undertaken.[47] This was the uniform he had helped create, and now it was to be captured in word and picture, not only for practical purposes of the moment, but also for reference far into the future.[48]

Captain John Bourke's aiguillettes for wear when serving as aide-de-camp to Brigadier General George Crook. NSM

In this 1883 image Captain Thomas McDougall, Seventh U.S. Cavalry (front row, far left) has on tall custom riding boots and holds an M1872 cavalry officer's saber. His fellow officers at Ft. Yates, Dakota Territory, are predominantly members of the Seventeenth U.S. Infantry (except the young subaltern at the far right with stylish gauntlets, who is also a Seventh Cavalry officer), including two field grade officers with white buffalo hair plumes, and a one-armed adjutant who wears the mounted helmet with white buffalo hair plume specified in 1881 (all in the front row center). The last mentioned officer has placed his aiguillette on the left shoulder, rather than the right. Most of the other officers wear 1881-pattern company grade infantry officers' spiked helmets and the dress coat without sleeve lace called for in 1879, except one man (back row, fourth from the left) who still has not removed the gold lace, despite the fact that this ornamentation was no longer to be permitted after January 1880, and this group portrait dates from at least 1881. The white whiskered officer in the front row with the chapeau de bras is the post surgeon. His trousers are dark blue to match the dress coat. The post chaplain likewise is present (back row, third from right) with his plain forage cap, somber black frock coat with shoulder straps, and black trousers. All the rest of the officers wear sky blue trousers with 1 1/2 dark blue leg stripes, with the exception of McDougall and the cavalry second lieutenant, who had 1 1/2 inch yellow leg stripes. GS

Even as the venerable quartermaster general's handiwork was being preserved for posterity, far from reaching equilibrium, military clothing remained in a state of flux. For one thing, the Quartermaster Department persevered in its efforts to cull old items from the inventory, including nearly 149,000 rubber blankets and over 105,000 rubber ponchos of Civil War vintage from its warehouses. These were sold in increments because they were no longer considered necessary. The deterioration of these items also prompted this move. So, too, did the department gain permission to dispose of the enlisted dress caps that became obsolete with the adoption of foot helmets.[49] Other outdated or substandard items were further removed from the rolls through distribution to Indian prisoners or for issue to the National Home for Disabled Veterans, as well as for supply of military prisoners incarcerated at Ft. Leavenworth.[50]

Captain Louis H. Carpenter, Tenth U.S. Cavalry, in the 1881 through 1902 period company grade cavalry officer's dress uniform. NA

At the last mentioned locale, shoes continued to be manufactured by inmates. Here again, the department sought improvements on past patterns, although in almost all other areas its official stand was: "No complaints have been received from the Army as to the quality and workmanship of the clothing and equipage now issued to the troops."

Supposedly, this condition existed because:

> The department, for years, has endeavored to improve both quality and patterns, and, it is thought, has succeeded in bringing the clothing to such perfection, as far as texture, warmth, and durability are concerned, that no cause for serious complaints can be found. In order to secure uniformity in the patterns and sizes of various articles of clothing and equipage manufactured at our depots, patterns of each size and each kind have been distributed from Philadelphia to the Jeffersonville and San Francisco depots, and suggestions invited to bring about such improvement in cutting as may suggest themselves to the officers concerned.[51]

In this light, Meigs rebutted a finding of the Inspector General's Department concerning "the want of uniformity in color complained of in uniform coats." He pointed out that this doubtlessly was a result of the mixing of old pattern coats that had been converted with new pattern coats. From 1875 forward, however, Meigs claimed all coats were made at the Philadelphia Depot, and were uniform in shade. Of course, sun did tend to fade the facings, which were of "high colors," thereby resulting in variations that Meigs dismissed as unimportant.[52]

With his characteristic pride of accomplishment Meigs went on with his defense. Perfection, while never possible, was nearly achieved because such complaints from five years earlier about the need to increase the waist length of dress coats had been attended to, while the comments that this garment ought to have larger straps to support the belt were not a general problem. If some men wanted larger loops "so as to accommodate the 'prairie' belt," rather than the regulation leather belt with cartridge box with which they originally had been designed to be worn, then all the enlisted man had to do was have larger straps made for this purpose locally. Meigs also stated the button that held these straps was attached "as firmly as it can be, but if any greater security is

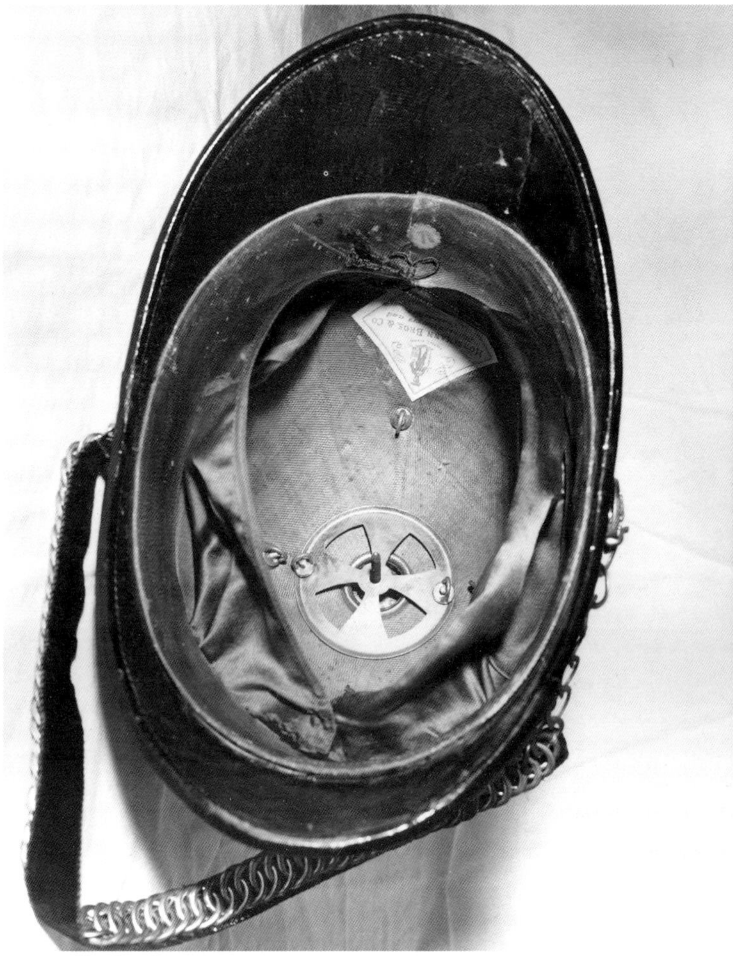

Three-quarter, side, and interior views of an 1881-pattern cavalry officer's helmet belonging to Captain M.M. Maxon, Tenth U.S. Cavalry. FDNHS

Enlisted men were to have a new helmet in 1881, as well, although mounted troops did not receive their's immediately. Instead, 1872-pattern helmets had their visors cut down to conform more closely to the new model, as this example for a cavalrymen indicates. Old insignia and fittings sometimes were retained during the transition from the pattern to the other. AHS

Five cavalry troopers serving at the U.S. Military Academy wear remodeled 1872-pattern helmets that have been altered to approximate the 1881-pattern, but all the fittings are the 1872 type. A company trumpeter stands to the left, while to his left is a first sergeant with the diamond device above the three stripes. In the center appears a sergeant, his six service chevrons being angled improperly, as opposed to the correct wearing of these "hash marks" by the first sergeant and the corporal second from left. The corporal's chevrons are the custom gullwing variety, which still were being worn occasionally by the early 1880s. The private to the far right has turned his back to reveal a Dyer cartridge pouch that carried rounds for the Springfield cavalry carbine. This firearm is attached to the black leather carbine sling via a large metal swivel snap. DPL

desired a prudent soldier can easily find time and opportunity to put a small 'stay' of light leather or canvas inside the coat to hold it [the belt] as well." The quartermaster general ended by pointing out the dress coats were designed to be worn "only in garrison, and not in the field," and therefore "the soldier could find time to attend to such little matters of their fit and finish as his fancy dictates."[53]

Although Meigs either denied or abrogated any responsibility for shortcomings in issue clothing, as noted previously he did admit to the imperfection of the footgear provided by his department.[54] He also acknowledged that the lining of enlisted cavalry capes for overcoats, "owing to the fugitive character of the dye" used to produce the correct hue for cape flannel sometimes caused an undesired effect. Here he mentioned "it appeared that in some cases greatcoats, while being packed under heavy pressure, became soiled by the yellow color."[55] The solution was to insert paper between the interior of the capes and the coats preparatory to shipment. In the meantime, the damaged coats could be salvaged by cleaning with oxalic acid and aqua ammonia. These stopgap measures were carried out while the department explored a fast dye that would "make further defects impossible."[56]

Following along similar lines to adjust certain minor defects, mention was made of how "the dark-blue overshirt adopted by the General of the Army on 3d February, 1881, did not meet with favor by the troops." As proof of this lack of appeal, nearly 30,000 of the shirts remained in stock, "which the enlisted men declined to receive."[57] One dissatisfied cavalryman summed up the lack of appeal when he stated:

> I shall never forget the despairing looks of the disgusted troopers as the dark blue shirt were dealt out to them. To this day the shirt—so-called—remains a mystery. It is not a shirt, nor a blouse, nor a surtout. To alter it is an impossibility; to wear it is an acknowledged misfortune; to pay for it is unhappily a reality.[58]

Alas, the distasteful article did not disappear. As a matter of economy, the remaining shirts were converted to blouses by recutting and the addition of a lining. This saved money by reducing the number of blouses that had to be produced, but the downside was the converted shirts did "not admit of being so readily altered as the regulation blouse."[59]

This situation did not mean that the idea of a dark-blue overshirt was abandoned. On the contrary, the Quartermaster Department developed what it considered to be an improved model. A standard was adopted on February 24, 1882, using the shirting flannel adopted during the previous February. The item resembled the earlier version in that it still was trimmed with branch colored worsted cord, in this case around the cuffs and falling collar, as in the past, but additionally around the front plait that formed part of the pattern, because this shirt was a pullover rather than a coat style. The cord likewise trimmed the tops of two breast pockets that represented other additions over the 1881-pattern. These were closed with hard rubber buttons, as was the plait.

Other specifications adopted in 1882 included updated details for metallic ornaments for helmets, forage caps, and uniform coats (April 21); enlisted dress helmets (May 6); and ornaments and trim for the helmets (September 23, 1882).[60] The first mentioned article generally complied with past descriptions, except in the instance of hospital stewards. The traditional silver metal "U.S." enclosed by a gold-colored wreath adopted in the 1850s was replaced by a dead or unburnished gilt wreath surrounding a German silver caduceus, for wear on the forage cap, although the original idea was to employ the caduceus without wreath. Furthermore, a German silver caduceus was called for as collar ornamentation for the dress coat. Previously, hospital stewards wore no devices on their coat collars, unlike amost all the other enlisted and non-commissioned personnel. This oversight was brought to Meigs' attention, and he had recommended the adoption of the caduceus as being in keeping with the overlay for the dress helmet issued to hospital stewards, thereby making their insignia consistent in all instances.[61]

Thus, by 1882 only Signal Corps personnel remained apart from these practices in that Brigadier General William B. Hazen, chief signal officer of the army, did not concur with Meigs' suggestion to place crossed flags on the forage cap and coat collars.[62] Insofar as the dress coat was concerned, the signalmen never sported the cross flag devices, although at least a few individuals seemingly took it upon themselves to

Side view of an altered 1872-pattern helmet cut to the approximate configuration of the 1881-pattern. The plume staff and base are of the 1872-pattern, but the plate is of the new 1881-pattern for cavalry. Photograph by Gordon Chappell.

Front and side views of the new 1881-pattern enlisted helmet. Foot troops, such as hospital stewards, as indicated by a German silver caduceus overlay and stamped sheet brass side buttons bearing a caduceus, were issued to dismounted men first, before being issued to mounted soldiers. WR

affix the overlay designed for the helmet plate to their forage cap, which otherwise would have been without an insignia on the front.

While such visible displays of branch affiliation were desirable to the military, the opposite case was true on campaign. For instance, word came from the District of New Mexico about the white cork helmet, which "in active warfare against the Indians" of the region "offered a conspicuous mark to the enemy." To rectify this flaw that potentially had deadly consequences, 1,000 cork helmets covered "with unbleached brown linen" were procured and sent out on a trial basis in the spring.[63] No immediate action followed this limited test, although more than a decade later khaki uniforms, including summer helmets in that shade, became the norm.

Conversely, another similar experiment had a more immediate, lasting impact. Once again, in reaction to considerable lobbying from the officers in the Southwest for a light colored campaign hat as a replacement for the black hat, a welcome response was forthcoming. In the summer of 1882 the Quartermaster Department purchased 1,000 drab campaign hats, which it intended to ship "to troops serving on the frontier or in active campaign" by the following spring.[64]

These samples were in many respects the result of Major J.C. Breckenridge, a member of the Inspector General's Department, official tour in the West where he found considerable desire for a fur hat rather than one of wool. Moreover, he indicated that there was a sustained interest in a light colored campaign hat for troops serving in hot climates, much as correspondence of the mid-1870s had indicated and been noted in Circular No. 8.[65] To this end the new quartermaster general, Rufus Ingalls, turned to Captain John F. Rodgers at Philadelphia for assistance. Rodgers was to obtain several colors and types of hats for review, to which the officer replied that he considered: "The only

An 1881-pattern enlisted ordnance dress helmet. Photograph by Gordon Chappell.

An example of an 1881-pattern enlisted base for the plume's staff or spike (right), and one of the varieties of bases available to officers (left). GS

An example of the "openwasher" inserted into mounted 1881-pattern enlisted helmets to provide support for the plume staff and plume. GS

proper substance to use in the manufacture of hats of this character is *fur* felt." He went on to admit: "They will cost considerable [sic] more to begin with than wool hats, but a reasonable [sic] careful man can make two of them last through a term of enlistment, whereas he would want five of the wool ones." As a partial offset to the increased price, a less costly eyelet was proposed as a replacement for Brasher ventilators.[66]

An artillery sergeant in the overcoat with branch lined cape authorized in 1879, and the 1881-pattern dress helmet. This combination was unusual, in that the helmet was designed to be worn with the dress coat. BU

The new quartermaster general, Rufus Ingalls, agreed with Rodgers. General Ingalls sought the secretary of war's permission to order 1,000 fur felt drab hats for trial issue, although the cost would be approximately $2.00 each as opposed to the $.67 for the 1876-pattern black wool hat.[67] With the secretary in agreement, in 1883, several units, including Troop I, Sixth Cavalry stationed at Ft. McDowell, Arizona Territory, were provided with the drab hat. The company commander and many of his comrades from other organizations who tested the hat responded favorably.[68] With these positive endorsements, another 1,000 hats were ordered, but these were to have "larger ventilators in the side" than the trial models.[69] In fact, the improved hat was so successful, as early as 1884 the hat no longer was considered experimental, and was issued extensively, proving more popular than the summer helmet, although this type of headgear remained in service for decades to come, as well.[70] In 1884, the Quartermaster Department indicated its intention to purchase the drab hat exclusively thereafter. During the next year the quartermaster general underscored this aim and asked the secretary of war to sanction the policy "to purchase no more of the present standard pattern black, all wool, hats." Instead, the quartermaster general proposed future contracts should be "confined entirely hats of drab colors." Therefore, samples of drab hats sent out for trial, and also of the 1876-pattern wool standard black hat, were submitted simultaneously for consideration by Secretary of War Robert Todd Lincoln.

Nevertheless, an alternative remained for those who still favored a dark hat, because as quartermaster representatives pointed out: "If a demand for black, instead of drab colored hats should be made hereafter, there will be no difficulty to procure them."[71] Under the circumstances, black and drab hats saw service side by side, although the latter type dominated, as indicated by ample photographic evidence from the late 1880s and early 1890s, as well as the many contracts let for the 1883-pattern.[72]

Other indications of the department's ongoing efforts to improve the lot of the soldier included the procurement of 2,000 head-nets for protection against mosquitoes. These were to be supplied to enlisted personnel in the Department of Dakota.[73]

Likewise, the Quartermaster Department continued to supply buffalo overcoats, fur caps and gauntlets, and arctic overshoes to troops stationed in similar cold climates. Another bit of data pointing toward the level of support being supplied to the rank and file, observations that right hand Berlin gloves wore out more rapidly than left hand gloves prompted a practical response. By 1882 two rights and one left-hand

Private William Hunt, Battery B, First U.S. Artillery, wears the 1881-pattern spiked helmet, which was to be worn in tandem with the dress coat first adopted in 1872 by heavy artillerymen. GS

glove were provided to the soldier as a set, a practice that allegedly met "with universal satisfaction."[74]

One other, albeit relatively minor gesture came about in that year, too. At the request of the governor of the military prison at Ft. Leavenworth for a distinctive prison guard uniform, the secretary of war agreed to a special version of the 1874-pattern enlisted blouse. This garment was to be adorned with white cord on the collar and cuffs, as were the trousers of the soldiers assigned to this duty. A unique forage cap badge consisting of a wreath encircling the letters "P.G.," both in white metal, was permitted for winter wear. In summer, "a straw hat with black band, and same badge as on the forage cap" was substituted. The clothing was to be altered from issue items by workers at the prison's tailor shops.[75]

But more wide sweeping additions than the prison guard outfit were on the horizon, when in 1883 several initiatives of the previous year were carried out and distributed. As noted previously, the drab campaign hat was one important example of this ongoing effort to produce the articles called for in 1881 and 1882.[76] Some of the new pullover shirts were made, too, but once again their distribution was limited in that yet another version of the overshirt was prescribed on April 12, 1883.[77] The chief external difference between the type prescribed in 1882 and its 1883 successor was the absence of cord. This meant that branch colored trim was no longer applied to the cuffs, collar, and pockets, making it less expensive to produce the shirts, and facilitating ease of issue. Furthermore, General Orders No. 45, Headquarters of the Army, June 20, 1883, not only eliminated the cord on shirts, but also did away with this trim on blouses. Thereafter, the five-button blouse would be devoid of cord or trim save for chevrons.[78] One means to achieve this new look was simply to remove the cord from 1874-pattern blouses and send these out to the field as requisitions were made.[79] At almost the same time, these rank indicators once more were described in general orders that amended those published in the prior year.[80] Indeed, refine-

An official Quartermaster Department photograph depicted prototypes of the base and spike adopted for the 1881-pattern enlisted helmet in the top row, along with the German silver castle overlay for enlisted engineers. The middle row of enlisted overlays from left to right were for the Ordnance Department, hospital stewards, commissary sergeants, and the Signal Corps. The complete plate with numeral is for a cavalry trooper, in this instance for the First U.S. Cavalry. A similar plate with crossed rifles was provided for infantrymen and with crossed cannon for artillerymen. The latter two branches are represented by the helmet side buttons on the left and right of the eagle, while the bottom row of side buttons from left to right were for engineers, signalmen, commissary sergeants, ordnance troops, hospital stewards, and cavalrymen. The hooks were not actually part of the side buttons when their final form was adopted. *ARSW 1881*

ment was the operative word by this point. As such, a test began whereby recruits in the Bay Area were taken to the San Francisco Depot to be measured and fitted for their uniforms. The same practice had been initiated previously in Philadelphia.[81]

One other option for a more tailored look was to obtain coats, trousers, and jackets, which the Quartermaster Department provided cut out but were sent unmade. The components came bundled securely with the cloth, buttons, thread, trimmings, and even needles to enable enlisted men detailed as tailors to assemble the garments for a fee. The kit was provided at the cost of materials to the soldiers who so elected to draw their clothing in this manner. Unmade blouses were charged at $2.72 each, while dress coats ranged from $5.65 for cavalry, light artillery, and signal men (without chevrons) to $5.94 for engineer musicians.[82] Another means to ensure a better fit, for trousers at least, was the adoption on September 4, 1883, of suspenders.[83] The secretary of war condoned the supply of suspenders in response to a "long-felt want" for this practical accessory. Previously, if men desired braces, they had to purchase them from private sources. During 1883, however, they were to be issued at one pair per year "as part of the soldier's clothing allowance...." Thus, the Quartermaster Department once again bowed to the wishes of the soldier, so that by mid-1884 distribution had been made throughout the army. Supposedly they gave "general satisfaction."[84]

Other instances of ongoing attempts to upgrade enlisted clothing also were in progress during 1883.[85] These labors brought about new specifications for cotton stockings, drawers, and blouses to replace the standards set in 1879.[86] The last mentioned article, as noted previously, no longer was trimmed in branch colors, and also had an interior that was lined in a new gray flannel, which had been selected on March 19, 1883.[87] Moreover, there were new standards set for dark-blue wool shirting and cape lining flannel, and for dark-blue indigo dyed coat cloth, the new specifications being approved on March 15 and April 4, 1883, respectively.[88]

An even more significant change was sanctioned on October 24, with the acceptance of a blanket-lined canvas overcoat that took its inspiration from the Miles overcoat made in limited quantities as requested by the equipment board.[89] This cold-weather garment was medium brown in color, and was the first of many items to be made of this material and hue for rugged articles of clothing. Even then, buffalo overcoats were retained, albeit in small numbers. Moreover, sky-blue kersey great coats dominated, these being double-breasted with removable capes that were held in place by small cuff buttons sewn underneath the collar and buttons holes that were provided at the top of the cap. The capes were lined in "facings to conform in color to the trim of the uniform, except infantry, in which case the linings" were to be dark-blue.[90]

A few minor adjustments to officer's uniforms also were undertaken in 1883.[91] One was the requirement for officers to wear a plain black leather belt on undress duty, marches, and campaigns. Prior to the pronouncement of General Orders No. 82, Headquarters of the Army,

A sergeant of the Twentieth U.S. Infantry appears in the 1881 through 1884 regulation dress uniform for his branch. The trouser stripes continued to be 1 inch wide of dark blue facing cloth. FAM

A group of non-commissioned officers of the Thirteenth U.S. Infantry in their 1881 through 1884 dress uniforms. The individual seated in the center is a first sergeant, as set off by the lozenge above his three stripes. Several of the men wear service stripes, as was regulation. FDNHS

November 6, 1883, the wearing of such a belt had been optional. This accoutrement was to be worn on the outside of the jacket because, after 1875, slashes were no longer available at the sides of the blouse to permit the belt being placed underneath the garment.[92]

Another choice made by some officers, although one not formerly permitted by regulations, was dispensing with the leather chin strap on the forage cap altogether, or the substitution of a gold wire cord in place of the leather strap. Such cap-straps proved popular, so that according to General Orders No. 102, Headquarters of the Army, December 26, 1883, they ultimately were required for all officers, becoming mandatory on or before March 1, 1884.[93]

One final modification of the officer's forage cap appeared in 1883, but in this case only impacted the few men holding commissions in the Adjutant General's Department. Since 1872 their cap badge had been mentioned in regulations simply as a solid silver shield with thirteen stars. Then, General Orders No. 79, Headquarters of the Army, November 2, 1883, provided further details in that a gold embroidered wreath on a dark-blue background was to encircle the shield, in keeping with the cap devices for all other officers of the staff and general staff.

By the next year, 1884, a more far-ranging change effected officers in all departments and corps. The 1872-pattern officers' overcoat had not been a resounding success. Indicative of this attitude was a question published in the *Army and Navy Register* asking why officers did "not have a winter dress that will distinguish them from the police force of our cities?" Because of its design, the writer even claimed some officers had been mistaken for coachmen. What was wanted was a design that would do away with these objectionable features and be comfortable, as well. The U.S. Navy had just obtained such a coat, and the suggestion was it also should be adopted by the U.S. Army.

In fact, the Quartermaster Department did obtain a pair of prototypes of overcoats for examination, including one with buttons similar to a style worn by the U.S. Navy.[94] After receiving the specimens, they were sent to the School of the Line at Ft. Leavenworth, Kansas, for examination and comment from the officers posted there from many cavalry and infantry regiments.[95] In this way, a fairly good survey sample could be obtained without a great expenditure of time and effort.[96] Even with this input, the process of determining whether a new style of overcoat would be adopted for officers continued into late summer.[97]

Toward the middle of October, however, a decision had been made to do away with the old model and substitute a replacement with "a long mohair loop at the throat" that had "three round knots and two slides between the knots."[98] The design being settled upon, the quartermaster general requested publication of a new general order announcing the change.[99] General Orders No. 117, Headquarters of the Army, October

Sergeant John Erickson of the Fourth U.S. Cavalry has obtained the new 1881-pattern helmet, and is in strict accordance with the regulations of the 1882 through 1884 period for the cavalry dress uniform, except he has altered his helmet cord by cutting the long yellow lines so as to make it possible to remove the helmet without disentangling himself from the cords. Note the reinforcing of his 1882-pattern trousers, which characterized mounted troops. NPS

Many regimental bands also adopted the 1881-pattern dress helmet, albeit in combination with special uniforms, such as the martial musician depicts at Ft. Leavenworth, Kansas, in the early 1880s. Although his helmet is an enlisted model, an officer's chin chain had been added. FAM

West Point bandsmen likewise donned the 1881-pattern helmet, but retained the uniform that had been is use for that group since the early 1870s, with its white facings and trim. NA

21, 1884, introduced "a double-breasted ulster of dark blue cloth lined with dark blue flannel," which in many respects was similar to the popular cloak coat that had been regulation from 1851 through 1872. *The Army and Navy Journal* published the order four days later, and in the November 15 issue provided interested parties with three views of the coat, revealing among other things that it had a slit on the left side so that the sword belt could protrude when worn under the somber overcoat. Additionally, a matching detachable hood "lined with black Italian cloth or other suitable material" was to be fastened by buttons under the collar. This was to be "large enough to cover the head and cap, to be worn at night or in inclement weather...."[100]

The idea of a hood for foul weather was not restricted to the new officers' overcoat, but additionally was linked to the 1883-pattern canvas overcoat, too. At first this winter item was worn with the muskrat cap. Soon, however, a matching brown "canvas cap" was espoused as having more warmth than fur headgear. According to Quartermaster Specification No. 109, adopted on April 17, 1884, these articles were to be "made of 6 ounce cotton duck, dyed brown, lined with light blanket cloth next to the duck, and with light-colored cotton jean in the inside...." A pair of buttons were to close the cap's cape around the throat, and a "vest size, brown 'lasting' button" was attached to "the top for finish." A visor, which could be folded upward and held in position by a hook and eye, was bound in 3/4 inch brown tape, as were the edges of the cap, although the first prototypes sent to the field for testing did not have this flap.[101]

Two years later, another evolution of the cap was in the offing when red wool lining replaced the cotton jean, this latter material be considered warmer.[102] Even this improvement did not produce the desired response, in that by 1887 the secretary of war allowed fur caps to be issued in lieu of the canvas cap, if commanders wished to request them.[103]

Even as actions to provide for adequate protection against cold moved ahead, Holabird instituted a permanent equipment review board within his department charged with considering suggestions, promising inventions, and other matters that might benefit "the welfare of the soldier" in terms of uniform articles or other gear.[104] As such, a proposition from a correspondent in McKavett, Texas, for a "jacket and pants designed for men of the prairie," which had been rejected while Meigs still was in charge, would be resurrected.[105] Holabird, unlike his former superior and other officers in the department, took an opposite stand. He had been interested in devising a canvas fatigue uniform "similar to the working clothes worn by miners in the western states."[106] When he came into office, he was predisposed toward the production of this no-nonsense garb, at least for fatigue purposes.

In this light, the Quartermaster Department announced the "experimental issue of canvas clothing dyed to a brown color to troops on fatigue duty, and especially to those stationed in hot climates."[107] The preliminary efforts toward this end called for 500 pairs of canvas trousers (formerly known as canvas overalls), 200 canvas sack coats, and 330 canvas plaited blouses to be shipped from Philadelphia direct to the Department of Arizona, while another 1,335 pairs of canvas trousers, 535 canvas sack coats, and 800 canvas plaited blouses were to be shipped to the San Francisco Depot "as soon as they could be completed." The costs were $1.20 for the blouse, $.87 for the sack coats, and $.70 for trousers. These were to be issued and recommendations made after a period of observation as to the outcome of the trial.[108] A similar directive required 500 pairs of trousers, 200 sack coats, and 300 plaited blouses to be sent to the Department of Texas, and another 2,663 pais of trousers, 1,065 sack coats, and 190 plaited blouses to be furnished to the St. Louis Depot, with additional quantities of all three of these articles to be supplied to that facility later.[109]

To fund his pet project Brigadier General Holabird noted that experiments had been undertaken to convert some of the 520,000 shelter halves in stock by dyeing the canvas and cutting the material up for fatigue clothing. This resulted in the expenditure of less than $1.50 per set of coat and trousers.

He reported this information to the secretary of war, then expanded on this theme, writing: "From trials we have heard from it appears that this move may be made a possible success by judicious exercise of a little liberality towards the men." Holabird emphatically elaborated: "The pay of the men is small. They are required to do much fatigue work that soiled their uniforms, and it would be a great boon to them could they be supplied gratis annually one suit (coat and trousers) of this canvas clothing."[110]

The cost could be partially offset by doing away with stable frocks and overalls, heretofore issued to mounted men, at an annual cost of $7008.48.[111] The secretary of war assented to this plan, and Holabird lost little time in asking the adjutant general to produce a general order announcing the new fatigue suit, albeit in final form this directive did not include the discontinuance of the stable uniform and overalls.[112]

Some of the other original permutations of the new canvas outfit likewise were to go by the wayside. For example, when complaints reached Holabird's department that the new fatigue clothing made no allowance for differentiating soldiers from civilians, or privates from non-commissioned officers, the development of distinguishing marks or insignia that could be removed while the garments were being laundered was pursued.[113] The cost of worsted chevrons was called for in the cases of corporals, sergeants, and first sergeants, and bids for these articles were sought, based upon the model of 3/8 inch worsted braid sewn on backings of the brown canvas.[114]

The drum major of the U.S. Military Academy Band, however, retained the towering bearskin that was traditional for his position. NA

Not all bands gave up their shakos, or caps, for the helmet, as seen in this group portrait of the musicians of the Fifth U.S. Infantry on September 8, 1883, with their old-cock feather topped headgear still in use. MHS

The idea of chevrons soon was dropped, and Captain Rodgers made it clear that the coats would not use metal buttons such as those on the old stable frock.[115] Further, the pleated version of the blouse that had been produced in limited quantities likewise ultimately was rejected.[116]

What Holabird at last settled on was a pattern he thought to be "as neat and as tasty as they can be made."[117] This was a simple fatigue suit in durable brown canvas, as described in Specifications 115 and 116, both adopted on May 31, 1884. One complete set was to be supplied per year. In the Departments of Dakota, the Platte, and the Columbia, the outfits also were to include a hood and mittens.[118] For troops stationed in all other areas only the blouse and trousers were provided.[119]

Ultimately, the blouses were similar to the flannel versions, but had two large exterior breast pockets, and closed with five hard rubber buttons. And like the wool blouse, they came in six sizes, following a policy established earlier in the year to produce coats and jackets in a more refined range, just as a new series of trouser sizes had been adopted too, with twelve different options becoming available.

The introduction of six rather than five blouse sizes and twelve instead of the previous five trouser sizes had come about as a result of a study by depot quartermasters in Philadelphia and San Francisco.[120] At the former locale recruits were measured as they entered the service to secure a better fit, while at the latter location the resident military storekeeper, Captain Gustavus A. Hull, was authorized to hire if necessary "a skillful and capable cutter" who possessed "the requisite taste and practice in the art of fitting Uniforms to soldiers," especially in regard to producing spring bottoms. Both recruits and troops stationed at the Presidio of San Francisco, California, could be used in this endeavor, and consultation was encouraged with "practical businessmen in the city, and the officers and old sergeants and soldiers" in an "endeavor to get the thing needed by the soldiers, neatly fitting Uniforms."[121] Hull later was invited to make comments on the number of sizes he thought to be optimum to settle the problem of ready to wear clothing that did not have to be altered extensively once the soldier received it.[122]

Dedicated to achieving this purpose, Holabird encouraged trial garments to be sent out in restricted numbers and prompted responses from the field. Comments tended to be positive. The idea was that the previous sizes made it nearly impossible for the department to fit men properly. It was pointed out that "an ordinary man can go into any ready-made clothing store and be fairly fitted." And so the question was raised: "Why should this not be done for the enlisted men of the Army...?"[123] All garments made thereafter, with a few exceptions, were to be produced in the new size range, although the existing stocks with old measurements followed the time honored practice of being issued first, until supplies were completely depleted.[124] Again, Holabird requested the Adjutant General's Department to provide a general order that made this innovation known.[125] General Orders No. 81, Headquarters of the Army, July 29, 1884, did do, but only mentioned trousers for the present, as well as issuing the remaining stocks of footgear with soles fastened by brass screws, despite the fact that defects related to this method of fastening continued to draw adverse commentary.[126] While reconciliation of this problem was being considered, trousers of a new style likewise were in the process of being adopted.[127] As adopted, the 1884-pattern trousers increased in price some $.25, so that they would cost $1.00 as opposed to the earlier issue.[128]

The trousers referred to in this order were to be slightly different from the pattern that was prescribed on October 9, 1882, the size variations being the chief variation based upon new specifications approved on January 16, 1884. On that day Holabird had consented to the new

The illustrations accompanying the uniform regulations of 1881 depicted double 1/2 inch stripes of facing material on the trousers of company musicians, although not until 1883 did a general order appear to indicate that this was to be the norm. As such, common practice and official approval did not always go hand in hand. This young engineer musician exhibits such stripes, but in the case of his branch the stripes were to be of scarlet piped in white, while those for artillery were of scarlet facing cloth, dark blue for infantry, and yellow for cavalry. JG

pattern, but indicated he wanted the reinforcing piece for mounted versions to be made larger before being sealed as the standard. Otherwise, the samples as made, with two side pockets and one right hip pocket were deemed proper for issue.[129]

For nearly the next nine months, however, there was little progress in providing the 1884-pattern, until sufficient existing stocks had been used up to permit general issue.[130] Nonetheless, a limited number of pairs evidently were made during this period, but they became part of the emergency reserve.[131] Similarly, an experiment to recut the reinforcing pieces on unmade trousers of the previous pattern was considered to provide for the twelve sizes of trousers, and with the waistband called for both in 1882 and 1884.[132] Toward the end of the year, however, supplies dwindled to the point that 1884-pattern trousers could be made in larger quantities, some 1,500 being called for in September as part of an anticipated 3,000 that would be required in the upcoming few months, because old sizes were running low.[133] Even at that juncture, old and new sizes were issued side by side, on a case by case basis, until all the on-hand inventory had been used up.[134]

The same situation existed for blouses throughout the year, and there were some other nuances that had to be considered, as well. For instance, in 1883 the blouse no longer was to display branch colored cord. This resulted in the trim being removed from 1874-pattern jackets, but for all intents and purposes, the basic design remained unchanged, although Specification 100 from January 16, 1884, included some subtle changes over the style adopted on May 19, 1883.[135] Quartermaster General Holabird underscored the state of development that then was in progress when he drew attention to the "discrepancy found to exist in the specifications and standard samples of blouses heretofore furnished the Jeffersonville Depot." A thorough examination of the topic led Holabird to conclude: "These new patterns must after all be looked upon as an experiment. Trial in active service may develop some further error, and suggestions of further improvements may arise." He thus concluded, "It is therefore deemed best to give the patterns as furnished to you as trial in active service."[136] After that he thought experience might dictate more refinements.

The chevrons for prison guards at Leavenworth also appeared to be specially made, being fashioned from white facing material, as indicated by this portrait of an unidentified sergeant. FAM

In 1882 the governor of the military prison at Ft. Leavenworth, Kansas, received permission for a uniform to be worn by guards at that martial penal facility. Troops assigned this duty were to don a customized 1874-pattern enlisted blouse with white cord on the collar and cuffs, the former element also was to be covered in black velvet. Trousers of these soldier-guards were to be trimmed with white piping, as well. FAM

This analysis both summarized Holabird's willingness to receive reactions from the field, as well as to acknowledge that change was ongoing. In fact, even as blouses in store were being doled out, some new made items were being provided in certain instances.[137]

To add to the confusion, yet another style of blouse was being called for, while the transition in sizes was underway. In September, blouses with three outside pockets were accepted as the latest requirement, in keeping with the quartermaster general's policy of experimentation based on perceived improvements of the soldier's outfit. During that month these garments were thereafter to be made, while in the meantime whatever items remained in the depots would be provided to fill orders from the field.[138]

Even then, prototypes with the three outside pockets were sealed as samples, and specifications were drafted late in 1884.[139] At that point, word went out to make nothing but the exterior pocket style, while the previous pattern pieces were recalled so that they could be issued.[140] Indeed, the pace moved so quickly in certain instances that a few of the exterior pocket blouses were furnished to troops before the end of 1884.[141] Regardless of which pattern was being provided, one senior officer, Lieutenant Colonel Nathan A.M. Dudely of the Ninth U.S. Cavalry, then commanding at Ft. Lyon, Colorado, expressly forbade altering clothing in violation of orders and regulations, because he contended the jackets worn by some of his men resembled "'cut away frock coats' or 'shagbellies' instead of regulation blouses."[142]

The concept of six sizes in part was designed to curtail such expressions of individual fancy, and also was carried over to dress coats. But the adjustment of measurements was not the only initiative taken relative to this garment. Once more, Captain Hull at the quartermaster depot in San Francisco entered the picture. He had continued to concentrate on improving the dress coat in general.[143] Hull sought a cut that would fit well and not require alteration after the soldier was given his coat. He indicated 111 men tried on the garments made from his new pattern. The result was that most conformed to the physique of the garment as made, or only required the movement of the buttons on the chest to make the coat tighter or looser as needed. Two men had to have their sleeves shortened, and one required his sleeves to be lengthened. Only one man could not be fitted at all from the selection of ready made coats.

In another test, thirty-nine artillerymen of Battery H, Fourth U.S. Artillery at the Presidio, were sent the coats with twenty-six of them not requiring additional tailoring, another eleven slight adjustments, and two not able to be fitted. The last pair of gunners required adjustments to the length of sleeves, the movement of buttons, and a loosening under the armpits in one of the two cases.

Three Third Cavalry troopers have exchanged their carbines for rifles and added extra Mills belts as bandoleers, plus display their Schofield .45 caliber revolvers. Two of them wear 1883-pattern shirts, while the man on the right retains the 1882-pattern shirt, although he had removed most of the piping, except for around the collar. He also continues to use 1876-pattern boots, in contrast to his comrade seated on the left who has on 1884-pattern boots. The brims on their headgear are wider than the 1883-pattern campaign as they came to be issued, indicating that they are either privately purchased cowboy style hats, or perhaps some of the prototypes of the drab hat, which may have been different in configuration to the final form of the hat. TT

In 1882, the U.S. Army surgeon general finally permitted the wearing of white metal caduceus devices on the collar of the dress coat for hospital stewards. By this point, the German silver "U.S." on hospital steward's forage caps also were to be replaced by a caduceus. Photograph by Jim Wertman. USA

Only five sizes had been provided for this trial. Hull felt this was sufficient in all but unusual cases, where an individual who was "peculiarly formed" necessitated measurements to be sent to the local depot for a special order. The captain shipped the five coats he had used in his study; along with skirt patterns for mounted coats, the samples all being for dismounted troops. Hull further called attention to suggestions he made on December 2, 1882, regarding the improvement of coats by "leaving off the 'belt straps' which seem to be useless, as these coats are only worn upon dress occasions when there is no weight of ammunition carried."

Hull then turned to the objection to light colored piping on the collar of the coat, the material close to the neck often being soiled quickly. As an alternative, Hull submitted a cavalry coat to Holabird with the plain facing sewn all the way around the collar, but leaving the dark blue cloth at the top edge exposed to protect the fragile cloth from becoming noticeably dirty in a short time after being issued. He concluded: "Coats made in this manner would require no more facing cloth, besides the collar is easily made, and the facing cloth when soiled, can be

The caduceus in wreath that replaced the old "U.S." within a wreath as the cap badge for hospital stewards. Photograph by Gordon Chappell.

replaced with less labor, as it can be attached on, without removing the collar.[144]

Much of what Hull had to say paralleled Holabird's desire to provide a uniform dress coat that would be "what its name implies." He wanted it to "be the best fitting and best made garment supplied by the [Quartermaster] Department." To achieve this intent he approved the lowering of the facings on coat collars to make them less susceptible to staining from perspiration, and easier to replace if required. Other matters of concern remained the complaint of the "shortness of the waist and skirts; collars too large and too low in the neck; and loops at the waist, which interfered with the cartridge box. Finally, the sleeves were "condemned as being too long for the size of the coats." He sent Philadelphia the sample coats and paper patterns furnished by Hull to illustrate the alterations he believed would eliminate these objections.[145]

Besides these deficiencies, criticism had been leveled at collar insignia for dress coats, which were seen as redundant because dress helmet plates bore the regimental designation on the front or branch insignia, thereby making them unnecessary appendages. Charges that the collar insignia likewise soiled the facings, had to be removed for cleaning, and because of their fragile nature regularly broke in the process, plus in the case of cavalrymen often were knocked off, damaged, or lost when the carbine sling caught on them. This last action sometimes even tore the fabric.[146]

One method to bring a halt to this annoyance was to discontinue the wearing of collar numbers. Although the Quartermaster General advocated omitting these devices, higher authorities originally declined to permit this change.[147]

Undaunted, Holabird pressed ahead with efforts to address some of the dress coat's other shortcomings, so more samples were prepared and a small group of officers and men gathered in the Washington, D.C., area to try on the experimental garments.[148] Another fifteen model coats were shipped to Ft. Leavenworth for examination there, including three with longer skirts, lengthened skirt facings, and pipings of "white" for infantry troops, the color change being contemplated because of continued charges that the medium blue dye used for that branch's color faded considerably. The idea was to determine what officers stationed there from around the country thought of the various designs, much as they had been polled in regard to officers' overcoats. Some of the questions that the quartermaster general was most anxious to answer were whether white piping was preferred; whether the skirt facings should be longer; what was considered the proper length of the skirt per se; and whether the loops (referred to as "dubbies" in the correspondence) at the waist should be removed or not. The coats were to be tried on men at that post, and opinions rendered as to which of the patterns (those provided by the San Francisco Depot or those from the Philadelphia Depot) were determined to be best. Ideas for further improvement also were solicited.[149]

Although some of these inquiries took time to consider, the last item in the list was decided sooner than the rest. Belt loops, a prolonged point of discourse, were pronounced obsolete. In May 1884 Holabird made this fact known, and ordered that all coats produced thereafter "should be without the straps which are let into the waist seams...."[150]

Although eliminating the belt loops was not costly, other contemplated changes were not as inexpensive or easy. With this in mind, Holabird sent a letter requesting the sentiments of the commanding general and the secretary of war before final actions were taken "in regard to improving the sizes, and, with it the patterns of the Uniform Dress Coats of the enlisted men of the Army." Submitting samples to his superiors, Holabird prefaced his request in the third person: "If any changes in the present standard trimmings are desirable, in the opinion of the Quartermaster General now would be the proper time to make them." To assist them in making an informed decision, Holabird provided a

Not only has this hospital steward from a New Mexico Territory garrison added the prescribed caduceus devices to his collar, but also he has borrowed a saber belt rig complete with heavy cavalry saber and an M1879 holster from a Sixth U.S. Cavalry trooper at the fort so he can appear more martial for the photographer. This is just one instance where even period photographs have to be carefully scrutinized to determine whether the image is representative or has been staged to suit individual whim. Other than that, he is strictly regulation for the 1882 through 1884 period, including the new trousers with waistband adopted in 1882. CBF

Among other features, trousers of the 1882-pattern had a waistband, belted-back, and slight spring at the cuffs. This pair is for a corporal of heavy artillery. SI

In 1883, a chevron was adopted for regimental and battalion color sergeants that had a circle in the center made of facing material in scarlet for artillery, white for engineers, blue for infantry, and yellow for cavalry. Pairs for the infantry overcoat were supposed to have a white circle as seen here. AMWH

dress coat of the standard then worn, and two samples of coats that were similar in style but with the facings extended all around the collar. He noted that in both instances the facings could be removed easily and replaced. The fact that the material did not reach the top of the collar, but had an edge of dark blue as Hull had suggested, also was underscored to demonstrate that the coats would be less subject to becoming visibly dirty. A fourth sample resembling the previous two had a longer skirt facing that extended to the bottom edge of the coat, rather than halting several inches above, as had been the design in use since 1872 for foot soldiers. Furthermore, all facings and piping were white. Holabird then noted that the belt loops had been omitted from all four examples, per the acting secretary of war's prior permission, "before proceeding any further in this matter," instructions were requested as to "whether any changes from the present standard shall be made and if so in what respect."

While waiting for a reply, Holabird pressed on with his efforts to reach a conclusion. This meant that he contacted the commanding colonel of the First U.S. Infantry, William "Pecos Bill" Shafter, who in October 1884 had sent along some prototype trousers with white stripes for non-commissioned officers. Holabird asked that these articles be returned for further consideration.[151]

Shafter responded quickly and dispatched the articles by registered mailed. He also advocated "that the stripe be made of white linen webbing instead of silk and cotton as the former material can easily be kept clean."[152] The Twenty-third Infantry's Captain George M. Randall echoed this advice, maintaining "the stripes made of white linen webbing...would be handsome and the most durable of all stripes. It would stand long usage and could easily be cleaned."[153] In his typical cooperative fashion, Holabird complied with the request and added one pair of trousers of the new pattern with stripes for a sergeant and another with stripes for a corporal in white linen webbing to his growing list of specimens.[154]

General Orders No. 92 of 1882 called for service in-war chevrons, which were bordered in red except for those issued to artillerymen, which were edged in white, to be worn closest to the cuff. The example seen here is for cavalry service, and above is a regular infantry service chevron signifying the completion of a five-year enlistment in that branch, also per the requirements of this general order. This coat belonged to First Sergeant Joseph W. Hunting, Company E, Fifth U.S. Infantry. DM

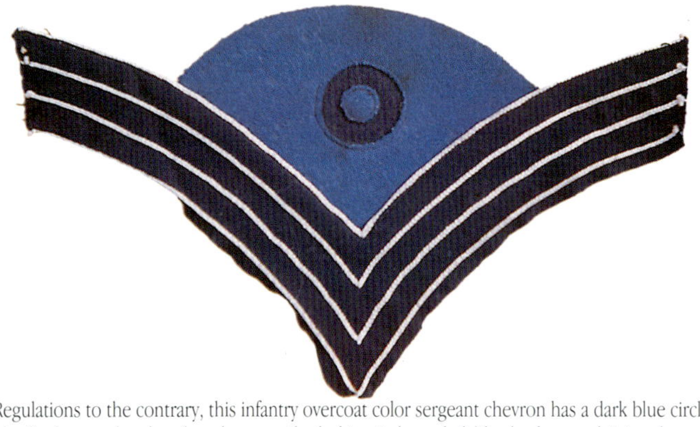

Regulations to the contrary, this infantry overcoat color sergeant chevron has a dark blue circle on a sky blue background, rather than the prescribed white circle on dark blue background. It is unknown whether this chevron is an unadopted prototype, or a custom made item. JG

With all these preliminaries attended to, Holabird was ready to return to his superiors with a recommendation. He approached them as follows:

> I have the honor to forward for the information and action of the Lieutenant General and the honorable Secretary of War, samples of Uniform Coats and Trousers having the sky blue facings as now in use, and also white facings and trimmings. It is recommended that the white be adopted in lieu of the sky blue, universal complaint being made about the latter color owing to its fugitive character, fades upon being exposed to the sun.[155]

He closed with a request that actions be taken on this matter as early as possible. Assuming that the response would favor his recommendation, he went so far as to instruct that preparations should be made to change the contract for sky blue facing material to white.[156] This preemptive action proved premature. Philip Sheridan, who had succeeded William Sherman in 1883 as the army's senior officer, wanted to have Colonel Elwell Otis, the commandant at Ft. Leavenworth's School of Application, review the bidding once more. In rejoinder to Lieutenant General Sheridan, a sergeant's coat with sky-blue piping, facings, and short skirt facings; a sergeant's uniform coat with white piping, white collar with facings all around, and long skirt facings; a corporal's uni-

In 1883, chevrons for overcoats of all branches were to be relocated from above the elbow to near the cuff so that they would no longer be obscured by the cape. In that same year, a new design of overcoat without turned up cuffs was adopted. The belt in the back likewise was discontinued, and the cape made separate from the coat so that it could be detached. This example is for an infantry private. JG

Detail of the cuff of an 1883-pattern enlisted overcoat. Cape linings continued to be in branch color, except for infantry, which remained dark blue. JG

As revealed by this photo of Private William J. Whelan of the Fourth U.S. Cavalry, beginning in 1883 the cape for enlisted overcoats could be removed and either garment worn separately. FAM

form with white piping, white collar having facings in front, and long skirt facings; and a pair of sergeant's trousers with dark blue stripes and the same with white stripes—all were to be furnished to Otis and other officers at the school.[157]

Meanwhile, Holabird forged ahead, so that by October 23, 1884, word was received that the secretary of war authorized a change in the facings for infantry from sky-blue to white. He further opted for the pattern with the facings that extended all around the collar, thereby causing the dictate that any coats made in the future would conform to this style. Another upshot was the recognition by quartermaster officials in Washington that the depot at Philadelphia would experience "an immediate demand for white facings and stripes for trousers...to replace those now in use." This triggered a reaction, calling for the Lieutenant Colonel M.I. Ludington, the quartermaster in charge at Philadelphia, to procure "a sufficient quantity of white facing cloth to commence issue." The material could be bought with the funds previously set aside for sky-blue cloth, and included both facing material and white webbing for trouser stripes.[158] The directive to Ludington then concluded:

> Now that the question of facings has been solved, it becomes the duty of the Department to devote its attention to the revision and improvements of patterns. The sample Coats made after patterns devised at the San Francisco and Philadelphia depots, forwarded by you on the 11" of April last, will be returned to you by the Depot Quartermaster in this City.

Front and back view of the blanket lined brown canvas overcoat approved in 1883. JG

Please study the subject once more, and after having fixed upon a desirable set of patterns, have one coat of each size made and forwarded to this office with accompanying specifications. It is needless to call your attention to the importance of the subject and the whole matter is entrusted to your consideration and judgment.[159]

Having placed the whole matter in Ludington's capable hands, a request went forward to release a general order notifying the change of infantry facings to white, and of the latest pattern of dress coat that would be issued to these foot soldiers.[160] To expedite issue, while awaiting the necessary order, instructions once more went out to make all infantry coats in the future according to this pattern, along with recalling the old coats with blue facing that were serviceable so that they might be remodeled by replacement of the trim with white, an alteration that was to cost $1.75 per coat, and that evidently was undertaken quickly in some cases, because ceratin garrisons were being furnished such garments by November.[161]

During this process, General Orders No. 120, Headquarters of the Army, October 24, 1884, ushered in the new infantry coat and white facings all around, that is, for enlisted men, because permission still had been withheld for officers to convert their trim as yet, in great part because of the economic impact this would have made on them.[162] As a related matter, this same general order spelled out the proper requirements for trouser stripes, which for sergeants continued to be 1-inch wide and those of corporals a 1/2 inch, and for field musicians two stripes on each side each measuring a 1/2 inch. Again, all were to be of cloth, save those for infantry, which were to be of white linen webbing.

While trouser stripes had provided a form of recognition for noncommissioned officers for some time, a new method to distinguish them was in the offing during 1884, as well. This was in keeping with a reform movement during the period throughout the federal government that would eventually impact on "the condition of the enlisted men, whenever practicable with a due regard to economy and efficiency."[163] Holabird, who was a leader in the army's efforts to enhance the rank

The 1879-pattern muskrat cap regularly was combined with the new 1883-pattern canvas overcoat. The collar has been turned up to protect the neck. JG

Late in 1883 a gold chin cord was prescribed for officers' forage caps. Several variations existed, a number of which had been used even prior to that time without official approval. KC

Front and side view of Captain Edmund Luff's Eighth U.S. Cavalry forage cap with the regulation gold cord strap. JM

An example of a variant gold cord used prior and subsequent to the adoption of a standard cord in 1883, in this case on the forage cap of a Seventh U.S. infantry officer. JB

Interior of Captain Luff's forage cap.

A Fourth U.S. Artillery officer's forage cap with the correct 1883-pattern cord. RB

and file's quality of life, sought among other things to elevate the status of non-commissioned officers by the introduction of gold lace chevrons and service stripes for all enlisted personnel.[164] The process began at the outset of the year with a request for samples of gold lace chevron material for estimating the number of yards needed to manufacture these insignia.[165] Then the quartermaster general asked for the cost in New York of English gold lace based upon some samples that had been obtained.[166] Sources for the material likewise were explored, including ascertaining who the contractor was who supplied cadets at the U.S. Military Academy. An example of his wares were requested, too.[167] Some military dealers even heard of the move and approached the Quartermaster Department to learn how they could bid on the lace.[168]

Even as the preliminary efforts moved along, the secretary of war authorized the issue of gold lace chevrons for non-commissioned officers. The first specifications drawings followed for a color sergeant chevrons with a 1 1/4 inch sphere instead of a star, which evidently had been suggested previously. White piping was to be used on engineer chevrons. The lace was to be applied to dark blue cloth with 4 1/2 inch devices, and the same measurement was to be used for the inside of the arc of chief trumpeter chevrons, whereas the logenze of first sergeants was to be about 2 1/4 inches long without piping and placed on a dark blue cloth background, as well. Specimens for the cavalry and infantry had been made in accordance with this plan, but the original artillery sample for first sergeants was disapproved at first. Instructions were given that

The new chin cord also could be applied to the non-regulation pillbox cap, as this example for a Sixth U.S. Cavalry officer demonstrates. EB

A medical officer's forage cap with the 1883-pattern cord and the proper silver embroidered "U.S." within a gold embroidered wreath, worn by most other staff officers, as well, except for the Adjutant General's Department, which adopted a shield within a wreath in 1883. The edged weapon is an M1840 Medical Department sword. Photograph by Gordon Chappell.

samples for all ranks were to be made, including for farriers, although these men were not considered non-commissioned officers, but conversely none were to be fashioned for principal musicians of the Signal Corps because the small number of men assigned to this organization precluded the establishment of a band, although there were trumpeters assigned to the corps at Ft. Myer. All the samples were to be sent to the depot quartermaster in Washington, D.C., except overcoat specimens. These were to remain with the quartermaster general. Three specimens, however, were to be placed in "better cases" and marked outside as to their contents.[169]

Then came a requirement for a detailed breakdown of costs attendant to manufacture gold lace chevrons so that the funds could be allotted for production.[170] Based upon the analysis of all this data, Holabird then sought revision of paragraph 2727 of army regulations, which would incorporate the use of gold lace chevrons for non-commissioned officers who could purchase them at cost for use "on their blouses and overcoats."[171] Holabird then called for "a War chevron for each arm of the service to be made and forwarded to this office." The quartermaster general further indicated: "It is thought that the service in peace chevrons might be made without piping on the edge, a plain piece of gold lace may answer the purpose. A few pieces of lace should also be forwarded."[172] After being provided these specimens, he concluded gold lace service chevrons with branch color facing as backing was the appropriate scheme, while for peace chevrons the background was to be dark blue cloth of the same material as the dress coat.[173] A few pieces of lace also were to be forwarded in order to determine if this material alone would be adequate for service stripes.[174] After being provided these specimens, he concluded gold lace service chevrons with branch color facing as backing was the appropriate scheme, while for peace chevrons the backing was to be dark blue cloth of the same material as the dress coat.[175] Satisfied as to the design, Holabird indicated that the production of gold lace chevrons in quantity would commence during the next fiscal year, once the budget was approved.[176] This meant that the Quartermaster Department was not yet ready to supply the fine items while awaiting funding. Once the resources were at hand, however, the intention was to assemble them at the Philadelphia depot, rather than by contract.[177] Still, the gold lace itself had to be purchased. Therefore, Holabird advised informal negotiations should be carried out for contracts to buy not only the lace, but also kersey, dark blue quality cloth of a finer quality for officers and non-commissioned officers, shirting flannel, and a number of other items that the quartermaster general deemed of value for the soldiers.[178]

Colonel Eugene A. Carr, who commanded the Sixth U.S. Cavalry, sports the gold forage cap cord, along with a Grand Army of the Republic (star-shaped device) medal and a medal from the Loyal Legion of the United States (Maltese cross), both veterans' organizations of the post Civil War era. NA

From late 1858 through the mid-1880 brass stadia were available for presentation to the best marksman of a company as a prize that he could wear attached to the uniform by means of a chain, as this sergeant of Company I, Twenty-fourth U.S. Infantry had done in conjunction with his 1874-pattern enlisted blouse. In all other respects his uniform is the typical garrison dress with forage cap as called for in regulations from 1874 through 1883. USAMHI, Bill Gladstone Collection

This meant that a standard for the gold lace had to be adopted, an action that took place on June 21.[179] By March, with all bids in hand, Horstmann was awarded a contract for 13,500 yards at $.93 a yard. The lace was "to be of the best English thread lace gold on silver, guaranteed to contain as stated in their bid, 89 to 90% silver, 1 to 2% gold and 8% alloy."[180]

During the months that followed, efforts at producing final designs occupied Holabird and some of his subordinates engaged in the process. For example, the original artillery color sergeant sample that did not meet with the quartermaster general's approval, and was reworked to display a 1 1/4 inch sphere made up of a 1/4 inch gold lace circle having a 3/4 inch center of coat cloth.[181] After this adjustment was completed, four complete sets of chevrons were required, with silver piping cord added to engineer stripes, rather than white silk stitching. The crescent for commissary sergeants also was to be made smaller than on the preliminary submission, and the points were to be worn up, not sideways.[182] With these actions being carried out, the time seemed appropriate to issue a general order authorizing the gold lace chevrons, with the idea that manufacture could move ahead in the near future, the artillery and ordnance versions being the first made, either in house or by contract.[183]

By late September the plan was advanced enough to announce the intention to issue the costly devices, and this was accomplished by the publication of General Orders No. 107, Headquarters of the Army, September 12, 1884, that not only introduced the gold lace devices, but also discontinued the wearing of service and campaign stripes on overcoats and blouses.[184] At that point only artillery gold lace chevrons were available, although those for engineers, which, incidentally, actually were to be outlined in white silk chain stitching as opposed to the silver trim Holabird had considered for a time, would be in stock by early fall. The prospect of cavalry and staff non-commissioned officer chevrons following shortly after that was viewed as the next phase. Only the infantry would have to wait, because the final decision as to whether there would be a change in the branch color still had not been determined.[185]

Rather than wait for the decision of what doughboys should wear, the department forged ahead in issuing the artillery, engineer, and staff chevrons, although it was made known that farrier's device would not be provided in gold, because these specialists were not deemed non-commissioned officers under General Orders No. 107. Further, the army no longer would provide U.S. Marine Corps service chevrons to the rank and file due to the fact that the army no longer was being furnished these hash marks. And in the case of commissary sergeants, the continuation of the crescent being placed with points up was dictated, although the prototype had been made with the device facing outward on the vertical, or in other words, "points front," as called for by General Orders No. 107. Notwithstanding some of the restrictions and contra-

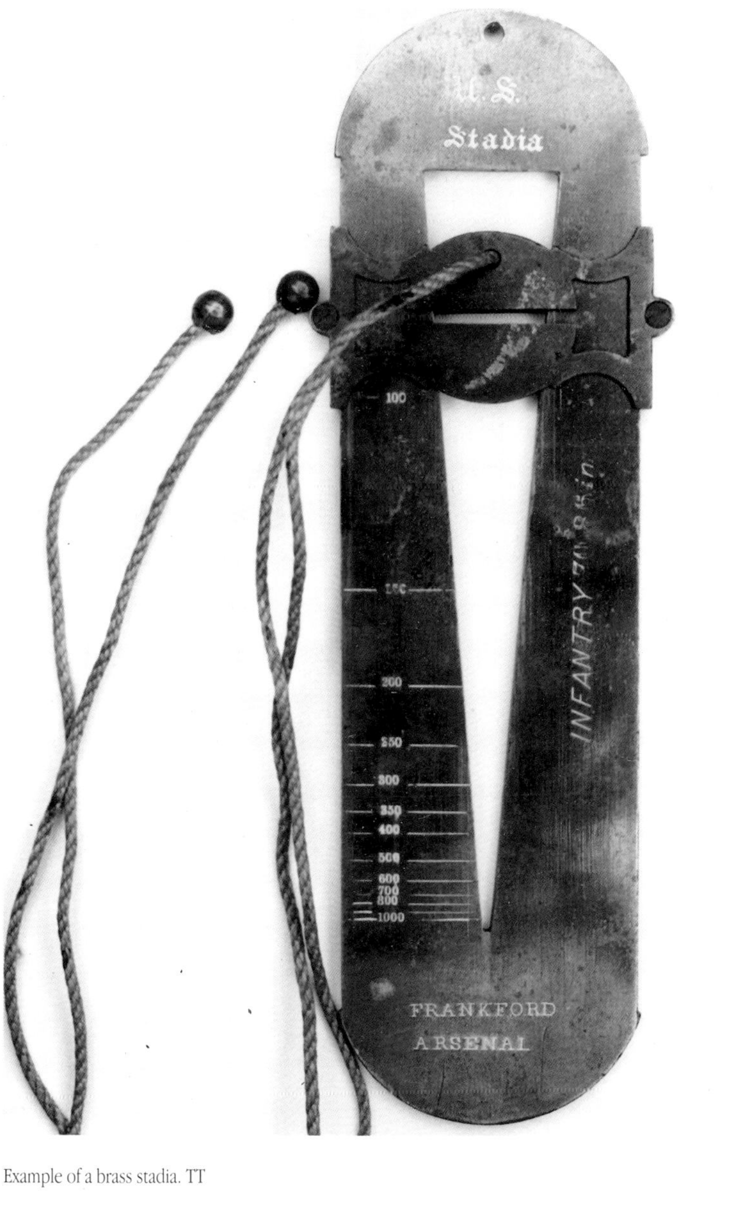

Example of a brass stadia. TT

By 1880, however, 3/4 inch sterling silver "Laidley" marksmanship devices were ushered in, and were to be worn in pairs, one on each side of the collar, as Private William Hunt of Battery B, First U.S. Artillery does on his 1874-pattern blouse. Private Hunt holds an 1876-pattern campaign hat. GS

Little Bighorn survivor Captain George D. Wallace, Seventh U.S. Cavalry, has affixed the 1883-pattern gold chin cord to his forage cap, as well as placed the 1880-pattern 3/4 inch sterling silver "Laidley" marksman buttons on his collar. FAM

dictions, all requests for supply were to be placed directly with Philadelphia, as no gold lace would be provided to any other distribution center, although this constraint was relaxed soon thereafter.[186]

The next few months were taken up with expanding the range of available types to cavalry, thereby causing Captain Rodgers to send a form letter on October 30 to all the posts in the Military Divisions of the Pacific and the Missouri to ascertain the quantities required once production began.[187] Soon he could declare "The Department is now prepared to supply all kinds of gold lace chevrons, except for the Infantry arm of the service."[188]

Just a few weeks earlier, however, the War Department had announced its intent to substitute white for blue as the facings for infantry. This meant no more blue chevrons in cloth or gold lace were to be produced henceforth.[189] Holabird quickly set to work to see that samples were made and closely monitored the development. He even cautioned that the bleaching of white facing cloth on the first sample resulted in good color, but care was to be taken that a high level of sulphur was not introduced in the process to tarnish the lace, which would happen if it were composed of too much copper and too little gold. With this advice, by the beginning of November the quartermaster general had reviewed the final infantry designs and pronounced them satisfactory.[190] Even then, the fabrication of infantry chevrons was not completed during 1884, thereby causing some orders to be detained until the following year.[191]

Another obstacle to universal distribution of gold lace was related to the proper insignia for chief musicians.[192] During 1884, the whole matter of band uniforms had been under consideration, and this was but one of many points being discussed after the quartermaster general sent a circular letter to all regimental commanders soliciting their opinions about bandsmen uniforms. This action resulted from a notion that the Quartermaster Department "provide all band uniforms, including the desired facings, trimmings & c. free of cost to the post funds or to the individual members of the band." Holabird went on to note: "This idea is believed to be a practical one which can readily be carried out." To do so, he thought it was advisable "to have regiments having bands indi-

In 1883, suspenders were approved for the first time as an item that would be provided by the Quartermaster Department. Photographs by Robert L. Sanders. JG

Cotton and woolen stockings both were available by the 1880s. Photographs by Robert L. Sanders. JG

cate what they wish the uniforms of their bands to be. It is desirable to have several arms of service have like facing and the same general groundwork for the dress." In order to achieve a degree of consensus, Holabird asked for "suggestions, plans of uniforms, and any ideas connected therewith" so that a successful solution of this measure could be achieved, with the proviso that "a moderate economy should be followed in so making recommendations."[193]

Here again, Holabird displayed his interest in dispensing a product that had been generated by requests from the field. Therefore, the input he received from many commanders, who availed themselves of the opportunity to make their views known, was considered in future deliberations within his department.

For instance, Colonel H.M. Black of the Twenty-third U.S. Infantry responded that his band wore the regulation uniform as "the *groundwork*" for both dress and undress, but supplemented this with regimental funds to trim the outfits in white, using opera cloth that cost $3.00 a yard. He also had white stripes added to the trousers and a white horsehair plume, along with worsted cords added to the dress helmet, the latter to replace the spike. These items cost $.75 and $1.00, respectively. For undress the men donned a forage cap ornamented with a gold lace band, and on the front appeared the regimental number embroidered in silver set in the center of a gold embroidered bugle, which in essence was the old 1851-pattern officers' cap device. Additionally, Black observed that all the bandsmen preferred to have their uniforms "altered by a co. tailor, so as to fit neatly." He also expressed the opinion that a white worsted or mohair knot be worn on the sleeves of the dress coat.[194] It is interesting to note that many of these practices were adopted as the blueprint for infantry bands soon thereafter.

Detail of the rear yoke and collar of an 1883-pattern field shirt. Photograph by Robert L. Sanders. JG

A dark blue flannel field shirt without piping was also introduced in 1883. Two versions were authorized, but the first design had only two buttons on the plait (one at the throat and one midway from the throat to the end of the opening) and proved short-lived. The front and back view of the second model, which remained in service virtually unchanged into the early twentieth century, is seen here. Photographs by Robert L. Sanders. JG

The interior of the yoke collar of 1883-pattern field shirts was lined front and back in muslin. Photograph by Robert L. Sanders. JG

These men of the Sixth U.S. Cavalry in New Mexico Territory depict the transitional garb of the mid 1880s. The trooper in the background with a forging (shotgun) gun held in the crook of his left arm has on an 1883-pattern shirt, while the young Navajo man to his left may have on one of the 1875 experimental dark blue flannel shirts. In turn, the soldier in the front row has on the 1878-pattern collarless gray shirt. The other two members of the hunting party wear enlisted sack coats, which beginning in 1883 were to have the branch cord removed and worn plain, as was the case with the shirt pattern adopted that year. Note that the man on the left in the front row has on an 1878-pattern muskrat cap. CBF

Numerous other infantry regiments were represented in the survey, too. For instance, word came from the Second Infantry that the band paraded in colorful attire. Their regulation dress helmet displayed "white fountain coque plumes with red tip for the men and all red for the bandleader." All members received white cotton front and back braids for the helmet and white cotton hat cords. The regulation dress coat had three rows of eleven bell buttons of silver plated white metal. Matching ones appeared on the skirt and cuffs. The coat still had many additional items to set it off from the common soldier. "Whale bone trimming" ornamented the chest, while white mohair braid appeared on the sleeves. All facings were white, and white cotton epaulets with fringe surmounted the shoulders. One inch wide white stripes accented the trousers. A white leather belt with sliding frog for the musician's sword completed the basic uniform, which had been worn since 1876, with the exception that the helmet replaced the old dress cap. Colonel Frank Wheaton, who commanded the Second Infantry, felt that his bandsmen required nothing more to complete their ensemble except for black leather music pouches with falling flaps, which fastened with a brass stud, much like the ones he had supplied for the Second Rhode Island Infantry, a unit he commanded during the Civil War. The colonel thought a harp or bugle emblem should appear on these accoutrements.[195]

In Arizona Territory Sergeant Neil Erickson (center) wears the 1882-pattern dark blue flannel overshirt, piped in yellow for cavalry, as does the fellow Sixth Cavalry comrade to his left. This latter trooper, however, has removed the collar and the piping from the plait of his shirt. The third soldier, a corporal, on the left has on an 1883-pattern field shirt. Other interesting details include the fact that both the corporal and Erickson have 1876-pattern campaign hats on, while the third member of the trio has opted for either a cowboy hat or an early version of the 1883-pattern campaign hat. Further, Erikson has obtained a pair of 1884-pattern gauntlets and 1884-pattern boots, while the other two individuals remain shod with 1876-pattern boots. NPS

In 1883 general orders dictated that cord in branch colors would no longer be worn on the collar or cuffs of enlisted blouses, either, as seen in the case of this example for a first sergeant of infantry from the period. Photographs by Robert L. Sanders. JG

In contrast, the privates of the Fourth U.S. Infantry band were decked out in dark blue coats trimmed with scarlet braid on the breast, sleeves, back, and collar. White epaulets with dark blue tops, presumably of worsted, along with a white waist belt and white cross belt added to the effect. Trousers were light blue with scarlet stripes, edged in dark blue. This was topped off by a helmet surmounted by a scarlet buffalo plume. In turn, the chief musician appeared in the same outfit, except for the addition of gold epaulets and dark blue trouser stripes edged in scarlet. The drum major also had light blue trousers, but the scarlet stripes were edged in gold. The dark blue coat contrasted with its scarlet cuffs, collar, trim on the back, and plastron. Gold epaulets and aiguillette, white belt, and bearskin shako with white and blue plume further set this figure apart. Finally, the chief musician had a uniform of the same length as officers, adorned with gold epaulets and a gold lace belt. All this was pleasing to Colonel William Carlin, who was then in command, although he desired dark blue or blue-black trousers rather than ones of "Saxony blue."[196] Colonel John D. Wilkins

of the Fifth U.S. Infantry disagreed. He preferred light blue kersey trousers, but wanted double white stripes to be sewn on the outer seams. White facings were desired for coats, as well. Mounted helmets without the breast cord, but with white mohair or woolen bands and a white fountain plume were deemed appropriate. The same overall arrangement was advocated for the principal musician and sergeant, but white sergeant stripes were to be substituted, and gold lace chevrons of the type recently adopted ought to be added, Wilkins wrote. His concept for the uniform of a chief musician was a single breasted dark blue frock coat, "the same as formerly worn by line officers," combined with sky blue trousers with black stripes that measured 1 1/4 inches wide. Gilt shoulder knots similar to those worn by officers in the U.S. Marine Corps, and the same helmet as he had described for the rest of the band would complete the chief musician's finery. The Seventh U.S. Infantry's commander, John Gibbon, departed further from the norm, supporting a proposed swallowtail coat with white facings proposed by Lieutenant C.A. Worden of his regiment. Gibbon added that "a tinge of yellow or orange would be better as giving a desirable contrast and less liable to become soiled.[197]

First Lieutenant Clarence M. Baily, the regimental adjutant who oversaw the Eighth U.S. Infantry's band, spoke for that unit. He preferred "a bright appropriate uniform," but acknowledged that it was difficult "to arrange a dress that would be economical and yet look well." Despite the challenge, he presented a tinted illustration depicting the crimson and white facings of the dress uniforms, which in his estimation was the best color combination. Moreover, he declared "a white cord aiguillette as worn by the West Point band would also be an improvement." As to the forage cap, he indicated "two pieces of narrow white braid around the bottom about one inch apart with a suitable ornament in front" would look well. The Eighth wore such a cap with a silver braid. Finally, he thought that whatever design was decided upon, the coats should be "furnished from the individual measurements taken from each man, but that the trousers should be sent *unmade*."[198]

Colonel Richard Dodge wanted his Eleventh U.S. Infantry band to have a spiked dress helmet with white worsted braid, and standard infantry dress coat trimmed with white facings and herringbone on the chest terminating in loops. One and a half inch white stripes seemed just the thing for the sky-blue trousers, while a white worsted belt or one of white leather without sword, held by a brass buckle was another

A half dozen enlisted men of Company I of the Battalion of Engineers depict the 1881 through 1884 dress uniform for that branch, including the dress helmet and trim of scarlet piped in white for coat, chevrons, and trouser stripes. The men at the far right and left are in the proper garrison uniform as it had evolved by 1884. DPL

Besides the muskrat cap and the forage cap, straw hats continued to be an optional item of wear with the five-button enlisted sack coat, as this cavalry sergeant portrays. The chevrons on his blouse have been customized to be curved, rather than straight as issued. FAM

This infantry sergeant has gone one step further and added tailor-made chevrons of sky blue facing cloth to his blouse of the 1883-pattern. He also has followed regulations by placing service chevrons on the blouse, a feature that does not appear frequently in photographs of the era, despite the fact that it was official policy to wear these marks of distinction. By 1884, however, orders were released prohibiting service marks to be worn, except in the case of the dress coat. The sergeant also has attached 1880-pattern collar marksmanship buttons to his collar. His belt and belt plate are part of the M1874 Palmer Brace system, which had been abandoned much earlier, but which was still being issued in part at this later date. HP

A corporal of engineers in the 1881-84 dress uniform. BU

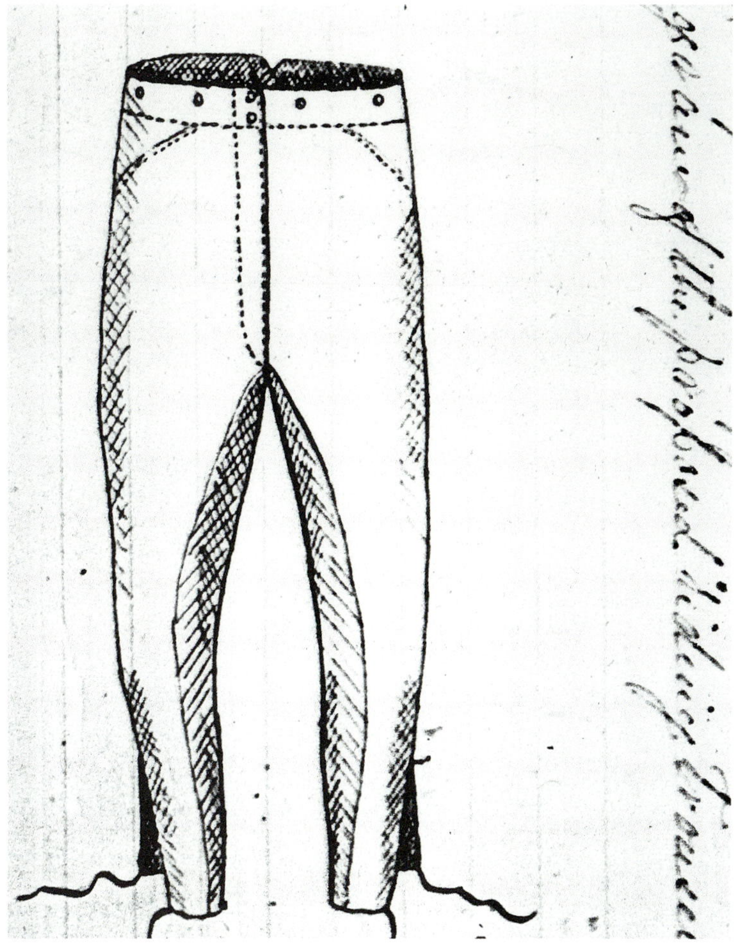

A suggestion to adopt breeches for mounted troops with tie-string at the bottom was considered in 1884, but not acted upon until more than a decade later, and then only for officers. NA

of his preferences. He submitted that a pouch should be attached to the belt that was similar in "shape to the old pattern cartridge boxes, for the purpose of carrying music."[199]

A far more detailed response came from First Lieutenant Frederick Smith, the regimental adjutant of the Twelfth U.S. Infantry. He provided a verbal description of the uniform worn by his unit's band, which he contended was "admired by both those in and out of the Army in regard to its general effect and appearance." During the previous half dozen years the lieutenant had given considerable thought to the band, and desired "to create as neat and showy a uniform as possible, as well as the least expensive, taking the full dress uniform of a private as the basis." What this entailed was the addition of two rows of buttons flanking the center buttons, and those on either side were to be placed in such a way as to provide "a curved appearance." All buttons were of better quality than those issued by the Quartermaster Department, however, and cost $6.00 per gross for coat size and $3.00 per gross for cuff size.

The front of the coat was "ornamented on the breast with two rows of white mohair braid 3/8 inch wide between each outside button terminating in a pointed fold at the outer button." Two rows of the same braid were sewn to the standing collar "extending back about two inches from" the opening of the collar and were applied over the facings. Three double rows of the same braid ran from the outer seam of the coat sleeve halfway around the cuff, where a small button was placed at the end of each row of braid. Sky-blue trousers with 1 1/2 inch white stripes, and a

The waistband, rear pocket, belted back, and watch pocket of a pair of 1884-pattern trousers, in this case for a sergeant of cavalry. Also evident is part of the "saddling" in the seat. SI

dress helmet with white horsehair plume completed the finery. The bandsmen likewise had a forage cap on which a gold embroidered wreath and lyre were displayed. Buff worsted and gilt epaulets, a buff leather waist belt with white metal plate, and a music pouch bearing the 1 1/2 inch long regimental numbers in white metal were provided, as well. The total cost for each man was $14.25.

As for the drum major, a white bearskin with brass scale chin strap set him off from the rest of the group. Three rows of buttons adorned the chest, which had a white plastron edged in narrow gold braid. Gold braid likewise trimmed the sleeves. The coat itself was a swallow tail, with the gold epaulets of the pattern worn prior to 1872 by officers. A blue baldric trimmed in gold along the edges and a gilt sword belt with sword were added as a final touch. The lieutenant particularly liked the appearance of the swallow tail, and favored the entire band wearing such a garment. He lamented that the regulation full dress, however, precluded alteration by cutting away the front panels "as the skirt of the present coat is too short to admit of altering to this style."[200]

Another infantry officer, Colonel J.H. Potter, who commanded the Twenty-fourth, likewise approved of the plastron, or "shield" front, with triple buttons. He wanted this to be of a bright color and match any other trim or facings on the coat.[201]

Cavalrymen had their say, as evidenced by a few representative replies. For instance, the Second Cavalry band wore the issue coat for dress, but also added "brass buttons at the ends of the herring-bones making three lines of buttons." Further, braid appeared at the back seams of the dress coat. These terminated in herring-bones at the shoulders. A single knot of braid appeared on the sleeves. Trousers displayed double yellow cavalry trumpeter stripes with a red stripe between the two. The Second retained standard cavalry dress helmets to top off their outfit. Their colonel, William Hatch, believed all these items should be furnished by the Quartermaster Department without additional cost. His final point was to call for the adoption of a small gilt lyre for the forage cap.[202]

The cuffs of the 1884-pattern trousers not only had a slight flare or spring to them, but also had two buttons on each inside for mounted versions that allowed a leather strap to be attached, making it possible for the trooper to keep the legs from riding up the calf when on horseback. The interior of the cuff was also lined. Once again, a portion of the saddling, or reinforcement, is evident, as is the 1/2 inch yellow facing cloth stripe of a cavalry corporal. SI

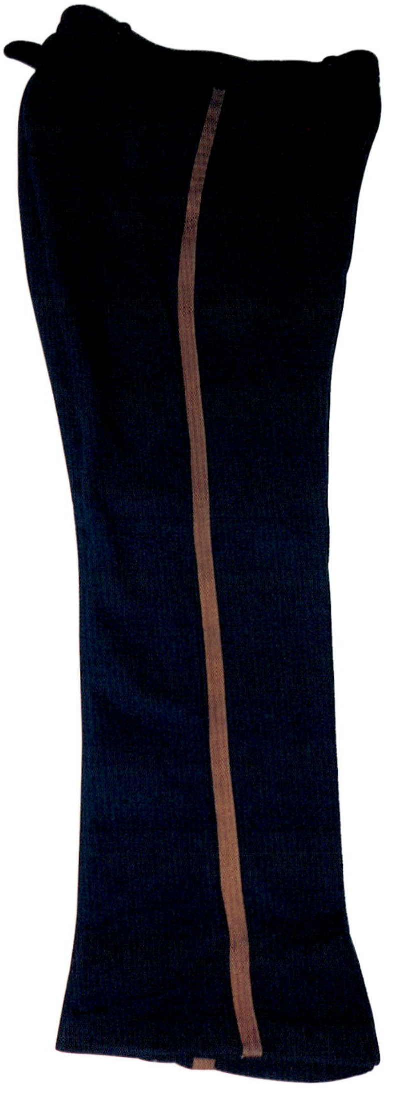

A pair of 1884-pattern corporal of cavalry trousers. SI

From the Fourth U.S. Cavalry, Colonel William B. Royall expressed a preference for the dress coat as issued, but with the addition of a lyre in the color of the facings being worn above each elbow, and below the elbow a knot of braid in the color of the facing. Interestingly, while several officers from dismounted regiments had been enamored with plumed helmet. Colonel Royall held an opposite point of view. He wanted to do away with the plume for bands and use the spike instead. This suggestion was "made because the plume is heavy; and, in windy weather interferes with the reading of music." Additionally, he fancied sky blue trousers trimmed with two-tone stripes, the centers being of some hue such as black and measuring 1/2 inch, while 1/2 inch trim of the facing color would appear on each side of the center stripe. In all cases he advocated the facing to be that of the branch color. As for blouses, the regulation issue was fine, but once more he suggested "a lyre chevron to be worn above the elbow." Colonel Royall then completed his list with the forage cap, which he thought should display as silver or gold metal lyre and 1 1/4 inch gilt cap cord.[203]

Colonel Horatio G. Gibson exhibited another method in arriving at what his Third U.S. Artillery Regiment saw as the ideal band ensemble. He convened a regimental council of three artillery company grade officers to review the subject. They judged "the full dress uniform of the band" should conform "with the uniform of the troops with which they are serving as nearly as possible." In their case the dress coat worn by artillery musicians was ideal, with sky blue trousers that had one inch stripes for sergeants and two half inch stripes for privates of the band, both in scarlet facing material. As additional marks of distinction, the spiked helmet could have an officer's style chin chain added, and the coat collar could be edged with quarter inch gold lace, as could the shoulder straps and sleeve facings. Another modification might be dark blue trousers with one inch gold lace stripes on the outer seams edged with half inch scarlet cloth on each. A music box that could be worn on a new type of belt also was deemed of merit.

As for the drum major, a bearskin with scarlet plume received a positive vote, to be combined with a double-breasted tunic having scarlet collar facings and a "breast shield trimmed with gold lace." Once more dark blue trousers with scarlet edged gold lace were viewed as optimum. The colonel agreed with most of the conclusions, but added that lyres would be appropriate cap ornaments, while plumes and aiguillettes could be added with good results.[204]

Colonel Jonathan Hamilton, Gibson's counterpart with the Fifth U.S. Artillery, made only one observation. He advanced a design for chevrons to be worn by drum majors. The concept was little more than two pairs of sergeant's stripes joined so as to form a more or less diamond shape, not unlike the regimental commissary sergeant's device that had been regulation from 1867 to 1870.[205]

In 1884, a new officer's overcoat that resembled the old cloak coat of pre-1872 design, became regulation. Rank continued to be depicted on the cuffs by braid, in this case for a major. Photograph by Glen Swanson. GS

A single braid on the cuff of the 1884-pattern officer's overcoat designated a first lieutenant, two braids a captain, and so forth as in the past, with second lieutenants, additional second lieutenants, and chaplains having no braid on the cuffs. GS

From these and other replies the Quartermaster Department eventually would prepare several additional items for issuance to regimental bands. Even then, a certain degree of latitude remained, most particularly in the cases of certain accessories and headgear. In the latter category, the pillbox cap, a style that had been adopted on a limited basis even before the Civil War and that had gained some credence, particularly among officers as a sort of walking out head dress, saw at least limited use with some bands.[206]

While the input related to band uniforms would not immediately bear fruit, another area of consideration again prompted action within the department. For some time the quartermaster general had lobbied to no avail for the appointment of staff non-commissioned officers analogous to post commissary sergeants, who would serve in the capacity of enlisted assistants to acting quartermaster officers stationed in various garrisons around the country. The officers so designated often were reassigned with frequency. For the most part they were not from the Quartermaster Department. These conditions made it attractive to have a full-time, dedicated senior NCO at the post to handle the daily operations and to provide continuity. Finally, Congress agreed, allowing for up to eighty men to be employed as post quartermaster sergeants.

With this addition to the ranks, Holabird moved ahead with his desire "to adopt a badge or insignia for the newly created Post Quartermaster Sergeants," along with appropriate chevrons that he ordered to have made in gold lace, one prototype pair to bear an acorn and another to have a trefoil embroidered in silk upon the cloth. He also called for "a pair of cloth chevrons (one with an acorn and one with a trefoil embroi-

The 1884-pattern officer's overcoat could be worn with or without cape. In turn, the cape could be worn without the overcoat. The lining was in the branch color. WC

Above and Opposite: Front, side, and rear views of the 1884-pattern officer's "ulster" overcoat, with the optional hood not being worn. NA

dered in silk of buff color)," and another "pair of chevrons (one with an acorn and one with a trefoil cut out) with the facing cloth stitched underneath, the same as for non-commissioned officers" to be made up for review. These designs were "to be of the 2" & 14" Army Corps as shown on the chart of Corps badges used during the late War." He further desired "a design for a badge for the forage cap (embroidered) and the helmet eagle, of both the acorn and the trefoil." Finally, Holabird opened the way to other suggestions for "any other design that may suggest itself...." Consultation with Horstmann and J. Wilson, who had "designers in their employ," was encouraged, as well, in the hope that something suitable might be developed.

In addition to the other designs, a crossed key and quill motif was considered "in gold thread or silk...for cloth chevrons," while another concept was advanced for gold lace chevrons embroidered in gold thread "which if properly raised will be quite effective. The design represents the ancient Roman fascine." One of these insignia might be used for the cap, as well, although it was still being discussed as to whether the devices for caps would be embroidered or of metal.[207] Even "the letters Q.D. embroidered either in silk, silver or gold" was presented as a possibility, which harkened back to the insignia proposed in 1872 for other non-commissioned staff officers who were to wear the "O.D." for Ordnance Department and the like.[208]

After all this discourse the crossed key and pen was selected for quartermaster sergeants. On the gold lace chevron it was to be "of gold thread and for cloth chevrons in yellow silk." Further, the first rendition of the device required the barrel of the key to "be lengthened somewhat

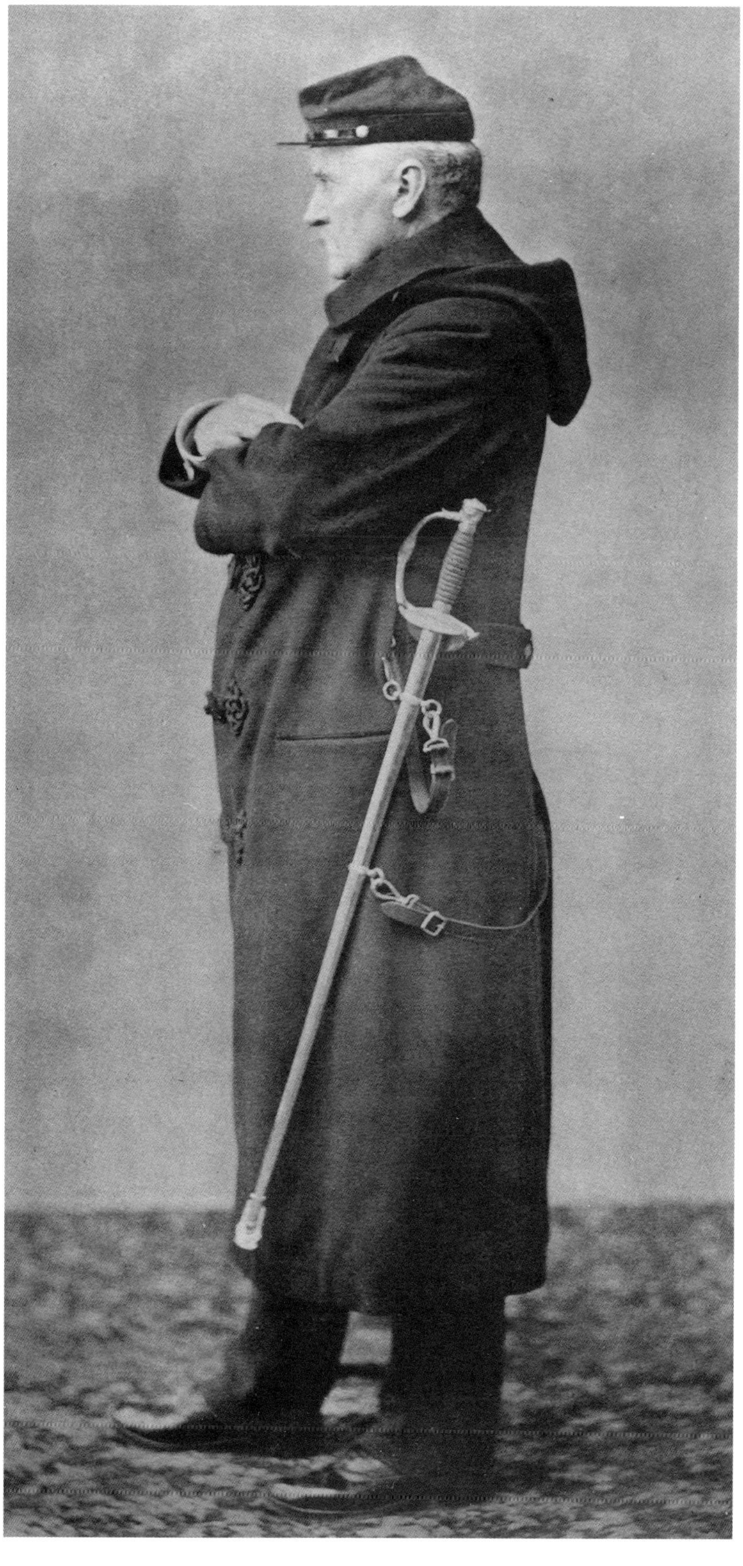

For inclement weather, the hood or cowl, which was of matching cloth to the coat, could be worn up over the forage cap. NA

Right: In 1884, a hood or canvas cap made of brown canvas on the outside and lined originally with light colored jean, then as of 1886 with red wool, was introduced. There was an abbreviated visor that could be unhooked and let down, or this could be worn in an up position against the forehead. This headgear could be combined with the fatigue suit in cold weather climates, or with the canvas overcoat. The matching brown canvas mittens also formed part of the foul weather kit. JG

Officers of the Fifth and Twenty-five U.S. Infantry regiments wear a variety of overcoat styles during the transitional period of the mid-1880s, including an 1872-pattern (far left with gilt buttons), buffalo overcoats, and several of the ulster overcoats introduced in 1884. NA

between the junction of the key, and the ring of the key, making the total length 2 inches instead of 2 1/2 inches as in pattern."[209]

Sufficient details had been attended for the quartermaster general to request a new general order be published for quartermaster sergeants' uniforms.[210] That information was contained in General Orders No. 107, Headquarters of the Army, September 12, 1884, which listed and briefly described both cloth chevrons and gold lace chevrons for all non-commissioned officers and specialists, including quartermaster sergeants, as well as stipulated that the dress uniform of a post quartermaster sergeant would be the same as for infantry, except that the facings were to be buff, as well as the leg stripes, which were to measure 1 1/4 inches wide and be of cloth.[211] Even then, word came from Washington that it was premature to order post quartermaster sergeant uniforms, because it was not certain to which installations they would be assigned.[212]

During this interim, the designation of the pen and key "surmounted by a wreath of the pattern worn by Hospital Stewards" as the device for the caps of quartermaster sergeants was established as proper, and eventually the crossed key and pen in German silver would be used as the helmet overlay with helmet side buttons of a similar style being prescribed, as well. These would require new dies to be made for fabrication, but one other detail related to post quartermaster sergeants could be obtained by purchase on the open market. This action grew from an idea that the newly prescribed dress coat for these men should bear staff buttons of the style worn by staff officers for generations. The cost of this undertaking was studied to ascertain how expensive implementation would be.[213]

Another innovation of 1884 was a brown canvas duck fatigue suit that consisted of a blouse and trousers, which could be combined with the 1883-pattern campaign hat or the canvas hood. NA

Circular No. 11, Headquarters of the Army, December 10, 1884, stated: "The only decorations allowed to be worn on occasion of ceremony are the 'army corps badge,' authorized by section 1227 of the Revised Statutes; the 'medal of honor;' and several distinctive marks given for excellence in rifle practice, as prescribed by existing regulations." As seen here, cavalry Sergeant Charles Dulkinbrager exhibits the marksmanship devices on the collar of his dress coat, the numerals and branch insignia having been discontinued in 1884 for troops, the year this portrait was taken. It also is likely that he had cut his helmet cords to separate them from the bands attached to the helmet. FAM

While new officers' overcoats were deemed appropriate for cold weather, white canvas forage cap covers seemed just the thing for junior officers during the summer while attending the Artillery School at Ft. Monroe, Virginia, in the mid-1880s. RB

In 1884, in addition to the Laidley collar devices, a marksmanship badge (bottom) that was to be worn on the left side of the chest, and a sharpshooter's cross, which was to be worn at the throat, were added to the decorations that could be displayed on the uniform. According to regulations, one of these devices could be worn by an individual, but the two were not to be combined. TT

The bill for such an undertaking was negligible in comparison to the decision that a totally "new and more clearly defined button" would replace the version adopted for enlisted in 1854.[214] While the two sizes for the chest and cuff remained pretty much the same, the eagle itself was very different, being somewhat more abstract than its predecessor in that it had an elongated neck and shortened wings. A specification would not be adopted until March 27, 1885, however, and even then the standard practice of issuing old buttons was instituted so that the fire gilded versions envisioned in 1884 were not available in large numbers for the time being.

Moreover, limited production of new dies resulted from an initiative to replace the frail, easily broken cap ornaments with stronger devices, although the quest would entail considerable expense if carried out on an army-wide basis. Nevertheless, under Holabird the Quartermaster Department acknowledged the various individual efforts by enlisted men to cope with this problem, and took up the challenge of finding a satisfactory solution.[215]

In one instance department officials replied to a series of suggestions that included the strengthening of cap insignia and the discontinuance of collar devices for the dress coat. Captain Rodgers assured the writer, Captain Robert Smith, who commanded a company of the Tenth U.S. Cavalry at Ft. Davis, Texas, that in the former case the matter was

Private C.M. Scaten's 1872-pattern dress coat no longer bears the sheet brass 1/2 inch regimental numbers, which were discontinued in 1884. FAM

Signal Corps personnel never wore collar insignia on their uniform coats, as substantiated by this mid-1880s photograph of First Class Private William Washington Neifert. The cords, plume, and facings on his coat are orange. The helmet is a recut 1872-pattern with the old style plume staff and base, but new 1881-pattern helmet plate. The saber belt may be a photographer's prop, because it is an officer's model. USAMHI

In 1884 gold lace service stripes and chevrons were introduced, and in due course replaced cloth ones on enlisted uniform coats, such as this example for a private of the Ordnance Department who had completed three enlistments. At the same time, service stripes were discontinued for use on blouses and overcoats.

The new gold lace chevrons for Signal Corps non-commissioned officers were to be combined with the crossed flag devices adopted in the previous decade as seen in the case of an 1872-pattern dress coat for a signal sergeant that has had the 1884-pattern gold lace chevrons added. SI

being pursued.[216] As part of these attempts to find a better insignia, Holabird sent word to First Lieutenant Sebree Smith of the Second U.S. Artillery asking if the young officer knew "of a suitable design for adoption for the Artillery arm of the service which can be worn in connections with the crossed cannon, leaving sufficient room for the letter of the company and number of the regiment...."[217] As a model, a design akin to Hancock's I Army Corps Veteran Volunteers badge (a septagon sunburst with the regimental number in white metal placed in the center) or Sheridan's Cavalry Corps (a glory in silver with gold crossed sabers in the center on a background in the color of the respective division—red for first, white for second, and blue for third) were mentioned to Lieutenant Smith.

Within a few days the range was expanded to include the preparation of cost estimates for cap badges required by cavalry, artillery, infantry, and ordnance personnel, along with hospital stewards. Jacob Jacobus, who had been responsible for producing the helmet eagle dies, was recommended as a potential source for ascertaining how much of an outlay would be required for steel dies for new cap insignia. Holabird further shared that while the badges themselves should be brass, the numbers, castles, flaming shell, and caduceus elements would be of white metal.[218]

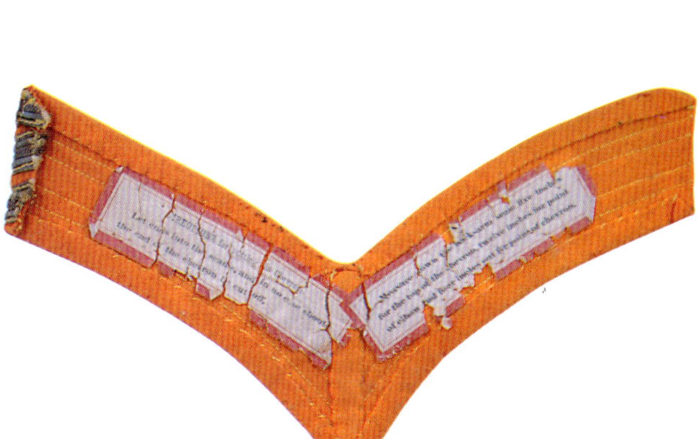

Back of a gold lace chevron, in this case for a Signal Corps sergeant. Printed instructions are visible as to care for these costly, easily tarnished insignia. JG

Front of a gold lace signal sergeant's chevron and a service in war stripe for a signalmen. JG

As another preliminary a "die for the cavalry arm of the service" was to be cut according to sketches furnished from the quartermaster general's office. The conceptual drawing featured a set of crossed sabers in bold relief upon a shield or background of a cluster of rays, again being something akin to the Sheridan Cavalry Corps badge, no doubt to the delight of the lieutenant general for whom the insignia was named. The cost estimate to produce this experimental design was $43.75 from the firm of Thomas Davis. Once the die was produced some samples in brass were to be struck, and white metal numbers and letters of the type then in use for helmet, collar, and forage cap insignia attached.[219] Then some inexpensive lead mockups were produced, which Holabird found to be suitable.[220] After that casts were made of cap ornaments from a composition of aluminum and cooper, and the quartermaster general even advanced the idea that some sample buttons of this material also should be produced.[221]

Taking yet a different tact, Captain Edmund L. Zalinski's submission of some cap ornaments made in imitation embroidery were "considered as great improvement over the metallic ornaments" then being issued to the men. Zalinski, who commanded a battery of the Fifth U.S. Artillery, therefore was invited to tell Rodgers "how and where they can be obtained and at what cost in quantity."[222]

In the final analysis, however, these details proved of little immediate value, because over a decade passed before the Quartermaster Department at last developed a replacement for the frail 1872-pattern cap devices.[223] Thus, only one aspect related to enlisted cap devices actually was resolved in 1884, when Sheridan announced his preference for cavalry trumpeters to wear crossed sabers rather than bugle devices, which had been adopted in the mid-1870s for field musicians.[224]

But this was not the only activity related to insignia in that year, because the Quartermaster Department sought examples of "the forage cap badge for officers of the Signal Corps which according to paragraph 2629 of the Regulations is deposited with the Chief Signal Officer of the Army."[225] Once that request had been attended to by the office of the chief of the Signal Corps, William B. Hazen, Holabird followed up with two samples of signal officers' badges. These were accompanied by a request for the chief signal officer to select the one that he desired as standard for his organization. The letter further noted: "The manufacturers state that the one attached to the card is frequently ordered by officers of the Signal Corps."[226] By May 9, 1884, this exchange prompted the printing of a memorandum that not only described the cap device, but also spelled out the helmet plate and shoulder knots that were to be worn for full dress by the second lieutenants of the corps. The description for the cap called for a gold and silver bullion device on a dark blue background that represented two square crossed flags and a burning torch in the center surrounded by a wreath. The shoulder knots were to bear the same device in size, but without the wreath. The background presumably was to be of orange facing cloth. Finally, the plate for the full dress helmet carried on the theme, with the torch and crossed flags being placed behind the breast shield on the eagle, much as crossed rifles, sabers, and cannon were for the infantry, cavalry, and artillery

Rear of the tail trim and belt loops of a Signal Corps sergeant's dress coat with the gold lace chevrons. The belt loops were to be removed from dress coats in 1884, as well, but this was not universally accomplished for some years. SI

The 1872-pattern infantry dress coat (left), along with its counterparts for other branches, remained relatively unchanged for nearly a dozen years. In 1884 the 1/2 inch sheet brass numerals on the collar were no longer to be worn, and the belt loops were to be removed. Further, gold lace service chevrons (as seen here) and non-commissioned officers' chevrons were to replace those of facing cloth. Photograph by Glen Swanson. JG

In late 1884 a circular order was sent to all regimental commanders requesting that they respond about the type of uniforms bandsmen wore in their unit, and soliciting suggestions about improvements or items that were deemed appropriate for supply by the Quartermaster Department. The response from headquarters of the Eighth U.S. Infantry stationed at Angel Island, California, included this watercolor, depicting a suggested uniform for bandsmen. NA

officers. Sketches accompanied the memorandum to make certain there was no misunderstanding, while an example of each of the three items was transmitted to the quartermaster general.

This material was timely in that a request from Horstmann regarding the design for the shoulder knots and cap device prescribed for signal officers by General Orders No. 30, Headquarters of the Army, April 14, 1884, could be clarified.[227] In fact, copies of the drawings provided by Hazen could be forwarded in reply to the firm's letter.[228]

Another directive published by the Adjutant General's Department, General Orders No. 12, Headquarters of the Army, February 20, 1884, established the grade of sharpshooter. Although the program was administered under the auspices of the Ordnance Department, the system established to recognize proficiency with carbines and rifles impacted on the uniform in that the marksmanship devices first proposed in 1880 became a regular feature of the outer wear. The scheme called for the wearing of a pair of marksmanship buttons on the collar of the coat and blouse for men who qualified during the current year. If an individual again qualified for a second year in a row, he could wear two pairs of the target-like devices. After qualifying three times (not necessarily in consecutive years) he was entitled to a marksmanship pin that was "to be worn on the left breast." At that point, no more than a pair of the buttons could be worn in tandem with the pin, which originally was a rather garish bronze bar with arabesque swirls that was very much a product of Gilded Age design. This was followed by a more stately sharpshooter's bronze cross that was to be pinned "below the opening of the coat collar as long as a man retained his status by a firing score of 88 percent or better at 200, 300, and 600 yards, and 76 percent or above at 800, 900, and 1,000 yards." Once a man ceased to make these scores, he retained the cross, but wore it on the left chest of the coat or blouse. There were also handsome medals in precious metals, which were awarded for departmental, divisional, and army-wide best shots.[229]

From the Seventeenth U.S. Infantry came a hand-tinted front, side, and rear view of a regimental bandsman from that unit. The idea was that the uniform already in use by the regiment was considered handsome and adequate for the purpose. NA

Many infantry bands, including this one from the Twenty-third U.S. Infantry stationed at Ft. Union, New Mexico Territory, in 1883, had white facings, despite the fact that the branch color was sky blue. FSHM

While the top prizes were fabricated at the U.S. Mint in Philadelphia and were costly as well as professionally rendered, the first permutation of the devices for regular marksmen and sharpshooters were not as distinguished. This provoked one soldier to send a letter to the editor of the *Army and Navy Journal* to decry the Ordnance Department's effort, expressing: "In this case I merely give utterance to a universal growl about those new decorations, the marksmanship pin and sharpshooter's cross. We are all disappointed, we expected something neat and tasty, something the wearer would not be ashamed of. The marksmanship pin looks more like a door-plate than anything else."[230]

Others evidently shared this disappointment, including the chief of the Ordnance Department, Brigadier General Stephen V. Benét. By 1885 refined designs replaced earlier versions, but regardless of the styles, both officers and men now had an outward means to recognize their proficiency with long arms.[231] Another 1884 general order that impacted both officers and men had to do with the final proclamation by President Chester A. Arthur announcing the United States' adherence to the Geneva Convention. General Orders No. 90, Headquarters of the Army, August 8, 1884, set forth the requirement that army regulations would be modified to include a distinguishable method accepted by all the signatories of the agreement to mark ambulances, hospitals, and noncombatants. In the latter instance, individuals were to wear a white brassard measuring sixteen inches long by three inches and bearing a red two inch by two inch cross in the center. From that point forward the device remained, and became famous as the symbol for medics in the American army, as well as in many other military forces. These were to be worn in addition to any military rank that the wearer might hold.[232] Thus, chevrons continued for non-commissioned officers, while shoulder straps remained in use for officers.

Nor was this the only undertaking during 1884 related to officers. In that year the idea for the Quartermaster Department to provide officers with dress helmets and cloth was investigated. While officers had been allowed to buy material from the department in the past, in late 1884 a plan was considered to stock dress helmets for them as well. Pursuant to this line of thinking, Holabird wanted to secure "150 helmets, of suitable sizes and in proportion to the officers of each arm of the service," while at the same time stockpiling 500 yards of various appropriate cloths needed to make all types of officers' clothing.[233] For several weeks he had his operatives particularly looking into the matter of the helmets. In the process, three officers' buffalo hair plumes were bought with sockets, one for each of the line organizations, and these were mounted on cards that were marked according to branch. At the same time, enlisted cavalry, artillery, and signal horsehair plumes and sheet brass sockets were to be attached to labeled cards and sent to Holabird.[234] Additionally, the costs of mounted and dismounted helmets were requested, although this was to be done discretely. Comparisons were to be obtained from Raymold and Whitlock, Warnock, Allien, and others, but caution was urged so as not to make Holabird's purpose public for fear that there would be "a certain amount of reticence and equivocation if not deceit among the dealers" if they learned why the information was gathered. The idea was to determine what an individual officer would pay versus a bulk order from the department.[235] Samples and prices were obtained, but in the end the conclusion that was reached demonstrated such a small savings to the individual officer as not to warrant the government incurring expenses to provide the service. With that, the specimens were either to be returned to the vendors, or if the dealers

In 1884, a helmet plate with burning torch and crossed signal flags was approved for the few Signal Corps officers then authorized for that small organization. This example was made by the firm of Henry V. Allien, and worn by Second Lieutenant Leroy E. Sebree. SI

wished to sell them, they could be bought for future reference and safekeeping at Philadelphia.[236]

Although it did not make economic sense to procure helmets for officers, the quartermaster general was willing to try to improve the enlisted forage caps. Although a contract for 12,000 forage caps was let early in 1884 to the firm of A. Wheeler for just under $53 per hundred, a small quantity of caps also were produced with leather rather than the traditional pasteboard interior tops. The was done in reply to complaints that the pasteboard did not have a great deal of strength and therefore broke. The secretary of war allowed some samples to be made up and given out at no charge to the enlisted men who were to wear them as a test. For this reason, these caps were supplied to troops at Forts Monroe, Hamilton, McHenry, and Washington Barracks.[237]

Even as the Quartermaster Department sought to strengthen the cap, it also moved forward on provisions for cold weather and other practical requirements. In this regard, the kersey lined "Miles overcoats" that had not been drawn by the men were sent to the Department of Dakota for gratuitous issue to the troops.[238] This was done with the realization that the coat was not as popular as some thought it might be with the rank and file. Besides, the new blanket-lined canvas overcoat was perceived as providing the necessary protection in extremely cold climates, by being both warm and resistent to moisture, while at the same time being less problematic than buffalo coats, given that the bison herds were nearly depleted.[239] Moreover, a new great coat had been adopted, one that not only was kersey-lined for warmth, but also featured several other advantages, including being made in the six new sizes rather than five, and that had the removable cape fitted with stout metal hooks, rather than button holes that were attached to metal eyes strongly sewn under the coat collar, rather than using the small cuff buttons as in the past. Other alterations included the widening of sleeves and the discontinuance of cuffs that had been standard on previous patterns.[240] There also was a provision for hooks fitted to the front of the skirts so that these could be folded back and attached to heavy thread loops if the foot soldier so wished when marching, giving a look often associated with the French Foreign Legion. Final specifications were completed in late September 1884, after some nine months of refining, and were to replace the interim standards adopted on March 8 of the same year.[241]

Leather gauntlets were another item that required standards to be prepared in 1884. Previously officers often bought such riding gloves in a variety of styles. The rank and file, however, usually had no such accessories to protect their hands on mounted service. Some enlisted men occasionally may have used some of their pay to acquire gauntlets, but finally the government saw fit to provide them, as the department's annual report recorded:

> A desideratum, long felt, has been supplied by obtaining the authority from the honorable Secretary of War to supply leather gauntlets to all mounted men of the Army. It has been possible to do this by rearranging the allowance of Berlin gloves. By giving the mounted men annually one pair of the latter, sufficient for parade purposes if deemed necessary, and three pairs of leather gauntlets during an enlistment of five years, this attractive and useful article has been added to the equipment of mounted men without additional cost to the Government.[242]

This fact was announced by General Orders No. 29, Headquarters of the Army, April 12, 1884.[243] While at first the supply was limited, the items were being issued to some units as early as the end of the summer of 1884.[244] This plan also contributed to the discontinuance of packaging Berlin gloves in sets of threes or providing them on an individual basis. The 1883 proposal simply failed, and the return to distributing the white gloves in pairs resumed.[245]

Conversely, another initiative from 1883, a study made by Captain Rodgers, concluded with a recommendation based upon a survey taken among many officers serving in the field that footgear with sewn soles should again be considered. Some respondents wanted brass screws and thread sewn soles, while others desired thread sewn soles only, and a few even proposed hobnails should be added for use in rugged terrain. Besides repeating the grievance about how the brass screws hurt the wearer's feet as they pushed through into the flesh, the stiffness of the leather used to make the issue shoe was another bone of contention. Rodgers compiled such remarks, then presented his remedies—sewn soles and a light garrison shoe made along the lines of an English model previously championed by the Miles Board. The captain went further. Besides a comfortable, flexible shoe for use on the post, a more rugged, high top type of footgear that rose about eight inches up over the ankle and lower leg seemed appropriate for the field.

While Ingalls was finishing his short term as quartermaster general, he indicated his sympathy to Rodgers' plan, and thought 500 test pairs should be made of both the "post" and the "field," as they came to be known, each type to be fastened with machine sewn thread rather than screws. He passed this opinion on to the secretary of war, who in turn agreed with the merit of the plan.[246]

Despite the fact that the process had started with Ingalls, the actual implementation of the project fell to Holabird, who then depended upon Captain Asa Blunt at Leavenworth to carry out the fabrication of the shoes, thereby triggering a series of exchanges between the two men.[247] Not surprising, Blunt voiced his own views on the matter, and succeeded in adding a third candidate to the list, a "campaign" shoe that laced up in front in keeping with past fashions, rather than the field shoe that was

Detail of Lieutenant Leroy E. Sebree's Signal Corps officer's helmet plate. SI

to be tried, which used a side buckle to close the uppers, somewhat like that used on Arctic overshoes.[248]

One of the features of the field shoe that was about to be issued was its promise of being "sufficiently high to cover and protect the ankle...." This meant that the custom of providing boots "to troops of all arms of service" would halt as soon as the brass screwed footgear had been used up and the new field shoe made available. Thereafter, the concept was to provide boots only to mounted troops, and here once again another style more conducive to wear exclusively on horseback was in the offing.[249]

In Rodgers' 1883 report, Captain Ada R. Chaffee of the Sixth U.S. Cavalry had been a proponent of not only light garrison shoes, but also of boots with a higher top. Earlier in January 1884 Holabird had examined five pairs of boots with "longer legs," and he was desirous of obtaining the secretary of war's reaction to experimental issue of the style.[250] The secretary had no objection. By the beginning of February Captain Blunt received word that 5,000 pairs with machine sewn soles were to be turned out by his convict work force. The uppers were to be of "wax uppers" similar to the field shoe, but the tops would be pebble grained leather. With this move, the hope was "that the difficult question of providing comfortable and serviceable foot-gear, suitable for Army purposes," would be attained.[251] The results of such wishful thinking were not to be known, however, until later, in that the various types of footgear generated in 1884 were not available in any numbers until the next year.[252]

This brief lag period did not detour Holabird's department from moving forward on other fronts, though. The day to day operations of letting contracts, publishing prices charged for articles as new items came into the system, and disposing of outdated goods all remained as part of the routine for his department.[253]

And ever cognoscente of details, the quartermaster general pointed out the requirement of a circular promulgated on May 7, 1877, requiring all clothes to be marked so as to identify them as government property. These were to bear the initials "USQMD."[254] As a further means of identifying the clothing, not only as official government issue, but also by unit and individual, the department expanded and improved the issuing of stencil plates for this purpose.[255] The practical ramifications that resulted from this process ranged from making it possible for items being returned from cleaning to reach the right men, as well as to root out theft if items were stolen, or in other instances sold illegally by soldiers.[256]

But what was near and dear to the quartermaster general's heart were efforts "to ascertain the value of whatever improvements" that could be made toward the betterment of the soldier's lot.[257] For instance, he had advocated sending clothing made of varying weights of material to the troops, as well as been supportive of a move to improve footgear.[258] One of the only places his department had not as yet managed to make inroads was the creation of "a special uniform for troops in the South," these attempts being thwarted by the Medical Department's strenuous objections based on the theory that woolen clothing and not cotton, which was under consideration, was the preferred material because of its absorbent qualities and other properties deemed to be more healthful by many military doctors of the era.[259]

Yet, all in all, by the end of 1884 the new quartermaster general must have been pleased with the progress made since the days when the old 1872-pattern uniform had somewhat grudgingly been implemented by his predecessor, the tireless but tradition bound Montgomery Meigs. Indeed, not long after his assumption of duties, Holabird had made significant inroads into achieving the objectives he had imposed on himself through "personnel attention and constant supervision to the improvements which he deemed advantageous and necessary for...comfort and efficiency" of the army. He had accomplished this by dedicating

Preliminary sketch of the Adjutant General's Department forage cap insignia rendered in 1884. NA

"much time and study to the needs of the enlisted men" with an aim "to ameliorate the conditions" in which they lived, as well as "to make them content, and awaken in them that soldierly pride so necessary to proper discipline."[260] While these were high-minded ends, the practicality of Holabird's work could not be denied after little more than eighteen months at the helm of the Quartermaster Department. Over the next several years Holabird's concepts and the labors of his department would undergo the acid test when troops braved the torrid deserts of the Southwest to the frigid Badlands of the high plains.

NOTES

1 In anticipation of this, Meigs let it be known that the dress cap would be replaced by a new helmet of a pattern submitted by Captain Rodgers; the discontinuance of the gray shirt for a dark blue one; and the abolishment of the unlined blouse. To be ready for these changes that were expected to be implemented on July 1, 1881, the department had to be prepared to have standards in place and preparations under way to make the clothing articles, as well as specifications drawn up and dies cut for the new helmets and insignia. M.D. Meigs to D.H. Rucker, January 9, 1881, LS, Clothing Br., Book A, 1881, OQMG, RG92, NA.

2 Chappell, *Brass Spikes and Horsetail Plumes*, 30-87, ably treats the evolution of the 1881-pattern dress helmet. As such, the discussion of this topic is kept to a minimum in the above text. Langellier, *Hats Off*, 64-99, provides a synopsis of the subject. Also see, M.C. Meigs to J.F. Rodgers, January 17, 1881; S.B. Holabird to Pettibone Manufacturers, January 19, 1881; M.C. Meigs to J. Tidball, February 1, 1881; M.C. Meigs to HQA, February 4, 1881; M.C. Meigs to D.H Rucker, February 12, 1881; M.C. Meigs to J.F. Rodgers, February 18, 1881; M.C. Meigs to D.H. Rucker, February 19, 1881; S.B. Holabird to D.H. Rucker, March 9, 1881; S.B. Holabird to J. F. Rodgers, March 9, 1881; M.C. Meigs to J.F. Rodgers, March 21, 1881; S.B. Holabird to D.H. Rucker, April 1, 1881; S.B. Holabird to J. Crane, April 2, 1881; and M.C. Meigs to D.H. Rucker, May 7, 1881, LS, Clothing Br., Book A, 1881, OQMG, RG92, NA.

3 General Sherman also indicated that regimental staff officers of infantry and heavy artillery, including adjutants, also were to wear the mounted helmet with plume. S.B. Holabird to J.F. Rodgers, March 25, 1881, ibid. This was an endorsement to an inquiry sent by a first lieutenant of the Fifteenth Infantry. See C.M. McKeever to J.S. Bishop, March 1881, ibid.

4 Chief Quartermaster Military Division of the Missouri; M.C. Meigs to Chief Quartermaster, Military Division of the Pacific; and M.C. Meigs to Chief Quartermaster Military Division of the Gulf, March 4, 1881, ibid.

Chapter Two: "No cause for serious complaint can be found," 1881-1884

5 Chappell, *Brass Spikes and Horsetail Plumes*, 31 and 34. It is possible some of the earliest dismounted helmets issued went to Colonel William Shafter's First U.S. Infantry in Texas. Five hundred were included in estimates for delivery. S.B. Holabird to Chief Quartermaster Military Division of Missouri, June 2, 1881, LS, Clothing Br., Book A, 1881, OQMG, RG, 92, NA. Ordnance enlisted personnel at the Springfield Arsenal also were acknowledged as having their estimates on hand for the new foot helmet according to S.B. Holabird to J.F. Rodgers, June 2, 1881, ibid.

6 M.C. Meigs to Secretary of War April 5, 1881, ibid. Despite the fiscal barriers, some 1,800 altered helmets with all components soon were on their way to the San Francisco Depot. S.B. Holabird to J.F. Rodgers, April 19, 1881, ibid.

7 M.C. Meigs to D.H. Rucker, May 12, 1881, ibid.

8 *ARSW, 1882*, Vol. I, 303, noted that this action took place as of February 7, 1882. Prior to that time, dress caps continued to be issued, while the new helmet was being made. As such, the pompons for these were not considered old pattern, nor were hat cords and tassels, which continued to be made available for issue with campaign hats. All other Civil War items in stock, however, were defined as old pattern. M.C. Meigs to J.A. Ekin, August 15, 1881, LS, Clothing Br., Book B, 1881, OQMG, RG92, NA. Old pattern clothing was to be held for issue to the National Home for Disabled Volunteers. M.C. Meigs to Secretary of War, August 18, 1881, ibid. his was in accordance with GO 113, WD, December 19, 1879, but this directive did not include surplus hat cords, cap covers, drawers, and shirts, which were to be sold at public auction. Somehow the Military Prison at Ft. Leavenworth had obtained many of these old pattern items slated for the home, including double-caped great coats, sack coats, trousers, and even new campaign hats. All but the latter were dyed blacked before issue to prisoners. These items were not permitted for convict use, causing the quartermaster general to request an explanation of how the material was received. M.C. Meigs to AGUSA, August 18, 1881, ibid.

9 M.C. Meigs to Major R.N. Batchelder, April 14, 1881, Book A, 1881, ibid. M.C. Meigs to J.F. Rodgers, May 23, 1881, ibid., required a telegraphic reply as to the cost of the staff corps devices. References to a request from one contractor for the eagle to be used so that bids could be made for their production are found in D.H. Rucker to S.B. Holabird, April 2, 1881; and S.B. Holabird to J. Crane, April 2, 1881, ibid. Some three thousand eagles were allowed to be purchased in open market at an estimated total cost of $168.75 as part of early efforts to provide these devices. S.B. Holabird to D.H. Rucker, September 27, 1881, Book B, 1881, ibid.

10 *ARSW, 1882*, Vol. I, 333. Another indication of the lack of funds for general distribution of the helmet is found in S.B. Holabird to A. Barrett, April 8, 1881, LS, Clothing Br., Book A, 1881, OQMG, RG92, NA, which included approval to send thirty infantry pompons to Columbus Barracks, thereby signifying caps were still in use while the helmet was not ready for distribution to all units. Elsewhere, cap eagles were being issued simultaneously with helmets for hospital stewards, cavalry, light artillery, ordnance, infantry, and commissary sergeants in the Department of Texas. Furthermore, the cords and bands for mounted helmets, along with scrolls, plumes, plume sockets, and side buttons, were to be taken from existing 1872-pattern stocks. M.C. Meigs to Chief Quartermaster Military Division of the Missouri, June 6, 1881, ibid.

11 M.C. Meigs to J. Rodgers, April 6, 1881, ibid.

12 S.B. Holabird to D.H. Rucker, April 19, 1881, ibid.

13 M.C. Meigs to J.F. Rodgers, March 29, 1881, ibid. Captain Rodgers was to visit the manufacturing establishments where the helmets and spikes were being made, as well as to inspect makers of campaign hats, arctic overshoes, woolen flannels, and kersey. M.C. Meigs to AGUSA, June 4, 1881, ibid.

14 M.C. Meigs to George W. Spencer, April 22, 1881, ibid.

15 M.C. Meigs to Chief Quartermaster Military Division of the Missouri, March 29, 1881; M.C. Meigs to R.W. Batchelder, April 14, 1881; S.B. Holabird to R.W. Batchelder, April 15, 1881; and S.B. Holabird to Chief Quartermaster Military Department of the South, June 10, 1881, ibid. S.B. Holabird to J.F. Rodgers, July 13, 1881, Book B, 1881, ibid., similarly indicated that no summer helmets would be sent to Ft. Keogh, Montana Territory. Nor at first was there money to provide summer helmets to the troops in Texas. S.B. Holabird to Chief Quartermaster Military Division of the Missouri, June 2, 1881, Book A, 1881, ibid. A complete list of items including summer helmets and dress helmets that were requested for the Department of Texas is contained in S.B. Holabird to Chief Quartermaster of the Military Division of the Missouri, June 6, 1881, ibid. Other indications of ongoing interest and issue of the summer helmet during this period are found in M.C. Meigs to D.H. Rucker, February 19, 1881; S.B. Holabird to Apple & Co., March 21, 1881, Book A, 1881; S.B. Holabird to M.I. Ludington, February 1, 1884, Book A, 1884; S.B. Holabird to M.I. Ludington, February 16, 1884, Book A, 1884; and J.F. Rodgers to Chief Quartermaster Military Division of the Atlantic, July 19, 1884, Book B, 1884, ibid.

16 M.C. Meigs to Secretary of War, January 28, 1881; and M.C. Meigs to AGUSA, June 7, 1881, Book A, 1881, ibid.

17 S.B. Holabird to Chief Quartermaster Military Division of the Missouri, June 2, 1881, ibid.

18 S.B. Holabird to J.F. Rodgers, July 13, 1881; and S.B. Holabird to Chief Quartermaster St. Louis Depot Quartermaster, July 19, 1881, Book B, 1881, ibid.

19 M.C. Meigs to Secretary of War, May 13, 1881, ibid. One of these emergency situations arose when flooding along the Missouri River resulted in the issue of military clothing to civilians who had be left destitute. M.C. Meigs to Secretary of War, August 6, 1881; M.C. Meigs to S. Breck, April 18, 1881; and M.C. Meigs to St. Louis Quartermaster Depot, April 18, 1881, Book B, 1881, ibid.

20 R.C. Drum to Commanding General Department of the South, August 24, 1881, ibid. As to the chapeau, the adjutant general of the Ohio National Guard sought clarification as to what the item looked like in so far as the side ornament was concerned. He was informed this decoration consisted "of a rosette of heavy black watered silk, crossed at an angle about 45 degrees to the base of the chapeau, by a gold bullion strap, on the lower end of which is a gilt staff button and near the upper end (slightly above the center of the rosette) the Arms of the U.S. in gilt metal." S.B. Holabird to Adjutant General State of Ohio, December 30, 1881, ibid.
The matter of accessories for the enlisted summer helmet seemed to cause some confusion, or at least raise certain questions. It in fact was designed to be worn without trimmings. Consequently, no insignia, spikes, or the like were provided by the Quartermaster Department when orders for such articles were received from the field. J.F. Rodgers to Chief Quartermaster Military Division of the Atlantic, July 19, 1884, Book B, 1884, ibid. Clarification of this point may have been the principal reason for the publication of Circular No. 9, HQA, October 11, 1887, which indicated the decision of the commanding general that "no cord is prescribed for the white or summer helmet, and none should be worn with it." Chappell, *Summer Helmets*, 21, speculates that the use of summer helmets for full dress, complete with trim, was the basis for this circular, but evidence to support this conclusion has not been found.

21 M.C. Meigs to Chief Quartermaster Military Division of the Atlantic, April 6, 1881, LS, Clothing Br., Book A, 1881, OQMG, RG92, NA.

22 S.B. Holabird to John Simpson, April 3, 1881, ibid. Nonetheless, many men had acquired the new great coat as indicated by M.C. Meigs to D.H. Rucker, April 6, 1881, Book A, 1881; S.B. Holabird to J.F. Rodgers, November 10, 1881; S.B. Holabird to F.M. Crandal, November 10, 1881; S.B. Holabird to J.F. Rodgers, November 11, 1881; M.C. Meigs to D.H. Rucker, December 28, 1881; S.B. Holabird to J. Garrard, December 29, 1881; and S.B. Holabird to Superintendent of General Recruiting Service, December 31, 1881, Book B, 1881, ibid. In other exchanges, the lining for capes of hospital stewards was confirmed as green. M.C. Meigs to Secretary of War, November 8, 1881, ibid. Meigs mused that the measurements might be expanded on overcoats of the new pattern to make them warmer and more comfortable, and would make it possible for a many to use the overcoat "as a comfortable cloak...." M.C. Meigs to J.F. Rodgers, November 22, 1881, ibid. These personal observations suggest that the quartermaster general did have the well being of the enlisted men in mind when his department produced articles of clothing, but often he seemed less concerned with this matter than other factors, such as economy.

23 M.C. Meigs to J.F. Rodgers, January 27, 1881, ibid. Use of fabric on hand to produce new patterns was not unusual, although this practice led to complaints as evidenced by a response to an inspection of Ft. Snelling, Minnesota where shoddy overcoats were found in service. Meigs retorted that his department had "not for many years bought or owned any shoddy overcoats." He did admit that during the Civil War such garments had come into the system, but he testified "after the soldiers came under the care of experienced and careful officers of the Quartermaster Department, they received good, strong, cloth garments...." Meigs completed his protestations with the remark: "Fashion has changed, probably tastes have improved, and the cloths and kerseys lately established as standards are of finer textures and probably even stronger than much bought and made up during the war." Thus, in one breadth he admitted of problems in the past, laid the blame to others outside his department, and lauded the improvements that had been wrought, which were so significant as to cause individuals to mistake slightly older garments made from earlier cloth specifications with Civil War cloth, even though this was not the case. M.C. Meigs to IGUSA, January 27, 1881, ibid.

24 M.C. Meigs to Chief Quartermaster Military Division of the Atlantic, February 16, 1881, ibid. The charge for old blanket-lined overcoats and for those lined in cloth were to be the same, as set forth in GO No. 72 of 1880. M.C. Meigs to Chief Quartermaster Military Division of the Missouri, November 10, 1881, Book B, 1881. Other reasons given for discontinuance of the blanket lined garments was the approval for half wool knit undershirts, and fur caps, gauntlets, and buffalo overcoats for "extremely cold climates." As to cape linings, Meigs personally believed that all of them should be lined in red, because he thought "of all the great coats worn by troops both regular and militia, none were so handsome as those worn by our regular artillery." M.C. Meigs to Secretary of War, March 9, 1881, Book A, 1881, ibid. The secretary evidently did not share this view, and traditional branch colors prevailed as linings.
Evidently, the new coat was desirable over the older pattern as demonstrated by an unfortunate artilleryman, who left behind his overcoat with lined cape, after completing sentry duty at Point San Jose, California, in the San Francisco Bay Area. When he returned to fetch the item, he found in its place an old pattern overcoat, while his "nearly new, cape lined with red, and stenciled on the lining...the figures 32" was gone. Commander Presidio of San Francisco, California to Commander Ft. Canby, Washington, July 19, 1881, Post Letter Book, Presidio of San Francisco, RUSACC, RG 393, NA.

25 S.B. Holabird to D.H. Rucker, April 8, 1881, LS, Clothing Br., Book A, 1881, OQMG, RG92, NA. Also see, M.C. Meigs to Secretary of War, April 3, 1881, and April 12, 1881, ibid. According to M.C. Meigs to Secretary of State, April 12, 1881, ibid., the items destined for France were as follows: 2 helmets, foot and mounted; 1 campaign hat; 1 forage cap; 1 blouse; 1 stable frock; 2 uniform coats, foot and mounted; 2 pairs trousers foot and mounted; 1 great coat; 1 wool blanket; 1 poncho; 1 rubber blanket; 1 shelter tent; 1 "Goodenough" horseshoe for summer and 1 for winter; 1 pair side lines; 1 aparajo; 1 riding saddle and bridle; and 1 six mule harness. The items of equipment were furnished by the Ordnance Department.

Just a few years later, France's rival, Germany, requested samples of American gear as well. Specifically, the German minister in Washington asked for examples of the U.S. infantry field uniform and equipment for shipment to his government. S.B. Holabird to Secretary of War, April 28, 1884, Book A, 1884, ibid.

26 *ARSW, 1882*, Vol. I, 302.

27 GO No. 4, HQA, January 7, 1881. Another element found in this order was the provision for "suitable knit undershirts, at the rate of three per year," to be supplied in addition to the flannel overshirt. The undershirts were described in Quartermaster Specification No. 77, adopted February 16, 1881.

28 S.B. Holabird to J.A. Ekin, and M.C. Meigs to R.N. Batchelder, January 26, 1881, LS, Clothing Br., Book A, 1881, OQMG, RG92, NA. Previously, M.C. Meigs to D.H. Rucker, January 9, 1881, ibid., provided advance information that a new general order would do away with the dress cap, gray shirts, and unlined blouses, with an effective date of July 1, 1881. Also see, *A&NJ*, August 27, 1881, 70.

29 S.B. Holabird to J.F. Rodgers, January 20, 1881, LS, Clothing Br., Book A, 1881, OQMG, RG92, NA. S.B. Holabird to D.H. Rucker, January 21, 1881, ibid.; and M.C. Meigs to J.F. Rodgers, February 4, 1881, ibid., made additional comments about the proposed shirts, and the later exchanges likewise made reference to dress helmets.

30 M.C. Meigs to General of the Army, February 7, 1881, ibid.

31 M.C. Meigs to D.H. Rucker, February 9, 1881, ibid.

32 S.B. Holabird to J.F. Rodgers April 5, 1881; M.C. Meigs to Captain G.A. Hull April 11, 1881; and M.C. Meigs to D.H. Rucker, April 11, 1881, ibid.

33 S.B. Holabird to L.L. Bruff, May 21, 1881, ibid. For two articles that provide some contemporary attitudes about the field shirt consult, *A&NJ*, January 1, 1881, 434; and January 7, 1882, 495. The earlier item also discussed the new headgear being adopted in early 1881, too.

34 M.C. Meigs to D.H. Rucker, May 20, 1881, LS, Clothing Br., Book A, 1881, and M.C. Meigs to D.H. Rucker, May 24, 1881, OQMG, RG92, NA. According to S.B. Holabird to Pippey & Co., June 14, 1881, ibid., the gray shirting flannel was rejected because of "lack of uniformity in color" which meant it could not be used for shirt manufacture. Even as the exchange took place, the gray shirt was being phased out. Directives were given to issue the 2,300 remaining ones in stocks located at posts around he country. These were needed because the "blue shirting flannel; could not be procured at once." S.B. Holabird to Chief Quartermaster Department of the Missouri, July 26, 1881, Book B, 1881, ibid.
West Point was one of the locales slated to receive the new shirts as soon as they could be provided. It is interesting to note that in the manifest for shirts to be provided to enlisted personnel there, a differentiation was made between the 175 artillery shirts and the 50 shirts for engineers. Probably there was no difference in the style, the red cord being applied to both as trim. As such, the letter perhaps only made separate references to indicate that the proper number and sizes were being delivered to the enlisted men at the Military Academy, rather than as an indication that there were two versions of the shirts with different cords for these branches. S.B. Holabird to J.F. Rodgers, September 23, 1881, ibid.
The fact that the blue flannel would not be available until winter also was mentioned in M.C. Meigs to Chief Quartermaster Military Division of Missouri, July 25, 1881, ibid. Instructions also were given to send grey shirts to the troops in Texas. This was to be the case for troops in the Department of the South. S.B. Holabird to J.F. Rodgers, August 5, 1881. ibid. Further, S.B. Holabird to Chief Quartermaster Military Division of the Atlantic, July 28, 1881, ibid., made it clear that gray shirts were not defined as "old pattern" this distinction being applied to Civil War surplus by the early 1880s. Therefore, they were to be supplied to the troops until none were left in stock. They would not be substituted for knit undershirts, however, because the new pattern of these undergarments were being delivered on schedule for distribution to the troops. M.C. Meigs to E.D. Baker, August 5, 1881, ibid.

35 Meigs to D.H. Rucker, May 13, 1881, Book A, 1881, ibid. Other evidence of the quartermaster general's desire to expedite the production of the blue shirt is found in a letter from S.B. Holabird to J.A. Ekin, October 3, 1881, Book B, 1881, ibid., which made arrangements for direct shipment of cloth as it became available from the mills in the "interests of the service."

36 G. Lawson to Quartermaster General (Through Post Headquarters), 1881, CCF, Box 66, File 870, ibid. The many endorsements as well as a sketch of the top of the 1876-pattern trousers versus the trousers with a waistband being requested formed part of this printed circular, which also was included in LS, Clothing Br., Book A, 1881, pp. 475-480.

37 M.C. Meigs to AGUSA, October 26, 1881, Book B, 1881, ibid. An attachment from the regimental quartermaster of the Nineteenth U.S. Infantry indicated that after examining the trousers of 140 men in the command he was "unable to find one who wears the trousers issued him by the Government without first having them made over in some way, most of them with spring bottoms and waistband tops, for which a company tailor charges from 2 to 3 dollars per pair." He went on to assert that "the trousers with springbottoms are the fashion for enlisted men, and have been so for many years...." He also revealed that there "were but few enlisted men in this command who wear suspenders...." R.W. Hoyt to Quartermaster General, July 29, 1881, as attachment R.H. Chandler to J.F. Rodgers, August 17, 1881, ibid.

38 M.C. Meigs to Chief of Ordnance, November 4, 1881, ibid. Sometimes unforseen circumstances impeded issue of trousers, such as in the isolated case of ten pairs being destroyed on purpose because the children of the woman who made them as part of the piece-work system still in place, had contracted smallpox. Rather than risk the spread of the disease, the trousers were burned, and the items stricken form the inventory. M.C. Meigs to D.H. Rucker, April 16, 1881, Book A, 1881, ibid.

39 S.B. Holabird to J.F. Rodgers, May 4, 1881, ibid.

40 M.C Meigs to A.C. Blunt, December 24, 1881; and S.B. Holabird to E.D. Baker, December 24, 1881, ibid.

41 More details were given in Quartermaster Specification No. 82, adopted October 9, 1882.

42 Of course, all trousers of previous patterns and sizes, made and unmade, were to be issued before the 1884-pattern was allowed to be issued, in keeping with past practices to exhaust stocks on hand. GO No. 81, HQA, July 29, 1884.

43 Endorsement S.B. Holabird to J.F. Rodgers, September 1, 1881 to J.B. Backus, "Report on Army Clothing," August 15, 1881, LS, Clothing Br., Book B, 1881, OQMG, RG92, NA. The tape drawstrings on drawers, which also was used for the same purposes on bed and pillow sacks, would be ordered in smaller quantities than previously during fiscal year 1884. The reason for this was that the drawstrings on drawers were to be dispensed with on pairs made after that time. R. Ingalls to S.B. Holabird, April 17, 1883, CCF, Box 58, Entry 2182, ibid.

44 S.B. Holabird, "Army Clothing," *Journal of the Military Service Institution of the United States*, II (1881): 379. Other opinions relative to trousers are revealed in *A&NJ*, April 14, 1877, 578; and May 21, 1881, 878.

45 Holabird, "Army Clothing": 382-3.

46 Ibid., 384.

47 Ibid., 387.

48 Risch, *Quartermaster Support of the Army*, 514.

49 *ARSW, 1882*, Vol. I, 303; M.C. Meigs to D.H. Rucker, October 25, 1881; M.C. Meigs to Secretary of War, November 14, 1881; and M.C. Meigs to D.H. Rucker, November 29, 1881, LS, Clothing Br., Book B, 1881, OQMG, RG92, NA. The last letter indicated the goal of printing and binding 1,000 sets, and also went on to request a copy of the 1851 regulations published by Horstmann be obtained to serve "as a guide in getting up the new illustrations, if practicable."

50 Barely two years after its publication, this work was out of print. J.F. Rodgers to W.L. Orr, February 20, 1884, Book A, 1884, ibid. Even so, a new volume was being considered as early as 1884. J.F. Rodgers to M.I. Ludington, August 6, 1884, Book B, ibid.

51 *ARSW, 1882*, Vol. I, 303.

52 Ibid., 304-5. S.B. Holabird to Secretary of War, September 27, 1881, LS, Clothing Br., Book B, 1881, OQMG, RG92, NA, also mentioned clothing to the National Home for Disabled Volunteers and clothing to Indians as requested by the Interior Department.

53 *ARSW, 1882*, Vol. I, 298.

54 M.C. Meigs to Inspector General of the Army, January 17, 1881, LS, Clothing Br., Book A, 1881, OQMG, RG92, NA.

55 Ibid. In another exchange, Meigs was told by Captain George B. Rodney, an officer serving with the Fourth U.S. Artillery in the Bay Area, that blouses and dress coats made at the San Francisco Depot were superior to those provided from Philadelphia and Jeffersonville. Endorsement S.B. Holabird to J.F. Rodgers, September 15, 1881, to G.B. Rodney to Quartermaster General, January 27, 1881, Book B, 1881, ibid. Meigs' response was that this could not be the case because the cloth used to make coats and blouses at San Francisco was shipped from the depots in the East. Because of this, the quality of the material could not be superior. S.B. Holabird to G.B. Rodney, September 29, 1881, ibid. That same day authority was given for the production of 1,150 cavalry blouses at San Francisco from materials on hand. S.B. Holabird to San Francisco Quartermaster Depot, September 29, 1881, ibid.

56 It should be noted that the "sewed boots and shoes of the pattern recommended by the Army equipment board of 1880 [Miles Board] had been received." These met with some favor among the rank and file, but extensive trials were not conducted immediately to determine whether they should replace screwed footgear or not. *ARSW, 1881*, Vol. I, 298. Even if improvements were required, the quartermaster general at least could point to the favorable reduction of cost for footgear made at the prison versus contract-made footgear from the past. Ft. Leavenworth produced boots for $2.90 a pair and shoes $1.85 a pair versus $2.37 for the last contract for boots let in 1878, and $2.55 for shoes in 1873 when the last outside source of manufacture was used. M.C. Meigs R. C. Drum, August 6, 1881, LS, Clothing Br., Book B, 1881, OQMG, RG92, NA. Conversely, a brief discussion of defective footgear is found in M.C. Meigs to A.P. Blunt, April 23, 1881, Book A, 1881; and Chief Quartermaster Military Division of the Missouri, July 28, 1881, ibid. As an aside, according to M.C. Meigs to A.P. Blunt, April 16, 1881, ibid., John McGowan was appointed the inspector of boots, shoes, and leather at the Military Prison, Ft. Leavenworth, where footgear continued to be produced by military inmates, while M.C. Meigs to A.P. Blunt, November 10, 1881, Book B, 1881, indicated that the "Standard Screw Machine" was in use at Ft. Leavenworth for the purposes of producing footgear.

57 *ARSW, 1882*, Vol. I, 298.

58 Ibid. The fugitive nature of yellow, as well as other hues persisted as a problem. For example, in 1884 a board of survey held by officers of the Fifth U.S. Cavalry made the same complaint about the dye rubbing off from great coat capes. The response was that these must have been from the 1880-1881 batch that were produced with faulty dyes. Very few incidents were reported, however, according to J.F. Rodgers to M.I. Ludington, March 12, 1884, LS, Clothing Br., Book A, 1884, OQMG, RG92, NA.

59 *ARSW, 1882*, Vol. I, 299.

60 *A&NJ*, January 7, 1882, 495. J.F. Rodgers to J. Summerhayes, September 3, 1884, LS, Clothing Br., Book B, 1884, OQMG, RG92, NA, also revealed dissatisfaction with the shirt-blouse.

61 *ARSW, 1882*, Vol. I, 299. Cir. No. 8, HQA, September 6, 1883, stated that the blouses

fashioned from the blue flannel shirting were to be issued at a charge of two dollars each. These garments were in the inventory until 1884, when the quartermaster general finally dictated that no more would be converted for issue. S.B. Holabird to M.I. Ludington, March 23, 1884, Book A, 1884; and J.F. Rodgers to G.H. Weeks, April 15, 1884, LS, Clothing Br., Book A, 1884, OQMG, RG92, NA. Instead, the remaining numbers were to "be set aside for such action as may hereafter be determined upon and issue therefrom should be made only when it is especially called for. J.F. Rodgers to R. Saxton, August 16, 1884, Book B, 1884, ibid. Thereafter a directive from the quartermaster general read: "Please cause all the gray flannel shirts and blouses made of obsolete dark blue shirts that may be on hand and not required for issue at various posts in the Division to be concentrated and shipped to the depot at San Francisco, Cal." S.B. Holabird to Chief Quartermaster Military Division of the Pacific, September 1, 1884, ibid. The depot then put sufficient numbers of these articles aside for prisoners and other potential use, then was to condemn and dispose of the items at auction. S.B. Holabird to San Francisco Quartermaster Depot; S.B. Holabird to Chief Quartermaster Military Division of the Atlantic; S.B. Holabird to Chief Quartermaster Military Division of the Missouri; S.B. Holabird to Philadelphia Quartermaster Depot; and S.B. Holabird to St. Louis Depot, September 1, 1884, ibid. These same letters required that existing stocks of trousers were to be issued until exhausted.

62 *ARSW, 1882*, Vol. I, 320-3.

63 M.C. Meigs to Inspector General, November 7, 1881, LS, Clothing Br., Book B, 1881, OQMG, RG92, NA. The secretary of war approved the idea, but the wreath was retained for the forage cap, despite Meigs' recommendation to the contrary. M.C. Meigs to D.H. Rucker; M.C. Meigs to Surgeon General of the Army; M.C. Meigs to Chief Quartermaster Military Division of the Atlantic; M.C. Meigs to Chief Quartermaster West Point; M.C. Meigs to Chief Quartermaster Military Division of the Pacific; and M.C. Meigs to Chief Quartermaster Military Division of the Missouri, December 8, 1881, ibid. The hospital steward collar devices are mentioned in several subsequent annual inventories and evidence of their issue exists in some cases, such as for Ft. Brady, Michigan. J.F. Rodgers to M.I. Ludington, August 15, 1884, Book B, 1884, ibid. Further, GO No. 9, HQA, January 27, 1882 reiterated the dress helmet styles and trimmings for enlisted men, and indicated the new caduceus within a wreath as the forage cap insignia of hospital stewards that replaced the former white metal "U.S." within a wreath. Overlays for staff and staff corps troops likewise were spelled out in GO No. 43, HQA, April 12, 1882. GO No. 43 represented an expansion of GO No. 96, WD, November 19, 1875, and GO No. 20, HQA, February 15, 1881.
At approximately the same time a recommendation to do away with metal insignia to replace it with cloth versions that had the devices printed on the fabric, was rejected as being too costly. This was in response to actual samples being sent from a private citizen for consideration. M.C. Meigs to Secretary of War, September 19, 1881, LS, Clothing Br., Book B, 1881, OQMG, RG92, NA.

64 M.C. Meigs to Inspector General of the Army, November 7, 1881, ibid., and *ARSW, 1882*, Vol. I, 298.

65 By 1884 an order bound for the signal school at Ft. Whipple requested 100 Signal Corps devices, presumably for use as hat ornaments, because several months later a separate order spelled out the requirement for 100 staff corps helmet eagles with crossed flag overlays, 100 plume staffs, 80 blouses, then went on to ask for 200 uniform dress coats, 300 crossed flag sleeve devices, 100 pairs of unmade foot trousers, 100 pairs of trouser stripes for sergeants and 50 pairs for corporals, along with 100 forage caps. J.F. Rodgers to M.I. Ludington, January 29, 1884; and B.C. Card to M.I. Ludington, May 14, 1884, LS, Clothing Br., Book A, 1884, OQMG, RG92, NA. The signalmen at Ft. Myer, Virginia (formerly Ft. Whipple) also would be sent 30 of the brown canvas suits adopted in 1884, as one of the first posts to be so supplied. B.C. Card to R.N. Batchelder, May 4, 1884, ibid.

66 *ARSW, 1882*, Vol. I, 299. Earlier, when an officer brought up the idea of gray coverings for the summer helmet, General Sherman vented his distaste for that hue, decrying that it was "not the fashionable color for National troops for obvious reasons...." The commanding general went on to state that "the helmet was designed to protect the head against the effect of the sun and ought not to be used when fighting Apaches." A better means to provide both protection against the solar heat and to avoid detection by enemy riflemen was a silk turn, which would take on the color of the locale after becoming soiled in the field. This was what Meigs had suggested, and Sherman through the idea had merit. Endorsement S.B. Holabird to Chief Quartermaster West Point, November 7, 1881, with attachment from R.C. Drum to Quartermaster General, November 3, 1881, LS, Clothing Br., Book B, 1881, OQMG, RG92, NA.

67 *ARSW, 1882*, Vol. I, 299.

68 Inspection Report, March 15, 1882, LS, Clothing Br., OQMG, RG92, NA.

69 J.C. Rodgers to Depot Quartermaster, April 29, 1882, CCF (Hats), ibid. It is interesting that the eyelet concept was resurrected with the adoption of the 1911-pattern "Montana Peak."

70 R. Ingalls to Secretary of War, July 18, 1882; and R. Ingalls to S.B. Holabird, July 17, 1882, LS, Clothing Br., Book B, 1882, OQMG, RG92, NA.

71 See for instance, CCF (hats), ibid.; S.B. Holabird to M.I. Ludington, July 19, 1883; and S.B. Holabird to Secretary of War, October 18, 1883; LS, Clothing Br., Book B, 1883, ibid.; *ARSW, 1883*, Vol. I, 56; and ibid., 1884, 311.

72 M.I. Ludington to S.B. Holabird, October 24, 1883; and November 17, 1883, LS, Clothing Br., Book B, 1883, OQMG, RG92, NA. The second letter required two hundred of the hats to be shipped to the depot at San Francisco, presumably for issue to troops in Arizona, but some remained in California according to Headquarters Department of California to Adjutant First Artillery, February 19, 1884, Post Endorsement Book, Presidio of San Francisco, Letter No. 129, RUSACC, RG393, NA, some of the trial hats were being provided, and as such the number of each of the six sizes needed were to be supplied. Within a few days, Major George Sanford of the Sixth U.S. Cavalry, noted that Troop I of his regiment had already been given some of the hats and "found them of good quality and generally satisfactory." But he continued: "They are not however adopted to use in garrison and I would respectfully suggest that they should not be issued to cavalry at this station [Presidio of San Francisco]. G.B. Sanford to Adjutant First U.S. Artillery, February 25, 1884, ibid.

73 Chief Quartermaster Military Division of the Missouri, August 9, 1884, LS, Clothing Br., Book, B, 1884, OQMG, RG92, NA, indicated that drab hats were not experimental and were to be charged for when drawn by the men. S.B. Holabird to Chief Quartermaster Department of Texas, December 18, 1884, Book C, ibid., related that drab hats were always to be furnished when requested, but when not specified, black hats were to be provided to fill orders. As another example of the popularity of the drab hat, a first lieutenant of the First U.S. Infantry went so far as to request this light colored head dress over the summer helmet. N.P. Phister to Quartermaster Ft. Mohave, Arizona Territory, LR, 1884, Letter Nos. 1601, 1615, and 1616, ibid.

74 *ARSW, 1884*, Vol I, 613.

75 S.B. Holabird, Endorsement 8 to Adjutant General, USA, October 28, 1885, "Endorsements on report of trial of Drab Colored hats made by Lieut. Frank West, Troop`I' 6th Cavalry, Fort McDowell, A.T., Aug. 31, 1883," LS, Clothing Br., Vol. 2, 1885, OQMG, RG92, NA. The 9th endorsement was the secretary of war's approval to adopt the drab hat.

76 For contracts to procure the 1883-pattern drab hat consult, Howell, *United States Army Headgear, 1855-1902*, 90. In spite of drab hats being in the majority, it should be noted that as late as the third edition (dated May 1, 1899) of *Regulations and Decisions Pertaining to the Uniform of the Army of the United States* (Washington, DC: Government Printing Office, 1899), paragraph 12, officers were permitted either a drab or a black campaign hat, except chaplains, who continued to be restricted to black ones only, through the early twentieth century. Paragraph 46 of this same document called out drab campaign hats for enlisted men, allowed straw hats during the warm season (if prescribed by the departmental commander), and required that "the color to be uniform for both officers and enlisted men in each troop, battery, or company." Previously, according to GO No. 72, WD, AGO, December 2, 1887, officers were to wear only the "black felt" campaign hat, but in practice usually donned the drab model. In turn, the same general order set forth enlisted hats as either: "Of black or drab-colored felt according to pattern in the office of the Quartermaster General; to be worn in garrison only on target practice, fatigue duty, and on marches and campaigns; the color to be uniform in each troop, battery, or company." As an example of continued availability of both colors see Chief Quartermaster Department of California to Post Adjutant, March 3, 1893, LR, Presidio of San Francisco, Letter No. 590, RUSACC, RG393, NA, that required the post quartermaster to specify which type of hat he desired in terms of drab or black color.

77 *ARSW, 1882*, Vol. I, 353.

78 Ibid, 298. Further, in accordance with GO No. 69, HQA, July 29, 1882, when division and departmental commanders so approved, one pair of arctic overshoes in the first and third year of enlistment and two pairs of woolen mittens each year were to be furnished the men at cost. So, too, were fur coats, fur caps, and gauntlets to be provided "in extremely cold climates." These would be surrendered at the end of each season by the soldier, who had been given the articles on temporary loan.
It is interesting to note that both GO No. 40, HQA, April 20, 1881, and later, GO No. 9, HQA, January 27, 1882, specified how post quartermasters were to treat the fur clothing, when enlisted men returned these items to officers charged with their keeping. The second version of this required the fur items were to be exposed to the sun, and beaten with light twigs or rattan to clean them and destroy any moth eggs. Thereafter, any necessary repairs were to be made "using for this purpose, as far as practicable, such articles of a corresponding character as cannot again be rendered unserviceable—and pack in boxes, well lined with petroleum and wrapping paper. The items did wear out, in spite of all precautions, as evidenced by orders for replacements, such as S.B. Holabird to M.I. Ludington, March 11, 1884, LS, Clothing Br., Book A, 1884, OQMG, RG 92, NA, referred to an advertisement for bids to obtain 5,000 pairs of fur gauntlets.

79 *ARSW, 1882*, Vol. I, 299. The sets of Berlin gloves with two rights and a left was a trial situation as indicated by M.C. Meigs to D.H. Rucker; M.C. Meigs to R. Saxton; M.C. Meigs to R.N.Batchelder; M.C. Meigs to Chief Quartermaster Military Division of the Pacific; and M.C. Meigs to Chief Quartermaster Military Division of the Atlantic, October 31, 1881, LS, Clothing Br., Book B, 1881, OQMG, RG92, NA. In another letter Meigs indicated that recruits normally were not issued the gloves, this item being provided once the enlistee arrived at his duty station. M.C. Meigs to Secretary of War, September 9, 1881, ibid. S.B. Holabird to J.F. Rodgers, September 30, 1881, ibid., seems to indicate that there were exceptions to this policy.
Another matter, although not related to uniforms per se, was the marking of personnel equipment. According to GO 20, HQA, February 25, 1882, all equipment was to be fitted to the men "under the direction of an officer" and "not otherwise be changed by cutting straps or punching holes" into the articles provided by the Ordnance Department. Further, knapsack, haversacks, and clothing bags were to be marked with crossed cannon for artillery, crossed sabers for cavalry, and crossed rifles for infantry, and "other corps, according to their respective devices, with the letter of

the company above the number of the regiment below the intersection." These were to be of black ink and applied by stencils that rendered five inch long devices and one inch high letters and numbers. The markings were to be located above the U.S. on the equipment, while the soldier's individual identification number was to "be placed at the bottom near the lower edge of the knapsack, &c." Additionally, GO No. 56, HQA, May 20, 1882, introduced another Ordnance Department related topic. Thereafter the revolver was to "form part of the equipment of each company sergeant of all arms of the service."

This action necessitated "a separate black leather cartridge belt, with a buckle and attachment for carrying revolver cartridges." In turn, the looped cartridge belts were to "be used only for carrying cartridges," for the rifle or carbine, "and not to be weighted with revolver or sabre" the latter weapon being issued to cavalry troopers and the gunners of mounted batteries. GO No. 128, HQA, November 14, 1882.

While company non-commissioned officers were receiving a sidearm and proper belt, a new edged weapon had been approved by the secretary of war. Light artillery officers were to carry sabers that resembled those prescribed for cavalry officers in 1872. The National Armory at Springfield, Massachusetts was to fabricate the saber for sale to officers. Originally a brown scabbard was provided for, but according to GO No. 121, HQA, October 11, 1882, a nickel-plated scabbard was to "be worn on all occasions."

80 *ARSW, 1882*, Vol. I, 303.

81 *ARSW, 1884*, Vol. I, 673, according to which the drab hat was adopted as standard on December 14, 1883.

82 Ibid., 672-3, and *ARSW, 1883*, Vol. I, 80.

83 Ibid., 81, indicated that the new standard for blouses was adopted on May 19, 1883. The removal of branch color trim came as a reversal of an action suggested by First Lieutenant J.A. Baldwin, Ninth U.S. Infantry, that faded cord on collars and cuffs of blouses could be replaced by purchase of cord in the proper branch colors. Balls of cord could be sent out and the men could buy the required trim at cost. S.B. Holabird to D.H. Rucker; S.B. Holabird to J.A. Ekin; S.B. Holabird to R.N. Batchelder; S.B. Holabird to Chief Quartermaster Military Division of the Missouri; and S.B. Holabird to Chief Quartermaster Military Division of the Atlantic, October 20, 1881, LS, Clothing Br., Book B, 1881, OQMG, RG92, NA.

84 See for instance, S.B. Holabird to M.I. Ludington, March 21, 1884, Book A, 1884; and J.F. Rodgers to Chief Quartermaster Military Division of the Pacific, July 22, 1884, Book B, 1884, ibid. The second letter also indicated that cord was to be removed from the 1882-pattern blue flannel pullover shirt.

85 GO No. 38, HQA, June 6, 1883, which revoked paragraphs 2728 to 2742 of U.S. Army Regulations, and paragraphs 2727, 2743, and 2746 as amended by GO No. 92 of 1882, and paragraph 2745, as amended by GO No. 129 of 1882, set forth the basics relative to non-commissioned officer and specialist insignia. Additionally, GO 58, HQA, July 31, 1883, clarified the trouser stripe arrangement, which remained 1 inch for sergeants and a 1/2 inch for corporals, but added double 1/2 inch wide stripes for musicians, thereby giving official blessing to a practice that had been used in certain instances in the past without being allowed by regulations. This same order indicated that a pair of suspenders would be provided each year for every enlisted man.

Another directive related to indications of non-commissioned status, GO 92, HQA, August 9, 1882, required paragraph 2441 of regulations was to be stricken, and paragraphs 2727, 2743, and 2746 (the latter as amended by General Orders No. 60, of 1882) were further amended. This order repeated that chevrons were to be worn points down above the elbow, but in this case made this a requirement for all garments, despite the fact that stripes on overcoats had been relocated to just above the cuff previously so that the cape would not obscure them. The new directive allowed service, service in war, or campaign chevrons to be worn on all coats, blouses, and overcoats. The remainder of the order detailed these diagonal "hash marks," setting an order of precedence as well, with the service in war (1/2 wide of the facing of the arm of service trimmed with a 1/8 inch red stripe on each side, except for artillerymen, who would have a white trim) being worn nearest the cuff, followed by campaign chevrons (the same as war stripes but of 1/2 inch aggregate width instead of 3/4 inch), then service chevrons for the completion of one term of enlistment (1/2 inch wide of the color of the facings). "But one campaign chevron for each enlistment" was permitted "not withstanding that the soldier may have served during such an enlistment in more than one campaign...."

Finally, GO No. 129, HQA, November 18, 1882, made one further clarification regarding the service, service in war, and campaign chevron. This document stated that these cloth marks would "conform in color to the facings of the arm of service in which the soldier served when earning the right to wear them."

86 S.B. Holabird to G.A. Hull, August 28, 1883, Roll 84, Microfilm Collection, USAMHI. Captain Hull was the military storekeeper in charge of the clothing depot at San Francisco. According to GO No. 37, HQA, June 5, 1883, "Such of the clothing, camp and garrison equipage for troops in the Military Division of the Pacific as is not procured or manufactured at the San Francisco depot will be forwarded in bulk to that depot for distribution." Troops at posts in all other divisions were to be supplied directly from the Philadelphia and Jeffersonville depots. For the entire table of clothing and equipment prices see, GO 45, HQA, June 26, 1883.

87 GO 62, HGQ, August 4, 1883.

88 *ARSW, 1884*, Vol. I, 614.

89 Ibid., 312. S.B. Holabird to M.I. Ludington, January 4, 1884, Book A, 1884; and S.B. Holabird to J.R. Michael, June 18, 1884, Book B, 1884, LS, Clothing Br., OQMG, RG92, NA, offer early evidence of procurement of suspenders. The January letter indicates the purchase of 10,000 pairs, while the June letter refers to another 5,000 pairs being bought at $2.04 per dozen.

90 Mention of this subject, including the desired improvement of the pattern for uniform dress coats is found in J.F. Rodgers to G.A. Hull, December 11, 1883, Microfilm Collections, USAMHI.

91 *ARSW, 1883*, Vol. I, 79 and 81; and S.B. Holabird to D.H. Rucker, September 21, 1881; S.B. Holabird to Chief Quartermaster Department of Dakota, September 30, 1881; M.C. Meigs to D.H. Rucker, December 7, 1881; M.C. Meigs to D.H. Rucker, December 24, 1881; and M.C. Meigs to D.H. Rucker; M.C. Meigs to J.A. Ekin; M.C. Meigs to R.N. Batchelder; M.C. Meigs to R. Ingalls, September 7, 1881, LS, Clothing Br., Book B, 1881, OQMG, RG92, NA.

92 *ARSW, 1883*, Vol. I, 79.

93 Ibid., 79-80.

94 *ARSW, 1884*, Vol. I, 672.

95 GO No. 7, HQA, February 6, 1883.

96 There were also some additional revisions for officers during the previous year, most notably in relation to uniforms worn by judge advocates and professors at West Point, which were discussed in GO No. 9, HQA, January 27, 1882.

97 Officers had to purchase these belts, but in another instance, drum-slings for drummers in companies or regimental bands, they would be issued to the musicians who played these instruments. These were adopted on January 15, 1883, and were made of 2 1/8 inch "cotton web. in two pieces, thirty-eight (38) an ten (10) inches long in the clear, held together by a leather frog, pear-shaped, three and five-eighths (3 5/8) inches long, two and five-eighths (2 5/8) inches wide at the broadest, and one and a half (1 1/2) at the lowest part." An oblong tongueless brass buckle, a brass slide, and a triangular brass wire to receive the hook of the drum were included as fittings. The following year, a color belt and slings were adopted for the carrying of standards and national colors by foot troops. Specifications for these were approved on October 9, 1884. S.B. Holabird to M.I. Ludington, September 12, 1884; and October 9, 1884, LS, Clothing Br., Book B, 1884, OQMG, RG92, NA.

98 S.B. Holabird to AGUSA, November 28, 1884, ibid., reiterated the removal of sleeve braid and the discontinuance of slashes at the hips of the officer's blouse in 1875, but noted that three buttons remained on the cuffs. As far as the belt was concerned, the Ordnance Department was the agency responsible for accoutrements and various other equipage. In an effort to ensure uniformity the chief of Ordnance directed the Rock Island Arsenal to produce 500 such belts, similar to another 100 ordered on July 22, 1884. S.V. Benét to Commanding Officer, Rock Island Arsenal, October 20, 1884, Letters to Ordnance Officers, Vol. 68, OCO, RG156, NA. H.W. Hovey to D.W. Flagler, March 31, 1884, with six endorsements; D.W. Flagler to Messrs. Brown, Pettibone & Kelly, July 25, 1885; J.G. Butler to F.E. Lacy, August 14, 1884; D.W. Flagler to P. Leary, October 13, 1884; and D.W. Flagler to H.C. Davis, October 31, 1884, LS, Rock Island Arsenal, RG156, NA, all of which trace the request for a standard belt through the actual manufacture, including 5 inch by 8 inch pasteboard boxes that were imprinted with the label "Officers Sword Belt Manufactured at Rock Island Arsenal 1884." These were ready for issue in late October 1884.

99 S.B. Holabird to M.I. Ludington, January 2, 1884, LS, Clothing Br., Book A, 1884, OQMG, RG92, NA, enclosed the sealed sample of the new cap cord, and further required the preparation of samples "of the various insignia now worn on the forage caps of all commissioned officers, properly labelled so as to identify them, to be kept in this office for reference, also the helmets for officers, both mounted and foot, together with the different trimmings for each arm or service." A few days later, S.B. Holabird to R. Saxton, January 12, 1884, ibid., conveyed the specifications for the new cap cord.

Not only the cap cord, but also the whole matter of the officers' forage cap was being studied at this time as indicated in S.B. Holabird to C. Chase, January 3, 1884 and S.B. Holabird to C. Chase, January 18, 1884, Book A, ibid., which were exchanges in response to First Lieutenant Constantine Chase of the Third U.S. Artillery, who shared his ideas about officers' head dress. He included a sample forage cap, which was rejected by Sherman, who although he thought the style had merit, determined change was not appropriate at the time. Nonetheless, the item had been furnished to one military outfitter, probably for cost analysis. J.F. Rodgers to Shannon, Miller, and Co., June 19, 1884, Book B, ibid. Also see J.F. Rodgers to Henry Allien, June 19, 1884; and J.F. Rodgers to J.H. McKenney, October 30, 1884, ibid., for contact with two other military suppliers on the matter. In the case of Allien, Rodgers had asked for plates, drawings, or samples of European fatigue caps for both officers and enlisted men.

100 *Army and Navy Register*, January 26, 1884, 5. Another officer disagreed with the proposition, especially if it meant that the old capote was reinstated. He felt the great coat adopted in 1872 was better than the antebellum design. As a matter of fact, he thought "The present uniform for all arms is the best and most soldierly that the U.S. Army has had in thirty years." The only change he proposed was the dis continuance of trouser stripes for sergeants. Instead, he believed silver cord should be used by all foot troops and gold cord by all mounted troops. Ibid., April 5, 1884, 2.

101 J.F. Rodgers to Hoyt and Gleason, Tailors, May 21, 1884, LS, Clothing Br., Book A, 1884, OQMG, RG92, NA.

102 S.B. Holabird to E.S. Otis, June 20, 1884, ibid.

103 GO No. 42, HQA, May 7, 1881, established the School for of Application for Infantry and Cavalry, which was to be "similar to the one in operation for the artillery at Fortress Monroe, Virginia...." The order went on to provide basis guidance for the institution, which was to consist of "three field officers of cavalry or infantry, with not less than four companies of infantry, four troops of cavalry, one light battery of

artillery and officers attached for instruction...." The organization laid the ground work for the eventual establishment of the U.S. Army Command and General Staff College. During its early existence, the post was one of the few U.S Army garrisons with a substantial number of troops representing all three combat arms of the time, and thus an ideal place to test new uniforms and equipments, as well as tactics and other military considerations with the emphasis on practical application. Colonel Elwell S. Otis of the Twelfth U.S. Infantry was tasked with organizing the school. Elvid Hunt, *History of Fort Leavenworth, 1827-1937* (Ft. Leavenworth: Command and General Staff College, 1937), 133-5. Timothy K. Nenninger, *The Leavenworth Schools and the old Army: education, professionalism, and the officer corps of the United States Army, 1881-1918* (Westport, CT: Greenwood Press, 1978), remains the single most important volume on the overall subject of Ft. Leavenworth's history during this period.

104 J.F. Rodgers to A.B. Johnson, September 25, 1884, LS, Clothing Br., Book B, 1884, OQMG, RG92, NA.

105 J.F. Rodgers to Henry Allien, October 29, 1884, ibid. Allien was but one of the military outfitters who supplied officers that showed an interest in the matter. In at least two more cases, other firms were told that photographs of the overcoats were forthcoming. J.F. Rodgers to Jacob Reeds' Sons, October 30, 1884; and J.F. Rodgers to John Earle, November 1, 1884, ibid.

106 S.B. Holabird to AGUSA, October 16, 1884, ibid.

107 GO No. 21, HQA, October 21, 1884.

108 The prototype had a slightly smaller visor than the final model of the hood that was adopted. S.B. Holabird to M.I. Ludington, March 22, 1884, LS, Clothing Br., Book A, 1884, OQMG, RG92, NA.

109 Quartermaster Specification No. 175, June 22, 1886; and *ARSW*, 1886, Vol. I, 6-7.

110 *ARSW, 1887*, Vol. I, 213; and GO No. 48, HQA, July 6, 1887.

111 Rodenbaugh and Haskins, *The Army of the United States*, 66. Also see, Jack D. Foner, *The United States Army Between Two Wars: Army Life and Reform, 1865-1898* (New York: Humanities Press, 1970), 83; 85-6.

112 While Meigs indicated he had knowledge of a type of dress "used to some extent on the frontier, generally made of canvas," he sought the reactions about such an outfit from several subordinates on duty in his office. He claimed none of them judged "it an improvement, for general use, upon the dress ordinarily worn by civilized people in and out of the Army...." Meigs expressed his own bias ending with the fiat that the soldier's dress is for general use. "It is the only one he should wear while in service." M.C. Meigs to Secretary of War, March 15, 1881, LS, Clothing Br., Book A, 1881, OQMG, RG92, NA.

113 Risch, *Quartermaster Support of the Army*, 504. Once again, this action was characteristic of the department's gradual move "in the direction of providing more comfortable clothing, adapted to particular needs." Ibid., 505.

114 J.G. Chandler to Chief Quartermaster Military Division of the Pacific, January 8, 1884, LS, Clothing Br., Book A, 1884, OQMG, RG92, NA

115 J.G. Chandler to M.I. Ludington, January 8, 1884, ibid.

116 J.B. Chandler to Chief Quartermaster Military Division of the Missouri, January 8, 1884, ibid.

117 S.B. Holabird to Secretary of War, March 19, 1884, ibid.

118 Ibid. S.B. Holabird to M.I. Ludington, May 5, 1884, ibid., began the process with 7,000 sack coats and trouser sets being slated for production at Philadelphia from redyed tents. All materials, including trimmings and buttons were to be provided for another 5,000 sets to be fabricated at San Francisco, while sufficient buttons, trim, and a sample of the dyed brown tent canvas was to be provided for another 15,000 sets that would be produced at Jeffersonville.

119 S.B. Holabird to AGUSA, March 24, 1884; and S.B. Holabird to AGUSA, April 4, 1884, ibid. The final form of this document included the reference to the wool field blouse with lining, and discontinued previous references to unlined blouses in that they no longer were being made. Further, the general order as finally issued did not do away with the stable duty outfit and engineer overalls as was proposed in the earlier version. This point was emphasized in J.G. Chandler to E.H. Liscum, August 20, 1884, and S.B. Holabird to AGUSA, September 16, 1884, Book B, 1884, ibid., a document that not only pointed out mounted men would continue to draw the stable frock and overalls, but also the only mounted and dismounted men alike were entitled to a canvas fatigue suit that was classified as "equipage," and therefore was to remain the property of the army, rather than be issued to individual soldier. Evidence of stable duty garb being retained is found in S.B. Holabird to R. Saxon, February 8, 1884, Book A, 1884, ibid., which called for 3,000 pairs of mounted overalls to be produced from surplus shelter halves.

120 J.F. Rodgers to M.I. Ludington, September 27, 1884, Book B, 1884, ibid. The matter of cleaning these and other articles, such as bed sheets and pillow cases led the Quartermaster Department to explore washing machines. S.B. Holabird to George Cook, September 3, 1884, Book B, 1884, ibid. In earlier times, women had been employed as laundresses to undertake such tasks, but in 1878 official recognition of these individuals was withdrawn, with the idea that this would save the government considerable sums of money. Nevertheless, in some instances, women continued to provide this service for several years after general orders discontinued their employment. Patricia Y. Stallard, *Glittering Misery Dependents of the Indian Fighting Army. (Ft. Collins, CO: Old Army Press, 1978), 65-6.*

121 J.F. Rodgers to M.I. Ludington, October 11, 1884; and November 3, 1884, LS, Clothing Br., Book B, 1884, OQMG, 92, NA.

122 J.F. Rodgers to M.I. Ludington, November 3, 1884, ind.

123 J.F. Rodgers to St. Louis Depot, September 16, 1884, ibid.

124 S.B. Holabird to M.I. Ludington, May 22, 1884, ibid.

125 At first a hood was considered, and some were sent to "northwestern posts" for trial. "The result was not favorable, the hood catching the wind, and a high standing collar has been adopted." Further a blanket lined cap was seen as an improvement over the hood. J.F. Rodgers to E.P. Vollum, March 8, 1884, Book A, 1884, ibid. Later that month the quartermaster general requested that the caps that were being tried in the Department of Dakota be studied as to the addition of a visor of the same material as the body that had waterproof stiffening inside and hooks and eyes so that it could be fastened or lowered at will. Some prototypes were requested that added this feature, which was to become standard once the cap was adopted. S.B. Holabird to M.I. Ludington, March 11, 1884, ibid. Mittens of matching material also were reviewed, and a style with a thumb, rather than with fingers, was adopted. J.F. Rodgers to M.I. Ludington, April 9, 1884; and S.B. Holabird to M.I. Ludington, April 29, 1884, ibid.

126 GO No. 32, HQA, April 16, 1884.

127 In fact, some fifteen sizes had even been provided on a limited basis at the San Francisco, before settling upon a final range and measurements. S.B. Holabird to G.H. Weeks, January 16, 1884, LS, Clothing Br., Book A, 1884, OQMG, RG92, NA. Also see, S.B. Holabird to R. Saxon, January 16, 1884, ibid; and two letters from J.F. Rodgers to R.N. Batchelder, January 16, 1884, ibid.

128 S.B. Holabird to G.A. Hull, August 28, 1883, Box 84, Microfilm Collections, USAMHI. The same letter reminded Hull that the recent allowance for suspenders hopefully would "aid in bringing about a neater fit in the trowsers."

129 S. B. Holabird to G.A. Hull, December 11, 1883, ibid.

130 *ARSW, 1884*, Vol. I, 610.

131 S.B. Holabird to Chief Quartermaster Military Division of the Missouri, January 18, 1884, Book A; J.F. Rodgers to W.S. Edgerly, March 18, 1884, Book A; S.B. Holabird to Chief Quartermaster Division of the Pacific, July 21, 1884, Book B; S.B. Holabird to G.H. Weeks, July 21, 1884, Book B, 1884, LS, Clothing Br., OQMG, RG92, NA. Also see GO No. 81, HQA, July 20, 1884, which required "the discarded sizes from one to five" to be issued by the Quartermaster Department from the large stocks of made and unmade trousers. "The same rule will govern the issue of boots and shoes made with brass screws" the order concluded.

132 S.B. Holabird to AGUSA, July 26, 1884, LS, Clothing Br., Book B, 1884, OQMG, RG92, NA.

133 The requirement to issue the footgear on hand no doubt was related to an inventory of existing stocks being provided. See S.B. Holabird to A.P. Blunt, July 2, 1884, ibid. A slightly earlier letter detailed some of the key issues concerning defective brass screwed shoes. S.B. Holabird to M.I. Ludington, June 27, 1884, Book A, 1884, ibid. This meant some enlisted men still bought shoes from private sources, although a salesman, who had previously been licensed to sell footgear at the Presidio of San Francisco, was denied permission to renew his pass to the post to do so. Commanding Officer Presidio of San Francisco to Joe Henry, September 3, 1885, LR, Presidio of San Francisco, June 30, 1885 to July 3, 1886, RUSACC, RG393, NA.

134 udington, February 4, 1884, Book B, 1884, LS, Clothing Br., OQMG, RG 92, NA.

135 J.F. Rodgers to M.I. Ludington, January 29, 1884, ibid.

136 S.B. Holabird to M.I. Ludington, January 16, 1884, Book A, 1884, ibid.

137 S.B. Holabird to M.I. Ludington, January 18, 1884; S.B. Holabird to G.H. Weeks, March 10, 1884; J.F. Rodgers to Chief Quartermaster Military Division of the Pacific, April 22, 1884, and June 19, 1884, Book A, 1884; B.C. Card to Chief Quartermaster Military Division of the Missouri, August 11, 1884 and August 15, 1884, Book B, 1884; and J.F. Rodgers to Chief Quartermaster Military Division of the Missouri, August 16, 1884, Book B, 1884, ibid. It should be noted that all this cor respondence likewise indicated no new blouses in the expanded size scheme were available either.

One factor prohibiting immediate issue of the new sizes was not only the stocks on hand, but also the fact that by early 1884 the entire army supposedly had been supplied with new uniforms, and would not require replacements for nearly another year. J.D. Bingham to AGUSA, January 2, 1884, Book A, 1884, ibid.

138 J.F. Rodgers to R. Saxon, April 22, 1884, Book A, 1884, ibid. S.B.Holabird to M.I. Ludington, January 18, 1884, ibid., required new blouses and trousers to be of patterns and sizes adopted in 1884, but once again old stocks were to be dispersed first.

139 J.F. Rodgers to M.I. Ludington, October 22, 1884, Book B, 1884, ibid. Several months earlier there was another trial in the Military Division of the Atlantic, which called for the substitution of shank buttons for sewn on buttons for trousers, but the concept was not universally applied until many years in the future. J.F. Rodgers to M.I. Ludington, June 9, 1884, Book A, 1884, ibid.

140 J.F. Rodgers to M.I. Ludington, September 16, 1884; S.B. Holabird to M.I. Ludington, September 23, 1884; J.F. Rodgers to M.I. Ludington, October 24, 1884; and S.B. Holabird to C.W. Foster, October 30, 1884, Book B, 1884, ibid. Stocks of blouses often ran low as did forage caps, on occasion, as indicated by M.C. Meigs to Secretary of War, December 31, 1882, Book B, 1882, ibid.

141 S.B. Holabird to C.W. Foster, December 15, 1884, Book C, 1884, ibid.

142 S.B. Holabird to M.I. Ludington, January 16, 1884; and S.B. Holabird to M.I. Ludington, March 21, 1884, Book A, 1884, ibid. The second letter indicated that the blouses made from the 1881-pattern shirts were not to be issued, but all others were to have the cord taken off, and sent for issue, while another 1,500 of the new pattern would be made up and set aside for the emergency reserve.

143 S.B. Holabird to R. Saxton, February 20, 1884, ibid.

144 B.C. Card to C. Bentzoni, March 2, 1884, ibid., indicates that this officer's request for supplying his company of the Twenty-fifth U.S. Infantry would be answered with blouses and trousers made in the five old sizes, whereas orders for Ft. Bayard, New Mexico Territory and Ft. Porter, New York, discussed in two letters both sent

by J.F. Rodgers to R. Saxton, June 5, 1884, ibid., noted that blouses in six sizes were being furnished. A number of letters from J.F. Rodgers to M.I. Ludington all dated June 13, 1884, ibid., also indicated that blouses in the six sizes and trousers in the twelve sizes were to be sent to Ft. Monroe, Virginia; and the following posts on the eastern seaboard and upstate New York: Fts. Columbus; Niagara; Preble; Schuyler; Trumball; Wadsworth; and Warren. So, too, were the garrisons of Washington Barracks; Little Rock Barracks; Mt. Vernon Barracks, Alabama; Newport Barracks, Kentucky; Jackson Barracks; and two installations in Florida, Ft. Barracas and St. Francis Barracks. J.F. Rodgers to Jeffersonville Quartermaster Depot, September 3, 1884, ibid., spelled out seventy-two blouses for Ft. D.A. Russell, Wyoming Territory were to be in the six sizes, too.

145 J.F. Rodgers to M.I. Ludington, September 18, 1884; and October 24, 1884; and S.B. Holabird to R. Saxton, September 25, 1884, Book B, 1884, ibid. The last letter required shipment of 1,000 blouses of the 1884-pattern and several types of equipment to the St. Louis Depot.

146 J.F. Rodgers to M.I. Ludington, October 18, 1884; and J.F. Rodgers to G.H. Weeks, October 24, 1884, ibid.

147 C.G. Suotelle to M.I. Ludington, October 24, 1884; and J.F. Rodgers to Chief Quartermaster Washington, DC, November 10, 1884, ibid. The action prompted by the second letter referenced here caused the old sealed standard blouses to be issued, and seemingly accounts for the fact that none of the mid-1880s blouses are found in the surviving quartermaster collection now held by the Smithsonian Institution. Conversely, specimens of the three exterior pocket model, at least from around 1886, are.

As a related aside, earlier in the year the quartermaster general directed that all but the current samples of uniforms were to be removed from the sample room at Philadelphia and these were to be packed up so that there would be no confusion between old and new items. Additionally, "The Continental and other historical uniforms" were to "be locked up in cases, sealed, and the keys forwarded to the Quartermaster General." S.B. Holabird to M.I. Ludington, January 19, 1884, Book A, 1884, ibid.

148 J.F. Rodgers to G.E. Sage, December 18, 1884, Book C, 1884, ibid. Men under First Lieutenant George Sage of the Fifth Artillery stationed at Ft. Schuyler, New York were among the first to receive the latest pattern blouses.

As part of the transition to the blouse with outside pockets, a question was raised as to the comparative cost of the blouses without pockets that were being produced in early 1884 versus the cost for the 1874-pattern blouses that had been piped. J.F. Rodgers to G.H. Weeks, November 17, 1884, Book B, 1884, ibid. One item of continuity throughout this transition was the use of gray blouse lining, in only one weight, for the interior of the various jackets being provided during the period. J.F. Rodgers to Chief Quartermaster Military Division of the Pacific, December 22, 1884, Book C, 1884, ibid.

149 *A&NJ*, June 7, 1884, 914.

150 J.G. Chandler to G.H. Weeks, January 8, 1884, LS, Clothing Br., Book A, 1884, OQMG, RG92, NA, noted that Hull had sent correspondence relative to this subject on December 11, 1883. Hull had also experimented with fifteen sizes of trousers during this period to determine if even further refinements in that area were worth while.

151 G.A. Hull to Quartermaster General, January 14, 1884, Box 84, Microfilm Collections, USAMHI. Captain Hull also reported that new pattern blouses conforming to the measurements he had used for the dress coats had been tried out with the same positive results. His intention was to send these on to the quartermaster general for review as well.

152 J.F. Rodgers to M.I. Ludington, February 1, 1884, LS, Clothing Br., Book A, 1884, OQMG, RG92, NA.

153 S.B. Holabird to AGUSA, February 26, 1884, ibid. As early as 1881, when the new helmet was adopted, a writer who signed himself FDB (probably Captain Frank D. Baldwin of the Fifth U.S. Infantry) encouraged the abandonment of the metallic insignia and its replacement by silk thread embroidery. Given that the individual was at that time in Nice, France, he no doubt had seen a similar practice in use by French troops.

154 As the *Army and Navy Register*, March 29, 1884, 1, indicated, "Much complaint is had by many in the Army that the metallic numbers and insignias of corps, now worn on the collars of the uniform coats, soil and tear the facings. The Quartermaster General's recommendation to do away with said ornaments has been disapproved by higher authority." Similar information is found in *ARSW, 1884*, Vol. I, 614.

155 J.F. Rodgers to R.B. Ayers, April 14, 1884, LS, CLothing Br., Book A, 1884, OQMG, RG92, NA. Ayers was the commanding colonel of the Second Artillery, and he and some of his regiment were stationed in the Washington, DC, area at the time.

156 S.B. Holabird to E.S. Otis, April 18, 1884, ibid. Colonel Elwell S. Otis served as commandant of the School of Application, and was the commanding officer of the Twentieth U.S. Infantry, as well.

157 S.B. Holabird to M.I. Ludington, May 21, 1884, ibid. *ARSW, 1884*, Vol. I, 611, reiterated this decision, as well as noted the frequent complaints about the fading of infantry facings, but the matter of whether white would replace these and "the mode of trimming, which suggested themselves, have thus far delayed final results." This was written in the early summer for the annual report to be made for the fiscal ending June 20, 1884. In actuality, some coats with straps were converted to the new pattern with the collar completely covered in facing material, but the straps were not removed.

158 S.B. Holabird to AGUSA, May 24, 1884, LS, Clothing Br., Book A, 1884, OQMG, RG92, NA.

159 S.B. Holabird to W. Shafter, June 2, 1884, ibid.

160 W. Shafter to S.B. Holabird, June 3, 1884, ibid. The samples had cotton and silk stripes on them, but Shafter noted these were "only put on to show how they would look."

161 G.M. Randall to Quartermaster General, June 4, 1884, ibid.

162 S.B.. Holabird to M.I. Ludington, June 5, 1884, ibid. Also see, J.F. Rodgers to M.I. Ludington, June 10, 1884, ibid., which refers to both Shafter's and Randall's letters. With these activities in the mill, Shafter's modified trousers were to be sent back, and "a good looking silk and cotton, or wool and cotton webbing to be purchased so that sample trousers could be made as ordered. J.F. Rogers to M.I. Ludington, June 19, 1884, ibid.

163 S.B. Holabird to AGUSA, June 25, 1884, ibid.

164 S.B. Holabird to M.I. Ludington, June 26, 1884, ibid.

165 S.B. Holabird to M.I. Ludington, July 9, 1884, Book B, 1884, ibid.

166 C.G. Sawtelle to M.I. Ludington, October 23, 1884, ibid. When asked later about the color of cloth chevrons and stripes for enlisted men from a military supplier, the response again was that white had been designated in both instances. J.F. Rodgers to Pettibone and Company, November 13, 1884, ibid.

167 C.G. Sawtelle to M.I. Ludington, October 23, 1884, ibid. As part of the process the seven coats and four paper patterns used in making up samples were to be sent to Lieutenant Colonel Ludington to facilitate his ongoing efforts. J.F. Rodgers to R.N. Batchelder, October 24, 1884, ibid. This was followed by an acknowledgement that the four sets of patterns prepared by a Mr. Heiberger, and four coats made at the San Francisco Depot, along with the approved pattern was being sent to provide the foundation for new standards. J.F. Rodgers to M.I. Ludington, October 24, 1884, ibid.

168 C.G. Sawtelle to AGUSA, October 23, 1884, ibid.

169 S.B. Holabird to San Francisco Depot, November 29, 1884, ibid., indicated that the old coats trimmed in sky-blue and sky-blue chevrons should be sent to Philadelphia for conversion. The same letter was written to all the depots. See also S.B. Holabird to G.H. Weeks, December 16, 1884; and S.B. Holabird to M.I. Ludington, December 16, 1884, Book C, 1884, ibid., and noted that new-made coat would conform to the white faced pattern, and that the old coats could be converted for the fee stated in the text above.

As to some garrisons being sent new white trimmed coats early on, see J.F. Rodgers to G.H. Weeks, November 7, 1884, Book B, 1884, ibid., indicating Ft. Klamath, Oregon was going to receive such coats. Three letters written by Rodgers on November 21, 1884, mention dress coats and trousers with white facing were bound for Fts. Yates, Missoula, and Fred Steele, on the Northern Great Plains, as well as Ft. Selden, New Mexico Territory. Yet another letter of November 22, 1884, indicates Ft. Hays, Kansas was going to be provided with the coats and trousers as was Ft. Laramie, Wyoming Territory, according to a fifth piece of correspondence on November 24, 1884, ibid.

170 J.F. Rodgers to A.B. Johnson, October 28, 1884, ibid. Johnson was a first lieutenant of the Seventh U.S. Infantry, who at the time was posted with his company at Ft. Snelling, Minnesota.

171 *ARSW, 1884*, Vol. I, 615. This quotation specifically referred to Holabird's efforts to obtain mattresses, pillows, bed sheets and pillow-cases for enlisted men, who previously were issued pillow sacks and bed sacks that they filled with straw. More on this subject is found in S.B. Holabird to Secretary of War, March 11, 1884; and March 24, 1884; and S.B. Holabird to M.I. Ludington, April 12, 1884, LS, Clothing Br., Book A, 1884, OQMG, RG92, NA. Another indication of the propensity to furnish soldiers with items that would better their lot was the adoption of a barrack bag of 8 ounce cotton duck, the forerunner of the duffle bags carried by generations of GIs to this day. These were to be marked with a US on the bottom. S.B. Holabird to M.I. Ludington, February 11, 1884, ibid. Also see Quartermaster Specification No. 109, adopted March 23, 1884.

Holabird's department also oversaw all construction at military posts, and as such a number of improvements were made in the late nineteenth century to barracks and mess halls. This included the introduction of steam heating, indoor plumbing with hot and cold water, and other efforts to modernize. The addition of such things as bowling alleys and the establishment of the post canteen system were further manifestations of reforms that hoped to curb the twin problems of the Victorian era army—desertion and alcoholism—by offering superior living conditions to the soldiers than in the past. Indication of these changes can be found by reviewing two studies by William L. Brown III, A Pictorial Hist*ory of Enlisted Men's Barracks of the U.S. Army, 1861-1895* (Harpers Ferry, VA: National Park Service, 1984) and *The Army Called it Home: Military Interiors of the 19th Century* (Gettysburg, PA: Thomas Publications, 1992). Also of note for comparative purposes is David A. Clary, These *Relics of Barbarism: A History of Furniture in Barracks and Guardhouses of the United States Army, 1800-1880* (Harpers Ferry, VA: National Park Service, n.d.).

172 Ernest F. Fisher, Jr., *Guardians of the Republic: A History of the Noncommissioned Officers Corps of the U.S.* Army (New York: Ballantine Books, 1994), 137, mentions Holabird's central role in army reform. This is not to imply that Holabird invented the metallic lace chevron. Its used had been advocated many years before, such as found in *A&NJ*, January 29, 1870, 371, where a correspondent wrote that such additions should "adorn the soldiers; they could be seen at a good distance, although dearer in price [to cloth], they would last for years." In truth, the Britain's military had employed chevrons of gold and silver lace, and in earlier times so had the U.S. Army.

173 J.F. Rodgers to M.I. Ludington, January 3, 1884, LS, Clothing Br., 1884, Book A, OQMG, RG92, NA.

174 S.B. Holabird to H.C. Hodges, January 5, 1884, ibid.

175 J.F. Rodgers to G.S. Hoyt, January 18, 1884, ibid.

176 Raymold and Whitlock wanted to bid on the lace and the firm was told that the date for this process was extended to February 28, 1884. S.B. Holabird to M.I. Ludington, January 17, 1884, ibid.

177 S.B. Holabird M.I. Ludington, January 23, 1884, ibid.

178 J.F. Rodgers to M.I. Ludington, February 9, 1884, ibid.

179 S.B. Holabird to M.I. Ludington, March 18, 1884, ibid.

180 S.B. Holabird to M.I. Ludington, March 22, 1884, ibid.

181 S.B. Holabird to M.I. Ludington, March 24, 1884, ibid.

182 S.B. Holabird to M.I. Ludington, March 22, 1884, ibid.

183 S.B. Holabird to M.I. Ludington, March 24, 1884, ibid.

184 S.B. Holabird to M.I. Ludington, April 3, 1884, ibid. No mention was made of Signal Corps chevrons as yet.

185 J.F. Rodgers to A. Sharke, June 2, 1884, ibid.

186 S.B. Holabird to M.I. Ludington, June 7, 1884, ibid. The other articles called for were bunks, mattresses, mattress covers, pillows, and pillow cases.

187 S.B. Holabird to M.I. Ludington, June 21, 1884, ibid.

188 S.B. Holabird to M.I. Ludington, May 5, 1884, ibid.

189 S.B. Holabird to M.I. Ludington, May 9, 1884, ibid.

190 S.B. Holabird to M.I. Ludington, May 25, 1884, ibid.

191 S.B. Holabird to AGUSA, May 26, 1884; and S.B. Holabird to M.I. Ludington, June 12, 1884, Book B, 1884, ibid.

192 After that, obsolete cloth campaign chevrons began to be recalled from the field. J.F. Rodgers to Chief Quartermaster Military Division of the Missouri, August 27, 1884, ibid.

193 J.F. Rodgers to St. Louis Depot, September 18, 1884; J.F. Rodgers to Chief Quartermaster Military Division of the Missouri, September 25, 1884; and J.F. Rodgers to M.I. Ludington, September 29, 1884, ibid. Several months before the quartermaster general had required a uniform coat with infantry gold lace chevrons for a sergeant and another for a corporal with blue facings to be prepared as well as trousers with the requisite dark blue stripes. He went on to order one uniform coat with white piping and facing and gold lace sergeant's stripes on a white background instead of sky-blue as the other prototypes had been made. A corporal's coat with the white-backed gold lace chevrons was to be fabricated as well. The skirts of both were to have facings that went all the way to the bottom edge, but one of the two samples was to have a collar that was covered in white facing all the way around while the other was to have only the front of the collar faced "as in the present pattern." Finally, he mandated that "until further orders the manufacture of infantry chevrons and Infantry Uniform Coats will cease." S.B. Holabird to M.I. Ludington, June 2, 1884, Book A, 1884, ibid.

194 J.F. Rodgers to M.I. Ludington, September 29, 1884, and October 1, 1884; J.F. Rodgers to Chief Quartermaster Military Division of the Atlantic, October 3, 1884; J.F. Rodgers to St. Louis Depot, October 10, 1884; S.B. Holabird to M.I. Ludington, November 1, 1884, ibid.; and S.B. Holabird to AGUSA, December 26, 1884, Book C, 1884, ibid. The last two letters discussed the position of the commissary sergeant's crescent, with the November 1 piece of correspondence also noting that samples for new gold lace overcoat chevrons were being returned to the depot because these had not been adopted as at first proposed. As one indication that gold lace chevrons were supplied from other sources than Philadelphia a special requisition from the Presidio of San Francisco to provide non-commissioned officers with their metallic thread stripes was to be handled by shipments from New York and the San Francisco Depot. G.H. Weeks to Post Adjutant Presidio of San Francisco, November 15, 1886, Letter No. 756, LR, Presidio of San Francisco, RUSACC, RG393, NA.

195 A typical reply is found in J.F. Rodgers to M.I. Ludington, November 15, 1884, LS, Clothing Br., Book B, 1884, OQMG, RG92, NA, detailing the needs of Ft. Riley, Kansas.

196 J.F. Rodgers to Chief Quartermaster Military Division of the Missouri, November 15, 1884, ibid. During the previous month it was made known that Signal Corps chevrons were not yet available, but this probably did not remain the case fore long given the rather limited numbers of men to be supplied in this small organization. J.F. Rodgers to Acting Assistant Quartermaster Ft. Myer, Virginia, October 7, 1884, ibid.

197 J.F. Rodgers to M.I. Ludington, October 17, 1884, ibid.

198 S.B. Holabird to M.I. Ludington, November 1, 1884, ibid.

199 J.F. Rodgers to Chief Quartermaster Military Division of the Missouri, December 8, 1884; and December 23, 188, Book C, 1884, ibid.

200 J.F. Rodgers to M.I. Ludington, November 7, 1884, Book B, 1884, ibid. In actuality a chevron was not adopted for this rank until 1899.

201 S.B. Holabird to Commander Willets Point, New York, October 3, 1884, ibid. This was for the engineer band, but the same letter went to all commanders of cavalry, artillery, and infantry regiments.

202 H.M. Black to Quartermaster General, October 14, 1884, Box 1171, CCF, RG92, NA. Previously the regimental musicians had red facings "that made the band look as it were borrowed from the artillery." At first, the martial music makers did not agree with the change that had been instituted by the regimental adjutant, Charles Fayette Roe, who also had reorganized the band in toto, including obtaining new instruments, which he had sent by none other than John Philip Sousa of the U.S. Marine Corps Band. Frances M.A. Roe, *Army Letters from an Officer's Wife* (Lincoln: University of Nebraska Press, 1981), 338. Additional background on regular army bands of the late Victorian era, along with a number of representative photographs, is found in, Thomas S. Railsback and John P. Langellier, *The Drums Would Roll: A Pictorial History of U.S. Army bands on the American Frontier 1866-1900* (London: Arms and Armour Press, 1987).

203 Frank Wheaton to Quartermaster General, March 1, 1884, LS, Clothing Br., Book B, 1884, OQMG, RG92, NA.

204 William P. Carlin to S.B. Holabird, November 5, 1884, ibid.

205 J. Gibbon to S.B. Holabird, December 20, 1884, ibid.

206 C.M. Baily to Quartermaster General, November 26, 1884, ibid.

207 R.I. Dodge to Quartermaster General, October 28, 1884, ibid.

208 F.A Smith to Quartermaster General, October 28, 1884, ibid.

209 J.H. Potter to Quartermaster General, October 31, 1884, ibid.

210 W.T. Hatch to Quartermaster General, October 24, 1884, ibid.

211 W.B. Royall to Quartermaster General, November 26, 1884, ibid.

212 H.G. Gibson to Quartermaster General, October 15, 1884, ibid.

213 J. Hamilton to S.B. Holabird, July 10, 1885, ibid. Emerson, *Chevrons*, 51, discusses the regimental commissary sergeant's chevron.

214 Gordon Chappell, "The 'Pillbox' Cap in the United States Army c. 1866-1902," *Military Collector and Historian* XXXII No. 1 (Spring 1980): 4-15, remains the best single source on this non-regulation headgear. Langellier, *Hats Off*, 102-5, offers some additional information, but does not expand on Chappell's concise article.

215 J.F. Rodgers to M.I. Ludington, July 26, 1884, LS, Clothing Br., Book B, 1884, OQMG, RG92, NA.

216 J.F. Rodgers to M.I. Ludington, August 4, 1884, ibid.

217 J.F. Rodgers to M.I. Ludington, August 18, 1884, ibid. A wreath of laurel rather than oak leaves evidently was considered at this point, with the letters "QD" being smooth and of the style worn as cap and coat ornaments. J.F. Rodgers to M.I. Ludington, June 16, 1884; and June 24, 1884, Book A, 1884, ibid.

218 S.B. Holabird to M.I. Ludington, September 11, 1884, Book B, 1884, ibid. The sample sent on September 9 was returned a few days later to be used as the sealed standard. S.B. Holabird to M.I. Ludington, October 9, 1884, ibid.

219 S.B. Holabird to AGUSA, September 20, 1884, ibid.

220 According to ibid., the new general order did not mention gold lace devices for farriers, because they were not considered as non-commissioned officers.

221 J.F. Rodgers to Chief Quartermaster Military Division of the Missouri, December 1, 1884, Book C, 1884, ibid.

222 S.B. Holabird to M.I. Ludington, December 19, 1884, ibid. Earlier efforts in 1884 were made to ensure that the helmets being issued conformed to the standards. For example, J.F. Rodgers to M.I. Ludington, February 7, 1884, Book A, 1884, ibid., required twelve each eagles with commissary sergeants, engineers, hospital stewards, and signal corpsmen overlays, along with a dozen sets of German silver numbers from 1 to 0, cap ornaments for each branch, and brass numbers from 1 to 0 to be provided to the office of the quartermaster general. J.F. Rodgers to M.I. Ludington, January 31, 1884, ibid., likewise requested six each of the enlisted helmet eagle types to be sent to the office. It should be noted that the trim for the post quartermaster sergeant helmets was not announced until GO No. 104, HQA, October 3, 1885.

223 S.B. Holabird to M.I. Ludington, October 18, 1884, LS, Clothing Br., Book B, 1884, OQMG, 92, NA.

224 *ARSW, 1884*, Vol. I, 614.

225 Ibid. For a brief discourse on enlisted initiatives to devise a means to over come these weaknesses read, T.J. Sperry, "1872 Enlisted Insignia Expedient Attachment Devices," *Military Collector and Historian* LXI No. 1 (Spring 1989): 43-5.

226 J.F. Rodgers to R. Smith, February 26, 1884, LS, Clothing Br., Book A, 1884, OQMG, RG92, NA. Later in the year, correspondence indicated that dispensing the far from popular collar numerals had been halted. J.F. Rodgers to Chief Quartermaster Military Division of the Missouri, November 1, 1884, Book B, 1884, ibid. As another related dictate, according to Cir. No. 11, HQA, December 10. 1884, "The only decorations allowed to be worn on occasions of ceremony are the 'army corps badge'..., the 'medal of honor;' and the several distinctive marks given for excellence in rifle practice...." This same circular noted that the summer helmet was permitted to be worn "on exceptional occasions, as a relief from the burning effects of the sun" in combination with the dress uniform, but was not considered "as part of the permanent dress uniform...."

227 J.F. Rodgers to S. Smith, February 16, 1884, Book A, 1884, OQMG, RG 92, NA. It is unclear while Smith was singled out for his opinion. Perhaps he had made some suggestions that Holabird was responding to through Rodgers.

22 J.F. Rodgers to M.I. Ludington, February 28, 1884, ibid.

229 S.B. Holabird to M.I. Ludington, March 6, 1884, ibid.

230 S.B. Holabird to M.I. Ludington, March 25, 1884, ibid.

231 S.B. Holabird to M.I. Ludington, May 24, 1884, ibid.

232 J.F. Rodgers to E.L. Zalinski, December 23, 1884, Book C, 1884, ibid.

233 The solution that eventually was adopted is treated in, William K. Emerson, "U.S. Army Enlisted Cap Insignia, 1896-1905," *Military Collector and Historian* XXIV No. 1 (Spring 1972): 11-15.

234 J.F. Rodgers to G.H. Weeks. August 2, 1884, LS, Clothing Br., Book B, 1884, OQMG, RG92, NA.

235 S.B. Holabird to Chief Signal Officer of the Army, February 4, 1884, ibid.

236 S.B. Holabird to Chief Signal Officer of the Army, February 11, 1884 , Book A, 1884, ibid.

237 June 10, 1884, handwritten note attached to a copy of the May 9, 1884, Memorandum from the Office of the Chief Signal Officer, CCF, Box 1171, File 278, OQMG, RG92, NA.

238 Horstmann Bros. to J.F. Rodgers, May 2, 1884, CCF, Box 1169, ibid.

239 B.C. Card to Horstmann Bros., May 19, 1884. LS, Clothing Br., Book A, 1884, ibid. GO No. 30 had stated the gold and silver embroidered cross flags and torch design was to be used, and even indicated that the patterns adopted were "deposited in the office of the Chief Signal Officer", but the descriptions were sufficiently vague as to require additional details to be sought not only by military outfitters, but also by the Quartermaster Department.

240 Carl W.A. Carlson, "U.S. Army Marksmanship Medals 1882-1897: A Critical Examination," *The Token and Medal Society* (February 1983): 4-10; and N. Neil Harris, ed., *Medals of the United States Mint The First Century 1792-1892* (N.P.: Token and Medal Society, n.d.), 337-52, provide useful data and images for the prizes awarded at the higher levels of competition.
As an indication of the serious efforts being made to promote the marksmanship program, those who were earned department or divisional awards were sent their medals via registered mail, and when received the garrison was to fall out "to participate in a ceremony attending the distribution of medals to those who were successful in winning places in the Division Rifle Team...." Inspector Rifle Practice Department of Arizona to Adjutant Presidio of San Francisco, August 3, 1886; and C. McKeever to Post Adjutant Presidio of San Francisco, September 8, 1886, LR, Presidio of San Francisco, RUSACC, RG393, NA.

241 *A&NJ*, November 15, 1884, 312.

242 *ARSW, 1885*, Vol. I, 627.

243 During the Civil War hospital corps and ambulance corps devices were developed, but these were not recognized on an international basis. See, Frederick P. Todd, *American Military Equipage 1851-1872,* Vol II (Providence, RI: The Company of Military Historians, 1977), 396-8.

244 This perquisite was not extended to enlisted personnel, however. S.B. Holabird to Chief Quartermaster Military Division of the Missouri, January 29, 1884, LS, Clothing Br., Book A, 1884, OQMG, RG92, NA. Nor was the suggestion that the department go beyond making material available for sale by providing coats for purchase as well, ever authorized. J.F Rodgers to E.P. Vollum, March 8, 1884, ibid.

245 S.B. Holabird to M.I. Ludington, September 13, 1884, Book B, 1884, ibid.

246 S.B. Holabird to M.I. Ludington, October 7, 1884, ibid.

247 J.F. Rodgers to H.C. Hodges, October 18, 1884, ibid.

248 J.F. Rodgers to M.I. Ludington, November 5, 1884, ibid. Horstmann also was involved in an exchange at this time related to a separate issue involving officers. The firm wanted to know whether infantry officers would adopt white as their facings in keeping with the change to that color for infantry enlisted men. This would mean new shoulder knots and straps for all officers, along with a new dress belt for company grade officers. The answer was that the action was pending. J.F. Rodgers to Horstmann Bros., October 25, 1884; and October 27, 1884, ibid. Immediately after this, Sheridan, to spare infantry officers the expense of such changes for the time being at least, determined that their facings would remain unchanged "at present." J.F. Rodgers to A.B.Johnson, October 28, 1884, ibid.

249 S.B. Holabird to M.I. Ludington, January 18, 1884, and January 29, 1884, Book A, 1884; J.F. Rodgers to M.I. Ludington, Book B, 1884, ibid; and *ARSW, 1884*, Vol. I, 613-4.

250 Ibid., 613.

251 Ibid., 610.

252 Ibid., 613.

253 Exchanges that led to the evolution and final version of this overcoat are found in S.B. Holabird to M.I. Ludington, January 16, 1884; January 31, 1884; and February 7, 1884, LS, Clothing Br., Book A, 1884, OQMG, RG92, NA. Also see, J.F. Rodgers to M.I. Ludington, September 27, 1884, Book B, 1884, ibid. While colorful, the - lining of capes in branch colors periodically required cloth to be furnished to recruits who had been issued great coats for one branch of the service, but who subsequently were transferred to another branch once their final assignments were made. One example of this is found in S.B. Holabird to Chief Quartermaster Military Division of the Atlantic, January 30, 1884, Book A, 1884, ibid., where men who had been given infantry overcoats had to remove their dark blue lining, which were to be returned to Philadelphia, while red cape lining was provided as a replacement for the new artillerymen. In another instance, enlisted men and officers at Ft. Lewis, Colorado were furnished dark blue cloth to line their great coats. S.B. Holabird to Chief Quartermaster Military Division of Missouri, February 7, 1884, ibid. This sort of requirement continued as indicated by a request for refunds to be made to men of the Fifth Artillery who had to pay for changes of their overcoat cape linings. F. Thorp to Post Adjutant Presidio of San Francisco, California, March 15, 1891, Letter No. 355, LR, Presidio of San Francisco, Letters February 20, 1891 to June 23, 1891, RUSACC, RG393, NA.

254 *ARSW, 1884*, Vol. I, 612. According to the *Army and Navy Register*, April 5, 1884, 7, the gauntlets were to be charged at $1.00 per pair. This was in lieu of the issue of fifteen pairs of Berlin gloves each year for enlisted men of the mounted service. S.B. Holabird to Chief Quartermaster Military Division of the Pacific, March 18, 1884, LS, Clothing Br., Book A, 1884, OQMG, RG92, NA. Again it appears that San Francisco played a leading role in this activity because personnel there were asked to provide four sample pairs to the quartermaster general, and later when the gauntlets supplied by the contract to James R. Michael were rejected, the San Francisco Depot officers were permitted to look into other sources, such as Raymold & Squire, with the proviso that the cost would be around $.95 per pair. S.B. Holabird to G.H Weeks, March 18, 1884; and S.B. Holabird to M.I. Ludington, May 26, 1884, ibid.

255 S.B. Holabird to AGUSA, March 18, 1884, ibid., requested that a general order be published amending regulations by adding paragraph 2778 1/2 permitting three pairs of gauntlets for each mounted enlisted man during a five year enlistment.

256 J.F. Rodgers to Chief Quartermaster Military Division of the Missouri, September 16, 1885, Book B, ibid., noted that the supply of gauntlets was "quite limited" and as such those ordered for Indian Scouts at Ft. Assiniboine, Montana Territory would not be shipped inasmuch as the scouts had been discharged on August 31.

257 *ARSW, 1884*, Vol. I, 614.

258 Rodgers' report on "The Military Shoe", and the process by which it was advanced to the quartermaster general then on to the secretary of war is found in, *ARSW, 1883*, Vol. I, 485-90.

259 S.B. Holabird to A.P. Blunt, January 18, 1884; January 28, 1884; April 12, 1884; and June 4, 1884, LS, Clothing Br., Book A, 1884, OQMG, RG92, NA.

260 *ARSW, 1884*, Vol. I, 612; and 682. In fact, a redesign of the "arctics" was undertaken in 1884, too. S.B. Holabird to A.P. Blunt, April 19, 1884, LS, Clothing Br., Book A, 1884, OQMG, RG92, NA; and *ARSW, 1885*, Vol. I, 604.

261 *ARSW, 1884*, Vol. I, 613.

262 S.B. Holabird to AGUSA, January 5, 1884, LS, Clothing Br., Book A, 1884, OQMG, RG92, NA.

263 S.B. Holabird to A.P. Blunt, January 25, 1884; and February 1, 1884, ibid.

264 *ARSW, 1884*, Vol. I, 613.

265 See for instance, J.F. Rodgers to J.A. Swift, January 15, 1884, Book A, 1884; and J.F. Rodgers to St. Louis Depot, September 18, 1884, Book B, 1884, LS, Clothing Br., OQMG, RG92, NA. In fact, specifications were not even adopted until April 24, 1884, for boots, post, and field shoes, while the first 500 prototype campaign shoes were not available for issue until 1885. Brinckerhoff, *Boots and Shoes of the Frontier Soldier*, 21.

266 S.B. Holabird to M.I. Ludington, June 7, 1884, LS, Clothing Br., Book A, 1884, OQMG, RG92, NA, offers an example of some typical contract awards in 1884. Information regarding price lists are found in S.B. Holabird to J.G.C. Lee, May 7, 1884, ibid. Surplus sales included old bugles that had been replaced by trumpets. S.B. Holabird to Secretary of War, January 24, 1884, ibid.

267 S.B. Holabird to M.I. Ludington, June 17, 1884, ibid.

268 *ARSW, 1884*, Vol. I, 615.

269 Living in open barracks did not preclude individuals from having their belongings pilfered, and there even was an instance in 1884 whereby a network had been set up to "fence" stolen U.S. Marine Corps uniforms. S.B. Holabird to M.I. Ludington, July 11, 1884, LS, Clothing Br., Book B, 1884, OQMG, RG92, NA. Sometimes military convicts even sold government clothing in order to buy liquor. Commanding Officer Ft. Mason, California to Post Adjutant Presidio of San Francisco, California, May 23, 1889, Letter No. 1262, LR, Presidio of San Francisco, March 11, 1889 to June 28, 1889, RUSACC, RG393, NA.

270 *ARSW, 1884*, Vol. I, 614-5.

271 See S.B. Holabird endorsement to a letter from Webster, J. M. Webster, July 12, 1884, Book B, 1884; and S.B. Holabird to Chief Quartermaster Department of Texas, December 18, 1884, Book C, 1884, LS, Clothing Br., OQMG, RG92, NA.

272 J.F. Rodgers to H.B. Osgood, September 3, 1884, Book B, 1884, ibid. Rodgers was not always as supportive When asked for his thoughts about leggings he retorted that in his experience they were "a useless appendage and most of them thrown away by the troops in the active campaigning during the Civil War." J.F. Rodgers to O.B. Mitcham September 3, 1884, ibid. Captain Mitcham was stationed at Cheyenne Depot, Wyoming Territory as an ordnance officer.

273 *ARSW, 1884*, Vol. I, 610.

3

"About as perfect as human thought can make them," 1885-1887

After considering several options, the Quartermaster Department settled on a new dress uniform design for infantrymen, with all white facings and trim and a fully covered collar. This 1884-pattern infantry coat was to be worn with the 1881 pattern dress helmet as seen in a full length portrait of Private Carter Huse, Twenty-fifth U.S Infantry. Huse wears one service in war or campaign chevron with its white backing on his coat nearest the cuff, as called for by orders, and regular service stripes of gold lace on dark blue cloth of the same material used to make the coat above these, indicating he had completed three five year terms of peacetime enlistment. SHSND

Quartermaster Department personnel spent much of 1885 laboring to make good the plans approved the previous year for such articles as gold lace chevrons.[1] Indeed, early in 1885 about half the gold lace stripes needed to supply the army were available. Nevertheless, instructions were given to buy sufficient yardage of lace to keep the manufacturing process on track—sound advice, in that the first batch of material that had been procured ran out during the summer.[2] Included in this scheme were service in war chevrons that were to be given to all soldiers, whether regulars or volunteers, who had been honorably discharged from duty "during the war of the rebellion."[3] Some of the first of these had been prepared for cavalry and artillery veterans, the backing being yellow and scarlet facing material, respectively. There was some discussion to cease this policy, evidently as a cost saving measure, but the quartermaster general could see no reason why there should be a reversal in this situation.[4] The provisions of General Orders No. 107, Headquarters of the Army, September 12, 1884, therefore remained in force, whereby service in war and campaign service chevrons were to be in the colors of the branch in which the veteran served, and were to be worn solely with the dress coat, rather than with the overcoat and blouse, as well.[5] Moreover, according to this original concept, service in peace hash marks were to be sewn above the cuff of the dress coat, but in this case the gold lace was to be attached to a dark blue backing.[6] In this latter instance, dark blue enlisted infantry trouser stripes, having been replaced by white webbing, were recalled to be salvaged where possible for the backgrounds of service in peace chevrons as a means to recycle material and save money.[7]

Clearly the intent was to forge ahead, and arrangements even were made for stripes to be provided to infantrymen.[8] Despite the initial delay, limited supplies were in hand to respond to some requisitions for gold lace chevrons for foot soldiers, although not every order was to be satisfied immediately.[9] Certain garrisons, though, including Ft. Reno. Indian Territory and Ft. Elliot, Texas, were given approval to have their supply sent in early February, while Ft. D.A. Russell, Wyoming Territory, had its request honored shortly thereafter.[10]

Of course, not everyone was satisfied with the rate which orders were filled. Because of the general press from the field to obtain gold lace chevrons, white infantry facings, and webbing trouser stripes, delays were inevitable, as was the resultant grumbling from some quarters.[11]

There also were some caveats, because the chevrons in particular were costly. This meant they were not to be ordered in amounts that would result in accumulation at various posts, where there were "no facilities to properly care for them." Unissued gold lace was subject to tarnishing, and thereby the formerly bright stripes would be rendered unserviceable.[12]

During the process, Lieutenant General Sheridan added one more ingredient to the mix, when he directed that thereafter the points of the crescent on commissary sergeant's chevrons should face forward, rather than upward, in accordance with General Orders No. 107 of 1884. This required four new standard patterns to be made conforming to the scheme, and alteration, if possible, of existing stocks based on the old "points up" design.[13] The same change eventually would follow for cloth chevrons, too.[14]

While toiling to turn out gold lace chevrons, quartermaster officials also expedited dispersement of the white faced infantry dress coat, and white cloth chevrons for blouses.[15] One method to quicken the pace was a requirement to convert sky blue-faced coats with white facings. This revamping was undertaken at the depots for unissued coats.[16] Once again there was a proviso. These remodeled coats were to be supplied first, before any new made ones reflecting changes in cloth and cut could be released.[17]

Similarly, under the previous provisions of General Orders No. 120, Headquarters of the Army, October 21, 1884, enlisted men could receive the new facings and chevrons without charge, and have the coats altered by a local tailor, a practice that was in full swing judging from the amount of precut white material being sent to the various garrisons early in the year, a procedure that would be repeated well into 1886 in some cases.[18]

But it was not just doughboys who were being re-outfitted by this point. It seems the quartermaster general was so pleased with the pattern coat selected for infantry, with its full faced collar and other changes, that he desired it to be adopted for all branches. Because of this, he had his office supplied with samples of the uniform dress coats and found them to be satisfactory. This meant four sets of mounted and dismounted coats for all branches were to be prepared, along with paper patterns of each size and correct specifications, which would be forwarded to Washington for final inspection.[19] The creation of new guidelines to replace those in use since February 27, 1880, would be required as part of the process.

Holabird gave the updated specifications his consent on March 7, 1885, and sealed samples for Signal Corps privates and musicians, post ordnance sergeants, ordnance enlisted men, light and foot artillery musicians, infantry musicians, engineers and engineer musicians, hospital

Infantry company musicians likewise were to be decked out in a dress coat with white facings, piping, and worsted herringbones on the chest according to the 1884 scheme. This bugler with his prodigious sideburns, who served in Company I, Twentieth U.S. Infantry, wears the coat adopted for infantry musicians in that year, and the 1884-pattern trousers, as well as a forage cap, rather than the spiked helmet that normally was associated with the dress uniform. Because he was having his picture taken in a studio, he could deviate from the regulations to suit his own tastes, but would not have done so on the parade ground. FAM

The survey conducted at the end of 1884 regarding band uniforms bore fruit by the following year when a mounted helmet with plume, bands, and cords was approved for infantrymen as dress wear. Additionally, bandsmen in all branches were to have a German silver lyre device for their helmets, music pouches, and shoulder knots with attached aiguillette in the branch color, as seen here for an infantry bandsmen about 1885 with the traditional herringbone trim on the chest of his uniform coat. GC

This infantry bandsman wears the regulation 1884-pattern dress coat for his branch, rather than the one specified for musicians with herringbone. All the other accessories are those adopted in 1885, including the 1/2 inch double trouser stripes. This is but one example that demonstrated, even after an effort to standardize, considerable latitude remained from one regimental band to the next in terms of dress and undress uniforms. FAM

An infantry color guard at Ft. Douglas, Utah Territory, in their 1884-pattern dress uniform. Note that the color sergeant in the center with the new chevron having a circle above the three gold lace stripes, which was adopted in 1883 for this honored position. This picture was taken circa 1885, as indicated by the marksmanship cross on the chest of the private standing to the left of the color sergeant. LDSA

stewards, commissary sergeants, and post quartermaster sergeants were to be prepared and sent to the general depots as models.[20] Thirteen other samples, presumably those not included in the original batch, were approved the following month.[21] The ever industrious Captain Hull in San Francisco suggested existing coats in the depot be transformed to match the new style as closely as possible, much as was being accomplished for infantry coats. As expected, Holabird concurred with this practical strategy.[22]

Even so, the coats for infantrymen were seen as a "radical change" from prior patterns, while alterations for all other branches at first only entailed new collar facings being added all around, a practice that accounts in part for some existent coats that have both fully faced collars and also retain belt loops, contrary to the discontinuance of this appendage as early as 1884.[23] This line of reasoning led the secretary of war to deny any addition to the clothing allowance for the other branches when their coats were revamped.[24] Nonetheless, the previous pattern coats for artillerymen began to be returned to the depot at San Francisco from Alcatraz for new facings to be applied.[25] Ultimately, all dress coats that were in stock for the artillery, engineers, and ordnance personnel "not in accordance with the latest patterns as regards trimmings on collar and skirts" were to be sent to Philadelphia for refurbishment.[26] Here it became evident that the replacement of collars was not the only change to be made, in that the longer skirt facings for dismounted coats now were added to the process.[27]

As another instance of this evolution, Holabird interpreted General Orders No. 120 as having dispensed with collar devices in that none were mentioned for use by the infantry.[28] To make this official, General Orders No. 104, Headquarters of the Army, October 3, 1885, published the secretary of war's directive to annul earlier regulations calling for

(Right) An 1884-pattern first sergeant of infantry uniform coat with bullion lace chevrons and the 1881-pattern infantry enlisted helmet of the body configuration that came into being in the late nineteenth-century. (Left) An infantry bandsman's uniform coat of the 1884-pattern with the worsted shoulder knots, aiguillette, and helmet cords adopted in 1885. The mounted style helmet with German silver lyre overlay also became regulation in 1885. Crossed rifle side buttons remained in use, however, and no lyre of bugle helmet side buttons are known to have been issued in the U.S. Army. Photograph by Glen Swanson. GS

Details of linings and interiors of 1884-pattern infantry dress coats. JB

Left top to bottom: Buff facing cloth formed the basis for the 1885-pattern post quartermaster sergeant chevrons, with yellow silk thread embroidered key and quill above on a piece of dark blue cloth of the same color as the enlisted blouse. These chevrons also were to be worn on the overcoat, which had a buff lined cape; 1872-1902 Ordnance Corps first sergeant; 1872-1902 Engineer sergeant; 1872-1887 pattern hospital steward; Right top to bottom: cavalry sergeant major 1872-1902; cavalry color sergeant 1883-1901 (both in the darker yellow adopted in 1887); infantry principal musician 1873-1884; and commissary sergeant 1872-1885. Bottom center: custom variant of a commissary sergeant chevron, c. 1880. Photograph by Susan Einstein. AMWH

collar devices. With the objectionable ornaments discontinued, a breast pin with the company letter and regimental number was seen as a possible replacement for use on the uniform coat. Designs were solicited from Philadelphia as part of an ongoing consideration of this topic.[29] The resulting sketches were not what had been envisioned, however, because while some of them were deemed "pretty," all were "too large." The services of a jeweler seemed appropriate at this point, in that someone with such experience might "be very apt to furnish proper designs." A horseshoe pin of approximately the scale being seen as optimum was furnished, too, which was viewed as a basis for a cavalry device, while crossed cannon could be incorporated into an artillery pin, and so forth.[30]

Eventually this idea was abandoned, but in the meantime, recently appointed post quartermaster sergeants would be granted their appropriate insignia. The crossed key and pen were adopted officially on February 24, 1885, for the forage cap and helmet plate, in keeping with the inserts for both the cloth and gold lace chevrons.[31] Once again, General Orders No. 104 sanctioned these German silver devices that doubled as the overlay on the helmet plate and the cap device, in the latter case being encircled by a burnished wreath. And when a post quartermaster sergeant elected to wear a campaign hat, he could add a cavalry hat cord if he desired, the existing stocks being surveyed for those "of the lightest shade" to answer this purpose, while those with more of an orange cast were regarded as adequate for the use of signal personnel.[32]

For the most part, however, the post quartermaster sergeants would be receiving newly-made insignia and uniform components fabricated at the depots so that they might turn out in their finery, including the fire-gilded staff buttons that had been procured for them by purchase on the open market from J.H. Wilson of Philadelphia.[33] With that, some of the earliest uniform requisitions would be approved for these non-commissioned staff officers at Ft. Fred Steele and Ft. Laramie, both in Wyoming Territory, along with Ft. Winfield Scott, California, and Ft. Bowie, Ft. Apache, and Camp Verde, Arizona Territory. In fact, at the first named garrison it was made clear that not only the dress coat, but also the overcoat, blouse, trousers, and all other elements of the basic outfit would be sent, with the chevrons attached where applicable.[34] While this seemed to be common practice, some orders were less encompassing, or made to special instructions via requests.[35]

Whatever the mode of supply, Holabird seemed willing to provide the new post quartermaster sergeants with their buff faced uniforms and crossed key with pen insignia.[36] Similarly, he wanted to set things in

During the mid-1880s the mixture of new items with old ones became common, as depicted by this sergeant of either the Ninth or Tenth U.S. Cavalry in the dress uniform of 1884-1885 with the new gold lace chevrons, boots, and gauntlets, but the old 1872-pattern uniform coat. Photograph by Eric Long. SI

motion for the manufacture of the fire gilded general service button that had been approved in 1884. This was in reaction to an observation "that the present buttons require constant cleaning and that in consequence the cloth becomes soiled; that the buttons in use in the U.S. Marine Corps can be worn without hardly tarnishing, &c." Thus, fire gilt was to be looked into, or some other method to provide this result, and the price for quantities was to be determined.[37]

In early March 1885, after examining samples of both large and small sizes provided by Allien and Company at an estimated $2.25 per gross, he was satisfied with the product. He then authorized the use of "this kind of button on all the uniform dress coats" made thereafter rather than continue with the 1854-pattern button. Lastly, he wanted "each coat having the new buttons" to bear "a tag indicating that the buttons are of fine gilt." With that Holabird called for the preparation of a specification accompanied by four sets of the samples to be provided to his office. Within a few weeks Colonel Ludington sent back the required items.[38] Once these had been bought, they were applied to both the new coats, as well as furnished in sets on occasion to modify old pattern coats already in the hands of the troops, such as for Ft. Concho, Texas, and Ft. Sisseton, Dakota Territory.[39] Once distributed these buttons required less care, thereby reducing one of the time consuming chores of troops to polish their brass buttons. Nonetheless, this practice was not completely eliminated, requiring the soldier to obtain a button board or come up with some other means to keep his uniform from being stained while he buffed his buttons.[40]

In certain instances the 1872-pattern dress coat was converted to approximate the new 1885-pattern by the addition of a fully-faced collar and the removal of the belt loops, as seen here in the case of a coat for a private of the light artillery. Photograph by Gordon Chappell. ES

Procurement of the gilt button was but one of many expenses incurred by the Quartermaster Department in 1885.[41] Consequently, the transfer of $4,823.69 worth of clothing to the Signal Corps and reimbursement for these items came as a welcome source of replenishment for Holabird's budget. This action came about as the result of a special congressional appropriation for the increased support of the Signal Corps.[42]

Despite a shaky relationship with the secretary of war, Brigadier General Hazen successfully sought additional funding for his highly restricted operations.[43] To his disappointment, however, this increase in resources failed to provide for additional officers to supplement the few second lieutenants that made up the organization, including provisions for a colonel, a lieutenant colonel, a major, a disbursing officer, and eight captains selected from long-service lieutenants were denied.[44]

Although Hazen did not have his way in terms of increased personnel, he did take it upon himself to customize the basic uniform, at least in so far as it was worn at Ft. Myer, Virginia, where signalmen received their training. He noted that while under instruction his men wore white linen cuffs and a plain white linen collar that stood one and one-half inches high, over which they placed a black stockband that was secured with a buckle, all of which was "intended to give the men in the school a neat appearance...." Likewise, the summer helmet was embraced, thereby rendering the formally authorized straw hat obsolete. Hazen related, though, that his was "not in any sense" to be construed as a "change of the prescribed uniform."[45] This was borne out by the fact that the special congressional allowance was applied to purchases of standard items from the Quartermaster Department.

The inventory of goods transferred to Hazen's corps included some seventy-five untrimmed helmet bodies with all the cords, plumes, and items necessary to complete them. He wanted thirty sets of canvas fatigue clothing sets (blouse and trousers) as well, but only three regular blouses and seven pairs of kersey trousers. Conversely, larger quantities of such practical items as underwear (200 shirts and drawers each) and overcoats (100) were called for, along with 300 pairs of wool stockings and 500 pairs of cotton stockings. To allow for production of other uniform items, Hazen's organization was furnished 100 yards of dark blue cloth, and nearly the same amount of kersey, along with 50 1/2 yards of dark blue flannel for blouses. There were four trumpets, too, and 900 pairs of Berlin gloves, 50 sets of facings for dress coats, plus 173 dress coats. To complete these coats, 151 pairs of gold lace sergeant chevrons, 30 for corporals, and 45 pairs of service in war stripes were applied for. One hundred and fifty crossed flag devices for sleeve markings rounded out the order.[46]

Early on Holabird made it known there would be no problem in providing these articles, including the full dress coats.[47] So, too, would gold lace chevrons be furnished as soon as requisitions had been received for them. Once the formal application was made "instructions for immediate manufacture and supply" would be given.[48] There also were ample plumes, helmet cords, overlays, and side buttons for shipment to the Signal Corps to fulfill a transfer of clothing items.[49]

Several 1872-pattern coats were converted to conform to the 1884-pattern infantry coat or the 1885-pattern uniform coat for other branches, such as this example for a cavalry private, which had its collar replaced or recovered in light yellow facing material to match the other trim. Note the two service stripes in gold lace on the sleeves above the cuff of the pattern adopted in 1884. WSHS

The belt loops were supposed to be discontinued as of 1884, but this cavalry trooper's coat retains the appendages as just one example of the many variations that existed during the transitional mid-1880s. WSHS

It did not take long before the bulk orders exhausted the funds available, however. By mid-May the Quartermaster Department ceased making signal devices and gold lace chevrons, realizing that the source of money was near an end. All other work for the Signal Corps was to stop for the same reason, and statements as to what items still remained from requisitions were to be reviewed.[50] Holabird contacted Hazen at this point, informing his colleague that only $256.19 was left in the special account, and this was before $25.76 had been deducted for helmet plumes. Then the quartermaster general enumerated the articles that could be provided before no more credit was available.[51]

Even under the circumstances, Holabird supported a change in enlisted insignia, which entailed the adding of a torch to the crossed flags in keeping with the design for officers of the Signal Corps. His only request was for a sample of the new device so that his department could provide them.[52] Over a month later, when the designs had not been received, he wrote to the chief signal officer asking that the style Hazen desired for helmet overlays and cap insignia be provided so that dies

An example of inspection stamp found inside an 1884-pattern and infantry uniform coat in size 2. AHS

Another example of the evolution of the dress coat in the mid-1880s is seen in this 1885-pattern cavalry musician's coat that conforms to all the standard specifications of the time, but has cloth chevrons for a principal musician, rather than gold lace chevrons per regulations as of 1884. This may be a prototype that was made up before the changeover to gold lace had been confirmed. SI

The sample pattern of the cavalry chief trumpeter's uniform coat as finally adopted in 1885. SI.

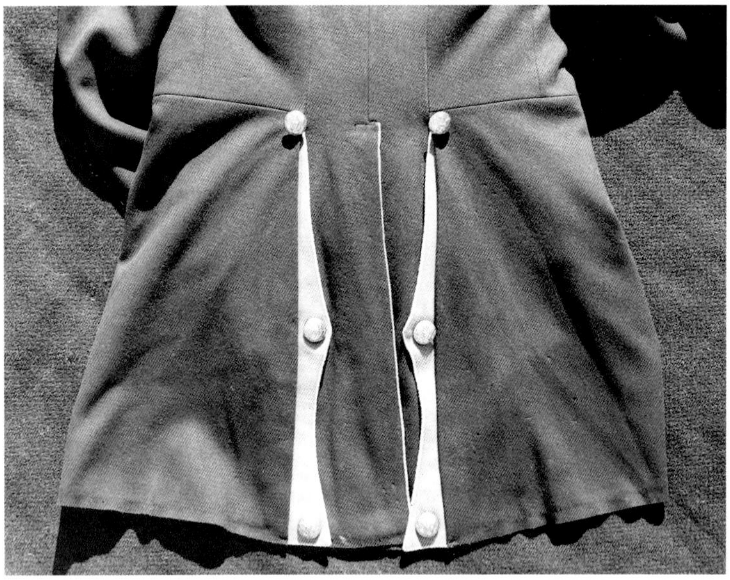

One of the changes to the uniform coat adopted for infantry in 1884, and for all other dismounted troops the following year was the lengthening of the facing decoration on the tails. SI

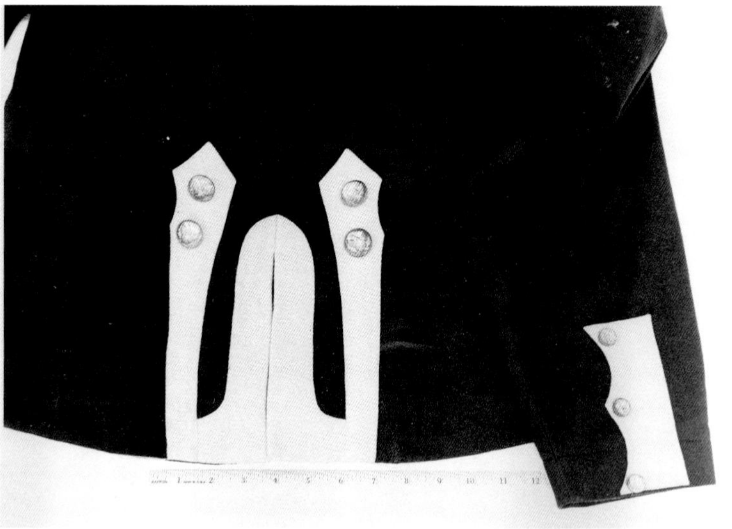

The rear tails of an 1872-pattern mounted dress coat (in this case for cavalry) with the belt loops removed per orders promulgated in 1884. BB

could be made.[53] This second piece of correspondence was prompted by General Order No. 77, Headquarters of the Army July 13, 1885, which changed regulations in so much as the torch was added to the signal flags for caps and helmets, but the devices were deposited in the office of the chief signal officer, which precluded quartermaster personnel from reacting to orders for the new insignia without having access to the prototype, from which they could have multiple copies produced. At the same time, for the sake of consistency, side buttons bearing a torch between the crossed flags would have to be manufactured, too.[54]

At least Holabird had somewhat better control over another byproduct of an earlier change to regulations that resulted from General Orders No. 62, Headquarters of the Army, June 4, 1885, which allowed for the detailing of an enlisted man at posts where there were no hospital stewards to fill such a position. The former group would be appointed by the secretary of war, be graded as first class hospital stewards, and distinguished by the traditional caduceus half chevrons. The latter category would be graded as second class, or acting hospital stewards, and would "wear upon the cuff of the left arm a *brassard* of white cloth sixteen inches by three inches, on which a red cross two inches by two inches" was placed. These were to be furnished by the Quartermaster Department without charge, unless lost, in which case the replacement price would be $.17 according to General Orders No. 71, Headquarters of the Army, June 23, 1885.

This directive caused little problem, in that the brassard was the same as set forth in General Orders No. 90 from the prior year. It took minimal effort to make these arm bands from facing cloth of the type provided for infantry uniforms and the scarlet used for the artillery. In this light, on June 30, 1885, the department was able to publish the simple specification for these devices, and in short order had them in stock to send in response to requests from the field.[55]

Provisions for acting hospital steward brassards represented a relatively small undertaking when compared to a slightly more challenging endeavor that resulted from the circular sent out in

The coats for heavy artillery enlisted men were the same as for infantrymen, except that all facings and piping were scarlet. The pouch is the McKeever cartridge box that came into common use for dress and garrison functions in the 1880s. WPM

1884 addressing the subject of regimental bands. With a considerable number of responses from the field favoring certain items, General Orders No. 23, Headquarters of the Army, March 10, 1885, disclosed that the band at West Point and the bandsmen of regiments would thereafter receive $45 per annum for their clothing allowance, except principal musicians, who were to be allotted $48. From these funds the men would be able to buy mounted helmets with plumes and cords, even if assigned to a dismounted organization, an aiguillette and shoulder knots, and a music pouch, in addition to a dress coat, blouse, the prerequisite number of Berlin gloves per year, and all the other regular items allowed to soldiers in general.

The order proved premature in that the Quartermaster Department did not have all the items spelled out in this document on hand. Thus, Holabird launched into further research and development in an attempt to deliver commanders what they wanted. After looking over samples of items provided for consideration as standards for military bands, the quartermaster general gave his seal of approval to cloth-covered music pouches with gold lace trim and a sling attached to the body by means of swivels. He wanted the branch color in silk to show through the lace, but otherwise there was to be no ornamentation on the flap. Silver plated lyres for cap devices and the helmet eagle of a medium size also were appealing.[56] So, too, were "worsted aiguillettes with suitable shoulder knots, white for Infantry, scarlet for Artillery, and yellow for Cavalry, of the pattern furnished by the Supt. Of the U.S. Military Academy at West Point."

Holabird wanted samples of all items selected submitted to him before any purchases were made. He particularly was keen on seeing the aiguillette and shoulder knots, because as he pointed out:

> The price paid by the Marine Corps for the aiguillette alone is given at $2.34. The cord and band for our mounted helmets costs only 49 cents, and it is not understood why the difference in price should be so great. It is suggested that you consult with Mr. Edward Eicke of New York, contractor for hat cords & c. He can doubtless make the aiguilette and shoulder knots. As the aiguilette for Cavalry and Artillery will be of worsted, the Infantry helmet cords and aiguilettes should also be, if possible, of worsted not of cotton.

Holabird closed with permission for Ludington "to invite proposals for such numbers of pouches, aiguillettes, shoulder knots, and lyres as may from time to time be required for this Department. Early action is desired so that there may be no unnecessary delay in filling orders."[57]

Although the quartermaster general did not wish to dally, requisitions for uniform articles to deck out bands were forthcoming before the inventory was on hand to respond with shipments. One early request came in April from St. Augustine, Florida. The garrison there was to receive the same disappointing reply sent to Ft. Concho, Texas, that "some of the articles" were "not ready for distribution," as well as awaited

The spiked 1881-pattern helmet was to be worn with the heavy artillery uniform coat. This example bears the German silver number for the Third U.S. Artillery. Photograph by Gordon Chappell.

The sealed standard sample of the heavy artillery first sergeant's 1885-pattern uniform coat. SI

Sergeant Benjamin Bowen has his portrait taken in the 1885-pattern light artillery uniform coat with gold lace chevrons and service stripes. FSHM

the approval of standard samples.[58] These and some preliminary contracts asking for the new accessories had to be put on hold temporarily.

The saga of the Eighth U.S. Infantry band stationed at Angel Island, California, offers what may well have been the typical pattern during this transitional phase. In late March, a requisition arrived for forty-five lyres, twenty-four pairs of shoulder knots with aiguillettes, twenty-four music pouches, and twenty-one white horsehair plumes, with a like number of helmets, cords, and bands, plus fittings. Immediate approval was given for twenty-one coats and the same number of complete helmets to be sent to the unit in San Francisco.[59] In reality, not until September 22 were the aiguillettes and knots, lyres, and white plumes packed and released, while at the end of the month the music pouches and helmet cords with bands still were not available, their delivery being promised "at the earliest possible date after their receipt from the contractors."[60]

These delays were not due to the quartermaster general's lack of diligence. Indeed, he urged speed. As early as May he had instructed that thirty sets of all the components authorized for bands should be kept on hand for each arm of service. Further orders were to be made upon requests from units. To permit this, Holabird stated that the shoulder knots with aiguillettes attached, along with the cords, bands, plumes, and lyres for both helmets and caps, which had been provided from the Philadelphia depot, were suitable. Specifications were to be created, and two sealed samples of the items were to be forwarded to the quartermaster general's office.

Even while details were being worked out for the designs and procurement of the new items, further clarification of who would be authorized to receive the materials, once available, was being addressed. For one thing, the quartermaster general indicated that General Orders No. 23 applied not only to West Point and regimental bands, but also to the Artillery School and at Ft. Monroe, Virginia, and to "any properly authorized Military band," but not to company musicians.[61] Furthermore, "enlisted men temporarily attached to Regimental bands though not actual members" were permitted to "draw the uniform established for

Front and rear of an 1885-pattern light artillery corporal's uniform coat made at the San Francisco Depot. Photographs by Gordon Chappell. USA

bandsmen," but were not entitled to the clothing allowance established for those permanently assigned to bands. In simple terms, this meant that the individuals attached to bands, but not assigned to the group, had to buy their own accessories rather than have them issued.

Another consideration was what the band for the battalion of engineers would wear in terms of colors. The quartermaster general informed the chief of engineers that bandsmen shoulder knots and aiguillettes, hair plumes, and helmet cords with bands, as well as music pouch trim, were white for infantry, scarlet for artillery, and yellow for cavalry. These colors were those assigned to the branches as a whole, inferring that the engineers might want to follow the same course of action, thereby adopting the red and white combination that had existed since 1872 for the corps.[62]

As a means to help solidify the particulars about these new embellishments, in late July Holabird provided a draft general order amending army regulations relative to band uniforms.[63] Although the idea was that the document would be released in August, not until late September did it make its way back to the quartermaster general for a final comment. At this point Holabird had nothing further to add.[64] Once again, in late October, General Orders No. 104 brought the regulations up to date.

Soon thereafter First Lieutenant A.C. Cowles of the Twenty-third U.S. Infantry suggested that the lyres of German silver called for in the general order might be replaced by ones made of brass coated in white metal. In fact, silver plated devices were bought on the open market from J.H. Wilson of Philadelphia, the first 500 being obtained on May 25, followed by the next 500 being bought on June 30, for a total cost of $35.00.

While these transactions were ongoing, another idea was promoted by Holabird himself, who came to the conclusion that another accessory had to be redesigned. The music pouches as first conceived were too small for the music books. In the future, he wanted the pouches to measure nine inches long by seven inches, with a thickness of one and one-half inches to eliminate this problem. To accommodate the desire for a smaller version, however, a second size with inside measurements of six and seven eighths by five and three-eights inches and having a depth of one and one-quarter inches also was available.[65]

At this point it seemed that everything was in place for supplying requisitions from the field. Although the desire to accommodate turned out to be hasty, the time was drawing near for the department to make good on the delivery of all band items, which as Colonel Nathan A.M. Dudely, commander of the First U.S. Cavalry, was told, would include complete mounted helmets, musicians' coats, double half-inch trouser stripes in branch colors, worsted shoulder knots with aiguillettes attached to the right knot, music pouches, and lyres for caps and helmet plates, plus white linen trousers.[66]

The last mentioned item had been a subject of discussion for considerable time, and not just in the context of bandsmen. While regulations had provided for these garments when commanders in extremely

Example of an 1885-pattern Engineer Corps private's uniform coat. These garments resembled the heavy artillery coat, except that the scarlet facing was piped in white. Note the service stripes. JG

Detail of the cuff ornament for an 1885-pattern Engineer Corps uniform coat. The campaign or service in war stripes for this branch were the only ones of the period to be made in two colors, the lace being sewn to scarlet facing material that was then chain-stitched in white silk. JG

hot climates so approved, enlisted men were on their own when it came to obtaining these substitutes for the issue kersey. General Orders No. 23 had paved the way for another course of action when it stipulated that bandsmen would be given white trousers, beginning with three pairs in the first year of their enlistment. Holabird wanted 3,000 pairs to be acquired in response, and mentioned that these should be similar to the ones already worn in the United States Marine Corps. He examined an existing pair, which he found satisfactory, except for the buckle at the back, which was used to secure the tightening strap commonly found on trousers of the era.[67]

A few days later the quartermaster general displayed his usual penchant for action. He realized that the marines obtained their trousers from abroad. This would result in a two or three month wait if European sources were to furnish the items. Holabird wanted to expedite the program, so he gave permission to purchase stocks from bidders in the United States based on the samples on hand. As another course to maintain momentum, he granted authority to buy 600 yards of white linen at $.51 a yard to supplement the 4,500 yards already on hand by early June.[68] But as before, he desired "a different stronger buckle" for the white trousers "similar in construction to the gilt buckles on kersey trousers."[69] When this one detail was resolved for both white metal buckles to be used with the linen trousers and brass versions for kersey trousers,

An 1881-pattern Engineer Corps enlisted dress helmet with German silver castle overlay. The helmet body is of the profile made late in the 1800s. Photograph by Gordon Chappell

Engineer non-commissioned officers' chevrons also were unique in the mid-1880s, in that the gold lace was sewn to the scarlet backing and then outlined in white silk chain-stitches, as in this case for a battalion quartermaster sergeant. SI

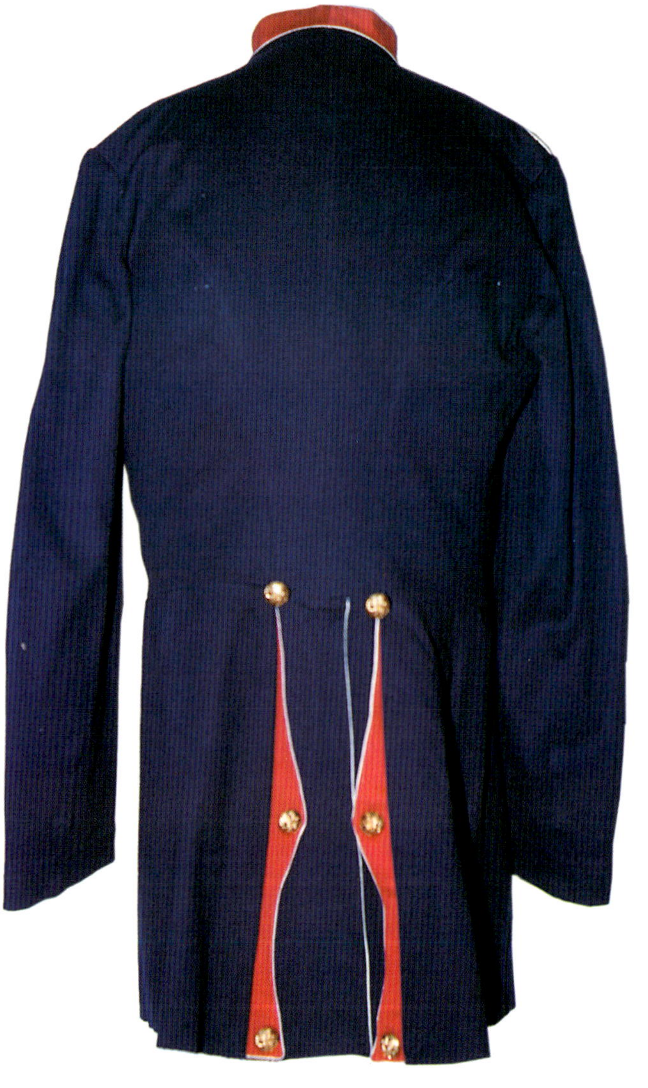

Rear of a sealed sample of the 1885-pattern Engineer Corps uniform coat with its scarlet facings piped in white. SI

Musician's uniform coats for the Engineer Corps had herringbone in two colors (white edged in scarlet) in keeping with the duel color scheme for that branch. SI

The 1885-pattern shoulder knots and aiguilettes for Battalion of Engineer bandsmen also carried out the same scarlet and white combination. JG

overalls, and drawers, paper patterns at last could be accepted as standard for the white trousers in September.[70]

But it was not just bandsmen who were of interest when it came to the white trousers. Colonel Otis, who was departing Ft. Leavenworth as commandant of the School of Application to accompany his regiment to Texas, had raised this subject anew on a broader scale when he inquired through military channels as follows:

> I have the honor to submit for your favorable consideration, the following facts under paragraph 2757 A.R. Commanding officers are authorized to sanction the use on duty of white pants in climates such as this command is serving in, the same to be bought out of the pay of the soldier. Under this regulation I desire next summer to have supplied for the troops at the Post of San Antonio, Texas, such quantities of white pants as a subsequent requisition may show, the probable number to be supplied would be about 1,050. I have tried to obtain these trousers from local merchants, and the price asked even in large quantities is one dollar and twenty-five cents per pair, which in my estimation is too high.

The chevrons for the 1885-pattern coat worn by post ordnance sergeants were to have a gold lace five-pointed star on a dark blue cloth background that matched the coat. In turn, the three gold lace stripes were to be sewn to a crimson background to match the facings on the coat. USAMNCO

If the Quartermaster General could make arrangements to furnish these trousers by April 30, 1885, to be paid for by the soldier on his June Muster and Pay Roll, I think they could be supplied at a rate commensurate with the soldiers' pay. The necessity of white trousers at a station such as this, is evident to any one who has served here, both as a matter of comfort and appearance.

In suggesting this I do not expect that the Quartermaster's Department will be put to any material expense for which it will not be reimbursed during the current fiscal year.

If this matter meets with the favorable consideration of the Department, I will cause estimates to be made at once, so that the matter can be taken in hand at an early date.

The commander of the Department of Texas, Brigadier General David L. Stanley, on December 20, 1884, endorsed the request "as a proper experiment." In turn, the Quartermaster Department made calculations and prepared a report detailing the costs of production for 1,000 pairs of summer trousers of either white cotton or linen duck, or brown linen duck in response to Colonel Otis' recommendation to quartermaster general of December 19, 1884.[71]

Nor did the matter of enhancements for trousers stop with white linen summer versions. Just as the buckle for the rear strap had been spelled out in specifications, a desire to provide a better type of suspender and fly button for kersey trousers was set into motion. Both brass and japanned versions were to be reviewed with an eye toward "improvement over those now in use."[72] It only took a few days for a reply advocating japanned buttons to be the preferred type, leading to the adoption of Specification No. 145 for these on April 14, 1885.[73]

Other endeavors related to trousers included the purchase of some darker blue kersey to make up trial trousers for the purpose of determining the merits, if any, for such garments. While Holabird admitted that darker shades of indigo tended to develop a "whitish tinge," he nevertheless thought that a "stable and satisfactory" alternative could be found.[74] As another possibility, a better quality of cloth than the kersey the department had adopted as standard might result as an outgrowth from such a study.[75]

The annual report to the secretary of war from the quartermaster general set forth the rationale for such actions. This account summarized the department's position:

The official sealed standard sample of the post ordnance sergeant 1885-pattern uniform coat. SI

Detail of the star and portions of an 1884-pattern gold lace post ordnance sergeant's chevron and service stripes below. FAM

The official sealed sample of the 1885-pattern commissary sergeant's uniform coat. SI

Owing to the great difficulty experienced by manufacturers to make kersey of a uniform color due to the peculiar action of the indigo, the Quartermaster-General directed that experiments be made to make goods of a somewhat darker and more serviceable color, less liable to result in the diversity of shades found in the deliveries of the various contracts.[76]

As a consequence, darker kersey in fact was procured, even though this meant that "the difference between the old and new shades" would be "quite marked," the final effect would be "a greater uniformity, once old stocks from the lighter shade of kersey had been depleted."[77] While specifications had not been changed to meet this goal, new standard samples had been sealed and sent off for future purchases.[78] In fact, official adoption would not be announced until the beginning of the new fiscal year (July 1886).[79]

Other suggestions came to the fore in regard to darker trousers, such as First Lieutenant Charles F. Roe's proposal that trousers in this shade exhibiting welts of white, scarlet, and yellow for infantry, artillery, and cavalry troops might replace the system then in vogue. Prototypes were made of each, but nothing more came of the project.[80]

In a separate action, late in December, the department made it clear that it had laid in a stock of 500 yards of dark blue doeskin cloth later in the year, which it retained at least for the moment as reference material, but ultimately it may have been provided to fulfill orders from non-commissioned officers, who were entitled to opt for superior material to that of privates from which to have their uniforms tailored.[81] Just over a week later this action was followed by the adoption of new standards for heavy kersey.[82] Finally, some thought was given to a return of trim on staff officers' trousers, as had been the case before 1872. A pair of dark blue trousers were to be modified with the addition of a three-sixteenth's gold cord "similar to that used on officers' helmets."[83] As another option, Holabird asked for a pair of the dark blue trousers to be decorated with gold lace.[84]

Once more, this course of action came to a dead end, which must have been of little surprise in that General Orders No. 113, Headquarters of the Army, October 31, 1885, had just a few weeks before continued to mandate plain dark blue trousers for all staff officers save those in the Signal Corps.[85] There were a number of other salient points covered in this order which bear repeating:

The crescents on both the gold lace chevrons for the dress coat and gray facing cloth chevrons for blouses and overcoats worn by commissary sergeants were to point forward and be worn vertically according to the specification adopted in 1885. Prior to that date, the crescent typically was worn with points up in a horizontal fashion. AMWH

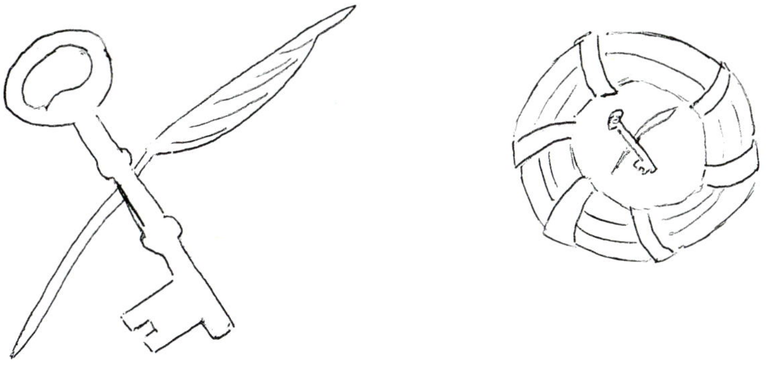

The creation of a new non-commissioned staff member in 1884, the post quartermaster sergeant, prompted the Quartermaster Department to select the design on the left for the final version of the post quartermaster sergeant's device, although the concept on the right was considered at first, according to correspondence from 1884, which contained this drawing of the two possible versions of insignia. NA

III. By direction of the Secretary of War Paragraphs 2726, 2749, (as amended by General Orders, No. 108, of 1882, from this office), and 2776 (as corrected by Gen'Orders, No. 64, of 1882, from this office) of the regulations are amended to read as follows:

BUTTONS.

2726. *For all enlisted men.*—To be of yellow metal, fire gilt and burnished, according to standard in the Quartermaster General's Office.

TROUSERS.

2749. *For enlisted men of all arms.*—Sky-blue mixture; to be cut and made in accordance with standard samples in the Quartermaster General's Office. Those for mounted troops to have a reinforce or saddle-piece of the same material on seat and legs.

FATIGUE HAT.

For all enlisted men.—Of black or drab-colored felt according to the pattern in the office of the Quartermaster General; to be worn in garrison only on fatigue duty, and on marches and campaigns; the color to be uniform in each troop, battery, or company.

IV. By direction of the Secretary of War paragraphs 2610, 2617, and 2641 of the Regulations are amended to read as follows:

2610. *For general officers, officers of the general staff, and staff corps (excepting the Signal Corps.)*—Dark blue cloth, plain, without stripe, welt, or cord.

2617. *Helmets for other mounted officers and officers of the Signal Corps.*—Same as above, except that for the Signal Corps the color of plume shall be orange, and the device two crossed signal flags and a burning torch in gilt.

2641. *For officers of other staff corps (excepting the Signal Corps).*—Same as above described, without the aiguillette.

V. By direction of the Secretary of War paragraph 2601 of the Regulations is annulled, and the following additional paragraphs are published to the Army, and will be numbered 2604 1/2 and 2610 1/2:

2604 1/2. *For all officers of the Signal Corps.*—Gilt, convex, and seven-eighths of an inch in exterior diameter, with plain border; device, two crossed signal flags and a burning torch; small buttons

Post quartermaster sergeants soon were authorized a dress coat with buff facings piped in white, and a gold embroidered key crossed by a quill as the basis for the chevrons. SI

I. By direction of the Secretary of War paragraph 2066 of the Regulations, as amended by General Orders No. 37, series of 1883, from this office [Adjutant General's Office] is annulled.

II. By direction of the Secretary of War the following is published for the information and guidance of all concerned:

Until publication of a new table of the price of clothing and equipage for the Army, the uniform clothing of finer quality procured exclusively for issue to the non-commissioned officers of the Army will be charged at the following prices:

Articles	**Price Made**	**Unmade**
Uniform dress coat, mounted, each	$8.59	$5.09
Uniform dress coat, mounted, chief trumpeter, each	$9.17	$5.67
Uniform dress coat, foot, each	$8.85	$5.35
Uniform dress coat, foot, principal musician, each	$9.43	$5.93
Uniform dress coat, staff corps, each	$8.90	$5.40
Uniform dress coat, staff corps, musician, each	$9.48	$5.98
Blouse, each	$4.19	$3.44
Trousers, mounted, per pair, each	$4.63	$3.38
Trousers, foot, per pair, each	$3.65	$2.65

Back of an 1885-pattern post quartermaster sergeant's coat. USAQM

of the same form and device, and one-half inch in diameter.

2610 1/2. *For all officers of the Signal Corps, except the Chief Signal Officer.*—Dark blue cloth, with stripe one and one-half inches wide, welted at the edges; color of the stripe, orange.

VI. By direction of the Secretary of War paragraphs 2771 and 2772 of the Regulations are annulled, and paragraphs 2765 to 2770, inclusive, are amended to read as follows:

FORAGE-CAP BADGES.

2765. The forage-cap badges, numbers or regiments, and letters of companies will be worn by the enlisted men of the Army in the following manner, viz:

2766. *For cavalry, artillery, and infantry.*—The numbers of their regiments in the upper, and the letters of their companies in the lower, angles of badges of their respective arms upon the forage cap, viz: Cavalry, crossed sabers; artillery, crossed cannon; infantry, crossed rifles.

2767. *For ordnance sergeants and soldiers.*—The shell and flame.

For hospital stewards.—The caduceus in white metal, inclosed by a wreath in yellow metal.

For commissary sergeants.—Crescent in white metal, the points in a vertical line.

For engineers.—The castle, with letter of company above it.

Although General Orders No. 113 codified many diverse elements that had been introduced during the prior year, the devices for the forage caps of enlisted men in the Signal Corps were not mentioned, nor did the requirement to wear the crescent for commissary sergeants with the points in a vertical line coincide with the common practice of applying the insignia to the cap with the points up on the horizontal. Clearly, orders and regulations were one thing, but certain elements were left up to individuals or officers outside of the Quartermaster Department, as they had been for generations.

The crossed key and pen motif carried over to the German silver overlay and side buttons adopted in 1885 for post quartermaster sergeants' helmets. Photograph by Gordon Chappell

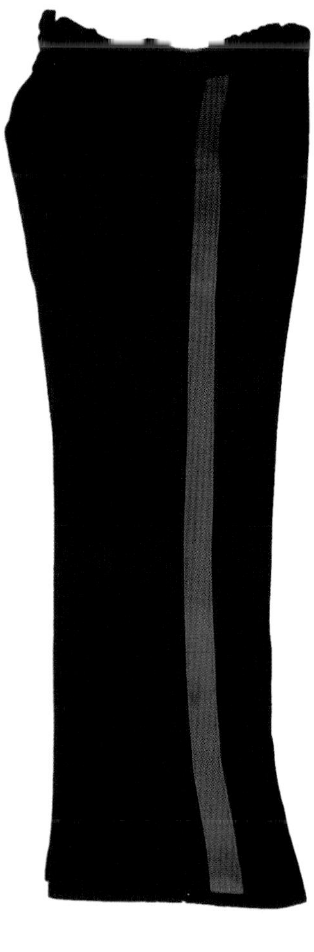

1884-pattern post quartermaster sergeant's trousers with 1 1/4 inch buff stripes of facing material authorized in 1885 for post quartermaster sergeants. SI

Another byproduct of this particular general order seems to have been some confusion about the color of campaign hats, at least for one military supplier. Representatives of Raymold and Whitlock of New York wrote for details about a new black campaign felt hat that allegedly had been adopted. Captain Rodgers could not oblige, stating that he knew nothing about this piece of headgear. The firm likewise wanted to know about the saddle cloth adopted for officers.[86] Here he could refer the firm to General Orders No. 95, Headquarters of the Army, August 14, 1884, and repeated in General Orders No. 8, Headquarters of the Army, January 21, 1885, both of which called for a dark blue cloth saddle pad edged in one and one-half inch cloth of the color of the arms of service, sky blue being for infantry, scarlet for artillery, and yellow for cavalry, although the color for infantry would be changed to white by the next year.[87]

This was but one of several miscellaneous elements of equipage overseen by Holabird's department. Whereas accoutrements and horse equipments was the province of the Ordnance Department, the Quartermaster Department was responsible for a variety of other items that did not necessarily form part of a soldier's personal outfit. Such items as color belts and slings for use to carry regimental standards and the national colors formed part of this diverse lot, as did the colors themselves.[88] In the latter instance, for many years after the Civil War the existing silken colors and guidons in stock were issued to regiments, companies, troops, and batteries. With the passage of time, many of these were sent to the various units around the country, while the remaining supply began to deteriorate, especially because the designs on them were painted rather than embroidered, contrary to regulations. All this prompted a series of changes, whereby embroidered versions were being manufactured exclusively. Moreover, the yellow silk background for artillery standards was replaced with scarlet in keeping with the branch color, and the blue backings used for both cavalry and infantry regimental standards came under scrutiny with the object of changing the cavalry version to yellow, once more to coincide with the branch color scheme of the time.[89] Once production began and the latest versions of the colors and standards were available, the past patterns were dropped from the rolls, but the secretary of war allowed them to be retained for decorative purposes.[90]

Even before this, a new guidon was considered for cavalry troops, with the upper half of the swallow-tail being red bearing the regimental number in white, while the lower half was white with the company letter in red. Artillery guidons, however, remained the same as in the past, until 1886.[91] That is, they were swallow-tails with thirteen alternating red and white stripes and a blue field in the corner, upon which two concentric rings of white stars were applied totaling the number of states in the Union.[92] As just one more precaution, cases were issued with the new guidons and standards "to protect them when not in use."[93] As with the surplus regimental standards, the Civil War version of guidons were dropped from the records, but could be employed for decorative purposes.[94]

This scheme included one new element, as well. Responding to a suggestion that silk markers and general guides be provided to infantry regiments, the Quartermaster Department followed through with a basic design that resembled a small national color (U.S. flag). The small twenty by eighteen inch silk marker would bear the number of the regiment in block letters. These would be hoisted on an eight feet long ash pole that had a ferule and spearhead. The general guides were similar, but had silk yellow fringe and measured fifteen by eighteen inches. They were to be fastened to brass tubing, which was nickel plated to prevent

A post quartermaster sergeant, standing on the left, displays his buff chevrons on a blouse without piping, as called for by May 19, 1883, specifications January 16, 1884, in lieu of specifications of May 19, 1883, when enlisted blouses were to no longer be trimmed in branch colors, although they still were to have a single button on the cuff (until that detail was discontinued in accordance with specifications released on January 14, 1884). By way of comparison, the seated commissary sergeant has on an 1874-pattern blouse piped in gray and the pre-1885 chevrons with the crescent worn points up. The third member of this group has elected to wear an 1883-pattern field shirt, and either a light colored civilian hat or an 1883-pattern campaign hat. He has added a non-regulation tie and waxed his long moustache to provide a devil-may-care look. CBF

The shoulder knots with attached aiguilettes became a common feature for the dress uniform of regimental bandsmen soon after the 1885-pattern became available. This musician has added the accessories to the special dress coat with heavy fogging to his uniform. BH

Infantry, artillery, and cavalry bandsmen's knots of the 1885-pattern were made in branch colors of white, scarlet, and yellow, as seen here. KC

oxidation, and inserted into the muzzle of a .45-70 caliber Springfield rifle.[95]

While the various field symbols were literally a matter of showing the colors, other products from the department were designed to be less visible. This especially was so for canvas fatigue clothing. These items became quite popular from Ft. McHenry in bustling Baltimore, Maryland, to remote garrisons in the Trans-Mississippi West.[96] In fact, a request was made for mounted troops to employ the garb on stable duty in lieu of the white canvas outfit long provided for this purpose.[97] Lieutenant General Sheridan, however, did not agree, denying the petition as noted in Circular No. 7, Headquarters of the Army, August 12, 1885. Following this same restrictive line of thinking, Holabird did not concur with a request made by First Lieutenant Thomas Connolly of the First U.S. Infantry, who wrote from Ft. Mohave, Arizona Territory, with a proposal to allow commissary sergeants and hospital stewards to draw the stout canvas outfits. The quartermaster general took a negative stance on the matter, but he had no objection to a request from the commanding general of the Department of Arizona, George Crook, who asked "for authority to sell government clothing" to the civilian packers who had been hired by the Quartermaster Department to support the troops "operating in Mexico" against Geronimo.[98]

One of the items that packers and others who were pursuing the Apaches South of the Border seemed to favor were the brown canvas fatigue trousers. Britton Davis, a Texas-born subaltern with the Third U.S. Cavalry, apparently found these preferable to blue wool when he took to the field in 1885. He recorded that his campaign kit consisted of: "brown canvas trousers, a western (semi-cowboy) hat, and blue flannel shirt. But I carried with me, strapped to my saddle, my army blouse with the insignia of a second lieutenant of cavalry. This I always donned before entering a town."[99] Even these bits of martial apparel went by the wayside as the campaign progressed. Again Davis recorded: "Thinking I would have no use for my army blouse before I rejoined the command, I left it with [Captain Emmet] Crawford, substituting a six-foot strip of canvas with a slit for my head as a better protection from the rain. I was thus without any insignia whatever. My brown canvas trousers, torn to

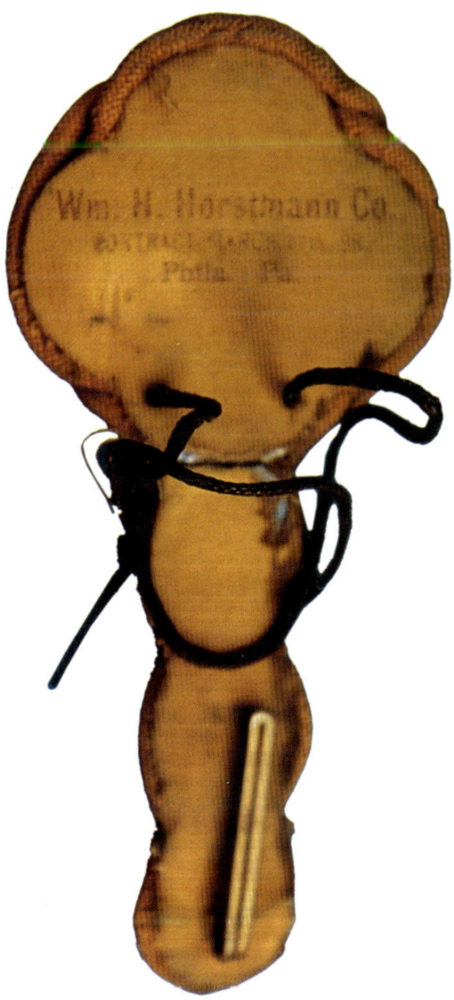

The knots were held on to the shoulder straps of the dress coat with strings that were attached to the underside. Originally the underside was made of cardboard covered in cloth, but this proved too flimsy, and thin tin foundations were adopted within a few years after the knots were introduced. KC

Sixth U.S. Cavalry musician Clarence Poole, at Ft. Wingate, New Mexico Territory, wearing the shoulder knots and aiguillettes adopted in 1885. BH

In 1885 the Laidley marksman's buttons (top) were replaced by the Blunt marksman's buttons (bottom). The rings could be run through eyelets on the back of the buttons to allow the insignia to be fastened to the collar. TT

shreds, had been replaced by a pair of black civilian trousers that by chance I had in my pack."[100]

Nor was the cavalry officer the only one to stray from regulations, because after being in the field for an extended period, he and his men "were in undershirts and torn overalls; hatless, dirty, unshaven for weeks, their feet swathed in bandages made from their flannel shirts." They had discarded their shoes for moccasins, but these had been soaked and became useless. The lieutenant was in the same state to the degree that his "shoes having given out," one of the Apache scouts in his command "had made a new pair of soles by tying on the bottom of the shoes strips of rawhide."[101] By the time Davis returned from his foray into Mexico he was anything but military in his appearance, being "ragged, dirty," and bristling with "a four months' beard," that along with his "old pair of black trousers that had been partially repaired with white thread blackened on the coffee pot, rawhide soles to my shoes," and hair poking through holes in his campaign hat, all of which created an effect that did not speak well for the Quartermaster Department's idea of rugged combat gear.[102]

Another officer, First Lieutenant Leonard Wood, certainly found much to be desired from the regulation issue, when he set aside his duties as a medical officer to pursue the Apaches in Mexico as Davis did. The young surgeon, who would eventually rise to the post of chief of staff of the U.S. Army, condemned the government issue, writing:

> The uniform is totally unfit for service in Sonora, or along our southern border, and troops on expeditions where hard work is to be done have got to have something lighter and cooler. Of course, a man can work under great disadvantages, but the wisdom of anything getting them in such a position is not evident. A cavalry soldier with his heavy clothing, clumsy boots, is unable to do more than a portion of the work he can do properly dressed.
> In the first place, he is carrying about twice the weight of clothing required. If instead of the heavy woolen clothing, something of the nature of stable or fatigue clothing were issued, and with this a pair of shoes with light uppers coming up to the ankle and having a medium thick Scotch sole with a few hob-nails around the edge,

During 1885 sharpshooters (the category above marksman) were to be designated a cross suspended from a bar reading "sharpshooter" that was to be worn on the chest, rather than at the throat, as had been the case for the earlier device. Both officers and enlisted men could earn these awards, which in this instance was presented to Captain Edmund Luff. JM

Subsequent awards of the 1885-pattern sharpshooter's device were designated by a small horizontal bar bearing the dates of qualification (below). The 1885-pattern marksman bar (above) was to be worn alone, and later qualifications designated by a maximum of two pairs of Blunt marksman's buttons, which were to be worn on either side of the collar. TT

Left: Up to two pairs of marksman's buttons could be worn on the collar, and a subsequent qualification indicated by a marksman's bar that also was adopted in 1885. This private of Company E, Fourth U.S. Infantry, wears all three according to regulations. TT

As with many other elements of the uniform, individual designs existed for marksmanship devices. For example, this custom specimen had three loops with single years suspended below and a marksman's bar attached above, despite the fact that wearing of both marksman bars and sharpshooter crosses in tandem was prohibited. TT

and in place of the heavy overcoat a rubber poncho. They would be in fair shape for as much work as their mount would stand.

As it is, a man is to all intents and purposes in a sweat box, and a subject for chafes, etc. Aside from this, it puts him at a great disadvantage when opposed to an enemy lightly and properly dressed. Infantry on this expedition marched in drawers and undershirts and found that they were much more comfortable, and could do more work, and do it with less exertion. I do not remember seeing a pair of blue pants put on after once wearing the lighter articles mentioned above.

As an indication of what was preferred to walk in, a number of men paid as high as 6 per pair [nearly a half a month's wages for a private] per pair for moccasins. The sewed shoe are totally unfit for field service (at least all we have had were) and they were the cause of much suffering, wearing out usually in six or seven days, and in some cases on the second. The stitching seems to have been poorly done, resulting in the whole sole falling off after a short time....

Even the old brass screwed models tended to hold up better, Wood contended. Civilian shoes made with American leather but after a fashion that was popular in Mexico and sewn with sinew "gave the best results" he concluded.

Thus, footgear particularly seemed to fall short of the mark when it came to the rigors of campaigning. For one thing, the much vaunted field shoe with its machine sewn soles received mixed reviews, besides which its production numbers were limited in that the nearly 26,000 pairs of the old brass-screw type shoes on hand by the end of fiscal year 1885 had to be supplied first before new items could replace them.[103]

It was not just the limited quantities that worked against the field shoe, if an account from First Lieutenant Jonathan Newton, then serving at Ft. McIntosh, Texas, expressed a common opinion about this style. He asserted: "The new field shoes are so clumsy, that no of the enlisted men want them."[104] This sort of reaction contributed to the suspension of field shoe manufacture in April 1885, except for any pairs that already had been cut out and were ready to be assembled at Leavenworth.[105] Whatever was left in the inventory at that point would be sent out to fill requisitions, but production never resumed after that.[106]

Despite this prohibition, period photographs show enlisted men combining both decorations, as in the case of Private Boyd Purdell from the Eleventh U.S. Infantry, Company G, serving at Whipple Barracks, Arizona Territory. He wears both the marksman and sharpshooter's devices on his chest. TT

This unidentified infantry bandsman also wears the two decorations in tandem. What is more, the gold lace sling with white grosgrain center stripe of his 1885-pattern music pouch is evident. TT

Sergeant Max Simon, Troop H, Sixth U.S. Cavalry, likewise displays both a marksman bar and a sharpshooter's medal, along with the prestigious distinguished marksman gold shield with white enameled center target (award worn highest on his chest) and one of the typical division type awards for marksmanship. Simon has also added a thin diameter gold cord to the collar of his 1885-pattern uniform coat, although nothing in regulations permitted this modification, but probably was an individual initiative to further distinguish this crack shot. TT

In like manner the cavalry boot suggested in 1884 with its wider top and sewn soles did not fare well, either. Again, Lieutenant Newton minced no words. He found:

The new cavalry boot...is too small just above the instep where the pebble leather is sewed on. In issuing forty-five pairs to a cavalry troop the other day, this complaint was general of both widths A and B lasts, and a majority of the men were forced to take their boots one size too large.[107]

Major George Sanford's battalion of the First U.S. Cavalry, then deployed to Kansas, found the new cavalry boot did not "seem to stand active service very well, the fault seeming to lie in the shape of the boot where the leg joins the lower portion so as to be obliged to be cut in order to be worn...."[108] Clearly something had to be done to rectify this shortcoming and one other source of irritation—the back seam of the boot was sewn on the inside, causing chafing against the wearer's rear calf—so an improved design was worked up and adopted in April 1886.[109]

Ultimately, the post shoe likewise would undergo a modification. For one thing, the instep was considered to be too small in certain instances, a disappointing finding reported by First Lieutenant Charles Humphreys based on the experience of Third U.S. Artillery personnel stationed at Ft. Barrancas, Florida.[110]

Another grievance lodged against post shoes was that they were of inferior quality. In this case a soldier had recourse.[111] The secretary of war set forth how an enlisted man could address this situation in a letter of September 17, 1885. Then the adjutant general published this guidance as Circular No. 9, Headquarters of the Army, October 24, 1885, which read in part:

Post shoes made at the Leavenworth Military Prison found by a board of survey, convened within thirty days after their issue, to have proved defective, through no fault of the wearer, may, upon approval of the post commander, be turned in to the post quartermaster, who is authorized to issue a new pair. The condemned shoes, as they accumulate, will be sent to the Military Prison and dropped from the returns of the officer responsible.

By the end of the year other details as to the replacement process for faulty footgear appeared in Circular No. 12, Headquarters of the Army, December 31, 1885, a document that called for the shoes to "be issued on receipt rolls as other clothing is issued, but their value" would not count against the clothing allowance of the soldier. Further, "The authority for the gratuitous issue and the approved proceedings of the board of survey" were to be appended to the document that indicated the issue of the replacement shoes. Afterwards, the imperfect footgear "turned in by the soldier" would be submitted by the man's company commander to the post quartermaster, who then would ship them to Ft. Leavenworth. Unfortunately, this same beneficence did not include imperfect boots, according to a decision the secretary of war signed on November 13.[112]

It should be noted that in certain instances the charges against the post shoes stemmed from the fact that the men were pressing them into service for daily fatigue wear or even for some field service, purposes for which these light weight articles were not intended. Their uppers of oak tanned American calfskin could not stand this sort of wear, but rather were meant only for dress occasions and light duty.[113]

A young cavalry sergeant has removed all the black enamel from his Blunt marksman's buttons and placed them at an angle on his 1885-pattern uniform coat, rather then wearing them squared as was the common practice. One of his gold lace chevrons is evident on the left sleeve. TT

Regardless of the source for objection, the quartermaster general again made an effort to satisfy the soldier by instructing Blunt to "procure the necessary laths and dies for making the post shoe based on the Walkenfast model," the English design that had inspired both this type of footwear and the campaign shoe, as well. The idea was to fabricate 1,000 pairs for trial on active service with the intent "to prevent failure."[114] A new means of stitching the uppers to the soles was developed in the course of this experiment, and canvas linings added, too. Once again, however, actions to upgrade the post shoe did not produce the desired results.[115]

One other form of protection for the feet, overshoes, evoked a somewhat better response. In 1884, the old "arctics" had been modified a bit from the original 1876-pattern, with the rearrangement of the fastening strap and buckle to the side of the shoe rather than in the front, as had been the situation with the "snow-excluder" of the past.[116] In either version, these evidently had been viewed as an improvement by the rank and file over the buffalo overshoes, which the troops declined to draw if given the option of the arctics. As a result, about 2,200 pairs of the buffalo overshoes were "on hand in the Saint Louis and San Francisco depots," causing Holabird to seek and receive permission from the secretary of war to distribute these at no cost to any men in the Department of Columbia (Pacific Northwest) and the Division of the Missouri who might so desire them.[117]

While in this instance the soldier might be ready to brave the elements, dealing with inclement weather still posed a question to which no easy answer was forthcoming. In 1884, when reviewing the topic, Holabird pointed out the pre-Civil War practice of issuing talmas (a large cape or cloak-like garment) to the enlisted men, but as a matter of economy rubber blankets and ponchos were substituted. There were so many of these articles on hand after Appomattox that the department persisted in issuing them, but time had taken its toll and the stocks were deteriorating.[118] The quartermaster general wanted to hand the ponchos and ground cloths out gratuitously, then sell whatever the men did not take. He suggested at that point to follow the advice of a cavalry board that met in 1884, the officers in that assembly recommending a rubber overcoat.[119] Samples had been obtained and the cost estimated at about three dollars if the garments were bought in quantity and issued to the men at one coat per year.[120]

Representative examples of the shooting awards given at the department, division, and army-wide levels. TT

The secretary of war was not in accord with the cavalry board or the quartermaster general on this subject. He disapproved the sale of such coats at cost to troops, but did give his blessing to the free issue of ponchos and rubber blankets.[121]

The secretary's non-concurrence for the adoption of rubber overcoats was in keeping with the experience of Lieutenant John Bigelow, Jr., of the Tenth U.S. Cavalry.[122] Bigelow, was another officer who sought out the Apaches in 1885 and 1886. As he set out to the field he had rolled up "a good quilt and a pair of blankets, a change of underclothing, a few toilet articles, and overcoat, and a light rubber coat." Bigelow soon reduced his load to one blanket, his great coat, and the light rubber slicker, along with a shelter half that served as a table cloth spread on the ground for meals, much as Davis had done with his oilcloth poncho. The next item to go was his woolen great coat, leaving him with the "light rubber overcoat, bought at Ft. Davis, Texas, that reached down below the tops of my boots, almost to my feet."

Bigelow revealed that he "had carried this garment hundreds of miles without having any serious occasion to use it, but ever hoping for that form of compensation for my trouble." Then came a torrential desert rain the "over-abundance with which this was dealt out to me by a northeast wind this afternoon militated against my enjoyment of it; and as I felt it creeping down my weather leg, so to speak, into my boot, I lost faith heavily in rubber overcoats and in post traders."[123]

Although the adoption of a suitable slicker was not forthcoming, quartermaster officials continued the quest for improved foul weather gear, including the acquisition of six black sheepskin overcoats and seven canvas covered overcoats, "the two kinds" having "been used to some extent by way of experiment"

While these efforts were abandoned, Holabird remained on course to improve the existing 1884-pattern overcoat. For one thing, he sought "the opinions of Company officers" to ascertain whether the coat was "sufficiently long to meet the needs of the Army...." The findings were affirmative, "except in isolated cases where the height and breast measurements of the wearer are not in symmetrical proportions." In the case of a tall, slender soldier, Holabird proposed a size No. 3 might be ordered to fit the upper torso, but then be too short. In this instance, quartermasters could be sent a request for a special order with the measurements provided so that a custom coat might be produced.[124] As one more possibility, the quartermaster general provided a sketch of the rear of the overcoat seams so that a reduction of the width in the coat's rear would be rendered to give a more tailored shape.[125]

Yet Holabird was not completely satisfied. He wanted to explore other options. In his quest he asked that a West Point cadet great coat be forwarded to him for which reimbursement would be made.[126] Probably his purpose was to examine this style to see what features might be applicable for the enlisted model. On that same day four sample overcoats, which had been made up for review as a possible successor for the 1884-pattern, were being returned to Philadelphia by the depot quartermaster in Washington, D.C. One of them with a gore was preferred, but a revised version with "six, instead of five buttons in front" was to

An extant example of an 1885-pattern cavalry sergeant's dress coat with the Blunt's marksman buttons still attached to the collar. WSHS

A corporal of Signal Corps 1885-pattern dress coat. SI

be fabricated, and as a further addition, hooks and eyes were to be placed on "the front parts of skirts, allowing the latter to be hooked back, thereby giving free play to the knees while marching...." Another distinctive detail called out for the prototype had to do with "the flaps created in hooking back" the front edge. These could "be turned under, thereby avoiding the exposure of the fastening on the outside of the skirt." Finally, care was to "be taken to bring the eye as close to the edge of the skirt as practicable."[127]

Soon thereafter an "overcoat having six buttons on each side in front, and hooks and eyes for looping the skirts" was received by the quartermaster general's office. The coat was found to be "satisfactory," but the front buttons were to be a "little closer together." Further, the hooks and eyes were to be placed as depicted by the quartermaster general, which he had marked on the sample with pins. With that, yet one more coat was to be made "having these modifications," and specifications were to be provided, along with the sample for another inspection by Holabird.[128]

As yet one more revision, a new blanket lining standard was adopted for the 1885-pattern overcoat and samples sent to Philadelphia, San Francisco, and Jeffersonville.[129] With all of these elements in place, Holabird wrote seeking permission to manufacture the new great coat for enlisted men thereafter, these having the dozen buttons on the chest and being of the darker blue kersey that also was adopted in 1885.[130]

The new standard was officially accepted on May 28, 1885, thereby replacing the short-lived standard from September 12, 1884. A request

The helmet overlay adopted for Signal Corps enlisted men in 1881 was a pair of crossed German silver flags. The same motif appeared on the side buttons. Photograph by Glen Swanson. GS

Three-quarter and front views of an 1885-pattern first class private of the Signal Corps uniform coat. SI

from First Lieutenant Thomas Woodruff of the Fifth U.S. Infantry at Ft. Leavenworth, Kansas, requested "authority to transfer all light blue overcoats and trowsers on hand," and in turn to replace these with dark blue versions followed almost as soon as news of the changeover had been announced. As always, this request had to be denied. The lighter shade coats and trousers were to be issued until there were no more in stock.

In still a further refinement of the overcoat, Holabird requested "one pair of cloth chevrons for first sergeants of Cavalry, Artillery, and Infantry" to be made from cloth conforming to the color of the kersey from which overcoats were made.[131] The intent was for these chevrons "if adopted at all, to be worn on the overcoat, and the groundcloth should match the color of the kersey of which the material is made as much as possible."[132] Although this was a reasonable goal aesthetically speaking, the adoption of such a policy would have meant three types of chevrons, cloth for blouses; gold lace for dress coats; and special overcoat chevrons with inserts of kersey for certain non-commissioned officers. The logistical details related to this plan evidently did not seem worth the effort, and nothing came of the proposal.

Only a few outstanding details remained in regard to enlisted greatcoats at that point. One of these factors was the cost of having overcoat capes relined for recruits who were issued one type of great coat at the beginning of their enlistment, only to be transferred to another arm of the service, thereby requiring a different color of lining. The secretary of war authorized the Quartermaster Department not only to provide the cloth, but also by Circular No. 6, Headquarters of the Army, July 3, 1886, permitted the reimbursement to the enlisted men, who had to have their capes relined, the sum of one dollar to defray costs of alteration.[133] As an aside, the branch color lined enlisted capes became so popular that requests were made to have them issued separately from the coats. In this situation the secretary of war gave a negative reply.[134]

Therefore, the overcoat and cape were to be issued as one unit, although they could be worn separately. Eventually it was decided that when they were worn, they would be combined with "the fatigue dress, including the fatigue cap," unless being worn in the field.

Similarly, officers were permitted to don enlisted overcoats on campaign, and at certain posts where rough duty was the rule. This did not excuse them from having the proper officers' overcoat, as well.[135] These were the dark blue ulsters introduced by General Orders No. 117, Headquarters of the Army, October 21, 1884, which were also covered during the next year by General Orders No. 8, Headquarters of the Army, January 21, 1885. The latter directive clarified that the slit on the left side of the overcoat was to permit the front sling and hook of the sword belt to be revealed so that the sword or saber could be worn with the coat. The leather sword belt itself, however, was to be placed under the overcoat. Additionally, General Orders No. 8 granted an optional cape of the same color and material of the overcoat, but with a three inch black velvet roll collar having rounded corners, and a black mohair loop and tassel plate closure.

During most of the 1880s, however, no forage cap insignia was called for in regulations for signalmen. This meant that some individuals, such as Second Class Private R.I. Sutton, who is seen here, took it upon themselves to add an appropriate device. Sutton simply pressed an 1881-pattern helmet overlay into service. JG

In turn, this unidentified Signal Corps private first class added a gilt wreath to encircle an 1881-pattern crossed flags overlay on his forage cap. The young man has further decked himself out with 1884-pattern gauntlets, and converted what appears to be the belt and plate for an 1884-pattern color belt (to be worn by soldiers bearing the regimental standard or national colors) into a saber belt! HO

In 1885 a torch was added to the overlay for the Signal Corps enlisted helmet. EB

The official forage cap device adopted in 1885, however, featured square flags that were larger than those on the helmet overlays. The cap with the correct 1885-pattern Signal Corps insignia is depicted being worn here in tandem with an overcoat of the 1885-86 period, the cape being lined in orange as required for the branch. JG

No mention of the cape's interior was made, an oversight corrected the following year by General Orders No. 6, Headquarters of the Army, February 1, 1886, which stated dark blue would designate general staff officers, while yellow would be used for cavalry, scarlet for artillery, and white for infantry, unlike enlisted infantrymen, who still kept their dark blue lined capes. The same order modified paragraph 2683 of army regulations, which stated that belts were to be worn on the outside of overcoats by officers below the rank of brigadier general. This was in conflict with General Orders No. 8, and the correction was made to set the record straight that sword belts went underneath the heavy coats. Of course, this did not apply to enlisted coats, whether worn by the rank and file or officers who opted for them under field conditions.

Once again, some enterprising signalman evidently opted for the helmet plate overlay as a cap device, this specimen having a tiny pin back added for such a purpose. The forage cap is of the 1889-pattern, as evidenced by the bound visor. GM

Another mainstay of the clothing allowance, besides overcoats, was also subject to the ebb and flow of change. In fact, blouses embodied the unsettled times when it came to issue articles. For nearly a decade after 1874 the enlisted five-button blouse had been a staple for the soldier. Then, in 1883, the discontinuance of branch colored cord started a process of constant revision, albeit subtle alterations in many cases. To begin with, Specification No. 92, adopted on May 19, 1883, differed little from the old jacket adopted as Specification No. 13 from March 13, 1879. The main dissimilarity between the two was that no cord was called for on the later version.

The next milestone was Specification No. 100 of January 16, 1884. While the official description was generally the same as its immediate predecessor, save for the lack of certain details, such as the button on the back seam placed at 1 3/4 inches from the edge of the cuff, and also there was no mention of padding in the collar, breast, and shoulders, nor a reference to a rounded collar, yet presumably all these elements were contained in the sealed sample used as the model for production. Other key distinctions were that the blouses made to match Specification 92 came in five sizes, while those fashioned in accordance with Specification No. 100 were produced in six sizes, and were of a slightly shorter length. This second point became a matter of some confusion, as revealed by a February 17 message from Lieutenant Colonel Ludington, who brought the discrepancy to the attention of the quartermaster general in regards to the lengths of the new blouse. When preparing Specification No. 122, the old lengths from Specification No. 100 were used. This was in error. Because the difference was slight, it was not seen as a major area for concern, although the variance ultimately was to be cor-

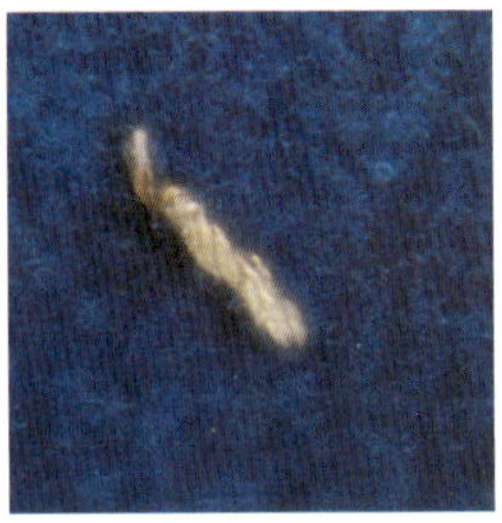

Detail of a black japanned hook added to great coats in 1885. JG

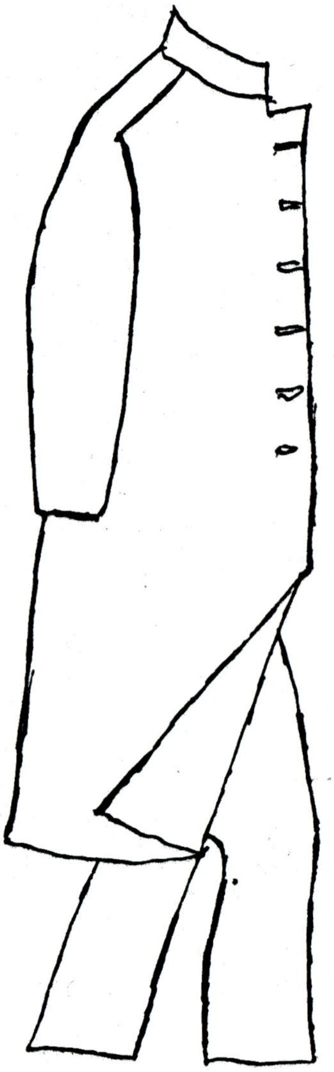

In 1885 more changes were considered to the overcoat, including replacing the buttons that once held the cape to the underside of the collar with metal hooks and eyes. A metal hook also was added toward the front edge of the skirt on both sides so that they could be secured back to facilitate marching or mounted wear, as this sketch from Quartermaster Department correspondence of 1885 depicts. NA

Captain Leefe's 1886-pattern dress knots of the Nineteenth U.S. Infantry and his 1881-pattern helmet, in this case made by the firm of Henry V. Allien. MK

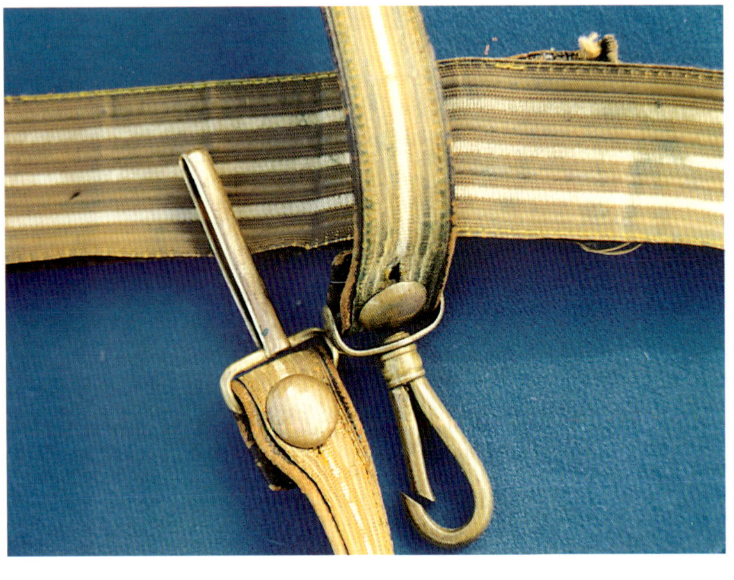

Although in 1884 white was adopted as the branch color for infantry, not until 1886 did officers of this arm of service convert their former medium blue facings and the grosgrain on company grade dress sword belts, as seen in this detail of Captain John Leefe's 1886-pattern belt. MK

rected from the original table when a new printing of the specification was released. Until then, Ludington noted the disparity in a chart that compared the incorrect printed version to the way the specifications should have been read:

Sizes	1	2	3	4	5	6
As Printed	28.	28 1/2.	29.	30.	31 3/4.	32 3/4.
Specifications	27.	27 1/2.	28.	29.	30 1/4.	30 1/2.[136]

Toward the end of the year, another series of permutations further complicated the picture. Rather than having two inside pockets, one on both sides of the chest, those blouses made following Specification No. 122 adopted on October 21, 1884, were to have only a single left interior pocket. This was more than offset by the fact that there were three outside pockets on the blouse, one on each side of the skirt, and the third "on the left breast." For the first time, exterior pockets had been officially introduced, although many types of civilian work wear had long been made with these features, as had the popular brown canvas fatigue blouse. As such, quartermaster officials saw these additions as a means of making the blouse "more serviceable and useful."[137]

Not content to let the matter rest, one more nuance was introduced late in the year with "the addition of three small buttons at the under seam of the sleeves at the cuffs of blouses" worn by enlisted men, being authorized as had long been the case for officers' blouses and coats.[138] This detail set into motion the fabrication of four sets of samples of the blouse with the sleeve buttons, although even then a further adjustment was called for because of the suggestion "...that a still further improvement of the fit of the blouses might be made if made a little more *comfortable under the arm*."[139]

This advice was one of two factors that required consideration before a final specification was released in 1886.[140] The other component that had to be included was a change in the blouse flannel itself.[141] This

An 1886-pattern shoulder knot for a captain of the Fourth U.S. Infantry. WSM

Shoulder knots for the colonel of the Twenty-fifth U.S. Infantry 1886-1902. JB

material was claimed to be of better quality, but it would not be available immediately, a realization that caused Ludington to worry. When a contract from S.M. Milliken was not forthcoming, he proposed purchase from the open market of cloth that might be "off color" from the army standard, but Holabird rejected such an option. Ludington was told to urge the contractor to hasten his production. Holabird also encouraged Ludington to keep looking for an existing cloth that met the army's criteria in case Milliken did not make good his delivery.[142] Even then, the quartermaster general was a stickler for maintaining standards, as he made known in a lengthy letter to Ludington. In this missive he decried "the looseness in regard to standard articles and samples; standard qualities, & c. of clothing and other articles manufactured or purchased for Army use" that had "long been tolerated" in the Quartermaster Department, which "thoroughly undermined...the moral soundness of the principal of adhering to standards, and to rules, regulations and instructions...." Now that he was quartermaster general, this would no longer be condoned. A man of high expectations, Holabird insisted that substandard items be rejected so that "improper or inferior articles" would never be issued to the enlisted men. To do so would be to "confess failure in just what the law appoints us to do," he preached. He steadfastly insisted: "The conclusion then is to reject every article below the standard and know that there is no power anywhere to receive an inferior thing in lieu of the regulation one."

Ever watchful, Holabird expressed his knowledge that there were other sources of the blouse flannel, with both Pippey & Co. and Thos. Kent receiving orders, the former source being judged to have a "better appearance" than the material of the latter purveyor.[143] Even then, quality control remained his modus operandi, as seen when he insisted on a preliminary inspection of 20,000 yards of blouse flannel scheduled for Jeffersonville from Pippey & Co. After that, a second and final inspection would take place at the facility in Indiana under the depot quartermaster there, who would be the ultimate approving authority to accept or reject the material.

For the moment, all this exertion to obtain the new cloth for production of the exterior pocket design blouse was academic, because "as a matter of economy" the traditional practice of issuing existing stocks

An infantry company grade officer in the 1886 through 1902 period dress uniform. NA

Front and side views of c. 1885 cavalry officer's trousers, in this case for Captain Edmund Luff. JM

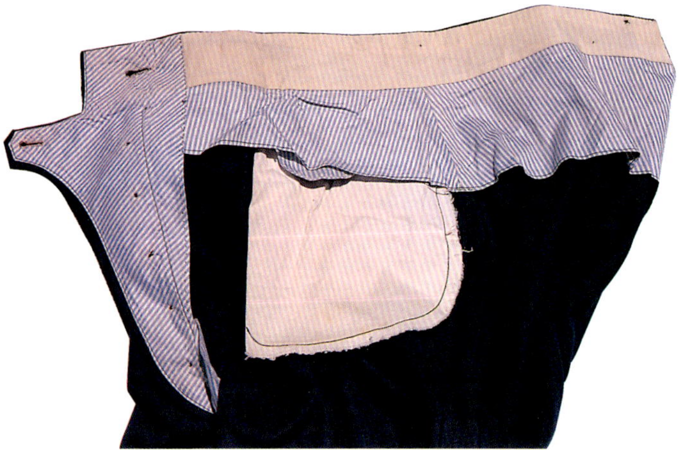

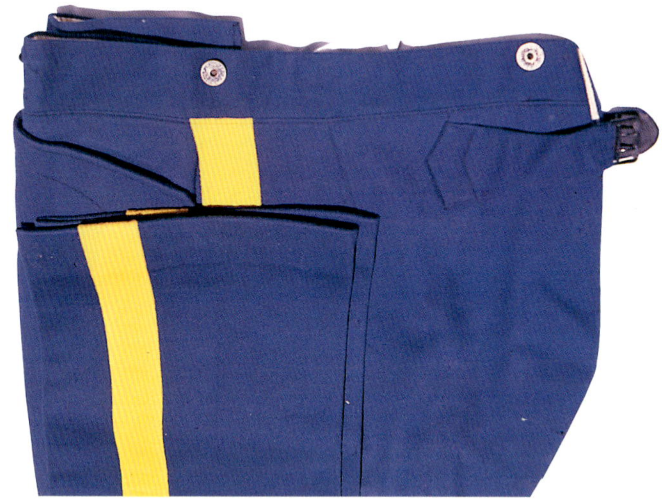

Cuff and waist of Captain Luff's trousers.

so as to "absorb the blouses of the old standard flannel" was set into motion. The reason for holding back the latest rendering of the blouse was stated in simple terms: "Owing to the disinclination on the part of the enlisted men to draw garments of older issues if articles of improved quality and finer grade can be procured," the Quartermaster Department would hold the updated models in reserve until the previous style had been distributed as completely as possible.[144] Interestingly enough, concerns that the men would be so enthusiastic about the new blouse that they would eschew the previous pattern were unfounded. Judging from photographic evidence of the era, men tended to wear the version of the five-button blouse made without exterior pockets.

Perhaps this situation was less a matter of taste than availability, though, because obsolete chevrons and old pattern blouses were to be issued exclusively in the far west, and those articles not dispensed to the men were to be sent back to the San Francisco Depot for further disposition. This is not to imply that no alternatives were pursued to convert serviceable blouses made of the old standard flannel. In November, after ordering all the blouses of the old flannel to St. Louis, including the reserve stock, and then directing that the blouses of the new standard would be set aside as the reserve, the question was raised whether "the blouses without pockets and those with cord" could be "altered to conform to the latest pattern?"[145]

It became apparent that only a partial transformation of the 1874-pattern blouses could be accomplished—the removal of the cord. This was considered satisfactory for the moment, so long as the cord was removed before issue.[146]

With that a disconcerting number of possibilities presented themselves when filling orders. By removing the cord from the collars and wrists, 1874-pattern blouses could be issued, or blouses made according to Specification No. 100, which were virtually identical to the model from the 1870s, could be shipped, albeit in both instances without exterior pockets. Then there were two renditions made according to Specification No. 122, which only differed in terms of the flannel being used to make the garment, one being produced form old standard fabric and the other from the new standard. Even then, there was a requirement to add the three buttons at the cuff, a component that probably was not officially incorporated until the Specification No. 164 replaced all previous forms of the blouse on March 12, 1886.[147] The only option that did not seem to come into play was in the case of the unpopular blouse made from "obsolete blouse shirts."[148]

Amidst the array of choices, the quartermaster in charge of the St. Louis Depot, Major C.W. Foster, was informed that all the blouses at

Left: Waist and lining at waist of Captain Luff's trousers. JM

Philadelphia and Jeffersonville were being transferred to his operation. These were "made of flannel of the former standard," and they were to be issued "before any of the blouses of the flannel made of the new standard." When particular sizes dwindled, replenishment would be made "from time to time as needed, a small supply of flannel having been reserved for that purpose." All other blouse flannel on hand at St. Louis was to be transferred to Jeffersonville. In turn, 2,000 yards of the new standard blouse flannel had been sent from the Indiana facility to the Missouri facility.

Preparatory to the transfer, a statement of made and unmade blouses on hand at Philadelphia, Jeffersonville, and St. Louis, along with all blouse flannel as of July 13, 1885, was called for, and which revealed most of the blouses already were in St. Louis awaiting distribution. The total number of blouses reported was 10,753 made and 286 unmade. There also was only 306 yards of blouse flannel in stock with outstanding contracts for another 7,641 yards.[149]

By mid-September the number of blouses had dropped to 9,047 made, but there were now 595 unmade blouses in the inventory, and some 4,561 yards of flannel was now available, with 57,721 1/2 yards awaiting delivery under existing contracts.[150] By the end of the next month there were 7,594 made blouses and 4,900 unmade blouses, almost all of which were at St. Louis, with 2,774 3/4 yards of flannel on hand, but none on order.[151]

What these figures did not divulge was the accumulation that appeared on the rolls partially stemmed from the lack of enthusiasm among the rank and file to accept the blouses on hand, especially those made in the old size 1 and 2 ranges. The troops were to "be encouraged to draw them." As an incentive, the price charged was dropped to $2.25 for each

A second lieutenant of infantry's blouse with the white back shoulder straps introduced in 1885. FAM

Second Lieutenant Carl Reichmann, a former enlisted man who received a commission in the Twenty-fourth U.S. Infantry in 1884, wears the white back shoulder straps adopted in 1886 and the 1883 pattern forage cap cord. FAM

Some shoulder straps were made with simulated embroidery borders made of gilt metal, as in this case for a second lieutenant of infantry. These were inexpensive to produce and fairly substantial for field service. The concept was introduced during the Civil War, although the popularity for such insignia was limited until late in the nineteenth-century with the outbreak of the Spanish American War. KC

of the old pattern size 1 and 2 blouses, resulting in a reduction of nearly twenty-five percent.[152] To press the matter, recruits ultimately were furnished with outmoded forms of the blouse in an effort to deplete the inventory on hand.[153] Another method was to provide military convicts and prisoners awaiting transfer to the penal facility at Ft. Leavenworth with old pattern garments.

Review of excess supplies from various posts around the country reinforced the appearance that the men refrained from accepting the old pattern blouses, along with trousers of both the previous size allocations, as well as those of the lighter shade of kersey.[154] Possibly Holabird saw these reactions as an inevitable part of change.

Certainly he was aware that the flurry of activities resulting after his assumption of the Quartermaster Department caused many revisions, along with the introduction of several new items. He felt that codification of these efforts required the printing of a specifications book to replace the out-of-date uniform regulations from 1882. Holabird noted: "owing to the frequent and necessary changes made in specifications of the various articles of clothing and equipage" the time had come to publish a new work containing all the most up-to-date information available. He desired this guide to "be as complete in every respect as it can be made, and as each officer of the QMDept cannot conveniently be furnished with a set of standards and samples, it has been decided to publish with each specification, a correct illustration of the article."[155]

At first Holabird intended to utilize the line drawing he had furnished for the annual reports in 1884 and 1885, "but upon a close comparison with the specifications" he thought otherwise, after discovering "that some of the drawings do not agree with the specifications, and *all* are lettered in an inartistic manner." In view of these faults, the quartermaster general wanted new drawings with "first class workmanship, and uniform size and style throughout," along with professional lettering so that the product would "be creditable to the Department." He further stipulated that he wanted all the illustrations to be executed "upon Bristol board or drawing paper, in order to obtain a better photolitho-

Major generals and above continued to be allowed the option of wearing the buff or gold sash across the chest of their dress coat. This example is for a major general, specifically Nelson A. Miles. WC

Shoulder straps for all staff corps, including engineers, medical corps, and ordnance continued to have dark blue centers with gold outer embroidery. This example is for a lieutenant colonel. JL

Typical officers' shoulder straps of the mid 1880s through the early twentieth century from left to right are: infantry second lieutenant; artillery second lieutenant; infantry lieutenant colonel; infantry captain (pre 1886); cavalry first lieutenant. JG

Nelson A. Miles as a major general. He wears a Grand Army of the Republic medal on the far right and several other badges from veterans' organizations, but not his Medal of Honor, the only regulation decoration allowed during the period, with the exception of various marksman and sharpshooter devices. USAMHI

See caption below.

graphic copy. Each plate should measure inside the lines 4 1/2 x 7 1/2 inches." He thought certain drawings should be "changed entirely, those for blouses, dress coats, canvas caps, stockings, and especially trousers being singled out, while guidon cases were to be added and "the stitching upon the cuffs of the leather gauntlets" brought into agreement with the standards in his office, which the illustration in the annual report were not.[156]

Ludington complied quickly and furnished some samples of new drawings. Holabird decided these were improvements over the ones that had appeared in the annual reports, but he still was not satisfied with the lettering. He indicated that the lack of uniformity in this detail might be overcome by the use of print in small type.[157]

All this caused the quartermaster general to seek an artist whose purpose it would be to execute "a complete set of drawings of each article of clothing for both officers and enlisted men, and of the various items of equipage." This, he told Ludington, would add to "the beauty and attractiveness of the book now being prepared by you."[158]

Efforts to meet the exacting goal set by Holabird in the production of the specifications and standards book were ongoing for some time to come. As work progressed on this combination practical tool and record

Above Right: While regulations called for gold epaulets with heavy bullion fringe to be worn by general officers for dress purposes, some individuals elected to wear specially made shoulder knots, as depicted on this brigadier general's dress coat. WC

Right: A painting of General Sherman in the dress uniform of the commanding general of the army from 1872 through 1884, with its twelve buttons in each row grouped in sets of four and the sash worn over the shoulder. Here the more common general officer's epaulets are depicted, rather than the shoulder knots. WPM

of his departments' efforts, a new general order set forth the basic issue as it had come to be provided by 1885, along with the associated prices charged against the enlisted man's account when he drew his clothing.[159] According to General Orders No. 71, Headquarters of the Army, June 23, 1885, the men were to receive their allowance at specific prices and quantities. (see Table 1)

TABLE 1

Statement of the price of which Clothing for the Army of the United States will be issued from July 1, 1885, until further orders.

CLOTHING

	Post Quarter-master Sgts.	Ordnance Sgts.	Hospital Stewards	Commissary Sgts.	Ordnance	Engineers	Artillery	Infantry	Light Artillery	Cavalry or Sig. Corps	
Helmet, without trimmings	$1.25	$1.25	$1.25	$1.25	$1.25	$1.25	$1.25	$1.25	$1.25	$1.25	each.
“ hair plume							.44	.44	.44	.44	“
“ cord and band							.47	.47	.47	.47	“
“ top piece of base	.02	.02	.02	.02	.02	.02.	.02	.02	.02	.02	“
“ socket for plume								.16	.16	.16	“
“ spike	.07	.07	.07	.07	.07	.07	.07	.07			“
“ scroll and rings							.02	.02	.02	.02	per pair
“ side buttons	.01	.01	.01	.01	.01	.01	.01	.01	.01	.01	“
“ device on shield	.02	.02	.02	.02	.02	.02	each				
“ number (white metal)							.01	.01	.01	.01	“
Cork helmet	1.25	1.25	1.25	1.25	1.25	1.25	1.25	1.25	1.25	1.25	“
Fatigue or campaign hat, black, wool	.65	.65	.65	.65	.65	.65	.65	.65	.65	.65	“
“ , drab, fur	1.40	1.40	1.40	1.40	1.40	1.40	1.40	1.40	1.40	1.40	“
“ cord and tassel	.67	.67	.67	.67	.67	.67	.67	.67	.67	.67	
Forage cap	.50	.50	.50	.50	.50	.50	.50	.50	.50	.50	“
Crossed sabers, cannon, or rifles, bugle, castle, pen and key, crescent, caduceus of forage caps	.02	.02	.02	.02	.02	.02	.02	.02	.02	.02	“
Wreaths for forage caps	.03		.03						“		
Fur cap	1.15	1.15	1.15	1.15	1.15	1.15	1.15	1.15	1.15	1.15	“
Letters, brass						.01	.01	.01	.01	.01	“
Numbers, brass							.01	.01	.01	.01	“
Overcoat, made	8.70	8.70	8.70	8.70	8.70	8.70	8.70	8.70	8.70	8.70"	
“ , unmade	6.70	6.70	6.70	6.70	6.70	6.70	6.70	6.70	6.70	6.70	“
Uniform coat, musicians, made						8.51	8.46	8.46	8.22	8.22	“
“ “, unmade						5.01	4.96	4.96	4.72	4.72	“
“ “ without chevrons, made	7.93	7.93.	7.93	7.93	7.93	7.93	7.88	7.88	7.64	7.64	“
“ “, unmade	4.93	4.93	4.93	4.93	4.93	4.93	4.88	4.88	4.64	4.64	
“ blouses, made	3.18	3.18	3.18	3.18	3.18	3.18	3.18	3.18	3.18	3.18	
“ “ “, unmade	2.43	2.43	2.43	2.43	2.43	2.43	2.43	2.43	2.43	2.43	“
Stable frocks									.50	.50	“
Overalls						1.19			.43	.43	per pair
Trousers, private heavy, made	2.66	2.66	2.66	2.66	2.66	2.66	2.66	2.66	3.43	3.43	
“ “ “ “ “, unmade	1.91	1.91	1.91	1.91	1.91	1.91	1.91	1.91	2.43	2.43	
“ “ “, light, made	2.51	2,51	2.51	2.51	2.51	2.51	2.51	2.51	3.24	3.24	
“ “ “, unmade	1.76.	1.76.	1.76	1.76	1.76	1.76	1.76	1.76	2.24	2.24	
“ Suspenders	.17	.17	17	.17	.17	.17	.17	.17	.17	.17	“
“ Shirt, dark-blue flannel	2.25	2.25	2.25	2.25	2.25	2.25	2.25	2.25	2.25	2.25	each
Knit undershirt	.54	.54	.54	.54	.54	.54	.54	.54	.54	.54	“
Drawers	.56	.56	.56	.56	.56	.56	.56	.56	.56	.56	per pair
Stockings, woolen	.24	.24	.24	.24	.24	.24	.24	.24	.24	.24	“
“ “, cotton, all colors	.10	.10	.10	.10	.10	.10	.10	.10	.10	.10	“
Berlin gloves	.12	.12	.12	.12	.12	.12	.12	.12	.12	.12	“
Gauntlets, leather									1.06	1.06	“
“, fur	1.52	1.52	1.52	1.52	1.52	1.52	1.52	1.52	1.52	1.52	“
Mittens, woolen	.27	.27	.27	.27	.27	.27	.27	.27	.27	.27	“
Boots, sewed									3.99	3.99	“
Shoes, sewed “post”	3.05	3.05	3.05	3.05	3.05	3.05	3.05	3.05	3.05	3.05	“
“ “ “field”	2.73	2.73	2.73	2.73	2.73	2.73	2.73	2.73	2.73	2.73	“
“campaign”	2.38	2.38	2.38	2.38	2.38	2.38	2.38	2.38	2.38	2.38	“
Arctic overshoes	3.40	3.40	3.40	3.40	3.40	3.40	3.40	3.40	3.40	3.40	“
Blanket, woolen	2.70	2.70	2.70	2.70	2.70	2.70	2.70	2.70	2.70	2.70	“
Chevrons, cloth N.C.S., color and lst sergeant's	2.31	.74	.74.	.74	.74	.74.	.74	.74	.74	.74	“
“ sergeant's					.40	.40	.40	.40	.40	.40	“
“ corporal's					.32	.32	.32	.32	.32	.32	“
“ pioneer's and farrier's					.72	.72	.72	.72	.72	.72	“
“ device for signal corps										.28	each

" gold lace	5.52	3.92	1.83	3.56							per pair
" " " sergeant major's						4.59	4.59	4.59		4.59	""""
" " " q.m. sergeant's						3.46	4.48	4.48		4.48	"
" " " chief trumpeter's										3.98	"
" " " principal musician's							3.76	3.76			"
" " " saddler sergeant's							3.98	"			
" " " color and lst sergeant's						3.50	3.50	3.50	3.50	3.50	"
" " " sergeant's					2.57	2.57	2.57	2.57	2.57	2.57	"
" " " corporal's					1.89	1.89	1.89	1.89	1.89	1.89	"
" " " service, peace and war	.60	.60	.60	.60	.60	.60	.60	.60	.60	.60	"
Stripes for trousers	.37	.37	.37	.37				"			
" sergeant's					.28	.65	.28	.21	.28	.28	"
" corporal's					.19	.55	.19	.13	.19	.19	"
" musician's						1.10	.38	.26	.38	.38	"
Facings for uniform coats, including silk	.63	.63	.63	.63	.63	.63	.58	.58	.60	.60	"

Prices at which articles of Equipage will be charged in case of loss or damage.

ARTICLES	AMOUNT		ARTICLES	AMOUNT
Barrack chair (rawhide seat)	$1.45		Canvas fatigue coat	$0.89
" " (poplar seat)	1.01		" " trousers	.85
Shoe-file	.25		" cap or hood	.93
Card-holder for bunks	.01		" mittens	.15
Buffalo overcoat	12..95		" Poncho, rubber	1.55
Canvas overcoat, blanket-lined	10.81		Blanket, rubber	1.13
Allowance of Clothing.				

A brigadier general's shoulder knot. WC

In addition to replacing epaulets with shoulder knots, Lieutenant General Sheridan also is bedecked with numerous corps badges and other unofficial veteran's symbols from his Civil War service in an image taken sometime after his ascent to the command of the army in 1884. GS

ARTICLES		YEAR 1st	2nd	3rd	4th	5th	Total for 5 yrs.
Helmets and trimmings, complete	no	1		1			2
Forage caps	no	1	1	1	1	1	5
Uniform coats	no	1	1		1		3
Trousers	pairs	3	2	3	2	2	12
Dark-blue flannel shirts	no	3	2	2	2	2	11
Knit undershirts	no	3	3	3	3	3	15
Drawers	no	3	3	3	3	3	15
Boots, sewed, for mounted men	pairs	1	1		1		3
"Post" shoes, sewed, for mounted men	pairs	1		1			2
"Field or "campaign" shoes, sewed, for mounted men	pairs	1	1	1	1	1	5
"Post" shoes, sewed, for footmen	pairs	1	1	1	1	*1*	*5*
"Field or "campaign" shoes, sewed, for footmen	pairs	2	1	2	1	1	7
Stockings, woolen	pairs	4	4	4	4	4	20
Stockings, cotton	pairs	2	2	2	2	2	10
Blouses	no	1	1	1	1	1	5
Overcoats	no	1					1
Chevrons, cloth	pairs	2	1	1	1	1	6
Chevrons, gold lace	pairs	1	1		1		3
Stripes, for trousers	pairs	3	2	3	2	2	12
Stable frock, for mounted men	no	1		1			2
Overalls, for engineers and m'ted men	pairs	1	1	1	1	1	5
Blankets, woolen		1		1			2
White Berlin gloves, for m'ted men	pairs	1	1	1	1	1	5
White Berlin gloves, for footmen	pairs	8	8	8	8	8	40
Suspenders	pairs	1	1	1	1	1	1
Gauntlets, leather, for mounted men	pairs	1	1		1		3
Helmets, mounted	no	1	1	2			
Forage caps	no	1	1	1	1	1	5
Lyres for forage caps	no	1	1	1	1	1	5
Uniform dress coats	no	1	1	1	3		
Blouses	no	1	1	1	1	1	5
Trousers and stripes, kersey	pairs	3	2	3	2	2	12
Trousers, white	pairs	3	2	3	2	1	11
Overcoat	no	1					1
Suspenders	pairs	1	1	1	1	1	5
Berlin gloves	pairs	8	8	8	8	8	40
Aiguillette and Shoulder-knots	sets	1	1		1		3
Shoes, "post"	pairs	1	1	1	1	1	5
Shoes, "field" or "campaign"	pairs	2	1	2	1	1	7
Wool-blankets	no	1		1			2
Dark-blue overshirts	no	3	2	2	2	2	11
Drawers	pairs	3	3	3	3	3	12
Woolen stockings	pairs	4	4	4	4	4	20
Cotton stockings	pairs	2	2	2	2	2	10
Music pouch	no	1					1

Three exterior pockets were added to the specifications for enlisted blouses on October 21, 1884, in lieu of specifications of January 16, 1884. In turn, by March 12, 1886, another change was made to specifications, in that three buttons were added to each cuff of the blouse (based upon a December 1885 decision of the secretary of war), and for the remainder of the century this basic garment was regulation. This example of the 1886-pattern with cuff buttons is the sealed sample for a cavalry farrier. SI

Cork helmets are supplied only to troops serving in extremely hot climates in the first and third years of their enlistment, and these only in lieu of the campaign hats. The necessity for such issue must in all cases be certified by the Department Commander.—*Par. 2763, Regulations.*

Fatigue or campaign hats are issued only to troops on the frontier or in active campaign at the rate of one per year.—Par. 2776 of the Regulations, amended by General Orders No. 64, H.Q.A., 1882.

Arctic overshoes and woolen mittens issued will be charged to the enlisted men at cost prices. The necessity of their issue must, however, be certified to by the Department and Division Commanders. The allowance for these articles is as follows: Arctic overshoes, one pair in each of the first and third years of enlistment, and woolen mittens, two pairs per annum. (G.O. No. 69, H.Q.A., 1882.)

Canvas fatigue coats and trousers will be furnished to each man who may be required to work on extra, daily, or fatigue duty at the rate of one suit per year, as part of his equipment. Troops serving in the Departments of Dakota, the Platte, and the Columbia are also permitted to draw one canvas cap or hood and one pair canvas mittens. All these articles will be issued free of charge and will remain public property until worn out or destroyed. (G.O. No. 69, H.Q.A., 1882; and G.O. No. 32, H.Q.A., 1883.)

Overcoats made of fur or other suitable material will be issued and accounted for in the manner prescribed by par. 2090 1/2 of the regulations published in G.G. No. 62, H.Q.A., 1883.

Text from Table 1 continued on p. 223.

Under the same paragraph enlisted men may draw annually one fur cap and one pair of fur gauntlets at the prices established in the annual price list; but these articles do not form part of the money allowances, and civilian employees may purchase, at the prices given in this list, fur clothing, when in the opinion of the Post Commanders their duties are such as they actually need them.

Under special authority of the War Department rubber blankets and ponchos may be issued gratuitously, at the rate of one per annum, to each man serving in the field or in active campaign, until the stock on hand shall have become exhausted. (Adjutant General's letter of Sept. 27, 1884.)

Enlisted men may draw, whenever in the opinion of the proper officer it may be necessary, during the first year's enlistment, the two woolen blankets to which they are entitled during their service of five years. (G.O. No. 139, H.Q.A., 1884.)

Besides defining the costs and numbers of articles to be issued over a five year enlistment, the Quartermaster Department set the tariff of how many articles of each size would be furnished per one hundred men when requisitions were made from the field. This formula was based upon averages, that may or may not have actually squared with the measurements of the men in a given command, but nevertheless department officials staunchly insisted this formula was to be adhered to without deviation, except in those instances where a man's measurements were larger or smaller than the ones provided for within the range of sizes. To ensure compliance General Orders No. 67, Headquarters of the Army, June 13, 1885, was promulgated. (see Table 2)

An 1886-pattern sack coat for a sergeant of the Signal Corps. The chevrons were orange, and the crossed flags were red and white. SI

The first sergeant of Company B, Twenty-fourth U.S. Infantry in the five-button enlisted blouse with exterior pockets adopted in 1884. The backgrounds for the diamond of his white cloth chevrons have been altered by cutting them in a triangular shape at the top, rather than leaving the arc of cloth above the stripes as originally issued. HP

TABLE 2

By direction of the Secretary of War paragraphs 2072 and 2073 of the regulations are amended to read as follows:

2072. All estimates or requisitions for clothing, whether special or annual, must conform strictly to the regulations prescribing the allowance, and the sizes. Exclusive issues of larger sizes than are worn by the men cannot be made. The following table show the proper proportions of sizes to the 100:

2073. Should any of the sizes of overcoats, uniform dress coats, blouses, and trousers specified in the foregoing paragraph prove inadequate, measurements will be sent with the estimate for those garments when required for men who cannot be fitted with the regular sizes.

	1	2	3	4	5	6	7	8	9	10	11	12	
Articles. *	6 3/4	6 7/8	7	7 1/8	71/4	7 3/8							
Boots					4	11	30	32	16	4	2	1	100
Shoes					4	11	30	32	16	4	2	1	100
Helmets	16	28	22	20	10	4							100
Campaign hats	16	28	22	20	10	4							100
Forage caps	16	28	22	20	10	4							100
Canvas caps	16	28	22	20	10	4							100
Uniform dress coats	10	25	30	25	6	4							100
Overcoats	10	25	30	25	6	4							100
Blouses	10	25	30	25	6	4							100
Canvas sack coats	10	20	30	20	15	5							100
Stable frocks	15	45	30	10									100
Undershirts, knit	8	36	38	15	3								100
Overshirts, dark blue flannel	8	36	38	15	3								100
Trousers, kersey	5	5	15	15	10	5	10	5	10	10	5	5	100
Trousers, white linen	10	20	30	20	15	5							100
Trousers, canvas	10	20	30	20	15	5							100
Drawers, Canton flannel	15	25	35	20	5								100
Canvas mittens	25	45	30										100
Fur gauntlets									30	50	20		100

*The figures on this line indicate the trade size of helmets, hats, and caps, corresponding to the sizes of the Quartermaster's Department.

Despite official pronouncements that the enlisted blouse was to have three exterior pockets, one on the left breast and on each side below the waist, nearly all extent examples and photographs from the period depict the earlier blouse's style without exterior pockets. Despite this fact, nothing in correspondence explains this situation, while specifications throughout the remainder of the 1880s and early 1890s continued to call for the outside pockets. This example (front and back) without pockets is typical, and bears quartermaster markings to indicate it is a Regular Army issue item from the late Victorian era. JB

Interior lining in the lighter gray twilled shirting typical of the 1874-1886 period for enlisted blouses. FAM

At this point the quartermaster general beamed with confidence over his department's labors. This prompted Holabird to provide a glowing estimate of these activities in the form of a letter he sent through the adjutant general to Sheridan, stating:

> The allowance for clothing is now so much greater than the enlisted man actually draws, a large saving appears to the credit of every moderately careful man at the termination of his enlistment; so that if some few of the minor article seem inadequate to his wants, they are largely supplemented, and more than balanced by other more costly garments. If therefore the allowance of gloves and stocking be increased, the issue of a compensating quantity of other clothing could be decreased. The clothing bill is now larger than ever before in the history of the Army, and any increase without an equalizing decrease should not be considered. With regard to keeping a supply at each post for sales to officers and enlisted men, the *Q.M. Genl.* is of the opinion that it would be neither wise nor expedient; certainly not economical. Officers can by regulations (par. 2087 of the regulations) purchase clothes for their own use, and when it is shown that the clothing supply at any post is inadequate, special requisitions can always be made and promptly filled.[160]

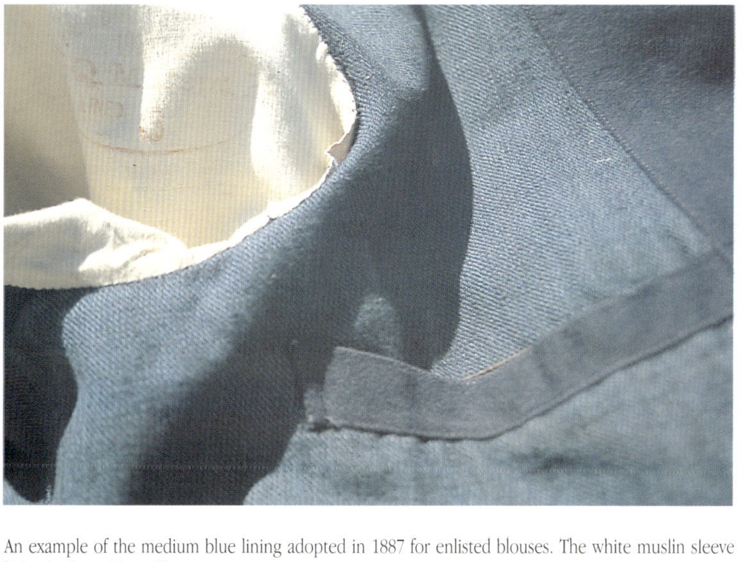

An example of the medium blue lining adopted in 1887 for enlisted blouses. The white muslin sleeve lining is also evident. JB

A typical enlisted man in the blouse prescribed in 1883 without cord, in this case for a cavalryman as evidenced by the insignia on his 1872-pattern forage cap and saber. This was the blouse commonly worn by the rank and file, in spite of official specifications calling for the garment to have three exterior pockets. MM

The quartermaster general also was effusive in his official remarks about the department's operation, and even reverted to an argument by silence in his annual report to the secretary of war for the fiscal year ending June 30, 1885 in which he proclaimed:

> Fewer complaints than ever before of the clothing and equipage issued to the Army during the last year have reached this office, and the impression seems to have obtained that but little fault can justly be found. The Army seems to be satisfied, and that is the best criterion by which the Department can be guided.[161]

During 1886 Quartermaster Department personnel attempted to sustain this momentum, although they candidly admitted there was room for improvement in certain sectors. One of the recognized shortcomings had to do with leather gauntlets. The department admitted that there was room for improvement. In a few instances the seams separated because chemicals used to dress the leather reacted adversely with the sewing silk. The specifications were changed so that linen rather than silk would be used in the future for stitching the fingers and thumbs, but silk was retained for the ornamental designs on the cuffs and the back of the hand. Troopers at Ft. Sill, Indian Territory, who had their gauntlets disintegrate because of this, were to be given replacements willingly, and the contractor was held responsible for the defect.[162]

The correction to gauntlets was followed by another initiative stemming from a suggestion that suspenders could be enhanced. The front

The five-button blouse commonly worn from the mid-1880s through the early twentieth century without pockets is seen in a smartly tailored version of the garment worn by an artillery first sergeant, who probably was a member of the garrison at Ft. McHenry, Maryland. It seems his chevrons have been altered by overstitching to make the stripes stand out. He likewise has elected to pose with both his sharpshooter and marksman devices, despite the fact that the two orders of qualification were not supposed to be worn together. JG

adjustment buckles warranted issue of extra tapes when the cloth wore out in this area, an observation Captain David J. Craigie, the acting quartermaster for Madison Barracks, New York, shared with the department. The idea seemed to have merit, but Lieutenant Colonel Ludington came up with another solution besides the one proposed by the captain. The front straps were to be reinforced with sheepskin leather, a change that Brigadier General Holabird thought suitable. He then directed that the specifications be amended to add this detail.[163]

Adjustment to gauntlets and suspenders was undertaken with relative ease, but imperfections related to footgear were not as easily addressed. One source of discontent was the narrowness of the instep for both shoes and boots.[164] As a remedy to this and other failings, the department obtained lasts known in the commercial trade as "Waukenphast" (also known as "Walkenfast"). These forms were procured to produce boots and shoes with broader insteps and a better shape. What is more, the number of widths was increased from two to three widths (A, B, and C) to give "the men a better selection" than in the past. The potential for heightened satisfaction was on the horizon, but only after the Waukenphast products became available. As was the norm, that would take time because furnishing footgear that had been made on the old lasts had to be undertaken to use up existing supplies before new models could be sent out to the soldiers.

Enlisted members of the Department of Dakota at the 1884 shooting competition are indicative of the prevalence of five-button blouses without pockets, a garment that resembled those worn by the officers in the picture by this time. Note the diversity of headgear, however, from forage caps to straw "boaters," campaign hats of both regulation and non-regulation styles, and even a summer helmet on the officer seated in the center front row. Even at this date uniformity was not achieved. TT

These three "bunkies" from the Sixth U.S. Cavalry serving at Ft. Stanton, New Mexico Territory, in 1885 represent the ultimate in nonconformity. Only their 1884 or 1886-pattern mounted gauntlets and their .45-55 cavalry carbines with pistol grip are the same. The rest of their outfits tend to be civilian garb, the fringed items possibly being costumes provided by the photographer at his studio. The kneeling trooper in the center has a shirt of the style favored by miners, firemen, and other non-military working men of the era. He seems to have on issue sky-blue kersey trousers, however, and 1876-pattern boots. The headgear may be 1883-pattern drab campaign hats, although the brims for the two standing men seem to be larger than issue hats. TT

Furthermore, Holabird discerned that certain more popular sizes would be depleted first, in which case the supply would have to be replenished with old patterns to preclude the men from seeking the latest shoe style. The number of post shoes, both with and without canvas linings, were to be determined, and the quantity required to furnish the army with its needs were looked at as part of the transition process.[165]

One means to accelerate the consumption of footgear made on the old lasts was the ongoing replenishment of boots and shoes that had worn out prematurely, especially as a consequence of the punishment that campaigning in the Southwest had caused.[166] Considerable numbers of replacements from the inventory, including brass screwed models, would heighten the pace of eliminating older styles so that those of the more recent pattern could be released. Moreover, the inability of sewn footwear to withstand the dry, hot, rough conditions of the borderlands actually caused a temporary reversion to brass screws on a limited basis for the troops serving in Arizona and New Mexico. These were made on the new lasts, however, so as to provide a better product to the men. Some 2,000 pairs of campaign shoes at $2.48 a pair, and 1,000 pairs of boots at $3.76 per pair, were made up for this purpose.[167]

The latter type of footgear had undergone change, as well. With the reaction that the back seams of boots, which had been sewn on the inside on the original model, rubbed the calf, the seam was sewn on the inside, then covered with a strip of leather as an added buffer. This provided a smooth interior. Additionally, the campaign shoe was enhanced. It was to be crimped at the back to insure "a more comfortable fit."[168] As 1886 approached an end, however, fabrication of these crimped campaign shoes halted so that the convict work force could concentrate on the output of post shoes made from the Waukenphast lasts, that style of footgear having run low. With all that, the subject of footwear still had not been closed. Evaluation of data brought about the conclusion that A width shoes and boots, plus those in sizes 5, 11, and 12 were required in lesser numbers than projected. With supporting statistics in hand, the governor of Leavenworth's prison enterprises was told to halt production of the unpopular sizes to "avoid an accumulation of boots and shoes" and "in the interest of economy."[169]

In March 1886 George Crook met to treat with Geronimo at Canyon de los Embudos, Mexico. Crook, seated second from the right in a pith helmet next to young Charles Roberts, wears a stout canvas suit and moccasins, while most of his subordinates follow suit by donning various civilian components of dress. Lieutenant Samson L. Faison, seated at the left foreground is as close to regulations as any in the group with his 1883-pattern campaign hat and outdated 1882-pattern piped field shirt. He, too, seems to have discarded kersey trousers for canvas ones, though, but the boots appear to be the issue 1884-pattern. Most of the other men have on shoes, however, and in the case of young Charley Roberts, a pair of civilian leggings have been obtained. NA

While not as flamboyant in their dress, these three troopers who have visited Goff's photo studio in Bismarck, Dakota Territory, still have modified their campaign kit to suit their tastes. The seated man and the one to his right have on civilian shirts, while the man standing with his gauntleted fist on his left hip wears an 1882-pattern piped shirt. He and the other standing figure wear 1884-pattern boots, while the seated man has on the higher topped 1886-pattern boots and a custom cartridge belt. The other two men wear Mills belts, and all have gauntlets, drab campaign hats, and mounted reinforced kersey trousers, the fellow in the center being set off by a 1/2 inch yellow stripe along the outer seam to indicate that he is a corporal. TT

Although Leavenworth remained the center for footgear production, a gradual return to contractors began after the secretary of war approved yet one more type of shoe. In the interest of adding "to the comfort of enlisted men" canvas barracks shoes were procured by purchase, and those men who wished could buy a pair per year at $.95 1/2. The first batch of 5,000 were offered with the understanding that if they were well received, more would be acquired from departmental funds.[170]

As one means to stretch those funds, leather scraps from prison footgear manufacturing funds were sold, and the money generated was reapplied to production.[171] Further evidence of frugality was the use of leftover cuttings from the fabrication of brown canvas fatigue wear as a substitute for the padding of kersey trousers. This saved just over two cents a pair. Given that thousands of pairs were produced each year, the move seemed to have merit, yet it may have been a matter of false economy in that some criticisms were made alleging that the canvas fragments strained "the garments so lined...."

Nor did efforts to ensure that resources were not squandered halt there. When "the enlisted men declined to draw the black wool campaign hats originally adopted, and preferred to draw only those of drab color," instructions were given "to issue the black hats until exhausted" to prevent waste. Even so, drab hats were furnished simultaneously so that troops at one post might have the black hat, while those at another would appear in the drab version.[172]

Leggings began to assume popularity for field service in the 1880s, sometimes being made of leather to be combined with shoes to provide a boot-like appearance, as this pair did for Captain Luff. JM

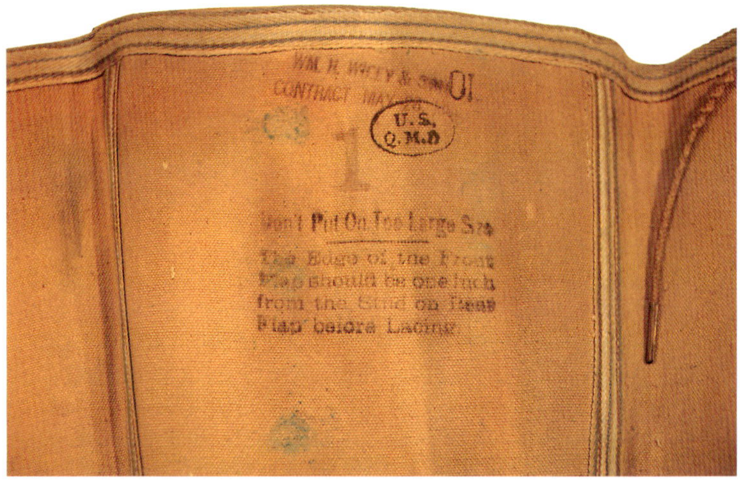

Contract markings in an official Quartermaster Department issue pair of brown canvas leggings. JM

The prior pattern of campaign hat was just one of the passe articles the rank and file shunned. Another were trousers of both the old sizes (1 through 5), and of the lighter shade of kersey. Men were to be encouraged to accept the former items by a nearly twenty-five percent reduction of the cost, as allowed for in Circular No. 2, Headquarters of the Army, March 12, 1886. At that point the rates were to be:

Trousers, mounted, made, heavy, sizes 1 to 5, each	$2.50
Trousers, mounted, unmade, heavy, sizes 1 and 2, each.	$1.75
Trousers, foot, made, heavy, sizes 2 and 3, each	$2.00
Trousers, foot, unmade, heavy, sizes 1 and 2, each	.$1.25
Trousers, mounted, made, light, sizes 1 to 4, each	$2.25
Trousers, mounted, unmade, light, sizes 1 to 3, each	$1.50
Trousers, foot, made, light, sizes 1 to 4, each	$1.75
Trousers, foot, unmade, light, sizes 1 and 2, each	$1.25

While the same circular noted that the men declined receipt of the lighter shade of trousers in twelve sizes "in the interest of economy," the secretary of war insisted that they be issued, and at that the full price be subtracted from the clothing allowance.[173] Given that some 18,632 pairs of the lighter shade of blue trousers were on hand, representing nearly $58,000 in expenditures, it was important not to have this clothing fall prey to the moths. The department contended they were "strong, durable, of good quality, and well made," as well as "equally serviceable as the latest shade, although not of the latest style."[174] Once more, recruits were viewed as a major outlet for moving the items from the depots to the troops.[175] Even then, a report was called for to determine how many pairs of trousers in the old sizes were still available, followed by a directive calling for unmade trousers of the lighter kersey to be "made up and issued whenever practicable" to any and all troops.[176]

Although trousers made in the former sizes and ones of the lighter shade of cloth were being dispensed as rapidly as possible, new standards with darker kersey and the suspender and fly buttons of the most up to date type were being produced concurrently as sealed samples. Many pairs of the latest trousers were fabricated at that point, and in July 1886 widely distributed to all the depots to serve as models for future production.[177] As part of the transition, all the sealed samples of former patterns of trousers were to be withdrawn and issued alongside all others in stock to deplete the entire inventory, an undertaking that was required before new darker shades and the latest patterns could be supplied.[178]

One means to expedite the draw down came late in the year with approval to sell 4,000 pairs of the lighter hue trousers in Kansas, Maine, Ohio, Virginia, and Wisconsin, where branches of the Soldiers' Home were located.[179]

Canvas leggings also were purchased privately by some individuals, such as this light tan pair made of material similar to shelter halves, which Captain Luff obtained for field service. JM

Beginning in 1887 brown canvas leggings began to be provided on a limited basis to troops, but not until January 10, 1888, were the first specifications adopted. This pair was obtained in the pre-Spanish-American War period by Captain Luff. JM

Front and back views of details of helmet bands for cavalry. Cord made from 1872 through the late 1880s were of the type on the left with loosely bundled threads. Those of later manufacture began to be made from more tightly bundled threads as seen on the right. KC

A cavalry trumpeter, corporal, and private in the regulation 1885 dress uniform. LC

There was yet one more outlet that withdrew not only trousers, but also many other items of clothing. Geronimo and many other Apaches had been relocated to San Augustine, Florida, where men, women, and children required some sort of attire in their far away place of incarceration.[180]

Another lot of former pattern items also had to be dispersed to the rank and file. Just as new darker blue kersey was being ushered in for trousers, the new criterion for flannel that had been adopted for blouses, including a finer quality for noncoms, created a fluid situation.[181] Once again, Holabird wanted to move the existing inventory before he would allow the release of the latest model. To hasten dispersion, he ordered Colonel Rufus Saxton, who was in charge at Jeffersonville, to "cause the immediate manufacture of five hundred blouses, size 3, old standard flannel, and forward them as soon as practicable to the St. Louis Depot."[182] Following this he sent a telegram to St. Louis to ascertain how many made and unmade old pattern blouses were at the depot there ready for issue.[183] The quartermaster in St. Louis then received notice to dispatch three hundred size 3, six hundred size 4, 400 size 5, and 400 size 6 unmade blouses and any old shade blouse flannel that was of the proper shade to Jeffersonville.[184] This requirement was proceeded by instructions to ship another 246 unmade and 700 made blouses in sizes 4 through 6 from St. Louis to Jeffersonville so they could be cut down into 446 size 2s and 500 size 3s. The reconfigured garments then were to be returned to Missouri for issue.[185]

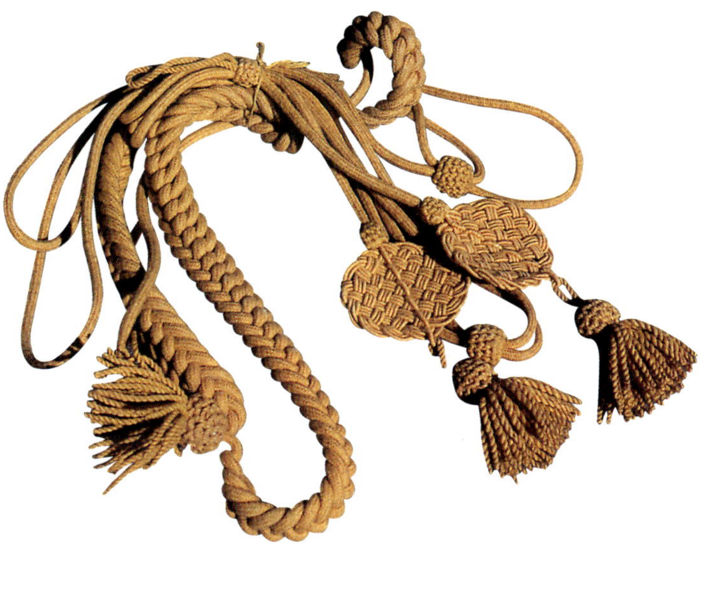

Helmet cords continued to be made in one piece for enlisted men throughout the nineteenth century, and issued bundled as seen here in this example for a cavalryman before attached to the helmet body. Photograph by Gordon Chappell. JG

As another means of making complete use of existing resources, word was sent to cancel a portion of an order for blouse lining. Instead, one thousand gray shirts were recalled from St. Louis for transferal to Jeffersonville, where they were to be pressed into service as blouse lining.[186]

All these machinations must have been confusing, but other subtle changes further contributed to continuance of a jumble of possibilities relative to blouses. For one thing, the December 10, 1885, decision by secretary of war to place three buttons on the sleeves of blouses had to be incorporated into the manufacturing process, as did another detail—the replacement of cotton thread with silk thread to make the blouses. Because the latter material tended to change color over time, usually fading to brown, silk was to be substituted, and this led to yet another

In 1887 ventilator tops no longer were to be made or issued with enlisted dress helmets, this accessory being considered superfluous. GS

new specification.[187] By late August sealed standard samples were sent to Philadelphia, Jeffersonville, and San Francisco.[188] This action coincided with notification to the superintendent of the recruiting service that all the old pattern blouses had been distributed, making it possible in early September 1886 to announce that those of the new pattern would be forthcoming in filling orders to inductees, and by inference to the rank and file at large in the not too distant future.[189]

This same news did not apply to trousers, nor overcoats. As a matter of fact, Quartermaster Captain Forrest H. Hathaway had made recommendations about distribution of the light shade overcoats for recruits and others that were taken into consideration.[190] The rule established was typical. If serviceable, old sky-blue stocks were to be issued before any other later shade coats would be released.[191] This basic dictum applied not only to overcoats, but also blouses and trousers.[192] Under this edict the supply of old great coats were to be used up. In fact, outmoded overcoats with sewed capes stored at Philadelphia were to be converted to have hooked capes. All ordnance, hospital stewards, commissary sergeants, artillery, cavalry, and Signal Service coats, of which there was a total in all categories and sizes of approximately 700. These were all to be made over into infantry overcoats.[193]

Likewise, a quantity of overcoats of the 1880-pattern on hand at St. Louis were to have the capes removed so that they could conform more closely to the newer style. Those that were not already lined with the dark blue for infantry were to have the facing cloth replaced with cavalry yellow. Furthermore, the 178 artillery great coats thus altered were to have their scarlet linings salvaged for reuse when overcoats of the darker shade were made for that branch. The concept seemed to be the restriction of old overcoats to infantry and cavalry, probably because these branches often served together in various garrisons, but to provide overcoats of the darker hue to other units.[194] Because the cost was minimal, this course of action was pursued. Many of these coats were to be sent to Columbus Barracks, Ohio, after they had been reworked.[195]

A first sergeant of cavalry in the dress uniform with the 1887 darker shade of yellow. Note the service in war stripes above the cuff flashes are backed in the darker yellow as well. Photograph by Glen Swanson. GS

Because of the fugitive nature of the dye used to obtain the shade of yellow for cavalry, in 1887 a darker hue was adopted for that branch., The plume on the left is of the type issued from 1872 through 1887, whereas the plume on the right is the color that was adopted in 1887 and remained regulation through 1903. KC

Not only were all helmet components to be made of the darker shade as of 1887, but also all trim on coats, blouses, and trousers were to conform to the new color as well. For example, on the left is the 1872-1887 yellow cuff trim for a cavalry dress uniform coat compared to the 1887-1903 darker shade. SI

Tail flashes of the design adopted in 1885 for mounted coats, and in this instance in the darker 1887 yellow. GL

In an effort to assure that the troops at Columbus Barracks would be furnished with some 428 reworked light shade overcoats, permission also was given for coats of larger sizes to be cut down to make up for any smaller coats that were needed, but which were not on hand. Some 525 pairs of foot trousers in the light shade were to be sent to fill the order for this Ohio post, as well.[196]

As part of the process, the quartermaster general wanted it made clear that lighter shades of coats were not to be returned from the field as excess so that darker ones would be supplied as replacements. The only men allowed to have the darker overcoats for the time being were non-commissioned officers, who could request garments made of finer quality dark kersey, both for great coats and trousers.

As an additional caveat, Brigadier General Holabird later directed that when overcoats were produced in the sky-blue using kersey from different contracts, shipments to the field should not mix one supplier's cloth with another's. The reason for this was that dissimilarity in shades was evident and could cause complaint for both overcoats and trousers of the varying hues of material. Although he recognized that "an exact shade" could rarely be matched "under two different contracts," he nevertheless urged how important it was to have the wool dyed "as nearly as possible to the standard."[197]

Although efforts to issue the inventory of obsolete blouses, shirts, trousers, and overcoats were undertaken, some items simply could not be utilized. This was the case for cloth service chevrons. Although these insignia were no longer regulation, on occasion some orders mistakenly called for them.[198] Eventually, this prompted a directive for all outdated chevrons at posts in the West to be sent to the San Francisco Depot.[199]

In a related area, the quartermaster general was resolved to make certain that gold lace chevrons, which had replaced the cloth service,

(right)A Fifth U.S. Cavalry officer's 1881-1887-pattern helmet with the light yellow buffalo plume compared to the 1887-1903-pattern cavalry officer's helmet (left) with the darker yellow plume, in this case for a member of the First U.S. Cavalry. Photograph by Glen Swanson. GS

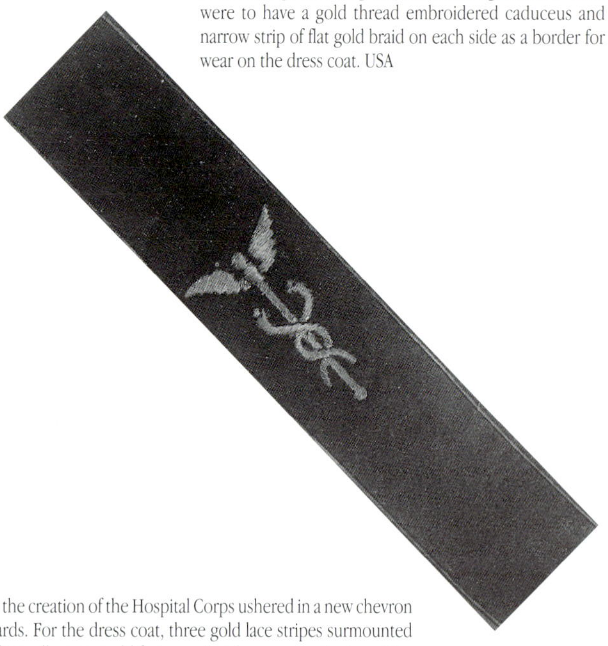

Right: Hospital steward's chevrons continued to be made of emerald green facing cloth as a backing, but as of 1885 were to have a gold thread embroidered caduceus and narrow strip of flat gold braid on each side as a border for wear on the dress coat. USA

Far Right: In 1887 the creation of the Hospital Corps ushered in a new chevron for hospital stewards. For the dress coat, three gold lace stripes surmounted by an arc of gold lace, all on emerald facing material, was prescribed, and the device was a Geneva cross of scarlet facing material. USA

service in war, and campaign chevrons were not provided recklessly. Since their adoption in 1884, 27,275 pairs of service in peace and 12,823 pairs of service in war chevrons had been provided by his department. He was concerned that these numbers far exceeded actual use. Perhaps the excessive requirements stemmed from the mistaken belief that the use of these chevrons was not restricted to the dress coat. As such, a circular was released to ensure that care was taken in future requisitions of these costly insignia.[200] Circular No. 12, Headquarters of the Army, December 31, 1886, defined the number of pairs of peace and war chevrons that could be allotted to the men without charge. After the number had been reached, the soldier would have to pay for any additional ones.[201]

Another detail that caught Holabird's attention was connected to the addition of a burning torch to the enlisted Signal Corps cap and helmet device. The quartermaster general wondered whether the same design should be incorporated into the insignia worn on the sleeves by privates and non-commissioned officers.[202] In this situation, the chief signal officer wanted to retain the crossed flags without torch. Thus, the device remained unchanged until after all existing supplies were gone,

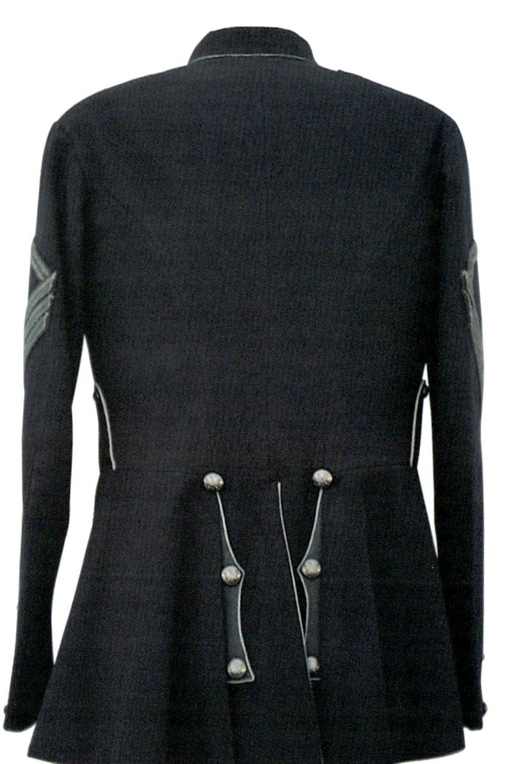

Front and back of an 1872-pattern hospital steward's coat that has had the new 1887-pattern first class hospital steward's chevrons added. FLNHS

by which point the color of the corps had been changed to black trimmed with white.[203]

In one more minor matter, band shoulder knots, the quartermaster general once again responded with his characteristic penchant for detail. When it was found that the pasteboard backings of these accessories were unsatisfactory, a tin frame was substituted in the interest of providing a more substantial foundation.[204]

A remaining element regarding the outfit of musicians was the trumpet cord and tassels for infantry buglers. As with all the facings for the branch, these had been previously made in blue. Now the quartermaster general required a white worsted version to be produced in keeping with the color change of 1884. He called for an estimate of cost for making these, followed by the adoption of a white version as the official color for trumpet cords for infantry and proposals for making 500 of them based upon a new specification and sealed sample set.[205]

Another initiative from the quartermaster general's office began with an inquiry expressing an interest in the possibility of obtaining large numbers of white neck bands made from linen or celluloid. The concept was to place these buffers inside the uniform dress coat collars of infantrymen, because the white facings soiled easily. Samples fastened to some dress coats were to be produced, and cost estimates were worked up to determine whether this was a realistic goal.[206]

Nearly eleven months later, during November, the concept was expanded to include all "the enlisted men of the Army at cost price of white linen collars or bands to be worn in connection with the Uniform Dress Coats." This was seen as a practical solution to the "frequent refacings of the collars of the coats," which became "necessary on account of the chin or neck of the men coming in contact with the facings, and as the collars will serve as a protection to the Coats, thereby making a savings to the enlisted men." The rationale was that they "should not form part of the annual money allowance." To this end, permission was sought to advertise for bids to produce an initial 5,000 collars. The expense was calculated at between $.84 to $.87 each when purchased in bulk.[207]

This increased proposal to provide removable collars to all enlisted personnel came from a joint discussion between the quartermaster general and the inspector general, Brigadier General Absalom Baird. These two men had conferred about the concept during the course of an exchange that took place after the secretary of war had tasked them to form a two man board to prepare a "new edition of the work entitled 'Uniform of the Army....'"[208] This appointment came about in recognition of the fact that "many changes and improvements had been made in the uniform of the enlisted men..." thereby rendering the previous publication illustrating army military attire "obsolete and misleading."[209]

As an interim measure a pamphlet had been printed with pertinent uniform regulations as they existed by 1886.[210] This undertaking bought time, as several factors were explored relative to publishing the uniform primer. Such factors as how much it would cost to print 1,000 copies; a

The collars of the first-class hospital steward's full dress coats were plain as another means of depicting the rank of the wearer. Furthermore, staff buttons were to be attached to the coat rather than the regular enlisted buttons adopted in the mid-1880s. FLNHS

In turn, the collars of the dress coats for acting hospital stewards were to bear a Geneva cross in scarlet facing material on each side, while the chevrons did not have an arc above them for this rank. SI

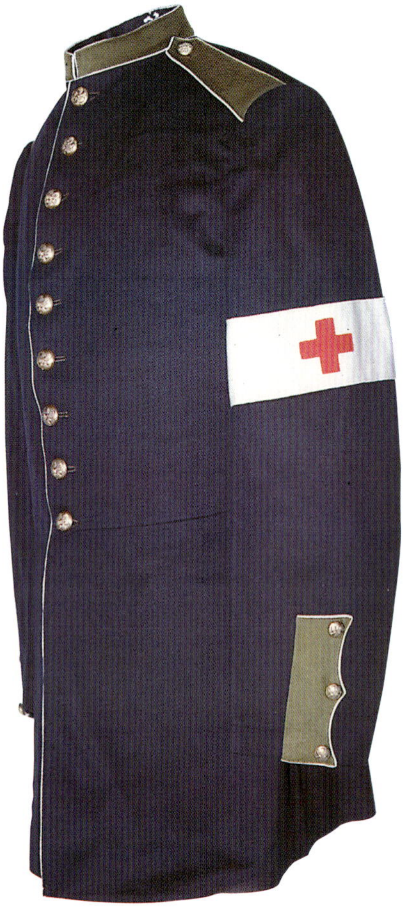

Privates of the Hospital Corps also had plain collars, but their coats bore the standard enlisted button and were made of a lesser quality cloth. Additionally, the white arm band with red Geneva cross was worn above the elbow on the left sleeve for these men. SI

projection of how long it would take to complete the assignment; and the feasibility of reusing some of the plates from the 1882 volume were all weighed. In every instance the mandate was "to have each article exact and correct, avoiding errors such as the omission of the herring-bones on the cadet coats and in the chapeau, and wreath for the Egnr. officers' forage cap." Conversely, no outdated items should be depicted, which meant an image of the general commanding the army with his twelve buttons in each row on the frock coat was to be eliminated, now that lieutenant general was the highest rank allowed. Plus, "all other articles no longer in force" were to be purged. Likewise, special attention was be given renderings of general officer attire.[211]

The original time-table was estimated at approximately six months, a schedule that proved unrealistic as the enterprise unfolded.[212] Perhaps some of the optimism was based on the belief that a number of the 1882 illustrations could be reused. This course of action, however, was not possible after it was learned that the masters of the old plates had been destroyed.[213]

At this point the secretary of war enabled the publication to be printed, once it was completed, by directing the expenditure of $2,600 for this purpose. This money, coupled with Holabird's vision of the product somewhat along the lines of the specification book already in progress, represented the next of many steps toward the completion of this volume.[214] As part of the procedure, once preliminary illustrations had been prepared, they were to be submitted to the inspector general for review, that officer having many suggestions to offer, which Holabird indicated he would "be glad to receive."[215]

Concurrently, the venture to turn out a specifications book accompanied by drawings of each article of clothing and equipage forged ahead.[216] This endeavor, like that for the uniform of the army guidebook, proved to take considerable time. Holabird ordered the original 130 drawings executed for the specification volume, which was seen as a handbook for quartermaster officers, and expressed mixed opinions about what he saw. Some of the mechanical drawings were suitable, but many of the images were stiff and looked unnatural, he said. Holabird wanted better shading and a more natural look to the renderings. He referred Ludington to the recently published regulations for the U.S. Navy for a model of what he sought.

The quartermaster general had consulted with B.I. Blauvelt, a proprietor of a New York electro engraving and printing company, and learned that negatives produced for photographs taken to scale could be used as the basis for etchings to be prepared. Some 500 copies of each then could be printed from the plates thus made, at about 1 1/4 cents per square inch. Armed with this information, Holabird informed Ludington that he wanted to experiment by having one garment "photographed in as many positions" as deemed necessary, and a sample etching produced. Further, lettering could be placed upon such printing plates, thereby overcoming Holabird's objection that the print on the copies he had reviewed was not up to par.[217]

Another similar undertaking entailed the assembling of a volume tracing designating flags from the Civil War.[218] As part of the research required to compile this study, several veterans and other knowledgeable individuals were contacted who had information of specific units.[219]

Quartermaster General Holabird was not one to dwell in the past, however. He was just as determined to look toward the future, as confirmed by his raising the ongoing question as to the merits of outfitting the men in "southern stations" with "cotton or linen clothing." The sur-

A private of the Hospital Corps wears the dress coat, but without the prescribed white arm band with red cross. His trousers, however, bear the correct 1/2 inch emerald green stripe piped on each side in white facing material as called for in 1887. Note that he wears the forage cap with correct Geneva cross device prescribed for privates and acting hospital stewards, however, the proper head dress called for by regulations for wear with this coat was the 1881-pattern spiked helmet. JG

geon general remained firm that light woolen garments "or an admixture of cotton and woolen" clothing was the most healthful.[220] Despite this contention from the army's most senior medical authority "that light woolen fabrics are more conducive to the preservation of sound health in warm climates than either linen or cotton," another military doctor, Captain W. Fitzhugh Carter, favorably commented upon white linen blouses and trousers for troops in Texas. Adding linen or cotton clothing to the supply list, however, would increase the budget, which already had been reduced $100,000 by Congress for fiscal year 1888.[221]

Dr. Carter was not the only one to champion a summer outfit. The *Army and Navy Journal* had periodically printed pro-summer uniform references, including one from a soldier who wondered "why the whole Army does not adopt a uniform of white during the summer months."[222] During May 1886, the Quartermaster Department took action toward answering this question by producing a limited number of white cotton duck sack coats to go along with trousers.[223] By early 1887, the response to this preliminary step had been positive, causing the department to seek the secretary of war's consent to distribute a warm climate outfit throughout Texas, especially after receiving correspondence in August 1887 from the Department of Texas' commanding officer, none other than Brigadier General David Stanley, who had brought up this topic earlier in the decade.

The forage cap badge prescribed in 1887 for first class hospital stewards was the traditional wreath surrounding the Geneva cross. EB

Taking Stanley's words to heart, and after receipt of an affirmative reply from the secretary of war, Holabird had several variants made up for review. These were expressed to Stanley's headquarters in San Antonio, where the general was to inspect nine pairs of trousers, four sack coats, and three pairs of overalls, and recommend the outfit that seemed most suited for summer wear in his command.[224] The packet contained a sack coat of 8 ounce cotton duck costing $.89; another sack coat of 6 1/2 to 7 ounce duck at $.98; still a third of cotton drilling as previously sent to the general, costing $.68; and a fourth version of 7 ounce bleached duck running $1.09 each, but with additional vest buttons on the sleeves the price would be $1.12, versus $1.00 if bone buttons were used. There was also a pair of bleached cotton duck trousers that had been purchased from the noted firm of John Wanamaker of Philadelphia for $1.25 per pair, and a 7 ounce bleached cotton duck pair of trousers made up by the Quartermaster Department at $.83 per pair, these being similar in construction to the Wanamaker trousers. Five other variations on the theme were inclosed, to wit: one of 8 ounce duck at $.81; 6 1/2 to 7 ounce duck at $.88; cotton drilling at $.65; a drilling model made after the pattern of the brown canvas fatigue trousers with pockets at $.55; and a similar pair without pockets at $.48. Finally, there were three pairs of overalls, one in cotton drilling at $.43 per pair, and two others of duck (a 6 1/2 to 7 ounce and an 8 ounce rendition), both costing $.59 per pair.

Starting in 1887 Hospital Corps enlisted personnel of all ranks were to have the dress helmet with large German silver Geneva cross overlay and the same device, but smaller, brazed to a stipple backed sheet brass side buttons. These were the only two-piece side buttons ever prescribed for enlisted men. WR

Holabird told Stanley that if the new summer issue was desired, the wool trousers and blouse allotment should be decreased accordingly. This would maintain the existing ceiling for the five-year enlisted clothing allotment as set by regulations, a foot solder being granted $19.15 for five years toward blouses and $37.32 for a five year period to provide for trousers.[225] After evaluation, two types were selected—bleached cotton blouses and trousers for non-commissioned officers, and unbleached cotton versions, these being slightly less costly, for privates.[226]

As early as April 1887 some 378 white canvas blouses were supplied to Ft. Brown, Texas. These were to be made of "the same material as used for stable frocks and invoiced as stable frocks." Further, the same order was to include 88 stable frocks for that post, as well as 55 for Ft. Davis and 26 for Ft. Hancock, also garrisons in the Lone Star State. In this instance, the stable frocks were to be "made to resemble canvas fatigue coats as nearly as possible." For one thing, this meant that they had rolling collars rather than standing collars.[227]

Another matter connected to hot weather also was raised in 1886. Colonel Jonathan Hamilton, commanding the Fifth U.S. Artillery at Ft. Hamilton, New York, maintained the chinstrap for the cork summer

A first class hospital steward (second from left) wears an M1840 NCO sword and the wreath around the Geneva cross on his cap, as well as the chevrons of his rank, three stripes points down with an arc above. The privates of his unit have no insignia on their blouses, and their caps bear only the German silver Geneva cross without wreath. These men served at Ft. Sill, Indian Territory. USAMHI

Overcoats for enlisted members of the Hospital Corps regularly were combined with the forage cap. Capes were lined in emerald green. JG

helmets were "abortions, and cannot be used." The colonel contended "the awkward men" of his command constantly knocked off this type of headgear or lost the item even in a light breeze. A better strap was required to correct this "evil."[228]

If this detail required consideration for improvement of the summer helmet, winter headgear likewise came under scrutiny. By this point the decision had been made for blanket lined caps to replace fur caps.[229] Some individuals expressed a reluctance to accept the hoods in that they were not deemed as effective in keeping out the cold as fur articles. One Captain Clarence E. Bennett of the Seventeenth U.S. Infantry at Ft. Totten, Dakota Territory, preferred fur caps. Captain Rodgers, however, furnished him some samples of the redesigned canvas caps in an effort to change the infantry officer's mind.[230]

The improved model that Captain Bennett received for examination may have been one that, rather than having the original jean interior, was lined with a scarlet wool to make it "still warmer."[231] Several versions of redesigned canvas hoods in fact had been prepared and one settled upon in late May as standard.[232]

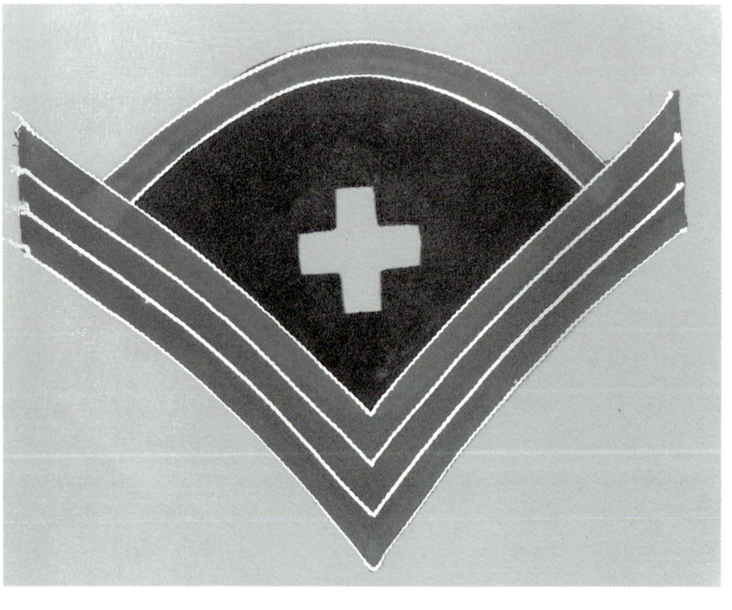

The 1887-pattern chevron of a first class hospital steward was to be worn on the blouse and overcoat. These were made of emerald green facing material with white silk thread chain stitching and a red cross on a dark blue background. The same device was prescribed for acting hospital stewards, except that the arc was omitted. AMWH

The cap, along with canvas mittens, were perceived to be a boon to the men.[233] This resulted in permission being given to expand distribution of the two items, free of charge, beyond the original Departments of Columbia, Dakota, and Platte to other locales.[234] With the approval of the secretary of war to allow David's Island, New York, and the garrison at West Point to obtain canvas caps or hoods, the quartermaster general asked for a revised general order to announce this decision. A draft of this directive was provided, amending the pertinent paragraphs of General Orders No. 32 of 1884 and General Orders No. 120 of 1885.[235] This then was the basis for General Orders No. 11, Headquarters of the Army, February 15, 1886, which increased the authorization for canvas suits to troops stationed in extremely cold climates, but not attached to any military department.

According to another general order released several months later, the plan was to provide these outfits "as a working dress...intended to save the regular uniform and to be worn on fatigue duty and at labor when these articles are more suitable than the woolen dress."[236] Further, company commanders had the authority to determine "whether the canvas fatigue clothing" was "actually required by the men or not," thereby enjoying great latitude at the local level to request such items.[237]

Nonetheless, while these tidings might have been welcomed by some, fur articles were not abandoned entirely. In fact, Captain Rodgers revealed that the Department of Dakota would be furnished "fur overcoats & fur caps" in lieu of the canvas blanket lined ones "as far as practicable" in an effort to "exhaust the former before sending out the latter." Consequently, fur caps continued to be dispensed, while buffalo overcoats were provided instead of the canvas versions until such a time as the selection of the latter fur items were depleted from stock.[238] In this light, the department even spent money to repair damaged articles, such

PLACE
STAMP
HERE

SCHIFFER PUBLISHING LTD
4880 LOWER VALLEY ROAD
ATGLEN, PA 19310-9717 USA

as buffalo overcoats at Ft. Brady, Michigan, and provided the petroleum paper used to store the items at the end of the cold season, as it had done in the past.[239]

Consequently, the inclination toward fur articles led the quartermaster general to bow to the wishes of the rank and file. This resulted in a policy to issue fur caps in lieu of the blanket lined canvas caps or hoods, "which are issued gratuitously to the enlisted men," after the quartermaster general recommended this action to the secretary of war on January 30, 1886. The secretary of war approved this recommendation, and "a paragraph was inserted in the annual price list just promulgated amending existing regulations by permitting the issue of fur caps in connection with fur gauntlets heretofore authorized."[240]

This did not mean that all canvas garments were rejected, however. Canvas blouses and trousers, for instance, were in ample supply, as the quartermaster general announced, when he wrote: "The manufacture of flannel shirts and canvas fatigue clothing in former years has been in excess of the requirements of the service. As a consequence less had to be made during this year to keep within the limits of appropriations."[241]

Under the circumstances there were sufficient canvas fatigue sets in the depots to respond to the French minister in Washington's request for a brown canvas coat and a pair of trousers to be shipped to his homeland for examination by the military there. France, once a major role model for martial fashion in the United States, reversed the role and now eyed the practical outfits developed for New World soldiers. The French minister was willing to reimburse the War Department for the garments, and Quartermaster General Holabird informed Secretary of War William C. Endicott of this factor, when asking whether or not his department should honor the request.[242]

Yet another instance of cost determining action came about from a suggestion to add a ribbed hem to undershirts. This proposed feature would result in an additional cost of five to six cents per garment, which when multiplied by the numbers of units required each year would increase the clothing budget as much as $4,500 per annum. The price was regarded as prohibitive; the idea rejected; and the knit undershirt adopted on February 10, 1881, continued to be made and issued.[243]

Nonetheless, specifications for many other items were updated or added during 1886. This included ones for the various buckles used on the rear straps of trousers; black japanned fly and suspender buttons for wool trousers; and white metal buttons for linen trousers, drawers, stable frocks, and overalls. There, likewise, were replacement standards for black silesia and black Italian cloth, which served to line dress coats; guidelines for dark blue cloth to fashion the non-commissioned dress coats; and new forage cap descriptions.[244] Additionally, trouser stripes for engineers, non-commissioned officers, and musicians were spelled out for the first time, rather than being left to the vague summary "according to the pattern in the office of the Quartermaster General" that had been the case in both the 1872 and 1881 regulations.[245] Similarly, the white linen webbing used to make infantry trouser stripes, once again for non-commissioned officers and musicians, were defined.[246] So, too, were post shoe models revamped.[247] Other footgear was further addressed, in that campaign shoes and sewn boots were once more the subject of adjusted patterns, as was cape lining flannel and sky blue kersey, both in heavy and fine quality versions.[248]

The last mentioned commodity induced Colonel Ludington to make a request of his superior in Washington. He asked permission to employ a dye from R. Mendell's firm to color 6,000 yards of the most recent

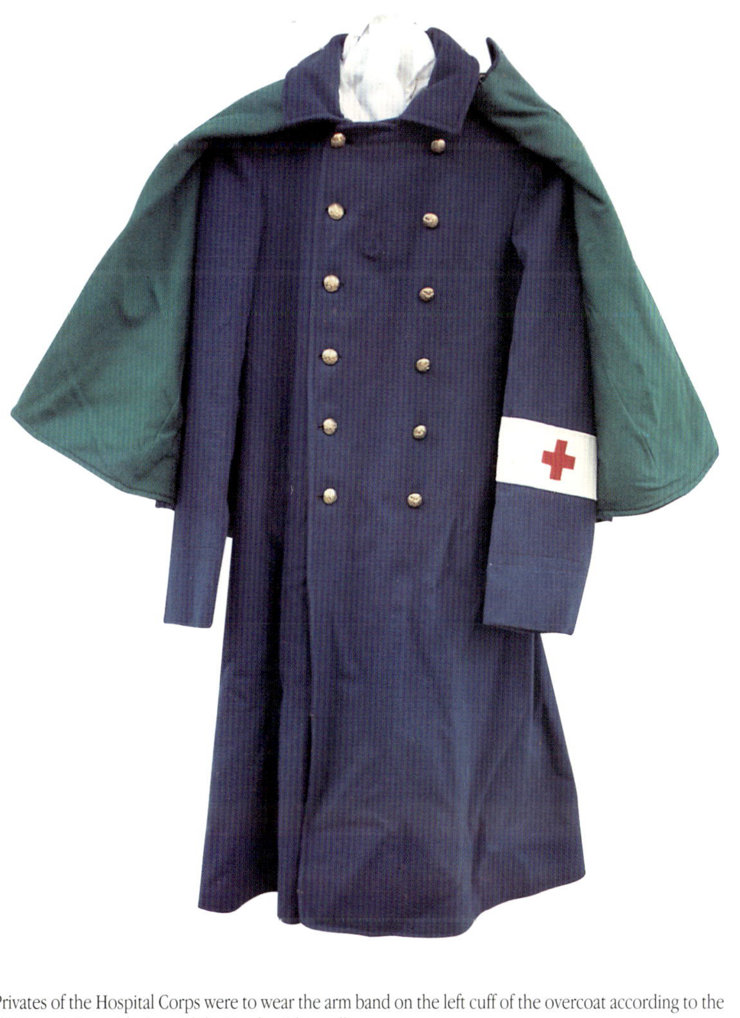

Privates of the Hospital Corps were to wear the arm band on the left cuff of the overcoat according to the 1887 regulations. Photograph by Gordon Chappell.

The new style of officers' aiguilettes that started to replace a slightly earlier type, beginning in 1887. This set is stored in a japanned tin case. JB

shade of dark blue for trousers and overcoats. The quartermaster general sanctioned the experiment in order "to determine the best dye to be used in Kerseys." Samples of cloth and trousers made from the test material resulted in the decision that the pure indigo dye material, such as the stock from Mendell's looms, offered the best course of action until a more satisfactory substitute could be discovered.[249]

Another problem that stemmed from imperfect dyes had to do with facing material. Holabird wrote that it was "a well known fact that the more brilliant the colors the more they" were subject to fading "upon exposure to the sun and air." He noted "yellow and sky blue were the most fugitive," but because the latter shade had been replaced by white for infantry, only the cavalry color required a solution as to how to produce a durable dye without sacrificing "the brilliancy desired."[250] The answer to that question remained elusive for the time being, but a related matter captured the quartermaster general's attention at nearly the same time his department considered the best course of action for the cavalry.

One more initiative connected to facings had to do with infantry officers. In order to bring their uniforms in line with those of their men, Holabird submitted a draft general order that would address this issue. A few days later General Orders No. 6, Headquarters of the Army, February 1, 1886, was circulated, and called for regimental officers to wear one and one-half inch cloth trouser stripes that were welted at the edges, and "in the color of the trimmings of their respective arms." There was little new here, except for the fact that infantry had abandoned blue for white, and the order thus underscored that officers were to follow suit. The telling portion of the document spelled out that the backings for

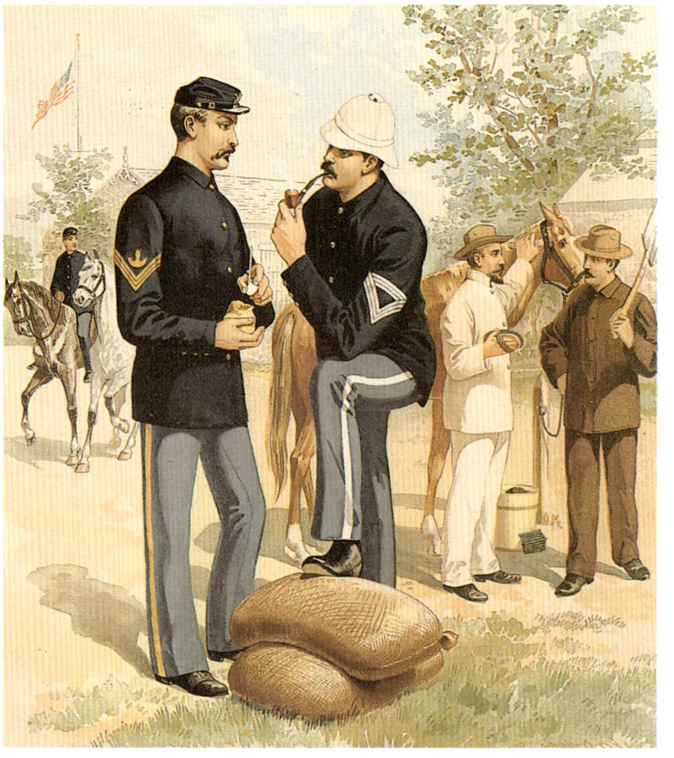

An infantry regimental quartermaster sergeant, so identified by the three tie bars above his chevrons, wears the 1880-pattern summer helmet with his five-button blouse. In this illustration painted by H.A. Ogden the other subjects include a cavalry saddler sergeant, a trooper in the stable frock and overalls, and another soldier in the 1884-pattern brown canvas fatigue uniform. GS

Second Lieutenant Kempke, the regimental adjutant of the Sixth U.S. Infantry, wears the newly adopted 1887-pattern officer's aiguilettes, which among other differences were made of cord of a larger diameter to the prior style. FAM

shoulder straps would be white, as would the linings of capes. By inference then, the background of shoulder knots and the silk grosgrain horizontal stripes for company grade officers' gold lace sword belts were to follow suit.[251]

This directive triggered several reactions. One was a concern that the sulphur that served as an agent to obtain a bright white woolen cloth would react detrimentally with the gold and silver bullion embroidery for shoulder straps and shoulder knots. Colonel George Andrews of the Twenty-fifth U.S. Infantry expressed this misgiving, and even sent a sample of white silk velvet as a proposed substitute to eliminate this perceived problem. The colonel was assured that there was "not sufficient sulphur in the white facing cloth used by first class manufacturers and dealers to have any marked or serious effect," therefore it was not necessary to be concerned about this issue. The quartermaster general further pointed out that the alternative of velvet was more problematical than good facing material, in that the silk-based cloth was nearly impossible to obtain in pure white; was subject to becoming dirty easily; caught and retained dust; and could be damaged by water, even a light rain being enough to leave water spots.[252]

Instead of velvet, Holabird proposed white flannel would be a more logical lining for officers' capes. He asked Lieutenant Colonel Ludington to procure samples and comparative costs. Likewise, he was to also buy a sufficient quantity to line one cape with white fabric for review.

After receipt of these items the quartermaster general selected the material that cost $1.90 a yard as the best suited for the purpose. Holabird further directed that no large quantities would be bought, given a limited budget. Additionally, all sales were "to be made only for cash," as was the practice for doeskin and fine cloth. He cautioned only one to two bolts were to be acquired at a time.[253]

In this Brigadier General Holabird looked to a middle ground that would allow "Officers of the Army every facility to purchase for their own personal use stock materials," but not to the detriment of his organization's budget. He therefore did not advocate even white facing cloth being provided, but once again because of a concern that this fabric would be subject to being soiled, thereby becoming "a total loss to the appropriations of the Quartermaster's Department," the amount on hand was to be limited.

Despite the possible pitfalls, as another courtesy, the quartermaster general informed the Philadelphia Depot's chief to maintain a store of stripes for officers' trousers, which could be purchased at $.30 per pair. Early in the year there was ample material on hand to make the stripes, as well as for other use relative to the ongoing conversion to white for infantry, especially because the quartermaster general had asked permission to accept seventy-one yards of white facing cloth that was available in excess of an order made with Horstmann & Bros.[254] Later, another twelve yards of white facing material were ordered. which officers could purchase, an option that by that point had been publicized in General Orders No. 46, Headquarters of the Army, July 7, 1886. Elsewhere it was reiterated that officers who required cloth trouser stripes could be supplied in the same manner as the requisition for cloth. But once again, the admonition remained in force against sending out "fine cloths in bulk to posts, especially white," because such a practice was viewed as a "waste of public property."[255]

This statement was not the last word emanating relative to officers' uniform items. Among other things, a new officers' aiguillette "in lieu of the pattern heretofore" prescribed was adopted, and therefore all future purchases would be of the most up to date style. The intention was "to introduce the new aiguilette gradually," however, so that no one would be compelled to "discard" the previous model immediately.[256]

While Sheridan had acquiesced on this matter, he spurned a proposition by First Lieutenant Charles F. Roe, the regimental adjutant of the Second Cavalry, to change the color of trousers of officers, especially after a darker blue had been settled upon at that stage.[257] The commanding general similarly refused an exhortation to replace the officers' forage cap.[258]

During 1886, although a new cap was not in the offing, there was a certain amount of activity related to another type of officers' head dress. In response to a question about "the *exact shape* of the chapeau for Officers of the Regular Army," Captain Rodgers dispatched a letter to the firm of Raymold & Whitlock asking: "Can you ascertain and inform this office from which source the late firm of Schuyler, Hartley & Graham obtained their model?" The captain went on to state: "The chapeau was adopted by the 'Marcy' Board in 1872 and it is desirable to ascertain whether the original chapeau (or model) was furnished to said Board by Messrs Schuyler, Hartley & Graham."[259]

Once he had received the required information, Rodgers requested a photographer from the Treasury Department to photograph an army officer's chapeau de bras to furnish the twelve prints made from each negative. The cost was to be borne by the Quartermaster Department.[260] Holabird then sent a photograph of the two versions of the chapeau, one that had a curved silhouette and one that was straight. Both had the same type of rosette fastened onto them. The former was "the standard chapeau," but Sheridan decided that officers could avail themselves of "the straight pattern" if they so desired. The same correspondence enclosed a photo of the Engineer Corps officer's badge that Sheridan also had approved.[261] Moreover, the quartermaster general sent the inspector general prints of the same "photographic illustrations of the officer's chapeaus and forage cap ornaments for officers of Engineers recently adopted by the Board on the publication of the book of uniforms of the U.S. Army."[262]

Ongoing efforts to settle upon the proper outfit for signal officers moved along, too. For instance, samples from a military outfitter for Signal Corps officers' buttons were examined and were decreed to be 7/8 inch in diameter for the coat size and 1/2 inch for the small cuff size, although the prototype for the smaller button was 7/16 of an inch. The company that made the model was to rectify this discrepancy, then make proper dies and furnish examples for final approval through the Quartermaster Department.[263] Some time passed, however, before a version of the button met with approval, when the chief signal officer submitted renditions worked up by Horstmann Bros. & Co. for the quartermaster general's opinion.[264]

Nor did the process of scrutinizing officers' garb halt in 1886. By the following year the quartermaster general took an active part in the design the officers' cape. A prototype that had been furnished for review featured a collar that Holabird felt did not "lie snug to the shoulders" and was "too round." He wanted to have it be more square and to lie close upon the shoulders, even if it meant sewing the collar down.[265]

On another topic, the fact that regulations "did not provide for the wearing of the helmet cords and tassels without the helmet" was a matter of interest, especially because "officers of the mounted service" were "in the habit of wearing the cords & tassels at receptions without the helmet, slung in the same manner, but fastened to the shoulder knots."[266] There was no objection to this custom, so long as the officer did not allow his breast cords to dangle once they had been detached from the helmet.

This particular applied only to mounted officers, but did not concern dismounted officers, who wore spiked helmets, or members of the various staff corps, who donned the chapeau. Most emphatically, it had no relation to chaplains, whose sole form of martial headgear was a plain black campaign hat. The somber outfit of these military clergymen was yet one more subject of discussion during 1887.

In point of fact, the ensemble resembled the regalia of many fraternal organizations of the period. Indeed, soon after Reverend Allen Allensworth accepted his appointment to the chaplaincy of the Twenty-fourth U.S. Infantry, he donned his new-bought martial attire and appeared in public. Upon seeing this man of the cloth in his new uniform,

A cavalry principal musician in the 1887 darker yellow chevrons and wearing the 1880-pattern enlisted summer helmet. JB

a local citizen was confused by Allensworth's garb. He asked to which fraternal society the chaplain belonged.[267]

Some chaplains took it upon themselves to add to their basic apparel. This gave rise to a prohibition contained in Circular No. 9, Headquarters of the Army, October 11, 1887, that existing regulations did "not permit the wearing of swords or regimental badges..." by these army churchmen.

In the meantime, the inspector general and the quartermaster general deliberated about the new uniform volume, they also seemed to think the chaplain's uniform was in need of some revamping. Their opinions, however, ran to less ornamentation, rather than more. The two suggested that the secretary of war allow existing regulations be changed so that a plain black frock coat would replace the previous form that had been ornamented on the chest with black herringbone trim. Additionally, the shepherd's crook shoulder straps could be worn with the coat, yet were not mandatory. Plain black trousers without welt or stripe continued to be worn, while a black and gold officers' hat cord was the only adornment for the black felt hat.[268]

But Chaplains were not the only ones to be singled out for black campaign hats. General Orders No. 72, Headquarters of the Army, December 3, 1887, announced one more amendment to regulations. Curiously, Paragraph 2634 provided for black felt campaign hats, "according to pattern, to be worn only on target practice, fatigue duty, and on marches and campaigns." Conversely, Paragraph 2776 stated that enlisted men could have either black or drab-colored felt hats, but the color was "to be uniform in each troop, battery, or company." Inexplicably, this general order represented a step backwards for those officers who preferred the drab headgear, plus set up a potential lack of uniformity when the enlisted men of a unit were issued the lighter head dress, while their officers appeared in the darker versions.[269] Photographs from the late Victorian era, however, tend to reveal a propensity for the drab hat among both men and their officers.

Other endeavors having to do with officers' regalia arose in 1887. There was, for instance, a new aiguillette that was to become the model for aides, adjutants, and the like in the future, but with "the proviso that Officers should not be required to make a corresponding change at once."[270]

Nor was it probable that an adjustment to Engineer Corps officers' shoulder knots was mandated immediately. In the 1881 regulations, the pattern was not illustrated, but at least described in paragraph 2651 as "a silver turreted castle of metal one and four-tenths inches in width by nine-tenths of an inch in height." A modified design for the castle was submitted and a representation furnished, along with a pad from the shoulder knot of the pattern that had been in use since General Orders No. 72 of 1872.[271] The castle device being proposed was slightly smaller than that spelled out in the regulations of 1881. The chief of engineers wanted this replacement to be ratified, an aim which both the adjutant general and quartermaster general embraced. This would entail striking out the verbiage about the size of the castle. If the secretary of war had no objections to this plan, a like adjustment to paragraph 2652 would be in order, in that the flaming bomb for officers of the Ordnance Department was to be of the same dimensions as those for engineers.[272] Several months passed before an affirmative answer was made to revoke these two paragraphs.

Additionally, an analogous revision of shoulder knots for members of the Adjutant General's Department was initiated. A small shield of the type worn on forage caps by officers of this organization was to be placed on the pad of the knots as of December 1887, although most probably a period of transition existed before the change over was completed.[273] This was an outgrowth of a slightly earlier effort to revise the forage cap badge for officers of the Adjutant General's Department. The shield was redesigned to add thirteen vertical stripes at the bottom surmounted by a horizontal line and a large central star with two rows of smaller stars.[274] Heretofore, the bottom of the shield had been plain.

One more initiative aimed at officers was the granting of permission to obtain between 150 and 200 yards of fine doeskin trouser material, which as had become the custom was obtained for sale to those who wished to avail themselves of this service. A circular letter was dispatched inviting bids that had to be submitted within thirty days.[275]

Not all additions to the existing scheme of things were aimed at the officer corps. For instance, on March 1, 1887, congress enacted legislation to create a U.S. Army Hospital Corps. This law expanded the enlisted strength of the Medical Department, added new duties and responsibilities, and created three classes of enlisted personnel—hospital stewards, acting hospital stewards, and privates.[276] This new structure triggered efforts by the Quartermaster Department to provide distinct uniform elements.

The first phase resulted in a forage cap, dress helmet, and campaign hat with cord and tassels being made up for hospital stewards, so that Lieutenant Colonel James R. Smith, the acting president of the board charged with drafting regulations for the new Hospital Corps, could review the items, presumably along with his fellow medical officers serving on this same body.[277] Following this preliminary step, some mock up chevrons were produced, but Holabird wanted another sample created, this time with the "greatest care and having a cross nicely cut out and the red material sewed underneath in the same manner as those for ordnance sergeants, saddler's sergeant, & c." Those for hospital stewards were to consist of "three bars and an arc of emerald green cloth piped with white enclosing a red Geneva Cross, all on a dark blue ground of [the] same shade as the dress coat."[278]

Trousers with green stripes edged in white were to be prepared, too, and an overcoat with staff buttons, rather than regular enlisted buttons, was called for, as well. Once again, these articles were for hospital stewards, as were gold lace chevron and cloth chevron prototypes. Furthermore, trouser stripes for acting hospital stewards and privates were to be turned out as samples. Additionally, coats for acting hospital stewards and privates were to be assembled, the former bearing red cloth Geneva crosses, one on each side of the collar, and further set off by chevrons similar to the hospital steward but omitting the arc. The coats were, in other regards, to be of the style of infantry enlisted men.

Infantrymen stand at parade rest in front of the band quarters at Ft. Sam Houston wearing the 1880-pattern white summer enlisted helmet, the dark blue wool five-button blouse, and white trousers, for which specification were first drawn up in 1885, but as early as the 1870s these items had been permitted for purchase by enlisted men, albeit with the approval of the department commander. FSHM

Blouses likewise were to be of the standard pattern, except that the ones for hospital stewards would have staff buttons. Stripes for blouses would be emerald green facing material with white silk chainstitching. Trousers were to be dark blue to match the shade of the coat, with green leg stripes piped in white for all ranks, starting with one and one quarter inch wide stripes for hospital stewards, one inch wide stripes for acting hospital stewards, and half inch wide stripes for privates.

The spiked helmet would be used, displaying a German silver Geneva cross overlay on a staff plate, with side buttons that had a smaller rendition of the cross affixed to a gilt button that has a stippled background. These details made the helmet side bottoms unique as compared to those for all other branches and corps. Forage caps would bear the same German silver cross as for the helmet plate. The device would be encircled by a white metal wreath for hospital stewards and worn without the wreath by the other men.[279] Overcoats had capes lined in emerald green, but the garments themselves would be "of Sky blue Kersey, Army standard, heavy quality," as they were for all enlisted men.[280]

The final form of most of these items was announced via General Orders No. 56, Headquarters of the Army, August 11, 1887.[281] Within a few days circulation of this order prompted another action, that of the preliminary efforts to incorporate these changes into existing uniform regulations; construct four sets of uniform dress coats and trousers, all from fine quality fabric, chevrons, leg stripes, helmet devices, and forage cap insignia; and provide costs of the items so they could be published in due course.[282] Soon thereafter, General Orders No. 68, Headquarters of the Army, October 24, 1887, spelled out the cash equivalents. (See Table 3)[283]

TABLE 3

Articles	Hospital Stewards	Acting Hospital Stewards	Privates
Uniform dress- each coats, made	$7.79	$7.81	$6.79
Uniform dress do coats, unmade	$5.29	$5.31	$5.04
Trousers, made do	$4.13	$4.13	$3.72
Trousers, unmade do	$3.13	$3.13	$2.97
Trousers stripes do	$.34	$.29	$.23
Geneva cross for do helmet eagle	$.03	$.03	$.03
Side buttons for helmet per pair	$.06	$.06	$.06
Geneva cross each for forage-cap	$03	$.03	$.03
Wreath for do forage-cap	$.04	————	
Chevrons, gold lace per pair	$3.56	$3.11	——
Chevrons, cloth do	$.70	$.70	
Facings for uniform dress-coats per set	$.68	$.68	$.68
Cloth crosses for uniform dress-coats per pair	——	$.02	——

A month after General Orders No. 68 was released, personnel of the Quartermaster Department proclaimed they were ready to issue clothing for the Hospital Corps. All that had to be done to initiate this action was for requisitions to be submitted.

Following the establishment of the Hospital Corps, recent changes for other non-commissioned staff officers also were taken in consideration. For instance, Captain Rodgers contacted Lieutenant Colonel Ludington conveying the quartermaster general's directive to have new standard sample dress coats for non-commissioned staff, "viz: Post Q.M. Sgts, Commissary Sgts, and Ordnance Sgts," manufactured of dark blue finer quality cloth rather than army standard coat wool, in order to bring the sealed samples in line with specifications.[284] The update likewise noted the replacement of standard enlisted buttons with staff buttons for the dress coats of these men, and for their blouses and overcoats, as well.[285]

Additionally, trouser stripes had to be realigned to address not only the Hospital Corps enlisted men, but also a decision to discontinue webbing for infantry. During the summer of 1887, officers of the Fifth U.S. Infantry successfully petitioned for a return to facing material leg stripes. They were informed that as soon as the linen webbing ran out, infantry non-commissioned officers and musicians would "be supplied with cloth stripes."[286] Within a matter of days, new specifications were drafted indicating the reversal of guidelines for webbing adopted on March 24 of the previous year, and the return to cloth, as well as underscoring the one-eighth inch white piping that was to outline each side of the trouser stripes for engineers and medical personnel. All copies of the previous specifications were to be mailed to the quartermaster general's office to avoid errors.[287] One more effort to set the record straight had to do with the linen collars, which had been adopted on March 24, 1887.[288] These were intended for issue "only in connection with the Uniform Dress Coats," although some requisitions had made it clear that in certain garrisons their use was interpreted more broadly.[289]

One other example of misconstruance of official intentions was evident in the case of enlisted blouses. When Specification No. 192, adopted on October 20, 1887, replaced the blouse specification of March 12, 1887, the supposition was that all details would fall into place. After all, the garment essentially was the same as in use for the past two years, with its three exterior pockets (two at the skirts and one on the left breast) and one inside pocket on the right breast. The addition of three small buttons on each cuff and the change to a blue rather than gray lining were the only particulars that required updating.[290]

Yet, somehow the system failed to work properly. After Holabird received what were to be the new sealed standards in mid-October, he found them at odds with the specifications. There were no buttons on the cuffs, and inexplicably there was a hook and eye applied to the collar to keep it closed. The former element was called for in specifications, yet omitted, while the latter addition was mentioned nowhere in regulations. The quartermaster general wanted the incorrect blouses modified to the extent that three buttons were to be sewn to each cuff. To avoid further bewilderment, the quartermaster general thought it prudent to make entirely "new standards of Blouses conforming to existing specifications," while the ones already sent to Jeffersonville and San Francisco would be put into stock and issued.[291] Early in December, the next iteration of samples arrived in Washington. These Holabird found to be satisfactory renditions, and gave his assent for them to become the sealed standard.[292]

Despite all these careful machinations, inexplicably photographs from the era seldom depict the blouse as defined by Specification No. 192. Rather, a version without exterior pockets predominated, as is the case with surviving specimens. To date, however, documents have not surfaced rescinding the October 20, 1887, pattern, nor explaining why the blouse did not seem to be issued as widely as official correspondence of the late Victorian period might lead one to believe!

While the matter of the proper blouse design was in a state of transition, footgear likewise persisted as a subject of ongoing deliberations. Warfare against the Apaches had demonstrated that machine sewn shoes did not stand up against the rigors of the Southwest environment. Consequently, boots and shoes on hand at Ft. Leavenworth were altered by adding brass screws. The concept was that this tap-soled footgear would be sufficiently fortified to withstand campaigning.[293]

In addition, a "thread known to the trade as 'metalin'" was acquired as a replacement for materials previously used for footgear production. This thread had a wire core that theoretically would provide a "stronger and more durable" product.[294]

One other step to address the challenge of rugged footgear was a comparative study to determine whether hand sewing versus machine sewing was best.[295] The secretary of war allowed funds to be expended for a contract to buy 2,500 pairs of boots and 5,000 pairs of shoes, which were hand sewn. Awards went to the lowest bidder for $3.94 and $2.45 per pair, respectively, the unit prices being somewhat higher because of the relatively limited quantities that were procured. The boots would be made on Waukenphast last, which were curved and which were in use at the military prison, but as an additional test the shoes would be fashioned on straight lasts, once again to ascertain what advantage one type might have over the other. This final experiment represented a reversal in the department's thinking, having observed that "field shoes and also posts shoes made upon the old straight lasts...never found favor with the enlisted men."[296] In fact, these shoes had been returned and were being reserved for prisoners only.[297] Furthermore, as of June 30, 1887, posts shoes had been discontinued altogether, despite their popularity, because the troops insisted on wearing them for all duties, including field service, for which they were not intended or substantial enough to survive.[298] Although the response was to halt production to avoid this situation, the department was in favor of the new barrack shoes introduced in 1886, and reacted by recommending 30,000 more be bought and offered to the soldiers at cost, which was $.95 per pair.[299]

As a further refinement, the form of mounted boots once again was revised, with new specifications being adopted on March 14, 1887, which brought the front height down to nineteen inches versus the back, which was to be fourteen inches high for a size 8. In order to accommodate trousers being tucked into them, the width of the leg at the top was to be fifteen inches. Two sealed samples of this pattern were sent via express for Ludington to make available to the quartermasters in New York and Boston.

Boots were championed by some, but others still promoted the idea of leggings, especially for foot troops. After considerable resistance at high levels within the army to permit leggings to be produced for field use, the Quartermaster Department at last gained a favorable decision from the secretary of war to add these accessories to the soldier's kit. A number of types available on the market were reviewed, and a preliminary purchase of 5,000 pairs was decided upon. Once obtained, the men would be able to buy them at cost, thereby not requiring an increase in the annual appropriations.[300]

An inexpensive suggestion from Colonel Ludington as an improvement for suspenders was entertained, as well. The idea was to lower "the strengthening straps" and narrow "the contab straps." Seven pairs of suspenders made in this manner were to be produced, with three being in the largest sizes. These would become the sealed standards, but no new specification would have to be written to accommodate this alteration.[301] With the stock of size 40 suspenders being nearly used up, and the substitution of other sizes in the offing, Ludington's improved model would be made available in due course.[302]

Holabird also was in accord with Captain Francis M. Gibson of the Seventh U.S. Cavalry regarding the cavalry branch color. This topic had come up on more than one occasion, but it was difficult to obtain a high color that would resist fading. Gibson had sent a dark shade as a sample. Soon thereafter department officials began steps to switch to a similar hue.[303]

At nearly the same time, the quartermaster general acknowledged receipt of a report prepared at Philadelphia relative to the "fugitive character of the yellow facings" for cavalry, and agreed that a darker yellow should be adopted. He went on to require four yards in the shade to be produced using the same basic specifications for the cloth. As a corollary, hair plumes, aiguillettes, bands and cords for helmets, and cords for trumpets would all have to be brought into line, so fours sets of these various items were to be made up to match so that Holabird could review them.[304] This directive was carried out by April 1887, and the quartermaster general found the results satisfactory.[305] With this, a new cavalry private's dress coat and one for a cavalry musician, both of which were the new sealed standards recently adopted to replace those adopted on March 5, 1885, were being sent out to San Francisco for future reference. Any cavalry coats in stock were to be made over with the darker shade of yellow. Less than three weeks later, however, the policy shifted to the extent that the change in cavalry facings was to take place on a gradual basis. Although estimations were to be made as to the quantity of darker yellow materials required for future use, all existing "cloth, braid and flannel, of the old shade" was to be utilized until the inventory ran out.[306]

In another instance, the quartermaster general again demonstrated his penchant for refinement when he learned that a Chicago manufacturer had furnished "a duck mitten with reversible thumb." He viewed these articles favorably enough to inform his operatives that when bids for such items were to be let, the contractor was to be invited to submit a proposal for them.[307] Later in the year, however, when these items actually were obtained under contract, they were rejected "as unserviceable or unfit for Army use."[308]

In an earlier exchange relative to hand wear, the quartermaster general pointed out the number of pairs of Berlin gloves had been reduced from the allowance tables for mounted men after the adoption of leather gauntlets. When a suggestion arose to increase the number of gloves provided, he countered that the allocation of gauntlets would have to be reduced accordingly to maintain budgetary levels.[309] Evidently that tradeoff did not seem appealing. For the moment, the idea went no further.

Neither did a movement toward improving the forage cap gain acceptance in 1887. After looking over representative samples from new contracts, Holabird remarked that the forage cap provided appeared "to be inferior as to quality of material, workmanship and general appearance...." He lamented that there had "been a falling off in the quality of the Caps," and in that light it seemed "wise to adopt new standards and perhaps new specifications, also." To further this project, he instructed that several samples be worked up in various qualities. Colonel Ludington was to forward these specially made items, along with his recommendations, to the quartermaster general's office for review.[310]

Independent of Brigadier General Holabird, First Lieutenant Stephen O'Connor of the Twenty-third U.S. Infantry recommended "improvements in the visors of the regulation Forage Caps." This advice was "duly noted," and "careful consideration" would be given to his suggestions.[311] The matter languished, however, until 1889, when new specifications were inaugurated, which among other things added a binding to strengthen the visor.[312]

Another discussion concerning headgear prompted Captain Rodgers to make a report in reply to comments from Ft. Wayne, Michigan, that dress helmets issued there were of inferior quality. After obtaining a sample helmet from that post, representatives from P. Herst, John B. Stetson, Raymold and Whitlock, and Allien and Co. all were consulted "with a view to correct any faults and to improve the present standard and specifications." The conclusion was that the helmet provided general satisfaction. Relatively few complaints had been made. The item was cheap, and usually wore well. It "unquestionably gave the enlisted men...the full value of the money paid for them." If circumstances were otherwise, Holabird indicated "it might be important to procure a costly article." This did not seem the case, however, and the sample sent to demonstrate faults was, in the opinion of the contractors who saw it, faulty because it had "been submitted to excessive rubbing or brushing to such a degree as to have removed all the nap and thus having brought to the surface the shellac stiffening."[313] For the moment, then, no other directives related to the helmet body were forthcoming.[314]

On the other hand, Holabird wished to ascertain that when making future purchases of enlisted helmets, was it advisable to "dispense with the round top piece covered with black cloth." The reason for this interrogative was that it seemed the top piece was "rarely if ever made use of by the enlisted men," and if eliminated would result in a savings to the clothing appropriations. The response was that the "black shell ventilator, or top piece" was superfluous, and in future specifications, as well as in the drawing for the handbook, it would be abolished. With this change it seemed an appropriate time to revise the specifications for metallic ornaments and helmet trimmings.[315]

The minor savings gained by eliminating the top piece offered some aid in the ongoing struggle to stretch the department's budget, but would in no way offset a new expenditure, that of furnishing items to various state governments. In a move toward attaining more professional standards that ultimately led to the creation of the national guard, Congress allowed clothing and materials procured by the U.S. Army's Quartermaster Department to be made available in the interest of "uniformity between the equipment of the militia of the several states and the troops of the United States."[316] To this end, requests were honored from several governors who wanted their citizen soldiers to be clothed as regulars.[317] Evidently, the volume was such as to draw down stocks faster than the Quartermaster Department was accustomed to, resulting in shortages. Once this hurdle was encountered, plans were made to plus up holdings to preclude the same situation from recurring in the future.[318] In the long run, this would provide an important means to keep inventories from stagnating, with the customary result of old pattern items blocking rapid availability of newer articles.

Another partial acceleration of moving existing stocks from storage came about when military prisoners at Ft. Leavenworth and Alcatraz were doled out surplus overcoats from quartermaster depots.[319] Similarly, the prisoners of war incarcerated at Forts Marion and Barrancas, Florida, and Mount Vernon Barracks, Alabama, would absorb another quantity of outmoded clothing articles. This requirement meant that the department decest itself of unwanted material, but it was not to be repaid for this service.

The quartermaster general made his case known in this matter when responding to his civilian superior's mandate. Despite the fact that no earmarked funds had been appropriated by congress, the responsibility to clothe the Apaches remained with the Quartermaster Department.[320] As such, in 1887 an order for canvas fatigue clothing for the adult males in the group was one of the first requirements that had to be honored.[321]

These fatigue sets were part of the secretary of war's requirement to furnish summer outfits that also included calico, stockings, and hats for the men. At first, the secretary requested that light canvas clothing fabricated not of the heavy duck that was salvaged from shelter tents and bedsacks, but rather "of light material found in all Southern towns, and which can be bought in New Orleans for $1.50 per suit" were to be furnished. Holabird pointed out that this was contrary to the articles issued to the enlisted men of the army, which in fact were manufactured from surplus shelter half material dyed brown. The quartermaster general stated "as no complaints" had been received by his "office that the garments are uncomfortable in southern stations," it did not make sense to provide the Indians with distinct apparel. Further, because Congress had mandated the distribution of clothing for the prisoners, but provided no special funds to do so, it behooved the Quartermaster Department to use obsolete articles to fill the orders so that no adverse impact would result on the restricted budget allotted to the military for issue to its forces. Major General John M. Schofield, who commanded the Division of the Atlantic, previously approved distribution of wool blouses and trousers of old patterns and sizes, and continuation of this practice was advocated. There was one problem in this instance; Colonel Loomis L. Langdon, the commanding officer of the Second Artillery remarked that he "considered it degrading to the enlisted men of the army to have their uniform worn by captives and therefor asked for the canvas suits, which if uniform, are not worn on parade or drill."[322]

Despite such objections, fiscal constraints drove the response.[323] Under the circumstances, the Apaches, for the most part, would have to be given material from existing stocks, regardless of whether the items were canvas fatigue clothing or old style wool uniforms.

It was this same need to conserve resources that prompted the quartermaster general to repeat that Circular No. 2 of 1886 was still in force in so far as the issuance of lighter shade overcoats and trousers were concerned.[324] As previously was the policy, the lighter shade of overcoats continued to be reworked into infantry models, so that there would be uniformity among the rank and file of what was the largest branch of the service until all the old coats had been furnished to the field.[325] So, too, were actions taken to determine the quantity of light shade kersey trousers at the posts around the country so that they could be recalled and gathered at the St. Louis Depot, where steps could "be taken to dispose of them...."[326] This idea seemed sound, but when lighter hues of the trousers were sent to some garrison, the local commander grumbled about the inferior quality of the cloth and the impact the varying shades had on destroying the uniformity of appearance when troops turned out in several colors of blue.[327]

That was the finding of Lieutenant Colonel Robert F. Hughes of the Inspector General's Department, who reported faulty kersey clothing articles being issued to the troops at Ft. Gaston, California. He provided samples of the cloth and was told "the sample of the light shade" seemed to have "been taken from a garment that was made during the last war, or more than twenty years ago." This surprised the quartermaster general, who "was not aware that any such Kersey was still in existence in the Army." Furthermore, it should never "have been issued at this late day," because "all garments of this material" were pronounced as "unfit for enlisted men." The items ought to be turned in at once for sale or to be issued as clothing for military convicts on Alacatraz. Conversely, while this fabric ought to have been condemned and reported as unserviceable years before, garments made from the up-to-date light shade of sky blue kersey. Holabird repeated they were to be given to the enlisted men, instead of the new darker color, under the requirements of Circular No. 2 of 1886.[328]

Light blue shade trousers received at the San Francisco Depot likewise came under scrutiny. If they were "damaged, stained, or otherwise unserviceable" they were to be reported as such, otherwise, they would be placed in stock for issue as directed.[329]

This practice extended to the bolts of kersey and blouse flannel stored in San Francisco.[330] The yardage was such that no new materials would be purchased during fiscal year 1887 for that depot. Holabird, however, provided for a contingency that if "a sudden demand for overcoats, trousers, or blouses" arose and a delay was foreseen in making such articles due to a lack of materials, the quartermaster general's office was to be sent a telegram immediately with notification of this situation. Under those circumstances, the additional costs of shipping material from the East Coast would be permitted, but otherwise the yard goods on hand in California would be used to fulfill all regular orders from western garrisons.[331]

Circular No. 2, Headquarters of the Army, March 12, 1887, also was indicative of efforts to depend on existing stocks, and in some instances to eliminate surplus, in this case by providing for the gratuitous issue of Civil War era hat cords and tassels with "each campaign hat drawn by men...until the stock of those" scattered at posts and depots were exhausted. Given that there were nearly 33,000 of these items in the inventory, and less than ten percent of the figure had been distributed during the prior fiscal year (July 1, 1885, to June 30, 1886), this plan seemed the only way to be rid the cords. Even then, there was "scarcely any demand for them."

The same March 1887 circular also addressed another component of the issue outfit—music pouches. These were only to be given out at the rate of one per each five year enlistment, and upon discharge the item was to be considered the personal property of the men to whom it was issued. As a corollary, helmet lyres, cords, bands, shoulder knots, music pouches, and other accessories adopted for regimental bandsmen required specifications and standards to be prepared. These were written, as were specifications for several other items during the year.[332]

All these permutations would be incorporated into the specification book that still was being prepared under the quartermaster general's watchful eye. Progress was slow, because he was not pleased with the "pepper and salt" appearance of the cloth in the illustrations rendered for the specifications handbook, and called attention to the quality of a similar article produced by the Navy Department, printed by Brett Lithographing Company of New York. He asked for detailed costs to be studied and reported to him, and underscored that he wanted "to make the publication a creditable one."[333]

Work toward the "Uniform of the United States Army" tome likewise was ongoing. Several details had to be attended to, however, before the release of this handsome volume of color plates and accompanying regulations was released, a goal that was not attained until 1888.[334] This important volume soon would be followed by a larger work with additional illustrations provided by artist Henry A. Ogden, depicting the army's ever changing outfit from the American Revolution to the late 1880s.[335]

And, as in the past, the department either made or contracted for all the clothing articles and several types of equipage required to outfit the army.[336] This required considerable time and attention to detail to ensure that the meager resources of the department were used to best purpose.[337]

All these endeavors had, in Holabird's estimation, been well received. And so he announced this in his report at the end of fiscal year 1887, when he wrote with pride:

Scarcely any, and certainly no general complaints upon the quality of the clothing and equipage furnished to the enlisted men of the Army has reached this office, and with the exception of the boots and shoes, the improvement of which still forms the subject of study, the clothing and equipage supplies are about as perfect as human thought and foresight can make them. Whenever an advantageous change is suggested, the Quartermaster General endeavors to comply with any judicious demands that may be made upon the Department.[338]

So it was that by the end of 1887, as the campaigns against the American Indian drew near to a close, the uniform of Uncle Sam's regulars had reached a milestone. The drab campaign hat, plain streamlined blouse, dark-blue shirt, springbottom trousers of a medium blue, and the branch colors for all save the Signal Corps were in place. A distinctly American look had been created. These articles, along with the adoption of suspenders, gauntlets, new footgear, sturdy brown canvas fatigue clothing, the basis for a summer uniform, and leggings had gone far in producing an outfit that kept "pace with national requirements"—one of Brigadier General Samuel Holabird's ambitious goals from the days just prior to his assumption of the leadership of the Quartermaster Department.

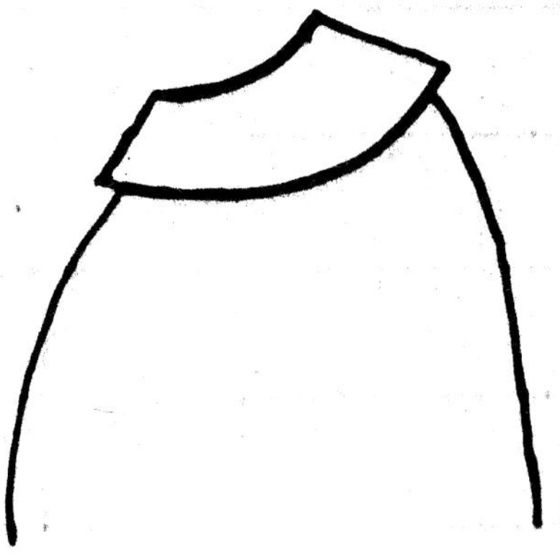

In 1887 the Quartermaster general turned his attention to the cut of the velvet collar for officers' capes, as indicated in this sketch from a letter on the subject written that year. NA

He had achieved this aim to a great extent because, after a decade and a half of agitation set into motion with the adoption of the 1872-pattern uniform, a state of equilibrium finally had been attained. Most changes over the next ten years would be gradual and comparably minor, at least until the United States Army was shaken from its peacetime stability in 1898, when war against Spain propelled it into a new arena as the military force behind a fledgling international power. That story, however, must be left to another telling.[339]

NOTES

1 Fifteen printed copies of the specifications for gold lace chevrons were sent to the Inspector General's Department and fifty copies each were distributed to the depots at Jeffersonville and San Francisco, along with another one hundred for Philadelphia. S.B. Holabird to Inspector General USA; S.B. Holabird to M.I. Ludington; S.B. Holabird to Depot Quartermaster San Francisco; and S.B. Holabird to Depot Quartermaster Jeffersonville, September 28, 1885, LS, Clothing Br., Vol. 4, 1885, OQMG, RG92, NA. Even before this, gold lace chevrons were being called for and supplied, such as for Ft. Winfield Scott, California at the southern side of the Golden Gate where eighteen pairs of chevrons (three pairs for first sergeants, six pairs for sergeants, and six pairs for corporals) along with two dozen service in peace and eighteen service in war (evenly divided among cavalry, artillery, and infantry) pairs. J.F. Rodgers to M.I. Ludington; and J.F. Rodgers to Chief Quartermaster Department of California, July 24, 1885, ibid.

2 J.F. Rodgers to M.I. Ludington, January 16, 1885, Vol. 1, 1885; and S.B. Holabird to M.I. Ludington, June 25, 1885, Vol. 2, 1885, ibid. Only hospital stewards were not provided gold lace, According to J.F. Rodgers to M.I. Ludington, January 3, 1886, Vol. 1, 1886, ibid., however, they did receive a new style of insignia made on the traditional green facing cloth material with gold embroidered caduceus and a thin gold cord border on each side. The chevrons for overcoats remained the green facing background with yellow silk chain stitching as the borders and the caduceus in yellow silk. It should be noted that previous dress coat chevrons for hospital stew-

ards were identical to the pattern retained for blouses and overcoats, but extent specimens have white silk rather than yellow silk embroidery.

3 S.B. Holabird to AGUSA, February 13, 1885, Vol. 2, 1885; and July 24, 1885, Vol. 4, 1885, ibid. Also see CCF, Box 209, OQMG, RG92, NA, for a March 25, 1885, discussion of the engineer service in peace chevron.

4 S.B. Holabird to AGUSA, January 21, 1885, LS, Clothing Br., Vol. 2, 1885, OQMG, RG92, NA.

5 As to campaign chevrons, from 1879 through 1884, these marks of distinction had been approved for wear on coats, blouses, and overcoats, their design being the same as those for service-in-war, except that they were narrower (one-half inch rather than three-quarter inch). The soldier would wear these until the end of an enlistment. At that time, if the man reenlisted, and the campaign had been decreed to have the magnitude of war service, the narrower stripe was to be replaced by the 3/4 inch version. In 1883, however, this became a moot point in that campaign chevrons, and a special "war stripe" authorized for Civil War duty, both were discontinued. Even after that, for a short period general orders continued to mention campaign stripes, which were to be placed at the top of all of these "hash marks." In addition, with the introduction of gold lace in 1884, service chevrons were to be worn only on the dress coat thereafter. Emerson, *Chevrons*, 75-6.

6 GO No. 49, HQA, April 18, 1885, slightly amended GO No. 107, HQA, September 12, 1884. The main difference was that the earlier order read in part: "The 'service in war' chevron will be worn next to the cuff; above this will be worn the 'service' chevron, and if more than one ascending in the order of time in which they were earned." The later version was clearer in the sequence of precedents stating: "The chevrons to indicate service and service in war, if more than one, will be worn one above the other in the order in which they were earned, one-fourth of an inch distance between." Additionally, GO No. 49 further articulated: "But one chevron will be worn for each enlistment, the 'service in war' chevron being worn in place of the 'service' chevron for each enlistment in which the right to wear it was earned." Circular No. 7, HQA, August 12, 1885, went on to explain that the service chevrons were not to be charged against the enlisted man's allowance. The only reason their costs were provided in the price list of clothing and equipment was for those cases when it became "necessary to charge them on account of loss or damage."

7 Quartermaster Military Division of the Missouri, July 2, 1885, Vol.1 , 1885; and J.F. Rodgers to M.I. Ludington, December 26, 1885, Vol. 4, 1885, LS, Clothing Br., OQMG, RG92, NA, both indicated that old dark blue infantry non-commissioned trousers stripes should be employed where possible to make chevrons.

8 J.F. Rodgers to Commanding Officer Ft. Leavenworth School of Application; and J.F. Rodgers to Chief of the Recruiting Service, January 27, 1885, Vol. 2, 1885, ibid., requested estimates for infantry gold lace chevrons required by these two organizations. On that same day Captain Rodgers sent similar letters to all posts, depots, and other facilities where Ordnance Department enlisted personnel or post ordnance sergeants were stationed, asking for the numbers of gold lace chevrons these men would require.

9 The chief quartermaster for the Division of the Atlantic was one of those who learned that infantry chevrons were not ready as yet. J.F. Rodgers to Chief Quartermaster Military Division of the Atlantic, January 15, 1885, Vol. 2, 1885, ibid. In a similar instance, a request for infantry gold lace chevrons and facings was denied to Ft. Bridger, Wyoming Territory, because none were in stock at the point. Conversely, blouses in the new six sizes were. These would be shipped to the post along with gold lace service chevrons and gold lace chevrons for the post commissary sergeant and hospital steward. Moreover, the order was to include buffalo overcoats in lieu of canvas ones. J.F. Rodgers to Chief Quartermaster Military Division of the Missouri, January 12, 1885, Vol. 1, 1885, ibid. Many months later, the Ninth U.S. Infantry enlisted men at that post would be sent eight unmade dress coats for privates, twenty-three sets of white facings to convert existing coats, twelve pairs of service in peace chevrons, versus eighty pairs of gold lace service in war chevrons for the sizable number of veterans in the unit including sixty for infantry, ten for cavalry, ten for artillery, and one for a former engineer. There were to be two pairs of infantry first sergeant chevrons, five pairs for sergeants, nine pairs for corporals, and 124 pairs of trouser stripes (54 for sergeants, 44 for corporals, and 26 for musicians). J.F. Rodgers to M.I. Ludington, July 6, 1885, Vol. 2, 1885, ibid. Sewn boots for Company C, Ninth U.S. Infantry were also turned down for Ft. Bridger because the new style with higher tops were to be provided exclusively to mounted troops, although a small quantity was furnished for purchase by officers and for certain contingencies. J.F. Rodgers to Chief Quartermaster Military Division of the Missouri, July 6, 1885, Vol. 1, 1885, ibid.

10 J.F. Rodgers to M.I. Ludington, February 10, 1885; and February 24, 1885, ibid. Two letters from Rodgers to Ludington on March 6, 1885, noted delivery of gold lace chevrons, white facings, and trousers stripes were being sent to two posts in Wyoming Territory, Ft. D.A. Russell and Ft. Washakie, respectively. During March and April numerous other pieces of correspondence repeated these directives for many posts around the country, thereby reflecting the relatively quick pace these materials were reaching the field. By August it is probable many other orders had been handled, such as for the Twenty-second U.S. Infantry at Ft. Lewis, Colorado, where thirty-seven pairs of non-commissioned infantry chevrons gold lace had been requested including for all the regimental non-commissioned staff, plus there were requirements for thirty pairs of service in war and fifty service in peace chevrons, along with the linen trouser stripes (fifty pairs for sergeants, forty pairs for corporals, and ten pairs for musicians). Other related items included ten sets of facings for infantry musicians' dress coats and fifty sets of facings for regular enlisted dress coats. J.G. Chandler to M.I. Ludington, August 18, 1885, Vol. 4, 1885, ibid. Through out the process, free issue of the chevrons for infantrymen remained until the preliminary supply reached the troops. Endorsement J.G. Chandler to AGUSA, August 10, 1885, ibid.

11 J.F. Rodgers to C. Hay, June 4, 1885, Vol. 1, 1885, ibid. Lieutenant Charles was a commissary officer, who was disgruntled when he did not receive his clothing and equipment allotment in a fashion that he considered timely, but Captain Rodgers explained the inability the Quartermaster Department to fill the orders "as fast as needed." Some of the holdup was connected to the white webbing, which was considered "more suitable and serviceable than facing cloth", but nonetheless suffered from the drawback of not being available domestically. Importing quantities of the material therefore caused considerable delay "in filling requisitions for the Army." To further complicate matters, the "webbing was liable to shrink;" hence it became necessary to cause all of it to be pre-shrunk before using it. *ARSW, 1885*, Vol. I, 602. This last factor probably explains why the white leg stripes sent for sergeants of the Eighth U.S. Infantry at Angel Island, California were found to be seven-eights of an inch wide rather than the one inch called for in the regulations. J.F. Rodgers to M.I. Ludington, October 24, 1885, LS, Clothing Br., Vol. 4, 1885, OQMG, RG92, NA. A 132 yard overrun from a later contract with Henry V. Allien for white webbing used for infantry sergeant's trouser stripes was accepted and issued according to S.B. Holabird to M.I. Ludington, January 8, 1886, Vol. 2, 1886, ibid. Later, when 132 yards of white webbing that over the original quantity contracted for from Allien was reported, a request was made to buy the additional material from the firm. S.B. Holabird to Secretary of War, January 4, 1886, ibid. It should be noted that the webbing purchased early in the year was obtained even before the specification was adopted, an action that did not take place until March 24, 1886, and was listed as Specification No. 169. S.B. Holabird to M.I. Ludington; and S.B. Holabird to R. Saxton, March 24, 1886, ibid.

12 S.B. Holabird to AGUSA, January 20, 1885, Vol. 1, 1885, ibid. Later in the year it again was necessary to point out another instance where gold lace chevrons would not be provided. This was in the case of farriers, who would have cloth brassards only, these specialists not being considered non-commissioned officers under regulations. J.F. Rodgers to Chief Quartermaster Military Division of the Missouri, September 28, 1885, Vol. 4, 1885, ibid.

13 S.B. Holabird to M.I. Ludington, January 28, 1885, Vol. 1, 1885, ibid.

14 S.B. Holabird to M.I. Ludington, February 13, 1885, Vol. 2, 1885, ibid.

15 J.F. Rodgers to M.I. Ludington, February 25, 1885, ibid., was among the earliest mentions of white cloth chevrons being shipped to garrisons, in this case for troops at Madison Barracks, New York. These were to be provided free of charge for the first issue to replace the blue chevrons for blouses. J.G. Chandler to AGUSA, August 10, 1885, Vol 4, 1885, ibid. For a later example of issuing white cloth infantry chevrons also see, J.F. Rodgers to M.I. Ludington, December 12, 1885, ibid, for Ft. Robinson, Nebraska. There were also thirty-two pairs of gold lace chevrons called for in the same order, but these were for troopers of the Tenth U.S. Cavalry.

16 Infanry Dress Coats with blue facings on hand at the General Depots are also altered by changing the facings of Coats from blue to white." S.B. Holabird to Secretary of War, February 19, 1885, Vol. 2, 1885, ibid. Also review, J.F. Rodgers to G.H. Weeks, February 18, 1885, Vol 1; S.B. Holabird to Chief Quartermaster Military Division of the Missouri, July 16, 1885, Vol 4, 1885; S.B. Holabird to AGUSA, July 30, 1885, Vol. 4, 1885; and S.B. Holabird to AGUSA, August 4, 1885, Vol. 4, 1885, ibid.

17 S.B. Holabird to AGUSA, May 4, 1885, Vol. 1, 1885, ibid. Over the ensuing months orders for coats were filled on an individual basis such as in the case of a requisition for two musicians' dress coats and twenty-seven coats for privates were being sent to the Twenty-fourth U.S. Infantry per B.C. Card to Chief Quartermaster Military Division of the Missouri; and B.C. Card to M.I. Ludington, August 26, 1885, Vol. 4, 1885, ibid. Unmade infantry coats with the white facings also were being sent out, as B.C. Card to M.I. Ludington, July 20, 1885, ibid., made known.

18 Replacement sets of gold lace chevrons with white backing likewise were to be provided at no charge during this transitional period, at least during the first year until every infantry non-commissioned officer entitled to the devices had received one set. S.B. Holabird to AGUSA, May 4, 1885, Vol 1, 1885; and S.B. Holabird to G.H. Weeks, September 13, 1885, Vol. 4, 1885, ibid. S.B. Holabird to AGUSA, November 28, 1885, ibid., and Circular No. 9, HQA, October 8, 1886, both made it clear, however, that gratuitous allowance for facing cloth was restricted to infantrymen, and did not apply to individuals on the post non-commissioned staff or other branches. For other indications from 1886 that white facings continued to be sent to units for the conversion of dress coats see, J.F. Rodgers to C.W. Foster; and J.F. Rodgers to C.W. Miller, January 29, 1886, LS, Clothing Br., Vol. 1, 1886, OQMG, RG92, NA. Miller was ordering forty-two sets of the facings for infantrymen at Ft. Custer, Montana Territory. Facings likewise were provided for the garrison of Boise Barracks, Idaho Territory. J.F. Rodgers to Chief Quartermaster Military Division of the Pacific, May 4, 1886, Vol. 2, 1886, ibid.

19 S.B. Holabird to M.I. Ludington, January 10, 1885, Vol I, 1885, ibid.

20 S.B. Holabird to M.I. Ludington, March 7, 1885; and J.F. Rodgers to M.I. Ludington, March 9, 1885, Vol. 2, 1885, ibid.

21 S.B. Holabird to M.I. Ludington, April 9, 1885, ibid.

22 S.B. Holabird to G.H. Weeks, April 7, 1885, ibid. Besides San Francisco, obsolete pattern coats also were to be returned to Jeffersonville and Philadelphia for potential conversion to new patterns. J.F. Rodgers to M.I. Ludington, February 24, 1885, Vol. 1, 1885; and S.B. Holabird to M.I. Ludington, September 22, 1885, Vol. 4, 1885, ibid. A paper pattern was to be furnished to assist in the reconditioning process. J.F. Rodgers to M.I. Ludington, July 13, 1885, Vol, 4, 1885, ibid. As an ex-

ample of this rehabilitation program Washington Barracks in the District of Columbia shipped back a dozen dress coats for reworking to Philadelphia. J.F. Rodgers to M.I. Ludington, May 9, 1885, Vol. 2, 1885, ibid. Captain Hull indicated he could convert cavalry and foot artillery coats for $1.00 and light artillery coats for $.50 each, which was acceptable to Holabird. S.B. Holabird to G.H. Weeks, September 12, 1885, Vol. 4, 1885, ibid.

23 These are not to be confused with some national guard coats of the period, which occasionally continued to be made with belt loops as just one deviation from Regular Army specifications.

24 S.B. Holabird to AGUSA, November 28, 1885, ibid. Cir. No. 11, HQA, December 8, 1885, repeated the secretary's November 9 decision restricting the allowance of the funds for alteration to the infantry only and not to any other arm of the service. In contrast, Circular No. 1, Headquarters of the Army, January 16, 1885, provided "the sum of two dollars for altering" infantry uniform dress coats and trousers "to conform to the requirements of General Orders No. 120...." In addition, Cir. No. 5, HQA, June 6, 1885, provided for "one pair of white cloth chevrons to each infantry non-commissioned officer, for use upon his blouse...." Those NCOs who because of their isolation from supply source did not receive the gratuitous issue of one pair of white chevrons were permitted to avail themselves of this same largesse by the authority of Cir. No. 8, HQA, September 10, 1885. Efforts to have coats converted for troops other than those in the infantry periodically were made by some commanders, such as Captain John W. Roder of the Fourth U.S. Artillery did to no avail. His request was denied as an expense that would add to the cost of operations if all soldiers were permitted this consideration. S.B. Holabird to AGUSA, October 18, 1886, LS, Clothing Br., Vol. 3, 1886, OQMG, RG92, NA. The cost of facing was set at $2.53 per yard for colored cloth and $2.55 per yard for white cloth. J.F. Rodgers to E.E. Hardin, April 23, 1886, Vol. 1, 1886, ibid.

25 J.F. Rodgers to Chief Quartermaster Military Division of the Pacific; and J.F. Rodgers to G.H. Weeks, November 28, 1885, ibid.

26 J.F. Rodgers to R. Saxton, December 8, 1885, ibid.

27 Cir. No. 10, HQA, November 13, 1885, reinforced the decision reached by Sheridan on October 1, that the "straps for waist-belts" no longer formed "a part of the uniform coat."

28 S.B. Holabird to Chief Quartermaster Military Division of the Atlantic, December 19, 1885, LS, Clothing Br., Vol. 2, 1885, OQMG, RG92, NA, not only indicated that no collar devices would be required in the future, but also service chevrons were no longer to worn on overcoats and blouses. Previously, Cir. No. 11, HQA, December 10, 1884, also had paved the way for discontinuance of collar numerals when it restricted the wearing of any decorations "on accessions of ceremony" to "the 'army corps badge,' authorized by section 1227 of the Revised Statutes, the 'medal of honor'; and several distinctive marks given for excellence in rife practice, as prescribed by existing orders." The last category was the key to collar numerals being displaced in that up to two square target devices could be worn on each side of the collar, leaving little room for numerals of branch insignia.

29 J.F. Rodgers to M.I. Ludington, January 26, LS, Clothing Br., 1885, Vol. 1, 1885, OQMG, RG92, NA.

30 J.F. Rodgers to M.I. Ludington, March 2, 1885, ibid.

31 S.B. Holabird to M.I. Ludington, February 24, 1885, ibid.

32 J.F. Rodgers to M.I. Ludington, July 23, 1885, Vol. 2, 1885, ibid. B.C. Card to M.I. Ludington, August 10, 1885, Vol. 4, 1885, ibid., included one such request for a post quartermaster hat cord and tassel, plus three dress coats for infantry privates and a pair of hospital steward's cloth chevrons, all bound for Ft. Bliss, Texas. The following year a order for Ft. Washakie, Wyoming Territory called for a quartermaster sergeant's campaign hat cord and tassels, along with blanket lined overcoats, gold lace chevrons and service chevrons, cloth chevrons, posts shoes, and a guidon case. J.F. Rodgers to M.I. Ludington, January 2, 1886, Vol. 2, 1886, ibid.

33 *ARSW, 1885*, Vol. I, 630-1.

34 J.F. Rodgers to M.I. Ludington, February 12, 1885; February 14, 1885; February 28, 1885; March 6, 1885; April 28, 1885; May 18, 1885, Vol. 1, 1885, and B.C. Card to M.I. Ludington, June 12, 1885, Vol. 4, LS, Clothing Br., OQMG, RG92, NA.

35 At Ft. Washakie, Wyoming Territory, for instance, facings and quartermaster sergeant chevrons were requested, rather than a completed coat, thereby indicating that the non-commissioned officer at this garrison must have had his new dress outfit assembled locally. J.F. Rodgers to M.I. Ludington, June 16, 1885, Vol. 1, 1885, ibid. The usual process in such an instance was to order cloth to make up the garments, which under GO No. 92, HQA, August 11, 1885, could be provided to non-commissioned officers, the fabric being of a better quality than that used for enlisted coats. This was evident at another garrison in today's Wyoming, Ft. Fred Steele, where the order for the post quartermaster sergeant's kit included one eagle device with overlay, two crossed pen and key cap devices, one set of uniform facings, one pair of cloth chevrons for the overcoat, three pairs of cloth chevrons for blouses, three pairs of trousers stripes, ten yards of dark blue cloth finest quality, and fifteen yards of sky-blue doeskin, once again indicative of the fact that the man was going to have most of his uniform custom tailored. J.F. Rodgers to M.I. Ludington, February 12, 1885, LS, Clothing Br., Vol. 1, 1885, OQMG, RG92, NA.
Alcatraz's request for the post quartermaster sergeant at the island fortress in San Francisco Bay included only two pairs of cloth chevrons, three sets of trouser stripes, and two forage cap devices. The reason became clear when another separate order was made the day for 1 3/4 yards dark blue fine quality cloth and 1 3/4 yards of dark blue flannel 6/4 fine quality cloth presumably to produce the coat and blouse for the newest member of the garrison's non-commissioned staff. J.F. Rodgers to M.I. Ludington, April 8, 1885, ibid. A year later, a dress coat was requested along with chevrons as separate items for the post quartermaster at Ft. Bayard, New Mexico Territory. Three pairs of trousers stripes and two sets of cloth chevrons completed the order. J.F. Rodgers to M.I. Ludington; and J.F. Rodgers to Chief Quartermaster Military Division of the Missouri, January 21, 1886, ibid.
In turn, the coat for the post quartermaster sergeant at Ft. Robinson, Nebraska, while made at Philadelphia, included a proviso for an "outlet" to "be left under the left arm", the purpose for which was not explained. B.C. Card to M.I. Ludington, August 6, 1885, Vol. 4, 1885, ibid. Applications for special made clothing were not uncommon, however, especially when sizes of unusual proportions were concerned. One such example was for a hospital steward's coat with a nineteen inch collar, forty-four inch chest, and forty-six inch waist ordered for Ft. Washakie, Wyoming Territory's rather rotund medic. B.C. Card to M.I. Ludington, August 26, 1885, Vol. 4, 1885, ibid. Previously a fair number of crossed key and pen insignia (forty each) had been sent to San Francisco along with fifty pairs of side buttons, and twenty helmet eagles. There were also twenty-five each helmet eagles for hospital stewards and commissary sergeants respectively in this same requisition. The fact that each type was singled out rather than as a bulk order for staff helmet plates indicates that the plates must have been shipped complete with their overlays applied. B.C. Card to M.I. Ludington, August 14, 1885, ibid.

36 *ASRW 1884*, Vol. I, 606.

37 J.F. Rodgers to M.I. Ludington, February 3, 1885, LS, Clothing Br., Vol. 1, 1885, OQMG, RG92, NA.

38 S.B. Holabird to M.I. Ludington, March 10, ibid.

39 M.I. Ludington, March 27, 1885, Vol 2, 1885, ibid.

40 J.F. Rodgers to M.I. Ludington, June 2, 1885, Vol. 1, 1885, ibid., sent 513 sets of gilt buttons to convert infantry dress coats, each set consisting of fifteen large and eight small buttons; whereas J.F. Rodgers to M.I. Ludington, November 30, 1885, Vol. 4, 1885, ibid., required 600 large and 300 small gilt buttons to be provided men of the Twenty-fifth U.S. Infantry as Ft. Sisseton, Dakota Territory.

41 Symptomatic of the relatively rapid rate of change that was taking place during the mid-1880s, when orders for forage caps were received one lot from Pippey had old buttons affixed to hold the chinstrap in place, while the contract filled by Hirschberg & Co., used the fire gilded buttons of the new pattern. S.B. Holabird to M.I. Ludington, October 28, 1885, ibid. Many such examples of old and new standards being worn side by side, or the mixture of the two, existed during this period of transition. To rectify future occurrences of this type, the new button was called for thereafter on all orders for forage capes. *ARSW, 1885*, Vol. I, 605.

42 By May 1886 a contract was let to Horstmann Bros. & Co. for 1,500 gross of large buttons and 1,000 gross of small buttons, followed in October of that same year by a contract to Thomas L. Hood of Philadelphia for 500 gross of large buttons and 300 gross of small buttons. The buttons were to be provided at "the cost price to enlisted men," which was determined to be $1.98 1/2 per gross for the coat size and $.99 1/2 per gross for the cuff size. S.B. Holabird to M.I. Ludington, May 27, 1886; and J.F. Rodgers to L.C. Allen, October 12, 1886, Vol. 1, 1886; J.F. Rodgers to M.I. Ludington; and S.B. Holabird to Chief Quartermaster Military Division of the Missouri, January 2, 1886; S.B. Holabird to Secretary of War; and J.F. Rodgers to G.H. Weeks, April 16, 1886, Vol. 2, 1886; and J.F. Rodgers to M.I. Ludington, October 28, 1886, Vol. 3, 1886, LS, Clothing Br., OQMG, RG92, NA. Over the ensuing years, various vendors continued to provide the fire gilded-buttons.

43 *ARSW, 1885*, Vol. I, 608.

44 When Secretary of War Lincoln attempted to add an African American enlisted man to the all-white Signal Corps, Robert Hazen was not supportive, but this move, according to *A History of the U.S. Signal Corps* (New York: G.P. Putnam's Sons, 1961), 70-2, was not the reason for the rift between the chief of the signal corps and his civilian superior. Hazen had criticized Lincoln for his handling of a relief expedition sent out to rescue Adolphus Greely's ill-fated arctic expedition of 1884. His outspoken and open disdain for the secretary of war led to a court martial and subsequent censure for "setting a pernicious example subversive of discipline and the interests of the service."

45 *ARSW, 1884*, Vol. IV, 29-30.

46 Ibid., 43.

47 Ibid., Vol. I, 658-9. Reference to the statement of clothing and equipment supplied to the Signal Corps also is found in J.F. Rodgers to R.N. Batchelder, August 28, 1885, LS, Clothing Br., Vol. 4, 1885, OQMG, RG92, NA.

48 S.B. Holabird to Chief Signal Officer, February 3, 1885, Vol. 2, 1885, ibid. Some of the dress coats would be altered in the process to conform to the new pattern. J.F. Rodgers to Acting Assistant Quartermaster Ft. Myer, July 6, 1885, Vol. 1, 1885, ibid. Some of the dress coats were of the old standard, which raised the specter that the cloth was inferior. In addition, the question as to whether the old coats should be altered to add the new full faced collar was discussed. S.B. Holabird to Chief Signal Officer, June 10, 1885, ibid.

49 S.B. Holabird to Chief Signal Officer, January 26, 1885, ibid. Among the orders was a dress coat for Sergeant Long with the gold lace chevrons applied. There also was another dress coat, two overcoats, and three pairs of trousers provided in this special order. J.F. Rodgers to M.I. Ludington, May 2, 1885, ibid.

50 J.F. Rodgers to M.I. Ludington; and J.F. Rodgers to G.H. Weeks, February 16, 1885, ibid.

51 J.F. Rodgers to M.I. Ludington, May 21, 1885, Vol. 2, 1885, ibid.

52 S.B. Holabird to Chief Signal Officer, May 29, 1885, ibid.

53 S.B. Holabird to AGUSA, June 18, 1885, Vol. 1, 1885, ibid.

54 S.B. Holabird to Chief Signal Officer, July 28, 1885, Vol. 4, 18885, ibid.

55 S.B. Holabird to M.I. Ludington, October 7, 1885, ibid. Further information about the appearance that Holabird had in mind for some of this insignia is revealed in an 1887 exchange. As part of preparation for an illustrated specifications handbook, during 1887, the quartermaster general suggested that the rendering of signal flags for the cap device should be redrawn because the spear-heads were not alike, nor were the flags square. The side buttons required reworking, too, in that the flame needed to be more pronounced and the flags made more uniform in size and be depicted as square. The shell and flame for ordnance helmet overlays looked more "like of bunch of flowers" than a flaming bomb. They were to be reworked to more closely resemble the forage cap device. S.B. Holabird to M.I. Ludington, December 28, 1887, Vol. 3, 1887, ibid.

56 o S.B. Holabird to M.I. Ludington, July 2, 1885, Vol. 1, ibid., the standard samples had been received and approved. Also see J.F. Rodgers to M.I. Ludington, August 14, 1885, Vol. 4, 1885, for the specifications. These were easy to make as indicated by stocks being available in July for distribution. For instance, three were to be sent for Ft. Davis, Texas in July and another two for Ft. Wingate, New Mexico Territory according to two letters from J.F. Rodgers to M.I. Ludington, July 20, 1885; and a third letter J.F. Rodgers to Chief Quartermaster Military Division of the Missouri, ibid. The order for Ft. Wingate likewise included two pairs of gold lace chevrons for the regimental color sergeant of the Thirteenth U.S. Infantry, along with two pairs of cloth chevrons, a blouse, and an overcoat for the same non-commissioned officer. By September a brassard was included in the order for Ft. Concho, Texas, as were gold lace chevrons, service chevrons, and infantry dress coats. J.F. Rodgers to M.I. Ludington, September 16, 1885, ibid.

57 It is interesting to note that Circular No. 6, HQA, June 8, 1884, already had provided for a lyre device for the helmet plate of bandsmen.

58 S.B. Holabird to M.I. Ludington, April 22, 1885, LS, Clothing Br., Vol. 1, 1885, OQMG, RG92, NA. Some of the materials the quartermaster general examined came from the West Point, as indicated in the above referenced letter. In fact, on two occasions he thanked the superintendent of the academy, Brigadier General Wesley Merritt, for sending photos of the musicians there, as well as loaning a lyre insignia, a music pouch, and an aiguillette as references for additional work on this project. S.B. Holabird to W. Merritt, April 21, 1885; and April 22, 1885, Vol. 2, 1885, ibid. During the earlier part of the year, the drum major was supplied a shako in lieu of a helmet, but otherwise the special items for bandsmen were supplied to the remainder of the musicians. This headgear appeared in the photographs furnished by General Merritt. S.I. Holabird to AGUSA, February 10, 1885, Vol. 1, 1885, ibid. It should be noted that Edward Eicke's of New York in received a purchase order on May 23, 1885 for 219 sets of shoulder knots with aiguillettes at $1.49 per set. Previously the firm had made helmet plumes and continued to do so, along with providing helmet cords and bands for purchases made on May 23 and June 30, 1885. See *ARSW, 1884*, Vol. I, 633, and 639. All major contracts and purchases on the open market for clothing and equipment undertaken by the Quartermaster Department in fiscal year 1884 also can be found in ibid., 626-57. Likewise see, S.B. Holabird to G.H. Weeks, March 11, 1885, Vol. 2, 1885; and June 2, 1885; J.F. Rodgers to .H. Weeks, June 2, 1885, Vol. 1, 1885; and S.B. Holabird to M.I. Ludington, February 3, 1885, Vol. 1, 1885; June 24, 1885; and July 24, 1885, Vol. 4, 1885, LS, Clothing Br., OQMG, RG92, NA.

59 S.B. Holabird to Chief Quartermaster Department of the East, April 6, 1885, Vol. 1, 1885; J.F. Rodgers to M.I. Ludington, April 6, 1885, and April 9, 1885; and S.B. Holabird to Chief Quartermaster Military Division of the Missouri, April 9, 1885, Vol. 2, 1885, ibid. The second letter from Rodgers to Ludington instructed delivery was to be made to the Sixteenth U.S. Infantry at Ft. Concho of twenty-five plumes, bands, cords, scrolls and rings, plus side buttons, cap lyres, and twenty unmade uniform dress coats. There also were to be forty pairs of trouser stripes. twenty-five aiguilettes and knots, and a like number of music pouches. Several weeks later similar requirements were made to supply the First U.S. Infantry Band at Ft. Grant, Arizona Territory with thirty music pouches, lyres, and aiguilettes with pairs of shoulder knots, as well as seventy-five pairs of white trousers. J.F. Rodgers to M.I. Ludington, May 15, 1885, Vol. 1, 1885, ibid. Several days later a directive came for a deliver of thirty lyres, thirty-one pairs of white trousers, and trouser stripes along with musicians' coats for the Twentieth U.S. Infantry band at Ft. Sidney, Nebraska. J.F. Rodgers to M.I. Ludington, June 26, 1885, ibid. On that same day twenty-four music pouches and twenty-four pairs of shoulder knots with aiguilettes were called for to outfit the Fourth U.S. Artillery Band at Ft. Adams, Rhode Island. J.F. Rodgers to M.I. Ludington, June 26, 1885, ibid.

60 J.F. Rodgers to M.I. Ludington, June 26, 1885, ibid.

61 J.F. Rodgers to G.H. Weeks, June 26, 1885, ibid.

62 J.F. Rodgers to C.M. Bailey, September 30, 1885, Vol. 4, 1885, ibid. A similar fate must have befallen a July order for bands and cords to deck out the helmets of the infantry musicians at Ft. Douglas, Utah, who in the past had worn mounted helmets before this became the norm. J.F. Rodgers to Chief Quartermaster Military Division of the Missouri, July 10, 1885, Vol. 1, 1885, ibid. At the end of fiscal year 1884 (June 30, 1885), the quartermaster general's office reported steps had been taken "to procure the additional articles" that had been approved by the secretary of war, and supposedly these items were "being issued to all bands in the Army upon proper requisition." *ARSW, 1884*, Vol. I. 602. In reality this claim was a bit optimistic to say the least, thereby indicating caution when accepting official statements about the matter of uniform from the agency charged with its development and supply. Certainly by early 1886 orders could be filled completely as divulged by a delivery of twenty-three sets of shoulder knots with aiguillettes, small sized music pouches, and all the components for mounted dress helmets including bands and plumes, but no bodies, probably because those already used by the men of the Twelfth U.S. Infantry were to have their spikes removed and the mounted trapping added. J.F. Rodgers to M.I. Ludington, January 6, 1886, LS, Clothing Br., Vol. 2, 1886, OQMG, RG92, NA. Later that year a small quantity of shoulder knots and aiguillettes were provided to the Third U.S. Cavalry band, while helmet lyres, large music pouches, shoulder knots with aiguillettes, white horsehair plumes, bands and cords were supplied to the Twenty-fourth U.S. Infantry band, and similar items delivered to the Ninth U.S. Infantry at Whipple Barracks, Arizona Territory, as but three more instances of the progress that had been made in this area. J.F. Rodgers to Philadelphia Depot Quartermaster, October 13, 1886, Vol. 1, 1886; J.F. Rodgers to M.I. Ludington, March 16, 1886, Vol. 2, 1886; and J.F. Rodgers to Depot Quartermaster Philadelphia, August 12, 1886, Vol. 3, 1886, ibid. To keep pace with requests for band articles periodic purchases were made, when funds were available, such as was the case in S.B. Holabird to M.I. Ludington, February 11, 1886, Vol. 1, 1886, ibid., in which among other things 96 white plumes, 108 shoulder knots with aiguillettes, 39 music pouches for infantry, 76 for cavalry, and 15 for artillery, were to be bought. Notably, the stores of bands articles did not necessary have to coincide with the ratio of infantry, cavalry, and artillery units in that there was some latitude about what could be ordered for issue. A prime example of this was the Fourth U.S. Infantry's band stationed at Fort Omaha, Nebraska (later renamed Ft. Crook). Artillery shoulder knots and aiguillettes, trouser stripes, plumes, and helmet bands with cords were substituted for infantry versions, although an infantry helmet plate with lyre was employed. J.F. Rodgers to M.I. Ludington, January 26, 1886, ibid.

63 S.B. Holabird to M.I. Ludington, May 13, 1885, Vol. 2, 1885, ibid.

64 S.B. Holabird to AGUSA, May 20, 1885; and S.B. Holabird to C.W. Foster, June 10,1885, Vol. 1, 1885, ibid. By the next summer, the quartermaster general recommended that the twenty-four musicians at the Military Academy, who formed the band, should all be granted the money clothing allowance of band sergeants of infantry, as but one example of the special status long enjoyed by West Point bandsmen. S.B. Holabird to AGUSA, August 11, 1886, ibid. Also see, J.F. Rodgers to M.I. Ludington, April 6, 1886; and May 12, 1886, Vol. 2, 1886, ibid., for an order to provide five uniform coats based on measurements and even naming the men to whom they were destined.

65 S.B. Holabird to AGUSA, June 16, 1885, ibid.

66 S.B. Holabird to Chief of Engineers, July 2, 1885, ibid.

67 S.B. Holabird to M.I. Ludington, July 9, 1885, ibid., was another example of dialogue related to band uniforms, in this case for the outfit that was being considered for chief musicians. The matter of white trousers, castle insignia, and the caduceus device for hospital steward's were other questions generated by the changes being introduced for bands in particular and the dress coat in general. The collar insignia were to be deleted, while ultimately white trousers were to be added. B.C. Card to J.L. Lusk, July 28, 1885, Vol. 4, 1885, ibid. First Lieutenant Lusk was an Engineer Corps officer serving at Willets Point, New York with the battalion of Engineers.

68 S.B. Holabird to AGUSA, July 30, 1885, ibid.

69 Endorsement S.B. Holabird to AGUSA, September 26, 1885, ibid. Early the next year the quartermaster general suggested a circular containing the exact definitions of the meanings set forth in GO Nos. 23 and 82 "relative to the clothing allowance for musicians and bandsmen" should be released. S.B. Holabird to AGUSA, January 8, 1886, Vol. 2, 1886, ibid.

70 S.B. Holabird to M.I. Ludington, October 26, 1885, ibid.

71 *ARSW, 1884*, Vol. 1, 638-9.

72 S.B. Holabird to M.I. Ludington, October 13, 1884, LS, Clothing Br., Vol. 3, 1885, OQMG, RG92, NA.

73 *ARSW, 1886*, Vol I, 508. Chief Quartermaster Military Division of the Pacific to Post Quartermaster Presidio of San Francisco, November 27, 1885, LR, Presidio of San Francisco, June 30, 1885 to July 30, 1886, RUSACC, RG393, NA. The money value was set at $5.75 for the pouches. S.B. Holabird to AGUSA, January 6, 1886, LS, Clothing Br., Vol. 2, 1886, OQMG, RG92, NA.

74 J.F. Rodgers to N.A.M. Dudely, September 3, 1885, LS, Clothing Br., Vol. 3, 1885, ibid. An order for the Eighteenth U.S.Infantry at Ft. Leavenworth from August 1885 included some of these items, most particularly the lyres for both the cap and helmet, shoulder knots and aiguillettes, and thirty pairs of "white linen trousers, of sizes supplied by the Q.M. Dept. conforming to kersey trousers...." There also were facings for ninety-nine infantry dress coats, some gold lace chevrons, and some cloth chevrons, including those for a principal musician and a post quarter master sergeant. B.C. Card to M.I. Ludington, August 14, 1885, Vol. 4, 1885, ibid. Later sixteen more unmade infantry dress coats were ordered, along with two more for infantry musicians that were made and sixteen privates' coats that likewise were premade. Additionally, there was to be a pair of cavalry musicians coats and ten cavalry privates' coats, the former being made and the latter being unmade. Twenty sets of cavalry facings were included as well, plus facings for two infantry musicians' coats and sixty-two privates' coats, all to be supplied by the Philadelphia Depot. J.F. Rodgers to M.I. Ludington, September 30, 1885, ibid. The Jeffersonville Depot among other things was to provide 103 unmade blouses, and 18 dark blue flannel shirts. Boots and post shoes rounded out the order. J.F. Rodgers to Depot Quartermaster Jeffersonville, September 30, 1885, ibid. The band for the Second U.S. Artillery took delivery of but four music pouches and sets of helmet cords, the low number perhaps representing an addition to a previous request for larger amounts. J.F. Rodgers to M.I. Ludington, November 6, 1885, ibid. By the next month, four dress coats for bandsmen at the U.S. Military Academy were to be made up, presumably also as additions to prior requisitions, perhaps for

men newly assigned to the organization. J.F. Rodgers to M.I. Ludington, December 8, 1885, ibid.

Meanwhile, in far away New Mexico Territory, Lieutenant W.H. Carter sought fifty pairs of old pattern trouser stripes for corporals, presumably for the use of regimental bandsmen at Ft. Bayard. J.F. Rodgers to Department Quartermaster St. Louis. September 16, 1885, ibid. The only old pattern at this point would have been the yellow worsted stripes issued since the 1860s, therefore it is unclear whether this is what Lieutenant Carter sought or not, and if so why any would be in stock at that late date.

75 S.B. Holabird to M.I. Ludington, April 21, 1885, Vol. 2, 1885, ibid.

76 S.B. Holabird to M.I. Ludington, April 25, 1885, ibid.

77 S.B. Holabird to M.I. Ludington, June 4, 1885, Vol. 1, 1885, ibid.

78 J.F. Rodgers to M.I. Ludington, June 20, 1885, ibid. Lewis S. Samuel's firm in New York received orders for 4,500 3/4 yards of white linen on May 2, 1885, and another 621 1/4 yards on June 8, 1885, *ARSW, 1884*, Vol. I, 626-7, thereby indicating the cloth was obtained and the trousers made by the Quartermaster Department rather than via contract. According to ibid., 630-1, some 700 gross of gilt buckles had been obtained by bid from Horstmann on June 30, 1884, for the kersey trousers, and just under 3,200 gross more delivered by purchase on the open market made during May 4, 1885, from Bombright Hood & Co. of Philadelphia. These were for kersey trousers.

79 Two letters from S.B. Holabird to M.I. Ludington, September 12, 1885, LS, Clothing Br., Vol. 4, 1885, OQMG, RG92, NA, were sent back to back, one regarding the acceptance of paper patterns for the trousers proper and the other indicating the buckles were to be the sealed samples, these measuring 7/8 inch by 1 1/4 inches outside, and having "two stout prongs, well let into the sides at a point five-sixteenths (5/16) of an inch from the outer bottom bar" according to the specifications.

80 J.F. Rodgers to M.I. Ludington, January 6, 1885, Vol. 2, 1885, ibid.

81 Ibid.

82 S.B. Holabird to M.I. Ludington, April 6, 1885, Vol. 1, 1885, ibid.

83 S.B. Holabird to M.I. Ludington, April 14, 1885, Vol. 2, 1885, ibid. In turn, similar white metal buttons soon were prescribed for stable frocks, overalls, and drawers. In the latter case, black buttons had been used previously, but were to be discontinued. S.B. Holabird to M.I. Ludington, August 26, 1885; and J.F. Rodgers to M.I. Ludington, November 18, 1885, Vol. 4, 1885, ibid. Also see, *ARSW, 1885*, Vol. I, 603, which stated: "Neat black japanned suspender and fly buttons, adding greatly to the appearance of the trousers, have been adopted, and are now being purchased and used on these garments. Similar buttons of white metal will be used on the drawers, stable frocks, and overalls."

84 S.B. Holabird to M.I. Ludington, March 2, 1885, LS, Clothing Br., Vol. I, 1885, OQMG, RG92, NA. Clothing and from this material was to be tracked carefully as to where it was shipped.

85 S.B. Holabird to Secretary of War, January 30, 1885, Vol. 1, 1885, ibid.

86 J.F. Rodgers to E.B. Bolton, February 2, 1885, ibid.

87 *ARSW, 1885*, Vol. I, 603.

88 Ibid.

89 Late in the year trousers were to be produced thereafter in the twelve regulation sizes and of the darker shade of kersey. J.F. Rodgers to M.I. Ludington, October 8, 1885, LS, Clothing Br., Vol. 4, 1885, OQMG, RG92, NA. Immediately after Christmas, specifications went to the depots to allow for production to be undertaken in compliance with this dictate. J.F. Rodgers to M.I. Ludington, December 26, 1885, ibid.

90 J.F. Rodgers to M.I. Ludington, May 17, 1886, Vol. 1, 1886, ibid., directed that darker trousers with the new style buttons be made to replace the previous standard. When this was accomplished they were furnished, and all the old standards were returned to be issued to the troops so that no confusion would result. S.B. Holabird to M.I. Ludington; S.B. Holabird to R. Saxton; S.B. Holabird to G.H. Weeks; and J.F. Rodgers to R.W. Batchelder, July 10, 1886, Vol. 3, 1886, ibid.

91 S.B. Holabird to M.I. Ludington, November 30, 1885, Vol. 4, 1885, ibid.

92 S.B. Holabird to M.I. Ludington, December 12, 1885, ibid. ARSW, 1885, Vol. I, 603, mentioned the finer quality kersey purchased for non-commissioned officers, and acknowledged that this cloth particularly had the "tendency, after being worn for a short while, to show at the parts most exposed a whitish tinge." The realization possibly accounts for the fact that three sources of supply were used in obtain the several hundred years of cloth so that the material could be tracked to determine which fared the best after issue and use. The privilege to buy the material had been made known in *ARSW, 1884*, Vol. I, 614.

93 S.B. Holabird to M.I. Ludington, December 26, 1885, LS, Clothing Br., Vol. 4, 1885, OQMG, RG92, NA.

94 S.B. Holabird to M.I. Ludington, November 6, 1885, ibid.

95 S.B. Holabird to M.I. Ludington; and J.F. Rodgers to M.I. Ludington, November 19, 1885, Vol. 3, 1885, ibid.

96 The elements of GO No. 113 related to enlisted cap insignia were repeated in S.B. Holabird to AGUSA, November 6, 1885, Vol. 4, 1885, ibid, along with a request to discontinue references to the obsolete dress cap in army regulations. Why this letter was sent, in that it the above noted general order already had tended to this matter, is unknown.

97 J.F. Rodgers to Raymold and Whitlock, March 2, 1885, Vol. 1, 1885, ibid.

98 GO No. 8, HQA, January 21, 1885, also noted that general officers and staff officers would have a dark blue cloth edged in gold lace measuring one inch in width. GO No. 44, HQA, July 9, 1886, added that the insignia which appeared on the forage caps for staff officers, likewise was to be affixed to the left and right rear corners of the saddle cloth. GO No. 6, HQA, February 1, 1886, again mentioned that the saddle cloths were to be trimmed in one and one-half inch wide cloth of the color of the branch and that a two inch number of the regiment would be in the same color and appear at the rear corner on each side. Given that this same order noted that capes for officers should be lined in white, it is inferred that by this point white had re placed light blue for infantry officers' saddle cloths. The Quartermaster Department prepared four sample pattern saddle cloths for the Ordnance Department, which had charge of horse equipage. S.B. Holabird to AGUSA, January 7, 1886, LS, Clothing Br., Vol. 1, 1886, OQMG, RG92, NA. Another letter from the quartermaster general written early the next year at least shed light on the 1883-pattern drab hat. It was noted that the standard was a brown hue, although a sample provided from Philadelphia was an incorrect shade that was nearly light gray. Further, the sample was "not so flexible and soft as the standard" and was heavier and "less sightly." S.B. Holabird to M.I. Ludington, January 3, 1887, ibid.

99 *ARSW, 1885*, Vol. I, 606, noted new crossed straps and a sling had been provided in order to bring "the weight of the color upon both shoulders of the carrier." Other items included drum covers, woolen blankets, barracks chairs, bunks, bedding, barracks bags, and company marking stamps that could be used to mark property with indelible ink for identification purposes. Ibid., 604-6. Stamps were widely used, and at least one even was made up for the Indian Scouts at Ft. Reno, Indian Territory. J.F. Rodgers to M.I. Ludington, April 15, 1886, LS, Clothing Br., Vol. 1, 1886, OQMG, RG92, NA. Specifications for barracks bags had been adopted on March 13, 1884, but were changed less than a year later by Specifications No. 132, March 9, 1885. J.F. Rodgers to M.I. Ludington, March 9, 1885, Vol. 2, 1885, ibid.

100 *ARSW, 1885*, Vol. I, 605-6. The quartermaster general shared his thoughts on this idea as early as 1884, writing: "The object is to bring up the subject and to endeavor to get scarlet for Artillery Colors and orange or yellow for Cavalry." S.B. Holabird to M.I. Ludington, September 16, 1884, LS, Clothing Br., Book 2, 1884, OQMG, RG92, NA. The cavalry yellow silk standards were adopted on February 4, 1884, and modified on July 7, 1886. The specifications for infantry colors followed on September 14, 1885. The scarlet artillery colors were adopted as official on April 29, 1886, the last date being noted in S.B. Holabird to IGUSA, June 8, 1886, Vol. 2, 1885, ibid. Prices for the new regimental colors eventually were set at $132.50 while the national colors, which infantry and artillery regiments also carried, were $69.00. J.F. Rodgers to E.H. Crowder, January 27, 1886, Vol. 1, ibid. The form of the national colors, which were the traditional thirteen stripe American flag, was adopted on September 14, 1885.

101 S.B. Holabird to R.W. Batchelder, April 13, 1886, ibid.

102 The prototype was being fashioned in mid-May 1886, and once it was completed, specifications followed on May 21, when the scarlet guidon with yellow crossed cannon and battery letter below and regimental number above became official. J.F. Rodgers to E.B. Williston, May 15, 1886, ibid.

103 *ARSW, 1886*, Vol. I, 605. This design harkened back to the guidons issued to the dragoons in the 1830s, and which were regulation until 1863, when they were changed to the striped swallow-tail. During 1884, a slight modification had been made based upon the suggestion of Colonel Ludington that the stars were to be yellow for cavalry guidons as was the company letter, while those for artillery were to be white. J.F. Rodgers to M.I. Ludington, October 21, 1884, LS, Clothing Br., Book B, 1884, OQMG, RG92, NA. A month later the resurrection of the concept for the red and white guidon appeared in correspondence. J.F. Rodgers to M.I. Ludington, November 14, 1884, ibid. Specification No. 129 was produced and forwarded early the next year, and a request made to include the new guidon in the regulations. S.B. Holabird to AGUSA, January 27, 1885; and S.B. Holabird to M.I. Ludington, January 28, 1885, Vol. 2, 1885, ibid.

104 *ARSW, 1885*, Vol. I, 695. For example, guidons with cases were supplied to Troop I, Sixth U.S. Cavalry at Ft. Wingate, New Mexico Territory, and to Troop M, Fourth U.S. Cavalry, at Ft. McDowell, Arizona Territory during fall 1885. J.F. Rodgers to M.I. Ludington, October 26, 1885; J.F. Rodgers to Depot Quartermaster St. Louis, October 26, 1885; and J.F. Rodgers to Chief Quartermaster Military Division of the Pacific, November 20, 1885, LS, Clothing Br., Vol. 4, 1885, OQMG, RG92, NA. By January 1886 more guidons were being prepared for cavalry troops. J.F. Rodgers to Chief Quartermaster Military Division of the Missouri, January 21, 1886, Vol. 1, 1886, ibid.

105 Both S.B. Holabird to Secretary of War, July 31, 1886, Vol. 1, 1886; and J.F. Rodgers to R.W. Batchelder, August 16, 1886, Vol. 3, 1886, ibid., directed that obsolete cavalry guidons were to be turned in to the office of the quartermaster general, per the secretary of war's authorization, where they could be recycled for purposes of decoration. New versions of the guidons were to be issued thereafter to artillery batteries and cavalry troops at one per unit. J.F. Rodgers to G.H. Weeks, October 8, 1886, Vol. 3, 1886, ibid.

106 *ARSW, 1885*, Vol. I, 606; S.B. Holabird to M.I. Ludington, January 20, 1885, Vol, 4, 1885; and March 30, 1885, Vol. 1, 1885, LS, Clothing Br., OQMG, RG92, NA.

107 J.F. Rodgers to Chief Quartermaster Department of the East, September 22, 1885, Vol. 4, 1885, ibid., acknowledged the order of canvas fatigue clothing for the garrison of venerable Ft. McHenry.

108 S.B. Holabird to AGUSA, June 26, 1885, Vol. 1, 1885, ibid.

109 S.B. Holabird to AGUSA, February 9, 1885, Vol. 2, 1885; and September 13, 1885, Vol. 4, 1885, ibid. Nor did the quartermaster general have any qualms about officers purchasing canvas fatigue clothing, so long as sufficient quantities were available to be spared. S.B. Holabird to W. Lassiter, January 26, 1886, Vol. 2, 1886, ibid.

110 Britton, Davis, *The Truth About Geronimo* (New Haven: Yale University Press, 1929), 165.

111 Ibid., 177.

112 Ibid., 174-5.

113 Ibid., 188.

114 Ibid., 192.

115 "Report of Assistant Surgeon Leonard Wood," September 9, 1886, Microfilm Collection M689, Roll 507, AGUSA, RG94, NA. Wood's findings and no doubt other complains led to the publication of Cir. No. 10, HQA, November 12, 1886, which stated in part: "In view of the rapid destruction of the boots and shoes worn by the U.S. troops during the scouting against Indians in Arizona and New Mexico, such boots and shoes will be replaced gratuitously when the fact is fully established by a board of survey that they have been thus destroyed through no fault of the men to whom they were issued.—[*Decision Sec. War, letter Oct. 30, 86—4124 A.G.O., 1886.*]"

116 Brinckerhoff, *Boots and Shoes*, 21-3. Both brass-screwed boots and shoes were to be used up, and these could be obtained from the general depots "upon proper requisition, until the supply on hand" was depleted. They were to be issued at $2.73 for a pair of boots and $1.76 for a pair of shoes. GO No. 71, HQA, June 23, 1885.

117 J. Newton to Quartermaster General, July 22, 1885, attached to an endorsement from B.C. Card to A.P. Blunt, July 22, 1885, LS, Clothing Br., Vol. 4, 1885, OQMG, RG92, NA.

118 S.B. Holabird to A.P. Blunt, April 22, 1885, Vol. 1, 1885, ibid.

119 J.F. Rodgers to R. Saxton, October 23, 1885, Vol. 4, 1885, ibid., provides what may be taken as a typical order of the period. Footgear bound for the Fifth U.S. Cavalry at Ft. Riley, Kansas included 35 pairs of field shoes, versus 180 pairs of post shoes, and 190 pairs of boots with sewn soles. Two previous orders, one destined for the Jeffersonville Depot and the other for the San Francisco Depot included no field shoes, but at the former installation 200 pairs of sewn soled boots and 1,306 pairs of campaign shoes were called for while at the later facility some 1,640 pairs of post shoes, 1,840 sewn pairs of boots, 190 pairs of boots with screws, and 280 pairs of shoes with the screwed soles were to be provided by the prison. J.F. Rodgers to Commanding Officer U.S Military Prison, October 23, 1885; and B.C. Card to R. Saxton, August 14, 1885, ibid.

120 J. Newton to Quartermaster General, July 22, 1885, attached to an endorsement from B.C. Card to A.P. Blunt, July 22, 1885, Vol. 2, 1885, ibid. The sewed boots still were being sent out despite such complaints as indicated by J.F. Rodgers to C.W. Foster, October 20, 1885, ibid., whereby twelve pairs of the sewn boots were ordered for the Eighth U.S. Cavalry in Texas.

121 J.P. Martin to A.P. Blunt, October 6, 1885, ibid. Martin with the acting assistant adjutant general for the Department of the Missouri.

122 Brinckerhoff, *Boots and Shoes*, 27.

123 Abstract from C. Humphreys' Annual Report in J.F. Rodgers to A.P. Blunt, July 21, 1885, LS, Clothing Br., Vol. 4, 1885, OQMG, RG92, NA. Some enlisted members of the Second U.S. Artillery registered dissatisfaction with the post shoe, too, according to a letter from their regimental quartermaster, Second Lieutenant Willoughby Walkc as transmitted in J.F. Rodgers to A.P. Blunt, September 22, 1885, ibid.

124 B.C. Drum to Quartermaster General, September 17, 1885, ibid.

125 Cir. No. 11, HQA, December 8, 1885. Cir. No. 3, HQA, April 14, 1886, slightly expanded upon the process by which defective post shoes could be replaced at no cost to the soldier.

126 Brinckerhoff, *Boots and Shoes*, 25-6.

127 S.B. Holabird to A.P. Blunt, November 12, 1885, LS, Clothing Br., Vol. 4, 1885, OQMG, RG92, NA. The quartermaster general also sent a lengthy letter on the matter of post shoes and campaign shoes to Blunt on July 14, 1885, ibid.

128 Because of the persistence of some soldiers to use the post shoes as a universal footwear rather than for the specific intention that brought them into being, fabrication of the model ceased in late June 1887. Brinckerhoff, *Boots and Shoes*, 23 and 26.

129 Ibid., 25.

130 *ARSW, 1885*, Vol. I, 607. Some 1,016 pairs of buffalo overshoes remained in stock at St. Louis by the following year according to, B.C. Card to Chief Quartermaster Military Division of the Missouri, August 10, 1886, LS, Clothing Br., Vol. 3, 1886, OQMG, RG92, NA.

131 The poncho issued during the Civil was described as: "Of good stout, unbleached muslin, coated with India rubber, vulcanized. To be sixty inches long. To be strengthened on the edge with an extra strip of rubber and to have an opening in the centre (lengthwise) of the poncho with edges lapping three inches wide and sixteen inches long, strengthened on the edge. Brass grommets same as in the rubber blankets, viz: one inch from their centres to the edge of blanket on one side and end, and two inches to the other side and end.They must be stayed and placed equidistant 14 inches apart so as to match." J.F. Rodgers to J.D. Billings, February 23, 1887, Vol. 1, 1887, ibid.

132 GO No. 73, HQA, July 1, 1885, provides a resume of the cavalry board's findings that had been recommended by the chief of ordnance and approved by the secretary of war.

133 S.B. Holabird to AGUSA, September 15, 1884, LS, Clothing Br., Book B, 1884, OQMG, RG92, NA. During May 1884, the quartermaster general had requested the purchase of rubber overcoat samples in lieu of the poncho for mounted troops, He asked that "some of the samples...have a slit behind, to be closed when the wearer is dismounted." The intent was to "combine lightness with durability and strength." S.B. Holabird to M.I. Ludington, May 22, 1884, Book A, 1884, ibid.

While Holabird was willing to pursue this course, he conversely rejected a patented process offered by F. Falenberg of Magdenburg, Germany, which supposedly could waterproof the uniform clothing. S.B. Holabird to Secretary of War, January 4, 1884, ibid. Even so, there was a limited attempt to replace the summer helmet with a water repellent version that came to naught after a brief trial proved prototypes supposedly having this property did not live up to expectations. J.F. Rodgers to Hirschberg & Co., New York City, November 19, 1885, Vol. 3, 1885, ibid.

134 S.B. Holabird to AGUSA, February 6, 1886, Vol. 2, 1886, ibid. The matter was not entirely forgotten, however, as one exchange between the quartermaster general and the attorney for the American Rubber Co. divulged in which Holabird stated that the matter of rubber clothing was under review by a board of officers late in 1886, and in the meantime he cited the general orders permitted the gratuitous issue of ponchos or ground cloths to the men. S.B. Holabird to A.F. Carman, November 24, 1886, Vol. 3, 1886, ibid.

135 On September 27, 1884 the Adjutant General was informed by the secretary of war of his concurrence with the issue of rubber goods in stock, and this was published in GO No. 71, HQA, June 23, 1885, which read: "Under special authority of the War Department rubber blankets and ponchos may be issued gratuitously, at a rate of one per annum, to each enlisted man serving in the field or in active campaign, until the stock on hand shall have become exhausted." Cir. 11, HQA, December 8, 1885, further indicated: "The gratuitous issue of rubber blankets or ponchos, provided for by General Orders No. 71, current series, from this office, can only be made to troops serving in the field or in active campaign."

Finally, Cir. 12. HQA, December 31, 1885 provided that: "Under existing orders rubber blankets and ponchos are issued only to enlisted men in the field or in active campaign. They are issued gratuitously in the same manner as canvas fatigue clothing, overcoats &c. The money value of the rubber goods does not form part of the money allowance of enlisted men. They are classed as 'equipage,' and their value is given at $1.55 and $1.13, respectively, so that if lost or misapplied they can be charged to the proper person."

136 John Bigelow, Jr., *On the Bloody Trail of Geronimo* (Los Angeles: Westernlore Press, 1968), 1; 3; and 16.

137 George Ruhlen to Chief Quartermaster Military Division of the Missouri, August 3, 1885, LS, Clothing Br., Vol. 3, 1885, OQMG, RG92, NA. J.F. Rodgers to Chief Quartermaster Military Division of the Missouri, January 3, 1887, Vol. 1, 1887, ibid., likewise noted that a few canvas coats lined with sheepskin had been "purchased and issued for trial."

138 J.F. Rodgers to P. Roemer, February 2, 1885, ibid.

139 J.F. Rodgers to M.I. Ludington, February 3, 1885, Vol. 2, 1885, ibid.

140 S.B. Holabird to Superintendent U.S. Military Academy, April 24, 1885, Vol. 1, 1885, ibid.

141 J.F. Rodgers to M.I. Ludington, April 24, 1885, ibid.

142 S.B. Holabird to M.I. Ludington, May 15, 1885, Vol. 2, 1885, ibid.

143 S.B. Holabird to M.I. Ludington, September 2, 1885, Vol. 4, 1885, ibid.

144 S.B. Holabird to Secretary of War, June 25, 1885, Vol. 2, 1885, ibid.

145 S.B. Holabird to T.M. Woodruff, July 22, 1885, Vol. 4, 1885, ibid. Reduced prices for old pattern trousers and blouses constituted one means to entice soldiers to accept the lighter shade and former sizes. S.B. Holabird to AGUSA; and S.B. Holabird to Chief Quartermaster Military Division of the Pacific, April 15, 1886, Vol. 1 , 1886, ibid.

146 J.F. Rodgers to M.I. Ludington, February 3, 1885, Vol. 2, 1885, ibid.

147 J.F. Rodgers to M.I. Ludington, February 10, 1885, Vol. 1, 1885, ibid.

148 S.B. Holabird to Chief of Engineers, September 22, 1885, Vol. 4, 1885, ibid. Actually, on March 22, 1884, the secretary of war had permitted men to receive $1 to defray the cost of changing their cape linings, but this was not made known generally until the publication of the circular in 1886. *ARSW, 1886*, Vol. I, 510.

149 Cir. No. 12, HQA, December 31, 1885. Even then, a request was made from Captain W.L. Haskins of the Fourth U.S. Artillery to permit this practice. Once more, authority was denied for this action. AGUSA to Commander Department of California, December 3, 1885, LR, Presidio of San Francisco, June 30, 1885-July 3, 1886, RUSACC, RG393, NA.

150 Cir. No. 3, HQA, April 14, 1886.

151 Ibid., which for the most part simply reinforced the same requirement that had been stated in Cir. No. 11, HQA, December 8, 1885, which in this regard directed: "The overcoat prescribed by General Orders No. 8, of 1885 is a part of the uniform, and all officers are required to own complete uniforms of their grade.—[*Decision Lieut. Gen., letter No. 24, 85—7092 A.G.O., 1885.*]" A captain in the U.S. Marine Corps had written about details relative to the officers' overcoat and was informed that the prototype had been made by Hoyt and Gleason. J.F. Rodgers to H. Lowry, January 13, 1885, LS, Clothing Br., Vol. 2, 1885, OQMG, RG92, NA.

152 J.F. Rodgers to M.I. Ludington, February 19, 1885, ibid.

153 *ARSW, 1885*, Vol. I, 603.

154 Per a December 2, 1885 letter from the secretary of war published in Cir. No. 12, HQA, December 31, 1885.

155 J.F. Rodgers to M.I. Ludington, January 3, 1886, LS, Clothing Br., Vol. 1, 1886, OQMG, RG92, NA. A private citizen, John Judge of New York, a tailor who had been engaged in altering uniforms for the men of Washington Barracks, wrote that he had knowledge of how to produce a better fit of trousers and blouses for the army, and Rodgers expressed an interest in meeting with him. J.F. Rodgers to J. Judge, May 15, 1886, ibid. For this reason it was agreed that Judge would be paid $3.00 per day for his time, including travel to Washington, DC, to present his scheme to improve the cut of military clothing and at the same time make "a savings in the materials in which they are cut." It should be indicated that Judge also was interested in securing "permanent employment as cutter" with the Quartermaster De-

partment. J.G. Chandler to M.I. Ludington, May 28, 1886, Vol. 3, 1886, ibid. As the various refinements were in progress, a request came for a sample of the latest version of the blouse to be sent to General M.R. Patrick governor of the National Home for Disabled Volunteers at Dayton, Ohio. The sample would be returned to Philadelphia. J.F. Rodgers to M.I. Ludington, January 29, 1886, Vol. 1, 1886, ibid. The same day, an acknowledgement was sent to indicate the sample was being forwarded to the home. J.F. Rodgers to M.R. Patrick, January 29, 1886, ibid.

156 On March 12, 1886, Specification No. 164 was adopted, and the following month one hundred copies of the specifications were sent to Philadelphia, fifty to San Francisco, along with the same number to Jeffersonville and the Inspector General's Department, the last referenced batch being provided per an October 1880 standing-request for such material. J.F. Rodgers to M.I. Ludington; J.F. Rodgers to G.H. Weeks; J.F. Rodgers to R. Saxton; and J.F. Rodgers to IGUSA, April 13, 1886, ibid.

157 *ARSW, 1885*, Vol. I, 604 and 609. Other new specifications besides blouse flannel adopted in fiscal year 1885, and which demonstrate the considerable activity afoot soon after Holabird became quartermaster general were as follows: blouses; color belts and slings; cavalry guidons; drum cases; silk and silk twist; gold and cloth chevrons; stripes for trousers; metallic helmet and forage cap insignia; canvas mittens; muskrat mittens; forage caps; facing cloth; cape-lining flannel; dark blue wool shirting; fly and suspender buttons; fire gilt uniform coat buttons; dress coats; markers and general guides; overcoats; brassards; mosquito bars; company marking stamps; conical wall tent stove pipes; barracks chairs; barracks bags; pillow cases; pillows; bed sheets; woolen blankets; and mattresses. Ibid., 609.

158 S.B. Holabird to M.I. Ludington, September 14, 1885, LS, Clothing Br., Vol. 4, 1885, OQMG, RG92, NA.

159 S.B. Holabird to M.I. Ludington, October 3, 1885, ibid.

160 S.B. Holabird to M.I. Ludington, October 28, 1885, ibid.

161 S.B. Holabird to B.Y. Pippey & Co., July 1, 1886, Vol. 1, 1886, ibid. Essentially the same letter was sent to Ludington as a matter of information. S.B. Holabird to M.I. Ludington, July 1, 1886, ibid. Yet another contract for 20,000 yards of gray blouse lining was to be awarded to Thos. G. Hood of Philadelphia, the firm being the lowest bidder at $.23 8/87 per yard. S.B. Holabird to M.I. Ludington, July 31, 1886, ibid. The same process of a preliminary inspection before shipping 5,000 yards of dark blue flannel of fine quality purchased from the San Francisco Woolen Mill Factory at $1.50 per yard, was employed before shipping the material east. J.F. Rodgers to G.H. Weeks, August 30, 1886, Vol. 3, 1886, ibid.

162 *ARSW, 1885*, Vol. I, 604.

163 S.B. Holabird to Chief Quartermaster Division of the Pacific, February 28, 1885, LS, Clothing Br., Vol. 1, 1885, OQMG, 92, NA. Representatives listings of items construed as excess at various posts prove informative. For instance, some 329 black campaign hats at Ft. Davis, Texas were unwanted along with 500 gray flannel shirts, 660 pairs of made heavy kersey mounted trousers in the old sizes, and 250 blouses in the old sizes. W.B. Hughes to St. Louis Depot Quartermaster, September 9, 1886, ibid. Among other things, 150 pairs of trousers of heavy kersey in the old sizes were not wanted at Ft. Laramie, Wyoming Territory. The same was true of 179 pairs at Ft. Robinson, Nebraska. J.F. Rodgers to Chief Quartermaster Military Division of the Missouri, July 17, 1886, ibid. Finally, many cloth service in peace, service in war, and campaign chevrons were ready to be turned in by the authorities at Ft. Wadsworth, New York, as were 185 right-handed Berlin glove left over from the abandoned experiment to issue more gloves for that hand than for the left. B.C. Card to Chief Quartermaster Department of the East, Vol. 4, 1886, ibid.

164 J.F. Rodgers to M.I. Ludington: and J.F. Rodgers to R. Saxon, November 13, 1885, Vol. 4, 1885, ibid., called for the shipment of all blouses of the old standards to be consolidated at St. Louis, while J.F. Rodgers to M.I. Ludington, November 30, 1885, ibid., sought information as to the feasibility to convert these garments to the new style.

165 As an example, 85 blouses without pockets, but that still had the cord attached, were to be sent for the recruiting officer in New York City. The cord was to be removed before issue. The same order was to include 141 cavalry overcoats of the old light blue shade of kersey and 150 pairs of mounted trousers made from the heavy weight old shade of kersey. J.F. Rodgers to St. Louis Depot, September 27, 1886, Vol. 1, 1886, ibid. Other portions of the order destined for recruits signed by Captain C.A. Stedman, Ninth U.S. Cavalry, were noted in J.F. Rodgers to Depot Quartermaster Philadelphia, September 27, 1886, ibid. The order included among other things 150 pairs of drawers, crossed sabers, and wool stockings, plus a like number of forage caps, dark blue flannel shirts, knit undershirts, and 65 blouses.

166 S.B. Holabird to M.I. Ludington; S.B. Holabird to R. Saxton; and S.B. Holabird to G.W. Weeks, March 12, 1886, Vol. 2, 1886, ibid.

167 B.C. Card to C.W. Foster, March 6, 1886, ibid.

168 J.F. Rodgers to C.W. Foster, November 16, 1885, Vol. 4, 1885, ibid.

169 B.C. Card to R. Saxton, August 28, 1885, ibid. See also J.F. Rodgers to M.I. Ludington, July 24, 1885, ibid., for the figures as of June 30, 1885.

170 J.F. Rodgers to M.I. Ludington, September 13, 1885, ibid.

171 J.F. Rodgers to M.I. Ludington and R. Saxton, November 16, 1885, ibid.

172 S.B. Holabird to AGUSA, February 16, 1886, Vol. 2, 1886, ibid. Further, according to Cir. No. 1, HQA, February 15, 1886, the old size trousers and blouses were to be offered to the men at a nearly twenty-five percent reduction in cost as follows: blouses sizes 1 and 2, $2.25; mounted trousers heavy kersey made sizes 1 to 5, $2.50; mounted trousers heavy kersey unmade sizes 1 and 2, $1.75; foot trousers heavy kersey made sizes 2 and 3, $2.00; foot trousers heavy kersey unmade sizes 1 and 2, 1.25; trousers mounted light kersey made sizes 1 to 4, $2.25; trousers light kersey unmade sizes 1 to 3, $1.50; trousers foot light kersey made sizes 1 to 4, $1.75; and trouser foot light kersey unmade sizes 1 and 2, $1.25. Cir. No. 2, HQA, March 12, 1886, repeated these prices, as well as stated that because of the disinclination of some enlisted men "to draw trousers of the new sizes 1 to 12) for the reason they are made of kersey of a lighter shade" it was required "in the interest of economy, to insist upon their being issued at the prices established for them...."

173 For instance, twenty size 2 blouses were being sent for the recruiter in Buffalo, New York of the old standard flannel as an example of the ongoing program to absorb the existing stocks. B.C. Card to R. Saxon, July 7, 1886, LS, Clothing Br., Vol. 1, 1886, OQMG, RG92, NA. Later, the quartermaster general disclosed that it became a matter of official policy to issue the obsolete patterns "to recruits at rendezvous and depots." This was to be done at a reduced charge to the incoming enlistee, which would save the new soldier money, along with being more cost effective for the government that if the outmoded items were placed for sale as surplus on the open market. That scenario would result in a net loss to the army under existing legislation that required funds thus obtained to be returned to the general fund, and not the War Department. Holabird further reasoned that once a man reported for duty, he - tended to draw one or two additional pairs of trousers before the end of his first year of enlistment, thereby assuring that he would have both old and new pattern trousers at least, and therefore uniformity, "except when off duty" would be achieved. What the quartermaster general did not indicate was how this process would work when it came to the many varieties of blouses being distributed. S.B. Holabird to Secretary of War, February 6, 1886, Vol. 2, 1886, ibid.

174 S.B. Holabird to AGUSA, September 28, 1885, Vol. 4, 1885, ibid.

175 Some representations of items ranging from 1872-pattern helmets, to gray flannel field shirts, blue infantry facings, cords and tassels for campaign hats (which elicited the remark in one instance that they "never [were] required"), old blouses, and old trousers are found in reports from Ft. Union, New Mexico Territory; Fort Washakie, Wyoming Territory; and Washington Barracks, Vancouver Territory, all of which are mentioned in the following respective correspondence: S.B.Holabird to Chief Quartermaster Military Division of the Missouri, July 22, 1885; J.A Goodin to Chief Quartermaster Military Division of the Missouri, July 1, 1885; and T.T. Patterson to Chief Quartermaster Military Division of the Pacific, June 30, 1885, ibid.

176 S.B. Holabird to M.I. Ludington, October 7, 1885, ibid.

177 Ibid. The letter also included copies of all specifications that had been published to date, along with any existing drawings. The drawings did not indicate one some times subtle difference, however, that of color. For instance, Newport Barracks' request included a quantity of stockings, but did not specify sizes of woolen stockings nor the sizes and colors of cotton stockings. J.F. Rodgers to Chief Quartermaster Department of the East, January 26, 1886, Vol. 2, 1886, ibid. Variations of the cotton stocking were indicated by this letter, too, a brown and white mixture and a black and white mixture being available.

178 J.F. Rodgers to M.I. Ludington, November 6, 1885, Vol. 4, 1885, ibid.

179 S.B. Holabird to M.I. Ludington, December 9, 1885, Vol. 3, 1885, ibid.

180 S.B. Holabird to AGUSA, April 8, 1885, Vol. 1 1885, ibid., requested the publication of a general order listing the quantities and prices of items to be issued to enlisted men and was published as GO No. 71.

181 S.B. Holabird to AGUSA, April 8, 1885, ibid.

182 *ARSW, 1885*, Vol. I, 601.

183 Ibid., 507. S.B. Holabird to G.H. Weeks, January 27, 1886; and March 5, 1886; LS, Clothing Br., Vol. 1, 1886, OQMG, RG92, NA; and S.B. Holabird to AGUSA, July 12, 1886, Vol. 3, 1886, ibid. On a related matter, the draft illustration of the enlisted gauntlets that were provided for the new specification publication did not match the actual article, and required redrawing. J.F. Rodgers to M.I. Ludington, August 16, 1886, ibid. Finally, a citizen writing from Richmond, Virginia wanted to know what the pattern for gauntlets was at this time. He was informed that regulations "did not prescribe the exact pattern of Gauntlets for mounted officers." Each individual was responsible for buying his own pair, although officers were allowed to purchase government issue ones at cost from the department. J.F. Rodgers to W.M. Evans, August 4, 1886, ibid.

184 J.F. Rodgers to M.I. Ludington, August 2, 1886, ibid.

185 S.B. Holabird to M.I. Ludington, November 13, 1886, Vol. 2, 1886, ibid. Ludington also suggested a snap buckle for the suspenders, but according to the same letter, Holabird did not favor the idea. Therefore it was disapproved.

186 S.B. Holabird to AGUSA, April 23, 1886, Vol. 1, 1886, ibid.

187 *ARSW, 1886*, Vol. I, 506. Ft. Davis, Texas was one of the installations where post shoes made on the old lasts were sent as revealed in, J.F. Rodgers to A.P. Blunt, March 16, 1886, LS, Clothing Br., Vol. 2, 1886, OQMG, RG92, NA.

188 S.B. Holabird to C.W. Foster; and S.B. Holabird to A.P. Blunt, January 25, 1886, Vol. 1, 1886, ibid. Sizes and widths of sewn shoes in stock at Philadelphia and Jeffersonville also were to be provided and all the pairs sent to St. Louis. B.C. Card to M.I. Ludington; and B.C. Card to R. Saxton, March 8, 1886, ibid.

189 Circular No. 10, HQA, November 12, 1886, reported the secretary of war's decision: "In view of the rapid destruction of boots and shoes worn by U.S. troops during the recent operations against Indians in Arizona and New Mexico, such boots and shoes will be replaced gratuitously" providing that they were "destroyed through no fault of the men to whom they were issued." Toe and heel plates were recommended for issue to troops at Ft. Mohave, Arizona Territory as a method to forestall such wear, but the quartermaster general disagreed. S.B. Holabird to AGUSA, January 7, 1886, Vol. 1, 1886, LS, Clothing Br., OQMG, RG92, NA.

190 S.B. Holabird to AGUSA, October 8, 1886, Vol. 3, 1886, ibid.; J.F. Rodgers to G.H. Weeks, October 19, 1886, Vol. 1, 1886, ibid.; and *ARSW, 1886*, Vol. I, 507. Issue of

brass screwed footwear was not restricted to Arizona Territory, however, with items on hand, rather than new made renderings also being sent as far north as Ft. Missoula, Montana Territory, and to the East Coast for Ft. Monroe, Virginia, Willets Point, New York, and Watervliet Arsenal, New York. J.F. Rodgers to R. Saxton, February 11, 1886, Vol. 1, 1886; J.F. Rodgers to A.P. Blunt; and J.F. Rodgers to St. Louis Depot, October 26, 1886; and J.F. Rodgers to Philadelphia Depot Quartermaster, August 20, 1886, Vol. 3, 1886, LS, Clothing Br., OQMG, RG92, NA.

191 *ARSW, 1886*, Vol. I, 507. S.B. Holabird to A.P. Blunt, August 9, 1886, LS, Clothing Br., Vol. 2, 1886, OQMG, RG 92, NA, provided information that the crimping forms as originally set up were altered to make improvements.

192 J.F. Rodgers to A.P. Blunt, September 16, 1886, ibid.

193 *ARSW, 1886*, Vol. I, 507.

194 Ibid., 507. GO No. 48, HQA, July 6, 1887, allowed one pair of barracks shoes to be drawn per year by a soldier, along with six linen collars. This same general order further stated that post shoes no longer would be manufactured because they were not considered "adapted to the military service...." Finally this general order allowed one fur cap and one pair of fur gauntlets to be issued annually to the men requiring them.

195 ers to A.P. Blunt, August 16, 1886, LS, Clothing Br., Vol. 3, 1886, OQMG, RG92, NA. This was an ongoing program as demonstrated by the question raised the following years as to when the next sale of scrap leather from Leavenworth was contemplated. J.F. Rodgers to A.P. Blunt, January 7, 1887, Vol. 1, 1887, ibid.

196 *ARSW, 1886*, Vol. I, 505; J.F. Rodgers to Chief Quartermaster Department of Dakota, January 12, 1886; and J.F. Rodgers to C.W. Foster, February 11, 1886, LS, Clothing Br., Vol. 1, 1886, OQMG, RG92, NA. J.F. Rodgers to Chief Quartermaster Department of Dakota, January 12, 1886, Vol. 2, 1886, ibid., repeated the requirement "that the black woolen campaign hats on hand must be used" before the other drab one could be put "into general use."

197 Seven drab campaign hats were included in the order for Camp Fairview, New Mexico Territory, and fifteen were shipped to Ft. Missoula, Montana Territory, while an other quantity went to Camp Sheridan, Wyoming Territory, as indications of the geographical spread where the lighter hats were worn in lieu of the black wool ones. J.F. Rodgers,to C.W. Foster, January 25, 1886, ibid.; and J.F. Rodgers to Depot Quartermaster St. Louis, October 26, 1886; and J.F. Rodgers to Chief Quartermaster Military Division of the Missouri, October 26, 1886, Vol. 3, 1886, ibid. Orders for the following year also remained consistent in that some 500 drab campaign hats were sent to the cavalry rendezvous at Jefferson Barracks, Missouri. There were 100 of size 2, 150 of size 3, and 50 of the remaining sizes 1, 4, 5, and 6. J.F. Rodgers to M.I. Ludington, April 19, 1887, Vol. 1, 1887, ibid. Several other orders for drab hats were filled for troops in the Department of Texas and other locations, too. When a certain decline in quality was observed, inspections resulted in improvement the campaign drab hats. S.B. Holabird to M.I. Ludington, November 22, 1887, Vol. 3, 1887, ibid.

198 Cir. No. 4, HQA, May 10, 1886, extended the price reduction to all blouses and trousers of the old sizes.

199 *ARSW, 1886*, Vol. I, 506. The quartermaster general repeated that the trousers adopted on January 16, 1884 were "equal in very respect both as to quality and make to those now being made" except for the fact that the kersey was a lighter shade of blue. He therefore requested that the secretary of war "as a matter or economy" require commanders to issue these trousers "before drawing or issuing any of the darker shade." S.B. Holabird to Secretary of War, February 6, 1886, LS, Clothing Br., Vol. 1, 1886, OQMG, RG92, NA.

200 That summer an order for recruits was made up of mounted trousers from heavy in the old sizes for recruits, and dismounted versions of the old sizes were supplied as well for foot troops. J.F. Rodgers to C.W. Foster, June 5, 1886; and B.C. Card to C.W. Foster, July 7, 1886, ibid. .

201 B.C. Card to M.I. Ludington, July 7, 1886, Vol. 1, 1886; and J.F. Rodgers to M.I. Ludington, August 16, 1886, Vol. 3, 1886, ibid.

202 J.F. Rodgers to M.I. Ludington, May 19, 1886, Vol. 1, 1886, ibid.

203 J.F. Rodgers to R.N. Batchelder, July 10, 1886, Vol. 3, 1886, ibid.

204 S.B. Holabird to M.I. Ludington; and S.B. Holabird to R. Saxton, July 10, 1886, ibid. Toward the end of 1886 a call for 500 cavalry and 4000 infantry overcoats, as well as 500 pairs of mounted trousers, and 1,000 dismounted trousers, both in the heavy weight kersey, were to be made at Philadelphia all of the "latest shades" and of the "latest patterns." This characterized Holabird's desire for the newer articles of wear to be ready for distribution in early 1887. J.F. Rodgers to Depot Quartermaster Philadelphia, November 24, 1886, ibid.

205 Holabird to M.I. Ludington; and J.F. Rodgers to W.B. Franklin, November 5, 1886, Vol. 2, 1886., ibid.

206 *ARSW, 1886*, Vol. I, 509. Among some of the first articles supplied were 144 pairs of cotton stockings, 17 drab campaign hats, and a like number of canvas blouses and trousers. Other issue items would be furnished later, but for the most part the earliest provisions were for specialty materials not in the Quartermaster Department's usual sphere, such as 600 yards of calico for women's dresses and 250 yards of the same type of cloth for girls' dresses, along with 33 pairs of women's shoes and 29 pairs of children's shoes. Another 600 yards of canton flannel was to be purchased for underclothing. J.F. Rodgers to M.I. Ludington, July 11, 1886; J.F. Rodgers to Chief Quartermaster Military Division of the Atlantic, July 14, 1886; J.F. Rodgers to M.I. Ludington, July 14, 1886, Vol. 3, 1886; and S.B. Holabird to Secretary of War, December 23, 1886, Vol. 2, 1886, LS, Clothing Br., OQMG, RG92, NA.

207 The blouses based on the new flannel were distributed as sealed pattern pieces and sent to the depots at Washington, DC, Philadelphia, Jeffersonville, and San Francisco. J.F. Rodgers to R.N. Batchelder; J.F. Rodgers to M.I. Ludington; J.F. Rodgers to R. Saxton; and J.F. Rodgers to G.H. Weeks, March 12, 1886, ibid.

208 S.B. Holabird to R. Saxton, March 6, 1886, ibid.

209 S.B. Holabird to C.W. Foster, April 9, 1886, Vol. 1, 1886, ibid.

210 S.B. Holabird to C.W. Foster, April 10, 1886, Vol. 2, 1886, ibid.

211 S.B. Holabird to C.W. Foster, May 10, 1886, Vol. 3, 1886, ibid.

212 J.F. Rodgers to M.I. Ludington, December 20, 1886, ibid. The remainder of the 1,216 gray flannel shirts in stock at St. Louis were being sent to Jeffersonville to be converted into blouse lining. J.F. Rodgers to R. Saxton; and J.F. Rodgers to C.W. Foster, February 1, 1887, Vol. 1, 1887, ibid. Besides the surplus shirts, gray lining flannel was still in stock, but the quartermaster general thought these goods "to be rather courser in grade than the standard sample," although he revealed that this did not cause him any real apprehension in that he reveled "little if any of this kind of flannel will be hereafter purchased." S.B. Holabird to M.I. Ludington, January 3, 1887, ibid. In fact, approval to change the color of the blouse lining from gray to blue came early in the next year with the publication of Specification No. 180, February 25, 1887. S.B. Holabird to M.I. Ludington, February 25, 1887, ibid.

213 *ARSW, 1886*, Vol. I, 505. As early as May 1886, the quartermaster general called for the purchase of 6,500 one hundred yard spools of machine silk thread, and four samples of blouses sewn with this thread were to be shipped to Jeffersonville. Because silk would be used to make blouses in the future, new specifications had to be written, and new standard samples made up, with four sets being required at the outset for approval by the quartermaster general. S.B. Holabird to M.I. Ludington, May 22, 1886, LS, Clothing Br., Vol. 2, 1886, OQMG, RG92, NA. Some complaints about the quality of linen thread used for sewing clothing also had been raised. This prompted cotton thread to be tested instead to see if this would be a better product. J.F. Rodgers to R. Saxton, February 15, 1887, Vol. 1, 1887, ibid.

214 W.B. Hughes to Depot Quartermaster Washington, DC; S.B. Holabird to M.I. Ludington; S.B. Holabird to G.H. Weeks, S.B. Holabird to R. Saxton, August 30, 1886, Vol. 3, 1886, ibid.

215 W.B. Hughes to Superintendent General Recruiting Service, September 1, 1886, Vol. 1, 1886, ibid.

216 J.F. Rodgers to C.W. Foster, September 16, 1886, Vol. 3, 1886, ibid.

217 J.F. Rodgers to Chief Quartermaster Division of the Pacific, February 3, 1886, Vol. 1, 1886, ibid.

218 J.F. Rodgers to G.H. Weeks, November 20, 1886, Vol. 3, 1886, ibid. As such Cir. No. 4, HQA, May 10, 1886, stated: "With a view to absorb the trousers and blouses, old sizes, on hand at posts, the reduction in price sanctioned in Circular No. 2, current series, from this office, is extended to all the sizes of the articles of clothing referred to.—[*Decision Sec. War, letter Apr. 24, 86—1740 A.G.O., 1886.*]

219 J.F. Rodgers to M.I. Ludington, November 9, 1886, LS, Clothing Br., Vol. 2, 1886, OQMG, RG92, NA. This letter further directed that trousers were to be used "regardless whether they are provided with shank buttons or not." Evidently not all the 1884 trial pairs with these rivet-like suspender and fly buttons that were akin to those still used on some modern "blue jeans" had not been distributed in toto. *ARSW, 1886*, Vol. I, 614.

220 J.F. Rodgers to M.I. Ludington, October 9, 1886, LS, Clothing Br., Vol. 1, 1886, OQMG, RG92, NA. Cloth also continued to be provided for lining capes as evidenced by a typical order to complete a great coat for a hospital steward and a post quartermaster sergeant respectively at Ft. Missoula, Montana Territory. J.F. Rodgers to Philadelphia Depot Quartermaster, October 26, 1886, Vol. 3, 1886, ibid.

221 J.G. Chandler to M.I. Ludington; and J.G. Chandler to Depot Quartermaster Philadelphia, October 13, 1886, ibid; Also see J.F. Rodgers to St. Louis Depot Quartermaster; and J.F. Rodgers to Philadelphia Depot Quartermaster, November 9, 1886, Vol. 2, 1886, ibid.

222 J.F. Rodgers to M.I. Ludington, October 13, 1886, Vol. 1, 1886; and J.F. Rodgers to St. Louis Depot Quartermaster, November 9, 1886, LS, Clothing Br., Vol. 2, 1886, ibid. Furthermore, a telegram instructed Major Foster in St. Louis to dispatch "all serviceable light shade overcoats, made and unmade, on hand, except those for infantry, with detachable capes." J.G. Chandler to C.W. Foster, October 13, 1886, Vol. 1, 1886, ibid.

223 J.F. Rodgers to Chief Quartermaster Military Division of the Missouri, September 30, 1886, Vol. 3, 1886, ibid.

224 S.B. Holabird to M.I. Ludington, January 3, 1887, Vol. 1, 1887, ibid. During the previous spring the quartermaster general had allowed an overrun of sky-blue kersey to be procured from Lewis Bros. & Co., which would differ from cloth made by other contractors. This was a necessity, although one not wholly embraced. S.B. Holabird to Secretary of War, March 9, 1886, Vol. 1, 1886, ibid. The approval from the secretary of war to buy the 442 yards of 6/4 heavy sky-blue kersey from Lewis Bros. was obtained. S.B. Holabird to M.I. Ludington, March 15, 1886, Vol. 1, 1886, ibid.

225 J.F. Rodgers to Superintendent General Recruiting Service, January 9, 1886, ibid.

226 Chief Quartermaster Military Department of California to Post Adjutant, Presidio of San Francisco, LR, April 8, 1887 to January 11, 1888, RUSACC, RG393, NA. Circular No. 1, HQA, February 3, 1887, extended this practice to "all obsolete coat facings, chevrons, and stripes" so that further action could be taken. Further, Cir. No. 1, HQA, February 3, 1887, used identical verbiage requiring every supply point to send back these same materials to the depots that served them so that these ar ticles could be inspected and proper actions taken. For examples of excess clothing being reported by this date review returns from Fort Wadsworth, New York; Ft. Robinson, Nebraska; Ft. Laramie, Wyoming Territory; and Ft. Davis, Texas see, G.N. Whistler to Chief Quartermaster Department of the East, June 30, 1886, Vol. 1,

1886; J.F. Rodgers to Chief Quartermaster Military Division of the Missouri, July 17, 1886; and W.B. Hughes to St. Louis Depot Quartermaster, September 9, 1886, LS, Clothing Br., Vol. 1, 1886, OQMG, RG92, NA, respectively.

227 S.B. Holabird to Secretary of War, December 20, 1886, Vol. 3, 1886, ibid.; and S.B. Holabird to AGUSA, July 24, 1886, Vol. 4, 1886, ibid. This did not mean that the gold lace chevrons were not available. For instance, instructions to send 150 pairs of gold lace service stripes, 74 pairs of first sergeants of artillery cloth chevrons, 10 pairs sergeants, 3 commissary sergeants, 7 hospital stewards, grey and green facing cloth, and other items were given to fulfill an order to the National Home for Disabled Volunteers. S.B. Holabird to M.I. Ludington, March 27, 1886, Vol. 1, 1886, ibid. The president of home received a response in March. J.F. Rodgers to W.B. Franklin, March 27, 1886, ibid. See also J.F. Rodgers to M.I. Ludington; and J.F. Rodgers to Chief Quartermaster Military Division of the Missouri, January 26, 1886, Vol. 2, 1886, ibid., for another example of ongoing orders of gold lace

228 *ARSW, 1887*, Vol. I, 512, repeated the restrictions placed on issuance of these chevrons, which could be stripped of their gold and the resultant product sold by some enlisted bent on adding a small increase to their pay.

229 S.B. Holabird to Chief Signal Officer, January 21, 1886, LS, Clothing Br., Vol. 1, 1886, OQMG, RG92, NA.

230 J.F. Rodgers to M.I. Ludington, January 26, 1886, Vol. 2, 1886, ibid. GO No. 18, HQA, February 16, 1889, and *Regulations for the Army of the United States 1889* (Washington, DC: Government Printing Office, 1889), 209-10, both announced the change from orange to black and white for Signal Corps, but according to Emerson, *Chevrons*, 64 and 94, the issue was not immediate, nor was a torch added in the specifications until 1891.

231 *ARSW*, 1886, Vol I, 508.

232 S.B. Holabird to M.I. Ludington, January 31, 1887, LS, Clothing Br., Vol. 1, 1887, OQMG, RG92, NA. S.B. Holabird to M.I. Ludington, February 5, 1887, ibid. The Quartermaster Department was to furnish field musicians their instruments as well and regulations were to be revised to reflect this point. S.B. Holabird to AGUSA, February 5, 1887, ibid.

233 J.F. Rodgers to M.I. Ludington, January 29, 1886, ibid. Two dress coats were altered in response and held for several months at the quartermaster general's office before being returned to Philadelphia, but the two "cellulized collars" that came with them were kept in Washington for a while longer. J.F. Rodgers to M.I. Ludington, November 24, 1886, Vol. 3, 1886, ibid.

234 S.B. Holabird to Secretary of War, November 24, 1886, ibid.

235 S.B. Holabird to Secretary of War, November 24, 1886, ibid. The two-man committee was constituted many months after the secretary of war had decided the new edition should be published, as one of the earliest references to the venture demonstrated. S.B. Holabird to AGUSA, January 21, 1886, Vol. 1, 1886, ibid. Also see, *ARSW, 1887*, Vol. I, 511.

236 *ARSW, 1886*, Vol. I, 510. J.F. Rodgers to C.B. Kohan, October 11, 1886, LS, Clothing Br., Vol. 1, 1886; and J.F. Rodgers to E.A. Armstrong, March 24, 1886, Vol, 2, 1886, OQMG, RG92, NA, repeated that the 1882 edition was no longer correct as the many changes in and additions made to the uniform of officers and had been added since the tome's release. Kohan was with the Boston *Courier*.
The journalist was not the only one asking questions about the uniform. Previously General Sherman had inquired whether the Quartermaster Department could furnish color illustrations of "various kinds of shoulder straps (natural size) and perhaps of Epaulettes of any Kind of Military trimmings, from Lieutenant up to General." Nothing like this was available and Ludington was tasked to look into obtain such a rendering. J.F. Rodgers to M.I. Ludington, January 31, 1885, Vol. 2, 1885, ibid.

237 As one example of the need to update the old uniform book published by the Quartermaster Department, which was no longer available, nor accurate, one military outfitter was supplied with a copy of current regulations. J.F. Rodgers to C.C. Dittrich & Co., March 15, 1887, Vol. 1, 1887, ibid. Later, when another firm asked for a copy of the new uniform book, the reply came that the book had not been produced as yet. When it was, the company would be so informed in order to obtain one. J.F. Rodgers to Browning, King and Company, January 7, 1887, ibid.

238 S.B. Holabird to M.I. Ludington, January 21, 1886, ibid. The last requirement must have referred to incorporating portraits of actual general officers into the art work judging from a request for a current picture of Lieutenant General Sheridan, and other solicitations for pictures of the adjutant general and inspector general. J.F. Rodgers to M.I. Ludington, March 5, 1886; and April 3, 1886, ibid. It should be noted that there had been two styles of shoulder straps for a "General of the Army". Those worn by Grant bore four silver stars on a dark blue field. J.F. Rodgers to Professor G. Brown Grode, March 29, 1887, Vol. 1, 1887, ibid. Sherman, when he succeeded his old comrade as general of the army, after Grant's election as president, ultimately had straps that displayed two silver stars flanking the arms of the United States.

239 S.B. Holabird to W.W. Phelps, January 25, 1886, ibid. Phelps, who was a member of the House of Representatives also was told that the 1882 work was no longer accurate.

240 J.F. Rodgers to M.I. Ludington, February 1, 1886, ibid.

241 S.B. Holabird to M.I. Ludington, February 8, 1886, Vol, 2, 1886, ibid.

242 S.B. Holabird to IGUSA, February 18, 1886, ibid.

243 *ARSW, 1886*, Vol. I, 510-11. J.F. Rodgers to S.R. Smith, August 2, 1886, Vol. 2, 1886; and J.F. Rodgers to Girat Gadchot, August 4, 1886, Vol. 3, 1886, LS, Clothing Br., OQMG, RG92, NA, indicated that the pamphlet included the uniform regulations of 1885, and subsequent updates to that time. Smith was the adjutant general of Connecticut, and his request for such information was indicative of a growing movement by state guards to follow the lead of the Regular Army in its uniform, insignia, and other aspects. Also see S.B. Holabird to IGUSA, January 6, 1886, Vol. 2, 1886, ibid., relative to the need for a pamphlet to answer such questions as one posed by members of Allien Co. as to the wearing of plumes and cords by infantry officers and enlisted men. J.F. Rodgers to M.I. Ludington, January 20, 1886, Vol 2, 1886; and August 16, 1886, Vol. 3, 1886, ibid., discuss illustrations for the specification volume, the later piece of correspondence underscoring that it was not required to depict sealskin caps and gauntlets, nor canvas lined Miles pattern over coats, because all these items no longer were regulation.

244 Rodgers to M.I. Ludington, October 18, Wol. 3, 1886, ibid.

245 S.B. Holabird to M.I. Ludington, April 2, 1886, Vol 2, 1886, ibid.

246 See for example, J.F. Rodgers to M.I. Ludington, February 15, 1887, Vol. 1, 1887; J.F. Rodgers to R.A. Mattison; J.F. Rodgers to Michael Myers; S.B. Holabird to W.B. Hazen; J.F. Rodgers to Charles Heckman; S.B. Holabird to James Stewart; S.B. Holabird to J.R. West; S.B. Holabird to Mrs. Captain Landers, June 14, 1886, Vol. 2, 1886; B.C. Card to M.I. Ludington, August 12, 1886, Vol. 3, 1886; J.F. Rodgers to J.D. Cox, April 7, 1887; J.F. Rodgers to Chief Signal Officer, April 13, 1887, Vol. 1, 1887; J.F. Rodgers to M.I. Ludington, April 2, 1887; J.F. Rodgers to Adjutant General State of New York, April 2, 1887; J.F. Rodgers to J.H. Guilding, April 2, 1887; J.F. Rodgers to M.I. Ludington, April 22, 1887, Vol. 2, 1887; J.F. Rodgers to M.I. Ludington, September 23, 1887, Vol. 3; and J.F. Rodgers to M.I. Ludington, October 7, 1887, ibid. Adding an index to the flag publication with the names of commanders and the similar details also was approved. J.F. Rodgers to M.I. Ludington, January 21, 1887, Vol. 1, 1887, ibid. The Government Printing Office was to undertake the printing of the index for the designating flag book. These would be bound into the book of color prints being produced by Burk and Fertridge. S.B. Holabird to M.I. Ludington, February 10, 1887, Vol. 2, 1887, ibid.

247 *ARSW, 1886*, Vol. I, 510.

248 S.B. Holabird to Surgeon General of the Army, February 1, 1887, LS, Clothing Br., Vol. 1, 1887, OQMG, RG92, NA.

249 *A&NJ*, August 18, 1888, 1115. Earlier the periodical had been supportive of universal issuance of summer helmets, regardless of the location of the garrison. Ibid., July 25, 1885, 1059.

250 *ARSW, 1886*, Vol. I, 510.

251 J.F. Rodgers to Washington, DC Depot Quartermaster, November 22, 1887, LS, Clothing Br., Vol. 3, 1887, OQMG, RG92, NA.

252 S.B. Holabird to D.S. Stanley, November 22, 1887, ibid.

253 *ARSW, 1888*, Vol. I, 526-7.

254 J.F. Rodgers to Philadelphia Depot Quartermaster, April 4, 1887, LS, Clothing Br., Vol. 2, 1887, OQMG, RG92, NA. Besides these trial items, standard stable frocks and mounted overalls were to be provided from Jeffersonville for Texas garrisons at San Antonio, Camp Del Rio, Camp Pena Colorado, Ft. Clark, Ft. Davis, Ft. Hancock, and Ft. McIntosh. J.F. Rodgers to Depot Quartermaster Jeffersonville, April 4, 1887, ibid. Moreover, summer helmets, drab campaign hats, and canvas fatigue coats with trousers were to be supplied to these same garrisons. J.F. Rodgers to St. Louis Depot Quartermaster, April 4, 1887, ibid. For comparative orders for all categories of clothing destined to posts in Dakota Territory, Montana Territory, and Wyoming Territory see, S.B. Holabird to M.I. Ludington, April 12, 1887, ibid. It also is notable that duck was purchased rather than drilling for stable frocks and overalls, as part of this ongoing effort to provide lightweight, durable outfits. S.B. Holabird to M.I. Ludington, August 24, 1887, Vol. 3, 1887, ibid.

255 J.F. Rodgers to M.I. Ludington, August 26, 1886, ibid. In another case Brigadier General Holabird expressed his opinion to Colonel Hamilton that Circular No. 11 of 1884 prohibited enlisted men from wearing a spike with their summer helmet, but not officers. That interpretation, however, was not final in that the Quartermaster Department exercised no supervision over the uniforms for officers of the Army." The Inspector General's Department had the ultimate say in this realm. S.B. Holabird to J. Hamilton, August 9, 1886, Vol. 1, 1886, ibid. During the prior year, "40 white helmets with trappings" were sold to Company A of the Arizona National Guard. While the other ranks serving in the regulars were to have plain summer helmets, that was evidently not the case for certain national guardsmen. S.B. Holabird to Secretary of War, September 12, 1885, Vol. 4, 1885, ibid. This was but one example of the department providing items to the national guard, a practice that increased considerably during the late 1880s. For other instances see S.B. Holabird to Secretary of War, September 12, 1885, ibid., for a request to borrow camp kettles and mess pans for an encampment being held in the Dakotas, and also see, J.F. Rodgers to S. Brown, February 19, 1885, Vol. 2, 1885, ibid., relative to the purchase of overcoat chevrons by the Fifth Maryland Infantry.

256 This decision was apparent from a response made to an order for the prison guard at Ft. Leavenworth. Instead of fur caps, cloth ones were to be sent. W.B. Hughes to Chief Quartermaster Military Division of the Missouri, September 4, 1886, Vol. 3, 1886; and in J.F. Rodgers to Chief Quartermaster Department of the East, January 8, 1886, Vol. 2, ibid.

257 J.F. Rodgers to Chief Quartermaster Department of Dakota, February 16, 1886, Vol. 2, 1886, ibid.

258 *ARSW, 1886*, Vol. I, 505.

259 J.G. Chandler to M.I. Ludington, May 28, 1886, LS, Clothing Br., Vol. 2, 1886, OQMG, RG92, NA. Several prototypes were provided, but sample no. 4 was selected as the new standard. Nevertheless, none of the new style were to be made until later. This was because the fiscal year was drawing to a close, and funds were limited. S.B. Holabird to Chief Quartermaster Department of Dakota, May 12, 1886,

ibid. That situation did not preclude specifications from being adopted and standard sealed models being made for shipment to the various depots in late June. S.B. Holabird to M.I. Ludington; S.B. Holabird to R. Saxton; ad S.B. Holabird to G.H. Weeks, June 22, 1886, ibid.

260 Even though certain restrictions were in force as far as canvas coats and trousers were concerned, permission to make up 1,000 pairs of canvas mittens was given later in 1886. S.B. Holabird to R. Saxton, October 22, 1886, Vol. 4, 1886, ibid.

261 *ARSW, 1886*, Vol. I, 505-6.

262 S.B. Holabird to AGUSA February 13, 1886, LS, Clothing Br., Vol. 1, 1886, OQMG, RG92, NA.

263 GO No. 46, HQA, July 7, 1886.

264 S.B. Holabird to A.C. Wildrick, July 16, 1886, LS, Clothing Br., Vol. 3, 1886, OQMG, RG92, NA.

265 J.F. Rodgers to C.W. Foster; and J.F. Rodgers to Chief Quartermaster Military Division of the Missouri, January 3, 1886, Vol. 1, 1886; J.F. Rodgers to F.H. Hathaway, April 24, 1886, Vol. 2, 1886; J.F. Rodgers to Chief Quartermaster Military Division of the Missouri, April 30, 1886, ibid; and W.B. Hughes to St. Louis Depot Quartermaster, September 4, 1886, Vol. 3, ibid.
The issue of muskrat caps in lieu of canvas caps when called for, would result in a charge of $1.15 each for the former headgear. It was noted "the officers and men prefer the fur cap and as the latter are cheaper it would be in the interest of economy to permit their being used." S.B. Holabird to Secretary of War, January 31, 1887, Vol. 1, 1887, ibid. As an aside, one of the last purchases of the buffalo coats had been made from M. Freytag of Chicago. J.F. Rodgers to Orville Nave, October 7, 1887, Vol. 1, 1886, Vol. 3, 1886, ibid. An order for the Department of Missouri called for fur caps in lieu of canvas hoods per the blanket permission of the secretary of war to do so when troops preferred the muskrat headgear. S.B. Holabird to C.W. Foster, June 27, 1887, Vol. 1, 1887, ibid. Later, fur caps and gloves were permitted for wear at the ordnance proving ground located at Sandy Hook, New Jersey. J.F. Rodgers to C.C. Morrison, December 5, 1887, Vol. 3, 1887, ibid. Likewise, fur caps and drab campaign hats that had been provided from Philadelphia would be deducted from a larger order placed with St. Louis for the various posts within the Department of Texas. J.F. Rodgers to Philadelphia Depot Quartermaster; and J.F. Rodgers to St. Louis Depot Quartermaster, December 2, 1887, ibid. Canvas hoods were provided to other posts simultaneously with fur caps, as demonstrated by several orders during the period including one for thirty-five canvas hoods slated for Ft. Abraham Lincoln, Dakota Territory. J.F. Rodgers to St. Louis Depot Quartermaster, December 21, 1887, Vol. 3, 1887, ibid.
Another alternative for cold weather—remaining Miles overcoats—did not seem to be an option, the few existing examples of these being turned in and presumably disposed of by sale or other means rather than being sent on to the troops, who seemed less than enthusiast with these trial garments. J.F. Rodgers to Chief Quartermaster Military Division of the Missouri; and J.F. Rodgers to Quartermaster St. Louis Depot, July 14, 1886, Vol. 1, 1886, ibid., notes for instance that twenty-five Miles overcoats were being turned in as surplus clothing from Ft. Bennett, Dakota Territory, along with ten cap bugles and twenty pairs of brass screwed shoes size 5 and another pair in size 16.

266 J.F. Rodgers to G.H. Weeks, January 7, 1886, Vol. 1, 1886; J.F. Rodgers to R.N. Batchelder, April 3, 1886, ibid; S.B. Holabird to Chief Quartermaster Department of the East, April 16, 1886, Vol. 2; and J.G. Chandler to M.I. Ludington, August 16, 1886, ibid.

267 *ARSW, 1887*, Vol. I, 511.

268 Some 5,000 sets of fatigue coats and trousers, however, were called for in the fiscal year 1887 to be made at Jeffersonville, along with 1,000 pairs of canvas gauntlets, 10,000 flannel shirts, and 18,000 blouses. S.B. Holabird to Secretary of War, April 24, 1886, LS, Clothing Br., Vol. 2, 1886, OQMG, RG92, NA. As an aside, unmade dark blue flannel shirts were to be charged to the enlisted men at $1.75 each. S.B. Holabird to J. Fornance, February 16, 1886, ibid.

269 J.F. Rodgers to Secretary of War, April 17, 1886, ibid.

270 ARSW, 1886, Vol. I, 508. J.G. Chandler to M.I. Ludington; J.G. Chandler to R. Saxton; and J.G. Chandler to G.H. Weeks, October 13, 1886, LS, Clothing Br., Vol. 1, 1886, OQMG, RG92, NA.

271 J.F. Rodgers to M.I. Ludington, January 7, 1886, ibid.

272 specifications for silesia and Italian cloth for those adopted on May 8, 1884, were announced in April 1886. S.B. Holabird to M.I. Ludington; S.B. Holabird to R. Saxton; S.B. Holabird to G.H. Weeks, April 16, 1886, Vol. 3, 1886, ibid. The new dark flannel specifications and a change in forage cap standards were noted by the quartermaster general in S.B. Holabird to M.I. Ludington; S.B. Holabird to R. Saxton; S.B. Holabird to G.H. Weeks, April 13, 1886, Vol. 1, 1886; S.B. Holabird to IGUSA, April 15, 1886; and June 8, 1886, Vol. 2, 1886, ibid.

273 Specifications were adopted as early as March 24, 1885, but standards had not be prepared and accepted until July 1, 1886. J.F. Rodgers to M.I. Ludington, July 1, 1886; and July 15, 1886, Vol. 1, 1886, ibid. Earlier in the year, however, 107 sets of five-eighth inch piping was shipped for engineer troops at Willets Point, New York. J.F. Rodgers to M.I. Ludington; and J.F. Rodgers to J.L. Lusk, January 11, 1886, ibid. It was not clear whether this material was for the battalion band, or for to be used for the trouser stripes of non-commissioned officers.

274 *ARSW, 1886*, Vol. I, 511.

275 J.F. Rodgers to A.P. Blunt, March 26, 1886, LS, Clothing Br., Vol. 2, 1886, OQMG, RG92, NA.

276 *ARSW, 1886*, Vol. I, 511. A slight adjustment also was made to light weight kersey, with the addition that the wool "must be one half blood" added to the requirement for contractors. S.B. Holabird to M.I. Ludington, April 20, 1886, LS, Clothing Br., Vol. 2, 1886, OQMG, RG92, NA.

277 The quartermaster general sent two letters regarding this subject to Philadelphia on the same day. See, S.B. Holabird to M.I. Ludington, January 4, 1886, ibid. This information was repeated in *ARSW, 1886*, Vol. I, 510.

278 S.B. Holabird to AGUSA, July 10, 1886, LS, Clothing Br., Vol. 3, 1886, OQMG, RG92, NA.

279 S.B. Holabird to AGUSA, January 29, 1886, Vol. 1, 1886, ibid.

280 After shoulder straps for the infantry were to be changed from blue to white, sample cards and the samples of officers' cap insignia likewise were to be corrected in those instances where the specimens were not strictly in conformance to the regulations, especially those for the Adjutant General's Department and the Signal Corps. J.F. Rodgers to M.I. Ludington March 15, 1887, Vol. 1, 1887, ibid.

281 S.B. Holabird to AGUSA, March 5, 1886, Vol. 1, 1886, ibid. If embroidery reacted adversely with inexpensive facing material, there was one means that would have eliminated this situation at least for shoulder straps. The use of pressed metal simulated borders and insignia in lieu of bullion had been introduced with the Smith patent shoulder straps of the Civil War. The same types of straps saw some use in the late Victorian era, but the real reason for this was the inexpensive nature of such straps that could be used in the field, especially during the Spanish American War. This still did not answer the question as to how to keep the white backings for shoulder straps from becoming soiled and thereby rendered unwearable. One method evidently was to employ a white enameled cloth field that "was easy to keep clean." Jacques Noel Jacobsen, Jr., *Military Antiques and Memorabilia Catalog 98* (Fall 1999), 19, depicts a pair of infantry captain's shoulder straps of this type. For more on James Smith's metallic straps consult, Howard G. Lanham, *Straps: The Evolution of United States Army Shoulder Straps* (Westminster, MD: Howard G. Lanham, 1998), 41-3.

282 S.B. Holabird to M.I. Ludington, March 16, 1886, LS, Clothing Br., Vol. 2, 1886, OQMG, 92, NA. The linings for enlisted infantry overcoat capes, however, remained dark blue and would not change. J.F. Rodgers to S. Cutchins, November 18, 1887, Vol. 3, 1887, ibid. There was one exception. In the early 1890s a brief, limited trial of white lined capes for enlisted men was undertaken, but soon abandoned.

283 S.B. Holabird to M.I. Ludington, March 27, 1886, Vol. 2, 1886, ibid.

284 S.B. Holabird to Chief Quartermaster Military Division of the Missouri, March 2, 1886, ibid. This exchange was the result of a request for fifty yards of white facing material for sale to officers at Ft. Lincoln, Dakota Territory. J.F. Rodgers to M.I. Ludington, March 2, 1886, ibid., repeated the quartermaster general's consent to provide trouser stripes and cape lining flannel to officers, this time as a reply for the articles from Ft. Douglas, Utah Territory. The practice was extended to all infantry officers. It is noteworthy that infantry officers continued to wear leg stripes of facing material, whereas non-commissioned officers were to have webbing, a differentiation that lasted for a short period until the return to the former fabric later in the decade. Consideration was given, however, to making officers' trouser stripes of either silk or linen webbing in that the quartermaster general requested one and one-half inch samples to be made of each for examination. J.F. Rodgers to M.I. Ludington, January 27, 1886, Vol. 1, 1886, ibid.
Even as stripes of facing material were settled upon for officers, contracts for white linen webbing were being let for enlisted men. For instance, 200 yards of one inch width was bought from Horstmann according to S.B. Holabird to M.I. Ludington, October 18, 1886, Vol. 3, 1886, ibid.
Some other representative contracts for 1886 included 20,000 yards of blouse flannel and 15,000 yards of gray blouse lining from B.Y. Pippey; 130,000 yards of Canton flannel from Thos. G. Hood; 800 aiguilettes and shoulder knots for bandsmen, 2,000 white metal trouser strap buckles, 20,000 forage caps, 1,000 quartermaster sergeants' pen and key devices, 1,000 hospital steward caduceus devices, 1,250 helmet cords and bands, 1,800 yards of facing cloth, 5,000 yards of mohair cord, and 16,000 yards of white linen webbing, all the last items coming from Horstmann. S.B. Holabird to M.I. Ludington, May 27, 1886, Vol. 1, 1886, ibid. Yet a second order featured 5,000 yards of dark blue fine quality flannel from the San Francisco Pioneer Woolen Factory; 50 large music pouches and 65 small from Henry V. Allien; 100 trumpet cords and 10 cavalry standards from Horstmann; and 5 artillery standards from C.A. Hart of Philadelphia. S.B. Holabird to M.I. Ludington, August 20, 1886, Vol. 3, 1886, ibid. For contract items bound for San Francisco see, S.B. Holabird to G.H. Weeks, June 4, 1886, Vol. 2, 1886, ibid.

285 S.B. Holabird to Secretary of War, January 14, 1886, ibid.

286 B.C. Card to Chief Quartermaster Division of the Pacific, August 12, 1886, Vol 3, ibid. In this climate of opinion, it is not surprising that Lieutenant William Lassiter of the Sixteenth U.S. Infantry, who wanted to acquire dark blue cloth for sale to officers on invoice rather than making a cash payment in advance, was informed that his request was denied. J.F. Rodgers to M.I. Ludington, January 14, 1886, Vol. 2, 1886, ibid.

287 S.B. Holabird to M.I. Ludington, May, 18, 1886, ibid.

288 J.F. Rodgers to First Lieutenant C.F. Roe, January 14, 1886, ibid.

289 During 1886, Howard Ackerman's New York firm had provided a sample of a new style forage cap for officers along with two officers coats, and a pair of trousers. He wanted these prototypes returned to him that. Captain Rodgers inquired as to whether these items of officers' wear were at Philadelphia. J.F. Rodgers to M.I. Ludington, January 17, 1887, Vol. 1, 1887, ibid. Rodgers also asked for a description of the cap and trousers to facilitate the search. J.F. Rodgers to Howard Ackerman, January 17, 1887, ibid.

290 J.R. Rodgers to Raymold & Whitlock, March 15, 1886, Vol. 1, 1886, ibid.

291 J.F. Rodgers to Supervising Architect of the Treasury, March 26, 1886, Vol. 2, 1886, ibid.

292 S.B. Holabird to M.I. Ludington, April 2, 1886, Vol. 3, 1886, ibid. Similarly, Holabird provided the chief of engineers with a photograph of the forage cap insignia for engineers. S.B. Holabird to Chief of Engineers, April 2, 1886, ibid.

293 S.B. Holabird to IGUSA, April 2, 1886; and April 15, 1886, Vol. 2, 1886, ibid.

294 S.B. Holabird to Shannon, Miller & Crane, April 22, 1886, ibid.

295 S.B. Holabird to Chief Signal Officer July 1, 1886, Vol. 1, 1886. ibid.

296 J.F. Rodgers to M.I. Ludington, February 11, 1887, ibid.

297 J.F. Rodgers to Colonel Edward H. Baker, March 15, 1887, ibid.

298 John P. Langellier and Alan M. Osur, *Chaplain Allen Allensworth and the Twenty-fourth U.S. Infantry, 1886-1906* (Tucson: Tucson Corral of the Westerners, 1980), 194.

299 A c. 1890 photograph of Thomas W. Barry, post chaplain at Ft. Riley, Kansas, demonstrated that at least this military clergyman ignored regulations, and added a chapeau de bras to his block frock coat.

300 S.B. Holabird to M.I. Ludington, April 22, 1887, LS, Clothing Br., Vol. 2, 1887, OQMG, RG92, NA.

301 These hats were to be of the same shape as the enlisted 1883-pattern drab campaign hat, and made of "black felt, composed of best coney and fine blown nutria." They were to have a sweat leather measuring two and one-quarter inches wide, and a three inch brim "all around, edged trimmed with narrow black silk braid. Black shade, and 5-3/4 inches deep to center of tip." There was to be no ventilator and the weight was to be four ounces. J.F. Rodgers to A.W. Corliss, May 15, 1888, Vol. 1, 1888, ibid. The hat was also to have a band (ribbon) attached to the base of the crown. J.F. Rodgers to Philadelphia Depot Quartermaster, June 7, 1888, Vol. 2, 1888, ibid.

302 S.B. Holabird to M.I. Ludington, November 30, 1887, Vol. 3, 1887, ibid.

303 J.G. Chandler to IGUSA. December 13, 1887, ibid. In this endorsement, the quartermaster general's office expressed its support for the chief of engineer's proposal to change the castle design.

304 J.G. Chandler to M.I. Ludington; and J.G. Chandler to Secretary of War, December 15, 1887, ibid.

305 GO No. 29, HQA, May 5, 1888. The knots for ordnance officers, however, were to remain the same. J.F. Rodgers to Philadelphia Depot Quartermaster, January 4, 1888, LS, Clothing Br., Vol. 1, 1888, OQMG, RG92, NA.

306 J.F. Rodgers to M.I. Ludington, December 6, 1887, Vol. 3, 1887, ibid. The cap badge had been redesigned and an approved form selected just a few months earlier. J.F. Rodgers to M.I. Ludington, September 21, 1887, ibid.

307 J.F. Rodgers to M.I. Ludington, August 22, 1887; and August 31, 1887, ibid.

308 S.B. Holabird to M.I. Ludington, April 2, 1887, Vol. 2, 1887, ibid.

309 Rodenbough and Haskins, *The Army of the United States*, 97-8.

310 S.B. Holabird to J.R. Smith, May 26, 1887, LS, Clothing Br., Vol. 2, 1887, OQMG, RG92, NA.

311 J.F. Rodgers to M.I. Ludington, June 1, 1887, ibid.

312 J.F. Rodgers to M.I. Ludington, June 2, 1887, ibid. The surgeon general approved the side buttons and helmet plate overlay in late August, and it was pointed out that the forage cap badge and the cross for helmets were to be the same. J.F. Rodgers to M.I. Ludington, August 22, 1887, Vol. 1, 1887, ibid. J.F. Rodgers to Chief Quartermaster Division of the Atlantic, October 26, 1887, Vol. 3, 1887, ibid., emphasized that no wreaths were to be worn on the forage caps of acting hospital stewards or privates.

313 J.F. Rodgers to Chief Quartermaster Military Division of the Missouri, November 29, 1887, ibid.

314 Not until October, however, were the gold lace and cloth chevron sealed samples approved for hospital stewards and acting hospital stewards. J.F. Rodgers to M.I. Ludington, October 11, 1887, ibid.

315 J.F. Rodgers to M.I. Ludington, August 15, 1887; and S.B. Holabird to M.I. Ludington, August 15, 1887, Vol. 2, 1887, ibid. The prices were worked out by Ludington, and information likewise provided to demonstrate the increased cost when men from other branches were transferred to the Hospital Corps, and furnished their first year allowance gratis. The total for a hospital steward would be $14.06, for an acting hospital steward $14.15, and for a private, $9.52. The Quartermaster Department had no funds to make such free issue, therefore, the Medical Department would have to provide money to permit gratis issue, if the surgeon general desired to do so. J.F. Rodgers to M.I. Ludington; and S.B. Holabird to Surgeon General, October 13, 1887, Vol. 3, 1887, ibid. Another impact of the formation of the Hospital Corps was the return of items made obsolete by the adoption of a new uniform, such as old hospital stewards' wreaths and devices, and half chevrons. J.F. Rodgers to Philadelphia Depot Quartermaster, December 20, 1887, ibid.

316 From this chart it is clear that coats, blouses, and trousers for hospital stewards and acting hospital stewards were of more expensive cloth than those produced for privates. Further the labor to apply the cross to the collar of acting hospital stewards' coats made his garment slightly higher than for hospital stewards. The fact that hospital stewards and acting hospital stewards were to have coats and trousers of finer quality cloth was confirmed by S.B. Holabird to M.I. Ludington, October 20, 1887, ibid.

317 S.B. Holabird to Surgeon General, November 23, 1887, ibid. Some of these items were available by early September. B.C. Card to Chief Quartermaster Military Division of Missouri, September 9, 1887, Vol. 2, 1887 ibid., indicated dark blue foot pattern trousers with stripes for hospital stewards and acting hospital stewards could be supplied to fill orders. Further, J.F. Rodgers to M.I. Ludington; and J.F. Rodgers to Chief Quartermaster Military Division of the Missouri, November 19, 1887, Vol. 3, 1887, ibid., acknowledged an order for Ft. Riley, Kansas, consisting of one cap wreath, seven cap crosses, eight helmet crosses and a like number of pairs of side buttons, seven sets of facings for dress coats for privates and one set for an acting hospital steward, along with trousers, trouser stripes, and chevrons, were being readied for shipment. What is more, J.F. Rodgers to Philadelphia Depot Quartermaster, December 28, 1887, Vol. 2, 1887, ibid., transmitted, among other things, four pairs of side buttons, four eagle devices, and four forage cap insignia to Ft. McDermit, Nevada Territory, for the Hospital Corps. Finally, an order for ten sets of clothing for Hospital Corps privates was sent out, including trousers, blouses, and coats, bound for Jefferson Barracks, Missouri. J.F. Rodgers to Depot Quartermaster Philadelphia, December 31, 1887, ibid.

318 M.I. Ludington, August 15, 1887, Vol. 1, ibid.

319 S.B. Holabird to M.I. Ludington, November 16, 1887, Vol. 3, 1887, ibid. That same day Holabird sent Ludington another letter asking for recommendations that would embody "all the changes made in the several articles of Uniform up to date" and any thoughts he might have to make "the new regulations more complete and definite." Previously requirements to revise various aspects of the regulations had been addressed by letters from Captain Rodgers in August and October respectively. J.F. Rodgers to M.I.Ludington, August 15, 1887; and October 10, 1887, ibid. These were followed by permission to order 100 gross of large and 75 gross of small staff buttons of the pattern submitted by Ludington to Holabird on November 16. S.B. Holabird to M.I. Ludington, November 21, 1887, ibid. As a related aside, GO No. 74, HQA, October 8, 1886, stipulated that "Whenever it" proved "necessary to issue metallic buttons to the enlisted men of the Army, to replace such as may have been previously supplied with the garments," they were "to be issued upon the clothing receipt roll and charged upon the soldier's clothing account at sixteen cents per dozen for large and eight cents per dozen for small sizes."

320 S.B. Holabird to Chief Quartermaster, Department of Dakota, August 9, 1887; and J.F. Rodgers to Philadelphia Depot Quartermaster, December 9, 1887, LS, Clothing Br., Vol. 3, 1887, OQMG, RG92, NA. The later piece of correspondence revealed that linen webbing was still on hand and being supplied late into the year, and probably into the next year.

321 S.B. Holabird to M.I. Ludington; and S.B. Holabird to San Francisco Depot Quartermaster, August 24, 1887, ibid.

322 *U.S. Army Uniforms and Equipment, 1889*, 150; and *ARSW, 1887*, Vol. I, 515. Even before the standards had been officially announced, the department had procured some 5,000 collars from Horstmann at $.75 per dozen, and a like number at the same cost from Charles F. Grosholz, another Philadelphia firm. S.B. Holabird to M.I. Ludington, January 26, 1887, LS, Clothing Br., Vol. 2, 1887, OQMG, RG92, NA.

323 J.F. Rodgers to Superintendent of the Recruiting Service, August 23, 1887, ibid. Too many collars had been ordered for recruits assembling at Columbus Barracks, Ohio, and trousers of finer quality were ordered for them in error as well. The latter garments were for non-commissioned officers only. The same letter indicated that trousers in old sizes of the unmade variety were no longer available. Finally, barracks shoes were not to be sent as this footgear was not intended for issue to recruits.

324 S.B. Holabird to M.I. Ludington; S.B. Holabird to San Francisco Depot Quartermaster; S.B. Holabird to Jeffersonville Depot Quartermaster; and J.F. Rodgers to Washington, DC Depot Quartermaster, October 20, 1887, Vol. 3, 1887, ibid. Also see, J.F Rodgers to Chief Quartermaster Military Division of the Missouri, December 13, 1887, ibid., which stated that gray blouse lining flannel was no longer on hand, and from that point forward "dark blue flannel of the same quality as the grey" was the standard. Specification No. 180 for blouse flannel lining (blue) was approved thereby canceling the specification adopted o February 25, 1886. S.B. Holabird to M.I. Ludington; and S.B. Holabird to R. Saxton, April 2, 1887, Vol. 2, 1887, ibid. During this interim period B.Y. Pippey received a contract for blouse lining, but this turned out to be darker than the new blue shade. Because the contract had been awarded before the new standard had been adopted, however, the 2,000 yards were accepted. S.B. Holabird to G.H. Weeks, August 3, 1887, Vol. 3, 1887; and S.B. Holabird to Depot Quartermaster Jeffersonville, and Depot Quartermaster Philadelphia, December 30, 1887, Vol. 2, 1887, ibid. In addition to the 10.0000 yards of blouse flannel, B.Y. Pippey also was given an order for 14,000 knit undershirts, 17,500 pairs of cotton stockings, 28,000 Berlin gloves, and 3,000 yards of sky-blue kersey of fine quality. S.B. Holabird to M.I. Ludington, August 3, 1887, Vol. 3, 1887, ibid.

In addition to a new form of blouse lining material, Specification No.189 was approved for fine quality dark blue flannel for the outside of blouses. This fabric was to be used for non-commissioned officers' and officers' blouses. S.B. Holabird to M.I. Ludington, April 16, 1887; and J.F. Rodgers to R. Saxton, April 16, 1887, Vol. 2, 1887, ibid. Permission was given to Philadelphia to pursue contracts for 18,000 yards of dark blue finished blouse flannel 6/4 and 8,000 yards of 6/4 shirting flannel. The Pioneer Woolen Mills of San Francisco received the order. S.B. Holabird to G.H. Weeks, March 31, 1887, Vol. 1, 1887. ibid. Some of the blouse flannel was inspected after it was made available, and was found to be "of good quality, color and finish." S.B. Holabird to M.I. Ludington, November 22, 1887, Vol. 3, 1887, ibid. Furthermore, specifications for finer quality blouse flannel and four sets of samples of light quality blue kersey were to be provided as soon as possible to the quartermaster general's office. J.F. Rodgers to M.I. Ludington, April 9, 1887, Vol. 1, 1887, ibid. The latter cloth when received from the contractors was marred because it had "a little too much finish" when compared to the standard sample. Otherwise, it was "of good color and apparently up to the standard and equally as serviceable."

S.B. Holabird to M.I. Ludington, November 22, 1887, Vol. 3, 1887, ibid.

325 J.F. Rodgers to M.I. Ludington; J.F. Rodgers to Jeffersonville Depot Quartermaster; and J.F. Rodgers to San Francisco Depot Quartermaster, October 31, 1887, ibid.

326 J.F. Rodgers to M.I. Ludington, November 3, 1887, ibid.

327 J.G. Chandler to M.I. Ludington, December 13, 1887, ibid. During the previous month, specifications had been distributed in quantity, and the sealed patterns now conformed to them. J.F. Rodgers to Philadelphia Depot Quartermaster, November 30, 1887, ibid.

328 Holabird acknowledged Blunt's recommendation that screwed boots and shoes for troops in Arizona and New Mexico be strengthened at Leavenworth, where they could be tap-soled with cable screw fastenings just inside the sewing. S.B. Holabird to A.P. Blunt, March 5, 1887, Vol. 1, 1887, ibid. Colonel Blunt was then asked how many boots and shoes could be so modified by his labor force for the next fiscal year, with it being understood that all sewing would be accomplished by hand, a method that was viewed as more stable than machine sewing. S.B. Holabird to A.P. Blunt, March 29, 1887, ibid. Later Blunt was told that if sewing "the soles to the welt of the Boots and Shoes by machines using metallic thread" resulted in a product "equally durable as work done exclusively by hand" there were no objections to using the labor saving equipment. Whatever the course of action taken, the prison was not to exceed $125,000 during the next fiscal year in its manufacturing operations, including purchase of materials, upkeep of equipment, pay of civilian employees, packing, and shipping, and all manner of costs. S.B. Holabird to A.P. Blunt, April 19, 1887, ibid.

329 *ARSW, 1887*, Vol., I, 512-13.

330 As part of this investigation Holabird wanted to find out the whereabouts of a J.W. DeCastro, who in 1882 had made some sample sewed shoes for the department. This investigation was to be undertaken in a discrete manner by someone not connected with the Quartermaster Department. J.F. Rodgers to M.I. Ludington, March 23, 1887, LS, Clothing Br., Vol. 1, 1887, OQMG, RG92, NA.

331 *ARSW, 1887*, Vol. I, 514.

332 Cir. No. 9, HQA, October 11, 1887 stated: "Until present supply of 'obsolete' field shoes on hand at depots and posts be exhausted, they will be issued at the reduced prices of $1.03 per pair. A supply of these shoes can be obtained by requisition made upon the Quartermaster General of the Army in the usual manner.—[*Decision Sec. War, June 27 and Sept, 22, 87—5501 A.G.O., 1887.*]" Further, because the secretary of war authorized the discontinuance of brass screwed post shoes, whatever ones were on hand at Leavenworth were to be sent to St. Louis, with the exception of "about a dozen pairs" that could be kept at the prison. The cost of the shoes per pair, with and without prison labor factored into the equation also was requested. S.B. Holabird to A.P. Blunt, April 26, 1887, LS, Clothing Br., Vol. 2, 1887, OQMG, RG92, 1887.

333 *ARSW, 1887*, Vol. I, 514; and *ARSW, 1888*, Vol. I, 528.

334 *ASRW, 1887*, 514 and 566. Other prices charged for clothing and equipment for this period appeared in ibid., 566-7. In another source the charge for obsolete post and field shoes was set at $1.03 per pair. S.B. Holabird to Secretary of War, September 21, 1887, LS, Clothing Br., Vol. 3, 1887, OQMG, RG92, NA.

335 S.B. Holabird to M.I. Ludington, April 28, 1887, Vol. 2, 1887, ibid. In addition, fifty copies of specifications for the sewed boots were sent to the commandant of the military prison at Leavenworth, and fifty copies of printed boot specifications, along with a like number of specifications for band shoulder knots, aiguillettes, and cavalry helmet cords and bands, all adopted on April 5, 1887, were sent to the various depots. J.F. Rodgers to A.P. Blunt; J.F. Rodgers to M.I. Ludington; J.F. Rodgers to R. Saxton; J.F. Rodgers to Quartermaster San Francisco Depot, May 18, 1887, ibid. Further copies of specification for sewed boots, cavalry bands, cords and plumes; dark blue flannel; music pouches; shoulder knots with aiguillettes; and linen collars were sent to the assistant quartermaster at Governor's Island, New York, the primary recruit rendezvous. J.F. Rodgers to C. Tompkins, June 1, 1887, ibid.
The quest for the perfect shoe did not end there. Research and experimentation continued for years as demonstrated by a letter from Rodgers asking where a copy of the work by Swiss military officer Major Salquin, titled The M*ilitary Shoe*, could be obtained. J.F. Rodgers to Arthur C. Johnson, January 17, 1887, Vol. 1, 1887, ibid. A supply of the publication was located as indicated by J.F. Rodgers to Warren Morse, November 13, 1888, Vol. 2, 1888, ibid., in which a copy of this pamphlet was being furnished per Morse's request. The ongoing efforts, through the early 1890s, relative to footwear are found in Brinckerhoff, *Boots and Shoes*, 29-44. Furthermore, Edward Lyman Munson, *The Soldier's Foot and the Military Shoe* (Menasha, WI: George Banta Publishing Company, 1917), reflects the fact that the quest continued well into the twentieth century. Dr. Munson was the president of the Army Shoe Board, among his other duties.

336 *ARSW, 1887*, Vol. I, 515.

337 S.B. Holabird to M.I. Ludington, July 8, 1887, LS, Clothing Br., Vol. 3, 1887, OQMG, RG92, NA.

338 S.B. Holabird to M.I. Ludington, September 7, 1887, ibid. The improved suspenders were adopted as Specification No. 179 on February 25, 1887 per S.B. Holabird to M.I. Ludington, February 25, 1887, Vol. 1, 1887, ibid. *ARSW, 1887*, Vol. I, 511-12.

339 J.F. Rodgers to F.M. Gibson, March 23, 1887, LS, Clothing Br., Vol. 1, 1887, OQMG, RG92, NA.

340 S.B. Holabird to M.I. Ludington, March 23, 1887, ibid.

341 S.B. Holabird to M.I. Ludington; and S.B. Holabird to R. Saxton, April 12, 1887, Vol. 2, 1887, ibid.

342 S.B. Holabird to San Francisco Depot Quartermaster, September 7, 1887, Vol. 3, 1887, ibid. In addition to the two coats for San Francisco, two others were sent to Jeffersonville and five to Philadelphia. J.F. Rodgers to Washington, DC Depot Quartermaster, September 7, 1887, ibid.

343 S.B. Holabird to G.H. Weeks, September 24, 1887, ibid. *ARSW, 1887*, Vol. I, 512, also mentions the incremental change to darker yellow for cavalry.

344 S.B. Holabird to M.I. Ludington; and S.B. Holabird to Chief Quartermaster Military Division of the Missouri, February 15, 1887, LS, Clothing Br., Vol. 1, 1887, OQMG, RG92, NA.

345 S.B. Holabird to M.I. Ludington, November 17, 1887, Vol. 3, 1887, ibid. As evidenced by First Lieutenant Henry W. Hovey order for forty-nine pairs of fur gauntlets for men of the Twenty-fourth U.S. Infantry from his office at Ft. Sill, Indian Territory, hand protection made from muskrat continued to be provided alongside canvas forms. J.F. Rodgers to C.W. Foster; and J.F. Rodgers to Chief Quartermaster Military Division of the Missouri, October 26, 1887, ibid. So, too, were arctic overshoes being procured and muskrat caps being manufactured or taken from stock for cold weather use. Indeed, both items were ordered in late 1887. Some 2,500 caps were to be obtained from Van Alstyn and Keck of Johnstown, New York, and 600 pairs of arctics were arranged for from Richard Levick's Son & Co., of Philadelphia. S.B. Holabird to M.I. Ludington, October 25, 1887, ibid.

346 S.B. Holabird to IGUSA, January 10, 1887, Vol. 2, 1887, ibid.

347 S.B, Holabird to M.I.Ludington, December 24, 1887, Vol. 3, 1887, ibid. By early 1888, the quartermaster general looked over some of the prototypes, but did not find any of them "satisfactory, being little, if any, better than the standard, both as to quality or workmanship." He did ask that for the present staff buttons should be added to future specifications for non-commissioned staff officers' forage caps. S.B. Holabird to Philadelphia Depot Quartermaster, February 15, 1888, Vol. 1, 1888, ibid. He repeated this remark in a March missive, and added that the gilt regulation button was to be retained for all other enlisted men. Moreover, he directed that future purchases of forage caps should be made using samples made by McKenney and another by Horstmann "marked #4, Nobby Pattern." S.B. Holabird to Philadelphia Depot Quartermaster, March 29, 1888, ibid.

348 J.F. Rodgers to S. O'Connor, October 12, 1887, Vol. 3, 1887, ibid.

349 Langellier, *Hats Off*, 89-94, briefly discusses the 1889-pattern forage cap and its 1895-pattern replacement.

350 S.B. Holabird to IGUSA, February 12, 1887, LS, Clothing Br., Vol. 2, 1887, OQMG, RG92, NA.

351 After looking at another specimen produced under a recent contract with Raymold and Whitlock, the quartermaster general concluded it was time "to raise the quality of the Helmet of the enlisted men of the Army." He observed: "the paste used in the manufacture shows through the felt, and that the black color fades into a brown or greenish tinge." S.B. Holabird to Philadelphia Depot Quartermaster, March 5, 1888, Vol. 1, 1888, ibid. Holabird also admitted that the helmet then being provided were "not of the very best grade that can be made" but they were adequate "for the price, equal to the standard sample." This did not mean that his department was content with what it offered, and efforts were underway to improve the item.S.B. Holabird to IGUSA, March 5, 1888, ibid. In fact, new specifications were adopted on January 13, 1888, and changed very soon thereafter, on February 12, 1889, in an ongoing effort to correct faults with the materials used. A slight change in the shape of the helmet shell also was evident during this transitional phase. *U.S. Army Uniforms and Equipment, 1889*, 292.

352 J.F. Rodgers to M.I. Ludington, November 25, 1887, LS, Clothing Br., Vol. 3, 1887, OQMG, RG92, NA.

353 J.F. Rodgers to Philadelphia Depot Quartermaster, December 22, 1887, Vol. 3, 1887, ibid. In another pronouncement relative to helmets, the summer helmet was not to be worn with cords. Cir. No. 9, HQA, October 11, 1887. The document declared: "No cord is prescribed for the white or summer helmet, and one should not be worn with it.—[*Decision Lieut. Gen., letter Sept, 24, 87—4546 A.G.O., 1887.*]" Evidently some confusion existed to prompt this prohibition, but it is not certain whether this was in response to questions about the propriety of decking the white helmet out with cords and bands, or instead was an injunction against instances where some individuals or units had adopted the trim without permission.
In relation to cords and bands for helmets, 1887 was the first year that they were given a more than cursory mention. In fact, Quartermaster Specification No. 188, April 5, 1887, offered significant particulars as to how these decorative drapes were to be made, while Specification No. 187, adopted April 5, 1887, described plumes in detail for the first time, whereas trumpet cords and tassels received their due on June 1, 1887. The last action resulted in part because of a change to white from light blue for infantry facings. *ARSW, 1887*, Vol. I, 515. See also, *U.S. Army Uniforms and Equipment, 1889*, 159-60, and 162; S.B. Holabird to M.I. Ludington, and S.B. Holabird to G.H. Weeks, June 1, 1887, LS, Clothing Br., Vol. 2, 1887, OQMG, RG92, NA; and B.C. Card to M.I. Ludington; B.C; Card to R. Saxton; and B.C. Card to G.H. Weeks, July 11, 1887, Vol. 3, 1887, ibid. While it may have seemed unnecessary to republish metallic insignia guidelines, the fact that some units still did not appear in the properly fitted out dress helmet was but one reason why the document required updating and circulation. For instance, an inspection of men of the Seventh U.S. Infantry at Ft. Laramie, Wyoming Territory, revealed that they did not wear the German silver regimental number on their helmet plates as long called for by regulations. R. Merrill to Assistant AG, Department of the Platte, September 3, 1887, RUSACC, Ft. Laramie, RG393, NA.

354 In most instances Congress set aside monies for transfer of clothing and equipment to the territorial and state militias, although there was no mechanism in place to credit the clothing appropriation directly. Even then, the quartermaster general thought it expedient to provide light shade overcoats and trousers, as well as trousers of the old sizes to the citizen soldiers, because these items were "classed as obsolete and unserviceable for troops after the latter ceased to be recruits." S.B. Holabird to Secretary of War, November 23, 1887, LS, Clothing Br., Vol. 3, 1887, OQMG, RG92, NA. Although he desired to rid the department of such items, Holabird by no means intended for every request to be filled from these outdated items as seen when a Boston firm asked to buy overcoats. The request was rejected with the statement that the department had no overcoats for sale and that there was "no likelihood that there ever will be a sale, unless a few" coats were deemed to be "worthless or otherwise unfit for issue." J.F. Rodgers to Boston Woven Hose Company, December 8, 1887, ibid.

355 *ARSW, 1887*, Vol. I, 510.

356 For examples see, S.B. Holabird to J.P. Richardson, Governor of South Carolina, July 15, 1887; J.F. Rodgers to A.D. Ayling, AG State of New Hampshire, October 29, 1887; S.B. Holabird to AG of Missouri, October 26, 1887; S.B. Holabird to M.I. Ludington, S.B. Holabird to Jeffersonville Depot Quartermaster, S.B. Holabird to S.B. Buckner, Governor of Kentucky; S.B. Holabird to Secretary of War, November 21, 1887; and J.F. Rodgers to M.I. Ludington, November 30, 1887, LS, Clothing Br., Vol. 3, 1887, OQMG, RG92, NA. An order for the Colorado state forces was covered by S.B. Holabird to Secretary of War, November 3, 1887, ibid.

357 *ARSW, 1887*, Vol. I, 509-10.

358 When there was a reluctance to draw lighter shade trousers for troops in some garrisons, the quartermaster general advocated sending these articles to Alcatraz Island for wear by military convicts. S.B. Holabird to Chief Quartermaster Division of the Pacific, October 26, 1887, LS, Clothing Br., Vol. 3, 1887, OQMG, RG92, NA. S.B. Holabird to M.I. Ludington; S.B. Holabird to Jeffersonville Depot Quartermaster; and S.B. Holabird to St Louis Depot Quartermaster, October 28, 1887, ibid., all carried information about sending overcoats to prisoners at Ft. Leavenworth.

359 *1887*, Vol. I, 510.

360 S.B. Holabird to Secretary of War, May 21, 1887, LS, Clothing Br., Vol. 1, 1887, OQMG, RG92, NA.

361 J.F. Rodgers to Chief Quartermaster Division of the Atlantic; and J.F. Rodgers to R. Saxton, April 26, 1887, Vol. 2, 1887, ibid.

362 S.B. Holabird to AGUSA, May 17, 1887, Vol. 1, 1887, ibid. This same letter also noted the requirement for women's and children's shoes, stockings, calico, and flannel, plus cloth coats for boys. Another exchange added more details as to the supplies that had to be bought for the women and youngsters. This included 100 hats for boys ranging from age four to thirteen; 200 wool suits for boys of the same age group; 492 pairs of cotton stockings brown mixed, which would be the only items of military issue on hand to fill the order; 825 pairs of women's stockings; 650 pairs of children's stockings; 420 pairs women's shoes; 150 pairs children's shoes for two through seven year olds; 175 pairs for eight through fourteen year olds; 7,000 yards of assorted calico; 2,500 yards of bright red flannel, medium weight; 1,500 spools of cotton thread in various colors; 10000 dozen assorted buttons for dresses and undergarments; and "500 papers assorted needles." S.B. Holabird to M.I. Ludington, May 21, 1887, ibid. Twenty-two women's shawls formed part of a subsequent order that also added more women's shoes and stockings, and some minor items for young boys. S.B. Holabird to M.I. Ludington, October 7, 1887, Vol. 3, 1887, ibid. Also see, J.F. Rodgers to Chief Quartermaster Division of the Atlantic, October, 7, 1887, ibid., for an acknowledgement that the supplies for Apaches at Ft. Pickens were being sent. Lastly, winter brought about other requirements, with 288 wool blankets being sent to the Apaches from those in stock considered unserviceable. J.F. Rodgers to Philadelphia Depot Quartermaster; and J.F. Rodgers to Chief Quartermaster Division of the Pacific, December 30, 1887, Vol. 2, 1887, ibid.

363 J.F. Rodgers to Chief Quartermaster Division of the Atlantic, June 1, 1887, ibid.

364 S.B. Holabird to AGUSA, April 19, 1887, ibid.; and *ARSW, 1887*, Vol. I, 512.

365 S.B. Holabird to Chief Quartermaster Division of the Atlantic; and S.B. Holabird to M.I. Ludington, August 24, 1887, LS, Clothing Br., Vol. 3, 1887, OQMG, RG92, NA.

366 S.B. Holabird to Chief Quartermaster Military Division of the Missouri; and J.F. Rodgers to St. Louis Depot Quartermaster, October 7, 1887, ibid.

367 S.B. Holabird to Chief Quartermaster Division of the Pacific, October 23, 1887, ibid.

368 J.G. Chandler to R.P. Hughes, December 5, 1887, ibid.

369 J.F. Rodgers to M.I. Ludington, November 16, 1887, ibid.

370 Five thousand yards of light shade kersey had been provided to San Francisco so that garments could be made up to take care of he needs of troops in the Southwest as they concluded the last operations against the Apaches. Trousers of this shade were to be used up in the interest of the service as well. S.B. Holabird to M.I. Ludington; S.B. Holabird to G.H. Weeks; and J.F. Rodgers to G.H. Weeks, June 14, 1887, Vol. 2, 1887, ibid.

371 S.B. Holabird to G.H. Weeks, April 19, 1887, ibid.

372 *ARSW, 1887*, Vol. I, 511. There were exceptions, as indicated by an order for hat cords called for by the post at San Antonio, Texas. J.F. Rodgers to Chief Quartermaster Military Division of the Missouri, April 2, 1887, LS, Clothing Br., Vol. 2, 1887, OQMG, RG92, NA.

373 J.F. Rodgers to M.I. Ludington, March 23, 1887, Vol. 1, 1887, ibid. Two sets of all components were to be prepared, but only one small music pouch was required, although gold lace for all arms were to be included for inspection by the quartermaster general. J.F. Rodgers to M.I. Ludington, March 25, 1887, ibid. In early April, an aiguilette and shoulder knot set for cavalry, plus large and small music pouches, the former for cavalry and the latter for artillery, along with a piece of infantry sling lace, were all approved as standard. S.B. Holabird to M.I. Ludington, April 12, 1887, Vol. 2, 1887, ibid. It should be noted that the supply of music pouches and gold lace chevrons remained small, and these items produced only as needed, the material being "highly perishable" S.B. Holabird to .H. Weeks, May 31, 1887, ibid. Other examples of new specification included those for heavy quality sky-blue kersey, which had been received and approved as standard, replacing that adopted on December 26, 1885. New sealed samples were supplied to the main depots per policy. S.B. Holabird to M.I. Ludington; S.B. Holabird to R. Saxton; S.B. Holabird to G.H. Weeks, April 9, 1887, Vol. 1, 1887; and S.B. Holabird to M.I. Ludington, June 3, 1887, Vol. 2, 1887, ibid. During the prior year dark blue cloth, fine quality specifications were adopted as No. 170. S.B. Holabird to M.I. Ludington; and S.B. Holabird to John Shillets Co., April 13, 1886, Vol 1, 1886, ibid. The secretary of war gave permission to extend the time for the John Shillets Company to produce 3,000 yards of this cloth. S.B. Holabird to M.I. Ludington, April 2, 1886, Vol. 3, 1886, ibid.

374 S.B. Holabird to M.I. Ludington, April 13, 1887, Vol. 1, 1887, ibid. Much later in the year he criticized the gauntlet and Berlin glove illustrations as unartistic. These looked "clumsy as compared to the original articles." Additionally, the shading for rubber ponchos, as well as woolen and rubber blankets was unsatisfactory, nor was some of the lettering. The ordnance cap device was not good, the side buttons for the Signal Corps "coarse", and the summer helmet needed to be shown in a some what bolder way with "a little more character." J.F. Rodgers to M.I. Ludington, November 5, 1887, Vol. 3, 1887, ibid. The paper used for printing at least met with approval, as was a target of 500 copies as a print run. S.B. Holabird to M.I. Ludington, November 30, 1887, ibid. Of the 500, some 200 were to be retained at the Philadelphia Depot, 100 were to go to San Francisco, and 200 were to be kept on hand at the quartermaster general's office. S.B. Holabird to Philadelphia Depot Quartermaster, July 18, 1888, Vol. 2, 1888, ibid. Thus, the original intention was not for public distribution, but rather for official Quartermaster Department use. J.F. Rodgers to Thomas F. Maloney, November 13, 1888, ibid. See also, J.F. Rodgers to Philadelphia Depot Quartermaster, March 1, 188, Vol. 1, 1888; and S.B. Holabird to Philadelphia Depot Quartermaster, July 13, 1888, Vol. 2, 1888, ibid. The publication was not released, however, until 1889. *U.S. Army Uniforms and Equipment, 1889*, viii.

375 For exchanges relative to the progress of the uniform book consult, S.B. Holabird to M.I. Ludington, December 29, 1887, Vol. 3, 1887, ibid.; J.F. Rodgers to W.H. Duff,

March 1, 1888, Vol. 1, 1888, ibid.; J.F. Rodgers to Philadelphia Depot Quartermaster, February 24, 1888, ibid; S.B. Holabird to Secretary of War, February 27, 1888, and April 19, 1888, ibid.; J.F. Rodgers to Messrs Schweitzer & Beer, April 28, 1888, ibid.; S.B. Holabird to George Berrie,May 17, 1888, Vol. 2, 1888, ibid.; J.F. Rodgers to Philadelphia Depot Quartermaster, July 3, 1888, ibid.; J.F. Rodgers to M.I. Ludington, July 3, 1888, ibid.; and C.G. Sawtelle to Philadelphia Depot Quartermaster, August 14, 1888, ibid. Permission was given for 1,000 copies to be published of the edition.

376 When John R. Nicholson, the recorder in chief for the Loyal Legion of the United States, requested a volume tracing the history of the "uniform of the U.S. Army since its organization" he was informed no such publication existed. S.B. Holabird to J.R. Nicholson, April 19, 1887, Vol. 1, 1887, ibid. In the late 1880s, *Uniform of the Army of the United States*, 1774-1889 (Philadelphia: Philadelphia Quartermaster Depot, 1889) was released with forty-four color plates by Henry A. Ogden and reprints of general orders and official regulations, to address this shortfall. For an early mention of this undertaking see, S.B. Holabird to Hon. James D. Richardson, July 26, 1888, Vol. 2, 1888, ibid.

377 For examples of the several articles made or assembled within the department see, S.B. Holabird to M.I. Ludington, and S.B. Holabird to R. Saxton, March 21, 1887, Vol. 1, 1887, ibid.; and J.F. Rodgers to M.I. Ludington, March 14, 1887, Vol. 2, 1887, ibid. These items were all produced through the depots or the military prison, as Congressman Frank Lawton was informed. Brigadier General Holabird told the congressmen clothing "was cut and made by piece work, and by tailors and sewing women, at the manufacturing depots of the Quartermaster's Department situated in Philadelphia, PA., Jeffersonville, Ind., and San Francisco, Cal." In turn, boots and shoes were turned out at the U.S. Military Prison, Ft. Leavenworth, Kansas. S.B. Holabird to Frank Lawton, February 12, 1887, ibid.
Once they arrived at a post, however, enlisted tailors continued to rework garments that did not fit properly. This was done at a cost set in 1880 of no more than $.25 for a coat, $.08 for a vest, and the same for overalls or breeches. S.B. Holabird to Secretary of War, November 11, 1887, Vol. 3, 1887, ibid.

378 For extensive examples of contracts let in 1887 see, S.B. Holabird to M.I. Ludington, March 31, 1887, Vol. 1, 1887; S.B. Holabird to M.I. Ludington, January 15, 1884, May 18, 1887, and May 20, 1887; S.B. Holabird to G.H. Weeks, May 26, 1887, Vol. 2, 1887; J.F. Rodgers to M.I. Ludington, July 9, 1887; S.B. Holabird to M.I. Ludington, July 13, 1887, July 13, 1887, August 9, 1887, September 26, 1887, and December 29, 1887; S.B. Holabird to San Francisco Depot Quartermaster, and S.B. Holabird to M.I. Ludington, October 10, 1887; J.F. Rodgers to L. Wilhelm, December 15, 1887, Vol. 3, 1887, ibid. Likewise an order for 10,000 yards of sky-blue kersey heavy quality at $1.87 per yard from B.Y. Pippey and 5,000 yards of blouse flannel at $1.19 34 per yard from the San Francisco Pioneer Woolen Factory as noted in S.B. Holabird to G.H. Weeks, January 29, 1887, Vol. 1, 1887, ibid. Further, Thomas Kent was the lowest bidder for 6/4 dark blue overcoat lining at one dollar per yard for four thousand yards of the material from this Clifton Heights, Pennsylvania manufacturer. S.B. Holabird to M.I. Ludington, January 7, 1887, ibid.

379 *ARSW, 1887*, Vol. I, 510-11.

380 Many aspects of the uniform for the late 1880s through the beginning of the twentieth century already have been covered. For instance, primary information contained in *U.S. Army Uniforms and Equipment 1889* is of great value. Two works by William Emerson, *Chevrons*, and *Encyclopedia of United States Army Insignia and Uniforms* (Norman: University of Oklahoma Press, 1996) likewise are musts. Head gear of the period is treated in Gordon Chappell's two monographs, *Brass Spikes*, 48-94, and *Summer Helmets*, 20-30; as well as by Langellier, *Hats Off*, 117-44. For pictorial references, two of the titles for Greenhill Books' GI series are germane, *Bluecoats: The U.S. Army in the West, 1848-1897* (London: Greenhill Books, 1995), and *Uncle Sam's Little Wars: The Spanish American War, Philippine Insurrection and Boxer Rebellion, 1898-1902* (London: Greenhill Books, 1999). Also consult J. Phillip Langellier, *They Continually Wear the Blues: U.S. Army Enlisted Dress 1865-1902* (San Francisco: Barnes McGee Publishing, 1976), 26-43.

APPENDIX A: Uniform Regulations, 1872

UNIFORM, DRESS, EQUIPMENTS, &c.

No officer or soldier of the Army shall wear any other than the prescribed uniform, when on duty.

COATS.

FULL DRESS FOR OFFICERS.

All officers shall wear a double-breasted frock coat of dark blue cloth, the skirt to extend from one-half to three-fourths the distance from the hip joint to the bend of the knee.

For a General: Two rows of buttons on the breast twelve in each row; placed by fours; the distance between each row five and one-half inches at top and three and one-half inches at bottom; stand-up collar, not less than one nor more than two inches in height, to hook in front at the bottom and slope thence up and backward at an angle of thirty degrees on each side, corners rounded; cuffs three inches deep, to go around the sleeves parallel to the lower edge, and with three small buttons at the under seam; pockets in the folds of the skirts, with two buttons at the hip and one at the lower end of each side-edge, making four buttons on the back and skirt of the coat; collar and cuffs to be of dark blue velvet; lining of the coat black.

For a Lieutenant General: The same as for a General, except that there will be ten buttons in each row, on the breast, the upper and lower groups by threes, and the middle groups by fours.

For a Major General: The same as for a General, except that there will be nine buttons in each row, on the breast, placed by threes.

For a Brigadier General: The same as for a General, except that there will be eight buttons in each rows on the breast, placed by pairs.

For a Colonel, Lieutenant Colonel, and Major: The same as for a General, except that there will be nine buttons in each row, on the breast, placed at equal distances; collars and cuffs of the same color and material as the coat. The upper half of the cuffs to be ornamented with three double stripes of gold braid running the length of the cuff, pointed at the upper ends, and with a small button below the point of each stripe, according to pattern.

For a Captain, 1st lieutenant, 2d lieutenant, and Additional 2d lieutenant: The same as for a Colonel, except that there will be seven buttons in each row, on the breast, and two stripes on the cuffs.

For all Storekeepers: A single-breasted coat, as lately worn by Captains of the staff, with staff shoulder-straps to indicate rank.

This coat shall be worn on all dress occasions, such as reviews, inspections, dress parades, guards, and courts-martial. It will be habitually worn at battalion drills, except in hot weather, or when otherwise exceptionally directed by the commanding officer.

UNDRESS FOR OFFICERS.

For fatigues, marches, squad and company drills, and other drills when authorized by the commanding officer, and for ordinary wear: A sack coat of dark blue cloth or serge; falling collar; single breasted, with five buttons in front, same as those worn on the dress coat; with black braid, one-fourth of an inch wide, extending from each button and button-hole back six inches and terminating in "herring-bone" loops.

The skirt to extend from one-third to two-thirds the distance from the hip joint to the bend of the knee, and to be slashed at the hip on each side; a knot of black braid, one-fourth of an inch wide, on the upper part of the cuff; according to pattern.

The shoulder-straps will always be worn with it. Black braid binding one-half of an inch wide, around edge of coat.

For Storekeepers: Of pattern above described, but without braid.

For Chaplain: Plain black frock coat with standing collar; one row of nine black buttons on the breast, with "herring-bone" of black braid around the buttons and button-holes.

COATS.

FOR ENLISTED MEN.

For Infantry: Single-breasted, dark blue basque, according to pattern deposited in Quartermaster General's Office, piped with sky-blue; collar same height as for officers' coat, faced with sly-blue cloth four inches back on each side, cut square to hook up close in front; number of regiment or badge of corps in yellows metal in middle of sky blue facing of collar on each side; skirt of coat on each side of opening behind to be faced with sky-blue cloth, ornamented with four buttons, as per pattern. Two straps of dark blue cloth, piped with the same color as the facings, let into the waist-seam on each side the coat and buttoning above the hip to sustain the waist-belt; shoulder-straps of cloth the color of the facings let into the shoulder-seam and to button over the shoulder-belts at the collar-seam with one button; shoulder-straps for Engineer soldiers to be scarlet, piped with white.

For Enlisted Men of Artillery, Engineers, and Ordnance: Same as for Infantry, except that the facings shall be scarlet for Artillery, scarlet and white for Engineers, and crimson for Ordnance.

For Cavalry and Light Artillery: Same as for Infantry, excepting that it is shorter in the skirt, and the facing upon the skirt put on differently, according to pattern in the Quartermaster General's Office; facings for Cavalry yellow, and for Light Artillery red.

Coats for Musicians: Ornamented on the breast with braid same color as the facings, running from the button as now worn, the outer extremities terminating in "herring-bones" and the braid returning back to the buttons.

Coats for Hospital Stewards: Same as for Infantry, except the facing to be of emerald green.
Coats for Ordnance Sergeants: Same as for enlisted men of Ordnance.
Whenever the dress coat is worn by enlisted men, it will invariably be buttoned up and hooked at the collar.
For fatigue purposes, for general wear, and on field service: A dark blue blouse of navy flannel, according to the pattern deposited in the Quartermaster General's Office.
Blouses for winter wear to be lined.

BUTTONS.

The same as now worn for all Officers and enlisted men. *Storekeepers*: General Staff button.

TROWSERS.

For General Officers, Officers of the General Staff, and Staff Corps: Dark blue cloth, plain, without stripe, welt, or cord.
For all Regimental Officers of Cavalry, Artillery, and Infantry. Light blue cloth, same shade of color as for enlisted men, with stripe one and one-half inches wide, welted at the edges; color, that of facings of their respective arms, except infantry, which will be dark blue.
Storekeepers: Dark blue cloth, with black stripe one and one-half inches wide.
For Chaplains: Plain black.
*For Enlisted Men of all Arms and of the Ordnance Depart*ment: Sky blue mixture, pattern now worn; waistband three and a half inches wide, to button with two buttons in front; pockets in front, opening at top.
Sergeants to wear a stripe one inch wide, color of facings; and Corporals to wear a stripe one-half inch wide, color of facings, except Infantry, which will be dark blue.
For Engineers: According to pattern in the Quartermaster General's Office.
For Ordnance Sergeants: Crimson stripe, one inch and one-quarter wide.
For Hospital Stewards: Emerald green stripe, one inch and one-quarter wide.
All stripes to be of cloth.
One-third of the trowsers of enlisted men issued on requisition shall be sent to posts cut out but not made up. The material of each pair of trowsers, with the buttons, thread, needles, and all necessary trimmings, shall be rolled up in a bundle, securely fastened and marked with the size of the trowsers.
Trowsers for all mounted men to be reenforced.
There shall be a 5th size, larger than No-4.

CRAVATS.

For all Officers: Black; the tie not to be visible at the opening of the collar.
Neither cravats nor stocks will be worn by enlisted men when on duty.

BOOTS AND SHOES.

For all Officers: Shall be of black leather and come above the ankle.
For Enlisted Men of Cavalry and Light Artillery: Boots, to come above the swell of the calf of the leg; shoes, Jefferson rights and lefts, according to pattern.
For Enlisted Men of Artillery, Infantry, Engineers, and Ordnance, and other Enlisted Men: Jefferson rights and lefts, according to pattern.
Top-boots may be worn by mounted men.

HAT OR CAP (FULL DRESS).

For General Officers, Officers of the General Staff and Staff Corps: Chapeau, according to pattern.
For Officers of Light Artillery and Cavalry: Black felt helmet, with gold cords and tassels, and gilt trimmings, according to pattern.
For all Storekeepers: Forage Cap of dark blue cloth, without braid; badge same as for General Officers.
For all other Officers: Of dark blue cloth, ornamented with gold braid and trimmings, according to pattern.
For Enlisted Men of Light Artillery and Cavalry: Black felt helmet, same pattern as for officers, with cords and tassels of mohair—red for Light Artillery and yellow for Cavalry. Helmet, ornamented with yellow metal trimmings, as per pattern.
For all other Enlisted Men: Of blue cloth, same pattern as for officers, ornamented with mohair braid of the same color as facings of the coat; trimmings of yellow metal, according to pattern.

FORAGE CAP.

For General Officers: Of dark blue cloth, chasseur pattern, with black velvet band and badge in front.
For all other Commissioned Officers: Of dark blue cloth, chasseur pattern, with badge of corps or regiment in front, top of badge to be even with top of cap, and according to pattern in Quartermaster General's Office.
For all Enlisted Men: Of plain blue cloth, same pattern as for officers, with badge of corps or letter of company of yellow metal worn in front as for officers.

FORAGE CAP BADGES.

For General Officers: A gold embroidered wreath on dark blue cloth ground, encircling the letters U.S. in silver, old English characters.
For Officers of General Staff, and Staff Corps: Same as General Officers, with the exception of those for Ordnance Officers, which will have a gold embroidered shell and flame on dark blue cloth ground.
For Officers of Engineers: A gold embroidered wreath of laurel and palm encircling a silver turretted castle on dark blue cloth ground.
For Officers of Cavalry: Two gold embroidered sabers, crossed, edges upward, on dark blue cloth ground, with number of regiment in silver in upper angle.
For Officers of Artillery: Two gold embroidered cannons, crossed, on dark blue cloth ground, with number of the regiment in silver at the intersection of the cross-cannon.
For Officers of Infantry: A gold embroidered bugle, on dark blue cloth ground, with number of the regiment in silver within the bend.

FATIGUE HAT.

For Officers and Enlisted Men: Of black felt, according to pattern, to be worn only on fatigue duty and on marches or campaigns.

PLUMES FOR OFFICERS.

For General-in-Chief: Three black ostrich feathers.
For other General Officers, for Officers of the General Staff, and Staff Corps: Two black ostrich feathers.
For Regimental Officers of Foot Artillery and Infantry: Of cocks' feathers, to rise five inches above the top of the cap, front feathers to reach the vizor, rear feathers to reach the top of the cap, with gilt ball and socket: color of plume to be red for Artillery and white for Infantry.
For Officers of Light Artillery and Cavalry: Horse-hair plume; gilt ball and socket, plume to be long enough to reach the front edge of the vizor of the helmet: color of the plume to be red for Light Artillery and yellow for Cavalry.

PLUMES AND POMPONS FOR ENLISTED MEN.

For Artillery: Red pompon, pattern shape; ball and socket of yellow metal.
For Infantry: White pompon, same shape and with same ball and socket as for Artillery.
For Ordnance: Crimson pompon, same ball and socket as for Artillery.
For Engineer Troops: Red pompon, with white top; same ball and socket as for Artillery.
For Light Artillery: Red; and for Cavalry, yellow horse-hair plume, same size and length as for officers; socket according to pattern.

SPURS.

For all Mounted Officers: Yellow metal or gilt.
For all Mounted Men: Of yellow metal, plain surface.

GLOVES.

For General Officers, Officers of the General Staff; and Staff Corps: Buff or white gauntlets or gloves.
For Field Officers of Artillery, Cavalry, and Infantry; for Officers of Light Artillery and Cavalry: White gauntlets or gloves. All other Officers, white gloves.

For all Enlisted Men: Of white Berlin, to be issued as clothing.

SASH.

For General Officers: Buff silk net, with silk bullion fringe ends; sash to go twice around the waist and to tie behind the left hip, pendent part not to extend more than eighteen inches below the tie.

SWORD-BELT.

For all Officers: A waist-belt, not less than one and one-half nor more than two inches wide, with slings of the same material as the belt, with a hook attached to the belt on which to hang the sword.
The belt to be worn outside the full dress coat and underneath the undress sack.
For General Officers: Of red Russia leather, with three stripes of gold embroidery, as per pattern now worn.
For all Field Officers: One broad stripe of gold lace on black enameled leather, according to pattern.
For all Officers of the General Staff, and Staff Corps, below the rank of Field Officers: Four stripes of gold, interwoven with black silk, lined with black enameled leather, according to pattern.
For Company Officers of Cavalry, Artillery and Infantry: Four stripes of gold lace, interwoven with silk of the same color as the facings of their arms of service, and lined with black enameled leather.
For all Storekeepers: Of black enameled leather, of patterns lately worn.
On undress duty, marches, and campaigns, officers may wear a plain black leather belt.
For all Non-Commissioned Officers: Plain black leather.

SWORD-BELT PLATE.

For all Officers and Enlisted Men: Gilt, rectangular, two inches wide, with a raised bright rim; a silver wreath of laurel encircling the "Arms of the United States;" eagle, shield, scroll, edge of cloud and rays bright. The motto "E pluribus unum" upon the scroll; stars also of silver, according to pattern.

SWORD AND SCABBARD.

General Officers: Straight sword, gilt hilt, silver grip; brass or steel scabbard, same as now worn.
For Officers of Light Artillery and Cavalry: Sabre and scabbard as now worn, and according to pattern in Ordnance Department.
For Officers of the Pay and Medical Departments: Small sword and scabbard, according to pattern in the Surgeon General's Office, as now worn.
For all other Officers: Same as the small, straight sword now worn by the officers of the General Staff, and according to pattern in the Ordnance Department.
The sword and sword-belt will be worn upon all occasions of duty, except stable and fatigue.
When not on military duty, officers may wear swords of honor, or the prescribed sword, with a scabbard, gilt, or of leather with gilt mountings.

SWORD-KNOT.

For General Officers: Gold cord, with acorn end.
For all other Officers: Gold lace strap, with gold bullion tassel, as now worn.

EPAULETTES.

For the General of the Army: Of gold, with solid crescent; device—two silver embroidered stars, with five rays each, one and one-half inches in diameter, and the "Arms of the United States" embroidered in gold placed between them.
For a Lieutenant General: Three silver embroidered stars of five rays each, respectively, one and one-half, one and one-quarter, one and one-eighth inches in diameter. The largest placed in the centre of the crescent; the others, placed longitudinally on the strap and equidistant, ranging in order of size from the crescent.
For Major General: Same as for Lieutenant General, omitting smallest star, and the smaller of time two remaining stars placed in the centre of the strap.
For a Brigadier General: Same as for a Lieutenant General, omitting all but the largest star.

SHOULDER-KNOTS.

For Officers of the Adjutant General's and Inspector General's Departments, and for Aides-de-Camp to General Officers:* Of gold cord, Russian pattern, on dark blue cloth ground; insignia of rank and letters of corps or designation of regiment embroidered on the cloth ground, according to pattern; an aiguillette of gold cord to be worn with the right shoulder- knot and permanently attached thereto, according to pattern.
For Officers of other Staff Corps: Same as above described, without the aiguillette.
For Officers of Cavalry, Artillery, and Infantry: Of the same pattern as for the Staff Corps, but on cloth of the same color as the facings of their arm, with insignia of rank and number of regiment embroidered on the cloth ground, according to pattern.
For Regimental Adjutants: Of the same pattern as for other officers of their arm, but with aiguillettes attached.
* See Miscellaneous.

INSIGNIA OF RANK ON SHOULDER-KNOTS.

For a Colonel: A silver embroidered eagle at the centre of the pad.
For a Lieutenant Colonel: Two silver embroidered leaves, one at each end of pad.
For a Major: Two gold embroidered leaves, one at each end of pad.
For a Captain: Two silver embroidered bars at each end of pad.
For a 1st Lieutenant: One silver embroidered bar at each end of pad.
For a 2d Lieutenant: Plain.
For an Additional 2d Lieutenant: Same as 2d Lieutenant.
The above insignia to be the *same* as prescribed for the shoulder-straps.

SHOULDER-STRAPS.

For the General of the Army: Dark blue cloth, one and three-eighths inches wide by four inches long, bordered with an embroidery of gold one-fourth of an inch wide; two silver embroidered stars of five rays each, and gold embroidered "Arms of the United States" between them.
For a Lieutenant General: The same as for the General, except that there will be three silver embroidered stars of five rays, one star on the centre of the strap, and one on each side, equidistant between the centre and outer edge of the strap, the centre star to be the largest.
For all Major Generals: The same as for the Lieutenant General except that there will be two stars instead of three; the centre of each star to be one inch from the outer edge of the gold embroidery on the ends of the strap; both stars of the same size.
For a Brigadier General: The same as for a Major General, except that there still be one star instead of two; the centre of the star to be equidistant from the outer edge of the embroidery on the ends of the strap.
For a Colonel: The same size as for a Major General, and bordered in like manner with an embroidery of gold; a silver embroidered spread eagle on the centre of the strap, two inches between the tips of the wings, having in the right talon an olive branch, and in the left a bundle of arrows; an escutcheon on the breast, as represented in the "Arms of the United States." Cloth of the strap as

follows: for the General Staff and Staff Corps, dark blue; Artillery, scarlet; Infantry, sky blue; Cavalry, yellow.

For a Lieutenant Colonel: The same as for Colonel, according to corps omitting the eagle, and introducing a silver embroidered leaf at each end, each leaf extending seven-eighths of an inch from the end border of the strap.

For a Major: The same as for a Colonel, according to corps, omitting the eagle and introducing a gold embroidered leaf at each end, each leaf extending seven-eighths of an inch from the end border of the strap.

For a Captain: The same as for a Colonel, according to corps, omitting the eagle, and introducing at each end two silver embroidered bars of the same width as the border, placed parallel to the ends of the strap, at a distance between them and from the border equal to the width of the border.

For a 1st Lieutenant: The same as for a Colonel, according to corps, omitting the eagle, and introducing at each end one silver embroidered bar of the same width as the border, placed parallel to the ends of the strap, at a distance from the border equal to its width.

For a 2d Lieutenant: The same as for a Colonel, according to corps, omitting the eagle.

For an Additional 2d Lieutenant: The same as for a 2d Lieutenant.

Officers serving in the field may dispense with the prescribed insignia of rank on their horse equipments, and may wear overcoats of the same color and shape as those of the enlisted men of their commands, and omit epaulettes, shoulder-knots, or other prominent marks likely to attract the fire of sharpshooters; but all officers must wear the prescribed buttons, stripes, and shoulder-straps to indicate their corps and rank.

The shoulder-strap will be worn whenever the epaulette or shoulder-knot is not.

CHEVRONS.

The rank of non-commissioned officers will be marked by chevrons upon both sleeves of the uniform coat and overcoat, above the elbow; of cloth of the same color as the facings of the uniform coat, divided into bars a half inch wide by black silk stitching, except for Engineers, which will be white stitching and piped with white, points down, according to new patterns in Quartermaster General's Office, as follows:

For a Sergeant Major: Three bars and an arc.

For a Quartermaster Sergeant: Three bars and a tie of three bars.

For a Principal Musician: Three bars and a bugle.

For an Ordnance Sergeant: Three bars and a star.

For a Hospital Steward: A half chevron of emerald green cloth one and three-fourths inches wide, piped with yellow cloth, running obliquely downward from the outer to the inner seam of the sleeve, and at an angle of about thirty degrees with a horizontal, and in the centre a "caduceus" two inches long, the head toward the outer seam of the sleeve.

For a 1st Sergeant: Three bars and a lozenge.

For a Battalion or Company Quartermaster Sergeant: Three bars and a tie of one bar.

For a Sergeant: Three bars.

For a Corporal: Two bars.

For a Pioneer: Two crossed hatchets, of cloth, same color and material as the facings of the uniform coat, to be sewed on each sleeve, above the elbow, in the place indicated for a chevron (those of a corporal to be just above and resting on the chevron), the head of the hatchet upward, its edge outward, of the following dimensions, viz:

Handle, four and one-half inches long, one-fourth to one-third of a inch wide.

Hatchet, two inches long,, one inch wide at the edge.

To indicate service: All non-commissioned officers, musicians, and privates, who have served faithfully for one term of enlistment, will wear as a mark of distinction upon both sleeves of the uniform coat, below the elbow, a diagonal half chevron, one-half inch wide, extending from seam to seam, the front end nearest the cuff, and one-half inch above the point of the cuff, to be of the same color as the edging of the coat.

In like manner an additional half chevron, above and parallel to the first, for every subsequent term of enlistment and faithful service. Distance between each chevron one-fourth of an inch.

Service in war will be indicated by a white stripe on each side of the chevron for Artillery, and a red stripe for all other corps, the stripe to be one-eighth of an inch wide.

OVERCOAT.

For General Officers: Of dark blue cloth, closing by means of four frog buttons of black silk and loops of black silk cord; cord down the breast, and at the throat by a long loop "à echelle," without tassel or plate, on the left side, and a black silk frog button on the right; cord for the loops fifteen hundredths of an inch in diameter; back, a single piece, slit up from the bottom from fifteen to seventeen inches, according to the height of the wearer, and closing at will by buttons, and button-holes cut in a concealed flap; collar of the same color and material as the coat, rounded at the edges, and to stand or fall; when standing to be about five inches high; sleeves loose, of a single piece and round at the bottom, without cuff or slit; lining woolen; around the front and lower borders, the edges of the pockets, the edges of the sleeves, collar, and slit in the back, a flat braid of black silk one-half an inch wide; and around each frog button on the breast a knot two and one-quarter inches in diameter, of black silk cord, seven hundredths of an inch in diameter, cape of the same color and material as the coat, removable at the pleasure of the wearer, and reaching to the cuff of the coat sleeve when the arm is extended; coat to extend down the leg from six to eight inches below the knee, according to height.

To indicate rank: There will be on both sleeves, near the lower edge, a knot of flat black silk braid, not exceeding one-eighth of an inch in width, and composed of five braids, double knot.

For all other Officers: Dark blue close fitting double-breasted surtout coat, with a cape made to detach from the coat and fall to the tips of the fingers when the arm and hand are extended; the skirt of the coat for mounted officers to reach half way between the knee and the sole of the foot; for dismounted officers, three inches below the knee.

The coat to have seven buttons on each breast of the same pattern as those on the uniform coat. The insignia of rank on the sleeve, as follows, viz:

Colonel, five braids, single knot.
Lieutenant Colonel, four braids, single knot.
Major, three braids, single knot.
Captain, two braids, single knot.
1st Lieutenant, one braid, single knot.

2d Lieutenant and Additional 2d Lieutenant, without braid. Military Storekeepers and Chaplains, without braid.

On the frontier and campaign, officers may wear the soldier's overcoat, with insignia of rank on the sleeve.

For Enlisted Men of all arms: Of sky blue cloth of the pattern now used in the mounted service.

OTHER ARTICLES OF CLOTHING AND EQUIPMENTS.

Flannel shirt, drawers, stockings, and stable-frock: The same as now furnished.

Stable-frocks for Mounted Men: Of white cotton, made loose and extending well down to the knee, without sleeve or body lining; to button in front.

Blanket: Woolen, gray, with letters U.S. in black, four inches long, in the centre; to be seven feet long and five and a half feet wide, and to weigh at least five pounds; to be made of wool; the blanket now issued to troops in California to be the standard.

Canvass overalls for Engineer Soldiers: Of white cotton; one garment to cover the whole of the body above the waist—the breast, the shoulders, and the arms; sleeves loose, to allow free play of the arms, with a narrow wristband buttoning with one button; overalls to fasten at the neck behind with two buttons, and at the waist behind with buckle and tongue.

For Cavalry and Light Artillery: White cotton overalls, to cover only the waist. These overalls are to be worn at all stable duties.

Sets of stencil plates of letters and numbers of two sizes (inch and half inch), for marking equipments, &c., shall be furnished lay the Quartermaster's Department to each company commander and regimental adjutant.

SIGNAL SERVICE

For the Chief Signal Officer: The same uniform as for the Adjutant General's Department, without the a aiguillettes.

The uniform of the Enlisted Men of the Signal Service shall be as follows:

The Cavalry uniform, except that the trimmings and facings be orange instead of yellow, bearing a device on the sleeve of the coat, as follows: crossed signal flags, red and white, on dark blue cloth; size of flags three-fourths of an inch square; length of staff three inches, after the pattern in the office of the Chief Signal Officer of the Army. This device to be worn by the non-commissioned officers above the chevrons; by privates of the first class on both arms; and by privates of the second class on the left arm only, in the same position as the chevron of non-commissioned officers.

HORSE FURNITURE.

FOR GENERAL OFFICERS AND THE GENERAL STAFF.

Housing for General Officers: To be worn over the saddle; off dark blue cloth, trimmed with two rows of gold lace. the outer row one inch and five-eighths wide, the inner row two inches and one-fourth; to be made full, so as to cover the horse's haunches and forehands, and to bear on each flank corner the following ornaments, distinctive of rank, to wit:

For the General of the Army: A gold embroidered spread eagle with two stars and "Arms of the United States" between them.

For Lieutenant General: A gold embroidered spread eagle and three stars.

For Major Generals: A gold embroidered spread eagle and two stars.

For Brigadier Generals: A gold embroidered spread eagle and one star.

Saddle-cloth for General Staff Officers, and Officers of the Staff Corps: Dark blue cloth, of sufficient length to cover the saddle and holsters, and one foot ten inches in depth, with edging of gold lace one inch wide.

For all other Officers: Dark blue felt, according to pattern; worn under the saddle and trimmed around the edges with cloth one and one-half inches wide, color as follows:

Infantry, sky blue.

Artillery, scarlet.

Cavalry, yellow.

For Infantry, Cavalry, and horse equipments, knapsacks, haversacks, c., and tools and materials for Cavalry, according to patterns in Ordnance Office. See Ordnance Memoranda No. 13, and General Orders No. 60, War Department, series of 1872.

MILITARY ACADEMY.

The uniform of the Professors and Sword Master at the West Point Military Academy shall be the same as now worn, excepting they will be permitted to wear the dark blue sack coat prescribed for Army officers, with the buttons of the General Staff to be worn on both coats.

FOR CADETS.

The same uniform as now worn.

MISCELLANEOUS

Aides-de-Camp and the Military Secretary, who have *increased* rank, will were the aiguillette with the uniform of the General Staff.

Aide-de-Camp to Major and Brigadier Generals will wear the aiguillette with the uniforms of their Regiments and Corps.

Whenever the full dress coat is worn by officers on duty the prescribed epaulettes or shoulder-knots will be attached. Letters to be embroidered on shoulder-knots in old English:

A.D.	Adjutant General's Department
I.D.	Inspector General's Department
J.A.	Bureau of Military Justice
S.S.	Signal Service
Q.D.	Quartermaster's Department
S.D.	Subsistence Department
M.D.	Medical Department
P.D.	Pay Department
E.C.	Engineer Corps
O.D.	Ordnance Department

Sashes will no longer be worn by officers below the grade of Brigadier General, or by non-commissioned officers.

Officers when not on duty are permitted to wear a buff, white, or blue vest, with the small button prescribed for them.

When trowsers and flannel shirts now in store shall have been issued or otherwise disposed of, the troops serving in warm climates will upon requisitions approved by commanding officers, be supplied with those articles of a lighter texture, but of the same material, cut, and color as those furnished the other troops of the Army.

Bands will wear the uniform of their Regiments or Corps. Commanding officers may at the expense of the Corps, sanctioned by the Councils of Administration, make such additions of ornaments as they may judge proper.

NOTE.—Swords of prescribed patterns will be distrbuted to Arsenals as soon as manufactured, for sale to officers.

A reasonable time after December 1 will be allowed to officers at remote stations to enable them to procure swords from the Ordnance Department.

APPENDIX B:
Officers' Uniform Specifications, 1876

The Board convened at Philadelphia, Pa., by Special Orders No. 264, paragraph 3, War Department, Adjutant General's Office, dated December 27, 1875, begs to submit the following description of articles of uniform clothing for officers of the Army.

FATIGUE HAT.

According to the pattern in the Quartermaster-General's Office.

Note.—A new pattern of fatigue hat having been recommended for adoption, a minute description of the present pattern is not thought necessary. The following description of the hat recommended by this Board is given instead:

Pattern and shape as shown in accompanying photographs numbered 1 and 2. Body of soft felt, either of fur or wool; crown lenticular shaped, so as to fold with a crease in center, lengthwise; 5 1/2 inches high on side; brim 2 3/4 inches wide, slightly curved, and unbound; revolving ventilator in each side 3 1/2 inches above brim; japanned or goat-skin sweat-leather.

FORAGE-CAP.

Chasseur pattern, as shown in accompanying plate numbered 3 and 4; of indigo-blue cloth; 3 inches high in front; 3 1/2 inches high on sides; 6 inches from edge of crown to bottom of band at back; crown 5 inches in diameter; depth at band about 1 1/4 inches; gild side or chin-strap buttons, vest size, according to arm of service; patent-leather chin-strap 1/8 of an inch wide; patent leather vizor unbound; japanned or goatskin sweat-leather, silk lining; embroidered badge of arm or corps in front; bottom of badge to be even with top of chin-strap.

For general officers, the band of the cap to be black velvet.

CHAPEAU.

According to pattern.

FULL-DRESS CAP.

Pattern as shown in accompanying cuts numbered 5, 6, and 7, felt shell, covered with indigo-blue cloth; 3 1/2 inches high in front; 4 1/2 high on sides; 6 1/2 inches high over the swell of the back, crown 5 1/2 inches long by 5 inches wide; revolving ventilator in crown; gold-wire braid 1/8 of an inch wide around the lower edge and around the crown at top, also, from top to bottom at each side and at back; patent-leather vizor unbound; patent leather chin-strap 1/2 of an inch wide with gilt slide; gilt side or chin-strap buttons, vest size, according to arm of service; japanned or goat-skin sweat-leather, silk lining; plume-socket of leather on inside at front with metallic guard at opening on top and front edge of crown; gold-embroidered eagle with shield on breast, surmounted by thirteen stars in silver; length from top of stars to end of tail, 1 3/8 inches; width from tip to tip of wings, 1 1/2 inches; tips of wings joined by an arc of rays, embroidered badge of arm or corps in front; bottom of badge to be even with top of chin-strap.

Plate 3 Forage Cap, Officer's, 1876 regulations. GC

Plate 4 Forage Cap, Officer's, 1876 regulations. GC

Plates 5-7, Full-Dress Cap, Officer's, 1876 regulations. GC

HELMET.

Pattern as shown in accompanying cuts numbered 8, 9, and 10; heavy body of fur bound with fine patent leather; measurements about as indicated on cuts; patent-leather chin-strap 5/8 of an inch wide with gilt slide; patent-leather vizor-strap folded 3/8 of an inch wide, double stitched, connecting chin-strap buttons; goat-skin sweat-leather.

Ornaments as follows:

Eagle.—Of yellow metal, gilt; pattern same as in coat of arms of the United States, with national shield on breast; head surmounted by scroll with motto "E Pluribus Unum" in relief letters, scroll extending downward and outward and joining olive branch and arrows in talons of eagle; whole height, 4 1/2 inches; greatest width between tips of wings, 4 inches; secured to helmet by wire stems.

Top piece and plume-socket.—Of yellow metal, gilt; base or foot a cross-piece made convex to fit top of helmet; ends of arms mitre-shaped and fastened to helmet by ornamental buttons; length between points of opposite arms, 5 1/4 inches; arms at widest part 1 1/4 inches, edges grooved and beveled; sphere one inch in diameter, on base surmounted by a short neck with ring, (neck 1/2 inch, ring 5/8 inch diameter,) from which is raised an inverted conical tube representing rays and displaying on front an heraldic eagle, the head of which is surmounted by a star, in relief; diameter of tube at top one inch; height, (including sphere at bottom,) three inches; the plume held in position at top of socket by a brass pin 4 3/4 inches long, having ornamental head, and a small brass disk; this pin enters through the socket top piece; the shell of helmet and concave brass disk, (1 7/8 inches in diameter,) on the inside, and is secured by a brass thumb-nut.

Scrolls and rings.—Of yellow metal, gilt, placed at sides near top, between the arms of the top piece; the scroll, (or button,) is ornamented to correspond with the fastenings of top piece, and is 3/4 of an inch in diameter; small eye and ring, (1/2 inch in diameter,) in center, to hold cords and bands; stem to enter shell of helmet and fasten on the inside.

Side or chin-strap buttons.—Of yellow metal, gilt, 7/8 of an inch in diameter, according to arm of service; edges beveled and grooved, surface slightly convex and chased; secured to helmet as scrolls are.

Plumes.—According to arm of service.

Cords and bands or braids.—Of gold-thread cord, 2 1/2 lines; the bands loop plaited and fastened to rings and scrolls at sides and festooned on front and back of helmet; the front festoon falls to the upper edge of vizor and the rear one to a corresponding depth behind; the loop plaiting is about 3/4 of an inch wide; at left ring and scroll a pendant tassel of sixty or seventy fringes where the cords are fastened; gilt cords about 5 feet 8 inches long with two netted slides of about 3/4 inch diameter; flat braided ornament 2 3/4 inches in diameter and tassels at each end of cord.

FORAGE-CAP BADGES.

For general officers.—A gold-embroidered wreath on dark-blue cloth ground, encircling the letters U.S. in silver, old English characters.

For officers of the general staff and staff corps.—Same as for general officers, with the exception of those for ordnance officers, which will have a gold-embroidered shell and flame on dark-blue cloth ground.

For officers of engineers.—A gold embroidered wreath of laurel and palm, encircling a silver-turreted castle on dark- blue cloth ground.

For officers of cavalry.—Two gold-embroidered sabres, crossed, edges upward, on dark-blue cloth ground, with number of regiment, in silver, in the upper angle.

For officers of artillery.—Two gold-embroidered cannons, crossed, on dark-blue cloth ground, with the number of the regiment, in silver, at the intersection of the cross-cannon.

For officers of infantry.—Two gold-embroidered rifles, without bayonets, barrels upward, on dark-blue ground, with the number of the regiment, in silver, in the upper angle.

PLUMES FOR OFFICERS.

For General-in-Chief.—Three white ostrich-feathers.

For other general officers, for officers of the general staff, and staff corps.—Two black ostrich-feathers.

For all regimental officers of foot artillery and infantry.—Of cock's feathers, to rise five inches above the top of the cap, front feathers to reach the vizor, rear

Plates 8-10, Helmet, Officer's, 1876 regulations. GC

Plates 11-13, Full-Dress Coat, Officer's, 1876, regulations. GC

feathers to reach the top of the cap, with gilt ball and socket; color of plume to be red for artillery and white for infantry.

For officers of light artillery and cavalry.—Horse-hair plume, gilt ball and socket, plume to be long enough to reach the front edge of the vizor of the helmet; color of the plume to be red for light artillery and yellow for cavalry.

FULL-DRESS COAT.

Double-breasted frock-coat of dark-blue broadcloth, as per accompanying plates numbered 11, 12, and 13, buttoning to the throat; standing collar, not less than one nor more than two inches in height, to hook in front at the bottom, and slope thence up and backward at an angle of thirty degrees on each side, corners rounded; sleeves to terminate in cuffs stitched down, cuffs 3 to 3 1/2 inches deep, to go around the sleeves parallel with the lower edge and close at the hand, with three buttons and buttonholes at the under seam, the lower bottom to be placed one inch from lower end of cuff; top one from 2 to 2 1/4 inches from lower one; the middle one midway between the top and bottom ones; buttons to be what is known as "vest size;" skirt to extend from one-half to three-quarters of the distance from the hip-joint to the bend of the knee; pockets in folds of skirts behind; folds to have "side edges;" two rows of buttons in front; the distance between the rows 5 1/2 inches at top and 3 1/2 inches at bottom; four buttons behind, two on waist seam at the top of the pocket folds, and two at bottom of the side edges; buttons on front and back to be what is known as "coat size;"' lining of coat, black.

For all general officers.—The collar and cuffs of coat to be of dark-blue velvet, and buttons on breast as follows: For the General, twelve in each row, placed by fours; for the Lieutenant General, ten in each row, the upper and lower groups by threes, and the middle by fours; for Major-Generals, nine buttons in each row, placed by threes; for Brigadier-Generals, eight in each row, placed by pairs.

For field-officers.—The collar and cuffs of the same color and material as the coat; buttons according to arm or corps of service, on breast, nine in each row, placed at equal distances; the upper half of the cuff to be ornamented with three double stripes of gold lace or braid, running up the sleeve parallel to the front edge, and at right angles with bottom of sleeve 3 to 3 1/2 inches; each double stripe to terminate in a point, within which to be placed a small button, known as "vest size," 1/4 of an inch below the top of the point, and on a line with the top of cuff-button; the braid to be of 1/2-inch gold lace, raised and stuffed so as to be 3/8 of an inch wide when finished; the double stripes of gold lace to be placed, the outre edge of each 1/2 inch distant from each other, and the inner edges 1/4 inch apart.

For captains and lieutenants.—The collar and cuffs of the same color and material as the coat; buttons on breast according to arm or corps of service, seven

Plates 14-15, Undress-Coats, Officer's, 1876 regulations. GC

The cuff braid was eliminated in 1875 along with the frogging on the chest and other braid for officer's jacket, yet the lithographs used by the Quartermaster Department to illustrate officers' uniform items in the mid-1870s inadvertently continued to depict the black mohair design on the sleeve. GS

in each row, placed at equal distances; the cuffs to be ornamented with two double stripes of gold lace placed as stripes of field officers.
For store-keepers.—A single-breasted coat, as lately worn by captains of the staff.

UNDRESS-COATS.

For all officers except chaplains.—A sack coat of dark-blue cloth or serge; as per accomanying plates numbered 14, 15, and 16; falling collar; single-breasted, with five buttons in front, same as those worn on dress-coats; skirt to extend from one-third to two-thirds the distance from the hip to the bend of the knee.
For chaplain.—Plain black frock-coat, with standing collar; one row of nine black buttons on the breast, with "herring-bone" of black braid around the buttons and button-holes.

COAT-BUTTONS.

Coat size, as now worn, according to corps or arm of service.

TROUSERS.

For all officers of the general staff and staff corps.—Dark-blue cloth, plain, without stripe, welt, or cord.
For all regimental officers of cavalry, artillery, and infantry.—Light-blue cloth, same shade of color as for enlisted men, with stripe 1 1/2 inches wide, welted at the edges; color of stripe that of facings of their respective arms, except infantry, which will be dark blue.
For store-keepers.—Dark-blue cloth, with black stripe 1 1/2 inches wide.
For chaplains.—Plain black.

CRAVATS.

For all officers.—Black. The tie not to be visible at the opening of the collar.

BOOTS AND SHOES.

For all officers.—Shall be of black leather and come above the ankles.

SPURS.

For all mounted officers.—Yellow metal or gilt.

GLOVES.

For general officers, officers of the general staff; and staff corps.—Buff or white gauntlets or gloves.
For field-officers of artillery, cavalry, and infantry; for officers light artillery and cavalry.—White gauntlets or gloves. All other officers, white gloves.

SASH.

For general officers.—Buff silk net, with silk bullion fringe ends; sash to go twice around the waist and to tie behind the left hip, pendant part not to extend more than eighteen inches below the tie.

SWORD-BELT.

As per annexed plates, numbered 17, 18, 19, and 20.
For all officers.—A waist-belt, not less than one and one-half nor more than two inches wide, with slings of the same material as the belt, with a hook attached to the belt on which to hang the sword.
For general officers.—Of red Russia leather, with three stripes of gold embroidery, as per pattern now worn.
For all field officers.—One broad stripe of gold-lace on black enameled leather, according to pattern.
For all officers of the general staff, and staff corps, below the rank of field officers.—Four stripes of gold, interwoven with black silk, lined with black enameled leather, according to pattern.
For company officers of cavalry, artillery and infantry.—Four stripes of gold lace, interwoven with silk of the same color as the facings of their arms of service, and lined with black enameled leather.
For undress duty, marches, and campaigns, a plain black leather belt of the same size and pattern as above.

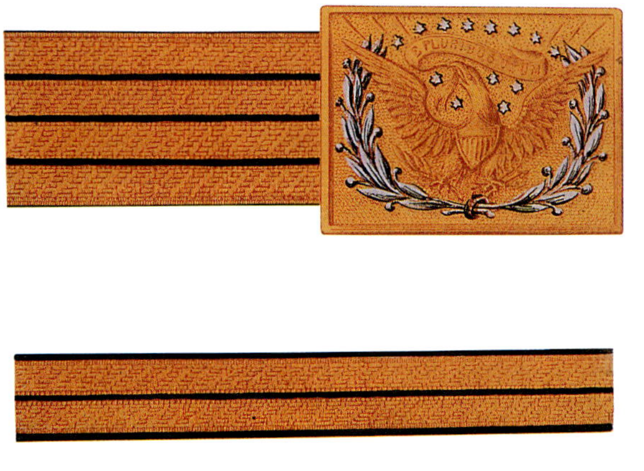

Plates 15-16, Sword-Belt and Sword-Belt Plate, Officer's, 1876 regulations. GC

Plates 21-24, Shoulder-Knots, 1876 regulations. GC

SWORD-BELT PLATE.

As per annexed plates, numbered 17 and 19.
For all officers.—Gilt, rectangular, two inches wide, with a raised bright rim; a silver wreath of laurel encircling the arms of the United States; eagle, shield, scroll, edge of cloud and rays bright. The motto "E pluribus unum" upon the scroll; stars also of silver, according to pattern.

SWORD-KNOT.

For general officers.—Gold cord with acorn end.
For all other officers.—Gold lace strap with bullion tassel, as now worn.

EPAULETS.

For the General of the Army.—Of gold, with solid crescent; device, two silver embroidered stars, with five rays each, one and one-half inches in diameter, and the arms of the United States embroidered in gold placed between them.
For a Lieutenant General.—Three Silver embroidered stars of five rays each, respectively, one and one-half, one and one-quarter, one and one-eighth inches in diameter. The largest placed in the center of the crescent; the others, placed longitudinally on the strap and equidistant, ranging in order of size from the crescent.
For a Major-General.—Same as for Lieutenant-General, omitting smallest star, and the smaller of time two remaining stars placed in the center of the strap.
For a Brigadier-General.—Same as for a Lieutenant-General, omitting all but the largest star.

SHOULDER-KNOTS.

As per annexed plates, numbered 21, 22, 23, and 24.
For officers of the Adjutant General's and Inspector General's Departments, and for aides-de-camp to general officers.—Of gold cord, Russian pattern, on dark-blue cloth ground; insignia of rank and letters of corps or designation of regiment embroidered on the cloth ground, according to pattern, an aiguillette of gold cord to be worn with the right shoulder- knot and permanently attached thereto, according to pattern.
For officers of other staff corps.—Same as above described, without the aiguillette.
For officers of cavalry, artillery, and infantry.—Of the same pattern as for the staff-corps, but on cloth of the same color as the facings of their arm, with insignia of rank and number of regiment embroidered on the cloth ground, according to pattern.
For regimental adjutants.—Of the same pattern as for other officers of their arm, but with aiguillettes attached.
Insignia of rank on shoulder-knots:
For a Colonel.—A silver embroidered eagle at the center of the pad.
For a Lieutenant Colonel.—Two silver embroidered leaves, one at each end of pad.
For a Major.—Two gold embroidered leaves, one at each end of pad.
For a Captain.—Two silver embroidered bars at each end of pad.
For a First Lieutenant.—One silver embroidered bar at each end of pad.
For a Second Lieutenant.—Plain.
For an additional Second Lieutenant.—Same as second lieutenant.
The above insignia to be the same as prescribed for the shoulder-straps.

SHOULDER-STRAPS.

For the General of the Army.—Dark-blue cloth, one and three-eighths inches wide by four inches long, bordered with an embroidery of gold one-fourth of an inch wide; two silver embroidered stars of five rays each, and gold embroidered arms of the United States between them.
For a Lieutenant-General.—The same as for the General, except that there will be three silver embroidered stars of five rays, one star on the center of the strap, and one on each side, equidistant between the center and outer edge of the strap, the center star to be the largest.
For all Major-Generals.—The same as for the Lieutenant- General except that there will be two stars instead of three; the center of each star to be one inch from the outer edge of the gold embroidery, on the ends of the strap, both stars of the same size.
For a Brigadier-General.—The same as for a major general, except that there still be one star instead of two; the center of the star to be equidistant from the outer edge of the embroidery on the ends of the strap.
For a Colonel.—The same size as for a major-general, and bordered in like manner with an embroidery of gold; a silver embroidered spread-eagle on the center of strap, two inches between the tips of the wings, having in the right talon an olive branch, and in the left a bundle of arrows; an escutcheon on the breast, as represented in the arms of the United States. Cloth of the strap as follows: for the general staff and staff corps, dark blue; artillery, scarlet; infantry, sky blue; cavalry, yellow.
For a Lieutenant-Colonel.—The same as for a colonel, according to corps, omitting the eagle, and introducing a silver embroidered leaf at each end. each leaf extending seven-eighths of an inch from the end border of the strap.

For a Major.—The same as for a colonel, according to corps, omitting the eagle and introducing a gold embroidered leaf at each end, each leaf extending seven-eighths of an inch from the end-border of the strap.

For a Captain.—The same as for a colonel, according to corps, omitting the eagle, and introducing at each end two silver embroidered bars of the same width as the border, placed parallel to the ends of the strap, at a distance between them and from the border equal to the width of the border.

For a First Lieutenant.—The same as for a colonel, according to corps, omitting the eagle, and introducing at each end one silver embroidered bar of the same width as the border, placed parallel to the ends of the strap, at a distance from the border equal to its width.

For a Second Lieutenant.—The same as for a colonel, according to corps, omitting the eagle.

For an additional Second Lieutenant.—The same as for a second lieutenant.

OVERCOAT.

For general officers.—Of dark-blue cloth, closing by means of four frog buttons of black silk; and loops of black silk cord; cord down the breast, and at the throat by a long loop "à l'échelle," without tassel or plate, on the left side, and a black silk frog button on the right; cord for the loops, fifteen- hundredths of an inch in diameter; back, a single piece, slit up from the bottom fifteen to seventeen inches, according to the height of the wearer, and closing at will by buttons and button-holes cut in a concealed flap; collar of the same color and material as the coat, rounded at the edges, and to stand or fall; when standing, to be about five inches high; sleeves loose, of a single piece and round at the bottom, without cuff or slit, lining woolen; around the front and lower borders, the edges of the pockets, the edges of the sleeves, collar, and slit in the back, a flat braid of black silk one-half an inch wide; and around each frog button on the breast a knot two and one-quarter inches in diameter, of black silk cord, seven-hundredths of an inch in diameter, cape of the same color and material as the coat, removable at the pleasure of the wearer, and reaching to the cuff of the coat-sleeve when the arm is extended; coat to extend down the leg from six to eight inches below the knee, according to height.

To indicate rank.—There will be on both sleeves, near the lower edge, a knot of flat black silk braid, not exceeding one-eighth of an inch in width, and composed of five braids, double knot.

For all other officers.—Dark-blue, close-fitting double-breasted surtout coat, with a cape, made to detach from the coat and fall to the tips of the fingers when the arm and hand are extended; the skirt of the coat for mounted officers to reach half way between the knee and the sole of the foot; for dismounted officers, three inches below the knee; edges to be stitched without braid.

The coat to have seven buttons on each breast of the same pattern as those on the uniform coat, arranged same as on full- dress coat; four buttonshehind, with side-edges same as on full-dress coat; no bottons on sleeves; lining to be of same color as facings for arm of service. The insignia of rank on the sleeve, as follows, viz.:

Colonel, five braids, single knot.

Lieutenant-colonel, four braids, single knot.

Major, three braids, single knot.

Captain, two braids, single knot.

First Lieutenant, one braid, single knot.

Second Lieutenant and Additional Second Lieutenant, without braid.

Military Store Keepers and Chaplains, without braid.

APPENDIX C:
Uniform Regulations, 1881

UNIFORM, DRESS, AND HORSE FURNITURE.
[*G.O.* No. 92, 1872.]

COATS.

Full Dress for Officers.

2587. All officers shall wear a double-breasted *frock* coat of dark blue cloth, the skirt to extend from one-half to three-fourths the distance from the hip joint to the bend of the knee.
2588. *For a General.*—Two rows of buttons on the breast, twelve in each row; placed by fours; the distance between each row five and one-half inches at top and three and one-half inches at bottom; standing collar, not less than one nor more than two inches in height, to hook in front at the bottom and slope thence up and backward at an angle of thirty degrees on each side, corners rounded; cuffs three inches deep, to go around the sleeves parallel with the lower edge, and with three small buttons at the under seam; pockets in the folds of the skirts, with two buttons at the hip and one at the lower end of each side-edge, making four buttons on the back and skirt of the coat; collar and cuffs to be of dark blue velvet; lining of the coat black.
2589. *For a Lieutenant General.*—The same as for a General, except that there will be ten buttons in each row, on the breast, the upper and lower groups by threes, and the middle groups by fours.
2590. *For a Major General.*—The same as for a General, except that there will be nine buttons in each row, on the breast, placed by threes.
2591. *For a Brigadier General.*-The same as for a General, except that there will be eight buttons in each row on the breast, placed by pairs.
2592. *For a Colonel, Lieutenant Colonel, and Major.*—The same as for a General, except that there will be nine buttons in each row, on the breast, placed at equal distances; collar and cuffs of the same color and material as the coat. Judge Advocates of the Army and Professors of the Military Academy are authorized to wear, when on duty, the plain dark blue body-coat prescribed in paragraph 2599; the buttons on the coat to be the same as for the general staff.—[*G.O.* 76, 1879; *G.O.* 9, 1882.]
2593. *For a Captain, 1st lieutenant, 2d lieutenant, and Additional 2d lieutenant.*—The same as for a Colonel, except that there will be seven buttons in each row, on the breast.
2594. *For all Storekeepers.*—The same as prescribed for officers of the same rank in the Quartermaster's, Medical and Ordnance Departments. [*G.O.* 23, 1878.]
2595. This coat shall be worn on all dress occasions, such as reviews, inspections, dress parades, guards, and courts-martial. It will be habitually worn at battalion drills, except in hot weather, or when otherwise exceptionally directed by the commanding officer. It may also be worn, with shoulder-straps, when on armed duty.—[*G.O.* 67, 1873.]

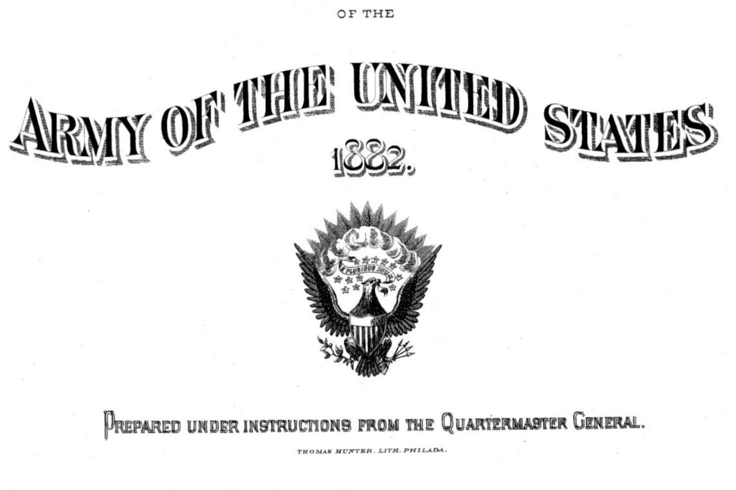

Helmets, Chapeau, and Helmet Plates, 1881 regulations. KC

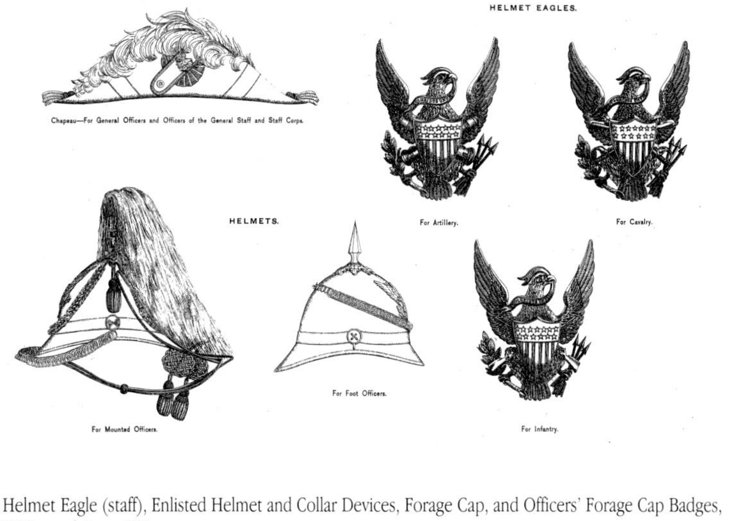

Helmet Eagle (staff), Enlisted Helmet and Collar Devices, Forage Cap, and Officers' Forage Cap Badges, 1881 regulations. KC

Helmet Eagle (staff), Enlisted Helmet and Collar Devices, Forage Cap, and Officers' Forage Cap Badges, 1881 regulations. KC

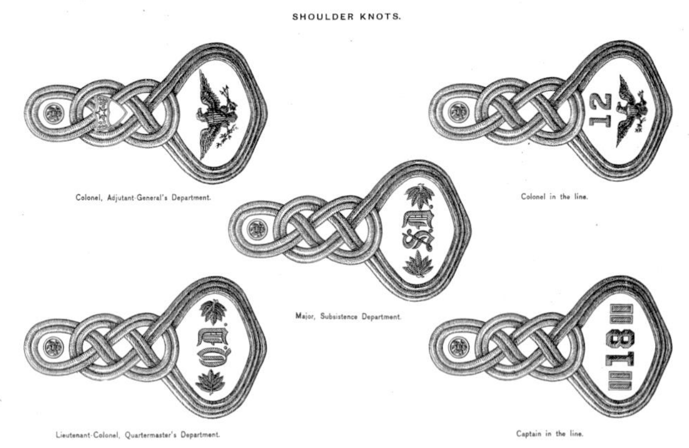

Shoulder Knots, 1881 regulations. KC

Undress for Officers.

2596. *For fatigues, marches, squad and company drills, and other drills when authorized by the commanding officer, and for ordinary wear.*—A sack coat of dark blue cloth or serge; falling collar; single breasted, with five buttons in front, same as those worn on the dress coat. The skirt to extend from one-third to two-thirds the distance from the hip-joint to the bend of the knee. The shoulder-straps will always be worn with this coat.—[G.O. 96, 1875.]
2597. *For all Storekeepers.*—Of pattern above described.
2598. *For a Chaplain.*—Plain black frock coat with standing collar; one row of nine black buttons on the breast, with "herring-bone" of black braid around the buttons and button-holes.
2595. Officers are permitted to wear a plain dark body-coat, with the button designating their respective corps, regiments, or departments, without any other mark or ornament upon it. This coat, however, is not to be considered as a dress for any military purpose.—[*G.O.* 96, 1875.]

Signal Service.

2600. *For the Chief Signal Officer.*—The same uniform as for a Brigadier General.
2601. *For other Officers of the Signal Corps.*—Same as that prescribed for the Adjutant General's Department, without the aiguillette, the usual distinction being made for the grades.—[*G.O.* 86, 1878.]

BUTTONS.

2602. *For General Officers and Officers of the General Staff.*—Gilt, convex with spread eagle and stars, and plain border; large size, seven-eights of an inch in the exterior diameter; small size, one-half inch.—[*Regs.* 1863, ¶ 1488.]
2603. *For Officers of the Corps of Engineers.*—Gilt, nine-tenths of an inch in exterior diameter, slightly convex; a raised bright rim one-thirteenth of an inch wide; device, an eagle holding in his beak a scroll, with the words "*Essayons*," a bastion with embrasures in the distance surrounded by water, with a rising sun—the figures to be dead gold upon a bright field. Small buttons of the same form and device, and fifty-five hundredths of an inch in extrior diameter.—[*Regs.* 1863, ¶ 1489.]
2604. *For Officers of the Ordnance Department.*—Gilt, convex, with plain border, cross cannon and bombshell, with circular scroll and across the cannon, containing the words "Ordnance Corps;" large size, seven-eights of an inch in exterior diameter; small size, one-half inch.—[*Regs.* 1863, ¶ 1491.]
2605. *For Officers of Artillery, Infantry, and Cavalry.*—Gilt, convex; a spread eagle with the letter A, for Artillery—I, for Infantry—C, for Cavalry, on the shield; large size, seven-eighths of an inch in exterior diameter; small size, one-half inch.—[*Regs.* 1863, ¶ 1492.]
2606. *Aides-de-Camp* may wear the button of the General Staff, or their regiment or corps, at their option.—[*Regs.* 1863, ¶ 1493.]
2607. *For Storekeepers.*—General Staff button.

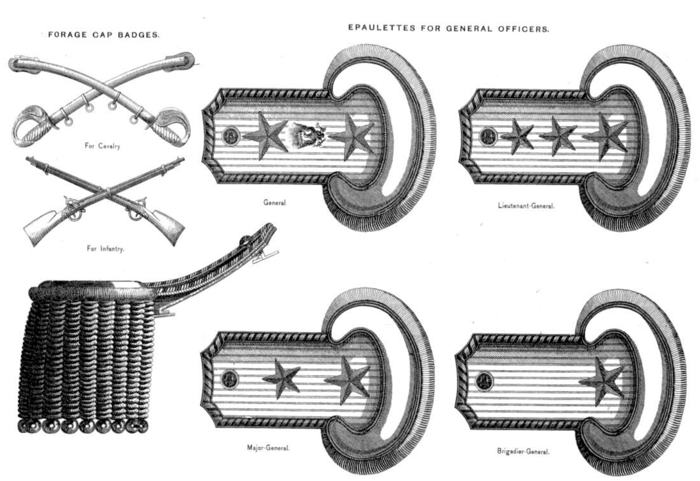

Enlisted Forage Cap Badges and Epaulets for General Officers, 1881 regulations. KC

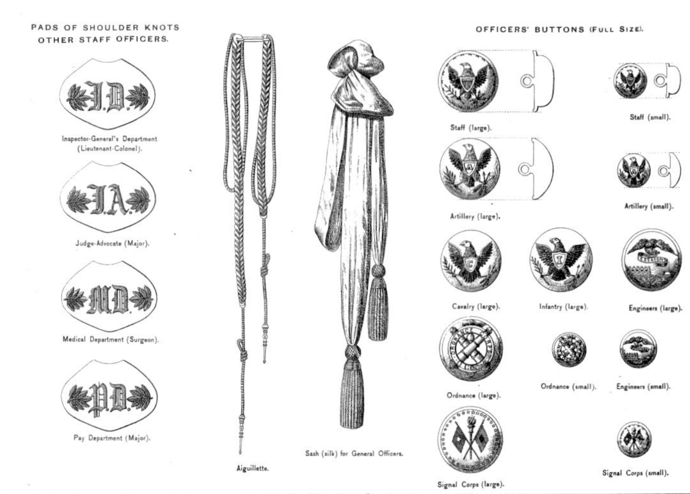

Shoulder Knot Pads,General Officer's Sash, and Officers' Buttons, 1881 regulations. KC

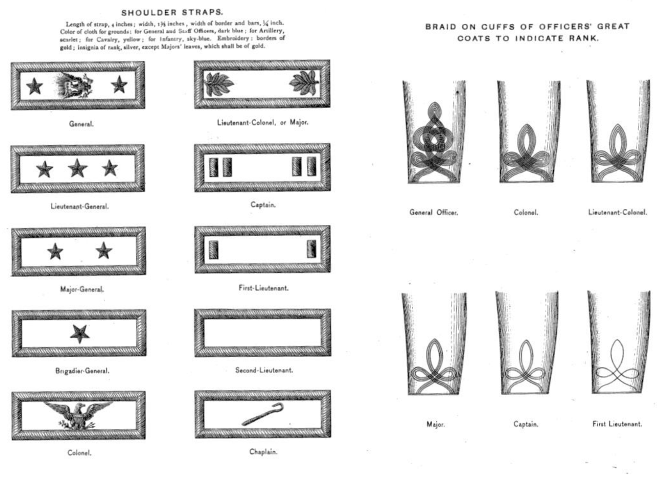

Shoulder Straps and Great Coat Braid, 1881 regulations. KC

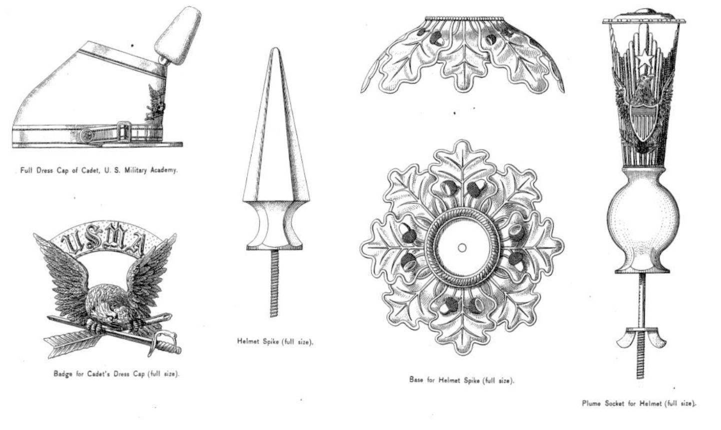

Cadet Full Dress Cap, Cadet Cap Badge, Helmet Spike, Helmet Base, Plume Socket, 1881 regulations. KC

CRAVATS.

2608. *For all Officers.*—Black; the tie not to be visible at the opening of the collar.

VESTS.

2609. Officers when on duty are permitted to wear a buff, white, or blue vest, with the small button prescribed for them.

TROUSERS.

2610. *For General Officers, Officers of the General Staff, and Staff Corps.*—Dark blue cloth, plain, without stripe, welt, or cord.
2611. *For all Regimental Officers of Cavalry, Artillery, and Infantry.*—Light blue cloth, same shade of color as for prescribed for enlisted men, with stripe one and one-half inches wide, welted at the edges; color, that of facings of their respective arms, except Infantry, which will be dark blue.
2612. *Storekeepers.*—Dark blue cloth, without stripe, welt, or cord.
2613. *For Chaplains.*-Plain black, with black cord on the outer seam.—[*G.O.* 10. 1880.]
2614. Whenever, in extreme southern latitudes, white trousers are worn by enlisted men, the officers must in like manner wear them.—[*G.O.* 76, 1879.]

HAT OR HELMET (FULL DRESS).

2615. *For General Officers, Officers of the General Staff and Staff Corps, except the Signal Corps.*—Chapeau, according to pattern, to be worn with the front peak turned slightly to the left, showing the gilt ornaments upon the right side.—[*G.O.* 67, 1873.]
2616. *Helmets for Field Officers.*—According to the pattern on file in the office of the Quartermaster General. Body: of cork or other suitable material covered with black cloth, or of black felt, at the option of the wearer. Trimmings: cords and tassels, top piece and plume-socket, chain chin-strap and hooks, eagle with motto, crossed cannon, crossed rifles, or sabres, all gilt, with the number of the regiment on the shield in white; plume of buffalo-hair, white for Infantry, yellow for Cavalry, and red for Artillery.
2617. *Helmets for all other Mounted Officers, and Officers of Signal Corps.*—Same as above, except that the color of the plume shall be orange for Signal Corps.
2618. *Helmets for other Officers of Foot Troops.*—Same as above, except that the trimmings are as follows: Top piece, spike, chain chin-strap with hooks and side buttons, eagle with motto, crossed rifles or cannon, all gilt, with the number of the regiment on the shield in white.
2619. *Officers' Summer Helmets.*—Body: of cork as per pattern in the office of the Quartermaster General, covered with white facing cloth; top piece, spike, chain chin-strap, and hooks, all gilt.—[*G.O.* 4, 1881.]

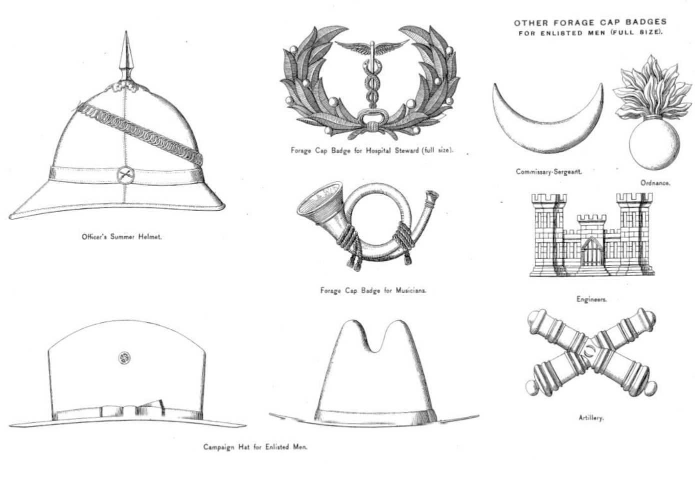

Officer's Summer Helmet, Campaign Hat, and Enlisted Forage Cap Badges, 1881 regulations. KC

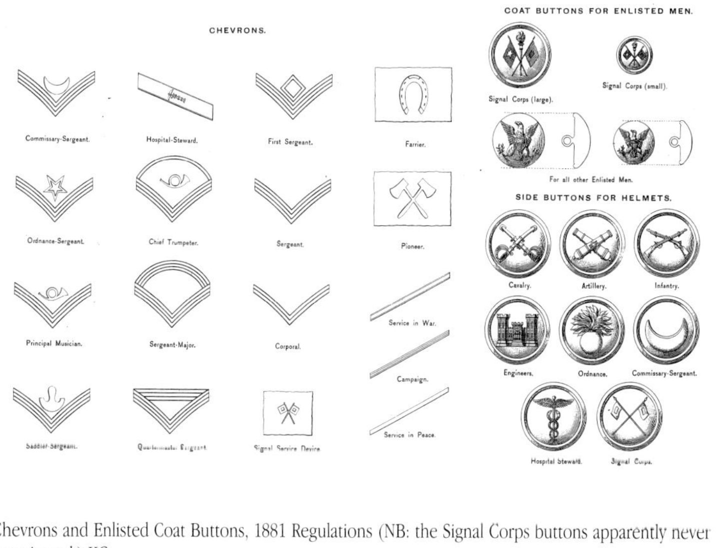

Chevrons and Enlisted Coat Buttons, 1881 Regulations (NB: the Signal Corps buttons apparently never were issued.) KC

General Officers' Full Dress, 1881 regulations. KC

Staff Officer Full Dress, Officer's Great Coat, Officer's Fatigue Dress, and Chaplain, 1881 regulations. KC

2620. The helmet cords will be attached to the left side of the helmet and come down to the let shoulder, where they are held together by a slide; one cord then passes to the front and the other to the rear of the neck, crossing upon the right shoulder and passing separately around to the front and rear of the right arm, where they are again united and held together by a slide under the arm; the united cords then cross the breast and are looped up to the upper button on the left side of the coat.—[*G.O.* 67, 1873.]

PLUMES FOR OFFICERS.

2621. *For General-in-Chief.*—Three black ostrich feathers.
2622. *For other General Officers, for Officers of the General Staff, and Staff Corps, except the Signal Corps.*—Two black ostrich feathers.

FORAGE CAP.

2623. *For General Officers.*—Of dark blue cloth, chasseur pattern, with black velvet band and badge in front.
2624. *For all other Commissioned Officers.*—Of dark blue cloth, chasseur pattern, with badge of corps or regiment in front, and top of badge to be even with top of cap.

FORAGE CAP BADGES.

2625. *For General Officers.*—A gold embroidered wreath on dark blue cloth ground, encircling the letters *U.S.* in silver, old English characters.
2626. *For Officers of Adjutant General's Department.*—A solid shield of silver bearing thirteen stars, according to the pattern in the Adjutant General's Office.—[*G.O.* 107, 1872; *G.O.* 67, 1873.]
2627. *For Officers of Engineers.*—A gold embroidered wreath of laurel and palm encircling a silver turreted castle on dark blue cloth ground.
2628. *For Officers of Ordnance.*—A gold embroidered shell and flame on dark blue cloth ground.
2629. *For Officers of the Signal Corps.*—According to the pattern deposited in the office of the Chief Signal Officer.—[*G.O.* 86, 1878.]
2630. *For all other Staff Officers.*—Same as for General Officers.
2631. *For Officers of Cavalry.*—Two gold embroidered sabres, crossed, edges upward, on dark blue cloth ground, with the number of regiment in silver in the upper angle.
2632. *For Officers of Artillery.*—Two gold embroidered cannons, crossed, on dark blue cloth ground, with the number of the regiment in silver at the intersection of the cross-cannon.
2633. *For Officers of Infantry.*—Two gold embroidered rifles without bayonets, barrels upwards, on dark blue cloth ground, with the number of the regiment in silver in the upper angle, according to pattern in the Quartermaster General's Office.—[*G.O.* 96. 1875.]

FATIGUE HAT.

2634. *For all Officers*: Of black felt, according to pattern, to be worn in garrison only on fatigue duty; and on marches and campaigns.—[G.O. 92, 1872; G.O. 67, 1873.]
2635. Whenever, in extreme southern latitudes, straw hats are worn by enlisted men, the officers must in like manner wear them.—[*G.O.* 76, 1879.]

EPAULETTES.

2636. *For the General of the Army.*—Of gold, with solid crescent; device.—two silver embroidered stars, with five rays each, one and one-half inches in

Officers' Full Dress and Cadet Dress uniform, 1881 regulations. KC

Signal Corps Enlisted Full Dress, Enlisted Fatigue Dress, and Stable Outfit, 1881 regulations. KC

Officers' Full Dress Uniforms, 1881 regulations. KC

diameter, and the "Arms of the United States" embroidered in gold placed between them.

2637. *For a Lieutenant General.*—Of gold, with solid crescent; device.—three silver embroidered stars of five rays each, respectively, one and one-half, one and one-quarter, and one and one-eighth inches in diameter. The largest placed in the centre of the crescent; the others, placed longitudinally on the strap and equidistant, ranging in order of size from the crescent.

2638. *For Major General.*—Same as for Lieutenant General, omitting smallest star, and the smaller of time two remaining stars placed in the centre of the strap.

2639. *For a Brigadier General.*—Same as for Lieutenant General, omitting all but the largest star.

SHOULDER-KNOTS.

2640. *For Officers of the Adjutant General's and Inspector General's Departments, and for Aides-de-Camp to General Officers.**—Of gold cord, Russian pattern, on dark blue cloth ground; insignia of rank and letters of corps or designation of regiment embroidered on the cloth ground, according to pattern; an aiguillette of gold cord to be worn with the right shoulder- knot, according to pattern.

The aiguillette, instead of being permanently attached to the shoulder-knot, may be made separate, so as to be attached to the coat underneath the knot by means of a strap or tongue passing through the lower fastening of he knot.—[*G.O.* 67, 1873.]

2641. *For Officers of other Staff Corps.*—Same as above described, without the aiguillette.

2642. For Officers of the Signal Corps.—Same as above described, without the aiguillette. The distinctive insignia will be according to the pattern deposited in the office of the Chief Signal Officer.—[*G.O.* 86, 1878.]

2643. Whenever the full dress coat is worn by officers on duty, the prescribed epaulettes or shoulder-knots will be attached. Letters to be embroidered in old English.

2644. *Adjutant General's Department.*—A solid shield of silver bearing thirteen stars, according to pattern in the Adjutant General's Office. For an Assistant Adjutant General with the rank of Colonel, it will be worn on the bullion of the knot, midway between the upper fastening and the pad.—[*G.O.* 67. 1863; *G.0.* 107, 1872.]

2645. *Inspector General's Bureau.*—I.D.

2646. *Bureau of Military Justice.*—J.D.

2647. *Quartermaster Department.*—Q.D.

2648. *Subsistence Department.*—S.D.

2649. *Medical Department.*—M.D.

2650. *Pay Department.*—P.D.

2651. *Engineer Corps.*—A silver turreted castle of metal one and four-tenths inches in width by nine-tenths of an inch in height.—[*G.O.* 107, 1872.]

2652. *Ordnance Department.*—A shell and flame in silver embroidery one and four-tenths inches in width by nine-tenths of an inch in height.—[*G.O.* 107, 1872.]

2653. *For Officers of Cavalry, Artillery, and Infantry.*—Of the same pattern as for the Staff Corps, but on cloth of the same color as the facings of their arm, with insignia of rank and number of regiment embroidered on the cloth ground, according to pattern.

2654. *For Regimental Adjutants.*—Of the same pattern as for other officers of their arm, but with aiguillettes attached.

Insignia of Rank on Shoulder-Knots.

*Aides-de-Camp and the Military Secretary, who have *increased* rank, will wear the aiguillette with the uniform of the General Staff.
Aides-de-Camp to Major and Brigadier Generals will wear the aiguillette with the uniform of their regiments an corps.

2655. *For a Colonel.*—A silver embroidered eagle at the centre of the pad.

2656. *For a Lieutenant Colonel.*—Two silver embroidered leaves, one at each end of pad.

2657. *For a Major.*—Two gold embroidered leaves, one at each end of pad.

2658. *For a Captain.*—Two silver embroidered bars at each end of pad.

2659. *For a 1st Lieutenant.*—One silver embroidered bar at each end of pad.

2660. *For a 2d Lieutenant.*—Plain.

2661. *For an additional 2d Lieutenant.*—Same as 2d Lieutenant.

2662. The above insignia to be the *same* as prescribed for the shoulder-strap.

SHOULDER-STRAPS.

2663. *For the General of the Army.*—Dark blue cloth, one and three-eighths inches wide by four inches long, bordered with an embroidery of gold one-fourth of an inch wide; two silver embroidered stars of five rays each, and gold embroidered "Arms of the United States" between them.

2664. *For a Lieutenant General.*—The same as for the General, except that there will be three silver embroidered stars of five rays, one star on the centre of the strap, and one on each side, equidistant between the centre and outer edge of the strap, the centre star to be the largest.

2665. *For all Major Generals.*—The same as for the Lieutenant General except that there will be two stars instead of three; the centre of each star to be one inch from the outer edge of the gold embroidery on the ends of the strap; both stars of the same size.

2666. *For a Brigadier General.*—The same as for a Major General, except that there still be one star instead of two; the centre of the star to be equidistant from the outer edge of the embroidery on the ends of the strap.

2667. *For a Colonel.*—The same size as for a Major General, and bordered in like manner with an embroidery of gold; a silver embroidered spread eagle on the centre of the strap, two inches between the tips of the wings, having in the right talon an olive branch, and in the left a bundle of arrows; an escutcheon on the breast, as represented in the "Arms of the United States." Cloth of the strap as follows: for the General Staff and Staff Corps, dark blue; Artillery, scarlet; Infantry, sky-blue; Cavalry, yellow.

2668. *For a Lieutenant Colonel.*—The same as for Colonel, according to corps omitting the eagle, and introducing a silver embroidered leaf at each end, each leaf extending seven-eighths of an inch from the end border of the strap.

2669. *For a Major.*—The same as for a Colonel, according to corps, omitting the eagle and introducing a gold embroidered leaf at each end, each leaf extending seven-eighths of an inch from the end border of the strap.

2670. *For a Captain.*—The same as for a Colonel, according to corps, omitting the eagle, and introducing at each end two silver embroidered bars of the same width as the border, placed parallel to the ends of the strap, at a distance between them and from the border equal to the width of the border.

2671. *For a 1st Lieutenant.*—The same as for a Colonel, according to corps, omitting the eagle, and introducing at each end one silver embroidered bar of the same width as the border, placed parallel to the ends of the strap, at a distance from the border equal to its width.

2672. *For a 2d Lieutenant.*—The same as for a Colonel, according to corps, omitting the eagle.

2673. *For an additional 2d Lieutenant.*—The same as for a 2d Lieutenant.
2674. *For Chaplains.*—A shoulder-strap of black velvet, with a shepherd's crook of frosted silver on the centre of the strap, may be worn.—[*G.O.* 10, 1880.]
2675. Officers serving in the field may dispense with prominent marks likely to attract fire of sharpshooters; but all officers must wear the prescribed shoulder-strap, to indicate their rank.
2676. The shoulder-strap will be worn whenever the epaulette or shoulder-knot is dispensed with.

GLOVES.

2677. *For General Officers, Officers of the General Staff; and Staff Corps.*—Buff or white gauntlets or gloves.
2678. *For Field Officers of Artillery, Cavalry, and Infantry; for Officers of Light Artillery and Cavalry.*—White gauntlets or gloves. All other officers, white gloves.

SASH.

2679. *For General Officers.*—Buff silk net, with silk bullion fringe ends; sash to go twice around the waist and to tie behind the left hip, pendent part not to extend more than eighteen inches below the tie.
2680. General officers above the grade of Brigadier General will be allowed, at their option, to wear the sash across the body from the left shoulder to the right side.
2681. The sash may be of buff silk and gold thread.—[*G.O.* 11, 1877.]

SWORD-BELT.

2682. *For all Officers.*—A waist-belt, not less than one and one-half nor more than two inches wide, with slings of the same material as the belt, with a hook attached to the belt on which to hang the sword.
2683. The sword and sword-belt will be worn outside the coat, and by all officers below the grade of Brigadier General, outside the overcoat.—[*G.O.* 107, 1872; *G.O.* 96, 1875.]
2684. *For General Officers.*—Of red Russia leather, with three stripes of gold embroidery, as per pattern.
2685. *For all Field Officers.*—One broad stripe of gold lace on black enameled leather, according to pattern.
2686. *For all Officers of the General Staff, and Staff Corps, below the rank of Field Officers.*—Four stripes of gold, interwoven with black silk, lined with black enameled leather, according to pattern.
2687. *For Company Officers of Cavalry, Artillery, and Infantry.*— Four stripes of gold lace, interwoven with silk of the same color as the facings of their arms of service, and lined with black enameled leather.
2688. *For all Storekeepers.*—Same as Officers of the General Staff of the same rank.—[*G.O.* 23, 1878.]
2689. On undress duty, marches, and campaigns, officers may wear a plain black leather belt.

SWORD-BELT PLATE.

2690. *For all Officers.*—Gilt, rectangular, two inches wide, with a raised bright rim; a silver wreath of laurel encircling the "Arms of the United States;" eagle, shield, scroll, edge of cloud and rays bright. The motto "*E pluribus unum*" upon the scroll; stars also of silver, according to pattern.

SWORD AND SCABBARD.

2691. *General Officers.*—Straight sword, gilt hilt, silver grip; brass or steel scabbard, same as now worn.
2692. *For Officers of Light Artillery and Cavalry.*—Sabre and scabbard as now worn, and according to pattern in Ordnance Department.
2693. *For Mounted Officers of Infantry.*—Sword and scabbard of the pattern prescribed for Cavalry Officers.
2694. *For Officers of the Pay and Medical Departments.*—Small sword and scabbard, according to pattern in the Surgeon General's Office, as now worn.
2695. *For all other Officers.*—Same as the small, straight sword now worn by the officers of the General Staff, and according to pattern in the Ordnance Department.
2996. Whenever the full dress coat is worn on armed duty and not in the field, by officers below the grade of Brigadier general, the nickel-plated sword scabbards will be worn by those officers for whom it is prescribed.—[*G.O.* 67, 1873.]
2997. Whenever the sack coat is worn on armed duty, the dark sword scabbard will be worn by those officers for whom it is prescribed.—[*G.O.* 67, 1873.]
2998. The sword and sword-belt will be worn upon all occasions of duty, except stable and fatigue.
2699. When not on military duty, officers may wear swords of honor, or the prescribed sword, with a scabbard, gilt, or of leather with gilt mountings.

SWORD-KNOT.

2700. *For General Officers.*—Gold cord, with acorn end.
2701. *For all other Officers.*—Gold lace strap, with gold bullion tassel.

SPURS.

2702. *For all Mounted Officers.*—Yellow metal or gilt.

OVERCOAT.

2703. *For General Officers.*—Of dark blue cloth, closing by means of four frog buttons of black silk cord and loops of black silk cord down the breast, and at the throat by a long loop "*à l'échelle*," without tassel or plate, on the left side, and a black silk frog button on the right; cord for the loops fifteen hundredths of an inch in diameter; back, a single piece, slit up from the bottom from fifteen to seventeen inches, according to the height of the wearer, and closing at will by buttons, and button-holes cut in a concealed flap; collar of the same color and material as the coat, rounded at the edges, and to stand or fall; when standing to

General Officer Fatigue Dress, Staff Officers' Full Dress, and General Officer's Great Coat. 1881 regulations. KC

Engineer and Ordnance Enlisted Full Dress, 1881 regulations. KC

be about five inches high; sleeves loose, of a single piece and round at the bottom, without cuff or slit; lining woolen, and with the facings, to correspond in color with the trimmings of the uniform (*G.O* 76, 1879); around the front and lower borders, the edges of the pockets, the edges of the sleeves, collar, and slit in the back, a flat braid of black silk one-half an inch wide; and around each frog button on the breast a knot two and one-quarter inches in diameter, of black silk cord, seven hundredths of an inch in diameter, cape of the same color and material as the coat, removable at the pleasure of the wearer, and reaching to the cuff of the coat sleeve when the arm is extended; coat to extend down the leg from six to eight inches below the knee, according to height.

2704. *To indicate Rank.*—There will be on both sleeves, near the lower edge, a knot of flat black silk braid, not exceeding one-eighth of an inch in width, and composed of five braids, double knot.

2705. *For all other Officers.*—Dark blue close-fitting double-breasted surtout-coat, with a cape, made to detach from the coat and fall to the tips of the fingers when the arm and hand are extended; the skirt of the coat for mounted officers to reach half-way between the knee and the sole of the foot; for dismounted officers, three inches below the knee.

The coat to have seven buttons on each breast of the same pattern as those on the uniform coat. The insignia of rank on the sleeve, as follows, viz:

Colonel, five braids, single knot.
Lieutenant Colonel, four braids, single knot.
Major, three braids, single knot.
Captain, two braids, single knot.
1st Lieutenant, one braid, single knot.
2d Lieutenant and Additional 2d Lieutenant, without braid. Military Storekeepers, same as officers of the General Staff of like rank.
Chaplains, without braid.

2706. On the frontier and campaign, officers may wear the soldier's overcoat, with insignia of rank on the sleeve.

HORSE FURNITURE

For General Officers and the General Staff.

2707. *Housing for General Officers.*—To be worn over the saddle; of dark blue cloth, trimmed with two rows of gold lace, the outer row one inch and five-eighths wide, the inner row two inches and one-fourth; to be made full, so as to cover the horse's haunches and forehands, and to bear one ach flank corner the following ornaments, distinctive of rank, to wit:

2708. *For the General of the Army.*—A gold embroidered spread eagle with two stars and "Arms if the United States" between them.

2709. *For Lieutenant General.*—A gold embroidered spread eagle and three stars.

2710. *For Major Generals.*—A gold embroidered spread eagle and two stars.

2711. *For Brigadier Generals.*—A gold embroidered spread eagle and one star.

2712. *Saddle-cloth for General Staff Officers, and Officers of the Staff Corps.*—Dark blue cloth, of sufficient length to cover the saddle and holsters, and one foot ten inches in depth, with edgings of gold lace one inch wide.

Hospital Steward, Ordnance Sergeant, Commissary Sergeant Full Dress, and Enlisted Great Coat, 1881 regulations. KC

2713. *For all other Officers.*—Dark blue felt, according to pattern; worn under the saddle and trimmed around the edges with cloth one and one-half inches wide, color as follows:
Infantry, sky-blue.
Artillery, scarlet.
Cavalry, yellow.

MILITARY ACADEMY.

2714. The uniform of the Professors and Sword Master at the West Point Military Academy shall be the same as now worn, excepting they will be permitted to wear the dark blue sack coat prescribed for Army officers, with the buttons of the general staff to be worn on both coats, and that professors are authorized to wear the coat prescribed in paragraph 2599.—[*G.O.* 9, 1882.]

2715. *For Cadets.*—The same uniform as now worn.

COATS.

2716. *For Enlisted Men of Infantry.*—Single-breasted, dark blue basque, according to pattern deposited in Quartermaster General's Office, piped with sky-blue; collar same height as for officers' coat, faced with sly-blue cloth four inches back on each side, cut square to hook up close in front; number of regiment or badge of corps in yellow metal in middle of sky-blue facing of collar on each side; skirt of coat on each side of opening behind to be faced with sky-blue cloth, ornamented with four buttons, as per pattern. Two straps of dark blue cloth, piped with the same color as the facings, let into the waist-seam on each side the coat and buttoning above the hip to sustain the waist-belt; shoulder-straps of cloth the color of the facings let into the shoulder-seam and to button over the shoulder-belts at the collar-seam with one button; shoulder-straps for Engineer soldiers to be scarlet, piped with white.

2717. *For Enlisted Men of Artillery, Engineers, and Ordnance.*—Same as for Infantry, except that the facings shall be scarlet for Artillery, scarlet and white for Engineers, and crimson for Ordnance.

2718. *For Enlisted Men of Cavalry and Light Artillery.*—Same as for Infantry, excepting that it is shorter in the skirts, and the facing upon the skirt put on differently, according to pattern in the Quartermaster General's Office; facings for Cavalry, yellow, and for Light Artillery, red.

2719. *For Musicians.*—Ornamented on the breast with braid same color as the facings, running from the button as now worn, the outer extremities terminating in "herring-bones" and the braid returning back to the buttons.

2720. *For Hospital Stewards.*—Same as for Infantry, except the facings to be of emerald green.

2721. *For Ordnance Sergeants.*—Same as for enlisted men of Ordnance.

2722. *For Commissary Sergeants.*—The same as Infantry, except that the facings will be cadet gray.

2723. *For Enlisted Men of the Signal Service.*—Same as Cavalry, except that the trimmings and facings will be orange.

2724. Whenever the dress coat is worn by enlisted men, it will invariably be buttoned up and hooked at the collar.

2725. *For Fatigue Purposes, for General Wear, and on Field Service.*—A dark blue blouse of navy flannel, according to the pattern deposited in the Quartermaster General's Office.

Blouses* for winter wear to be lined.

---

*Only one blouse will hereafter annually be issued to each enlisted man. This will be lined.—[*G.O.* 4, 1881.]

BUTTONS.

2726. *For all Enlisted Men.*—Yellow, the same as is used by the Artillery, etc., omitting the letter in the shield.—[*Regs.* 1863, ¶ 1495.]

CHEVRONS.

2727. The rank of non-commissioned officers will be marked by chevrons, points down, upon both sleeves of the uniform coat, blouse, and overcoat, above the elbow; of cloth of the same color as the facings of the uniform coat, divided into

bars a half inch wide by black silk stitching, except for Engineers, which will be white stitching and piped with white, and for Infantry [overcoat], which will be dark blue, according to pattern in Quartermaster General's Office, as follows:
2728. *For a Sergeant Major.*—Three bars and an arc.
2729. *For a Quartermaster Sergeant.*—Three bars and a tie of three bars.
2730. *For a Saddler Sergeant.*—According to pattern in the Quartermaster General' Office.—[*G.O.* 67, 1873.]
2731. *For a Chief Trumpeter.*—According to the pattern in the Quartermaster General's Office.—[*G.O.* 67, 1873.]
2732. *For a Principal Musician.*—Three bars and a bugle.
2733. *For an Ordnance Sergeant.*—Three bars and a star.
2734. *For a Commissary Sergeant.*—Three bars and a crescent (point up) of same color as chevron and above it.—[*G.O.* 38, 1873.]
2735. *For a Hospital Steward.*—A half chevron of emerald green cloth one and three-fourths inches wide, piped with yellow cloth, running obliquely downward from the outer to the inner seam of the sleeve, and at an angle of about thirty degrees with a horizontal, and in the centre a "caduceus" two inches long, the head toward the outer seam of the sleeve.
2736. *For a 1st Sergeant.*—Three bars and a lozenge.
2737. *For a Battalion or Company Quartermaster Sergeant.*—Three bars and a tie of one bar.
2738. *For a Sergeant.*—Three bars.
2739. *For a Corporal.*—Two bars.
2740. *For a Pioneer.*—Two crossed hatchets, of cloth, same color and material as the facings of the uniform coat, to be sewed on each sleeve, above the elbow, in the place indicated for a chevron (those of a Corporal to be just above and resting on the chevron), the head of the hatchet upward, its edge outward, of the following dimensions, viz.:
Handle, four and one-half inches long, one-fourth to one-third of a inch wide.
Hatchet, two inches long,, one inch wide at the edge.
2741. [Revoked by *G.O.* 92, 1882.]
2742. *For Enlisted Men of the Signal Corps.*—Crossed signal flags, red and white, on dark blue cloth; size of flags, three-fourths of an inch square; length of staff, three inches, after pattern in the office of the Chief Signal Officer of the Army. This device to be worn by the non-commissioned officers above the chevrons; by privates of the first class on both arms; and by privates of the second class on the left arm only, in the same position as the chevron of non-commissioned officers.
2743. *To Indicate Service.*—All non-commissioned officers, musicians, and privates, who have served faithfully for one term of enlistment, will wear as a mark of distinction upon both sleeves of the uniform coat, overcoat, and blouse, below the elbow, a diagonal half chevron, one-half inch wide, extending from seam to seam, the front end nearest the cuff, and one-half inch above the point of the cuff, to be of the same color as the facing on the uniform coat.—[*G.O.* 92 1882.]
2744. In like manner an additional half chevron, above and parallel to the first, for every subsequent term of enlistment and faithful service. Distance between each chevron one-fourth of an inch.
2745. Each chevron will conform in color to the arm of service in which the soldier served.—[*G.O.* 92 1873.]
2746. The *service-in-war* chevron will be one-half and inch wide, of the same color as the facings, with piping, on each side of the stripe, one-eighth of an inch,—white for Artillery and red for all other arms,—thus making the chevron three-fourths of an inch in width in the aggregate, and will be worn by enlisted men on the uniform coat, overcoat, and blouse, as soon as the right to wear it has been earned.
The *campaign* chevron will be identical with the war chevron, except that it will be one-half of an inch instead of three-quarters of an inch in width in the aggregate, and will also be worn by enlisted men on the uniform coat, overcoat, and blouse, as soon as the right to wear it has been earned. But one campaign chevron for each enlistment will be allowed, not withstanding that the soldier may have served during such enlistment in more than one campaign for which chevrons are authorized.
All soldiers who, during the war of the rebellion, were in the volunteer service are entitled to wear the war chevron, provided they served in one or more campaigns in the field.
The *service-in-war* chevron will be worn next the cuff; above this will be worn the *service* chevron or chevrons; and next above this the *campaign* chevron.—[*G.O.* 92, 1882.]
2747. War and service chevrons are issued without charge.

CRAVATS.

2748. Neither cravats nor stocks will be worn by enlisted men when on duty.

TROUSERS.

2749. *For Enlisted Men of all Arms, of the Signal Service, and the Ordnance Depart*ment.—Sky blue mixture; waistband, two inches wide, to button with two buttons in front; pockets in front, opening at top.—[G.O. 108, 1882.]
2750. Sergeants to wear a stripe one inch wide, color of facings; and Corporals to wear a stripe one-half inch wide, color of facings, except Infantry, which will be dark blue.
2751. *For Engineers.*—According to pattern in the Quartermaster General's Office.
2752. *For Ordnance Sergeants.*—Crimson stripe, one inch and one-quarter wide.
2753. *For Hospital Stewards.*—Emerald green stripe, one inch and one-quarter wide.
2754. *For Commissary Sergeants.*—Cadet gray stripe, one and one-quarter inch wide.—[*G.O.* 38, 1873.]
2755. All stripes to be of cloth.
2756. Trousers for all mounted men to be reinforced.
2757. In extreme southern latitudes, in summer, commanding officers are authorized to sanction the use, on duty, of white trousers, to be bought, out of pay of the soldier, of the local merchant or trader.—[*G.O.* 76, 1879.]

BOOTS AND SHOES.

2758. The Quartermaster's Department manufactures (at the Leavenworth Military Prison) the shoes for the Army of the best materials and patterns possible. No particular shoe is adopted as *uniform.*—[*G.O.* 76, 1879.]

HAT OR HELMET (FULL DRESS).

2759. *Helmets for Mounted Troops.*—Body of black felt, or other suitable material, as per pattern in the office of the Quartermaster General, with leather chin-strap. Brass eagle, with motto, shield, and crossed arms, according to arm of service. Number of regiment or device of corps in white metal (German silver) on shield. Brass side buttons bearing device of corps or arm of service. Top-piece, plume-socket, and rings, all brass. Horse-hair plume, and cords and bands of color according to arm of service.
2760. *Helmets for all Foot Troops.*—Of same pattern as for mounted troops, with chin-strap, brass eagle, and side buttons as described. The top ornament to consist of a spike and base of brass as per pattern, instead of plume-socket. No rings.

Enlisted Artillery Full Dress, 1881 regulations. KC

2761. *Trimmings.*—Devices in white metal (German silver) for staff and staff corps. Commissary sergeants, a crescent; hospital stewards, a caduceus; engineers, a castle; ordnance, a shell and flame; signal corps, crossed flags. To be worn on the shield.—[*G.O.* 43, 1882.]
2762. The helmet cords will be attached to the left side of the helmet and come down to the left shoulder, where they are held together by a slide; one cord then passes to the front and the other to the rear of the neck, crossing under the right shoulder and passing separately around the front and rear of the right arm, where they are again united and held together by a slide under the arm; the united cords then cross the breast and are looped up to the upper button on the left side of the coat.—[*G.O.* 67, 1873.]
2763. Cork helmets will be supplied only to troops serving in extremely hot climates, in the first and third years of their enlistment, and these only in lieu of the campaign hat. The necessity for such issue must in all cases be certified by the Department Commander.—[*G.O.* 72, 1880.]

FORAGE CAP.

2764. *For all Enlisted Men.*—Of plain blue cloth, same pattern as for officers, with badge of corps or letter of company of yellow metal, according to patterns in the Quartermaster General's Office, worn in front as for officers.

FORAGE CAP BADGES.

2765. The cap badges, numbers of regiments, and letters of companies will be worn by enlisted men of the Army in the following manner, viz.:
2766. *For Light Artillery and Cavalry Soldiers.*—The numbers of their regiments in the upper, and the letters of their companies in the lower, angles of the badges of their respective arms upon the forage caps; the helmets and trimmings according to the pattern now worn.
2767. *For Ordnance Sergeants and Soldiers.*—The "shell and flame" on forage caps.
2768. *For Hospital Stewards.*—The caduceus in white metal, enclosed by a wreath, on forage cap.—[*G.O.* 9, 1882.]
2769. *For Commissary Sergeants.*—Crescent in white metal, the points in a vertical line, on forage caps.
2770. *For Engineers.*—The castle, with letter of company above it, on forage caps.
2771. *For Artillery.*—The crossed cannons, with number of regiment in upper, and letters of company in lower, angles, on forage cap.
2772. *For Infantry.*—The crossed rifles with the numbers of regiment and letters of company placed as for Artillery, upon forage caps.
2773. *For Field and Band Musicians.*—Bugle, with numbers of regiment in the centre, and the letters of the company above the bugle.
2774. *The cap trimmings* for enlisted men of all arms and crops will be of yellow metal, unless otherwise specified.—[*G.O.* 8, 1877.]
2775. This regulation does not dispense with nor prohibit the wearing on the collar of the coat the number of the regiment or badge of corps.

FATIGUE HAT.

2776. *For Enlisted Men.*—Of black felt, according to pattern; only to be issued to troops on the frontier or in active campaign, at the rate of one per year.—[*G.O.* 64, 1882.]

Cavalry and Infantry Enlisted Full Dress, 1881 regulations. KC

2777. In extreme southern latitudes, in summer, commanding officers are authorized to sanction, on duty, the straw hat, to be bought, out of pay of the soldier, of local the merchant or trader.—[*G.O.* 76, 1879.]

GLOVES.

2778. *For all Enlisted Men.*—Of white berlin.

SPURS.

2779. *For all Mounted Men.*—Of yellow metal, plain surface.

OVERCOATS.

2780. *For all Enlisted.*—Of sky-blue cloth, double breasted, according to pattern; the linings and facings to conform [in color]* to the trimmings of the uniform.—[*G.O.* 67, 1873; *G.O.* 76, 1879.]

REGIMENTAL BANDS.

2781. Bands will wear the uniforms, generally, of their regiments. Commanding officers may, upon appropriations made by the councils of administration, add such ornaments as they deem proper to the uniforms for chief musicians and bands.—[*G.O.* 107, 1872.]

WEST POINT BAND.

The uniform as now worn.—[*G.O.* 107, 1872.]

*The lining for Infantry great coat capes to be dark blue.

APPENDIX D: Select Quartermaster Specifications, 1884-1887

Sky-blue Kersey

[Adopted before assignment of specification numbers commenced.]

To be 6-4 wide; to be pure long-staple, American fleece wool, free from shoddy or flocks, and dyed with pure indigo to color of standard sample; the nap to be slightly raised; to weigh not less than twenty-two ounces per linear yard; to have thirty-four threads of filling and forty threads of chain in each square inch; the breaking-strain to be not less than fifty-five (55) pounds to one inch width of warp in the piece, and forty-five (45) pounds to one inch in width of filling in the piece.

Adopted November 12, 1874.

Helmets Specification No. 1

To be made of felt composed of one part each of Russia, best coneyback, musk-rat, extra coney, and a half part of wash-blow. The body approaches in shape the helmets as seen in antique Greek sculpture—top spherical, side vertical, front and back gently sloping outward to the point where the helmet is to rest on the head; thence, in a more diverging line extending in front to a vizor, in back to a cape for the protection of the neck. From center of top along the sides to have lower edge about eight (8) inches, to extreme point of vizor eleven and one-half (11 1/2) inches, to extreme point of back eleven (11) inches.

Vizor is gradually narrowing, and rounded at the front; length about three and one-half (3 1/2) inches, width across the forehead about twelve (12) to twelve and one-fourth (12 1/4) inches, across the front (one inch above the extreme point) about five (5) inches.

The neck-cape is about seven and one-fourth (7 1/4) inches wide, three and one-fourth (3 1/4) inches long, corners rounded.

The edge of helmet, vizor, and cape is bound with fine enameled leather. On either side, about three and one-half (3 1/2) inches above the lower edge, is a ventilator.

At the lower edge, on either side, is a button fastening for chin-strap.

The latter consists of two parts made of enameled leather five-eighth (5/8) of an inch wide, each about nine and one-half (9 1/2) inches long. These parts are united, and can be lengthened or shortened by means of a loop (same material as strap) at the end of one, and a brass bar-buckle one (1) by three-fourths (3/4) of an inch at the end of the other part. From one side button to the other, straight across the front, is another strap of enameled leather, five-eighth (5/8) of an inch wide, stitched to the body of the helmet.

Sweat-leather, two and one-half (2 1/2) inches wide, of Belgium sheepskin.

The helmet is ornamented with eagle, top piece, and plume-socket, scrolls and rings, and side buttons, and is trimmed with hair plume and cords and bands.

Helmet ornaments are made of sheet-brass, No. 24.

Hair Plumes for Helmets.—Made of good horse-hair dyed.

To droop from top of socket over back and sides of helmet.

The hairs are woven and sewed together at one end, giving the latter the form of a flattened knob about one and five-eighth (1 5/8) inch diameter, with star-

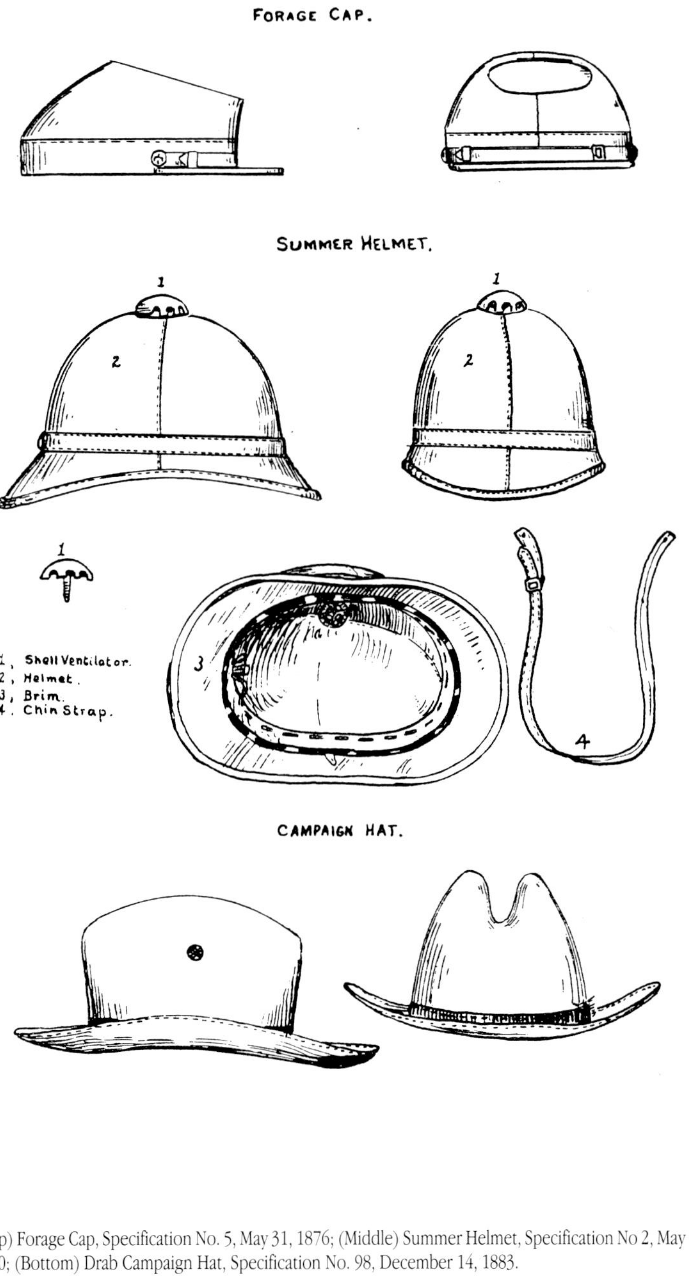

(Top) Forage Cap, Specification No. 5, May 31, 1876; (Middle) Summer Helmet, Specification No 2, May 5, 1880; (Bottom) Drab Campaign Hat, Specification No. 98, December 14, 1883.

shaped brass eyelet in center to admit the pen of the top piece. Length of plume from eyelet to end, fourteen (14) inches.

Cords and Bands for Helmets.—Made of worsted, No. 26, and "machined" gold-thread cord. The bands are loop-plaited, fastened to the scroll rings, and festooned on front and back of helmet, the festoons reaching in front to the upper edge of chin-strap, approaching the lower edge of back within two (2) inches. The loop-plaiting is about one (1) inch wide, and ends under scrolls on the left side in a tassel of sixty (60) to seventy (70) fringes one and three-fourths (1 3/4) inch long. Through the braided head, about three-fourths inch diameter, passes the continuation of the bands in the form of two cord, each five (5) feet eight (8) inches long, with two (2) netted slides netted over a fuller's board three-fourth (3/4) inch in diameter, five eighths (5/8) of an inch high. Three inches from lower end the cords are fastened together by a braided knot holding a loop about two and three-fourths (2 3/4) inches long. At the end of each cord also is a small braided knot and an aiguillette, plaited flat in three strands of smaller cord, in oval shape, two and three-eighth(2 3/8) inches long, two and three-fourths (2 3/4) inches wide. From lower end of each aiguillette is suspended another tassel of from sixty (60) to seventy (70) fringes one and three-fourths (1 3/4) inch long, with braided head three-eighth(3/8) of an inch high, three-fourths (3/4) inch diameter.

Adopted May 31, 1876.

Cork Helmets Specification No. 2

Shape and weight.—To be shape according to standard sample, and to weigh about seven and one-fourth (7 1/4) ounces when finished; reasonable variations from this weight) due to sizes to be allowed.

Material, etc.—The shell to be composed of two thicknesses of the best quality cork, laminated or scarf-seamed, and securely cemented together with shellac. The linings to be firmly shellaced to the inside shell; that for the dome to be of slate-colored drilling, and that for the visor or shade to be of emerald-green merino or cashmere. Sweat-leather to be on frame or hoop as in sample, well separated from the shell (for ventilation) by ten (10) small cork studs securely fastened; sweat to be about one and three-eighth (1 3/8) inch deep, an to be provided with a drawing string. Outside covering to be made of the best quality bleached cotton-drilling in four (4) sections, welt seamed and secured to the shell with shellac. Band of same material, about three-fourths (3/4) of an inch deep. Edge to be bound with stout bleached stay-binding. Adjustable ventilator at top as in sample. Chin-strap of white enameled leather, and brass hooks for same, as in sample.

Adopted by the Secretary of War May 5, 1880.

Dress Caps Specification No. 3

The body or shell is made of felt, composed of equal parts of Russia, best coney-backs, muskrat, extra coney, and one-half (1/2) part of wash-blow. Its weight, uncovered, two and three-fourths (2 3/) to three (3) ounces, according to size. Front vertical about three and one-half (3 1/2) inches high; back five and one-half (5 1/2) inches long; rises upward and forward in a convex sweep, and meets the crown at a point one and one-eighth (1 1/8) to one and one-fourth (1 1/4) inch higher than the point where it meets the upper edge of the front.

The crown is slight oval, five and one-fourth (5 1/4) inches in diameter from front to back, four and one-half (4 1/2) inches across. Ventilator in center of crown. At the front edge is an opening, bound with a thin strap of enameled metal, to admit the stem of the pompon, which is also held in position by a small leather socket sewed to the inside of the cap-front, about one-half (1/2) inch below the crown.

The body is covered with fine wool-dyed indigo-blue cloth, braided around the upper edge immediately below the crown, around the lower edge one-fourth (1/4) to five-sixteenths (5/16) of an inch above the latter; also straight down the back, and in a straight slanting line on both sides, equidistant from back and front seam. This braiding is worsted three-sixteenths (3/16) of an inch wide, and of the following colors: for infantry, sky-blue; engineers and artillery, scarlet; ordnance, crimson; commissary sergeants, gray; hospital stewards, emerald green. A visor of heavy enameled leather, straight and horizontal, front edge slightly convex, sides straight corner rounded, inner edge following the shape of the cap on both sides, ending in a point about five (5) inches from the front seam.

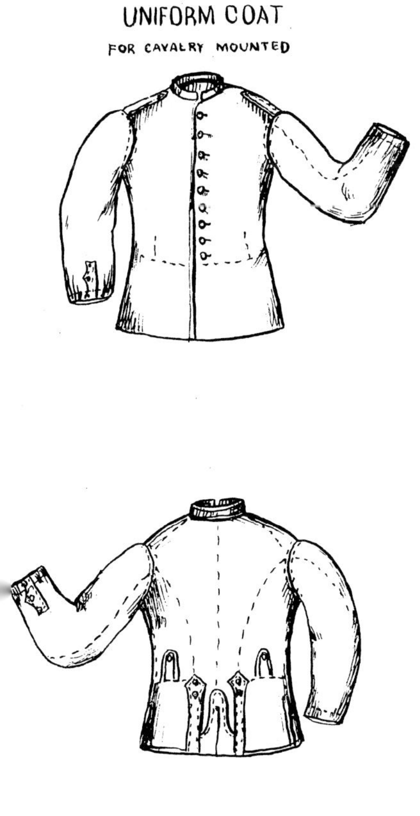

Mounted Uniform Coat, Specification No. 11, February 27, 1880.

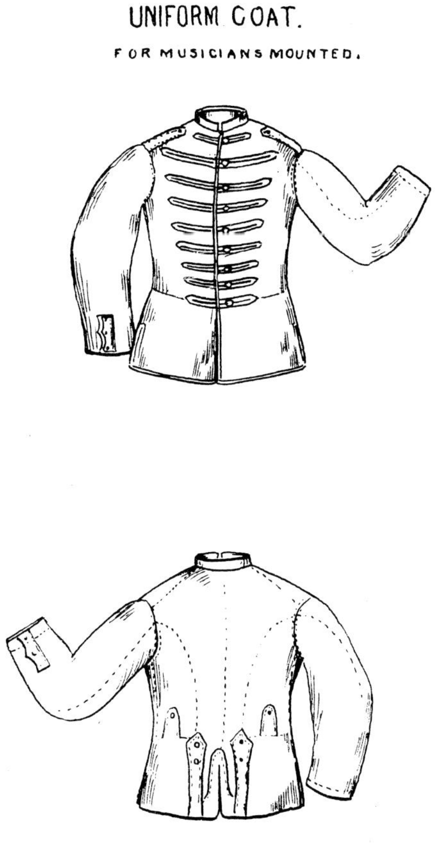

Mounted Musician Uniform Coat, Specification No. 11, February 27, 1880.

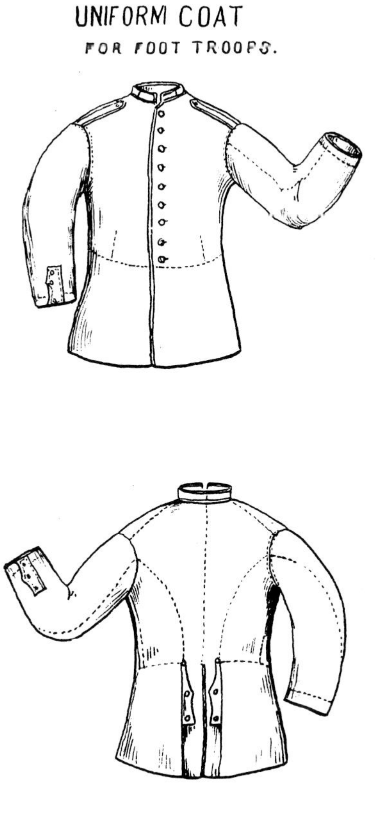

Foot Troops Uniform Coat, Specification No. 11, February 27, 1880.

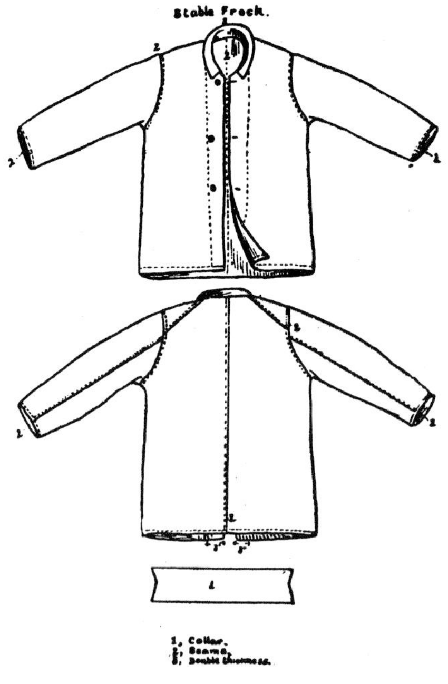

Stable Frock, Specification No. 15, March 12, 1879.

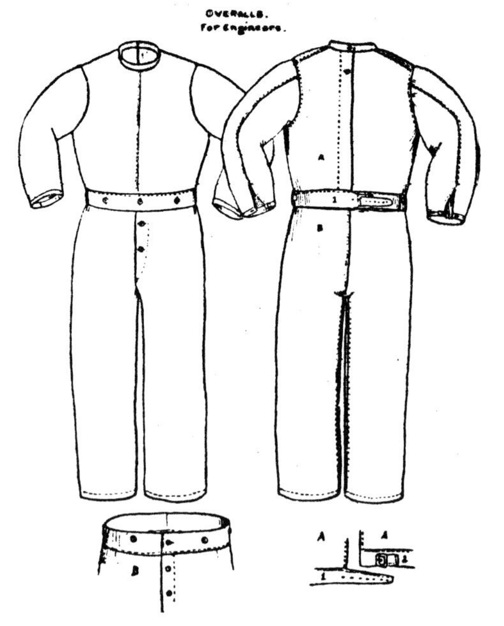

Engineer Overalls, Specification No. 16, March 12, 1879.

On each side, immediately behind the end of vizor, is a small regulation button for chin-strap.

The latter is made of thin enameled leather, five-eighth (5/8) of an inch wide, in two parts, eight and one-half to nine (9) inches each, and arranged to be lengthened and shortened, as described for helmet chin-strap. Sweat-leather, one and three-fourths (1 3/4) to two (2) inches wide, of Belgium leather. In front, immediately below the crown, is a brass eagle, and below the latter the badge of the corps or arm of service.

Sizes same as helmets.

Adopted May 31, 1876.

Pompons for Dress Caps.—Of fine worsted, firmly made on a wood-block. Nap well raised and close. To be pear-shaped, three (3) inches long, one and three-fourths (1 3/4) inch in diameter at bottom, and one (1) inch at top. Under the center of the bottom is a brass half sphere about eleven-sixteenths (11/16) of an inch in diameter, from which protrudes a stem three (3) inches long, made of strong copper wire.

Color of pompons for infantry, sky-blue; artillery, scarlet; engineers, lower half scarlet, upper half white; ordnance, crimson; commissary sergeants, gray; hospital stewards, emerald green.

Adopted May 31, 1876.

Wool Campaign Hats Specification No. 4

Mixture.—To be clean wool, of fine grade, equal in quality to XXX Ohio fleece. No waste or shoddy to be used in mixture.

Weight.—Hat bodies to be weighed out, five and one-half (5 1/2) ounces heavy, of clean wool.

Shape.—The 7 1/8-size to be six (6) inches deep to center of tip, and five and one-half (5 1/2) inches deep at front and rear. Other sizes in proportion, varying one-sixteenth (1/16) of an inch to each size.

Brim.—Edge of brim to be tuned over three-eighth3/8) of an inch on the upper side, and stitched down with two (2) rows of stitching, and to measure two and one-half (2 1/2) inches in front and rear and two and five-eighth (2 5/8) inches in width at sides.

Trimming.—Trimmed with eight (8) ligne Union braid, same quality as on sample hat; to be sewed on by sewing machine. Sweat to be of brown Japanned leather, turned on top, one and three-quarters (3/4) inch wide, and sewed in hat by sewing machine. Two "Brashers" Patent Ventilators, one on each side of crown, three and one-half (3 1/2) inches from brim.

The hat to be velvet finished, soft and pliable, same as standard sample.

No more than six (6) hats to be packed in each band-box. Adopted June 14, 1876.

Forage Caps Specification No. 5

Made of best wool-dyed indigo blue cloth. Band about one and one-fourth (1 1/4) inch wide, strengthened by a strip of strong split-leather of the same width, sewed in between the cloth and the sweat-leather. The front rises straight and vertical one and one-half (1 1/2) to one and five-eighths (1 5/8) inch above the band, sides straight and slightly converging toward the crown. The back about

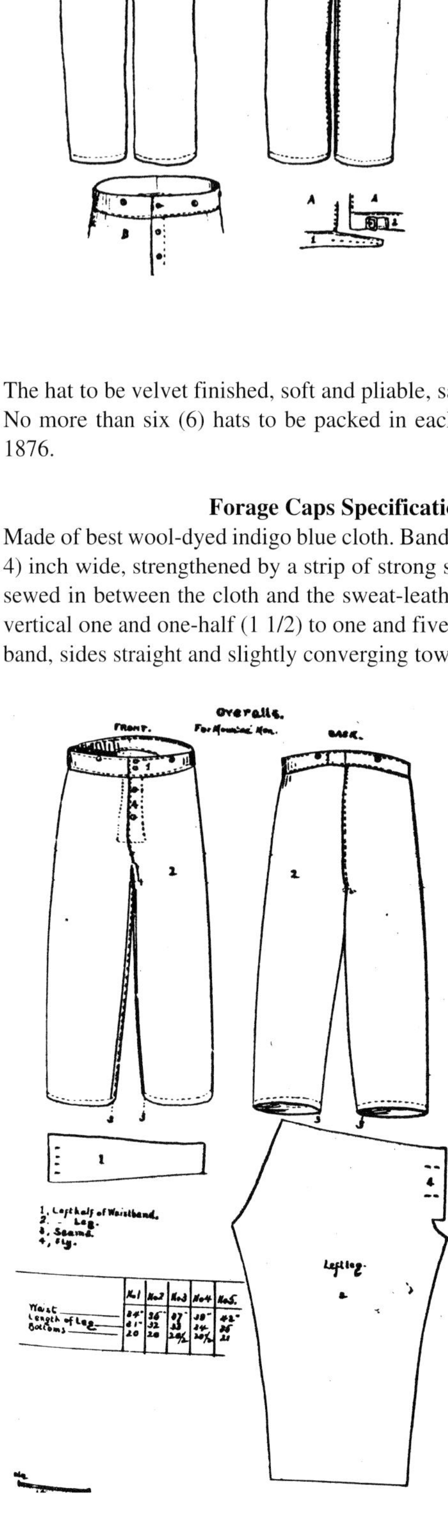

Overalls for Mounted Men, Specification No. 16, March 12, 1879.

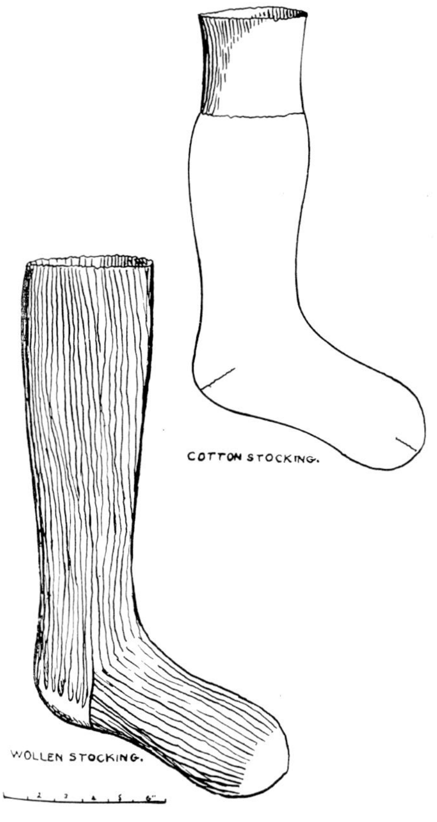

(Left) Woolen Stockings, Specification No. 21, June 4, 1877 (Right) Cotton Stockings, Specification No. 22, October 17, 1879.

five (5) inches long, rises from band forward at an angle of 45 degrees, slightly convex.
The crown is circular, about four and three-fourths (4 3/4) inches in diameter, made upon strong "tarred board." The shape of the cape would thus give an incline to the crown of one (1) to one and one-fourth (1 1/4) inch from rear to front.
A straight horizontal vizor of patent leather, about three-sixteenths (3/16) of an inch thick, shaped as described for dress-caps. A small brass regulation button on each side, immediately behind the end of the vizor, for chin-strap.

The latter is made in two parts, of fine enameled leather about one-half (1/2) inch wide, each part about nine (9) inches long, and arranged, as on dress-cap, to be lengthened and shortened at will.
Sweat-leather of Belgium leather, one and one-half (1 1/2) inch wide.
Lining of glazed muslin, fastened by its lower edge only to the inner stiffening of the band, the upper edge gathered with strong thread.
<adopted>May 31, 1876.

Muskrat Caps Specification No. 6

To be made according to standard sample of muskrat skin, with ear-flaps, cape, and visor, according to pattern. Lining of brown chintz or silesia, padded with cotton wadding.
Sizes same as for dress and forage caps.
Adopted March 12, 1879.

Seal-skin Caps Specification No. 7

To be made of the "wool seal" skin, with ear-flaps, cape, and vizor, according to pattern. Lining of Turkey red chintz, padded with cotton wadding.
Sizes same as for dress and forage caps.
Adopted May 23, 1876.

Metallic Uniform-Coat, Helmet, Dress, and Forage-Cap Ornaments Specification No. 8

Cap Bugles.—For field and band musicians: Of sheet bass, No. 28, representing an old-style bugle with circular crook, and a cord slung three (3) fold around the lower part, terminating in two (2) tassels on one, and one (1) tassel on the other side.
Height across crook one and one-fourth (1 1/4) inch; width from mouth-piece to outer edge of bowl, two and one-fourth (2 1/4) inches. Brass wire loops same as on letters [Adopted May 31, 1876.]
Side Buttons for Helmet.—One on each side, a little above the lower edge of helmet.
The are one (1) inch diameter, edge beveled and grooved, surface slightly convex, and chased.
They are secured to helmet by double brass-wire loops, as the scrolls are.
Design for Cavalry and Signal Service: Two crossed sabers, hilts downward and outward. For Light Artillery: Two cannon crossed at the trunnions. [Adopted May 31, 1876.]

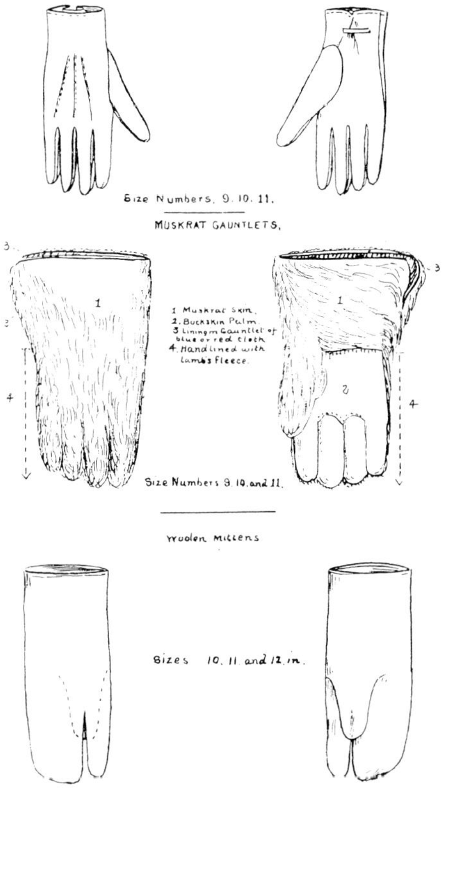

(Top) Berlin Gloves, Specification No. 23, May 31, 1876 (Middle) Muskrat Gauntlets, Specification No. 25, March 12, 1879 (Bottom) Woolen Mittens, Specification No. 24, May 31, 1876

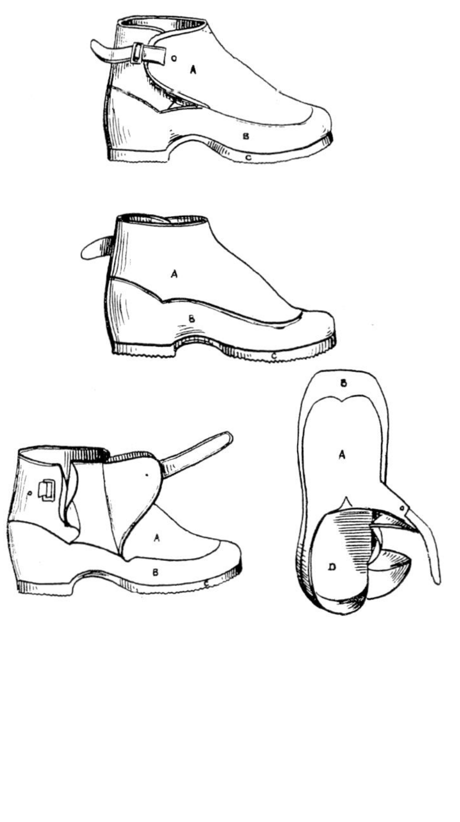

Arctic Over Shoes, Specification No. 30, May 5, 1876.

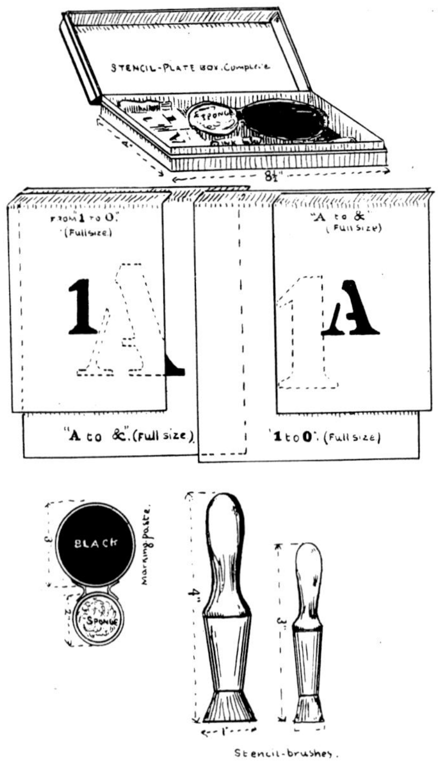

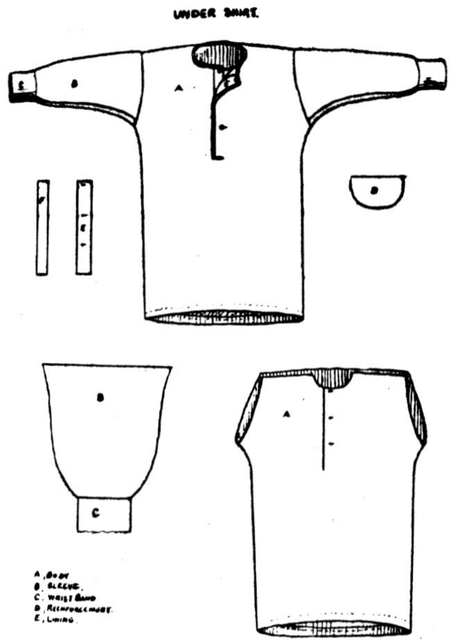

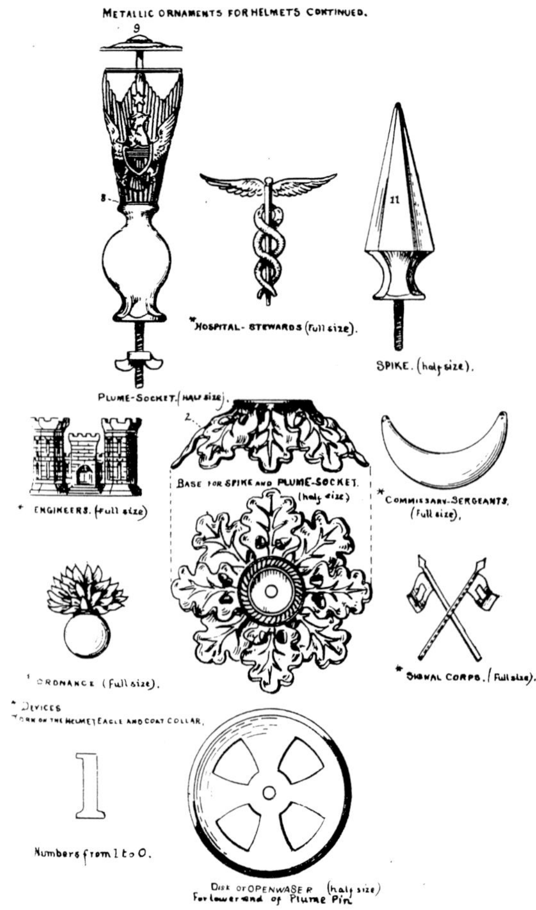

Above Left: Stencil Kit, Specification No. 55, May 31, 1876. Above Center: Under Shirt, Specification No. 77, February 11, 1881. Above and Below Right: Metallic Ornaments for Helmets, Specification No. 80, April 12, 1882.

Castles for Cap.—Of sheet brass, No. 28, representing an ancient castle with three (3) towers. Height of center tower, seven-eighth (7/8) of an inch; of side towers, one and one-fourth (1 1/4) inch each; of battlements between towers, five-eighths (5/8) of an inch. Width at base, one and seven-eighth (1 7/8) inch; at top of side towers, one and three-fourths (1 3/4) inch. Two small brass-wire loops soldered to back to fasten to cap. [Adopted May 31, 1876.]

Castles for Coat.—To be of sheet brass, No. 28, representing an ancient castle with three (3) towers. Height of battlements tree-eighth (3/8) of an inch; of center tower, one-half (1/2) inch; of side towers, five-eighth (5/8) of an inch each; breadth at base and top, one (1) inch. Two small brass-wire loops soldered to back to fasten to coat collar. [Adopted May 31, 1876.]

Crescents for Cap.—For Commissary Sergeants: Of sheet white metal, crescent shaped.

Width from point to point, one and five-eighth (1 5/8) inch; height of arc one (1) inch; greatest width in center one-half (1/2) inch. Brass wire loops on back same as letters. [Adopted May 31, 1876.]

Crescents for Coat.—For Commissary Sergeants' coats: Made of white metal, crescent shaped. From point to point, one (1) inch.

Height of arc nine-sixteenths (9/16) inch; greatest width in center one-half (1/2) inch. Brass wire loops on back same as letters. [Adopted May 31, 1876.]

Crossed Cannon.—For Artillery Caps: Of sheet brass No. 28 representing two cannon crossing each other at the trunnions, muzzles upward; length two and one-eighthh (2 1/8) inches; breadth at breeches two (2) inches; at muzzles, one and seven-eighth (1 7/8) inch. Four brass-wire loops strongly soldered on back to fasten to cap. [Adopted May 31, 1876.]

Crossed Sabers.—For Cavalry Caps of sheet-brass, No 20, representing two cavalry crossed sabers in scabbards, crossed in the middle, with hilts and edges downward. To be shaped or curved as to fit the front of the cap.

Length of sabers, three (3) inches; height from hilt of one to point of other, one and one-fourth (1 1/4) inch; from point to point, two and three-fourths (2 3/4) inches.

Four small brass-wire loops same as on crossed cannon. [Adopted May 31, 1876.]

Crossed Rifles.—Of sheet-brass, No. 20: Two rifles crossing each other at a point equidistant from butt and muzzle.

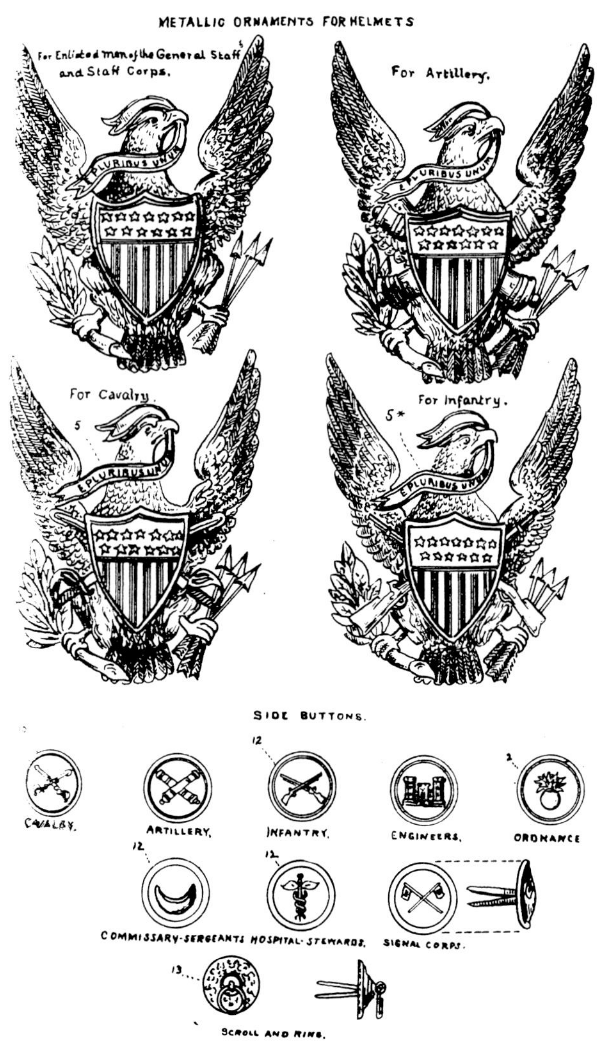

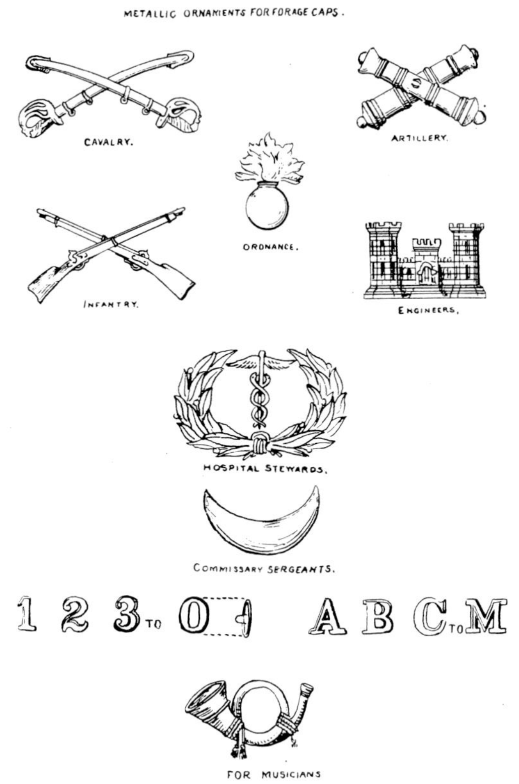

Metallic Ornaments for Forage Caps, Specification No. 80, April 21, 1882.

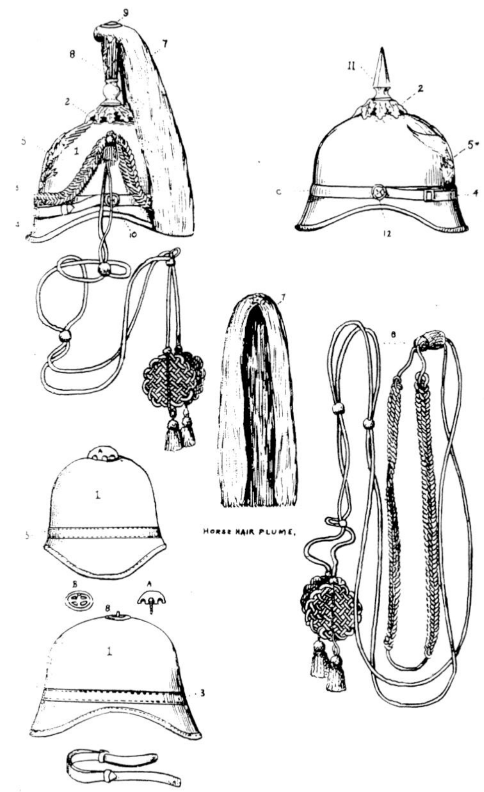

Helmets, Specification No. 81, May 6, 1882.

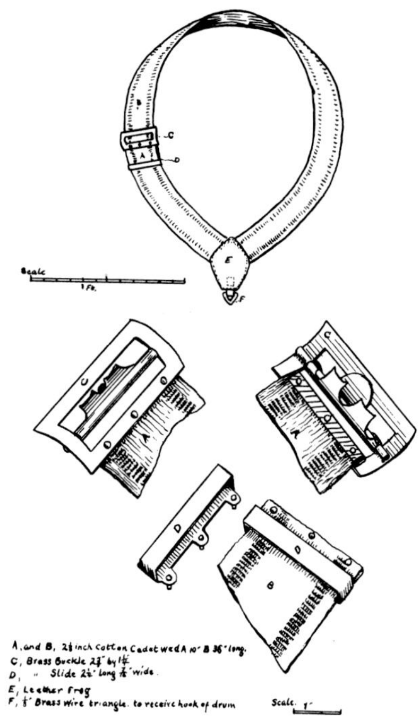

Drum Slings, Specification No. 85, June 15, 1883.

Muzzles pointing upward and outward, hammers upward, their position crossed making the upper space form an angle of 137°. Length of rifle, two,and five-cighth (2 5/8) inches; diameter at point of crossing, about one-eighthh (1/8) on an inch. To be shaped or curved as to fit the front of cap.

The whole ornament occupying a rectangular space about two and seven-sixteenths (2 7/16) inches wide by one and three-eighth (1 3/8) inch high

Fastenings: Four brass-wire loops firmly soldered, opening horizontally with the rifles, and placed about one-half (1/2) inch from muzzles and butts. [Adopted May 31. 1876.]

Eagles for Cap.—To be worn on caps of all arms of the service. Of sheet-bras No. 23, representing an eagle with national shield on breast, head surmounted by a scroll bearing the motto "E pluribus unum," extending downward and meeting olive branch, and arrows in talons of eagle. Height one and one-half (1 1/2) inch; greatest width between tips of wings,one and one-half (1 1/2) inch. Brass-wire loops soldered at back of each wing. be shaped or curved so as to fit the front of cap. [Adopted May 31, 1876. Amended July 19, 1877.]

Eagles for Helmet.—Made of sheet-brass No. 24, of the shape of the eagle in the coat of arms of the of the United States, with a national shield on breast, head surmounted by a scroll bearing the motto "E pluribus unum;" scroll extending downward and meeting olive branch and arrows in talons of the eagle. Whole height, four and one-half (4 1/2) inches; greatest width between tips of wings, three and seven-eighth (3 7/8) inches to four (4) inches. Two loops of strong wire-soldered on the back to fasten to helmet by means of two small pieces of leather. [Adopted May 31, 1876.]

Brass Letters for Cap.—"A" to "M:" Roman capitals five-eighth (5/8) of an inch, to be made of sheet-brass. No. 28, edged beveled. Two small brass-wire loops strongly soldered on the back of letter to fasten it to cap. [Adopted May 31, 1876.]

Letters "U.S". of white metal.—Of white metal, chased: Roman capitals one-half (1/2) inch high, to be placed within the wreath. To have wire loops soldered on back to fasten to cap. [Adopted May 31, 1876.]

Numbers for Cap.—Nos. "1" to "0" inclusive; five-eighths (5/8) of an inch long, to be made of sheet-brass, No, 28; edges beveled. Small brass-wire loops same as on letters. [Adopted May 31, 1876.]

Numbers for Coat.—Nos. "1" to "0" inclusive: Each number to be made of sheet-brass, No. 28, one-half (1/2) inch long, edges beveled. Two brass-wire loops soldered on back of number to fasten it to coat collar. [Adopted May 31, 1876.]

Scrolls and Rings for Helmet.—One on each side, between the leaf-shaped points of the top piece, its lower edge one-half (1/2) inch below these points.

The scroll is three-fourths (3/4) inch in diameter, ornamented to correspond with the fastening of the top piece.

On the top of the scroll, in the center, is an eye of thin wire three-sixteenths (3/16) of an inch high, holding a thin brad ring one-half (1/2 inch in diameter, to keep the cords and bands in position.

The stem of scroll formed of two pieces of thin brass wire to fasten inside the helmet. [Adopted May 31, 1876.]

Shells and Flames for Cap.—Of sheet brass, No. 28, representing a shell and flame. Diameter height of shell, three-quarters (3/4) of an inch; height of flame from upper edge of shell, seven-eighth (7/8) of an inch; greatest width of flame, one and one-eighth (1 1/8)inch.

Brass-wire loops the same as on numbers. [Adopted May 31, 1876.]

Shells and Flames for Coat.—To be of sheet brass, No. 28, representing a shell and flame.

Shell, one-half (1/2) inch diameter, flames rising one-half (1/2) inch above upper edge of shell; greatest breadth of flame nearest to shell. three-quarters (3/4) of an inch.

Brass-wire loops the same as on numbers. [Adopted May 31, 1876.]

Plume-sockets for Helmet.—A crossed-foot, with convex bend, to fit exactly the surface of the helmet top.

Each leaf-shaped point of the cross ends is fastened by means of an ornamental button with stem of two thin wires.

Length of cross between alternate points, five and a quarter (5 1/4) inches; each leaf one and a quarter (1 1/4) inch, at widest, three-quarters (3/4) of an inch at narrowest part; edge beveled and grooved.

On the center of the cross rests a sphere one (1) inch in diameter, surmounted by a short neck with ring, the former one-half (1/2) inch, the latter five-eighth (5/8) inch diameter, combined about one-half (1/2) inch high, from which arises an

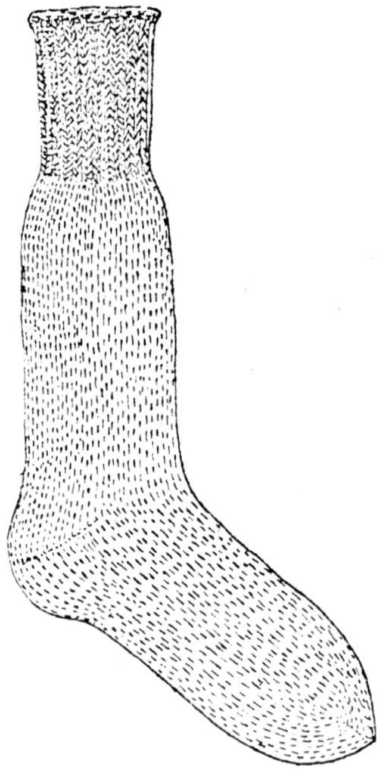

Cotton Stockings, Specification No. 87, February 23, 1883.

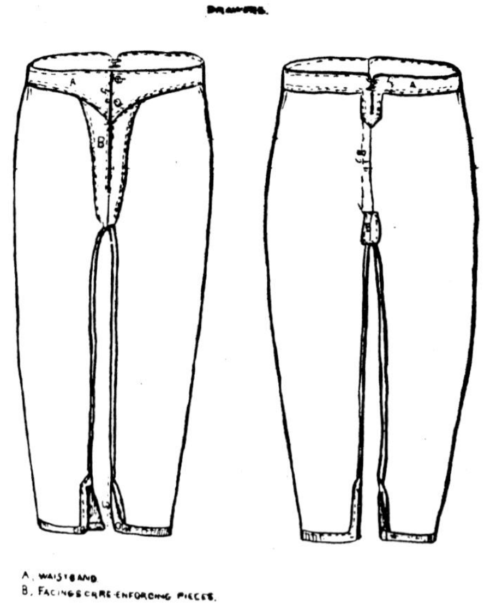

Drawers, Specification No. 93, May 25, 1883.

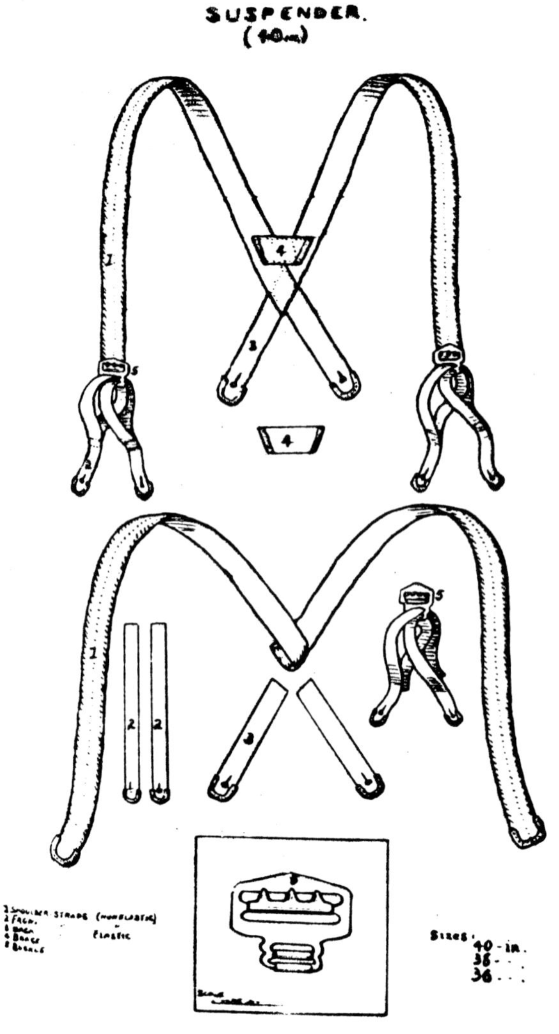

Suspenders, Specification No. 94, September 4, 1883.

inverted conical tube, fluted, ornamented by an heraldic eagle, with star above the head.

The top of the tube ends in four triangular points. Width of tube across top one (1) inch. The plume is fastened to the top of this socket by means of a brass pin one-fourth (1/4) of an inch thick, four and three-quarters (4 3/4) inches long, with ornamented button at upper and screw thread at lower end.

The latter enters through the socket and helmet, and is fastened at the inside ny means of a brass washer one and seven-eighth (1 7/8) inch diameter, and a thumb-nut. The plume is held in a drooping position by the head of the above-mentioned brass pin, and a brass disk, one and one-fourth (1 1/4) inch diameter, laid under the woven top part of the plume and resting on the points of the socket. [Adopted May 31, 1876.]

Wreaths for Hospital Stewards' Caps.—Wreath made of dead or unburnished gilt-metal, representing two olive branches, held at the bottom by a loop and knot, turning upward and bending in an oval shape, approaching each other at the top. Height one and one-half (1 1/2) inch; greatest distance between outer edges, two and five-eighth (2 5/8) inches; greatest width of single branch five-eighth (5/8) inch.

Brass-wire loops same as on back of letters. [Adopted May 31, 1876.]

Great Coats Specification No. 9

Material.—Sky-blue kersey, twenty-two (22) ounce Army standard; Lining: for body 6/4 dark-blue flannel, to weigh eleven and one-half (11 1/2) ounces to the linear yard, or 6/4 to weigh five and three-quarters (5 3/4) ounces to the linear yard; for capes, colored flannel, Army standard, 6/4 to weigh ten (10) ounces to the linear yard, or 8/6 to weigh five (5) ounces to the linear yard; for sleeves, unbleached muslin.

Shape and dimensions.—To be according to standard sample, double-breasted, with two rows of five (5) buttons each, and with full cape extending to end of sleeve when arm is extended. Eight (8) to ten (10) buttons (small regulation) and button holes in cape, according to size. Skirt straight and to reach below the knee of wearer; slit in back of skirt to be from sixteen (16) to nineteen and one-half (19 1/2) inches long, according to size of coat. Falling collar from four and one-half (4 1/2) to five (5) inches high when up. Cuff of double thickness of material, and to be from five (5) to five and one-quarter (5 1/4) inches deep when turned up. Back strap to consist of two straps seven (7) to ten (10) inches long, three and one-quarter (3 1/4) inches wide at end joining coat, and one and one-half (1 1/2) inch at bottom end. Left-hand strap to have two button holes; right-hand strap two buttons, held in place by small straps stitched to back seam. Lining of body to extend down to top opening in back. Two inside breast pockets.

Color for cape linings to be: For hospital stewards, emerald green; for commissary sergeants, gray; for ordnance, crimson; for engineers and artillery, scarlet; for signal corps, orange; for infantry, dark-blue; for cavalry, yellow.

Adopted February 6, 1880.

Great Coats, Canvas Lined Specification No. 10

Pattern.—To be according to pattern, with two (2) outside pockets and a waist belt, and to be of two (2) sizes corresponding to the Regulation great coats of sizes 3 and 4.

Materials.—The outside to be of cotton duck weighing nine and one-half (9 1/2) ounces to the square yard, dyed blue to the shade of standard sample. The inside or lining to be of Army standard twenty-two (22) ounce 6/4 sky-blue kersey. The cords and tassels to be of blue worsted according to pattern—one for the neck to be sixty (60) inches long, and two (2) for the hood to be each forty-two (42) inches long; the latter to be fastened at the outer edge of neck and drawn at the center of the hood or cape. Seven (7) rubber buttons on front and two on belt, as on sample. Adopted August 18, 1880.

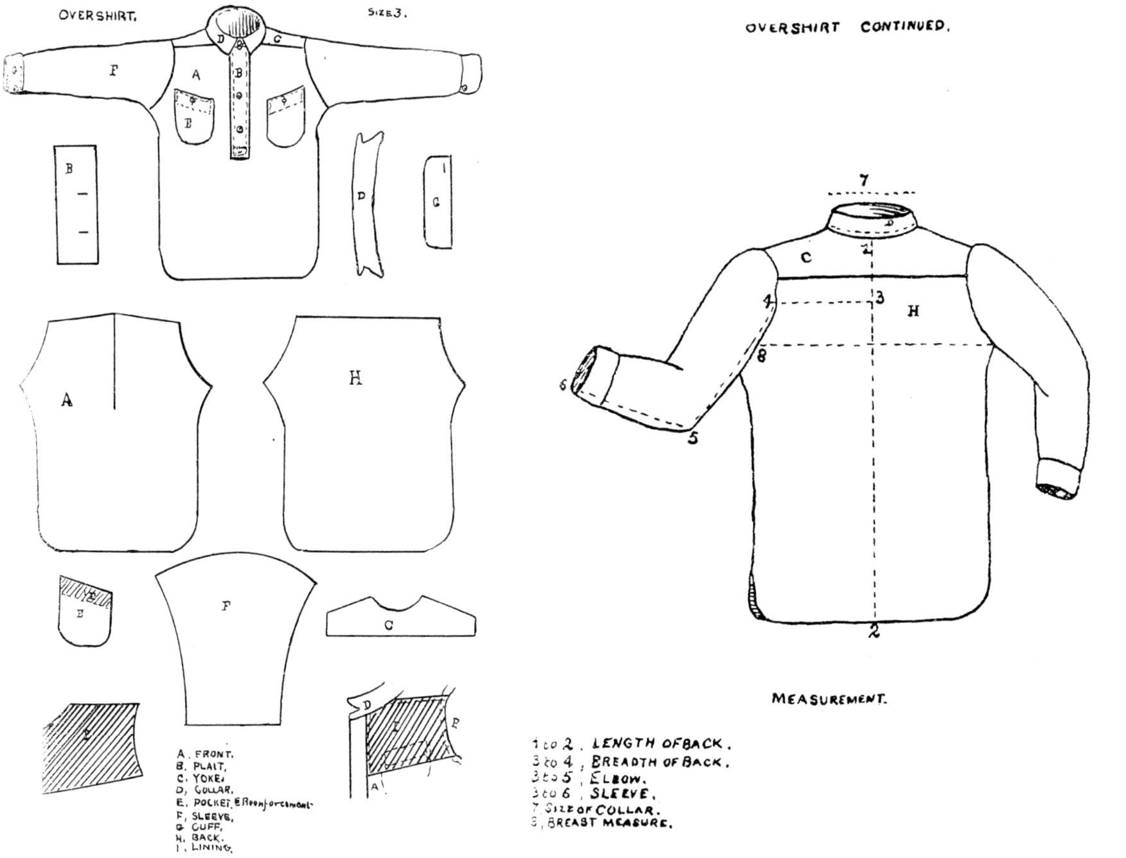

Overshirts, Specification No. 97, November 26, 1883.

Uniform Coats Specification No. 11

Material.—Dark-blue cloth (Army standard.) Linings: For body and sleeves, slate-colored cotton jeans; for skirt, black Italian cloth. Regulation brass buttons.

Pattern and Dimensions.—For Foot Troops.—Single-breasted dark-blue basque according to standard sample. Nine (9) buttons in front. Standing collar, one and one—quarter (1 1/4) to one and one-half (1 1/2) inch high, cut square to hook in front. Cloth facings and piping, of color of the various arms of service, on collar, cuff, and back of skirt according to pattern. Shoulder straps of facing cloth let into seam at point of shoulder, and to button at collar with one button. Two belt straps or supporters three (3) to three and one-half (3 1/2) inches high, of cloth same as coat, piped with facing cloth, rising from waist seam at each side and buttoning above with single button. Inside pocket in left breast, opening perpendicularly.

For Mounted Troops.—To be similar to the above, except that the skirts be two (2) to two and three-quarters (2 3/4) inches shorter, and slashed and piped at sides to within two (2) inches of the waist, and the back facings according to standard sample. *For Musicians.* To be the same as the above, with the addition of the breast facings (according to pattern) of one-eighth (1/8) inch worsted braid, of proper color of arm of service.

For enlisted men of Staff Corps.—To be the same as the above, except that the piping be white for all corps, and edges of all facings and straps be piped with white cloth according to sample.

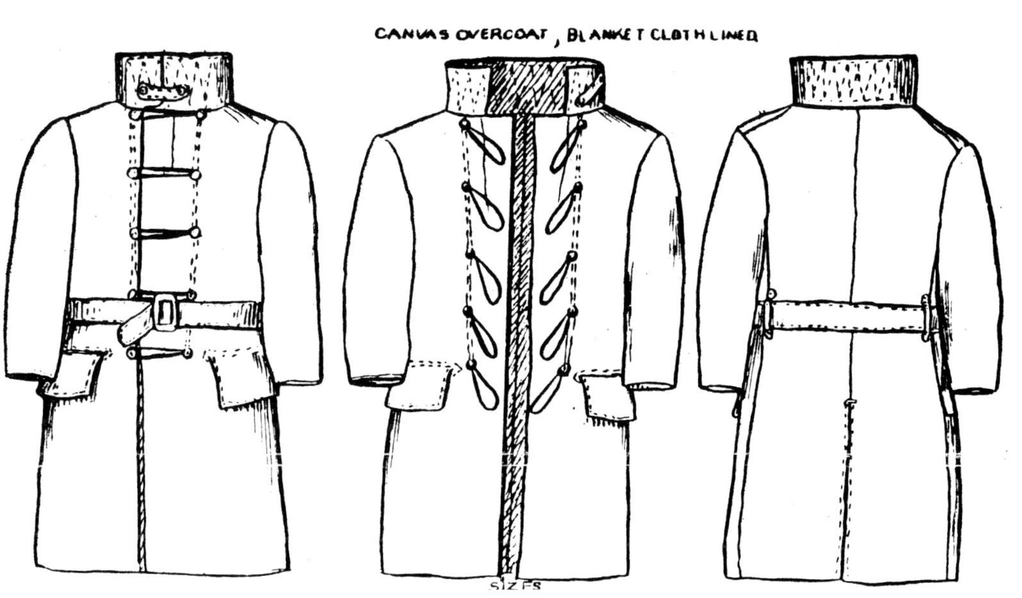

Canvas Overcoats, Specification No. 95. October 24, 1883.

	No.1 Inches.	No. 2 Inches.	No. 3 Inches.	No. 4 Inches.	No. 5 Inches.
Length of Waist	18	18 1/2	19	20	21
Length of coat, foot	29 1/2	30	31	32	33
Length of coat, mounted	26	27	28	29	30
Collar	15	15 1/2	16	16 1/2	17
Breast	35	36 1/2	39 1/2	42	44
Waist	31 1/2	33	35	37	41
Sleeve, Hand	5 1/2	6	6	6 1/2	6 1/2

Adopted February 27, 1880.

Chevrons Specification No. 12

Chevrons, to indicate rank of all non-commissioned officers of all arms, shall be made of cloth the color of the facings on their respective uniform coats (except that those for great coats be of dark-blue for Infantry.) The bars to be divided by a heavy stitching of No. 8 silk, and the upper and lower angles to be finished or bound with similar stitching.

White silk stitching for Engineers and for great coats Infantry; black for all others.

The arms of the chevron bars to be six (6) to seven (7) inches long, to be the arc of a circle of about twenty-five (25) inches radius, and to meet at an angle of about ninety-six (96) degrees. Distance between extreme outer ends about nine (9) inches.

One chevron to be worn on each sleeve of the uniform coat and great coat, above the elbow, point downward.

Design for Chevrons.—For a Sergeant major, three (3) bars and an arc of three (3) bars.

For a Quarter-master Sergeant, three (3) bars and a tie of three (3) bars.

For a Principal Musician, three (3) bars and a bugle of the pattern worn on caps.

For an Ordnance Sergeant, three (3) bars and an outlined star.

For a Commissary Sergeant, three (3) bars and a crescent.

For a Hospital Steward, a half chevron of emerald-green cloth, one and three-fourths (1 3/4) inch wide, piped with yellow cloth, running obliquely downward from the outer to the inner seam of the sleeve, and at an angle of about thirty (30) degrees to the horizontal, an in the center a "Caduceus" two (2) inches long, the head toward the outer seam of the sleeves.

For a First Sergeant, three (3) bars and a lozenge, (white lozenge for Engineers.)

For a Battalion or Company Quartermaster Sergeant, three (3) bars and a tie of one (1) bar.

For a Sergeant, three (3) bars.

For a Corporal, two (2)bars.

*For a Saddler Sergeant, three (3) bars and a saddler's round knife, handle upward. Knife of the following dimensions: handle one and three-quarters (1 3/4) inches long, three-quarters (3/4) inch wide near top; five-eighth (5/8) inch near blade; blade one and one-eighthh (1 1/8) inches deep in center; from point to point of blade, three and one-quarter (3 1/4) inches; center of edge, one and one-fourth (1 1/4) inch above inner angle of chevron.

*For a Pioneer, two crossed hatchets, of cloth, same color and material as the facings of the uniform coat, to be sewed on each sleeve, above the elbow, in the place indicated for a chevron (those of a Corporal to be just above and resting on the chevron), the head of the hatchet upward, its edge outward, of the following dimensions, viz.: Handle, four and one-half (4 1/2) inches long, one-quarter (1/4) to one-third (1/3) of a inch wide; hatchet, two (2) inches long, one (1) inch wide at edge.

*For a Farrier, horseshoe, same color and material as the facing on uniform coat, with toe piece one and three-quarters (1 3/4) of an inch long, one-half (1/2) inch deep, and two heel-pieces about one-half (1/2) by three-quarters (3/4) inch each, of *gray* facing cloth. Four (4) nail holes, showing the underlying blue coat-cloth, on each side of the shoe at equal distances from each other. To be worn above the elbow, heels pointing downward. Dimensions of horseshoe: three-quarters (3/4) of an inch wide, four and one-half (4 1/2) inches long from outer edge of toe piece to a line between extreme points of heels; between outer lines across center, three and three-quarters (3 3/4) inches; between extreme points of heels about two (2) inches.

To indicate service, a diagonal half chevron, one-half (1/2) inch wide, extending from seam to seam, the front end nearest the cuff, one and one-half (1 1/2) inch above the cuff; to be made of the same color as the facings, except for Engineers, which shall be white. Service in war will be indicated by a white

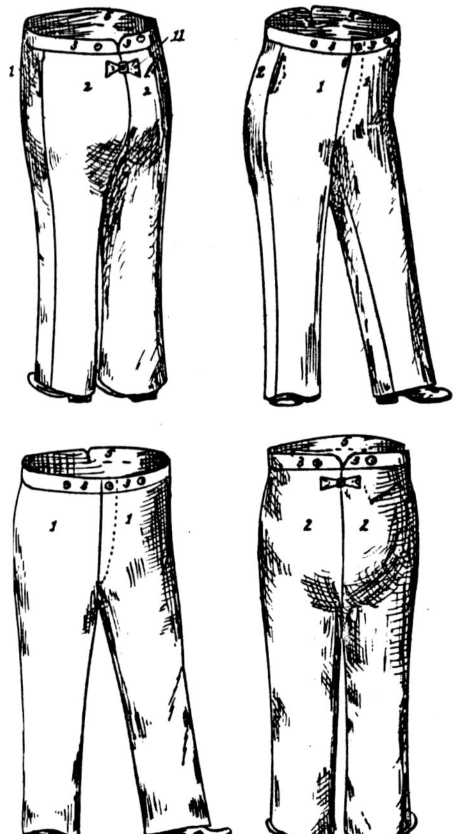

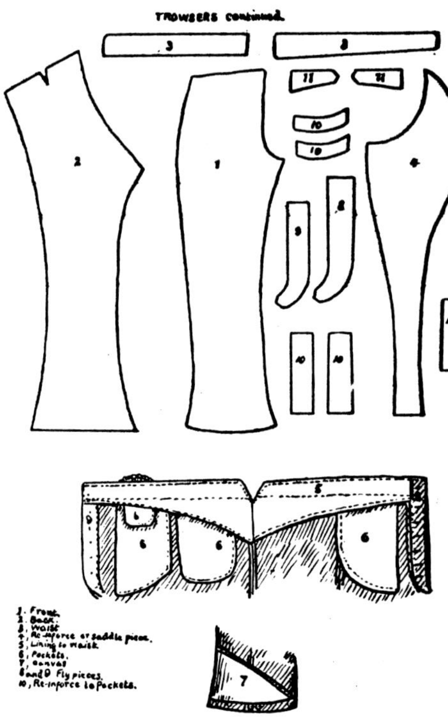

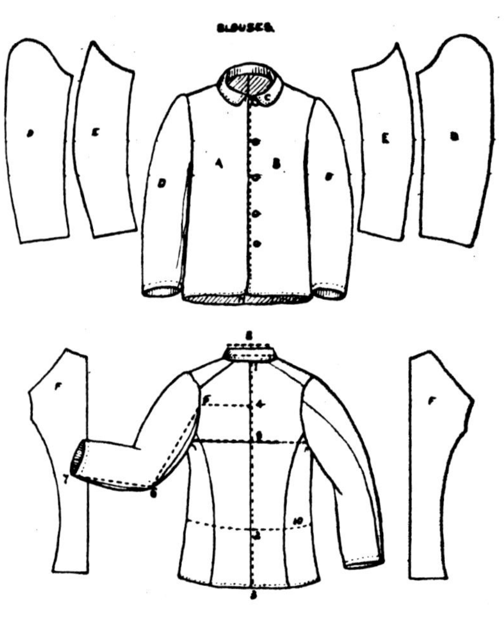

Trowsers, Specification No. 99, January 16, 1884.

Right: Blouses, Specification No. 100, January 26, 1884.

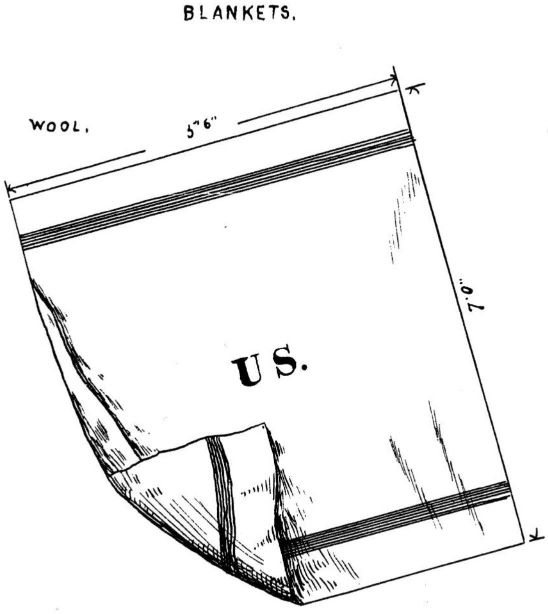

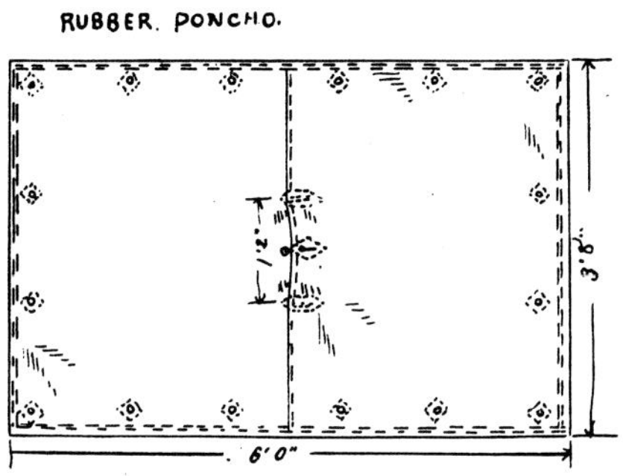

(Top) Wool Blankets, Specification No. 101, February 5, 1884; (Bottom) Rubber Ponchos, Specification No 223, January 5, 1889 (in use since the Civil War but adopted specification not previously published).

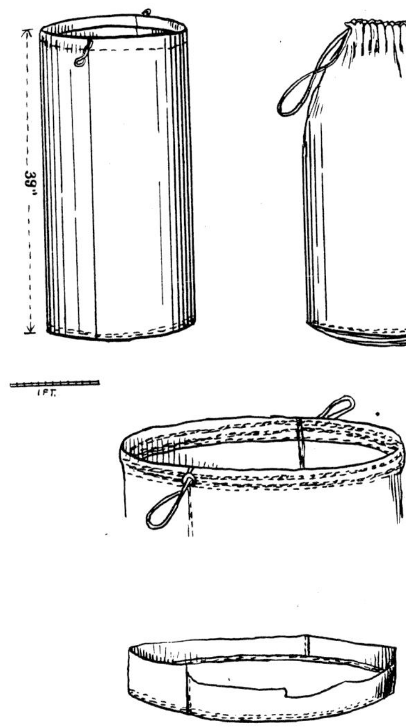

Barracks Bag, No Specification No. Assigned, March 13, 1884.

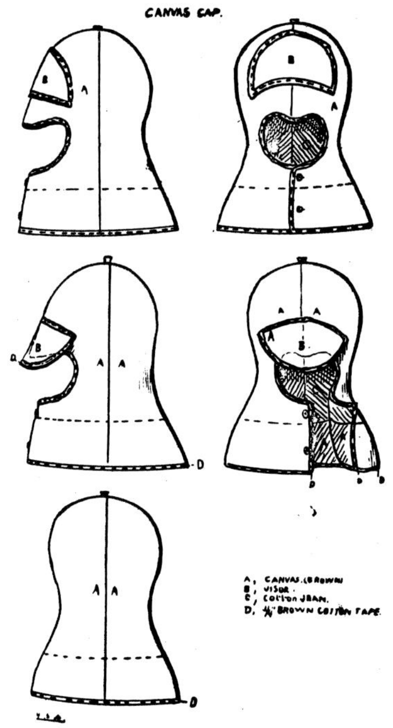

Canvas Cap, Specification No. 109, April 17, 1884.

stripe on each side of the chevron for Artillery, and a red stripe for all other corps. The stripes to be one-eighth (1/8) of an inch wide. Distance between each service chevron one-quarter (1/4) of an inch.

In great coat chevrons, Infantry, for First Sergeants, Principal Musicians, and Pioneer, the center design as described above shall be of white cloth.

Signal Service device, two embroidered signal flags crossed, each three-quarters (3/4) of an inch square, bearing in the center a square one-quarter (1/4) of an inch. One flag white with red inner square; the other red with white inner square. Flags and squares bullion edged; staffs three (3) inches long, with silver spears, made upon a piece of dark-blue coat-cloth three (3) inches square, with the corners rounded off. To be worn by non-commissioned officers above the chevrons; by privates of the first class on both sleeves above the elbow, and by privates of the second class on the left arm only.

NOTE.—Chevrons marked (*) require to be made on a groundwork of dark-blue cloth.

Adopted March 12, 1879.

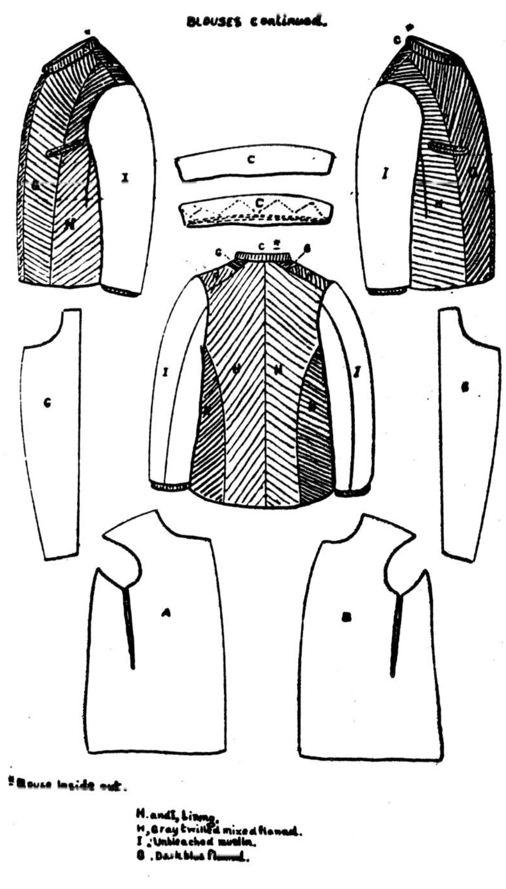

Lined Blouses Specification No. 13

Material.—Dark-blue wool flannel, Army standard. Gray twilled mixed flannel lining for body, and unbleached muslin lining for sleeves.

Pattern.—To be a single-breasted sack coat, with falling collar, and having five (5) regulation buttons in front, from neck to waist, similar to standard sample. Depth of collar two and a half (2 1/2) to three (3) inches according to size. Collar rounded at corners and trimmed on outer edge with worsted cord, corresponding in color to the facing cloths for the various arms of the service. The cuffs are also trimmed with cord (similar to that on collar), forming an inverted ^ on upper side of sleeve and straight across the lower side. Point of angle four and one-half (4 1/2) inches from edge of cuff; distance of cord above edge of under side of cuff, about one and three-quarters (1 34/) inch. Small regulation button on outer seam of cuff, one and three-quarters (1 3.4) inch from edge. Two inside pockets. Canvas or vest padding in shoulders, breast, and collar.

	Breast measure.	Length. measure.	Waist measure.	Collar	Length of sleeve.
	Inches.	*Inches.*	*Inches.*	*Inches.*	*Inches.*
Size 1—	34	29	32	15 1/2	32
Size 2—	36	29 1/2	34	16	32 1/2
Size 3—	38	30	36	16 1/2	33 1/2
Size 4—	40	31	38	17	34
Size 5—	44	32 1/2	42	18	35

Adopted March 15, 1879.

Unlined Blouses Specification No. 14

To be the same material and pattern as the lined blouse, except that there will be no lining. The seams, where exposed, to be turned down and stitched.
Adopted March 12, 1879.

Stable Frocks Specification No. 15

Material.—Light canvas or unbleached drilling, equal in quality to that of the standard sample. Metal (trowsers) buttons.
Pattern and dimensions.—To be made in a shape of a loose sack coat, single breasted with three (3) buttons, and a standing collar from two (2) to three (3) inches high, according to size. Measures for four (4) sizes to be as follows:

	Breast measure. Inches.	Length. measure. Inches.	Collar Inches.	Length of sleeve. Inches.
Size 1—	38	33	17	33
Size 2—	39	34	18	33 1/2
Size 3—	40	35	19	34
Size 4—	42	36	20	34 1/2

Adopted March 12, 1879.

Overalls Specification No. 16

Material.—Six (60 or seven (7 ounce cotton, or linen duck or drilling. White metal (trowsers) buttons.

Pattern and Dimensions.—For Engineers.—

To consist of two parts, a body or jacket and a pair of trowsers. The body loose, without yoke, slightly gathered at waistband, opening at back, and fastening at top with two (2) buttons, and a waist strap with strap and strong brass buckle, the strap being a continuation of the waistband. Sleeves loose, with narrow cuff- band to button. Waistband about one and three-quarter (1 3/4) inch wide, and to have five (5) button-holes, about five (5) inches apart. worked in front, to button the leg overalls to.
The lower part to form a loose pair of trowsers, with waistband, three (3) buttons in fly, and buttons in front, on waistband, corresponding to the button-holes in that of body.
For Mounted Troops.—To be similar to the lower or trowsers part of those for engineers, except that the arrangement of buttons on waistband be the same as on trowsers, that is, for suspenders.

	No. 1 Inches	No. 2. Inches	No. 3 Inches	No. 4 Inches	No.5 Inches
BODY Breast Measure	38	39	41	43	45
Waist	34	35	37	39	42
Collar	17	18	18 1/2	19	20
Length of Sleeve	32 1/2	33	33 1/2	34	35
Length of Body	18	18 1/2	19	19 1/2	21
LEG					
Length of side Seam	42	43	44	45	46
Length of Leg	31	32	33	34	35
Waist	32	34	36	38	40
Bottoms	20	20	20 1/2	20 1/2	21

Adopted March 12, 1879.

Trousers Specification No. 17

Material.—Sky-blue kersey, Army Standard.

Pattern and Dimensions.

For Foot Troops.—To be cut according to standard sample, loose, without lining or plaits and without waistband. Bottoms to spread well over shoe.
For Mounted Troops.—To be similar in pattern to those for foot-men, with the addition of a re-inforce or saddle piece of same material on seat and legs. Four buttons at bottom of each leg, two on each side, for straps.

	No. 1 Inches	No. 2. Inches	No. 3 Inches	No. 4 Inches	No.5 Inches
Length of side Seam	41 1/2	42 1/2	43 1/2	45 1/2	47 1/2
Length of Leg	31 1/2	32	33 1/4	34 1/2	36
Waist	32	34	36	37 1/2	42
Bottoms	19	19 1/2	20	20 1/2	20 1/2

Adopted March 12, 1879.

Stripes for Trousers Specification No. 18

Material.—To be made of facing cloth, same color as facings for uniform coat, except for infantry, which will be dark blue, and with the addition of white piping one-eighthh (1/8) inch wide for engineers.

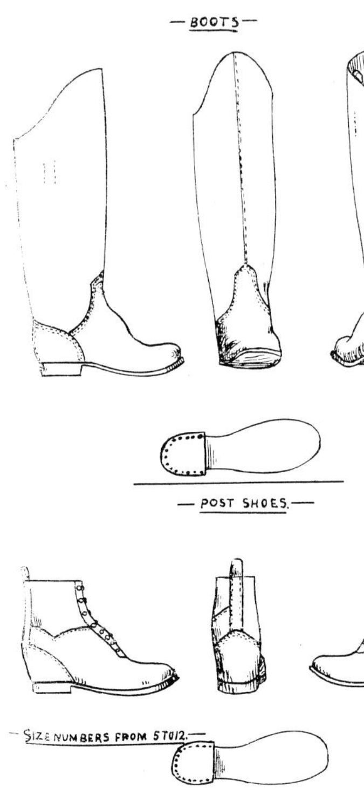

(Top) Boots, Specification No. 110, April 24, 1884; (Bottom) Post Shoes, Specification No. 111, April 24, 1884.

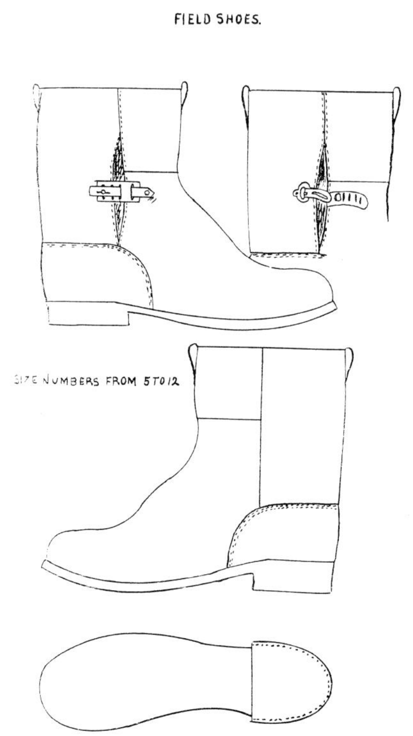

Field Shoes, Specification No. 112, April 24, 1884.

Dimensions.—For non-commissioned Staff, one and one-quarter (1 1/4) inch wide.
For Sergeants, one (1) inch wide.
For Corporals, one-half (1/2) inch wide.
All stripes are cut forty-five (45) inches long, and wide enough to be turned in one-quarter (1/4) of an inch on either side.
To be worn along the outer seam of the trowsers, the rear edge following the seam.
Adopted February 27, 1880.

Gray Flannel Shirts without Collar Specification No. 19

To be made of Army standard gray shirting flannel. Loose, with shoulder yoke, collar band, and one (1) plait two (2) inches wide, and about twelve (12) inches long, in the front. Collar band to be about seven-eighth (7/8) of an inch deep. Two buttons and button-holes in front plait, one at the end of collar band, and one at each wristband. The yoke to be lined with gray flannel, same quality as shirt is made of. A slit eight (8) inches long, at lower edge of each side seam, rounded off at front edges.
To be four (4) sizes.
Adopted January 16, 1878.

Drawers Specification No. 20

Material.—To be of unbleached Canton flannel, Army standard.
To be made loose, like standard sample, with waistband three (3) inches wide, buttoning in front with two (2) buttons. Opening at back of waist with four (4) worked eyelet-holes, and lacing- string of white cotton tape. A slit four and a half (4 1/2) inches long at bottom of each leg. Two strings or ties of white tape about nine (9) inches long at bottom of each leg. The bottoms of legs and slits in legs and at back of waist to be neatly faced with white cotton tape.

DIMENSIONS.

	No.1 Inches.	No.2 *Inches.*	No. 3 *Inches.*	No.4 *Inches.*	No. 5 *Inches.*
Length of side seams 40	41	42	43	44	
Length of leg seams	30	31	32	33	34
Waist	32	34	36	38	40

Adopted September 25, 1879.

Woolen Stockings Specification No. 21

Wool.—To be about one-half (1/2) each of good super-pulled wool and fine medium or X fleece wool, and to be mixed in the proportion of forty to fifty per cent (40 to 50%) of black and fifty to sixty percent (50 to 60%) of white, according to the shade required.
Yarn.—To be spun three-and a-half (3 1/2) run, with eighteen to twenty (18 to 20) holes of twist.

Leather Gauntlets, Specification No. 113, May 21, 1884.

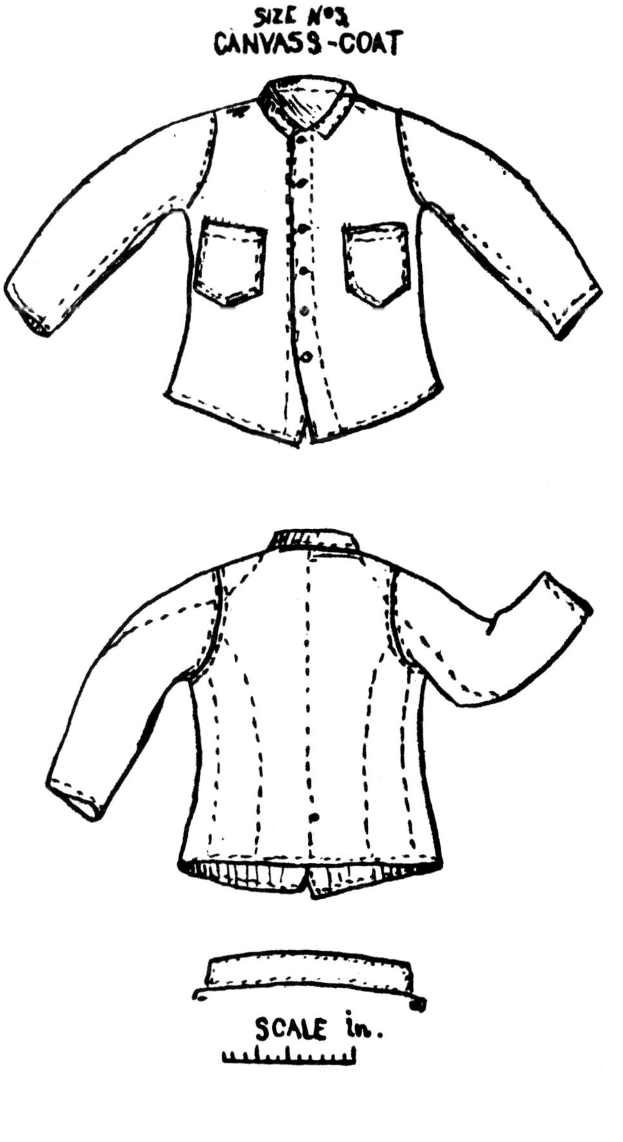

Canvas Coat, Specification No. 115, May 31, 1884.

Legs.—To be knit two-thread on a regular two and one (2 and 1) ribbed "Aiken" twelve (12) gauge machine.
Heels.—To be knot four-thread eighteen (18) ribs wide, about three (3) inches long, plain on bottom, and four (4) narrowings. In joining the heel to the foot every stitch must be taken up singly.
Toes.—To be knit four-thread of white yarn of corresponding quality to the other, and to be regularly narrowed.
Top of Legs.—To be fastened or bound off twice around.
The stockings to be well fulled and shaped, and when finished to weigh three (3) pounds to the dozen pairs.
The legs to be not less than fourteen (14) inches long; the feet to be of three (3) sizes, viz: 9 1/2, 10 1/2, and 11 1/2 inches, and to be assorted in the following proportion of sizes to the dozen: 5, 9 1/2; 4 10 1/2; and 3 11 1/2. Size to be plainly stamped on the toe of each stocking.
Adopted June 4, 1877.

Cotton Stockings Specification No. 22

Colors.—To be of three (3) colors, viz: Gray mixed, Brown mixed, and White (unbleached), and to be put up in dozens of one color.
Material.—The brown and gray mixed to be of good long-staple American cotton, free from impurities, of a grade not lower than "New Orleans middling," double corded; and the white to be of good long-staple American cotton, free from impurities, single corded.
Workmanship.—The brown and gray mixed to be "full regular," made according to the standard sample, with fashioned heels and toes and to be knit with the "Shaw" machine, the yarn to be spun from two (2) rovings in the regular hosiery twist for cotton. The top to be ribbed to a depth of about four and a half (4 1/2) inches and to be joined to the leg without seam or linking, forming an integral part of the stocking, to be knitted from two (2) No. 9 yarns and have the upper edge welted. The leg to be knitted of two (2) No. 8 yarns. The substance of the heel to be increased by additional yarn of No. 23. Length of leg from lower edge of ribbed top to be not less than seven and one-half (7 1/2) inches.
The white (unbleached) to be similar to the above, except that the yarn be spun from a single roving.

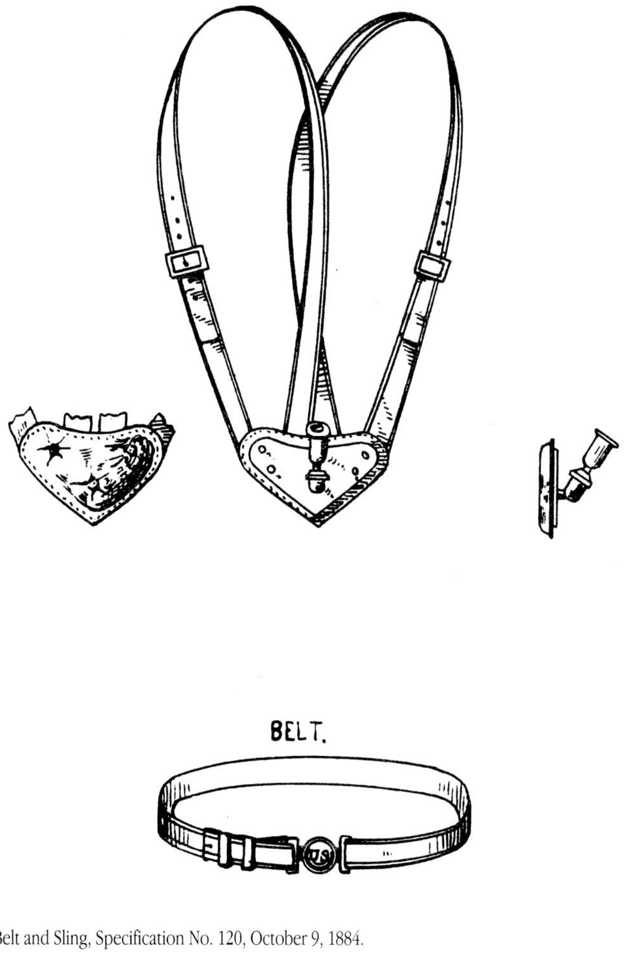

Color Belt and Sling, Specification No. 120, October 9, 1884.

Sizes.—To be of five (5) sizes, viz: 9 1/2-inch, 10-inch, 10 1/2-inch, 11-inch, and 11 1/2-inch, put up separate, in the following proportions: two 9 1/2, four 10, three 10 1/2, two 11, and one 11 1/2 to the dozen pairs.
Weight.—To weigh not less that two (2) pounds to the dozen pairs.
Adopted October 17, 1879.
NB: Amended per *ARSW, 1882*, Vol. I, 519 as follows: "Please amend the specifications for cotton stockings (No. 22) heretofore furnished you by erasing the word 'and to be knit on the "Shaw" machine,' and writing beneath the words 'Adopted October 17, 1879,' the following 'Amended by the Secretary of War, September 5, 1881.'"

White Gloves Specification No. 23

Made of strong white cotton known commonly as "Berlin cotton wool." Gored between the fingers. Three (3) welts stitched along the back of the hand.
A white elastic band, one-fourth (1/4) inc wide, about one (1) inch long, fastened to the inner side of the wrist.
Stitched hem around the wrist. To be of three size: No. 9, 10, and 11.
Adopted May 13, 1876.

Woolen Mittens Specification No. 24

To be made of pure gray woolen yarn, double and twisted; thumb and forefinger formed. To be of three (3) sizes, viz: 10, 11, and 12 inches in length,
Each dozen pairs to have five pairs if the smallest, four pairs of the medium, and three pairs of the largest size, and to weigh two and one-quarter (2 1/4) pounds.
Adopted May 31, 1876.

Muskrat Gauntlets Specification No. 25

To be made of muskrat skin, according to standard sample. Lining of lamb's fleece in hand, and blue or red cloth in gauntlet. Gauntlets to be at least five (5) inches deep, and of sufficient fullness to admit cuff of dress-coat or blouse. Palms of buckskin.
To be of three (3) sizes, viz: 9, 10. and 111.
Adopted March 12, 1879.

Boots Specification No. 27

To be worked square with the last on which they are made; the edges to be finished with shoulder-sticks, without heel-ball, and must measure at least half a size (outside) more than they are marked.
The upper leather to be the best oak-tanned from slaughter-hides. The soles to be best oak-tanned from "straight" Texas hides, or from South American (commonly called "Spanish") dry hides. No split leather to be used.
The width of the soles across the ball of the foot to be graduated as follows, and to be in proportion throughout: No. 5, 3 5/8 inches; No. 6, 3 3/4 inches; No. 7, 3 7/8 inches; No. 8, 4 inches; No. 9, 4 1/8 inches; No. 10, 4 1/4 inches; No. 11, 4 3/8 inches; No. 12, 4 1/2 inches.
The insteps and toes to measure as follows: No. 5, 9 1/4, 9 inches; No. 6, 9 3/4, 9 1/8 inches; No. 7, 9 3/4, 9 1/2 inches; No. 8, 10, 9 7/8 inches; No. 9, 10 1/8, 10 inches; No. 10, 10 5/8, 10 1/8 inches; No. 11, 10 7/8, 10 1/2 inches; No. 12, 11, 10 3/4 inches.
The measurement for a No. 8 boot, standard is as follows, viz: Heel, 13 1/2 inches; instep 10 inches; ball or toe, 9 7/8 inches; length of legs, 15 1/2 inches in front, 14 inches back; width of leg at top, 14 3/4 inches; width of strap, 1 3/8 inches; length of strap, 9 inches; height of counter, 2 1/2 inches. (counter to be sewed over side seam;) length and width of heel, 3 inches; width of sole or ball, 4 inches. They are to have not less than six (6) stitches to the inch in the side seam, and not less than nine (9) stitches to the inch on counters and straps.
To have double soles, fastened to the upper leather and inner soles firmly with brass screws (the thread of which will be cleanly cut by the machine on 12 1/2 brass wire) well clinched inside, so as to render the inner sole perfectly smooth. The screws to be at no greater distance apart than will afford five (5) spaces to every two (2) inches.
Adopted February 25, 1878, in lieu of those adopted May 31, 1876, as modified August 24, 1876.
Change in number of stitches on counters and straps from 10 to 9 made November 21, 1878.

Felt Boots Specification No. 28

To be made of heavy wool-felt, molded to shape of last. Heavy single sole and slip sole of hemlock lather fastened to upper with heavy brass screws, same as Army standard boot. Upper leather (split) to cover front, sides, and back, rising well upon the instep in form of tongue, and at back to a height of from three to three and a half (3 to 3 1/2) inches from the top of the heel; stay piece of leather at back to rise from upper to a height of not less than three (3) inches, and to be sufficiently wide to protect the felt from the more than usual friction and wear at that part of the leg. The leather upper to be secured to the felt boot by a double row of stitching, as on sample, and the upper edge if side seams to be fastened with copper rivets and burs. Stay-strap and buckle to rise from front part of heel, at sides, and fasten over the instep to relieve the strain on the felt at that point.

Dimensions.—For feet, to be as described for Army boots.

Height of leg to be fifteen (15) inches in front and fourteen (14) in back for size 8, and to vary proportionally for the other sizes.

Outside circumference of leg at fullest part to be not less than seventeen and a half (17 1/2) inches for size 8, and to vary according to the sizes. Top of leg to be bound with leather put on with a double row of stitching. Straps (to pull on by) to be similar to those on Army boots, except that where stitched to the leg they shall expand to an oval of about 2 1/4 to 2 12 inches, and be fastened to leg with a double row of stitching, so as to distribute as widely the strain of the felt.

Adopted July 20, 1878.

Shoes Specification No. 29

To be worked square with the last on which they are made; the edges to be finished with shoulder-sticks, without heel-ball, and to measure at least half a size outside more than they are marked. Upper leather to be of the best oak-tanned from slaughter hides; soles of best quality oak-tanned South American (commonly called Spanish) dry hides. No split leather to be used. Width of the soles across the ball of the foot to be graduated as follows, and to be in proportion: No. 5, 3 5/8 inches; No. 6, 3 6/8 inches; No. 7, 3 4/8 inches; No. 8, 4 inches; No. 9, 4 1/8 inches; No. 10, 4 1/4 inches; No. 11, 4 3/8 inches; No. 12, 4 1/2 inches.

The instep and toe to measure as follows: No. 5, 9 1/4, 9; No. 6, 9 1/2, 9 1/4; No. 7, 9 3/4, 9 1/2; No. 8, 10, 9 3/4; No. 9, 10 1/4, 10; No. 10, 10 1/2, 10 1/4; No. 11, 10 3/4, 10 1/2 inches; No. 12, 11, 10 3/4 inches.

Double soles to be fastened to upper leather and inner sole with brass crews made of No. 12 1/2 brass wire, the thread of which must be cleanly cut by the machines.

Screws to be well clinched inside, so as to render inner sole perfectly smooth.

Tongues to rise one-half (1/2) inch above uppers when on the foot, and to measure at least two (2) inches across top; to be joined at the upper front by a flat seam at a point just above the thong-holes, and cut so as to mold to instep.

To have as least nine (9) stitches to the inch in the fitting.

Adopted March 8, 1876.

Arctic Overshoes Specification No. 30

Fronts and quarters made of black tweed waterproof, with coarse gray felt lining, held together by an inner coating of India rubber. Vulcanized rubber foxing around the entire shoe, to rise at heel sufficiently to cover counter; to be about one (1) inch deep at sides forward of heel, and to rise at toe of a height is about two (2) inches at center; single sole and heel of vulcanized rubber, bottoms rough; average height about seven and a half (7 1/2) inches from heel to top of upper; average weight three pounds and ten ounces (3 lbs. 10 oz.) per pair.

Front and quarter joined by a gore of same material, so as to exclude snow, water, c.

Sizes to cover Army boots and shoes of two numbers smaller, and to be of a corresponding tariff, thus: No. 7 overshoe to cover No. 5 boot or so, and so forth on through the scale of sizes.

The tariff for overshoes would, therefore, be 3/7, 10/8, 39/9, 35/10, 14/11, 4/12, 3/13, 1/14 = 100.

Fastening at front, a buckle and strap, as on sample. Front quarter secured by rivet on each side.

Adopted May 5, 1876.

Stencil Plate Specification No. 55

A complete set of stencil plates consists of two full alphabets, Roman capitals, and including the usual mark for "&," and two series of numbers from "1 to 0" One set of letter and numbers to be one (1) inch, the other one-half (1/2) inch high. They are cut on plate os sheet-brass, No. 28, the larger two and a quarter (2 1/4) by two (2) inches, the smaller one and three-quarters (1 3/4) by one and a half (1 1/2) inch. The upper edge of each plate is turned up so as to form a rim about one-half (1/2) inch high.

These plates are issued in Japanned tin boxes eight and a half (8 1/2) inches long, four (4) inches wide, and one and three-quarters (1 3/4) inch high, with hinged lids. Each box contains, besides the full sets of stencils, a cake of marking paste in tin box, a sponge, and a stencil-brush. Printed directions for the use of the latter materials are fastened to the inside of the lid.

Adopted May 31, 1876.

Dark-blue Cloth, Specification No. 61

To be six-quarter (6-4) wide; to be pure long-staple, American fleece-wool, dyed with pure indigo to color of the standard sample; to be free from shoddy or flocks, and the nap to be very slightly raised; to have fifty-six (56) threads of filling, and sixty (60) threads of chain in each square inch; to weigh not less than twenty-one (21) ounces per linear yard; the breaking-strain to be not less than sixty-eighth (68) pounds to one (1) inch width of warp; and fifty (50) pounds each to one (1) inch width of filling in the piece. All cloth to be of the standard strength here given, with allowance of three (3) pounds for variation in samples;

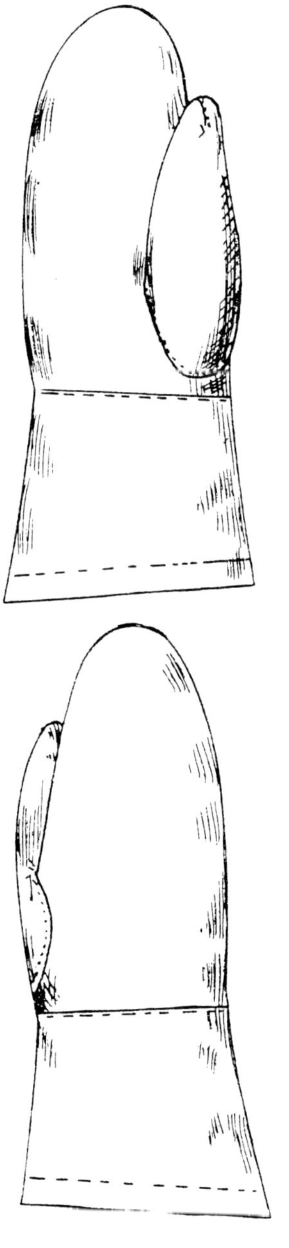

Canvas Mittens, Specification No. 121, October 13, 1884.

but no cloth breaking under a strain four (4) pounds less than the standard will be accepted from contractors.
May 31, 1876 [Originally adopted on November 12, 1874, according to LS, Clothing Br. Vol. A, 1874.]

Sky-blue Kersey Heavy Quality Specification No. 62

To be six-quarter (6-4) wide, and made of pure long-staple American fleece-wool, free from shoddy, flocks. or other impurities; wool dyed with pure indigo to color of standard sample; nap very slightly raised. To contain forty-eighth (48) threads of warp and forty-two (42) threads of filling to the square inch, and to weigh not less than twenty-two (22) ounces per linear yard of fifty-four inches (54) inches in width.
To be capable of sustaining not less than fifty-eighth (58) pounds to one inch width of warp in pieces, and fifty (50) pounds to one inch width of filling in pieces, but no kersey breaking under a strain four (4) pounds less than the standard.
Adopted July 2, 1876.

Sky-blue Kersey Light Quality Specification No. 63

To be fifty-four (54) inches wide, and made of pure long-staple American fleece wool, free from shoddy, flocks, or other impurities; wool dyed with pure indigo to color of standard sample; nap very slightly raised. To contain forty-eighth (48) threads of warp and forty-six (46) threads of filling to the square inch, and weigh eighteen (18) ounces to the linear yard.
To be capable of sustaining the following strain to the inch, viz: thirty-three (33) pounds for warp and thirty-six (36) pounds for filling to the inch.
Adopted May 23, 1876.

Facing-cloth Specification No. 64

To be made six-quarter (6/4) of a yard wide, of best American fleece-wool, free from shoddy, flocks, or other impurities; twilled; all wool, dyed in the following colors, viz: sky-blue, scarlet, yellow, crimson, orange, gray, emerald-green, and white.
To contain sixty-four (64) threads in the chain, sixty (60) threads in the filling to the square inch, and to weigh sixteen (16) ounces to the linear yard.
Capable of sustaining the following strain to the inch, viz: thirty (30) pounds for chain, twenty (20) pounds for filling.
Adopted May 31, 1876.

Dark-blue Wool Flannel Specification No. 65

To be fifty-four (54) inches, or 6/4, wide, and to be made of pure, long staple American fleece-wool, not less than full one-half blood, free from shoddy, flocks, or other impurities.
To be twilled, and the nap slightly raised. To contain not less than fifty-six (56) threads of warp and forty-eighth (48) threads of filling in each square inch. To weigh not less than eleven and one-half (11 1/2) ounces to the linear yard. To be capable of sustaining a strain of thirty-two (32) pounds to the inch in width of warp, and twenty-five (25) pounds to the inch in width of filling.
All flannel to be of the strength given, with allowance of two (2) pounds for variation in samples; but no flannel breaking under a strain three (3) pounds less than the standard will be accepted from contractors.
The color to be dark-blue, of same shade as the standard sample, and to be dyed in the wool with pure indigo.
Approved September 29, 1877.

Cape Lining Flannel Specification No. 66

To be fifty-four (54) inches, or 6/4 wide and to be made of pure, long staple, American fleece wool, not less than full one half blood, free from shoddy, flocks, or other impurities. To contain not less than fifty-four (54) threads of warp and fifty (50) threads of filling in each square inch.
To be capable of sustaining a strain of twenty (20) pounds to the inch in width of warp, twenty-two (22) pounds to the inch in width of filling. To be twilled and to weight not less than ten ounces (10 oz) to the linear yard.
All flannel to be of the strength herein given with an allowance of two (2) pounds for variation in samples; but no flannel which breaks under a strain of three (3) or more pounds less than the standard will be accepted from contractors.
The colors to be green, gray, crimson, scarlet, orange, dark blue and yellow of the standard shades, to be dyed fast color. The blue to be pure Indigo dyed.
Adopted February 10, 1880.

Canton Flannel Specification No. 67

To be made of long-staple American cotton, free from dirt or imperfections, and a grade not inferior to that known commercially as "low middling." To be thirty (30) inches wide, and nap raised. To weigh six (6) ounces to the linear yard; to contain not less than seventy (70) thread of warp and fifty (50) threads of filling to the inch, and to be capable of sustaining a strain, to the inch (tested in piece), of sixty (60) pounds on the warp an fifty pounds on the filling. Flannel to be unbleached.
Approved July 24, 1877.

Gray Shirting Flannel Light Quality Specification No. 68

To be three-quarters (3/4) wide. To have forty-eighth (48) threads of chain and fifty-six (56) threads of filling in each square inch. The chain to be made of the best long staple American cotton, No. 46 thread, doubled and twisted, dyed pure indigo blue, and to weigh one and one-half ounces to the yard.
The filling to be composed of good quality American fleece-wool, at least one-half blood, free from shoddy, flocks or other imperfections; to be dyed with indigo and logwood to color of filling of standard sample; and to weigh three and one-half ounces to the yard.

Cloth Chevrons, Specification No. 127, January 28, 1885.

To weigh not to be less than five (5) ounces to the linear yard of twenty-seven (27) inches in width.

The breaking strain to be not less than thirty-four (34) pounds to one inch width of warp in the piece and thirty-one (31) pounds to one inch width of filling in the piece.

The flannel will be neither hot nor cold pressed. None but unpressed flannel will be accepted from contractors.

The flannel must be properly fulled, and the shades of color of the sealed standard sample will be adhered to.

Adopted January 5, 1876.

Gray Shirting Flannel Heavy Quality Specification No. 69

To be three-quarters (3/4) wide. To have forty-eighth (48) threads of chain and fifty-six (56) threads of filling in each square inch. The chain to be made of the best long staple American cotton, No. 40 thread, doubled and twisted, dyed pure indigo blue, and to weigh one and three-quarters ounces to the yard.

The filling to be composed of good quality American fleece-wool, at least one-half blood, free from shoddy, flocks or other imperfections; to be dyed with indigo and logwood to color of filling of standard sample; and to weigh four and one-quarter ounces to the yard.

To weigh not to be less than six (6) ounces to the linear yard of twenty-seven (27) inches in width.

The breaking strain to be not less than thirty-four (34) pounds to one inch width of warp in the piece and thirty-six (36) pounds to one inch width of filling in the piece.

The flannel will be neither hot nor cold pressed. None but unpressed flannel will be accepted from contractors.

The flannel must be properly fulled, and the shades of color of the sealed standard sample will be adhered to.

Adopted January 5, 1876.

Twelve-ounce Duck Specification No. 70

To be made of American cotton, of a grade not inferior to "low middling," and woven ins s workmanlike manner, free from imperfections. To be full twenty-eighth and one-half (28 1/2) inches wide when finished, and to weigh not less than twelve (12) ounces to the linear yard. To contain not less than forty-four (44) threads of warp, nor less than thirty (30) threads of filling to the inch, and to be capable of sustaining a strain of not less than one hundred and twenty-eighth (128) pounds in the warp and eighty-four (84) pounds in the filling to the half (1/2) inch tested in the piece. To be entirely free from sizing, and not to be "hot finished."

Adopted March 12, 1879, in lieu of those adopted February 25, 1875.

Ten-ounce Duck Specification No. 71

To be made of American cotton, of a grade not inferior to "low middling," and woven in a workmanlike manner, free from imperfections. To be full twenty-eighth and one-half (28 1/2) inches wide when finished, and to weigh not less than ten (10) ounces to the linear yard. To contain not less than forty-six (46) threads of warp, nor less than thirty-two (32) threads of filling to the inch, and to be capable of sustaining a strain of not less than one hundred and eight (108) pounds in the warp and sixty-four (64) pounds in the filling to the half (1/2) inch tested in the piece. To be entirely free from sizing, and not to be "hot finished."

Adopted March 12, 1879.

Eight-ounce Cotton Duck Specification No. 72

To be made of American cotton, of a grade not inferior to "low middling," and woven in a workmanlike manner, free from imperfections. To be full twenty-eighth and one-half (28 1/2) inches wide when finished, and to weigh not less than eight (8) ounces to the linear yard. To contain not less than fifty (50) threads of warp, nor less than thirty-two (32) threads of filling to the inch, and to be capable of sustaining a strain of not less than seventy-eighth (78) pounds in the warp and forty-five (45) pounds in the filling to the half (1/2) inch tested in the piece. To be entirely free from sizing and not to be "hot finished."

Adopted March 12, 1879.

Dark-Blue Wool Shirting Flannel Specification No. 75

To be fifty-four (54) inches, or 6/4, wide, and to be made of pure, long staple American fleece-wool, not less than one-half blood, free from shoddy, flocks, or other impurities, and to weigh not less than ten (10) ounces to the linear yard. To be twilled, and the nap slightly raised; to contain not less than fifty-six (56) threads of warp and forty-eighth (48) threads of filling to each square inch, and to be capable of sustaining a strain of not less than twenty-six (26) pounds to the inch in width of warp, and not less than twenty-two (22) pounds in the inch in width of filling, tested in the piece.

The color to be dark-blue, similar in shade to the standard sample, and to be dyed in the wool with pure indigo.

Adopted February 9, 1881

Overshirts Specification No. 76

Materials.—Dark-blue wool-flannel, Army standard, ten (10) ounce, shoulder lining, light-gray cotton jeans.

Pattern.—To be according to sample, single breasted, with falling collar and coat sleeves, and without yoke or alite at sides. The front to open all the way down and be fastened with five (5) small regulation brass buttons. The collar and cuffs to be trimmed with worst cord of color according to arm of service, as shown on pattern. To be made without pockets or lining (except the small stay or lining in the shoulder, as in sample.)

To be of five (5) sizes of the following dimensions:

	Breast Measure.	Length Measure.	Collar	Length of Sleeve.
Size 1	36	29	15	31
Size 2	38	30	15 1/4	32
Size 3	40	31	16	33
Size 4	42	32 16 1/2	33 1/2	
Size 5	44 33	17	34 1/2	

Adopted February 16, 1881.

Undershirts Specification No. 77

Materials.—The mixture to consist of fifty per centum, (50%) of super-pulled natural sheeps grey and fine medium or X fleece wool, mixed to the shade of standard sample, and fifty per centum (50%) of good middling cotton, and to be free from shoddy, flock, reworked wool or other impurities. The whole mixture to be thoroughly carded.

Workmanship.—To be firmly knit on a sixteen (16) gauge machine; to be t"taken up" on the shoulder, self-finish, with "regular" cuffs; to be bound with drab Prussian binding around the neck and down the breast opening.

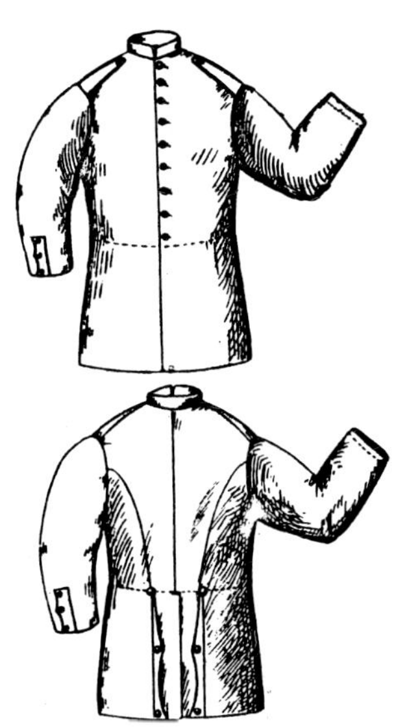

Uniform Dress Coats Foot, Specification No. 131, March 5, 1885.

To have three (3) eighteen (18) line pearl buttons on front, and corresponding button-holes properly made; to be scoured in garment, and dried on forms. To be finished like, and equal in all respects to, the standard sample.
To be six (6) sizes, the breast measures and lengths of which shall be as described, and the weights not less than the figures given below:

Size Numbers——	1	2	3	4	5	6
Breast Measure—	36 ins.	38 ins.	40 ins.	42 ins.	44 ins.	46 ins.
Length of Shirt—	31 ins.	32 ins.	33 ins.	34 ins.	34 ins.	35 ins.
Weight——	14 ozs.	15 1/2 ozs.	15 1/2 ozs.	18 ozs.	19 ozs.	20 ozs.

To be manufactured in the following proportion of sizes to the one hundred:

	5	25	35	20	10	5 = 100

Adopted February 16, 1881.

Overshirts Specification No. 79

Materials.—Dark-blue wool-flannel, Army standard; worsted cord, and hard-rubber buttons, 23 ligne.
Pattern.—To be according to sample, loose, with falling collar (without band), single plait two inches (2") wide on front, and with cuffs. Two (2) outside "patch" breast pockets, about seven inches (7") deep by six inches (6") wide, rounded at bottoms. The side seams open about nine inches (9") from bottom, and secured at top of opening with a stay of white cotton binding well stitched on the inside. A button and button-hole to be at each of the following places, viz, at the throat; at the middle of front plait; at the center of the mouth of each pocket, and on each cuff, making six in all. Worsted cord, of color according to arm of service, to be stitched around the edges of collar and of front plait, upon the upper edge of each pocket, and around each cuff where it joins the sleeve. Corners of cuffs and bottom of shirt to be rounded off.
Dimensions.—Depth of collar for average size about three and one-half inches (3 1/2") in front and two and three-quarters inches (2 3/4") behind; of cuff about two and one-half inches (2 1/2"); of front plait about ten inches (10"). To be of four sizes, measures as follows:

	Length of shirt. Inches.	Length of sleeve. Inches.	Collar. Inches.	Cuff. Inches.
Size 1	30	32 1/2	15	8 1/2
Size 2	31	33	15 1/2	9
Size 3	32	34	16 1/2	9 1/2
Size 4	33	35	17	10

Adopted February 24, 1882, in lieu of the specifications adopted February 16, 1881, which are hereby canceled.

Metallic Ornaments for Helmets, Forage Caps, and Uniform Coats Specification No. 80

FOR HELMETS.

Eagles.—Eagles according to pattern made of No. 24 sheet-brass (high); American eagle displayed proper with national shield on breast and bearing in beak a scroll with motto "E pluribus unum;" olive branch in dexter talon and branch of arrows in sinister. For troops of the line the distinguishing arms are displayed under the shield, viz: Artillery, the crossed cannon; cavalry, crossed sabers; infantry, crossed rifles, and upon the lower part of the shield is borne the regimental number in German silver. For the staff and staff corps, the crossed arms are omitted and the distinguishing badge, in German silver, is borne upon the lower part of shield, viz: For hospital stewards, the caduceus; for commissary sergeants, the crescent; for engineers, the castle; for ordnance and ordnance sergeants, the shell and flame, and for Signal Service, the crossed flags. When flat the eagle is about the following dimension: Greatest width between tips of wings four and one-quarter (4 1/4") inches; from upper edge of scroll to tip of tail three and seven-eighth (3 7/8") inches. It shall be molded to the form of helmet shell and be provided with three (3) wire loops by which to fasten it on.
Spike and base (foot troops).—Spike to be of polished high brass, according to pattern, hexagonal, fluted surface, with screw of brass to fit socket in top of helmet. Height of spike three (3") inches; widest diameter one (1") inch; length of screw (in the clear) three-fourths (3/4") of an inch; base of No. 24 sheet-brass (high); oak-leaf design according to pattern, eight (8) points, bed in center to receive base of spike and hole cut for spike-screw.
Plume socket (for mounted men's helmets).—To be of high brass, according to pattern. An inverted fluted cone and mitered top (four points), front ornamented with the national eagle and shield and a single star surmounting eagle head.

Uniform Dress Coats Mounted, Specification No. 131, March 5, 1885.

Spherical base, into the mouth of which the cone is securely brazed, and which is formed into a hexagonal pedestal at the bottom similar to that of spike so far as to rest firmly upon the oak-leaf base and be bored for the plume pin. Height of spherical base (including mouth and pedestal) about one and one-half (1 1/2") inches; of cone two (2") inches; diameter of cone at top one (1") inch, at bottom five-eighth (5/8") of an inch; diameter of spherical base one (1") inch. Plume pin, with ornamental head and plain washer (each about one and one-fourth (1 1/4") inches in diameter), about four and three-quarters (4 3/4") inches in length, the thread of which shall be cut so as to screw into the ventilator socket in top of helmet. For the lower end of pin a large open washer or disk with beveled edge to bear against the inside of helmet shell for better security of the top piece, and be kept in place by a small brass thumb nut. Diameter of disk, about two and one-half (2 1/2") inches.
The oak-leaf base to be the same as described for foot helmets.
Side buttons.—Side buttons to be of high brass, according to pattern, with flat brass double stems. Devices on buttons in high relief: For engineers, the castle; for ordnance, the shell and flame; for hospital stewards, the caduceus; for commissary sergeants, the crescent; for Signal Corps, the crossed flags; for artillery, the crossed cannon; for cavalry, the crossed sabers; for infantry, the crossed rifles.
Numbers.—Numbers to be one-half (1/2") inch in height and made of No. 18 German silver, according to pattern, with two soft copper wire stems to hold them to shield.
Devices.—Devices for staff and staff corps to be German silver, according to pattern. Designs are mentioned in description of eagle, and stems as for numbers.
Scrolls and rings (mounted troops).—Scrolls and rings. One on each side, between the leaf-shaped points of top piece, its lower edge one-half (1/2") inch below these points. The scroll is three-fourths (3/4") inch diameter, ornamented to correspond with the fastening on the top piece. On the top of the scroll, in the center, is an eye of thin wire three-sixteenths (3/16") of an inch high, holding a thin brass ring one-half (1/2") inch in diameter, to keep the cords and bands in position. The stem of the scroll is formed in two pieces of thin brass wire to fasten to it at the inside of the helmet. All to be high brass.

FOR FORAGE CAPS.

Bugles for musicians.—Bugles for field and band musicians: Of sheet brass (high) No. 28, representing an old-style bugle with circular crook, and a cord slung three (3) fold around the lower part, terminating in two (2) tassels on one, and one (1) tassel on the other side. Height across crook one and one-fourth (1 1/4") inch; width from mouth-piece to outer edge of bowl, two and one-fourth (2 1/4") inches. Brass-wire loops same as on letters.

Castles (engineers).—Castles: Of sheet-brass (high) No. 28, representing an ancient castle with three (3) towers. Height of center tower, seven-eighth (7/8") of an inch; of side towers, one and one-fourth (1 1/4") inches each; of battlements between towers, five-eighths (5/8") of an inch; width at base, one and seven-eighth (1 7/8") inches; at top of side towers, one and three-fourths (1 3/4") inches. Two small brass-wire loops strongly soldered to back to fasten to cap.

Shells and flames (ordnance).—Shells and flames: Of sheet- brass (high) No. 28, representing a shell and flame. Diameter height of shell, three-quarters (3/4") of an inch; height of flame from upper edge of shell, seven-eighth (7/8") of an inch; greatest width of flame, one and one-eighth (1 1/8")inches. Brass-wire loops the same as on letters.

Crescents (commissary sergeants).—Crescents: Of sheet white metal (German silver), crescent shaped. Width from point to point, one and five-eighth (1 5/8") inches; height of arc one (1") inch; greatest width in center one-half (1/2") inch. Brass wire loops on back same as letters.

Wreaths and caduceus (hospital stewards).—Wreaths made of dead or unburnished gilt-metal, representing two olive branches, held at the bottom by a loop and knot, turning upward and bending in an oval shape, approaching each other at the top. Height one and one-half (1 1/2") inch; greatest distance between outer edges, two and five-eighth (2 5/8") inches; greatest width of single branch five-eighth (5/8") of an inch. Brass-wire loops as on back of letters.

A caduceus of German silver, similar to that on helmet eagle, to be worn within wreath.

Crossed cannon (artillery).—Crossed cannon: Of sheet-brass (high) No. 20, representing two cannon crossing each other at the trunnions, muzzles upward; length two and one-eighthh (2 1/8") inches; breadth at breeches two (2") inches; at muzzles, one and seven-eighth (1 7/8") inches. Four brass-wire loops strongly soldered on back to fasten to cap.

Crossed sabers (cavalry).—Crossed sabers: Of sheet-brass (high) No 20, representing two cavalry sabers in scabbards, crossed in the middle, with hilts and edges upward. To be shaped or curved so as to fit the front of the cap. Length of sabers, three (3") inches; height from hilt of one to point of other one and one-fourth (1 1/4") inches; from point to point, two and three-fourths (2 3/4") inches. Four brass-wire loops same as on crossed cannon.

Crossed Rifles (infantry).—Crossed rifles: Of sheet-brass (high) No. 20; two rifles crossing each other at a point equidistant from butt and muzzle; muzzles pointing upward and outward; hammers upward, their position crossed, making the upper space form an angle of 137°; length of rifle, two and five-eighth (2 5/8") inches; diameter at point of crossing, about one-eighthh (1/8") of an inch. To be shaped or curved so as to fit the front of cap; the whole ornament occupying a rectangular space about two and seven-sixteenths (2 7/16") inches wide by one and three-eighth (1 3/8") inches high. Fastenings: Four brass-wire loops firmly soldered, opening horizontally with the rifles, and placed about one-half (1/2") inch from muzzles and butts.

Letters "A" to "M."—Brass letters "A" to "M": Roman capitals, one-half (1/2) inch long, to be made of sheet-brass (high) No. 28; edges beveled. Two small brass-wire loops strongly soldered on the back of letter to fasten it to the cap.

Numbers "1" to "0.""—Brass Numbers: Nos. "1" to "0," inclusive; one-half (1/2") of an inch long, to be made of sheet-brass (high) No, 28; edges beveled. Small brass-wire loops, same as on letters.

FOR UNIFORM COATS

Caduceus (hospital stewards).—Caduceus of German silver, similar to adopted for helmet and forage cap, to be worn on each facing of the collar.

Castles (engineers).—Castles: To be of sheet brass (high) No. 28, showing an ancient castle with three (3) towers; height of battlements three-eighth (3/8") of an inch; of center tower, one-half (1/2") inch; of side towers, five-eighth (5/8") of an inch each; breadth at base and top, one (1") inch. Two small brass-wire loops soldered to back to fasten to coat collar.

Shells and Flames (ordnance).—Shells and flames: To be of sheet-brass (high) No. 28, representing a shell and flame; shell one-half (1/2") inch diameter, flames rising one-half (1/2") inch above upper edge of shell; greatest breadth of flame nearest to shell, three-quarters (3/4") of an inch. Brass-wire loops same as on numbers.

Crescents (commissary sergeants).—Crescents: To be made of white metal (German silver) crescent-shaped; from point to point, one (1") inch; height of arc nine sixteenths (9/16") of an inch; greatest width in center one-half (1/4") inch. Brass wire loops on back same as on numbers.

Numbers (troops of the line).—Numbers: Nos. "1" to "0" inclusive; each number to be made of sheet-brass (high) No. 28, one-half (1/2") inch long; edges beveled. Two brass-wire loops soldered on the back of number to fasten it to coat collar.

Adopted April 21, 1882, in lieu of specifications No. 8, of Book of Specifications, and conforming to standard samples this day adopted.

Helmets for all Troops Specification No. 81

Material.—To be black: To be made of felt composed of one part each of "Russia" and best "coney," and one-half part of short stock nutria or beaver; wine stiffened. Such other suitable material besides felt of the above composition as may from time to time be determined upon bids received in response to advertisement may be used if approved; in which case the character and quality of such material, as shown in the sample submitted and accepted, will govern the contract.

Shape, & c.—To be in shape according to standard sample. Black enameled leather band, about seven-eighth (7/8) of an inch wide, to surround the helmet at base of crown, as on sample. The lower edge of helmet to be bound with black enameled leather, and the inside of visor all around to be lined with green morocco leather, pasted to the body with rubber cement. The sweat to be of Belgium sheepskin, about two (2) inches wide; inside the sweat a band about an inch wide of heavy enameled leather or cloth. All to be well stitched in place. A shell ventilator, according to pattern, to take the place of the top-piece or spike when desired.

Sizes.—To be of six (6) standard sizes from one (1) to six (6) inclusive, corresponding to the trade sizes of 6 3/4 to 7 3/8 inclusive.

The standard sample to be followed in all respects as to shape, quality of materials, & c.

Adopted May 6, 1882, in lieu of specifications (No. 1) adopted May 31, 1876, which are hereby canceled.

NOTE—*Ornaments and trimmings for foot troops.*—The top-piece to consist of a spike on a base of oak leaves, according to sample, and to be made to screw into the base of ventilator, as shown in sample. Eagle with shield and motto, and side buttons, according to pattern, for each arm of service. All to be of yellow metal.

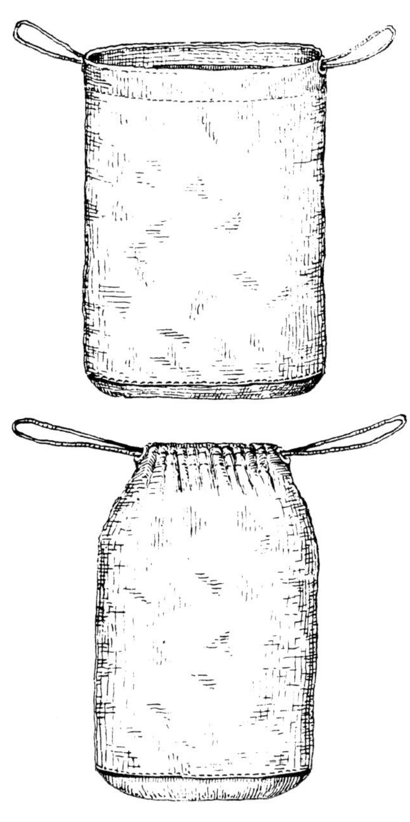

Barrack Bags, Specification No. 132, March 9, 1885.

The number of the regiment or device of corps to be in white metal (German silver) and be borne on the lower half of shield on eagle's breast, according to pattern.
For mounted troops. The top ornament to consist of a horse-hair plume (color according to arm of service) and a yellow-metal plume-socket, as described in specifications, which rests upon the oak-leaf base. Eagle with shield and motto, and side buttons, according to arm of service. All to be yellow metal.
The number of the regiment or device of corps, in German silver, to be borne on the shield, as described for foot troops.
Adopted May 6, 1882.

Trowsers Specification No. 82

Material.—Sky-blue kersey, Army Standard.

Pattern and Dimensions.

For Foot Troops.—To be cut according to standard sample, loose, without lining or plaits; waistband two inches wide, to button with one button in front; pockets in front, opening at top. Bottoms to spread well over shoe.
For Mounted Troops.—To be similar in pattern to those for foot-men, with the addition of a reinforce or saddle-piece of same material on seat and legs. Four buttons at bottom of each leg, two on each side, for straps.

	No. 1 Inches	No. 2. Inches	No. 3 Inches	No. 4 Inches	No.5 Inches
Length of side Seam	41 1/2	42 1/2	43 1/2	45 1/2	47 1/2
Length of Leg	31 1/2	32	33 1/2	34 1/2	36
Waist	32	34	36	37 1/2	42
Bottoms	19	19	20	20 1/2	20 1/2

Adopted October 9, 1882, in lieu of specifications adopted March 12, 1879, which are hereby canceled.

Helmets for all Troops Specification No. 84

Material.—To be black: To be made of felt composed of one part each of "Russia" and best "coney," and one-half part of short-stock nutria or beaver; wine stiffened. Such other suitable material besides felt of the above composition as may from time to time be determined upon bids received in response to advertisement may be used if approved; in which case the character and quality of such material, as shown in the sample submitted and accepted, will govern the contract. Suitable hoes must be made in the the sides of the helmet for inserting of the side buttons, and in proper places on the helmet for all other trimmings.
Shape, & c.—To be in shape according to standard sample. Black enameled leather band, about seven-eighths (7/8) of an inch wide, to surround the helmet at base of crown, amd to have an adjustable chin strap, each part ten and one-half (10 1/2) long. of the same material, with brass sliding-buckle, as on sample. The lower edge of helmet to be bound with black enameled leather, and the inside of visor all around to be lined with green Morocco leather, pasted to the body with rubber cement. The sweat-leather to be of Belgium sheep-skin, two (2) inches wide; inside the sweat-leather a band one (1) inch wide of heavy enameled leather. All to be well stitched in place. A shell ventilator, according to pattern, to take the place of the top-piece or spike when desired.
Sizes.—To be of six (6) standard sizes, numbered from one (1) to six (6) inclusive, corresponding to the trade sizes of 6 3/4 to 7 3/8 inclusive.
The standard sample to be followed in all respects as to shape, quality of materials, workmanship, & c.
Adopted November 10, 1882, in lieu of specifications adopted May 6, 1882, which are hereby canceled.
NOTE—
Ornaments and Trimmings for Foot Troops.—The top-piece to consist of a spike on a base of oak leaves, according to sample, and to be made to screw into the base of ventilator, as shown in sample. Eagle with shield and motto, and side buttons, according to pattern, for each arm of the service. All to be of yellow metal.
The number of the regiment or device of corps to be in white metal (German silver) and be borne on the lower half of shield on eagle's breast, according to pattern.
For Mounted Troops.—The top ornament to consist of a horse-hair plume (color according to arm of service) and a yellow-metal plume-socket, as described in specifications, which rests upon the oak-leaf base. Eagle with shield and motto, and side buttons, according to arm of service. All to be yellow metal.
The number of the regiment or device of corps, in German silver, to be borne on the shield, as described for foot troops.

Drum-slings Specification No. 85

To be made of heavy two and one-eighthh (2 1/8) inch cotton cadet web, in two pieces, thirty-eighth (38) and ten (10) inches long in the clear, held together by a leather frog, pear-shaped, three and five-eighth (3 5/8) inches long, two and five-eighth (2 5/8) inches wide at the broadest, and one and one-half (1 1/2) at the lowest part. The webbing to be let into the frog in such a way that the long part passes under the right breast of wearer, and at such angle that, when worn, it hangs perfectly smooth.
AN OBLONG TONGUELESS BUCKLE, two and five-eighth (2 5/8) inches by one and a quarter (1 1/4) inches of strong brass, five-sixteenths (5/16) of an inch wide, with catch on inner side at the end of shorter part, and a slide of the same material seven- sixteenth (7/16) of an inch wide at the end of longer part, for the purpose of lengthening or shortening the sling. Buckle and slide both to be neatly fastened by webbing three (3) rivets each.
A TRIANGLE of one-eighthh (1/8) inch brass-wire, to receive hook of drum at the lower end of frog, to which it is fastened by a leather loop let into the frog and securely stitched. Each side of triangle to be one (1) inch long.
Adopted January 15, 1883.

Cotton Stockings Specification No. 87

Colors.—To be of three (3) colors, viz, gray mixed, brown mixed, and white (unbleached), and to be put up in dozens of one color.
Material.—The brown and gray mixed to be of good long-staple American cotton, free from impurities, of a grade not lower than "New Orleans middling," double corded; and the white to be of good long-staple American cotton, free from impurities.
Workmanship.—The brown and gray mixed to be "full regular," made according to the standard sample, with fashioned heels and toes; the yarn to be spun from two (2) rovings in the regular hosiery twist for cotton. The top to be ribbed to a depth of about four and a half (4 1/2) inches, and to be joined to the leg without seam or linking, forming an integral part of the stocking; to be knitted from three (3) No. 14 yarns and have the upper edge welted. The leg and the foot to be knitted of three (3) No. 13 yarns. The substance of the heel to be increased by additional yarn of No. 25. Length of leg from lower edge of ribbed top to be not less than seven and one-half (7 1/2) inches. The white (unbleached) to be similar to the above, except that the yarn be spun from a single roving.
Sizes.—To be of five (5) sizes, viz, 9 1/2-inch, 10-inch, 10 1/2-inch, 11-inch, and 11 1/2-inch. Each size to be put up separate, in the following proportions:

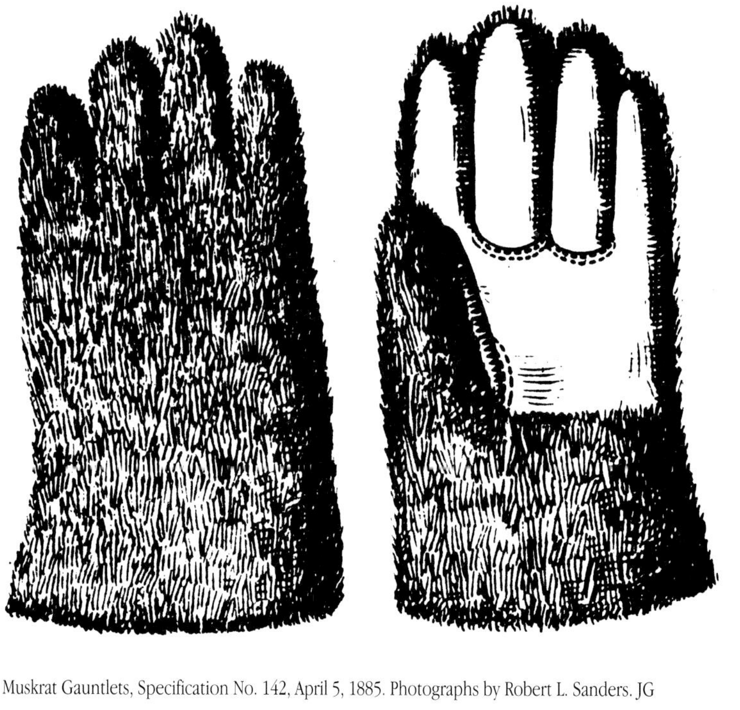

Muskrat Gauntlets, Specification No. 142, April 5, 1885. Photographs by Robert L. Sanders. JG

Sixteen 9 1/2, thirty-two 10, twenty 10 1/2, sixteen 11, and eight 11 1/2 to the one hundred pairs.
Weight.—To weigh not less that two (2) pounds to the dozen pairs.
Adopted February 23, 1883, in lieu of specifications adopted October 17, 1879 (No. 22), which are hereby canceled.

Gray Blouse Lining Flannel Specification No. 88

To be twenty-seven (27) inches wide when finished. To have fifty-six (56) threads of chain and forty-eighth (48) threads of filling in the inch (square).
The chain to be made of the best long-staple American cotton yarn, No. 40, doubled and twisted, dyed pure indigo blue, and to weigh one and three-quarter (1 3/4) ounce to the yard. The filling to be composed of good quality American fleece-wool, at least one-quarter blood, and of the best long-staple American cotton, in the proportion of seventy-five (75) parts wool to twenty-five (25) parts cotton, and to be free from shoddy, flocks, or other impurities. To be dyed with indigo and logwood to color of filling of standard sample; and to weigh four and one-quarter (4 1/4) ounces to the yard. Weight not to be less than six (6) ounces to the linear yard.
The breaking strain to be not less than forty (40) pounds to one inch width of warp, and thirty-eighth (38) pounds to one inch width of filling in the piece.
To be neither hot nor cold pressed. To be properly fulled, and of the shade of the standard sample.
Adopted March 19, 1883.

Dark-blue Wool Shirting and Cape Lining Flannel Specification No. 89

To be fifty-four (54) inches, or 6/4 wide and to be made of pure, long-staple, American fleece wool, not less than one half- blood, free from shoddy, flocks, or other impurities, and to weigh not less than ten (10) ounces to the linear yard. To be twilled and the nap very slightly raised; to contain not less than fifty-six (56) threads of warp and forty-eighth (48) threads of filling in each square inch, and to be capable of sustaining a strain of not less than twenty-six (26) pounds to the inch in width of warp and not less than twenty-two (22) pounds to the inch in width of filling, tested in the piece.
The colors to be dark-blue, green, gray, crimson, scarlet, orange, and yellow, of the standard shades, to be dyed with fast colors. The blue to be dyed in the wool with pure indigo.
Adopted March 15, 1883 in lieu of the Specifications for Dark-Blue Wool Shirting Flannel adopted February 9, 1881, and of the Specifications for Cape Lining Flannel adopted February 10, 1880, both of which are hereby canceled.

Dark-blue Indigo Coat Cloth Specification No. 90

To be fifty-four (54) inches, or 6/4 wide, and to be of pure American fleece wool, not to be less than three-quarter to full blood, free from shoddy, flocks, or other impurities. To be twilled, and to be finished to the standard sample.
To contain not less than sixty-six (66) threads of warp and sixty (60) threads of filling in each square inch. To weigh not less than twenty (20) ounces to the linear yard. To be capable of sustaining a strain fifty (50) pounds to the inch in width of warp and forty-two (42) pounds to the inch in width of filling. The color to be same shade of dark blue as the standard sample, and to be dyed in the wool with pure indigo, and to have a yellow or white woolen list.
Adopted April 4, 1883, in lieu of specifications adopted May 31, 1876, which are hereby canceled.

Fly and Suspender Buttons, Specification No. 145, April 14, 1885.

Overshirts Specification No. 91

Materials.—Dark-blue wool-flannel, Army standard; worsted cord, and hard-rubber buttons, 23 ligne.
Pattern.—To be according to sample, loose, with falling collar (without band), single plait two inches (2") wide on front, and with cuffs. Two (2) outside "patch" breast pockets, about seven inches (7") deep by six inches (6") wide, rounded at bottoms. The side seams open about nine inches (9") from bottom, and secured at top of opening with a stay of white cotton binding well stitched on the inside. Buttons and button-holes to be at each of the following places, viz: One (1) at the throat; two (2) on the front plait, equidistant between the throat and bottom of opening; one (1) at the center of the mouth of each pocket, and one (1) on each cuff, making seven in all. Corners of cuffs and bottom of shirt to be rounded off.
Dimensions.—Depth of collar for average size about three and one-half inches (3 1/2") in front and two and three-quarters inches (2 3/4") behind; of cuff about two and one-half inches (2 1/2"); of front plait about fourteen inches (14"). To be of four sizes, measuring as follows: [all dimensions in inches]

	Length of shirt.	Length of sleeve.	Collar.	Cuff.
Size 1	30	32 1/2	15	8 1/2
Size 2	31	33	15 1/2	9
Size 3	32	34	16 1/2	9 1/2
Size 4	33	35	17	10

Adopted April 12, 1882, in lieu of specification (No. 79) adopted February 24, 1882, which are hereby canceled.

Blouses Specification No. 92

Material.—Dark-blue wool flannel, Army standard. Gray twilled mixed flannel lining for body, and unbleached muslin lining for sleeves.
Pattern.—To be a singled-breasted sack coat, with falling collar, and having five (5) regulation buttons in front from neck to waist similar to standard sample. Depth of collar two and a half (2 1/2) to three (3) inches according to size. Collar to be rounded at corners. Small regulation button on outer seam of cuff, one and three-quarters (1 3/4) inch from edge. Two inside breast pockets. Canvas or vest padding in shoulders, breast, and collar.

	Breast measure. Inches.	Length. measure. Inches.	Waist measure. Inches.	Collar Inches.	Length of Sleeve Inches.
Size 1	34	29	32	15 1/2	32
Size 2	36	29 1/2	34	16	33 1/2
Size 3	38	30	36	16 1/2	33 1/2
Size 4	40	31	38	17	33 1/2
Size 5	44	32 1/2	42	18	35

Adopted May 10, 1883 in lieu of specifications (No. 13) approved March 12, 1879, which are hereby canceled.

Drawers Specification No. 93

Material.—To be unbleached Canton flannel, Army standard.
Drawers to be made to conform to standard sample. Waistband two (2) inches wide at back, increasing to five (5) inches wide in front, as in standard, buttoning with two (2) buttons about two and one-half (2 1/2) inches apart.
To have facings, or reinforcing pieces, each about two (2) inches wide, double stitched on as in standard, extending from point of waistband in front to within eight and one-half (8 1/2) inches of opening at back of waist; this opening to be four (4) inches long, with four work eyelet-holes, and lacing strings of three-quarter (3/4) inch white cotton tape.
To have opening at bottom of each leg five (5) inches long, and bottom bands one (1) inch wide, with one (1) button-hole and two (2) buttons on each leg, one (1) inch apart.

The openings in back of waist and in legs to be neatly faced with Canton flannel about one (1) inch wide; all openings to be secured by button-hole stitch.

Dimensions of each size to be as follows:

	No. 1 Inches.	No. 2 Inches.	No. 3 Inches.	No. 4 Inches.	No. 5 Inches.
Length of side seam	29	40 1/2	41 1/2	43	45
Length of leg seam	29	30	31	32	33
Waist	31	32	34	36	38

Adopted May 25, 1883, in lieu of specifications approved September 25, 1879 (No. 20) approved March 12, 1879.

Suspenders Specification No. 94

Front straps.—The front straps are to be made of non-elastic webbing 3/4 inch broad, to have thirteen cords, and to be of weight and quality of the standard sample. They are to be attached directly to the buckle in the manner known as "cantab," and before they are sewed together; to be 9 1/2 inches long, and overlap each other to an extent that they will give sufficient "play" or change of length of the two straps that are fastened together. The button-hole is to be woven into the strap and must be at least half an inch from the extremity of the strap.

Shoulder-straps.—The shoulder straps are to be made of one continuous piece of non-elastic webbing folded and bent upon itself in the middle, as per sample. They are to be 1 3/8 inches broad, of same weight, and equal in quality in every respect to the standard sample; to be regular in width and weaving, and to have a figure woven on them equal to sample. The extremities to be neatly bound.

Back straps.—The back straps are to be made of elastic rubber web, to have twenty-two cords and to be 1 1/4 inches broad. The rubber thread is to be that made by the East Hampton Rubber Co., or other equally as good, of the size known to the trade as No. 28, and to be freshly manufactured. The button-holes are to be woven into the strap and to be at least 7/8 of an inch from the extremity of the strap or end. The straps are to be neatly woven, with a smooth even face, and edges to be neatly bound at the ends, the binding to extend up one-half the length of the button-hole on each side.

Buckle.—The buckle is to be made in one piece and be stamped from sheet-brass of weight equal to that on sample, and to have three prongs. It must have an opening sufficient to accommodate the shoulder-straps, and two similar openings or slots of a size that will allow the cantab straps to freely play or move through it. Each slot must have an anti-friction roller to prevent the wear of the strap upon the buckle, as on sample. Both the friction rollers and the prongs must be made from brass, well nickel-plated.

Re-inforce straps.—The back straps to be united to the shoulder-straps by two rows of stitching, as shown on sample. The shoulder-straps are also to be fastened together in back by a re-enforce or strengthening piece made from web similar to the shoulder-straps, of the size and shape of sample, with its cut-edges bound, the strengthening-piece securely sewed to the shoulder-straps, as in sample. The front strap will be sewed by four lines of stitching nearly forming a square, as per sample. *Button-hole strengthening*.—All the button-holes are to be strengthened by being whipped or oversewed at their wearing extremities, to the extent of the sample.

Lengths.—The suspenders are to be of three lengths, and to measure from button-hole to button-hole 36 inches, 38 inches, and 40 inches, respectively, in the following proportions per 100 pairs; 60 pairs 36-inch, 20 pairs 38-inch, and 20 pairs 40-inch, measuring from the extremes of the front and back button-holes.

Thread.—All the thread used in sewing the suspenders must be from the sea-island cotton and be of the best quality.

Color.—All the parts of the suspender must be of the same color and must be "fast" color, and as per samples.

Packing.—The suspenders must be neatly packed in paper boxes, one dozen of same size in a box.

Each pair of suspenders is to have the length of same stamped or stenciled in black or blue color on the reverse side of the strengthening-strap (without, however, defacing the outer side) in letters and figures 3/8 of inch long, as follows: 40-in., 38-in., 36-in.

Adopted September 4, 1883.

Canvas Overcoats, blanket-lined Specification No. 95

Materials.—The Overcoats to be made of ten (10) ounce brown cotton duck, lined throughout (body, sleeves, and collar) with heavy blanket cloth.

Shape.—To be double-breasted, frock skirt; slashed at back to within about eight (8) inches of the waist-belt; pockets on both side covered with flaps four (4) inches by eight (8) inches; lined with blanket cloth, to be worn either inside or out. Large collar, fastened by a strap (of brown duck) about 5 1/2 inches by 1 3/4 inches, with button-hole at each end.

Buttons.—The coats to have ten (10) rubber buttons 1 1/8 inches in diameter, five on each breast, placed equidistant. starting one inch below the collar seam. The collar to have three (3) rubber buttons 3/4-inch in diameter, one on each side, to fasten the collar when turned up, and one to take up the strap of collar when turned down,

Loops.—The loops by which the coat is buttons across the breast to be about six (6) inches long made of 1/4-inch black mohair cord, and secured to the coat under buttons.

Waist-belt

Waist-belt.—To be made of the same material as the body of the coat, three (3) inches wide, to fasten with a japanned-iron buckle or slide, and to be supported on each sid of the coat by supporters, made of the same material, placed at the side seams.

SIZES.

	No. 1 Inches.	No. 2 Inches.	No. 3. Inches.	No. 4. Inches.
Length of coat	50	52	54	56
Breadth of back	9 1/4	9 1/2	10	10 1/2
Length of sleeve	33	34	35	36
Width of collar	5 1/2	5 3/4	6	6 1/2
Width of breast	40	42	44	46
Width of waist	36	38	40	42

Adopted October 24, 1883, and conforming to the standard sample approved October 13, 1883.

Overshirts Specification No. 97

Materials.—Dark-blue wool-flannel, Army standard; worsted cord, and hard-rubber buttons, 23 ligne.

Pattern.—To be according to sample, loose, with falling collar (without band), single plait two inches (2") wide on front, and with cuffs. Two (2) outside "patch" breast pockets, about seven inches (7") deep by six inches (6") wide, rounded at bottoms. The side seams open about nine inches (9") from bottom, and secured at top of opening with a stay of white cotton binding well stitched on the inside. Buttons and button-holes to be at each of the following places, viz: One (1) at the throat; two (2) on the front plait, equidistant between the throat and bottom of opening; one (1) at the center of the mouth of each pocket, and one (1) on each cuff, making seven in all. Corners of cuffs and bottom of shirt to be rounded off.

Dimensions.—Depth of collar for average size about three (3") inches in front and two and one-quarter inches (2 1/4") behind; of cuff about two and one-half inches (2 1/2"); of front plait about fourteen inches (14"). To be of five (5) sizes, measuring as follows:

Length of	No. 1	No. 2	No. 3	No. 4	No. 5
shirt	33 inches	33 inches	34 Inches	35 inches	36 inches
Length of					
Sleeve	32 1/2"	33"	34"	35"	36"
Collar	15"	15 1/2"	16 1/2"	17"	17 1/2"
Cuff	7 1/2"	8"	8 1/2"	9"	9 1/2"

Adopted November 26, 1883, in lieu of specifications adopted February 12, 1883, which are hereby canceled.

Fur Campaign Hats Specification No. 98

Mixture.—To be composed of two-thirds best coney and one-third fine blown nutria.

Weight.—Hat bodies to be weighed 4 3/4 ounces heavy.

Shape.—Block to be 5 3/4 inches deep to cent of tip.

Brim.—To be 2 3/4 inches wide in front and rear, and 3 inches wide at sides; to be of double thickness, and to have two rows of stitching, as shown on sample.
Color.—To be drab or other suitable color, as per sample.
Trimmings.—To be trimmed with 8-ligne union band—same quality as on sample hat—to be sewed on by hand. Sweat to be of imported lined leather, 2 1/4 inches wide, sewed to the reed by zigzag stitch. A wire-gauze ventilator to be on each side of the hat, 3 1/2 inches from brim—to be the size as on sample hat.
The hats to be doe finished, as per sample.
To be packed thee hats in each box.
Adopted December 14, 1883.

Trousers Specification No. 99

Material.—Sky-blue kersey, Army standard.
For foot troops.—To be cut and made in accordance with the standard patters and samples approved January 16, 1884. To have side pockets, and a hip pocket on the rights side. He bottoms to be lined with canvas.
For mounted troops.—To be similar to those for foot-men, with the addition of a reinforce or saddle-piece of the same material on seat and legs. Four buttons at bottom of each leg, two on each aide, for straps.

Size.	Waist.	Seat.	Crotch.	Outside Seam.	Inside Seam.	Knee.	Bottom.
	Inches.	Inches.	Inches.	Inches.	Inches.	Inches.	Inches.
1	31	35	23	41	31	17 1/2	19
2	32	36	23	40	30	17 1/2	19
3	32	37	23	43	33	17 3/4	19 1/4
4	32	38	24	42	32	18	19 3/4
5	33	38	24	41 1/4	31	18 1/4	19 3/4
6	33	39	24	44 1/2	34	18 1/4	19 3/4
7	34	39	25	42 1/2	32	18 1/2	20 1/4
8	34	40	25 1/2	45 1/2	35	18 1/2	20 1/4
9	36	41	26	42 3/4	32	19	20 1/2
10	36	41	26	44	33	19	20 1/2
11	38	43	26	45	34	19 1/2	21
12	40	44	26 1/2	44 1/4	33	19 1/2	21

Adopted January 16, 1884, in lieu of specifications of October 8, 1882, which are hereby canceled.

Blouses Specification No. 100

Material.—Dark-blue flannel, Army standard; gray twilled mixed flannel lining for body, and unbleached muslin lining for sleeves.
Pattern.—To be a singled-breasted sack coat, with falling collar, and having five (5) regulation buttons, large, in front from neck to waist. To have two (2) inside breast pockets.
To be cut and made in accordance with the standard patterns and samples approved January 16, 1884.

Size	Breast.	Length.	Waist.	Collar.	Length of Sleeve
	Inches.	Inches.	Inches.	Inches.	Inches.
1	34	29	32	16	31
2	35	29 1/2	33	16 1/2	31 1/2
3	36	29	34	17	32
4	38	30	36	18	33
5	40	31 1/2	38	19	34
6	42	32 1/2	40	19 1/2	34 1/2

Adopted January 16, 1884 in lieu of specifications of May 19, 1883, which are hereby canceled.

Woolen Blankets Specification No. 101

Each blanket to be 7 feet long and 5 feet 6 inches wide, and to weigh not less than 5 pounds. To be gray in color, and made of pure long-staple wool, free from shoddy, reworked wool or cotton, or any other impure materials. The warp to be of not lower grade than three-eighths blood-bred wool; the filling or woof to be of not lower grade than one-half blood-bred wool; to have the letters "U.S." in dark blue, 4 inches long, in the center; to bear a strain of not less than 25 pounds per inch for the warp, and 30 pounds per inch for the woof, without tearing, and to have not less than 22 threads of warp and 25 threads of filling or woof to the inch. The threads to be well driven up. The stripes at ends of blanket to be dark blue, of pure indigo dye.

Overcoats, Specification No. 148, May 28, 1885.

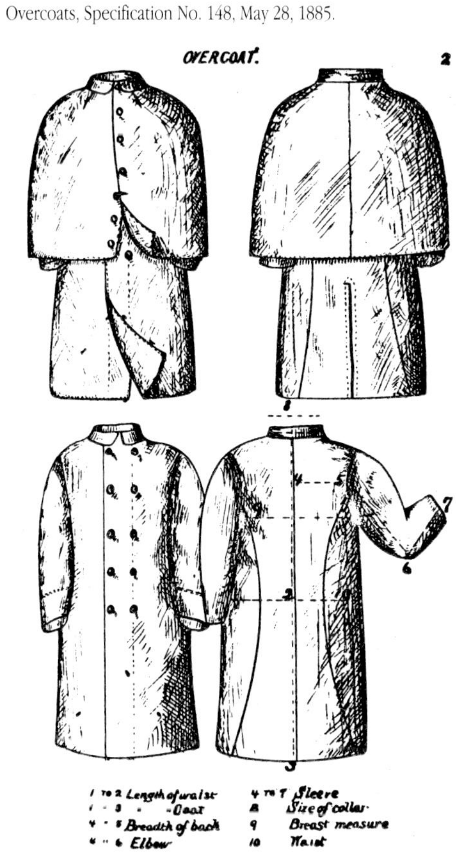

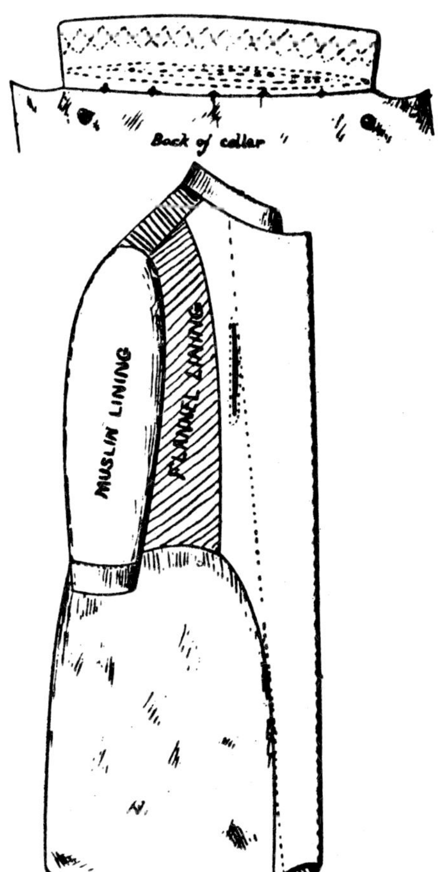

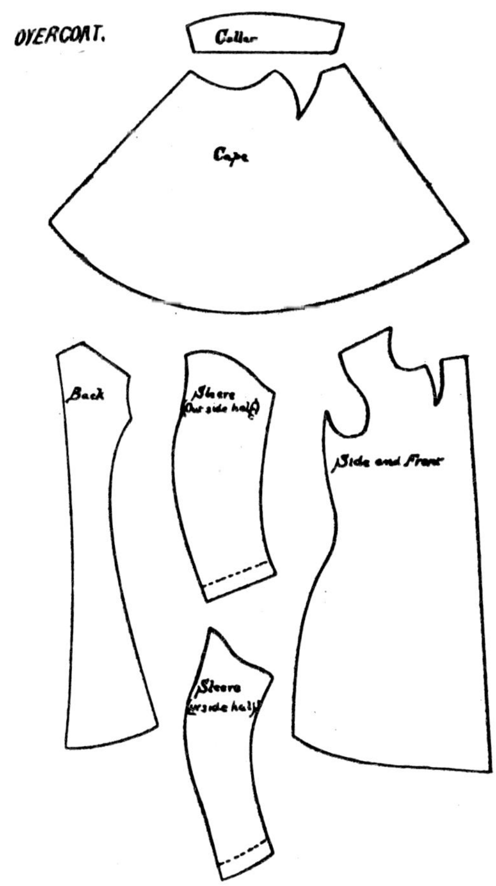

Note.—It is immaterial whether the letters "U.S." be stamped on the blanket or woven into the fabric; their color must be pure indigo dye.

Adopted February 5, 1884, in lieu of specifications adopted August 23, 1876, which are hereby canceled.

Cavalry Standards Specification No. 102

Material.—To be of a single thickness of seamless blue banner silk.

Dimensions.—To be 2 feet 5 inches long (exclusive of casing for the lance of the same material) by 2 feet 3 inches long on the lance.

Design.—To bear the coat of arms of the United States as on the design sketch for cavalry standard approved by the Quartermaster-General, and which may be described as follows:

An eagle with outstretched wings, on its breast a U.S. shield; in the right talon an olive branch with red berries, and in his left ten arrows bunched. A red scroll held in eagle's beak, with the letters "E Pluribus Unum" in yellow; over the scroll a group of thirteen stars surmounted by an arc of diverging sun-ray. Below the eagle a red scroll with the figures and letters "U.S. Cavalry" in yellow.

Embroidery.—The design, letters, and figures to be embroidered in silk, the same on both sides of the standard.

The standard to be trimmed on three sides with United States silk knitted fringe 2 1/2 inches deep.

The lance to be 9 feet long, including metal spear and ferrule.

Adopted February 4, 1884.

Barrack Bags Specification No. ?

Material.—To be made of eight (8) ounce cotton duck, thirty-three and one-half (33 1/2) inches wide, dyed brown; to have drawing strings sixty-six (66) inches long, made of No. 3 Gilling line passing through two (2) sheet brass grommets, one (1) on each side. To be sewed with No. 24 and No. 30 black cotton.

Size.—Thirty-nine (39) inches deep and seventeen and one-half (17 1/2) inches in diameter.

Workmanship.—To be made flat stitched in the bottom and side seams; to have a tab ring at the top, one and one-half (1 1/2) inches wide for draw strings, and conform to the sealed standard sample, adopted this date.

Adopted March 13, 1884.

Overcoats Specification No. 108

Material.—Sky-blue kersey, 22 ounce, Army standard. Lining for body, dark-blue flannel, to weigh 11 1/2 ounces to the 6/4 linear yard. Flannel for cape lining, Army standard, to weigh 10 ounces to the linear yard and to be of the following colors, viz: For hospital stewards, emerald green; for commissary sergeants, gray; for ordnance, crimson; for engineers and artillery, scarlet; for signal service, orange; for infantry, dark-blue; for cavalry, yellow. Sleeve lining colored jean.

Pattern.—To be double-breasted, with cape and having two rows of five regulation brass buttons, large, on each breast. The cape to be adjustable by means of seven hooks beneath the collar of the coat, and seven eyes upon the cape; to have seven regulation brass buttons, small.

Workmanship.—To be cut and made in conformity with the standard patterns and samples.

Sizes.	Length of Coat	Length of Cape	Breast Measure	Waist Measure	Length of Sleeve	Length of Collar
1	44 1/2	24 1/2	36	34	32 1/2	17
2	45	25 1/2	38	36	33	17 1/2
3	46	26 1/2	41	39	33 1/2	18 1/2
4	47	27 1/2	44	42	34	19 1/2
5	48	28 1/2	45	44	34 1/2	20
6	49	29	46	46	35	20 1/2

Adopted March 8, 1884, in lieu of specifications of February 6, 1880, which are hereby canceled.

Canvas Cap Specification No. 109

Material.—To be made of 6-ounce cotton duck, dyed brown, lined with light blanket cloth next the duck, and with light- colored cotton jean in the inside; to have two buttons on the cape to button at the throat; and one vest size brown "lasting" button on the top for finish. The visor and edges bound with 3/4 brown cotton tape.

Style.—Scull cap with extension, forming a cape reaching to the shoulders and meeting in front, covering the throat and buttoning together with two buttons. A visor of the same material bound with 3/4 brown cotton tape sewed in the forehead (to be worn up or down as desired), and having hook and eye to fasten it when turned up.

Workmanship.—To be cut and made in conformity with the sealed standard sampled adopted this date.

Adopted April 17, 1884.

Boots Specification No. 110

To be worked square with the last on which they are made; the edges to be finished with pressers, without heel-ball, and must measure at least half a size (outside) more than they are marked.

The upper leather to be made of best oak-tanned from slaughter-hides. The leg to be finished on the grain, and the foot to be wax upper. The soles to be best oak-tanned from "straight" Texas hides, or from South American (commonly called "Spanish") dry hides. No split leather to be used.

The width of the soles across the ball of the foot to be graduated as follows, and to be in proportion throughout: No. 5, 3 4/8 inches; No. 6, 3 5/8 inches; No. 7, 3 6/8 inches; No. 8, 3 7/8 inches; No. 9, 4 inches; No. 10, 4 1/8 inches; No. 11, 4 2/8 inches; No. 12, 4 3/8 inches.

The insteps and toes to measure as follows: No. 5, 9 1/8, 8 7/8 inches; No. 6, 9 5/8, 9 inches; No. 7, 9 5/8, 9 3/8 inches; No. 8, 9 7/8, 9 6/8 inches; No. 9, 10, 9 7/8 inches; No. 10, 10 4/8, 10 inches; No. 11, 10 6/8, 10 3/8 inches; No. 12, 10 7/8, 10 5/8 inches.

The measurement for a No. 8 boot, standard, letter "A," is as follows, viz: Heel, 13 1/8 inches; instep 9 6/8 inches; ball or toe, 9 5/8 inches; length of legs, 20 inches in front, 14 1/2 inches in back; width at leg top, 16 inches; width of strap, 1 1/4 inches; length of strap, 7 inches; height of counter, 3 inches at back; length of heel, 3 inches; width of heel, 2 7/8 inches; width of sole or ball, 3 7/8 inches.

Straps to be made of calfskin leather and sewed on to the inside of the leg. They are to have not less than six stitches to the inch in the back seam, and to be stitched with three rows of silk on the front and counter.

To have the sole sewed with seven stitches to the inch on the welt, and four stitches to the inch on the inner sole; with not less than 12-cord flax thread on the inner sole, nor less than 10-cord flax thread on the welt.

Measurement for a No. 8 boot, standard made on "B" last, is, with the following exceptions, the same as that made on the "A" last; Heel, 13 1/4 inches; instep, 9 7/8 inches; ball or toe, 9 6/8 inches.

Adopted April 24, 1884, in lieu of those of February 25, 1878, which are hereby canceled.

"Post" Shoes Specification No. 111

To be worked square with the last on which they are made; the edges to be finished with pressers, without heel-ball, and to measure at least half a size (outside) more than they are marked.

The upper leather to be of the best oak-tanned American calfskin, and to weigh 4 pounds to the skin. Soles of best quality oak-tanned, from straight Texas hides, or from South America (commonly called "Spanish") dry hides. No split leather to be used.

The width of the soles across the ball of the foot to be graduated as follows, and to be in proportion throughout: No. 5, 3 3/8 inches; No. 6, 3 4/8 inches; No. 7, 3 5/8 inches; No. 8, 3 6/8 inches; No. 9, 3 7/8 inches; No. 10, 4 inches; No. 11, 4 1/8 inches; No. 12, 4 3/8 inches.

The instep and toe to measure as follows: For letter "A," No. 5, 8 5/8, 8 1/8 inches; No. 6, 8 7/8, 8 1/8 inches; No. 7, 9 1/8, 8 5/8 inches; No. 8, 9 3/8, 8 7/8 inches; No. 9, 9 5/8, 9 1/8 inches; No. 10, 9 7/8, 9 3/8 inches; No. 11, 10 1/8, 9 5/8 inches; No. 12, 10 3/8, 9 7/8 inches. For letter "B" 1/8 inch more.

The height of the leg for a No. 8 shoe to be 6 1/4 inches. The upper to be cut without side seam; to have counter, side piece, strap, and crimped tongue stitched on with silk. To be laced in front, and to have metallic eyelets and hooks; to have soles sewed with seven stitches to the inch welt, and four stitches to the inch on the inner sole, with not less than 12-cord flax thread on the inner sole nor less than 10-cord flax thread on the welt.

Adopted April 24, 1884, in lieu of those of March 8, 1876, which are hereby canceled.

"Field" Shoes Specification No. 112

To be worked square with the last on which they are made; the edges to be finished with pressers, without heel-ball, and to measure at least half a size (outside) more than they are marked.

The upper leather to be of the best oak-tanned American calfskin, and to weigh 4 pounds to the skin. Soles of best quality oak-tanned, from straight Texas hides, or from South America (commonly called "Spanish) dry hides. No split leather to be used.

The width of the soles across the ball of the foot to be graduated as follows, and to be in proportion throughout: No. 5, 3 4/8 inches; No. 6, 3 5/8 inches; No. 7, 3 6/8 inches; No. 8, 3 7/8 inches; No. 9, 4 inches; No. 10, 4 1/8 inches; No. 11, 4 2/8 inches; No. 12, 4 3/8 inches.

The instep and toe to measure as follows: For letter "A," No. 5, 9, 8 6/8 inches; No. 6, 9 4/8, 8 7/8 inches; No. 7, 9 4/8, 9 2/8 inches; No. 8, 9 6/8, 9 5/8 inches; No. 9, 9 7/8, 9 6/8 inches; No. 10, 10 3/8, 9 7/8 inches; No. 11, 10 5/8, 10 2/8 inches; No. 12, 10 6/8, 10 4/8 inches. For letter "B" 1/8 inch more.

The height of the leg for a No. 8 shoe to be 8 inches, width of leg at top 6 1/2 inches, to have crimped front, with calfskin straps 2 1/2 inches long and 1/2 inch wide at back and front; to have close seam on the inside, and light calfskin gusset 5 inches long; to be closed with automatic buckle on the outside; the counter to be 2 1/2 inches high and to extend across side seams; to have counter, side piece, strap, and crimped tongue stitched on with silk. To have not less than nine stitches to the inch on the counter and straps. To have soles sewed with seven stitches to the inch on the welt and four stitches to the inch on the inner sole, with not less than 12-cord flax thread on the inner sole nor less than 10-cord flax thread on the welt.

Adopted April 24, 1884, in lieu of those of March 8, 1876, which are hereby canceled.

Leather Gauntlets Specification No. 113

To be made of Angora goat-skin.

The gauntlet or cuff to be at least 4 1/2 inches deep, and of sufficient fullness to admit the cuff of coat.

The cuff to be lined in russet leather.

The gloves to be "table cut," and well stitched throughout with silk, and in quality of material and workmanship they must conform to the standard sample.

To be os five sizes, and put up in the following proportion to 100 pairs: 10, 8; 30, 8 1/2; 30, 9; 20, 9 1/2; 10, 10.

Adopted May 21, 1884.

Canvas Sack Coats Specification No. 115

Material.—Six ounce cotton duck dyed brown.

Pattern.—To be a singled-breasted sack coat, with falling collar, and having six india-rubber buttons in front from waist to neck; to have an outside pocket sewed on each breast. *Workmanship.*—To be cut and made in accordance with the standard patterns and samples.

SIZES	Breast Measure. Inches.	Waist Measure Inches.	Length of Coat. Inches.	Length of of Sleeve. Inches.	Length of Collar. Inches.
1	36	34	28	31 1/2	17
2	37	35	28 1/2	32 1/2	17 1/2
3	39	37	29	33	18
4	41	39	29 1/2	34	19
5	42	40	30 1/2	34 3/4	20
6	44	43	31 1/2	35	20 1/4

Adopted May 31, 1884.

Canvas Trousers Specification No. 116

Material.—Six ounce cotton duck dyed brown.

Pattern.—To have slating top pockets, a watch pocket, and a hip pocket on the right side, straps and buckle; waist-band and flies faced with the same material the trousers are made of.

Workmanship.—To be cut and made in accordance with the standard patterns and samples.

SIZES	Waist. Inches.	Seat. Inches.	Inside seam. Inches.	Outside seam. Inches.	Bottom. Inches.
1	31	36	30 1/2	40 1/2	19 1/2
2	32	38	31	41 1/2	20
3	33	40	32	43 1/2	20 1/2
4	34	42	33	44 1/2	20 1/2
5	36	44	34	45 1/2	21
6	40	45	35	46 1/2	21

Adopted May 31, 1884.

Overcoats Specification No. 118

Material.—Sky-blue kersey, 22 ounce, Army standard. Lining for body, dark-blue flannel, to weigh 11 1/2 ounces to the 6/4 linear yard. Flannel for cape lining, Army standard, to weigh 10 ounces to the linear yard and to be of the following colors, viz: For hospital stewards, emerald green; for post quartermaster sergeants, buff; for commissary sergeants, gray; for ordnance, crimson; for engineers and artillery, scarlet; for signal service, orange; for infantry, dark-blue; for cavalry, yellow. Sleeve lining corset jeans. Eight (8) white metal hooks and eyes, large viz: seven (7) for adjusting cape to the coat and one (1) on the collar; one (1) black japanned hook and eye at the bottom front skirt to hook it back.

Pattern.—To be double-breasted, with cape, and having five (5) regulation brass buttons, large, on each breast. The cape to be adjustable by means of seven (7) hooks beneath the collar of the coat and seven (7) eyes upon the cape. To have seven regulation brass buttons, small, on (1) inside pocket on the left breast, opening perpendicularly.

Workmanship.—To be cut and made in conformity with the standard patterns and samples.

Sizes.	Length of Coat	Length of Cape	Breast Measure	Waist Measure	Length of Sleeve	Length of Collar
1	44 1/2	24 1/2	36	34	32 1/2	17
2	45	25 1/2	38	36	33	17 1/2
3	46	26 1/2	41	39	33 1/2	18 1/2
4	47	27 1/2	44	42	34	19 1/2
5	48	28 1/2	45	44	34 1/2	20
6	49	29	46	46	35	20 1/2

Adopted September 12, 1884, in lieu of specifications of March 8, 1884, which are hereby canceled.

Color Belt and Sling Specification No. 120

Belt.—To be of the best quality of black bridle leather, one and three-fourths (1 3/4) inches, full, in width, with a girth of forty (40) inches exclusive of clasp fastenings, and to be finished with a cast-brass plate having the letters "U.S." raised in center an a brass outlet buckle.

Sling.—The cylindrical cup to receive the end of the pike to be of cast-brass, one and one-eighthh (1 1/8) inches inside diameter, with rim around top edge, and to be firmly attached by a movable ball-socket to a heart-shaped plate of

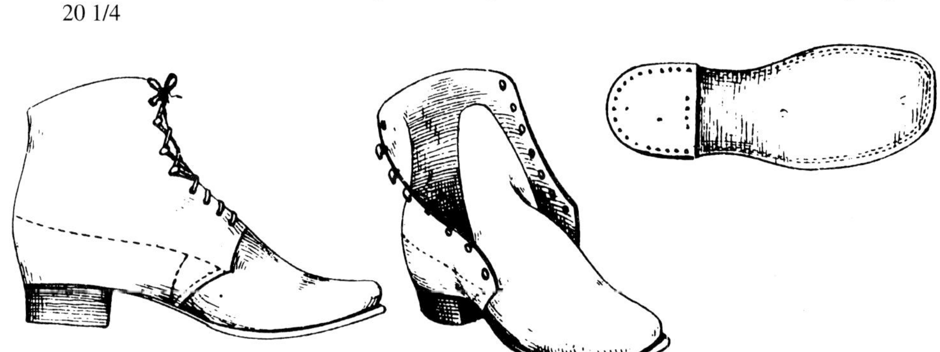

Crimped Campaign Shoes, Specification No. 150, April 15, 1885.

brass of No. 19 Government standard, in the manner shown by sample in the office of the Quartermaster General, U.S.A.
The brass plate to be securely fastened by six (6) rivets to a leather base of the same shape and double thickness, and having on its under side a tufted [[ad covered with pebble leather and stuffed with curled hair of best quality. All of the leathers to be well sewed together around the edge.
Two (2) leather straps one and seven-eighth (1 7/8) inches wide and twelve (12) inches long, and two (2) leather straps one and seven-eighth (1 7/8) and fifty-two (52) inches long, to be securely sewed to the upper sides and top of the leather heart-shaped base in the manner shown by sample in the office of the Quartermaster General, U.S.A.
The shorter straps to be finished with a cast-brass buckle having an opening of one and seven-eighth (1 7/8) inches wide, and the long to have hole punched in the ends to receive the tongue of buckle.
When in use the long strap on the right to be buckled to the short one on the left, and the short strap on the left to the long one on the right.
All leather, except covering of pad, to be of best quality bridle leather.
Adopted October 9, 1884.

Canvas Mittens Specification No. 121

Material.—The mitten to be made of six (6) oz. cotton duck, dyed brown.
Style.—Plain mitten with thumb only, and having gauntlet cuff neatly stitched on at the wrist.
Sizes and Workmanship.—Length of mittens from tip of the hand to the wrist at the point where the cuff is joined: for No. 1., (9) nine inches; for No. 3, (9 1/2) nine and one-half inches; for No. 3, (10) ten inches. Width across the palm of the hand: No. 1, (4 1/4) four and one-quarter inches; No. 2, (4 1/2) four and one-half inches; No. 3, (5) five inches.
Depth of cuff when finished (4 3/4) four and three-quarters inches. Length of thumbs from tip to wrist: for No., 1, 4 3/4) four and three-quarters inches; No. 2, (5) five inches; No. 3, (5 1/2) five and one-half inches; to be neatly and securely stitched to mitten.
The cuff to be formed and neatly stitched to mitten, and finished with one-half inch turned in at the edge, and securely and neatly stitched.
The entire mitten to be made in a neat and workmanlike manner, and to conform to the sealed standard samples.
Adopted October 14, 1884.

Blouses Specification No. 122

Material.—Dark-blue wool flannel, Army standard; gray twilled mixed flannel lining for body, and unbleached muslin lining for sleeves.
Pattern.—To be a singled-breasted sack coat, with falling collar, and having five (5) regulation buttons in front from neck to waist. To have three (3) outside pockets, one on each side of skirt and one on the left breast, and one inside pocket on the right breast.
To be cut and made in accordance with the standard patterns and samples adopted January 16, 1884, and to be made and finished in accordance with the standard samples adopted this date.

Size	Breast. Inches.	Length. Inches.	Waist. Inches.	Collar. Inches.	Length of Sleeve Inches.
1	34	27	32	16	31
2	35	27 1/2	33	16 1/2	31 1/2
3	36	28	34	17	32
4	38	29	36	18	33
5	40	30 1/4	38	19	34
6	42	32 1/2	40	19 1/2	34 1/2

Adopted October 21, 1884, in lieu of specifications of January 16, 1884, which are hereby canceled.

Woolen Mittens Specification No. 124

To be of color of standard sample. To be made of gray woolen yarn, spun from long-staple wool of not less than one-half blood bred, free from shoddy, re-worked wool, and other impurities, spun to weigh about seventy-three (73) grains for each twenty-five (25) yards of single thread; the yarn to be doubled and twisted.
The mittens to be woven from sixteen (16) to eighteen (18) inches in length according to size, and fulled to the representative size, viz: 10, 11, and 12 inches in length, and from 5 1/4 to 6 inches in width before being fulled.
To be manufactured in the following proportion of sizes to the one hundred—

40	36	21 = 100.
10	11	12

The mittens when finished to weigh an average of three (3) pounds and six (6) ounces per dozen pairs.
Adopted November 6, 1884, in lieu of specifications of May 31, 1876, which are hereby canceled.

Company Marking Stamps Specification No. 125

The stamp to be of brass, 1/2 inch high. 11/16 of an inch wide, and of sufficient length for the inscription.
The face of stamps to bear the necessary inscription in letters and figures cut 3/32 of an inch deep; the prominent letters and figures to be 1/2 inch long, and other letters 1/4 inch long.
The stamp to be firmly connected by a rod to a walnut handle 4 1/4 inches long, mounted with a brass cap and ferrule.
The stamp to have a mortised end of sufficient size to contain two numeral types, with a screw fitted in it to hold the types in place.
Two sets of brass numerals, from 0 to 9, inclusive, of such dimensions and finish as to properly fit to the mortise of the stamps and give an even impression with the stamp inscription, and to be furnished with each stamp, as also one marking pad, 2 1/2 inches wide and 4 1/4 inches long, and 1 2-ounce bottle of warranted indelible ink.
The stamp, ad, bottle of ink, and sets of numerals to be put up in a substantial hinged-lid, japanned tin box 4 1/4 inches wide, 8 inches long, and 1 1/4 inches deep, arranged and finished according to sample in office of the Quartermaster-General, U.S.A.
Adopted November 29, 1884.

Gold Lace Chevrons Specification No. 126

Lace.—To be of best quality gold on silver, to contain not less than 89 to 90 per cent. Silver and one and eight-tenths (1 8/10) to two (2) per cent. Gold: to be full one-half (1/2) inch wide, and in weight, weave, and finish to conform to standard sample.
Cloths.—The cloth forming the groundwork for arms, arcs, and ties of chevrons to be of facing cloth (conforming to published specifications) of the same color as the facings of the uniform coat.
The cloth forming the groundwork for chevron devices (except that for Hospital Stewards) to be the same as that for the uniform coat. To be cut in shape of a quadrant of a circle having a radius of from five (5) to six (6) inches (as size of device may require), the straight sides of pieces to be neatly stitched to the

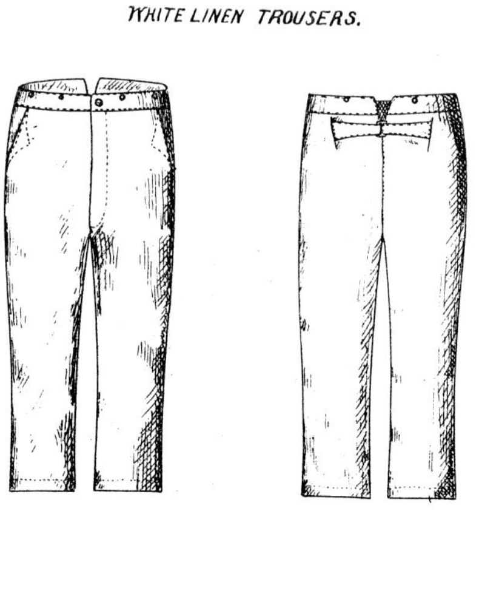

White Linen Trousers, Specification No. 153, May 5, 1885.

under side of the upper edge of cloth of arms; the nap of the cloth to run downward when the chevron is on the sleeve.

Bars and Arms.—The bars of the chevron to be a single width of lace, to be neatly joined at the angles and stitched with gold-colored silk upon the facing cloth on each border of the lace, and also at the outer ends, which are to be turned under. The bars are to be placed about one-eighthh (1/8) of an inch apart, and a border of facing cloth of about one-eighthh (1/8) of an inch to show on all sides.

The chevrons for Engineers to have a stitching of white silk upon each side of the lace bars.

The arms of the chevron bars to be six (6) to seven (7) inches long, to be the arcs of a circle of about twenty-five (25) inches radius, and to meet at an angle of about ninety-six (96) degrees; distance between extreme outer ends about nine (9) inches.

Design for Chevrons.—Sergeant Major: Three bars and an arc of three bars. The upper edge of outer bar of arc to be the arc of a circle of about seven and one-fourth (7 1/4) inches radius.

Quartermaster Sergeant: Three bars and a tie of three bars. The upper tie to extend horizontally from the extreme outer end of one arm of the chevron to that of the other.

Saddler Sergeant: Three bars and a saddler's round knife, handle upward. Knife of the following dimensions: handle one and three-fourths (1 3/4) inches long, three-fourths (3/4) inch wide near top; five-eighth (5/8) inch near blade; blade one and one-eighthh (1 1/8) inches deep in center; from point to point of blade, three and one-fourth (3 1/4) inches; center of edge, one and one-fourth (1 1/4) inches above inner angle of chevron. Lace of handle to run vertically, or ferrule about horizontally, and of blade to be crimped to shape of same.

Chief Trumpeter: Three bars and an arc of one bar, with bugle of pattern worn on cap about one and one-half (1 1/2) inches above inner angle of chevron. The upper edge of bar of arc to be the arc of a circle of about seven and one-fourth (7 1/4) inches radius. Bugle to be of form, dimensions, and finish of standard sample chevron.

Principal Musician: Three bars and a bugle. The bugle to be the same as for Chief Trumpeter chevrons.

Ordnance Sergeant: Three bars and an outlined star of lace. Lower point of star to be about one (1) inch above inner angle of chevron. Star to be of dimensions and finish as standard sample chevron.

Post Quartermaster Sergeant: Three bars, and a crossed key and pen. The latter device to be embroidered on gold bullion. The key and pen to cross about two and one-half (2 1/2) inches above the inner angle of the chevron, and to be of form, dimensions, and finish of standard sample chevron.

Commissary Sergeant: Three bars and a crescent (points front). Distance from point to point of crescent, two(2) inches; width in center, three-fourths (3/4) of an inch; center of lower edge to be about one and three-fourths (1 3/4) inches above inner angle of chevron

Hospital Steward: A half chevron of emerald-green cloth, one and three-fourths (1 3/4) inches wide and about nine and one-half (9 1/2) inches long, bound with gold tracing braid one-eighthh (1/8) of an inch wide. In the center a caduceus, embroidered in gold thread, to form dimensions, and finish of standard sample chevrons.

1st Sergeants: Three bars and an outlined lozenge, having side about one-fourth (1/4) of an inch wide. Lozenge about two and one-half (2 1/2) inches long and two (2) inches wide, placed lengthwise about one and one-fourth (1 1/4) inches above inner angle of chevron.

Sergeants: Three bars.

Regimental and Battalion Color Sergeant: Three bars and a ring one-fourth (1/4) of an inch wide, one and one-fourth (1 1/4) inches in inside diameter, and placed one and three-fourths (1 3/4) inches above inner angle of chevron.

Corporal: Two bars.

To indicate service: A single width of lace stitched upon a piece of cloth of the color of uniform coat, the ends of lace to be turned under; a bordering of the cloth one-eighthh (1/8) of an inch wide to appear on all sides. Length of chevron, about nine and one-fourth (9 1/4) inches.

To indicate service in war: The same as above, except that facing cloth of the color of the facings of the particular arm of services will be substituted for the outer cloth.

Workmanship.—To be in accordance with the standard samples adopted this day.

Adopted January 28, 1885.

Cloth Chevrons Specification No. 127

Cloth.—The cloth forming the groundwork for arms, arcs, and ties of chevrons to be of facing cloth (conforming to published specifications) of the same color as the facings of the uniform coat, except in the case of the Infantry overcoat chevron, when it will be of dark-blue cloth.

The cloth forming the groundwork for chevron devices (except that for Hospital Stewards) to be the same as that for the uniform coat. For Pioneers and Farriers device to be cut about nine (9) by five and one-half (5 1/2) inches; Signal Corps device three (3) inches square with corners rounded off, and for all other devices to be cut in shape of a quadrant of a circle having a radius of from four (4) to six (6) inches (as size of device may require), the straight sides of pieces to be neatly stitched to the under side of the upper edge of cloth of arms; the nap of the cloth to run downward when the chevron is on the sleeve.

The cloth forming the background of devices to be of facing cloth of same color of facings as the uniform coat.

Bars and Arms.—The bars of the chevron to be outlined on the groundwork of facing cloth in rows of heavy stitching of No. 8 silk, the upper and lower edged to be finished with similar stitching.

White stitching for Engineers and for overcoats for Infantry, and black for all others.

The arms of the chevron bars to be six (6) to seven (7) inches long, to be the arcs of a circle of about twenty-five (25) inches radius, and to meet at an angle of about ninety-six (96) degrees; distance between extreme outer ends about nine (9) inches.

Design for Chevrons.—Sergeant Major: Three bars and an arc of three bars. The upper edge of outer bar of arc to be the arc of a circle of about seven and one-fourth (7 1/4) inches radius.

Quartermaster Sergeant: Three bars and a tie of three bars. The upper tie to extend horizontally from the extreme outer end of one arm of the chevron to that of the other.

Saddler Sergeant: Three bars and a saddler's round knife, handle upward. Knife of the following dimensions: handle one and three-fourths (1 3/4) inches long, three-fourth (3/4) inch wide near top; five-eighthh (5/8) inch near blade; blade one and one-eighthh (1 1/8) inches deep in center; from point to point of blade, three and one-fourth (3 1/4) inches; center of edge, one and one-fourth (1 1/4) inches above inner angle of chevron.

Chief Trumpeter: Three bars and an arc of one bar, with bugle of pattern worn on cap about one and one-half (1 1/2) inches above inner angle of chevron. The upper edge of bar of arc to be the arc of a circle of about seven and one-fourth (7 1/4) inches radius. Bugle to be of form, dimensions, and finish of standard sample chevron.

Principal Musician: Three bars and a bugle. The bugle to be the same as for Chief Trumpeter chevrons.

Ordnance Sergeant: Three bars and an outlined star. Lower point of star to be about one (1) inch above inner angle of chevron. Star to be of dimensions and finish as standard sample chevron.

Post Quartermaster Sergeant: Three bars, and a crossed pen and key, embroidered in gold-colored silk. The key and pen to cross about two and one-half (2 1/2) inches above the inner angle of the chevron, and to be of form, dimensions, and finish of standard sample chevron.

Commissary Sergeant: Three bars and a crescent (points front). Distance from point to point of crescent, two (2) inches; width in center, three-fourths (3/4) of an inch; center of lower edge to be about one and three-fourths (1 3/4) inches above inner angle of chevron.

Hospital Steward: A half chevron of emerald-green cloth, one and three-fourths (1 3/4) inches wide and about nine and one-half (9 1/2) inches long, piped around the edge with yellow silk. In the center a caduceus embroidered in yellow silk.

1st Sergeant: Three bars and a lozenge, having side about one-fourth (1/4) of an inch wide. Lozenge about two and one-half (2 1/2) inches long and two (2) inches wide, placed lengthwise about one and one-fourth (1 1/4) inches above inner angle of chevron.

Sergeant: Three bars.

Regimental and Battalion Color Sergeant: Three bars and a ring one-fourth (1/4) of an inch wide, one and one-fourth (1 1/4) inches in inside diameter, and placed one and three-fourths (1 3/4) inches above inner angle of chevron.
Corporal: Two bars.
Farrier: A horseshoe three-fourths (3/4) of an inch wide, about four and one-half (4 1/2) inches long from outer edge of toe-piece to a line between extreme points of heels; between outer lines across center about three and three-fourths (3 3/4) inches; between extreme points of heels about two (2) inches. A toe-piece about one and three-fourth (1 3/4) inches long, one-half (1/2) inch deep, and two heel-pieces about one-half (1/2) by three-fourths (3/4) inch each, of gray facing cloth, to be stitched on. Four (4) nail holes on each side f the shoe, at equal distances from each other, to be underlaid with blue cloth.
Pioneer: Two crossed axes of the following dimensions: Handles, four and one-half (4 1/2) inches long, one-fourth (1/4) to one-third (1/3) of a inch wide. Hatchet, two (2) inches long, one (1) inch wide; ax two (2) inches long and about one (1) inch wide at the edge.
Signal Service device: Two embroidered signal flags crossed, each 3/4 of an inch square, bearing in the center a square one-fourth (1/4) of an inch; one flag white with red inner square, the other red with white inner square. Flags and squares to be edged with bullion; staff about three (3) inches long, with silver spear-heads.
Workmanship.—To be in accordance with standard samples adopted this day.
Adopted January 28, 1885, in lieu of specifications of March 12, 1879, which are hereby canceled.

Woolen Blankets Specification No. 128

Material.—To be pure long staple, free from shoddy, reworked wool or cotton, or any other impure materials. The warp to be of not lower grade than three-eighths blood bred wool; the filling or woof to be of not lower grade than one-half blood-bred wool.
Size.—To be 7 feet long and 5 feet 6 inches wide.
Color.—To be blue and white mixed, conforming strictly to standard sample, with a dark-blue stripe 2 1/2 to 3 inches wide, across each end about 6 inches from edge, the color of stripes to conform to those of the standard sample. The blue color in both the warp and woof filling to be of *pure indigo dye* of best quality indigo.
Weight.— To weigh not less than 5 pounds.
Threads.—To have not less than 22 threads of warp and 25 threads of filling or woof to the inch. The threads to be well driven up.
Strength.—To bear a strain of not less than 25 pounds per inch for the warp and 30 pounds per inch for the woof without tearing
U.S. brand.—Each blanket to have the letters "U.S."4 inches long in the center, placed lengthwise with the blanket. The letters to be of pure indigo and to conform in color to stripes, and may be either woven into the fabric or stamped on the blanket.
Finish.—To conform in all respects to the standard sample adopted this day.
Adopted January 9, 1885, in lieu of specifications of February 5, 1884, which are hereby canceled.

Cavalry Guidons Specification No. 129

Silk.—To be of best quality of banner silk.
Size.—To be 3 feet 5 inches on the lance; to be cut swallow-tailed, 15 inches to the fork.
Design.—Two horizontal stripes, each one-half the width of flag, the upper to be red and the lower white. The upper stripe to have on both sides, in the center, the number of regiment in white silk, and the lower the letter of troop, in red silk. The letter and number to be block-shaped, 4 3/4 inches high, and held in place by a border of needle-work embroidery three-sixteenths of an inch wide, of same color.
Lance.—To be 1 1/4 inches in diameter, and 9 feet long, including spear and ferrule.
Case or cover.—To be of water-proof material, to protect the guidon when furled.
Workmanship.—To conform to standard sample on file in the Quartermaster-General's Office.
Adopted January 27, 1885.

Metallic Ornaments for Helmets and Forage Caps Specification No. 130
FOR HELMETS.

Eagles.—Eagles according to pattern made of No. 24 sheet-brass (high); American eagle displayed proper with national shield on breast and bearing in beak a scroll with motto "*E pluribus unum*;" olive branch in dexter talon and branch of arrows in sinister. For troops of the line the distinguishing arms are displayed under the shield, viz: Artillery, the crossed cannon; cavalry, crossed sabers; infantry, crossed rifles, and upon the lower part of the shield is borne the regimental number in German silver. For the staff and staff corps, the crossed arms are omitted and the distinguishing badge, in German silver, is borne upon the lower part of shield, viz: For post quartermaster sergeants, the crossed pen and key; hospital stewards, the caduceus; for commissary sergeants, the crescent; for engineers, the castle; for ordnance and ordnance sergeants, the shell and flame, and for signal service, the crossed flags. When flat the eagle is about the following dimensions: Greatest width between tips of wings 4 1/4 inches; from upper edge of scroll to tip of tail 3 7/8 inches. It shall be molded to the form of helmet shell and be provided with three wire loops by which to fasten it on.
Spike and base (foot troops).—Spike to be of polished high brass, according to pattern, hexagonal, fluted surface, with screw of brass to fit socket in top of helmet. Height of spike 3 inches; widest diameter 1 inch; length of screw (in the clear) 3/4 of an inch; base of No. 24 sheet-brass (high); oak-leaf design according to pattern, 8 points, bed in center to receive base of spike and hole cut for spike-screw.
Plume socket (for mounted men's helmets).—To be of high brass, according to pattern. An inverted fluted cone and mitered top (four points), front ornamented with the national eagle and shield and a single star surmounting eagle head. Spherical base, into the mouth of which the cone is securely brazed, and which is formed into a hexagonal pedestal at the bottom similar to that of spike so far as to rest firmly upon the oak-leaf base and be bored for the plume pin. Height of spherical base (including mouth and pedestal) about 1 1/2 inches; of cone 2 inches; diameter of cone at top 1 inch, at bottom 5/8 of an inch; diameter of spherical base 1 inch. Plume pin, with ornamental head and plain washer (each about 1 1/4 inches in diameter), about 4 3/4 inches in length, the thread of which

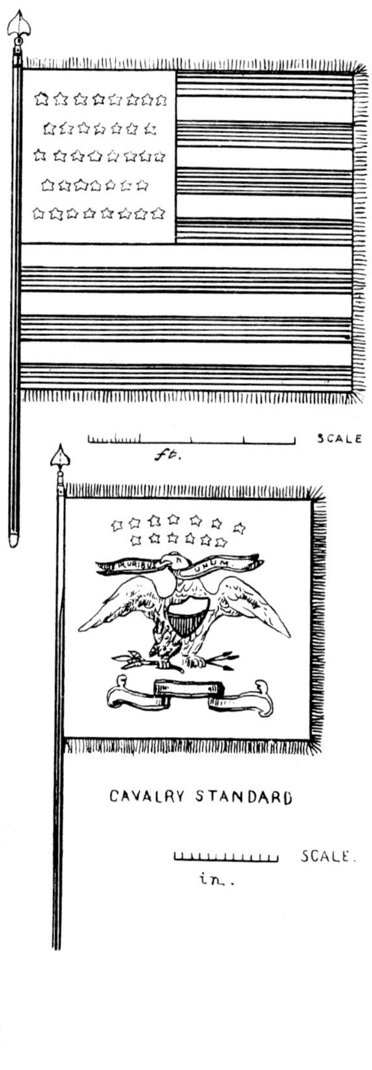

(Top) National Colors (Flag), Specification 159, September 14, 1885; (Bottom) Cavalry Standard Specification No. 102, February 4, 1884.

shall be cut so as to screw into the ventilator socket in top of helmet. For the lower end of pin a large open washer or disk with beveled edge to bear against the inside of helmet shell for better security of the top piece, and be kept in place by a small brass thumb nut. Diameter of disk, about 2 1/2 inches.

The oak-leaf base to be the same as described for foot helmets.

Side buttons.—Side buttons to be of high brass, according to pattern, with flat brass double stems. Devices on buttons in high relief: For engineers, the castle; for ordnance, the shell and flame; for post quartermaster sergeants, the crossed pen and key; for hospital stewards, the caduceus; for commissary sergeants, the crescent; for Signal Corps, the crossed flags; for artillery, the crossed cannon; for cavalry, the crossed sabers; for infantry, the crossed rifles.

Numbers.—Numbers to be 1/2 inch in height and made of No. 18 German silver, according to pattern, with two soft copper wire stems to hold them on shield.

Devices.—Devices for staff and staff corps to be German silver, according to pattern. Designs are mentioned in description of eagle, and stems as for numbers.

Scrolls and rings (mounted troops).—Scrolls and rings. One on each side, between the leaf-shaped points of top piece, its lower edge 1/2 inch below these points. The scroll is 3/4 inch diameter, ornamented to correspond with the fastening on the top piece. On the top of the scroll, in the center, is an eye of thin wire 3/16 of an inch high, holding a thin brass ring 1/2 inch in diameter, to keep the cords and bands in position. The stem of the scroll is formed in two pieces of thin brass wire to fasten to it at the inside of the helmet. All to be high brass.

FOR FORAGE CAPS.

Bugles for musicians.—Bugles for field and band musicians: Of sheet brass (high) No. 28, representing an old-style bugle with circular crook, and a cord slung three fold around the lower part, terminating in 2 tassels on one, and 1 tassel on the other side. Height across crook one and 1 1/4 inch; width from mouth-piece to outer edge of bowl, 2 1/4 inches. Brass-wire loops same as on letters.

Castles (engineers).—Castles: Of sheet-brass (high) No. 28, representing an ancient castle with three towers. Height of center tower, 7/8 of an inch; of side towers, 1 1/4 inches each; of battlements between towers, 5/8 of an inch; width at base, 1 7/8 inches; at top of side towers, 1 3/4 inches. Two small brass-wire loops strongly soldered to back to fasten to cap.

Shells and flames (ordnance).—Shells and flames: Of sheet- brass (high) No. 28, representing a shell and flame. Diameter height of shell, 3/4 of an inch; height of flame from upper edge of shell, 7/8 of an inch; greatest width of flame, 1 1/8 inches. Brass-wire loops the same as on letters.

Crescents (commissary sergeants).—Crescents: Of sheet white metal (German silver), crescent shaped. Width from point to point, 1 5/8 inches; height of arc 1 inch; greatest width in center 1/2 inch. Brass wire loops on back same as letters.

Wreaths and caduceus (hospital stewards).—Wreaths made of dead or unburnished gilt-metal, representing two olive branches, held at the bottom by a loop and knot, turning upward and bending in an oval shape, approaching each other at the top. Height 1 1/2 inch; greatest distance between outer edges, 2 5/8 inches; greatest width of single branch 5/8 of an inch. Brass-wire loops as on back of letters.

A caduceus of German silver, similar to that on helmet eagle, to be worn within wreath.

Wreaths and crossed pen and key (post quartermaster sergeants).—Wreath: same as above, a crossed pen and key of German silver, similar to that on the helmet eagle, to be worn within the wreath.

Crossed cannon (artillery).—Crossed cannon: Of sheet-brass (high) No. 20, representing two cannon crossing each other at the trunnions, muzzles upward; length 2 1/8 inches; breadth at breeches 2 inches; at muzzles, 1 7/8 inches. Four brass-wire loops strongly soldered on back to fasten to cap.

Crossed sabers (cavalry).—Crossed sabers: Of sheet-brass (high) No 20, representing two cavalry sabers in scabbards, crossed in the middle, with hilts and edges upward. To be shaped or curved so as to fit the front of the cap. Length of sabers, 3 inches; height from hilt of one to point of other 1 1/4 inches; from point to point, 2 3/4 inches. Four brass-wire loops same as on crossed cannon.

Crossed Rifles (infantry).—Crossed rifles: Of sheet-brass (high) No. 20; two rifles crossing each other at a point equidistant from butt and muzzle; muzzles pointing upward and outward; hammers upward, their position crossed, making the upper space form an angle of 137°; length of rifle, 2 5/8 inches; diameter at point of crossing, about 1/8 of an inch. To be shaped or curved so as to fit the front of cap; the whole ornament occupying a rectangular space about 2 7/16 inches wide by 1 3/8 inches high. Fastenings: Four brass-wire loops firmly soldered, opening horizontally with the rifles, and placed about 1/2 inch from muzzles and butts.

Letters "A" to "M."—Brass letters "A" to "M": Roman capitals, 1/2 inch long, to be made of sheet-brass (high) No. 28; edges beveled. Two small brass-wire loops strongly soldered on the back of letter to fasten it to the cap.

Numbers "1" to "0."—Brass Numbers: Nos. "1" to "0," inclusive; 1/2 of an inch long, to be made of sheet-brass (high) No, 28; edges beveled. Small brass-wire loops, same as on letters.

Adopted February 24, 1885, in lieu of those of April 21, 1882, which are hereby canceled.

Uniform Coats Specification No. 131

Material.—Dark-blue cloth, Army standard. Linings for body and sleeves, corset jeans; for skirt, black Italian cloth; regulation brass buttons.

Pattern and Dimensions.—for foot troops.—Single-breasted dark-blue frock-coat according to standard sample; nine buttons in front; standing collar, cut square to hook in front; cloth facings and pipings, of color for the various arms of service on collar, cuff, and back of skirt, according to pattern; shoulder-straps of facing-cloth let into seam at point of shoulder, and to button at collar with one button; inside pocket in left breast, opening perpendicularly.

For mounted troops.—To be similar to the above, except that the skirt be 3 inches shorter, and slashed and piped at sides to within about 3 inches of the waist, and the back facings to be according to standard sample.

For musicians.—To be the same as the above, with the addition of the breast-facings (according to pattern) of 1/4-inch worsted braid, of proper color of arm of service.

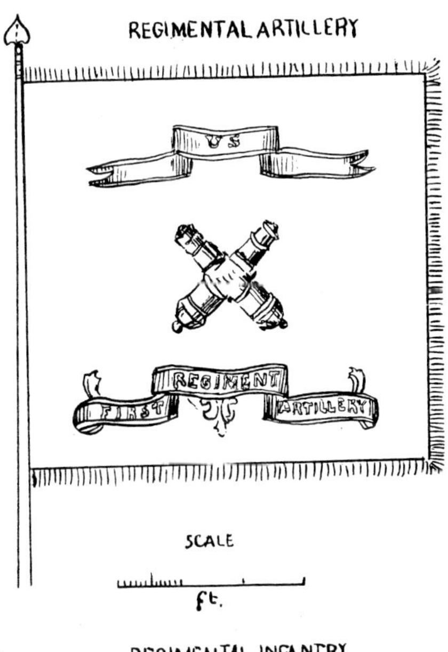

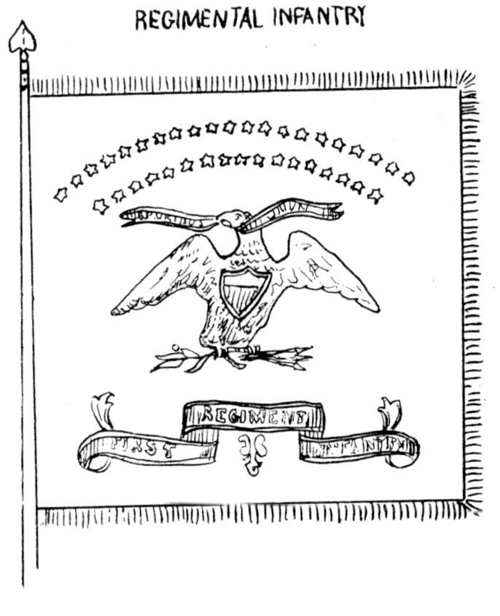

(Top) Artillery Regimental Standard, Specification No. 172, April 29, 1886; (Bottom) Infantry Regimental Standard, Specification No. 158, September 14, 1885.

For enlisted men of staff corps.—To be the same as the above, except that the piping be white for all corps, and edges of all facings and straps be piped with white cloth, according to sample.

Measurements for uniform coats, foot.

SIZES.	1	2	3	4	5	6
	Inches.	Inches	Inches	Inches.	Inches.	Inches.
From collar seam to waist	18	18 1/2	19 1/4	19 1/2	20 1/4	20 1/4
Full length of Coat	32	32 1/2	33 1/4	33 1/2	34 1/4	34 1/4
Full length of Sleeve	31	31 3/4	32 1/2	34	35	35 1/2
Width of back	7	7 1/4	7 3/4	8	8 1/4	8 3/8
Collar at neck	15 1/4	15 3/4	16	17	17 1/2	18 3/8
Height of Collar, front	1	1	1	1	1	1
" " back	1 1/4	1 1/4	1 1/4	1 1/4	1 1/4	1 1/4
Width of sleeve at hand	5 1/2	5 1/2	6	6 1/4	6 1/4	6 1/2
Breast measure	35	36 1/2	38	40	41	43
Waist measure	32	34	36	38	39	41

Measurements for uniform coats, mounted.

SIZES.	1	2	3	4	5	6
	Inches.	Inches	Inches	Inches.	Inches.	Inches.
From collar seam to waist	17 1/2	18	18 3/4	19	19 3/4	20 1/4
Full length of Coat	28 1/2	29	29 3/4	30	30 3/4	31 1/4
Full length of Sleeve	31	31 3/4	32 1/2	34	35	35 1/2
Width of back	7	7 1/4	7 3/4	8	8 1/4	8 3/8
Collar at neck	15 1/4	15 3/4	16	17	17 1/2	18 3/8
Height of Collar, front	1	1	1	1	1	1
" " back	1 1/4	1 1/4	1 1/4	1 1/4	1 1/4	1 1/4
Width of sleeve at hand	5 1/2	5 1/2	6	6 1/4	6 1/4	6 1/2
Breast measure	35	36 1/2	38	40	41	43
Waist measure	32	34	36	38	49	41

Adopted March 5, 1885, conforming to standard samples adopted his day. The specifications of February 27, 1880, are hereby canceled.

Barrack Bags Specification No. 132

Material.—To be made of six (6) ounce cotton duck, twenty-eighth and one-half (28 1/2) inches wide, dyed brown; to have drawing strings sixty (60) inches long, made of one-quarter (1/4) inch braided cotton cord passing through two (2) sheet brass grommets, one (1) on each side. To be sewed with No. 24.
Size.—Thirty-two (32) inches deep and fifteen (15) inches in diameter.
Workmanship.—To be made flat stitched in the bottom and side seams; to have a tabling at top two (2) inches wide for drawing strings, and conform to the sealed standard sample, adopted this date.
Adopted March 9, 1885, in lieu of those of March 13, 1884, which are hereby canceled.

Dark-blue Cloth-finished Blouse Flannel Specification No. 133

Wool.—To be pure, long-staple American fleece wool of one-half (1/2) and three-quarters (3/4) full blood, mixed in equal proportions, and free from shoddy, flocks, or other impurities.
Width.—To be fifty-four (54) inches, or six-fourths (6/4) of a yard wide.
Threads.—To contain not less than sixty (60) threads of warp and fifty-two (52) threads of filling in each square inch.
Weight.—To weigh not less than thirteen (13) ounces to the linear yard.
Strength.—To be capable of sustaining a strain of twenty-eighth (28) pounds to the inch in width of warp, and twenty-three (23) pounds to the inch in width of filling.
Color.—To be of the same shade of dark blue as the standard sample, and to be dyed in the wool with pure indigo, best quality, unless otherwise authorized in writing by the contracting officer.
Finish.—To be twilled (kersey twill) nap well raised, cropped. steamed, closely shorn, well pressed, and finished in every way equal to the standard sample.
Adopted March 21, 1885, in lieu of specifications of September 29, 1877, which are hereby canceled.

Stripes for Trousers Specification No. 134

Materials.—To be of facing cloth of same color as facings for uniform dress coat except for infantry, which will be of white linen webbing. Stripes for engineers to have in addition a white piping one-eighthh of an inch wide.
Dimensions.—For non-commissioned staff, 1 1/4 inch wide.
For sergeants, 1 inch wide.
For corporal, one-half inch wide.
For musicians, two stripes, one-half inch wide, placed one-quarter of an inch apart.
All stripes to be cut 45 inches long, and cloth stripes wide enough to be turned in one-quarter of an inch on either side.
To be worn along the outer seam of the trowsers, the rear edge following the seam.
Adopted March 24, 1885, in lieu of specifications of February 27, 1880, which are hereby canceled.

Facing Cloth Specification No. 135

To be 54 inches or 6/4 wide, of best American fleece wool, free from shoddy, flocks, or other impurities.
To be dyed in the following colors, viz: dark blue, scarlet, yellow, crimson, orange, gray, emerald-green, white, and buff.
To contain 64 threads in the chain, 60 threads in the filling to the square inch, and to weigh from 14 1/2 to 15 1/2 ounces to the linear yard, but not to fall below 14 1/2 ounces.

Artillery Guidon, Specification No. 174, May 21, 1886.

To be capable of sustaining the a strain of 30 pounds to the inch in width of warp, and 20 pounds to the inch in width of filling.

Adopted March 25, 1885, in lieu of specifications of May 31, 1876, which are hereby canceled.

Uniform Coat Buttons Specification No. 136

Size.—To be of two (2) sizes, designated as large and small. The large size to be thirty-two and one-half (32 1/2) lignes, and the small size twenty-five (25) lignes.

Shell.—The shell of the large size buttons to be made from gilding metal, number twenty-six (26) gauge. The small size to be made of same metal twenty-eighth (28) gauge.

Backs.—The backs of both large and small size to be of soldering brass, number twenty-six (26) gauge.

Eye.—The eye of the large size buttons to be copper, number thirteen (13) gauge, and the small size of same metal, number fifteen (15) gauge.

Gilding.—To be done by fire process, and shell to be so treated that all gold shall be on outside surface. The weight of gold on each shell of large size buttons to be not less than four-fifths (4/5) of a pennyweight for each gross, and for small size two-fifths (2/5) of a pennyweight for each gross.

Burnishing.—The burnishing to be done in the best manner know to the trade.

Stamping.—To be done with sharp, bright dies, free from any imperfections.

Solder.—The eye to be soldered into the back of the button with best quality spelter solder, and no backs to be used that show an abrasion around the eye.

Color.—To conform to standard sample.

Acid test.—To stand an acid test equal to standard samples.

Packing.—The buttons to be put up in gross boxes on cards of two (2) dozen each. Each card to be protected by two (2) thicknesses of tissue paper.

Adopted March 27, 1885.

Silk and Silk Twist Specification No. 141

Silk.—Black machine silk size "B." One ounce spools to contain 750 yards each, to stand a tensile strength of 8 pounds; to be of strictly pure dye and clear black color. Spool silk, size "B" on 20 yards, 30 yards, 70 yards, and 100 yards spools , to stand a tensile strength of 8 pounds and contain full measurements, and to be of strictly pure dye.

Twist.—Button-hole twist, size No. 10, No. 12, and No. 14, on 1-ounce spools, to be 8 strands, braided. Size No. 10 to stand a tensile strength of 19 pounds, and each spool to contain 39 yards. Size No. 12 to stand a tensile strength of 16 pounds, and each spool to contain 46 yards. Size No. 14 to stand a tensile strength of 14 pounds, and each spool to contain 53 yards. Seven-yard, 10-yard, and 24-yard spools to be same size, strength, and quality of twist as the 1-ounce spools. All button-hole twist to be of strictly pure dye, a clear black color, and full measurement.

Raw stock.—All silk and silk twist to be of best "Tsatlee" or "Japan" raw stock, or other equally good, thoroughly cleaned, free from knots and slugs.

Stamping of spools, packing, & c.—All spools of silk or twist to be indelibly stamped on one end of spool "Property of United States," and on other end the quantity and size of silk the spool contains.

The silk to be put up in boxes of 1 dozen spools and silk twist in boxes of 8 spools, and marked with the name of the contractor and date of contract.

Adopted April 2, 1885.

Muskrat Gauntlets Specification No. 142

To be made if muskrat skin, according to standard sample. Lining of lamb's fleece in hand, and blue or red cloth in gauntlet. Gauntlets to be at least five (5) inches deep, and of sufficient fullness to admit cuff of dress-coat or blouse. Palms sheepskin conforming in quality to standard sample.

To be three (3) size, viz: 9, 10, and 11.

Adopted April 3, 1885, in lieu of those of March 12, 1879, which are hereby canceled.

Forage Caps Specification No. 143

Made of best wool-dyed indigo-blue cloth, conforming in quality and color with the standard sample. Band about one and one-fourth (1 1/4) inch wide, strengthened by a strip of strong split-leather of the same width, sewed in between the cloth and the sweat-leather. The front rises straight and vertical one and one-half (1 1/2) to one and five-eighth (1 5/8) inch above the band, sides straight and slightly converging toward the crown. The back, about five (5) inches long, rises from the band forward at an angle of 45 degrees, slightly convex.

The crown is circular, about four and three-fourths (4 3/4) inches in diameter, made upon strong "tarred board" covered on the inside with black silesia. The shape of the cape would thus give an incline to the crown of one (1) to one and one-fourth (1 1/4) inch from rear to front.

A straight horizontal vizor of patent leather, about three-sixteenths (3/16) of an inch thick, shaped as described for dress-caps. A small brass regulation button on each side, immediately behind the end of the vizor, for chin-strap.

The latter is made in two parts, of fine enameled leather about one-half (1/2) inch wide, each part about nine (9) inches long, and arranged, as on dress-cap, to be lengthened and shortened at will.

Sweat-leather of Belgium leather, one and one-half (1 1/2) inch wide.

Lining of glazed muslin, fastened by its lower edge only to the inner stiffening of the band, the upper edge gathered with strong thread.

Adopted April 3, 1885, in lieu of those of May 31, 1876, which are hereby canceled.

Dark-blue Wool Shirting and Cape Lining Flannel Specification No. 144

To be fifty-four (54) inches, or 6/4 wide, and to be made of pure, long-staple, American fleece wool, not less than one half- blood, free from shoddy, flocks, or other impurities, and to weigh not less than 10 ounces to the linear yard.

To be twilled and the nap very slightly raised; to contain not less than fifty-six threads of warp and 48 threads of filling in each square inch, and to be capable of sustaining a strain of not less than 26 pounds to the inch in width of warp, and not less than 22 pounds to the inch in width of filling, tested in the piece.

The colors to be dark-blue, green, gray, crimson, scarlet, orange, yellow, and buff of the standard shades, to be dyed with fast colors. The blue to be dyed in the wool with pure indigo.

Adopted March 3, 1885, in lieu of those of March 15, 1883, which are hereby canceled.

Fly and Suspender Buttons Specification No. 145

To be equal in all respects to the sealed standard samples.

Size.—The fly button to be twenty-two (22) lignes; the suspender buttons to be twenty-seven (27) lignes.

Style.—To be what is called in the trade four (4) hole metal back, japanned fly and suspender buttons.

Packing.—To be put up in five (5) gross boxes.

Adopted April 14, 1885.

"Markers" and "General Guides" for Foot Regiments Specification No. 146

Marker.

Silk.—To be of best quality banner silk.

Size.—To be 20 inches by fly and 18 inches on the pike.

Design.—To be same as national color, except that the stars are to be two circles, with one star in each corner of the field. In the inner circles of stars, the number of regiment in solid block figure. Stars and figures to be in white silk needle-work embroidery on a single thickness of silk.

Pike.—To be of ash, and finished with brass spear-head and ferrule. Total length, 8 feet.

Case or cover.—To be of water-proof material, to protect the color when furled.

Workmanship.—To conform to standard sample in the office of the Quartermaster-General, U.S.A.

General Guide.

Silk.—Same as for marker.

Size.—To be 18 inches fly from the rod-casing and 15 inches on the rod.

Design.—Same as marker.

Trimming.—To be trimmed with yellow silk cut fringes 1/2 inches deep.

Metal rod and spear-head.—Rod to be of brass tubing, nickel-plated, and diameter to exactly fit inside the bore of a 45/100- inch caliber rifle. To be 28 1/2 inches long, with a collar fitted 10 inch from the bottom to rest on the muzzle of the gun. To be finished at the proper places with two nickel-plated knobs for fastening the flag, and at the top with a nickel-plated spear-head 3 1/2 inches long, conforming to the standards sample.

Case or cover.—Same as for marker.
Workmanship.—To conform to standard sample in the office of the Quartermaster-General, U.S.A.
Adopted April 25, 1885.

Overcoats Specification No. 148

Material.—Sky-blue kersey, 22 ounce, Army standard. Lining for body, dark-blue flannel, to weigh 11 1/2 ounces to the 6/4 linear yard. Flannel for cape lining, Army standard, to weigh 10 ounces to the 6/4 linear yard and to be of the following colors, viz: For hospital stewards, emerald green; for post quartermaster sergeants, buff; for commissary sergeants, gray; for ordnance, crimson; for engineers and artillery, scarlet; for signal service, orange; for infantry, dark-blue; for cavalry, yellow. Sleeve lining corset jeans. Eight white metal hooks and eyes, large, viz, seven for adjusting the cape to the coat, and one on the collar; one black japanned hook and eye at the bottom of front of skirt to hook it back, and four black japanned hooks, two on each edge, the upper hook placed 11 inches below the lower button-hole, and the lower hook 13 inches from the upper hook; four worked eyes, two on each side of skirt, placed in a position to hook up each front corner of skirt at an angle which will show 12 inches if the bottom of the skirt turned up.
Pattern.—To be double-breasted, with cape, and having 6 regulation brass buttons, large, on each breast. The cape to be adjustable by means of 7 hooks beneath the collar of the coat, and 7 eyes upon the cape. To have 7 regulation brass buttons, small, 1 inside pocket on the left breast, opening perpendicularly.
Workmanship.—To be cut and made in conformity with the standard patterns and samples.

Sizes.	Length of Coat	Length of Cape	Breast Measure	Waist Measure	Length of Sleeve	Length of Collar
1	44 1/2	24 1/2	36	34	32 1/2	17
2	45	25 1/2	38	36	33	17 1/2
3	46	26 1/2	41	39	33 1/2	18 1/2
4	47	27 1/2	44	42	34	19 1/2
5	48	28 1/2	45	44	34 1/2	20
6	49	29	46	46	35	20 1/2

Adopted May 28, 1885, in lieu of specifications of September 14, 1884, which are hereby canceled.

Music Pouches, Specification No. 184, April 5, 1887.

Brassards Specification No. 149

Material.—To be made of white facing cloth, of Army standard quality.
Dimensions.—To be 16 inches long and 3 inches wide when finished.
Design.—To be a strip of white cloth with sides turned under and stitched down with white silk. To have in the center a Greek cross 2 inches by 2 inches, made of scarlet facing cloth, edges of same to be stitched all around with scarlet silk.
Workmanship.—To conform with to standard sample adopted this day.
Adopted June 30, 1885.

Crimped Campaign Shoes Specification No. 150

To be worked square with the last on which they are made; the edges to be finished with pressers, without heel-ball, and to measure at least half a size outside more than they are marked.
Upper leather to be of the best oak-tanned from slaughter hides. The soles to be best quality oak-tanned, from Texas hides, or from South America (commonly called "Spanish") dry hides.
No split leather to be used.
The width of the soles across the ball of the foot to be as follows: No. 5, 3 4/8 inches; No. 6, 3 5/8 inches; No. 7, 3 6/8 inches; No. 8, 3 7/8 inches; No. 9, 4 inches; No. 10, 4 1/8 inches; No. 11, 4 2/8 inches; No. 12, 4 3/8 inches.
Other measurements to be as follows: letter "A"

Last.	Toes.	Instep.	Heel.	Ankle.	Height.
5	8 5/8	8 7/8	12 5/8	8 3/4	5 5/16
6	8 7/8	9 1/8	12 7/8	9	5 3/8
7	9 1/8	9 3/8	13 1/8	9 1/4	5 7/16
8	9 3/8	9 5/8	13 3/8	9 1/2	5 1/2
9	9 5/8	9 7/8	13 5/8	9 3/4	5 9/16
10	9 7/8	10 1/8	13 7/8	10	5 3/4
11	10 1/8	10 3/8	14 1/8	10 1/4	5 11/16
12	10 3/8	10 5/8	14 3/8	10 1/2	6

For letter "B," one-fourth of an inch more on instep and toes.
The middle counter to be made of skirting leather; the inner counter or lining to be of wax upper, neatly skived around the upper edged and fastened with three (3) cord wax thread, to have not less than nine (9) stitches to the inch on the counter and side seams. To have soles sewed with seven (7) stitches to the inch on the soles, and four (4) stitches to the inch on the welt inner solves, with twelve (12) cord flax thread on the inner seam and ten (10) cord flax thread on the outer seam or sole.
Adopted July 14, 1885.

"Post" Shoes Specification No. 151

To be worked square with the last on which they are made; the edges to be finished with pressers, without heel-ball, and to measure at least half a size (outside) more than they are marked.
The upper leather to be of the best oak-tanned American calfskin, and to weigh 4 pounds to the skin. Soles of best quality oak-tanned, from straight Texas hides, or from South America (commonly called "Spanish") dry hides. No split leather to be used.
The width of the soles across the ball of the foot to be graduated as follows, and to be in proportion throughout: No. 5, 3 3/8 inches; No. 6, 3 4/8 inches; No. 7, 3 5/8 inches; No. 8, 3 6/8 inches; No. 9, 3 7/8 inches; No. 10, 4 inches; No. 11, 4 1/8 inches; No. 12, 4 3/8 inches.
The instep and toe to measure as follows: For letter "A," No. 5, 8 13/16, 8 1/8 inches; No. 6, 9 1/16, 8 1/8 inches; No. 7, 9 5/16, 8 5/8 inches; No. 8, 9 9/16, 8 7/8 inches; No. 9, 9 13/16, 9 1/8 inches; No. 10, 10 1/16, 9 3/8 inches; No. 11, 10 5/16, 9 5/8 inches; No. 12, 10 9/16, 9 7/8 inches. For letter "B" 1/8 inch more.
The height of the leg for a No. 8 shoe to be 6 1/4 inches. The upper to be cut without side seam; to have counter, side piece, strap, and crimped tongue stitched on with silk. To be laced in front, and to have metallic eyelets and hooks; to have soles sewed with seven (7) stitches to the inch welt, and four (4) stitches to the inch on the inner sole, with not less than twelve (12) cord flax thread on the inner sole nor less than ten (10) cord flax thread on the welt.
Adopted July 14, 1885, in lieu of specifications if April 24, 1884, which are hereby canceled.

6/4 Sky-blue Kersey—Fine Quality Specification No. 152

To be fifty-four (54) inches wide and to be made of not less than three-quarters (3/4) blood bred wool, free from shoddy, flocks, or other impurities; to contain not less than seventy-six (76) threads of warp and sixty-eighth (68) threads of filling to each square inch; to be capable of sustaining a strain of no less than fifty-eighth (58) pounds to one inch width of warp and fifty (50) pounds to one inch width of filling.

To be woven like and finished equal to the standard sample.

The color to be the same shade of sky-blue as the standard sample, and to be dyed in the wool with pure indigo (unless otherwise authorized in writing by the contracting officer), and to have a yellow or white woolen list.

The kersey to weigh twenty-two (22) ounces pre linear yard.

Adopted July 25, 1885.

White Linen Trousers Specification No. 153

Material.—To be made of white linen equal to the approved sample pair of trousers. The buttons, suspender and fly, to be white bone, of good quality. Buckle for back strap to be strong and neat.

Pattern.—To be made with waist-band, side pockets, plain buttons, and in conformity with the following measurements:

Workmanship.—To be cut and made in accordance with the standard patterns and samples.

SIZES	Waist. Inches.	Seat. Inches.	Inside seam. Inches.	Outside seam. Inches.	Bottom. Inches.
1	32	36	31	41	19 1/2
2	34	38	31 1/2	41 1/2	20
3	36	40	32	42	20 1/2
4	38	42	33	43	20 1/2
5	40	44	34	44	21
6	42	45	35	45	21

Adopted May 5, 1885.

Gold Lace Specification No. 154

To be of the best quality gold on silver, the wire to weigh not less than ninety (90) grains to the linear yard of lace and to contain not less than 89 to 90 per cent. of silver and 1 8/10 to 2 per cent. gold.

To be full one-half (1/2) inch wide, and in weight, weave, finish, and all other respects to conform to standard sample.

The United States Mint assay to be standard.

Adopted August 25, 1885, in lieu of specifications of January 28, 1885.

Gold Lace Chevrons Specification No. 155

Lace.—To be of gold lace of Army standard.

Cloths.—The cloth forming the groundwork for arms, arcs, and ties of chevrons to be of facing cloth (conforming to published specifications) of the same color as the facings of the uniform coat.

The cloth forming the ground work for chevron devices (except that for Hospital Stewards) to be the same as that for the uniform coat. To be cut in shape of a quadrant of a circle having a radius of from five (5) to six (6) inches (as size of device may require), the straight sides of pieces to be neatly stitched to the under side of the upper edge of cloth of arms, the nap of the cloth to run downward when the chevron is on the sleeve.

Bars and Arms.—The bars of the chevron to be a single width of lace, to be neatly joined at the angles and stitched with gold-colored silk upon the facing cloth, on each border of the lace, and also at the outer ends, which are to be turned under. The bars are to be placed about one-eighthh (1/8) of an inch apart, and a bordering of facing cloth of about one-eighthh (1/8) of an inch to show on all sides.

The chevrons for Engineers to have a stitching of white silk upon each side of the lace bars.

The arms of the chevron bars to be six (6) to seven (7) inches long, to be the arcs of a circle of about twenty-five (25) inches radius, and to meet at an angle of about ninety-six (96) degrees; distance between extreme outer ends about nine (9) inches.

Design for Chevrons.—Sergeant Major: Three bars and an arc of three bars. The upper edge of outer bar of arc to be the arc of a circle of about seven and one-fourth (7 1/4) inches radius.

Quartermaster Sergeant: Three bars and a tie of three bars. The upper tie to extend horizontally from the extreme outer end of one arm of the chevron to that of the other.

Saddler Sergeant: Three bars and a saddler's round knife, handle upward. Knife of the following dimensions: handle one and three-fourths (1 3/4) inches long, three-fourths (3/4) inch wide near top; five-eighth (5/8) inch near blade; blade one and one-eighthh (1 1/8) inches deep in center; from point to point of blade, three and one-fourth (3 1/4) inches; center of edge, one and one-fourth (1 1/4) inches above inner angle of chevron. Lace of handle to run vertically, or ferrule about horizontally, and of blade to be crimped to shape of same.

Chief Trumpeter: Three bars and an arc of one bar, with bugle of pattern worn on cap about one and one-half (1 1/2) inches above inner angle of chevron. The upper edge of bar of arc to be the arc of a circle of about seven and one-fourth (7 1/4) inches radius. Bugle to be of form, dimensions, and finish of standard sample chevron.

Principal Musician: Three bars and a bugle. The bugle to be the same as for Chief Trumpeter chevrons.

Ordnance Sergeant: Three bars and an outlined star of lace. Lower point of star to be about one (1) inch above inner angle of chevron. Star to be of dimensions and finish as standard sample chevron.

Post Quartermaster Sergeant: Three bars, and a crossed key and pen. The latter device to be embroidered on gold bullion. The key and pen to cross about two and one-half (2 1/2) inches above the inner angle of the chevron, and to be of form, dimensions, and finish of standard sample chevron.

Commissary Sergeant: Three bars and a crescent (points front). Distance from point to point of crescent, two(2) inches; width in center, three-fourths (3/4) of an inch; center of lower edge to be about one and three-fourths (1 3/4) inches above inner angle of chevron

Hospital Steward: A half chevron of emerald-green cloth, one and three-fourths (1 3/4) inches wide and about nine and one-half (9 1/2) inches long, bound with gold tracing braid one-eighthh (1/8) of an inch wide. In the center a caduceus, embroidered in gold thread, to form dimensions, and finish of standard sample chevrons.

1st Sergeants: Three bars and an outlined lozenge, having side about one-fourth (1/4) of an inch wide. Lozenge about two and one-half (2 1/2) inches long and two (2) inches wide, placed lengthwise about one and one-fourth (1 1/4) inches above inner angle of chevron.

Sergeants: Three bars.

Regimental and Battalion Color Sergeant: Three bars and a ring one-fourth (1/4) of an inch wide, one and one-fourth (1 1/4) inches in inside diameter, and placed one and three-fourths (1 3/4) inches above inner angle of chevron.

Corporal: Two bars.

To indicate service: A single width of lace stitched upon a piece of cloth of the color of uniform coat, the ends of lace to be turned under; a bordering of the cloth one-eighthh (1/8) of an inch wide to appear on all sides. Length of chevron, about nine and one-fourth (9 1/4) inches.

To indicate service in war: The same as above, except that facing cloth of the color of the facings of the particular arm of services will be substituted for the outer cloth.

Workmanship.—To be in accordance with the standard samples adopted this day.

Adopted August 25, 1885, in lieu of specifications of January 28, 1885, which are hereby canceled.

Blanket-lining Cloth Specification No. 156

To be fifty-four (54) inches of 6/4 wide, and made of pure long stable American fleece wool or full one-quarter blood, combed and spun into soft yarn.

To contain not less than forty-four (44) threads in the filling and thirty (30) threads in the warp to each square inch, and to weigh not less than forty (40) ounces to the linear yard.

The cloth to be capable of standing a strain of not less than forty-five (45) pounds to the inch in width of warp, and fifty-four (54) pounds to the inch in width of filling.

To be dyed a fast black color, and nap raised equal to the standard sample.

Adopted September 2, 1883.

Buckles Specification No. 157

The buckle for Kersey trousers, overalls, and drawers to be of brass, seven-eighth (7/8) by one and one-quarter (1 1/4) inches outside measure; the revolving bar carrying two (2) stout prongs, well let into the sides at a point five-sixteenths (5/16) of an inch from the outer bottom bar.

The buckle for White Linen trousers to be made ow white metal, and to conform in size to the brass buckle above described.

Both to be equal in all respects to the sealed standard samples adopted this date.

Adopted September 12, 1885.

Regimental Colors, Infantry Specification No. 158

Material.—To be of a single thickness of seamless blue banner silk of best quality.

Dimensions.—To be six (6) feet six (6) inches fly, by six (6) feet deep on the pike.

Design.—To bear in the center the coat of arms of the United States (as described in specifications for Cavalry standards). Underneath the eagle a red scroll with the number and name of regiment (as, for example, "1st Regiment U.S. Infantry") in white.

The coat of arms, scroll, numbers, and letters to be embroidered (needle work) in silk, the same on both sides of the Color, and in size, pattern, shades of color, and all other particulars to conform to standard sample in office of the Quartermaster General of the Army.

Trimmings.— The color to be trimmed on three sides with yellow silk knotted fringe, two and one-half (2 1/2) inches deep. One cord and tassels (total length to be not less than eleven and one-half (11 1/2) feet) to accompany each Color, to be of blue and white silk intermixed.

Pike.—To be of the best quality of ash, straight-grained, and free from knots. To have a brass spear-head, and at the foot a brass ferule to fit easily into the socket of the color sling. Total length nine (9) feet and ten (10) inches long.

Cover.—To have an oil-cloth cover to fit easily over the Color when rolled on pike.

Workmanship.—To conform to the standard sample in the office of the Quartermaster General of the Army.

Adopted September 14, 1885.

National Colors Infantry and Artillery Specification No. 159

Material.—To be of a best quality banner silk.

Dimensions.—To be six (6) feet six (6) inches fly, by six (6) feet deep on the pike.

Design.—Thirteen horizontal stripes od equal breadth, alternately red and white, beginning with red. N the upper quarter next to the pike, a blue field of seamless banner silk thirty-one (31) inches long from the pike casing and extending down to lower edge of the fourth red stripe from the top, with stars (one for each State) arranged horizontally in five (5) rows. The stars to be embroidered (needle work) in white silk, on both sides, and to be two and one-half (2 1/2) inches from point to point.

Trimmings.— The Colors to be trimmed on three sides with yellow silk knotted fringe two and one-half (2 1/2) inches deep. One silk cord and tassels (total length to be not less than eleven and one-half (11 1/2) feet to accompany each Color, to be of blue and white silk intermixed for Infantry and red and yellow for Artillery.

Lettering.—The number of name of regiment as for example. "1st Regiment U.S. Infantry," "2d Regiment U.S. Artillery" to be embroidered in silk (needle work) on the center stripe in letters and figures two and one-half (2 1/2) inches high. White for infantry, and yellow for Artillery.

Pike.—To be of the best quality of ash, straight-grained, and free from knots. To have a brass spear-head, and at the foot a brass ferule to fit easily into the socket of the color sling. Total length nine (9) feet and ten (10) inches long.

Cover.—To have an oil-cloth cover to fit easily over the Color when rolled on pike.

Workmanship.—To conform to the standard sample in the office of the Quartermaster General of the Army.

Adopted September 14, 1885.

Sky-blue Kersey Heavy Quality Specification No. 160

Wool.—To be of fine American fleece-wool of not less than one-half blood bred and free from shoddy, flocks, or other impurities.

Width.—To be fifty-four (54) inches or 6/4 yards.

Threads.—To contain not less than fifty (50) threads of warp, and fifty-five (55) threads of filling to the square inch.

Weight.—To weigh not less than twenty-two (22) ounces to the linear yard.

Strength.—To be capable of sustaining a strain of sixty-five (65) pounds to the inch in width of warp, and sixty (60) pounds to the inch in width of filling.

Color.—To be of the same shade of blue as the standard sample, and be dyed in the wool with pure indigo of the best quality, unless otherwise authorized by the contracting officer.

Finish.—The nap to be slightly raised. The finish to be equal in every respect to the standard samples.

Adopted December 26, 1885, in lieu of specifications of July 2, 1876, which are hereby canceled.

White Metal Buttons for White Linen Trousers, Drawers, Overalls, Stable Frocks, etc. Specification No. 161

To be equal in all respects to the sealed standard samples. *Size.*—The small or fly buttons to be twenty-two (22) lignes, the large suspender buttons to be twenty-seven lines. *Style.*—To be what is called in the trade four (4) hole metal back, white metal fly and suspender buttons.

Packing.—To be put up in five (5) gross boxes.

Adopted January 12, 1886.

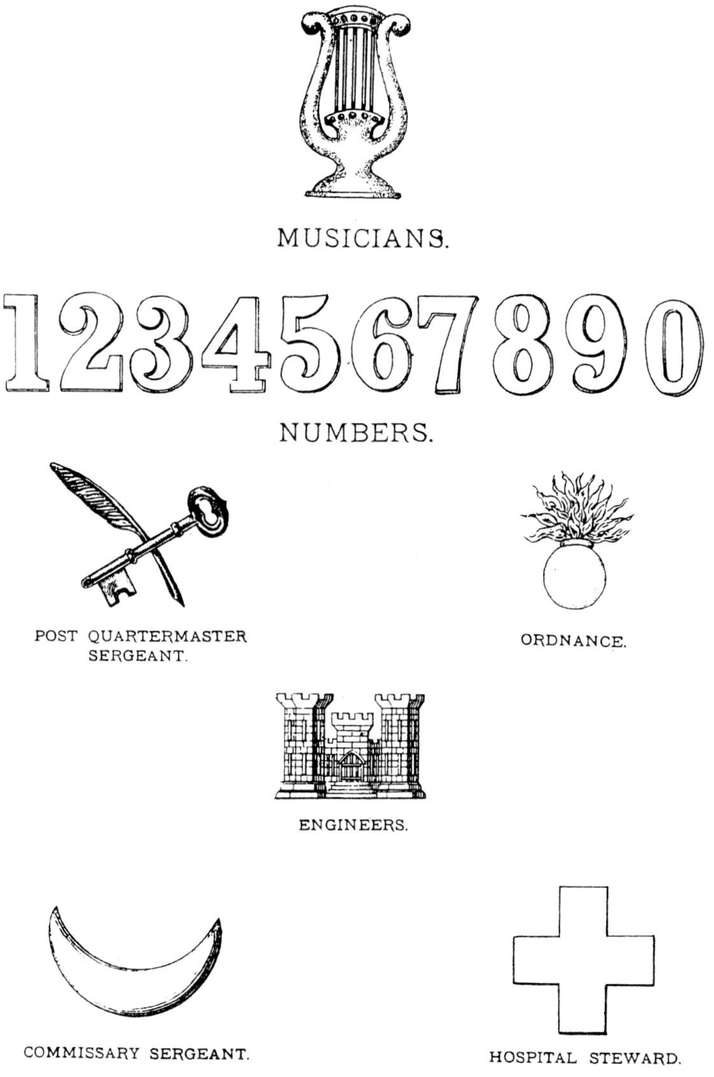

Metallic Helmet Ornaments, Specification No. 186, April 5, 1887.

Blouses Specification No. 164

Material.—Dark-blue flannel, Army standard; grey twilled mixed flannel lining for body, and unbleached muslin lining for sleeves.

Pattern.—To be singled-breasted sack coat with falling collar, and having five (5) regulation buttons, large, in front from neck to waist, and three (3) regulation buttons, small, on the cuff of each sleeve. To have three (3) outside pockets, one (1) on each side of skirt, and one (1) on the left breast, and one (1) inside pocket on the right breast.

Workmanship.—To be cut in accordance with the standard patterns adopted January 16, 1884, and to be made and finished in accordance with the standard samples adopted this date.

Measurements:

Sizes.	Length of Blouse.	Length of Sleeve.	Width of Hand.	Size of Neck.	Width of Collar.	Width of Back.	Size of Armhole.	Size of Breast.	Size of Waist.
	Inches.								
1	27	31	12	16	3	7	16	34	32
2	27 1/2	31 1/2	12	16 1/2	3	7 1/2	17	35	33
3	28	32 1/2	12	17	3	7 3/4	18	36	34
4	29	33	12	18	3 1/2	8	19	38	36
5	30 1/4	34	12 1/2	19	3 1/2	8	20	40	38
6	30 1/2	34 1/2	13	19 1/2	3 1/2	8 1/4	21	42	40

Adopted March 12, 1886, in lieu of specifications of October 21, 1884, which are hereby canceled.

Campaign Shoes (with partly Machined Sewed Bottoms) Specification No. 167

Material.—Uppers to be the best quality of leather, oak-tanned, from slaughter hides.

Vamp, back, and *tongue* to be wax-upper.

Inner counter to be of smooth wax-upper.

Middle counter to be of slaughter leather.

Soles to be of the best quality oak-tanned, from straight Texas hides, or from South American (commonly called "Spanish") dry hides.

Thread to be the best quality linen thread.

Nails used in heels to be 10/8 Swede No. 12, 10 lbs. to the 100 pairs shoes, and 5/8 American iron, 5 lbs. to the 100 pairs shoes.

Sizes—Nos. 5 to 12, inclusive.

The *width of the soles* the ball of the foot to be as follows and to be in proportion throughout:—

SIZES.	5	6	7	8	9	10	11	12
Letter "A"	3 5/16	3 7/16	3 9/16	3 11/16	3 13/16	3 15/16	4 1/16	4 3/16
Letter "B"	3 3/8	3 1/2	3 5/8	3 3/4	3 7/8	4	4 1/8	4 1/4
Letter "C"	3 7/16	3 9/16	3 11/16	3 13/16	3 15/16	4 1/16	4 3/16	4

5/16 The *instep and ball of the foot to measure* as follows:—

SIZES	5	6	7	8	9	10	11	12
Letter "A"								
Instep	8 3/4	9	9 1/4	9 1/2	9 3/4	10	10 1/4	10 1/2
Ball	8 1/2	8 3/4	9	9 1/4	9 1/2	9 3/4	10	10 1/4
Letter "B"								
Instep	9	9 1/4	9 1/2	9 3/4	10	10 1/4	10 1/2	10 3/4
Ball	8 3/4	9	9 1/4	9 1/2	9 3/4	10	10 1/4	10 1/2
Letter "C"								
Instep	9 1/4	9 1/2	9 3/4	10	10 1/4	10 1/2	10 3/4	11
Ball	9	9 1/4	9 1/2	9 3/4	10	10 1/4	10 1/2	10 3/4

Measurement for a No. 8 shoe, standard, *Letter "A,"* is as follows: *Heel*, 13 1/8 inches; *instep* 9 1/2 inches, *ball and toe* 9 1/4 inches, heigh*t of back* at rear 5 1/2 inches, *length of heel* 3 inches, *width of heel* 2 7/8 inches, *height of heel* 1 1/4 inches, *width of sole or ball*, 3 11/16 inches.

Measurement for a No. 8 shoe, standard, *Letter "B,"* to be as Letter "A," with the following exceptions:—

Heel 13 3/8 inches, *instep* 9 3/4 inches, *ball or toe* 9 1/2 inches, *width of sole or ball* 3 3/4 inches.

Measurement for a No. 8 shoe, standard, *Letter "C,"* to be as Letter "A," with the following exceptions:—

Heel 13 5/8 inches, *instep* 10 inches, *ball or toe* 9 3/4 inches, *width of sole or ball* 3 13/16 inches.

Workmanship.—Vamp and back to be crimped; tongue to be handsewed to vamp, with flat seam; *inner counter* to be neatly skived around the upper edge and to be fastened to the back with 3-cord waxed linen thread, nine (9) stitches to the inch. The *inner sole*, *upper*, and *welt* to be fastened together with twelve (12) cord wax sole thread, four (4) stitches to the inch. *Outer sole and welt* to be fastened together with ten (10) cord wax sole thread, seven (7) stitches to the inch. To be worked square with the last. The edges to be finished with pressers without heel-ball, and to measure at least half a size (outside) more than they are marked.

Adopted April 27, 1886, in lieu of those of July 14, 1885, which are hereby canceled.

White linen webbing for trouser stripes Specification No. 169

To be made of bleached white-linen, No. 100 3 fold high grade. To be woven in check pattern, with rounded edges.

To be one inch webbing to have one hundred and sixty-three (163) ends in the warp and fifty-six (56) shots to the inch.

The half-inch webbing to have seventy-two (72) ends in the warp and fifty-six (56) shots to the inch.

The webbing to be thoroughly shrunk after weaving and equal in every respect to the sealed standard sample.

Adopted March, 24 1886.

Dark-blue cloth, fine quality Specification No. 170

Wool.—To be pure American fleece wool of not less than three quarters (3/4) blood to full blood, and free from shoddy, flocks, or other impurities.

Width.—To be fifty-four (54) inches, or six fourths (6/4) of a yard wide.

Threads.—To contain not less than eighty (80) threads of warp, and seventy-four (74) threads of filling to the square inch.

Weight.—To weigh not less than nineteen (19) ounces to the linear yard.

Strength.—To be capable of sustaining a strain of forty-two (42) pounds to the inch in width of warp and thirty (30) pounds to the inch in width of filling.

Color.—To be the same shade of dark blue as the standard sample, and to be dyed in the wool with pure indigo, best quality (unless otherwise authorized in writing by the contracting officer.)

Finish.—To be equal in all respects to the standard sample.

Adopted April 13, 1886.

Forage Caps Specification No. 171

Made of best wool-dyed indigo-blue cloth, conforming in quality and color with the standard sample. Band about one and one-fourth (1 1/4) inch wide, strengthened by a strip of strong split-leather of the same width, sewed in between the cloth and the sweat-leather. The front rises straight and vertical one and one-half (1 1/2) to one and five-eighth (1 5/8) inch above the band, sides straight and slightly converging toward the crown. The back, about five (5) inches long, rises from the band forward at an angle of 45 degrees, slightly convex.

The crown is circular, about four and three-fourths (4 3/4) inches in diameter, made upon strong "tarred board" covered on the inside with black silesia. The shape of the cape would thus give an incline to the crown of one (1) to one and one-fourth (1 1/4) inch from rear to front.

A straight horizontal vizor of patent leather, about three-sixteenths (3/16) of an inch thick, shaped as in standard sample. A small brass regulation button on each side, immediately behind the end of the vizor, for chin-strap. the side buttons and slide on chin-strap to be fire-gilt.

The latter is made in two parts, of fine enameled leather about one-half (1/2) inch wide, each part about nine (9) inches long, and arranged, as on dress-cap, to be lengthened and shortened at will.

Sweat-leather of Belgium leather, one and one-half (1 1/2) inch wide.

Lining of glazed muslin, fastened by its lower edge only to the inner stiffening of the band, the upper edge gathered with strong thread.

Adopted April 15, 1886, in lieu of those of April 3, 1885, which are hereby canceled.

Regimental Colors, Artillery Specification No. 172

Material.—To be of a single thickness of seamless scarlet silk, of quality and exact shade of color to that in the sealed standard sample.

Dimensions.—To be six (6) feet six (6) inches fly by six (6) feet on the pike.
Design.—To bear in the center two cannons crossing, with the letters "U.S." above in a scroll, and underneath, the number of regiment (as, for example, "First Regiment Artillery"), also in a scroll. The scrolls to be of yellow and the letters of scarlet.
The crossed cannon, scrolls and letters to be embroidered (needlework) in silk, the same on both sides of the color, and in size, pattern, shades of color and all other particulars to conform to standard sample in Office of the Quartermaster-General of the Army.
Trimmings.—The color to be trimmed on three sides with yellow silk knotted-fringe, two and one-half (2 1/2) inches deep. One cord and tassels (total length to be not less than eleven and one-half (11 1/2) feet) to accompany each color, to be of scarlet and yellow silk intermixed.
Pike.—To be of the best quality of ash, straight grained, and free from knots. To have a brass spear-head, and at the foot a brass ferule to fit easily into the socket of the color sling. Total length nine (9) feet and ten (10) inches long.
Cover.—To have an oil-cloth cover to fit easily over the color when rolled on pike.
Workmanship.—To conform to the sealed standard sample in the Office of the Quartermaster General of the Army.
Adopted April 29, 1886.

Leather Gauntlets Specification No. 173

To be of Angora goat-skin. The gauntlet or cuff to be at least four and one-half (4 1/2) inches deep, and of sufficient fullness to admit cuff of coat.
Cuff to be lined with russet leather.
The glove to be "table cut," and the seams well stitched throughout with linen thread. The seams in the thumb and between the finger welted.
The cuff and back of glove to be stitched with silk, as in standard sample.
In quality of material and workmanship they must conform to the standard sample.
To be of five sizes, and put up in the following proportion to the 100 pairs: Ten, 8; twenty-three, 8 1/2; thirty, 9; twenty-two, 9 1/2; fifteen, 10.
Adopted May 11, 1886, in lieu of specifications of May 21, 1884, which are hereby canceled.

Artillery Guidons Specification No. 174

Silk.—To be a single piece of best quality of banner silk of exact shade of scarlet as the standard sample.
Size.—To be three (3) feet five (5) inches fly from the lance, and two (2) feet three (3) inches on the lance; to be cut swallow-tailed, fifteen (15) inches to the fork.
Design.—To bear in the center, on both sides of the guidon, two cannon crossing (about fourteen and one-half (14 1/2) inches in length), with the number of regiment above and letter of battery below. The crossed cannon, letter, and number to be yellow silk, and to be held in pace by a border of needle-work embroidery three-sixteenth (3/16) of an inch, of same color. The letter and number to be block-shaped, four and one-half (4 1/2) inches high.
Lance.—To be one and one-fourth (1 1/4) inches in diameter, and nine (9) feet long, including spear and ferrule.
Case or Cover.—To be of waterproof material, to protect the guidon when furled.
Workmanship.—To conform to standard sample on file in the Quartermaster General's Office.
Adopted May 21, 1886.

Canvas Cap Specification No. 175

Material.—To be made of six (6) ounce cotton duck dyed brown, lined with light blanket cloth next the duck, and with scarlet flannel in the inside; to have two buttons on the cape to button at the throat; and one vest size brown "lasting" button on the top for finish. The visor and edges bound with 3/4 brown cotton tape.
Style.—Scull cap with extension forming a cape reaching to the shoulders and meeting in front, covering the throat, and buttoning together with two (2) buttons. A visor of the same material bound with 3/4 brown cotton tape sewed in the forehead (to be worn up or down as desired), and having hook and eye to fasten it when turned up.
Workmanship.—To be cut and made in conformity with the sealed standard sample adopted this date.
Adopted June 22, 1886, in lieu of specifications of April 17, 1884, which are hereby canceled.

Cavalry Standards Specification No. 176

Material.—To be of a single thickness of seamless yellow banner silk.
Dimensions.—To be four (4) feet fly, and three (3) feet on the lance.
Design.—To have the Coat of Arms of the United States as on the standard sample, and which may be described as follows:
An eagle with outstretched wings; on its breast a U.S. shield; in the right talon an olive branch with red berries, and in his left ten (10) arrows bunched. A red scroll held in eagle's beak, with the motto "E Pluribus Unum," in yellow; over the scroll a group of thirteen (13) white stars, surmounted by an arc of diverging sun-ray, also in white.
Below the eagle a red scroll with the number and name of Regiment in yellow, for example "3d U.S. Cavalry."
Embroidery.—The design, letters, and figures to be embroidered in silk, the same on both sides of the standard.
Trimmings.—The standard to be trimmed on three (3) sides with United States silk-knotted fringe, two and one-half (2 1/2) inches deep.
Lance.—To be nine (9) feet, six (6) inches long, including metal spear and ferrule.
Case or Cover.—To be of waterproof material to protect the Standard when furled.
Workmanship.—To conform in all respects to the standard sample on file in the Quartermaster-General's Office.
Adopted July 7, 1886, in lieu of those of February 4, 1884, which are hereby canceled.

Suspenders Specification No. 179

Front straps.—The front straps are to be made of non-elastic webbing 3/4 inch broad, to have thirteen cords, and to be of weight and quality of the standard sample. They are to be attached directly to the buckle in the manner known as "Cantab," and before they are sewed together; to be 9 1/2 inches long, and overlap each other to an extent that they will give sufficient "play" or change of length of the two straps that are fastened together. The button-hole is to be woven into the strap and must be at least half an inch from the extremity of the strap.
Shoulder-straps.—The shoulder straps are to be made of one continuous piece of non-elastic webbing folded and bent upon itself in the middle, as per sample. They are to be 1 3/8 inches broad, of same weight, and equal in quality in every respect to the standard sample; to be regular in width and weaving, and to have a figure woven on them equal to sample. The extremities to be neatly bound.
Back straps.—The back straps are to be made of elastic rubber web, to have twenty-two cords and to be 1 1/4 inches broad. The rubber thread is to be that made by the East Hampton Rubber Co., or other quality equally as good, of the size known to the trade as No. 28, and to be freshly manufactured. The button-holes are to be woven into the strap and to be at least 7/8 of an inch from the extremity of the strap or end. The straps are to be neatly woven, with a smooth even face, and edges to be neatly bound at the ends, the binding to extend up one-half the length of the button-hole on each side.
Buckle.—The buckle is to be made in one piece and be stamped from sheet-brass of weight equal to that on sample, and to have three prongs. It must have an opening sufficient to accommodate the shoulder-straps, and two similar openings or slots of a size that will allow the cantab straps to freely play or move through it. Each slot must have an anti-friction roller to prevent the wear of the strap upon the buckle, as on sample. Both the friction rollers and the prongs must be made from brass, well nickel plated.
Re-inforce straps.—The back straps to be united to the shoulder-straps by two rows of stitching, as shown on sample. The shoulder-straps are also to be fastened together in back by a re-inforce or strengthening piece made from web similar to the shoulder-straps, of the size and shape of sample, with its cut edges bound, the strengthening-piece securely sewed to the shoulder-straps, as in sample. The front strap will be sewed by four lines of stitching nearly forming a square, as per sample. *Button-hole strengthening.*—All the button-holes are to

be strengthened by being whipped or over-sewed at their wearing extremities, to the extent of the sample.

Lengths.—The suspenders are to be of three lengths, and to measure from the extremes of the front and back button-holes 36 inches, 38 inches, and 40 inches, respectively.

Thread.—All thread used in sewing the suspenders must be from the Sea-island cotton and be of the best quality.

Color.—All the parts of the suspender must be of the same color and must be "fast" color, and as per samples.

Packing.—The suspenders must be neatly packed in paper boxes, one dozen of the same size in a box.

Each pair of suspenders is to have the length of same stamped or stenciled in black or blue color on the reverse side of the strengthening-strap (without however defacing the outer side) in letters and figures 3/8 inch long, as follows:—40-in., 38-in., 36-in.

Adopted February 25, 1887, in lieu of those of September 4, 1883, which are hereby canceled.

Blouse-lining Flannel Specification No. 180

Wool.—The warp to be made of the best long-staple American cotton yarn, No. 40, doubled and twisted, dyed pure indigo blue, and to weigh one and three-quarters (1 3/4) ounces to the yard. The filling to weigh four and one-quarter (4 1/4) ounces to the yard, and be composed of good American fleece wool, at least one-quarter blood, and if the best long-staple American cotton, in the proportion of seventy-five (75) parts wool to twenty-five (25) parts cotton, and to be free from shoddy, flocks, or other impurities. The wool of the filling to be dyed with pure indigo, and the cotton with a fast dye.

Width.—To be full twenty-seven (27) inches wide when finished.

Threads.—To have fifty-six (56) threads of warp and forty-eighth (48) threads of filling in the inch (square).

Strength.—To be capable of sustaining a strain to be not less than forty (40) pounds to one inch width of warp and thirty-eighth (38) pounds to one inch of filling in the piece.

Weight.—The good when finished to weigh not less than six (6) ounces to the linear yard.

Color.—To conform to the standard sample.

Finish.—To be neither hot or cold pressed, and to be properly fulled.

Adopted April 2, 1887, in lieu of specifications of March 19, 1883, which are hereby canceled.

Boots (with partly machine sewed bottoms) Specification No. 182

Material.—Uppers to be the best quality oak-tanned from slaughter hides, the leg to be finished on the grain.

Straps to be made of calf-skin to smooth-wax upper.

Vamp and outside *counter* to be of wax-upper.

Soles of best quality oak-tanned, from straight Texas hides, or from South American (commonly called "Spanish") dry hides; no split leather to be used.

Thread to be of the best quality silk and linen thread.

Nails used in heels to be 11/8 Swede No. 12, 10 lbs. to the 100 pairs boots, and 5/8 American iron, 5 lbs. to the 100 pairs boots.

Sizes—Nos. 5 to 12, inclusive.

The width of the sole across the ball of the foot to be as follows and to be in proportion throughout:

SIZES.	5	6	7	8	9	10	11	12
Letter "A"	3 5/16	3 7/16	3 9/16	3 11/16	3 13/16	3 15/16	4 1/16	4 3/16
Letter "B"	3 3/8	3 1/2	3 5/8	3 3/4	3 7/8	4	4 1/8	4 1/4
Letter "C"	3 7/16	3 9/16	3 11/16	3 13/16	3 15/16	4 1/16	4 3/16	4

5/16 *The instep and ball of the foot to measure* as follows:

SIZES	5	6	7	8	9	10	11	12
Letter "A"								
Instep	8 3/4	9	9 1/4	9 1/2	9 3/4	10	10 1/4	10 1/2
Ball	8 1/2	8 3/4	9	9 1/4	9 1/2	9 3/4	10	10 1/4
Letter "B"								
Instep	9	9 1/4	9 1/2	9 3/4	10	10 1/4	10 1/2	10 3/4
Ball	8 3/4	9	9 1/4	9 1/2	9 3/4	10	10 1/4	10 1/2
Letter "C"								
Instep	9 1/4	9 1/2	9 3/4	10	10 1/4	10 1/2	10 3/4	11
Ball	9	9 1/4	9 1/2	9 3/4	10	10 1/4	10 1/2	10 3/4

Measurement for a No. 8 boot, standard, *Letter "A,"* is as follows: *Heel*, 13 1/8 inches; *instep* 9 1/2 inches, *ball or toe* 9 1/4 inches, *length of leg* 19 inches in front, 14 inches in back, *width of leg* at top 15 inches, *width of strap*, 1 1/4 inches, *length of strap*, 7 inches; *height of counter*, 3 inches, *length of heel* 3 inches, *width of heel* 2 7/8 inches, *height of heel* 1 1/4 inches, *width of sole or ball*, 3 11/16 inches.

Measurement for a No. 8 boot, standard, *Letter "B,"*
to be as Letter "A," with the following exceptions:
Heel 13 3/8 inches, *instep* 9 3/4 inches, *ball or toe* 9 1/2 inches, *width of sole or ball* 3 3/4 inches.

Measurement for a No. 8 boot, standard, *Letter "C,"*
to be as Letter "A," with the following exceptions:
Heel 13 5/8 inches, *instep* 10 inches, *ball or toe* 9 3/4 inches, *width of sole or ball* 3 13/16 inches.

Workmanship.—The leg to be cut in two pieces, with the lap seam in front; to be stitched with three (3) rows of stitching, ten (10) stitches to the inch; the upper stitching to be heavy silk thread, the under stitching to be of best quality linen thread. Back seam to be covered with a strip of same material as leg, to measure one (1) inch in width at top and two (2) inches in width at counter. Counter to be stitched to leg with five (5) cord waxed linen thread, six (6) stitches to the inch. The strap to be sewed to the inside of the leg with five (5) cord waxed linen

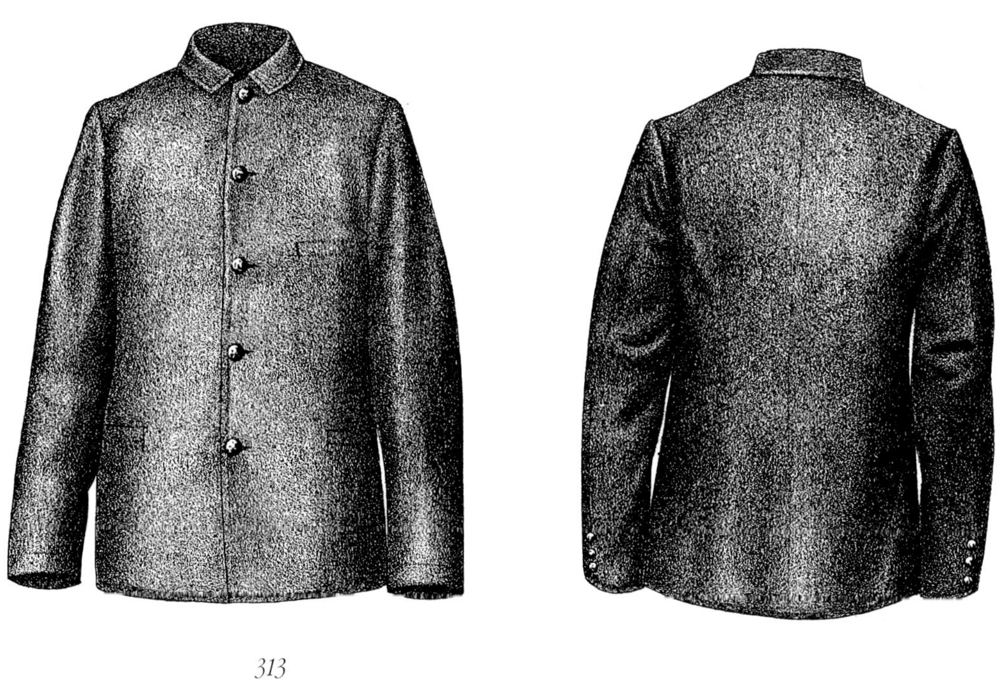

Blouses, Specification No. 192, October 20, 1887.

thread, six (6) stitches to the inch. The vamp and outside counter to be stitched on the leg with three (3) rows of stitching, ten (10) stitches to the inch, the upper stitching to be of the best quality linen thread. The back seam to be sewed with five (5) cord waxed linen thread, six (6) stitches to the inch. The inner sole, welt, and upper to be fastened together with twelve (12) cord wax sole thread, four (4) stitches to the inch. The outer sole and welt to be fastened together with ten (10) cord wax sole thread, seven stitches to the inch. To be worked square with the last, the edges to be finished with pressers without heel-ball, and to measure at least half a size (outside) more than they are marked. The feather of the inner sole to be rounded.
Adopted March 14, 1887, in lieu of those of April 27, 1886, which are hereby canceled.

Linen Collars Specification No. 183

To be four-ply standing collar, conforming in height and shape to sealed sample.
Materials.—The outside surface to be of pure Irish linen. The two inner-linings and facing to be made of material like and equal to that of the sealed standard sample.
Workmanship and Finish.—The stitching to be 22 to the inch. The collars to be "Combination" turned, to be properly laundried, and to conform in all other respects to the sealed standard sample.
Sizes.—To run from 14 to 18, inclusive, in such proportions as required.
Adopted March 24, 1887.

Music Pouches—Large and Small Specification No. 184

Sizes.—To be made in two sizes, known as large and small. The pouch or box part if the large size to be seven (7) inches long, nine (9) inches wide, one and one-half (1 1/2) inches deep. The pouch or box part of the small size to be six and three-quarters (6 3/4) inches long, five and one-quarter (5 1/4) inches wide, and one and one-quarter (1 1/4) inches deep.
Material and Make.—The body to be made off black enameled leather, first quality, covered with dark blue cloth weighing 16 ounces to the yard, firmly glued and stitched to the leather; the cloth to be turned over the edge of the leather in the box part 3/4 of an inch and on the flap 3/8 of an inch; the flap to have two rows of stitching—one row close to the outer edge of the "turn in," the other row 3/16 of an inch apart from the first row. The flap to be fashioned and finished with an edging of (real) gold lace 9/32 of an inch wide (known in the trade as No. 1962), in accordance with the standard sample. The ends to be of black patent leather 1/8 of an inch thick, firmly and neatly stitched to the body of the pouch, eight stitches to the inch, this stitching forming a finish to the back part of the pouch. In the center of the rounded bottom of the pouch a brass "nib," with a shoulder, is to be rivetted over a cooper burr on the inside, the nib to be 3/16 inch stem, having an oval head 5/16 inch, the flap to be furnished with a leather strap 3 1/2 x 1 1/4 inches, securely stitched to the underside of the same with a hole punched therein to receive the nib. On the back near the top, and at proper angles, are to be placed two triangles, brass 7/8 inch, held in place by black enameled leather straps securely and neatly stitched to the pouch.
Carrying Strap or Sling.—The carrying strap to be made of first quality black enameled leather, one (1) inch wide, rounded edges, and made in two parts; the long part 41 1/2 inches long, the short part 13 inches long, including the "turn-in" for snaps and buckle; each part to be furnished with a gilt spring-snap on one end, and put on with gilt screw studs with 1/2-inch heads; the other end of the long part to have five eyelet-holes for tongue of buckle, the first hole 3 1/2 inches from the end and the others 1 inch from centers; one end of the short or adjusting end part of the strap to be furnished with a gilt buckle 1 inch square. The face of the carrying strap to be finished with a band of (real) gold 13/16 inch wide (known in the trade as No. 2043), neatly stitched on with yellow silk. The center of this band of gold lace to have a row of stitching 1/8 inch wide, of the various colors denoting the arms of service, in the proportion for each arm, as may be required.
Adopted April 5, 1887.

Shoulder-knot and Aiguillette Specification No. 185

KNOTS.

Cord.—To be U.S. gauge 5, made on 16 carrier machine, of two-end No. 26, two-fold worsted 3/4 blood stock, filling of cotton.
Tin.—Tin from 6 1/4 2 3/4 inches, extremes. Brass hook, 1 3/4 inches, No. 14 wire, double.
Upper.—Twilled cloth.
Lining.—Twilled muslin or chintz.
Button.—Small, coat, Army standard. The Knot to be fashioned over the cushioned tin form in three-cord net work, in accordance with the standard sample.

AIGUILLETTE.

Cord.—To be U.S. gauge 3, made on 24 carrier machine, of two-end No. 26, two-fold worsted 3/4 blood stock, filling of cotton. To be passed over the plate and under the net work of the right shoulder-knot; a loop to be formed on each side, the back loop to be 15 inches long, and the front loop 17 inches long, clear of knot. The back part of aiguillette to be loop-plaited for 30 inches of its length from the knot, then extending in single cord 5 inches from plait, at which point a coil of five laps is made and the end passed through this coil and extended in single cord 4 1/2 inches, and finished with a brass tip 3 1/4 inches long; at top of coil is a small worsted cord-loop for button. The front part of aiguillette is to be made in the same manner as the back part except that the portion to be loop-plaited is 22 inches, from which the single cord extension is six inches to the coil. The knots and aiguilettes to be dyed fast colors, and to conform in all respects to the sealed standard sample.
Adopted April 5, 1887.

Lyres Specification No. 186

To be made of German silver, fifteen per cent, fine, with two brass-wire prongs 3/4 inch long securely soldered on the back of the device.
To be one and three-sixteenths (1 3/16) inches by eleven-sixteenths (11/16) of an inch at the extreme.
To conform in all respects to the standard sample.
Adopted April 5, 1887.

Hair Plumes for Helmets Specification No. 187

To be made of good horse-hair dyed a fast color to shade of standard sample.
To droop from the top of socket over back and sides of helmet.
The hairs are woven and sewed together at one end, giving the latter the form of a flattened knob about one and five-eighth (1 5/8) inches diameter, with star-shaped brass eyelet in center to admit the pen of the top piece. Length of plume from eyelet to end fourteen (14) inches.
Adopted April 5, 1887.

Cords and bands for Helmets Specification No. 188

To be made of worsted No. 26, and "machined cord," dyed a fast color to shade of sample.
The bands are loop-plaited, fastened to the scroll-ring, and festooned on front and back of helmet, the festoons reaching in front to the upper edge of chin-strap, and approaching the lower edge of back within two (2) inches.
The loop-plaiting is about one (1) inch wide, and ends under the scrolls on the left side in a tassel of sixty (60) to seventy (70) fringes one and three-fourth (1 3/4) inches long. Through the braided head, about three-fourths (3/4) inch diameter, passes the continuation of the bands in the form of two cords, each five (5) feet eight (8) inches long, with two (2) slides netted over a fuller's board three-fourth (3/4) inch in diameter, five-eighth (5/8) of an inch high. Three inches from the lower end the cords are fastened together by a braided knot, holding a loop about two and three-fourths (2 3/4) inches long. At the end of each cord is also a small braided knot, and an aiguillette, plated flat in three strands of smaller cord, in oval shape, two and three-eighth(2 3/8) inches long, two and three-fourths (2 3/4) inches wide. From the lower end of each aiguillette is suspended another tassel of from sixty (60) to seventy (70) fringes, one and three-fourths

(1 3/4) inches long, with braided head three-eighthof an inch high, three-fourths inch diameter.
Adopted April 5, 1887.

Dark-blue flannel, fine quality Specification No. 189

Wool.—To be pure long staple American fleece wool of not less than three quarters (3/4) blood, free from shoddy, flocks, or other impurities.
Width.—To be fifty-four (54) inches, or six fourths (6/4) of a yard wide.
Threads.—To contain not less than sixty-eighth (68) threads of warp, and seventy-two (72) threads of filling in each inch.
Weight.—To weigh not less than thirteen (13) ounces to the linear yard.
Strength.—To be capable of sustaining a strain of not less than twenty-seven (27) pounds to the inch of warp, and twenty-five (25) pounds to the inch of filling.
Color.—To be the same shade of dark blue as the standard sample, and to be dyed in the wool with pure indigo of best quality (unless otherwise authorized in writing by the contracting officer.)
Finish.—To be equal in all respects to the standard sample.
Adopted April 16, 1887.

Trumpet-cords and Tassels Specification No. 190

Material.—Cord: U.S. Gauge No. 5 made on 16 Carrier machine one end of No. 18 four-fold Genappe best-quality, filling cotton.
Tassel.—Hard wood mold. Two (2) inches covered on 48 Carrier machine, one end No. 18, four-fold Genappe. *Skirt.*—Seven ends No. 25, two fold worsted, single twist, 3-8 blood stock, three (3) inches deep, about 80 bullions to tassel.
Gimp.—Brass wire and cotton open with one end No. 18 four-fold Genappe, six rows.
Length.—Length of cord to be twenty-one (21) feet.
Dyeing.—To be fast color.
Colors.—To be white for Infantry, scarlet for Artillery, and yellow for Cavalry conforming in shade to that of the standard samples.
Adopted June 1, 1887.

Trouser Stripes Specification No. 191

Materials.—To be of facing cloth of the same color as facings for Uniform Dress Coats. Those for Engineers and the Hospital Corps to have, in addition, a white piping on each side one-eighth of an inch wide.
Dimensions.—For non-commissioned staff, one and one-quarter (1 1/4) inches wide.
For Sergeants and Acting Hospital Stewards, one (1) inch wide.
For Corporals and Privates of the Hospital Corps, one-half (1/2) inch wide.
For Musicians, two stripes, one-half (1/2) inch wide, placed one-quarter (1/4) inch apart.
All stripes to be cut forty-five (45) inches long, and wide enough to be turned under in one-quarter (1/4) of an inch on either side.
To be worn along the outer seam of the trousers, the rear edge following the seam.
Adopted August 24, 1887, in lieu of specifications of March 24, 1885, which are hereby canceled.
The specifications for Linen Webbing, adopted March 14, 1886, are also canceled.

Blouses Specification No. 192

Material.—Dark-blue flannel, Army standard; blue twilled mix flannel lining for body, and unbleached muslin lining for sleeves.
Pattern.—To be singled breasted sack coat with falling collar, and having five (5) regulation buttons, large, in front from neck to waist, and three (3) regulation buttons, small, on the cuff of each sleeve. To have three (3) outside pockets, one (1) on each side of skirt, and one (1) on the left breast, and one (1) inside pocket on the right breast.
Workmanship.—To be cut, made, and finished in accordance with the standard samples adopted this date.

Measurements:

Sizes.	Length of Blouse.	Length of Sleeve.	Width of Hand.	Size of Neck.	Width of Collar.	Width of Back.	Size of Armhole.	Size of Breast.	Size of Waist.
	Inches.								
1	27	31	12	16	3	7	16	34	32
2	27 1/2	31 1/2	12	16 1/2	3	7 1/2	17	35	33
3	28	32 1/2	12	17	3	7 3/4	18	36	34
4	29	33	12	18	3 1/2	8	19	38	36
5	30 1/4	34	12 1/2	19	3 1/2	8	20	40	38
6	30 1/2	34 1/2	13	19 1/2	3 1/2	8 1/4	21	42	40

Adopted October 20, 1887 in lieu of specifications of March 12, 1886, which are hereby canceled.

BIBLIOGRAPHY

Primary

Unpublished

E.M. Coughlin Correspondence. Glen Swanson Collection.

Ft. Fetterman. Letters and Telegrams Received, Circulars and Orders. Wyoming Territory Records, April 1874-July 1880. Wyoming State Museum, Cheyenne, WY.

Microfilm Collections, Heraldry, Boxes 83-85. U.S. Army Military History Institute, Carlisle Barracks, PA.

Post Letters Sent. Old Ft. Niagara MSS Collections. Ft. Niagara, NY.

Record Group 92. Office of the Quartermaster General. National Archives, Washington, DC.

Combined Correspondence Files, Boxes 76; 77; 82; 137; 1170- 1171.

General & Misc. Correspondence, Vol. A, 1872.

Letters Received, Office of the Quartermaster

General, 1874-1887.

Letters Sent, Clothing Branch, 1874-1888.

Register of Letters Received. Philadelphia Depot.

Record Group 94. Letters Received, 1874-1887. Adjutant General's Office. National Archives, Washington DC.

Record Group 107. Abstract from Register of War Office, 1872, Even Numbers. Office of the Secretary of War. National Archives, Washington, DC.

Record Group 112. Letters Received. U.S. Army Surgeon General's Office. National Archives, Washington, DC.

Record Group 156. Office of the Chief of Ordnance. National Archives, Washington, DC.

Letters Sent, Rock Island Arsenal.

Letters to Ordnance Officers.

Record Group 371. Post Returns, Ft. Concho, Texas. National Archives, Washington, DC.

Record Group 391. Special Order No. 76, November 17, 1873, Headquarters Seventh Cavalry, Ft. Abraham Lincoln, Dakota Territory. Records US Army Mobile Units, 1821-1942, National Archives, Washington, DC.

Record Groups 393. Records of U.S. Army Continental Commands. National Archives, Washington, DC.

Ft. Sanders, Wyoming Territory.

Presidio of San Francisco, California.

Published

Annual Report of the Secretary of War, 1874-1887. Vol. I. Washington, DC: Government Printing Office, 1874-1887.

Army and Navy Journal. 1874-1885.

Army and Navy Register. 1880 and 1884.

Bourke, John G., *On The Border With Crook*. New York; Charles Scribner's Sons, 1891.

Circular No. 8 Report on Hygiene of the United States Army With Descriptions of Military Posts and Circular No. 9 Report of the Surgeon General on the Transport of Sick and Wounded by Pack Animals. New York: Sol Lewis, 1974.

"Clothing For Soldiers." Philadelphia *Inquirer* (January 7, 1888), 1.

Everett, John P. "Bullets, Boots, and Saddles. Being Personal Recollections of Men Who Took Part in the Battle of the Big Horn in Montana Territory June 25, 1876, as Told to John P. Everett." *The Sunshine Magazine* IX (September 1930), 4-10.

Exec. Doc. 56 Senate. 46th Cong. 2d Sess.

Finerty, John F. *War-Path and Bivouac*. Chicago: M.A. Donohue, 1890.

Fuller, Ezra B. "Recollections of an Old Cavalryman." *Journal of the United States Cavalry Association* XXVI (January 1916): 413-433.

General Orders. War Department, 1872-1875.

General Orders and Circulars. Headquarters of the Army, 1875- 1888.

Graham, W.A. *The Custer Myth*. Mechanicsburg, PA: Stackpole Books, 1995.

_____., Ed. *Official Record of a Court of Inquiry convened...upon request of Major Marcus A. Reno...to investigate his conduct at...the Little Bighorn, June 25-26, 1876*. Pacific Palisades, CA: 1951.

Hammer, Kenneth, Ed. *Custer in '76: Walter Camp's Notes on the Custer Fight*. Provo, UT: Brigham Young University Press, 1976.

Hill, Michael D. and Innis, Ben., Eds. "The Ft. Buford Diary of Private Sanford, 1876-1877." *North Dakota History* LII No. 3 (Summer 1985): 2-40.

Holabird, S.B. "Army Clothing." *Journal of the Military Service Institution of the United States* II (1881): 355-387.

Hunt, Frazier and Robert. *I Fought With Custer: The Story of Sergeant Windolph*. New York: Charles Scribner's Sons, 1947.

King, Charles. *An Apache Princess*. New York: Grossett and Dunlap, 1903.

_____. Campaigning With Crook and Stories of Army Life. New York: Harper and Brothers, 1890.

_____. *Captain Blake*. Philadelphia: Lippincott, 1891.

_____. "George Crook." *War Papers Read Before the Commandary of the State of Wisconsin, Military Order of the Loyal Legion of the United States*, Vol. I, 260-8.

_____. *Marion's Faith*. Philadelphia: Lippincott, 1889.

Magnussen, Daniel O., Ed. *Peter Thompson's Narrative of the Little Bighorn Campaign 1876*. Glendale, CA: The Arthur H. Clark Co., 1974.

Munson, Edward Lyman. *The Soldier's Foot and the Military Shoe*. Menasha, WI: George Banta Publishing Company, 1917.

Nelson, Henry Loomis. *The Army of the United States*. New York: B.M. Whitlock, 1890.

Partoll, Albert J., Ed. *After the Custer Battles: Sources of Northwest History No. 29*. Missoula: Montana State University, 1939.

Regulations and Decisions Pertaining to the Uniform of the Army of the United States. Washington, DC: Government Printing Office, 1899.

Regulations for the Uniform of the Army of United States With Illustrations, 1888. Philadelphia: Quartermaster Department, 1888.

Regulations for the Army of the United States 1889. Washington, DC: Government Printing Office, 1889.

Roe, Frances M.A. *Army Letters from an Officer's Wife*. Lincoln: University of Nebraska Press, 1981.

Taylor, William O. *With Custer on the Little Bighorn*. New York: Viking, 1996.

Uniform of the Army of the United States 1882. Philadelphia: Thomas Hunter, 1882.

Uniform of the Army of the United States, Illustrated from 1774 to 1889. Philadelphia: Quartermaster General, 1889.

U.S. Army Uniforms and Equipment, 1889: Specifications for Clothing, Camp and Garrison Equipage, and Clothing and Equipage Materials. Lincoln: University of Nebraska Press, 1986.

Utley, Robert M., Ed. *Life in Custer's Cavalry: Diaries and Letters of Albert and Jennie Barnitz, 1867-1868*. New Haven: Yale University Press, 1977.

Woodruff, Charles A. "Battle of the Bighole." *Contributions to the Historical Society of Montana* VII (1911): 95-108.

Woodhull, Alfred A. *A Medical Report upon the Uniform and Clothing of the Soldiers of the U.S. Army*. Washington, DC: Surgeon General's Office, 1868.

Zogbaum, Rufus Fairchild, "Army Uniform." *Harper's Weekly* (May 4, 1895), 417.

Secondary

Books and Monographs

Ambrose, Stephen. *Upton and the Army*. Baton Rouge: Louisiana State University, 1964.

Bibliography

Ashburn, P.M. *History of the Medical Department of the United States Army*. Cambridge, MA: Houghton Mifflin Co., 1929.

Brinckerhoff, Sidney B. *Boots and Shoes of the Frontier Soldier*. Tucson: Arizona Historical Society Museum Monograph No. 7, 1976.

Brown, William L. III. *The Army Called it Home: Military Interiors of the 19th Century*. Gettysburg, PA: Thomas Publications, 1992.

_____. *A Pictorial History of Enlisted Men's Barracks of the U.S. Army, 1861-1895*. Harpers Ferry, VA: National Park Service, 1984.

Chappell, Gordon. *Brass Spikes & Horsehair Plumes: A Study of U.S. Army Dress Helmet, 1872-1903*. Tucson: Arizona Pioneers Historical Society, 1966.

_____. *Brass Spikes and Horsetail Plumes: A Study of the U.S. Army Dress Helmet, 1872-1904*. Gettysburg: Thomas Publications, 1997.

_____. *The Search For The Well-Dressed Soldier, 1865-1890*. Tucson: Arizona Historical Society, 1972.

_____. *Summer Helmets of the U.S. Army 1875-1910*. Cheyenne: Wyoming State Archives and Historical Department, 1967.

Clary, David A. *These Relics of Barbarism: A History of Furniture in Barracks and Guardhouses of the United States Army, 1800- 1880*. Harpers Ferry, VA: National Park Service, n.d.

Cox, Kurt Hamilton. *Custer and His Commands: From West Point to Little Bighorn*. London: Greenhill Books, 1999.

Emerson, William K. *Chevrons: Illustrated History and Catalog of U.S. Army Insignia*. Washington, DC: Smithsonian Institution Press, 1983.

_____. *Encyclopedia of United States Army Insignia and Uniforms*. Norman: University of Oklahoma Press, 1996.

Fisher, Ernest F., Jr. *Guardians of the Republic: A History of the Noncommissioned Officer Corps of the U.S. Army*. New York: Ballantine Books, 1994.

Foner, Jack D. *The United States Army Between Two Wars: Army Life and Reform, 1865-1898*. New York: Humanities Press, 1970.

Gray, John S. *Centennial Campaign: The Sioux War of 1876*. Norman: University of Oklahoma Press, 1988.

Greene, Jerome A. *Yellowstone Command: Colonel Nelson A. Miles and the Great Sioux War*. Lincoln: University of Nebraska Press, 1991.

Harris, N. Neil, Ed., *Medals of the United States Mint: The First Century 1792-1892*. N.P.: Token and Medal Society, n.d.

Hedren, Paul L. *With Crook in the Black Hills: Stanley J. Morrow's 1876 Photographic Legacy*. Boulder: Pruett Publishing Company, 1985.

A History of the Signal Corps. New York: G.P. Putnam's Sons. 1961.

Howell, Edgar M. *United States Army Headgear, 1855-1902: Catalog of United States Army Uniforms in the Collections of the Smithsonian Institution, II*. Washington, DC: Smithsonian Institution, 1975.

Hunt, Elvid. *History of Fort Leavenworth, 1827-1937*. Ft. Leavenworth: Command and General Staff College, 1937.

Hutchins, James S. *Boots & Saddles at the Little Bighorn* (Ft. Collins, CO: The Old Army Press, 1976.

Important Custer, Indian Wars and Western Memorabilia. San Francisco: Butterfield Butterfield, 1995.

Jacobsen, Jacques Noel, Jr. *Military Antiques and Memorabilia Catalog 98 Fall 1999*. Staten Island. J.N. Jacobsen, Jr. 1999.

Julian, R.W. *Medals of the United States Mint: The First Century, 1792-1892*. Neil Harris, Ed., N.P.: The Token and Medal Society, Inc., n.d.

Katz, D. Mark. *Custer in Photographs: A Visual Portrait of one of America's Most Intriguing Civil War Heroes*. New York: Bonanza Books 1985.

Knight, Oliver. *Life and Manners in the Frontier Army*. Norman: University of Oklahoma Press, 1978.

Landreth, Marsha. *Great American Generals: William T. Sherman*. New York: Gallery Books, 1990.

Langellier, John P. *American Indians in the U.S Military, 1866- 1945*. London: Greenhill Books, 2000.

_____. *Army Blue: The Uniform of Uncle Sam's Regulars, 1848- 1873*. Atglen, PA: Schiffer Military History, 1998.

_____. *Bluecoats: The U.S. Army in the West, 1848-1897*. London: Greenhill Press, 1995.

_____. *Hats Off: U.S. Army Head Dress, 1872-1912*. Atglen, PA: Schiffer Military History, 1999.

_____. *They Continually Wear the Blue: U.S. Army Enlisted Dress Uniforms, 1865-1902*. San Francisco: Barnes-McGee, 1976.

_____. *Uncle Sam's Little Wars: The Spanish-American War, Philippine Insurrection, and Boxer Rebellion, 1898-1902*. London: Greenhill Books, 1999.

_____., and Osur, Alan M. *Chaplain Allen Allensworth and the 24th Infantry 1886-1906*. Tucson: Tucson Corral of the Westerners, 1980.

Lanham, Howard G. *The Evolution of United States Army Shoulder Straps*. Westminster, MD: Howard G. Lanham, 1998.

McChristian, Douglas C. *An Army of Marksmen: The Development of United States Army Marksmanship in the 19th Century*. Ft. Collins, CO: Old Army Press, 1981.

_____. *The U.S. Army in the West, 1870-1880: Uniforms, Weapons, and Equipment*. Norman: University of Oklahoma Press, 1995.

Marszalek, John F. *Sherman: Soldier's Passion for Order*. New York: The Free Press, 1993.

Nenninger, Timothy K. *The Leavenworth Schools and the old Army: education, professionalism, and the officers corps of the United States Army, 1881-1918*. Westport, CT; Greenwood Press, 1978.

Railsback, Thomas S., and Langellier, John P. *The Drums Would Roll: A Pictorial History of U.S. Army Bands on the American Frontier, 1866-1900*. London: Arms and Armour Press, 1987.

Risch, Erna. *Quartermaster Support of the Army: A History of the Corps, 1775-1939*. Washington, DC: Office of the Quartermaster General's Office, 1962.

Rodenbough Theo. F., and Haskin, William L., Eds. *The Army of the United States: Historical Sketches of Staff and Line With Portraits of Generals-in-Chief*. New York: Argonaut Press, 1966.

Stallard, Patricia Y. *Glittering Misery Dependents of the Indian Fighting Army*. Ft. Collins, CO: Old Army Press, 1978.

Steffen, Randy. *The Horse Soldier, 1776-1943*. Vol. II. Norman: University of Oklahoma Press, 1979.

Todd, Frederick P. *American Military Equipage 1851-1872*. Vol II Providence: The Company of Military Historians, 1977.

Weigley, Russell F. *Quartermaster General of the Union Army: A Biography of M.C. Meigs*. New York: Columbia University Press, 1959.

Articles

Baird, L.C. "The Philadelphia Quartermaster Intermediate Depot." *Quartermaster Review* VI, No. 6 (May-June 1927): 18-23.

Carlson, Carl W.A. "U.S. Army Marksmanship Medals 1882-1897: A Critical Examination." *The Token and Medal Society* (February 1983): 4-10.

Chappell, Gordon. "The 'Pillbox' Cap in the United States Army c. 1866-1902." *Military Collector and Historian* XXXII, No. 1 (Spring 1980): 4-15.

Emerson, William K. "Guides for Military Research." *Trading Post* XXXVI, No. 2 (January-March 1977): 4.

_____. "U.S. Army Enlisted Cap Insignia, 1896-1905." *Military Collector and Historian* XXIV, No. 1 (Spring 1972): 11-15.

Greene, Jerome A. "The U.S. Army Buffalo Overcoat and M1883 Canvas Blanket-Lined Overcoat on the Northern Plains Frontier, 1876-1891." *Military Collector and Historian* XLIV, No. 2 (Summer 1992): 73-75.

Hamilton, C.S. "Jeffersonville Intermediate Depot History and Functions." *Quartermaster Review* VII, No. 1 (July-August 1927): 3-9.

Hutchins, James S. "The Army Campaign Hat of 1872," *Military Collector and Historian* XVI, No. 3 (Fall 1964): 65-73.

Sperry, T.J. "1872 Insignia Expedient Attachment Devices." *Military Collector and Historian* XLI, No. 1 (Spring 1989): 43-45.

_____. "Winter Clothing on the Northern Plains." *Military Collector and Historian* XLIV, No. 3 (Fall 1992): 116-120.

Williams, W.T. "History of Jeffersonville Quartermaster Intermediate Depot." *Quartermaster Review* V, No. 4 (January-February 1926): 10-20.

Winners of the West (January 30, 1928), 6.

Unpublished

Andrews, R.A. "Years of Frustration: William T. Sherman, The Army and Reform." Unpublished MA Thesis, Department of History, Northwestern University, 1968.

Thomas, Donna M.E., "Army Reform in America: The Crucial Years, 1876-1881." Unpublished Ph.D. Dissertation, Department of History, University of Florida, 1980.

INDEX